1970	1971	1972	1973	1974	1975	1976	1977	1978	1979	1980	1981	1982
2.1	2.1	2.3	3.2	2.8	2.7	2.3	2.0	2.1	2.2	1.8	2.0	1.8
1.0	1.0	1.0	1.0	1.4	1.5	1.4	1.6	1.5	1.7	2.4	2.9	2.5
4.6	4.7	4.7	4.8	4.7	4.3	4.4	4.4	4.6	4.7	4.4	3.9	3.7
12.7	12.4	12.7	13.0	12.3	11.5	12.1	12.5	12.7	12.3	11.3	11.0	10.0
9.4	9.1	8.9	8.7	8.8	8.8	8.9	8.8	8.6	8.6	8.5	8.5	8.2
4.0	4.0	4.0	3.9	3.8	4.1	4.1	4.1	4.1	3.8	4.0	4.1	4.5
6.6	6.5	6.6	6.6	6.9	6.9	6.6	6.5	6.6	6.6	6.5	6.4	6.3
9.2	9.2	9.1	9.0	8.7	8.9	9.0	9.0	8.9	8.6	8.3	8.2	8.3
3.2	3.2	3.3	3.3	3.3	3.0	3.2	3.2	3.2	3.2	3.1	2.9	2.7
11.9	12.1	12.0	11.7	11.8	12.0	11.7	11.8	11.9	11.8	12.3	12.5	13.1
—	—	—	—	—	—	—	—	—	—	—	—	—
—	—	—	—	—	—	—	—	—	—	—	—	—
—	—	—	—	—	—	—	—	—	—	—	—	—
—	—	—	—	—	—	—	—	—	—	—	—	—
—	—	—	—	—	—	—	—	—	—	—	—	—
37	36.8	36.9	36.9	36.4	36	36.1	35.9	35.8	35.6	35.2	35.2	34.7
5.7	5.6	5.3	5.1	5.1	5.0	4.9	4.5	4.1	3.8	3.7	3.6	3.5
0.8	0.7	0.7	0.7	0.8	0.8	0.8	0.8	0.9	0.9	1.0	1.1	1.1
4.6	4.8	4.8	4.9	4.7	4.2	4.1	4.3	4.5	4.6	4.5	4.3	4.0
22.7	21.6	21.5	21.9	21.3	19.7	19.8	19.7	19.7	19.7	18.9	18.6	17.4
62.1	62.7	62.7	62.8	63.4	64.9	64.8	64.8	65.2	65.7	66.7	66.9	67.4
4.1	4.6	4.9	4.6	4.7	5.3	5.6	5.8	5.6	5.3	5.2	5.6	6.5
3.40	3.63	3.90	4.14	4.43	4.73	5.06	5.44	5.87	6.33	6.84	7.43	7.86
12.35	12.56	12.93	13.00	12.76	12.45	12.59	12.72	12.83	12.78	12.66	12.57	12.53
753	885	951	924	759	802	975	895	820	844	891	933	884
2,735	3,060	3,152	2,901	2,187	2,112	2,425	2,093	1,793	1,704	1,649	1,578	1,410
8.0	7.4	7.2	7.4	8.6	8.8	8.4	8.0	8.7	9.6	11.9	14.2	13.8
2.7	2.4	2.9	1.9	-0.5	-0.6	2.7	1.7	1.7	1.3	2.9	4.8	7.7
292	309	354	397	438	448	513	576	653	736	807	927	949
313	340	370	400	453	533	573	620	682	760	879	996	1,106
-21	-31	-16	-3	-15	-85	-61	-44	-29	-24	-73	-70	-158
283	303	322	341	344	395	477	549	607	640	712	789	925

Foundations of
MICROECONOMICS

Foundations of
MICROECONOMICS

Robin Bade

Michael Parkin
University of Western Ontario

THIRD EDITION

PEARSON

Addison
Wesley

Boston San Francisco New York
London Toronto Sydney Tokyo Singapore Madrid
Mexico City Munich Paris Cape Town Hong Kong Montreal

Editor-in-Chief	Denise Clinton
Senior Acquisitions Editor	Adrienne D'Ambrosio
Editorial Assistant	Jennifer Moquin
Senior Project Manager	Mary Clare McEwing
Supplements Editor	Marianne Groth
Senior Administrative Assistant	Dottie Dennis
Executive Media Producer	Michelle Neil
Senior Media Producer	Melissa Honig
Executive Marketing Manager	Stephen Frail
Marketing Assistant	Kate MacLean
Managing Editor	Nancy Fenton
Senior Design Manager	Charles Spaulding
Technical Illustrator	Richard Parkin
Senior Manufacturing Buyer	Carol Melville
Copy Editor	Barbara Willette
Project Management, Page Makeup	Elm Street Publishing Services, Inc.

Library of Congress Cataloging-in-Publication Data

Bade, Robin.
    Foundations of microeconomics / Robin Bade, Michael Parkin.--3rd ed.
      p. cm.
    Includes index.
    ISBN 0-321-36503-8
    1. Economics. I. Parkin, Michael, 1939–   II. Title
    HB171.5 .B155 2007
    330—dc21

Printed in the United States of America.

1 2 3 4 5 6 7 8 9 10—QWT—09 08 07 06 05

Text and photo credits appear on page C–1, which constitutes a continuation of the copyright page.

To Erin, Tessa, Jack, Abby, and Sophie

About the Authors

Robin Bade was an undergraduate at the University of Queensland, Australia, where she earned degrees in mathematics and economics. After a spell teaching high school math and physics, she enrolled in the Ph.D. program at the Australian National University, from which she graduated in 1970. She has held faculty appointments at the University of Edinburgh in Scotland, at Bond University in Australia, and at the Universities of Manitoba, Toronto, and Western Ontario in Canada. Her research on international capital flows appears in the *International Economic Review* and the *Economic Record*.

Robin first taught the principles of economics course in 1970 and has taught it (alongside intermediate macroeconomics and international trade and finance) most years since then. She developed many of the ideas found in this text while conducting tutorials with her students at the University of Western Ontario.

Michael Parkin studied economics in England and began his university teaching career immediately after graduating with a B.A. from the University of Leicester. He learned the subject on the job at the University of Essex, England's most exciting new university of the 1960s, and at the age of 30 became one of the youngest full professors. He is a past president of the Canadian Economics Association and has served on the editorial boards of the *American Economic Review* and the *Journal of Monetary Economics*. His research on macroeconomics, monetary economics, and international economics has resulted in more than 160 publications in journals and edited volumes, including the *American Economic Review*, the *Journal of Political Economy*, the *Review of Economic Studies*, the *Journal of Monetary Economics*, and the *Journal of Money, Credit, and Banking*. He is author of the best-selling textbook, *Economics* (Addison-Wesley), now entering its Seventh Edition.

Robin and Michael are a wife-and-husband duo. Their most notable joint research created the Bade-Parkin Index of central bank independence and spawned a vast amount of research on that topic. They don't claim credit for the independence of the new European Central Bank, but its constitution and the movement toward greater independence of central banks around the world were aided by their pioneering work. Their joint textbooks include *Macroeconomics* (Prentice-Hall), *Modern Macroeconomics* (Pearson Education Canada), and *Economics: Canada in the Global Environment*, the Canadian adaptation of Parkin, *Economics* (Addison-Wesley). They are dedicated to the challenge of explaining economics ever more clearly to an ever-growing body of students.

Music, the theater, art, walking on the beach, and five fast-growing grandchildren provide their relaxation and fun.

Microeconomics

Brief Contents

Contents

PART 4   A CLOSER LOOK AT DECISION MAKERS   261

PART 6   HOW INCOMES ARE DETERMINED   441

PART 7   THE GLOBAL ECONOMY   493

Preface

Students know that no matter what major or career they choose, they will encounter economics at many points throughout their lives. They will make economic decisions and be influenced by economic forces. They want to understand the principles of economics that can guide their decisions and help them understand the economic forces they encounter.

Foundations of Microeconomics is inspired by the special place that economics occupies in every student's education and is our attempt to meet the challenges that all students face.

As we publish the Third Edition of *Foundations*, we are gratified by the tremendous response of the economics community to our approach. Clearly, many of you agree with our view that to achieve its goals, the principles course must:

- Focus on core concepts;
- Steer a path between an overload of detail that swamps the student and a minimalist approach that leaves the student dangling with too much unsaid;
- Encourage learning-by-doing.

We have encountered this view from our own students, and we have heard it echoed by hundreds of colleagues across the United States and throughout the world. *Foundations of Microeconomics* is our best effort to take these challenges seriously and to help students see economics in the clearest possible light.

The *Foundations* icon with its four blocks (on the cover and through the book) symbolizes our four paths to that clarity: (1) continuous practice and immediate reinforcement of core concepts; (2) seamless integration of print and online resources for different learning styles; (3) diagrams that step students through the action and that use color logically and consistently; and (4) real-world applications that bring theory to life.

LOWERING THE BARRIERS TO ENTRY

Most of us want to teach a serious, analytical course that explains the core principles of our subject and helps students apply these principles in their lives and jobs. We are not content to teach "dumbed-down" economics. But we know that most students drown rather than learn to swim when thrown into the deep end of the pool. In this book and its MyEconLab and Study Guide, we make painstaking efforts to lower the barriers to learning and to reach out to the beginning student.

We focus on core concepts; provide a variety of learning tools to match diversity of learning styles; use diagrams in conjunction with captions that tell a complete story; and illustrate theory with examples and issues that students encounter in their lives.

■ Focus on Core Concepts

Each chapter of *Foundations* concentrates on a manageable number of main ideas (most commonly three or four) and reinforces each idea several times throughout the chapter. This patient, confidence-building approach guides students through unfamiliar terrain and helps them to focus their efforts on the most important tools and concepts of our discipline.

■ Many Learning Tools for Many Learning Styles

Foundations' integrated print and electronic package builds on the basic fact that students have a variety of learning styles. In MyEconLab students have a powerful tool at their fingertips—they can complete all Checkpoint exercises and end-of-chapter exercises online, work interactive graphs, assess their skills by taking Practice Tests, receive a customized Study Plan, and step through Guided Solutions.

■ Diagrams That Tell the Whole Story

We developed the style of our diagrams with extensive feedback from faculty focus group participants and student reviewers. All figures make consistent use of color to show the direction of shifts and contain detailed, numbered captions designed to direct students' attention step by step through the action. Because beginning students of economics are often apprehensive about working with graphs, we have made a special effort to present material in as many as three ways—with graphs, words, and tables—in the same figure. And in an innovation that seems necessary but is to our knowledge unmatched, nearly all of the information supporting a figure appears on the same page as the figure itself. No more flipping pages back and forth!

■ Real-World Connections That Bring Theory to Life

Students learn best when they can see the point of what they are studying. In the Third Edition, we have made a major effort to focus on the *why* behind the presentation. How often have instructors heard students ask, "What use is all this theory, anyway?" To answer this perennial question, we have added a new feature entitled *Reality Check*, which explores commonsense applications of economics in the everyday life of the student.

In addition, our popular Eye On features continue, with many fresh new examples. Current and recent events appear in Eye on the U.S. Economy boxes. We place our experience in global and historical perspectives with Eye on the Global Economy and Eye on the Past boxes. All our Eye On. . . boxes connect theory with reality.

PRACTICE MAKES PERFECT

Everyone agrees that the only way to learn economics is to do it! Reading and remembering don't work. Active involvement, working problems, repeated self-testing: These are the ingredients to success in this subject. We have structured this text and its accompanying electronic and print tools to encourage learning by doing. The central device that accomplishes this goal is a tightly knit learning system based on our innovative *Checklist-Checkpoints* structure.

■ Checklists

Each chapter opens with a *Chapter Checklist*—a list of (usually) three or four tasks the student will be able to perform after completing the chapter. Each Checklist item corresponds to a section of the chapter that engages the student with a conversational writing style, well-chosen examples, and carefully designed illustrations.

■ Checkpoints

The best time to review material is when it's fresh in students' minds. That's where Checkpoints come in. A full-page *Checkpoint*—containing a Practice Problem with solution and a parallel Exercise—immediately follows each chapter section. The Checkpoints serve as stopping points and encourage students to review the concept and to practice using it before moving on to new ideas. Diagrams and tables bring added clarity to the Checkpoint problems and solutions.

Each Checkpoint also contains a section reference to the corresponding material in MyEconLab.

■ Chapter Checkpoints

At the end of each chapter, a *Chapter Checkpoint* summarizes what the student has just learned with a set of key points and a list of key terms. It also contains a further set of questions divided into three groups: exercises, critical thinking, and Web exercises.

WHAT'S NEW IN THE THIRD EDITION

Much has happened in the world since the second edition of *Foundations* was written. The U.S. government's expenditures on the Iraq war and homeland security turned a small budget surplus into a large and growing budget deficit.

Hurricanes Katrina and Rita ripped holes in the fabric of the U.S. economy and posed challenges for government agencies. A tsunami in Indonesia and an earthquake in Pakistan stretched the capacity of the world's disaster relief resources. The ongoing march of technological change continued to bring ever rising living standards for most but costly adjustments for many.

Foundations of Microeconomics, Third Edition, seeks to make sense of these and other major events of the early 2000s. Examples and data have been thoroughly updated to provide students with a compelling and current text that reflects the world that they live in.

In addition, we have made a number of improvements in coverage, organization, and structure, the most important of which we explain here.

■ Major Content Changes in Introductory Chapters

Chapter 1 (Getting Started) focuses more explicitly and sharply on the core question: When does the self-interest promote the social interest? This theme is illustrated with eight big global or national issues: globalization, the new economy, disappearing rain forests, water shortages, global warming, natural disasters, unemployment, and the social security "time bomb." Related themes of efficiency and equity as dimensions of the social interest are sounded and are revisited throughout the book.

Chapter 2 (The U.S. and Global Economies) features a new section on the global economy, in which the rise of Asia and changes in global inequality are discussed. This descriptive chapter lays a solid base from which the student can build an understanding of the forces that shape our economic lives.

Chapter 3 (The Economic Problem) simplifies the explanation of how to calculate opportunity cost from the *PPF* and clarifies even further the principle of increasing opportunity cost. The distinction between allocative and productive efficiency is sharpened, as is comparative and absolute advantage. This chapter has a new and more effective explanation of the gains from specialization and exchange.

■ Major Content Changes in Micro Chapters

Chapter 6 (Efficiency and Fairness of Markets) now places the market in the broader context of alternative methods of allocating scarce resources—market price, command, majority rule, contest, first-come-first-served, sharing equally, lottery, personal characteristics, and force—and evaluates the efficiency and fairness of the market against its alternatives.

Chapter 7 (Government Influences on Markets) features a new section on price supports in agricultural markets.

Chapter 8 (Taxes) improves the flow by reversing the order of the discussion of the inefficiency of a tax and the explanation of the relationship between incidence and the elasticities of demand and supply.

Chapter 13 (Perfect Competition) echoes the overarching themes of efficiency and fairness by showing in a new section why perfect competition is efficient and fair.

Chapter 14 (Monopoly) incorporates a new discussion of monopoly policy issues, with an explanation of the role of patents.

Chapter 19 (Inequality and Poverty) receives major revision. The discussion of income distribution now includes material on the dynamics of the distribution and the movement of individuals through the income quintiles. Similarly, the discussion of poverty examines the duration of poverty spells and the extent of chronic long-term poverty. Income redistribution is discussed from both a positive and normative perspective.

■ Major Content Changes in Global Economy Chapters

Chapter 20 (International Trade) features a new discussion of offshoring.

Chapter 21 (International Finance) showcases new material on fixed exchange rates, with extended discussion of the Chinese yuan and the effects of fixing the yuan at too low a level on China's foreign exchange reserves.

ORGANIZATION

Our text focuses on core topics with maximum flexibility. We cover all the standard topics of the principles of economics curriculum. And we do so in the order that is increasingly finding favor in the principles course. We believe that a powerful case can be made for teaching the subject in the order in which we present it here.

We introduce and explain the core ideas about efficiency and fairness early and then cover major policy issues in a series of chapters that use only the tools of demand and supply and the ideas of marginal benefit, marginal cost, and consumer and producer surplus. Topics such as consumer choice and cost curves, which are more technical, are covered later.

Extensive reviewing suggests that most teachers agree with us. But we recognize that there is a range of opinion about sequencing, and we have structured our text so that it works equally well if other sequences are preferred.

Deciding the order in which to teach the components of microeconomics involves a tradeoff between building all the foundations and getting to policy issues early in the course. There is little disagreement that the place to begin is with production possibilities and demand and supply. We provide a carefully paced and thoroughly modern treatment of these topics.

Following the order of this text, the course quickly gets to interesting policy issues. Two further chapters lay the foundation: elasticity in Chapter 5 and a discussion of the efficiency and fairness of markets in Chapter 6. Introducing students to both efficiency and fairness (equity) issues early in the course enables a more complete and engaging discussion of topics such as price floors, price ceilings, production quotas, taxes, externalities, public goods, and common resources, all of which we cover in Chapters 7 through 10. Teaching this material early in the course maintains student interest, directly serves the role of the principles course as a foundation for citizenship, and provides an immediate payoff from learning the demand-supply and related tools. Only when these policy issues have been covered do we dig more deeply behind the consumption and production decisions.

Teachers who prefer to cover policy issues later in the course can skip Chapters 6 through 10 and move straight from elasticity to consumer choice (Chapter 11) and then on to the economics of the firm. The policy-related chapters can be covered at any chosen point later in the course.

The flexibility chart on p. xxxix provides detailed information that enables you to rearrange the chapters in a variety of ways. And the alternative course chart on p. xl offers some suggestions of other possible paths through the book.

A RICH ARRAY OF SUPPORT MATERIALS FOR THE STUDENT

Foundations of Microeconomics is accompanied by the most comprehensive set of learning tools ever assembled. All the components of our package are organized by Checkpoint topic so that the student may move easily among the textbook, MyEconLab, and the Study Guide, while mastering a single core concept.

The variety of tools that we provide enables students to select the path through the material that best suits their individual learning styles. The package is technology-enabled, not technology-dependent. Active learners will make extensive use of the MyEconLab personalized Study Plan and tutorial instruction and the animated graphics of eText, our online version of the textbook. Reflective learners may follow a print-only path if they prefer.

■ MyEconLab

MyEconLab—the online homework and tutorial system that is packaged with every new copy of *Foundations*—puts students in control of their own learning through a suite of study and practice tools correlated with the online, interactive version of the textbook and other media tools. Within MyEconLab's structured environment, students practice what they learn, test their understanding, and then pursue a Study Plan that MyEconLab generates for them based on their performance on practice tests.

At the core of MyEconLab are the following features:

- **Practice Tests**—Practice tests for every Checkpoint enable students to test their understanding and identify the areas in which they need to do further work. Practice Test questions based directly on the Practice Problem and Exercise in each Checkpoint and end-of-chapter problems ask students to work with graphs: interpreting them, manipulating them, and even drawing them. Instructors can let students use the supplied pre-built tests or create their own tests.
- **Personalized Study Plan**—Based on a student's performance on practice or assigned tests, MyEconLab generates a Personalized Study Plan that shows where further study is needed. The correlation between the text and MyEconLab is perfect and seamless.
- **Additional Practice Exercises**—The Personalized Study Plans direct students to additional exercises for each topic. Additional practice exercises are keyed to each section of the textbook and link students to the eText with animated graphs.
- **Tutorial Instruction**—Launched from the additional practice exercises, tutorial instruction is provided in the form of solutions to problems, step-by-step explanations, and other media-based explanations.
- **Powerful Graphing Tool**—Integrated into the practice tests and additional practice exercises, the graphing tool lets students manipulate and even draw graphs so that they grasp how the concepts, numbers, and graphs are connected.

- ## Three Types of Graphing Problems:

Draw Graphs—MyEconLab's Draw Graph problems automatically grade the graphs students draw.

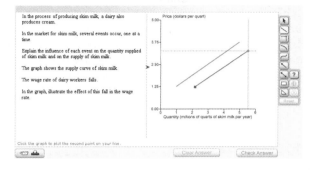

Model-based Graphs—Students can change data inputs and watch graphs shift. Multiple-choice, true/false, and short-answer questions quiz students on their interpretations of the graph.

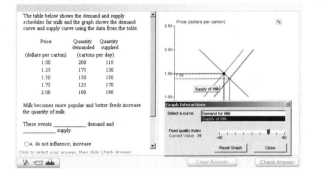

Data Graphs—Students can plot up to five variables against each other, giving them a clear picture of how economic indicators relate to each other.

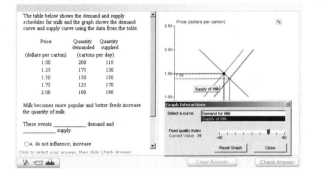

MyEconLab Study Plan links to the following resources:

- **eText**—Quick reference to specific pages of the textbook that correspond to each Study Plan exercise. (MyEconLab is also available in a version that contains a full, searchable online textbook. Ask your Addison-Wesley representative for details.)
- **eStudy Guide**—The entire Study Guide in electronic format and printable.
- **Animated Figures**—Every figure from the textbook is presented in step-by-step animations with audio explanations of the action.
- **Glossary**—A searchable version of the textbook glossary with additional examples and links to related terms.

Additional MyEconLab Resources

- **Ask the Author**—Virtual office hours with Robin Bade and Michael Parkin.
- **Econ Tutor Center**—Staffed by qualified, experienced college economics instructors! The Econ Tutor Center is open five days a week, seven hours a day. Tutors can be reached by phone, fax, e-mail, or White Board technology. The Econ Tutor Center hours are designed to meet your students' study schedules, with evening hours Sunday through Thursday. Students receive one-on-one tutoring on examples, related exercises, and problems.
- **Glossary Flashcards**—Every key term is available as a flashcard, allowing students to quiz themselves on vocabulary from one or more chapters at a time.
- **Economics in the News**—Updated most weekdays during the school year, news items with links to sources for further reading and discussion questions. Once per week, we post a quiz which instructors may assign to test student comprehension of the week's news.
- **eThemes of the Times**—Archived articles from *The New York Times*, correlated to each chapter of the textbook and paired with critical thinking questions.
- **Research Navigator**—(CourseCompass version only) Extensive help on the research process and four exclusive databases of accredited and reliable source material including *The New York Times*, *The Financial Times*, and peer-reviewed journals.

■ Study Guide

Mark Rush of the University of Florida and Tom Meyer of Patrick Henry Community College have prepared the Study Guide. The Study Guide is available in both print and electronic formats. It provides an expanded Chapter Checklist that enables the student to break the learning tasks down into smaller, bite-sized pieces; self-test materials; and additional practice problems. To ensure consistency across the entire package, the authors who wrote the questions for the Test Bank also wrote the self-test questions for the Study Guide.

▌ The Econ Tutor Center

Staffed by qualified, experienced college economics instructors, the Econ Tutor Center is open five days a week, seven hours a day. Tutors can be reached by phone, fax, and e-mail. The Econ Tutor Center hours are designed to meet your students' study schedules, with evening hours Sunday through Thursday. Students receive one-on-one tutoring on examples, related exercises, and problems. Please contact your Addison-Wesley representative for information on how to make this service available to your students.

A QUALITY-ASSURED SUPPORT SYSTEM FOR THE INSTRUCTOR

Our instructor resource tools are the most comprehensive, carefully developed, and accurate materials ever made available. MyEconLab, the Study Guide, the PowerPoint lecture notes, the Instructor's Manual, and the Test Banks all key off the Checkpoints in the textbook. The entire package has a tight integrity. We are the authors of the MyEconLab content and PowerPoint notes. We have paid close attention to the design, structure, and organization of MyEconLab. And we have helped in the reviewing and revising of the Study Guide, Instructor's Manual, and Test Banks to ensure that every element of the package achieves the consistency that students and teachers need.

▌ MyEconLab Instructor Resources

MyEconLab provides flexible tools that allow instructors to easily and effectively customize online course materials to suit their needs. Instructors can create and assign tests, quizzes, or graded homework assignments. MyEconLab saves time by automatically grading all questions and tracking results—including student practice—in an online gradebook. MyEconLab can even grade assignments that require students to draw a graph.

After registering for MyEconLab, instructors have access to downloadable supplements such as Instructor's Manuals, PowerPoint lecture notes, and Test Banks. Test Banks can also be used within MyEconLab, giving instructors ample material from which they can create assignments.

For more information about MyEconLab, or to request an Instructor Access Code, visit www.myeconlab.com.

▌ Instructor's Manual

The Instructor's Manual contains chapter outlines and road maps, answers to in-text exercises, additional exercises with solutions, and a virtual encyclopedia of suggestions on how to enrich class presentation and use class time efficiently. The third edition is particularly enhanced with the addition of many new and lively Lecture Launchers, which were written by Mark Rush, University of Florida; Carol Dole, State University of West Georgia; and Margaret Anne Shannon, Gordon College.

■ Three Test Banks

Three separate Test Banks are available for *Foundations of Microeconomics*, with more than 5,000 multiple-choice, numerical, fill-in-the-blank, short-answer, essay questions, and integrative questions that build on material from more than one Checkpoint or more than one chapter. This edition features the addition of a fifth choice to all multiple-choice questions. Mark Rush reviewed and edited questions from seven dedicated principles instructors and added all fifth choices to form one of the most comprehensive testing systems on the market. Our questions authors are Seemi Ahmad (Dutchess Community College), Sue Bartlett (University of South Florida), Jack Chambless (Valencia Community College), Carol Dole (State University of West Georgia), Paul Harris (Camden County Community College), William Mosher (College of the Holy Cross), and Terry Sutton (Rogers State University). These Test Bank authors also wrote questions for the Study Guide to ensure consistency.

■ PowerPoint Resources

We have created the PowerPoint resources based on our 10 years of experience using this tool in our own classrooms. Every figure and table—every single one, even those used in Checkpoint questions and solutions—is included in the PowerPoint lecture notes. Many of the figures and tables are animated so that you can build them gradually in the classroom. Key figures can be expanded to full-screen size or shrunk to make space for text explanations at a single mouse click during a lecture. We have determined the optimal build sequence for the animated figures and have produced them with the same degree of clarity and precision as the figures in the text.

The speaking notes sections of the PowerPoint files provide material from the Instructor's Manual on teaching tips and suggestions.

■ Overhead Transparencies

Full-color overhead transparencies of *all* figures from the text will improve the clarity of your lectures. They are available to qualified adopters of the text (contact your Addison-Wesley sales representative).

■ Instructor's Resource Disk with Computerized Test Banks

This CD-ROM contains Computerized Test Bank files, Test Bank and Instructor's Manual files in Microsoft Word, and PowerPoint files. All three Test Banks are available in Test Generator Software (TestGen with QuizMaster). Fully networkable, the CD-ROM is available for Windows and Macintosh. TestGen's graphical interface enables instructors to view, edit, and add questions; transfer questions to tests; and print different forms of tests. Tests can be formatted by varying fonts and styles, margins, and headers and footers, as in any word-processing document. Search and sort features let the instructor quickly locate questions and arrange them in a preferred order. QuizMaster, working with your school's computer network, automatically grades the exams, stores the results on disk, and allows the instructor to view and print a variety of reports.

■ FastFax Testing

FastFax Testing is designed for instructors who do not have access to a computer or an assistant who can help prepare tests for students. Simply choose from a large pool of questions in the print Test Banks and include custom headers, if you like. Fill out the test information sheet that lists instructor-selected questions and test preferences that describe how the test should be generated. You may even request multiple forms of a test and receive answer keys for each one.

Turnaround time is usually 48 hours or less and test pages can be mailed or faxed back to you by the date the test is needed. FastFax Testing is fast, reliable, and free to qualified adopters of this text.

■ Economist.com Edition

The premier online source of economic news analysis, economist.com provides your students with insight and opinion on current economic events. Through an agreement between Addison-Wesley and *The Economist*, your students can receive a low-cost subscription to this premium Web site for three months, including the complete text of the current issue of *The Economist* and access to *The Economist's* searchable archives. Other features include Web-only weekly articles, news feeds with current world and business news, and stock market and currency data. Professors who adopt this special edition will receive a complimentary one-year subscription to economist.com.

■ The Wall Street Journal Edition

Addison-Wesley is also pleased to provide your students with access to *The Wall Street Journal*, the most respected and trusted daily source for information on business and economics. For a small additional charge, Addison-Wesley offers your students a reduced cost, 10- or 15-week subscription to *The Wall Street Journal* print edition and *The Wall Street Journal Interactive Edition*. Adopting professors will receive a complimentary one-year subscription of both the print and interactive versions.

■ Financial Times Edition

Featuring international news and analysis from journalists in more than 50 countries, the *Financial Times* will provide your students with insights and perspectives on economic developments around the world. The *Financial Times Edition* provides your students with a 15-week subscription to one of the world's leading business publications. Adopting professors will receive a complimentary one-year subscription to the *Financial Times* as well as access to the Online Edition at FT.com.

■ The Dismal Scientist Edition

The Dismal Scientist provides real-time monitoring of the global economy, allowing your students to go beyond theory and into application. For a nominal fee, a 3-month subscription to The Dismal Scientist can be included with each new textbook. Each subscription includes complete access to all The Dismal Scientist's award-winning features. Adopting professors receive a complimentary one-year subscription.

■ PearsonChoices Alternative Editions . . . your text, your way!

With ever-increasing demands on time and resources, today's college faculty and students want greater value, innovation, and flexibility in products designed to meet teaching and learning goals. We've responded to that need by creating PearsonChoices, a unique program that allows faculty and students to choose from a range of text and media formats that match their teaching and learning styles and students' budgets.

■ Books à la Carte Edition

For today's student on the go, we've created a highly portable version of *Foundations* that is three-hole punched. Students can take only what they need to class, incorporate their own notes, and save money! Each Books à la Carte text arrives with a laminated study card, perfect for students to use when preparing for exams, plus access to MyEconLab.

■ SafariX Textbooks Online

SafariX Textbooks Online is an exciting new service for college students looking to save money on required or recommended textbooks for academic courses. By subscribing to Web Books through SafariX Textbooks Online, students can save up to 50 percent off the suggested list price of print textbooks. Log on to www.safarix.com for details about purchasing *Foundations*.

ACKNOWLEDGMENTS

Working on a project such as this generates many debts that can never be repaid. But they can be acknowledged, and it is a special pleasure to be able to do so here and to express our heartfelt thanks to each and every one of the following long list, without whose contributions we could not have produced *Foundations*.

Mark Rush again coordinated, managed, and contributed to our Study Guide, Instructor's Manual, and Test Bank. He assembled, polished, wrote, and rewrote these materials to ensure their close consistency with the text. He and we were in constant contact as all the elements of our text and package came together. Mark also made many valuable suggestions for improving the text and the Checkpoints. His contribution went well beyond that of a reviewer. And his effervescent sense of humor kept us all in good spirits along the way.

Working closely with Mark, Tom Meyer wrote content for the Study Guide and Carol Dole and Margaret Anne Shannon wrote content for the Instructor's Manual. Maggy Shannon also inspired and energized us with her innovative ideas for chapter openers and Reality Check box content.

Seemi Ahmad, Sue Bartlett, Jack Chambless, Carol Dole, Paul Harris, William Mosher, and Terry Sutton, provided questions for the Study Guide and Test Banks.

The ideas that ultimately became *Foundations* began to form over dinner at the Andover Inn in Andover, Massachusetts, with Denise Clinton and Sylvia Mallory. We gratefully acknowledge Sylvia's role not only at the birth of this project but also in managing its initial development team. Denise has been our ongoing inspiration for more than 10 years. She is the most knowledgeable economics editor in the business, and we are privileged to have the benefit of her enormous experience.

The success of *Foundations* owes much to its outstanding sponsoring editor, Adrienne D'Ambrosio. Adrienne's acute intelligence and sensitive understanding of the market have helped sharpen our vision of this text and package. Her value-added on this project is huge. It has been, and we hope it will for many future editions remain, a joy to work with her.

Once again, Mary Clare McEwing has been our indomitable development editor, ably assisted by Dottie Dennis. We said in the preface to the first edition and repeated in the second that Mary Clare had rounded up the best group of reviewers we'd ever worked with. Perhaps we should stop being astounded! She has done it again. Mary Clare has steered the revision along through several redrafts and polishes.

Charles Spaulding oversaw the new impressive cover design and with Gina Kolenda converted the raw ideas of our brainstorms into an outstandingly designed text. Meredith Nightingale provided the detailed figure designs.

Marianne Groth did an excellent job as editor of our print supplements.

Michelle Neil, Executive Media Producer, and Melissa Honig, Senior Media Producer, have set a new standard for online learning and teaching resources. Michelle spearheaded the effort to set up MyEconLab, worked creatively to improve our technology systems, and worked with our editors and us to develop our media strategy. Melissa managed the building of MyEconLab. They have both been sources of high energy, good sense, and level-headed advice, and quickly found creative solutions to all our technology problems.

Nancy Fenton, our ever cheerful, never stressed production supervisor, worked with a talented team at Elm Street Publishing Services—project editor Ingrid Benson, typesetter Debbie Kubiak, art coordinators Angel Chavez and Angela Gelsomino, and the best proofreader we have ever encountered. Our photo researcher, Beth Anderson, provided us with an outstanding selection of images from which to choose.

Our marketing manager, Stephen Frail, has been a constant source of good judgment and sound advice on content and design issues ranging over the entire package from text to print and electronic supplements.

Our copy editor, Barbara Willette, and supplements copy editor, Kirsten Dickerson, gave our work a thorough review and helpful polish.

Richard Parkin, our technical illustrator, created the figures in the text, the dynamic figures in the eText, and the animated figures in the PowerPoint presentations and contributed many ideas to improve the clarity of our illustrations. Laurel Davies provided painstakingly careful work on MyEconLab questions and acted as one of its accuracy checkers.

Jeannie Gillmore, our personal assistant, worked closely with us in creating MyEconLab Exercises and Guided Solutions. She also served as a meticulous accuracy checker on the text, Study Guide, and Instructor's Manual. John Graham of Rutgers University and Constantin Ogloblin of Georgia Southern University provided careful accuracy reviews of the Test Banks.

Jane McAndrew, economics librarian at the University of Western Ontario, went the extra mile on many occasions to help us track down the data and references we needed.

Finally, our reviewers, whose names appear on the following pages, have made an enormous contribution to this text. Once again we find ourselves using superlatives. But they are called for. In the many texts that we've written, we've not seen reviewing of the quality that we enjoyed on this revision. It has been a pleasure (if at times a challenge) to respond constructively to their many excellent suggestions.

Robin Bade
Michael Parkin
London, Ontario, Canada
robin@econ100.com
michael.parkin@uwo.ca

Reviewers

Charles Aguilar, El Paso Community College
Seemi Ahmad, Dutchess Community College
William Aldridge, Shelton State Community College
Rashid B. Al-Hmoud, Texas Tech University
Ali Ataiifar, Delaware County Community College
John Baffoe-Bonnie, Pennsylvania State University, Delaware County Campus
A. Paul Ballantyne, University of Colorado
Sue Bartlett, University of South Florida
Klaus Becker, Texas Tech University
John Bethune, Barton College
Gautam Bhattacharya, University of Kansas
Gerald W. Bialka, University of North Florida
David Bivin, Indiana University–Purdue University at Indianapolis
Geoffrey Black, Boise State University
Carey Anne Borkoski, Arundel Community College
Barbara Brogan, Northern Virginia Community College
Christopher Brown, Arkansas State University
Donald Bumpass, Sam Houston State University
Seewoonundun Bunjun, East Stroudsburg University
Nancy Burnett, University of Wisconsin at Oshkosh
James L. Butkiewicz, University of Delaware
Barbara Caldwell, University of South Florida
Bruce Caldwell, University of North Carolina, Greensboro
Robert Carlsson, University of South Carolina
Shawn Carter, Jacksonville State University
Jack Chambless, Valencia Community College
Joni Charles, Southwest Texas State University
Robert Cherry, Brooklyn College
Chi-Young Choi, University of New Hampshire
Paul Cichello, Xavier University
Quentin Ciolfi, Brevard Community College
Jim Cobbe, Florida State University
John Cochran, Metropolitan State College
Ludovic Comeau, De Paul University
Carol Conrad, Cerro Coso Community College
Christopher Cornell, Fordham University
Richard Cornwall, University of California, Davis
Kevin Cotter, Wayne State University
Tom Creahan, Morehead State University
Elizabeth Crowell, University of Michigan at Dearborn
Susan Dadres, Southern Methodist University
Troy Davig, College of William and Mary
Jeffrey Davis, ITT Technical Institute (Utah)
Dennis Debrecht, Carroll College
Al DeCooke, Broward Community College
Vince DiMartino, University of Texas at San Antonio
Carol Dole, State University of West Georgia

Kathleen Dorsainvil, Winston-Salem University
John Dorsey, University of Maryland, College Park
Amrik Singh Dua, Mt. San Antonio College
Marie Duggan, Keene State College
David Eaton, Murray State University
Harold W. Elder, University of Alabama
Harry Ellis, University of North Texas
Stephen Ellis, North Central Texas College
Carl Enomoto, New Mexico State University
Chuen-mei Fan, Colorado State University
Gary Ferrier, University of Arkansas
Rudy Fichtenbaum, Wright State University
Kaya Ford, Northern Virginia Community College
Robert Francis, Shoreline Community College
Roger Frantz, San Diego State University
Arthur Friedberg, Mohawk Valley Community College
Julie Gallaway, Southwest Missouri State University
Byron Gangnes, University of Hawaii
Gay Garesché, Glendale Community College
Neil Garston, California State University at Los Angeles
Lisa Geib-Gunderson, University of Maryland
Linda Ghent, Eastern Illinois University
Kirk Gifford, Ricks College
Maria Giuili, Diablo Valley Community College
Mark Gius, Quinnipiac College
Randall Glover, Brevard Community College
Stephan Gohmann, University of Louisville
Richard Gosselin, Houston Community College
John Graham, Rutgers University
Warren Graham, Tulsa Community College
Jang-Ting Guo, University of California, Riverside
Dennis Hammett, University of Texas at El Paso
Leo Hardwick, Macomb Community College
Mehdi Haririan, Bloomsburg University
Paul Harris, Camden County Community College
Gus Herring, Brookhaven College
Michael Heslop, Northern Virginia Community College
Steven Hickerson, Mankato State University
Andy Howard, Rio Hondo College
Yu Hsing, Southeastern Louisiana University
Matthew Hyle, Winona State University
Todd Idson, Boston University
Harvey James, University of Hartford
Russell Janis, University of Massachusetts at Amherst
Ted Joyce, City University of New York, Baruch College
Arthur Kartman, San Diego State University
Chris Kauffman, University of Tennessee
Diane Keenan, Cerritos College
Brian Kench, University of Tampa
John Keith, Utah State University
Joe Kerkvliet, Oregon State University

Douglas Kinnear, Colorado State University
Morris Knapp, Miami Dade Community College
Steven Koch, Georgia Southern University
Kate Krause, University of New Mexico
Stephan Kroll, California State University—Sacramento
Joyce Lapping, University of Southern Maine
Tom Larson, California State University, Los Angeles
Robert Lemke, Florida International University
Tony Lima, California State University at Hayward
Kenneth Long, New River Community College
Marty Ludlum, Oklahoma City Community College
Roger Mack, De Anza College
Michael Magura, University of Toledo
Mark Maier, Glendale College
Paula Manns, Atlantic Cape Community College
Dan Marburger, Arkansas State University
Kathryn Marshall, Ohio State University
Drew E. Mattson, Anoka-Ramsey Community College
Stephen McCafferty, Ohio State University
Thomas McCaleb, Florida State University
Diego Mendez-Carbajo, Illinois Wesleyan University
Thomas Meyer, Patrick Henry Community College
Meghan Millea, Mississippi State University
Michael Milligan, Front Range Community College
Jenny Minier, University of Miami
David Mitchell, Valdosta State University
William Mosher, Clark University
Kevin Murphy, Oakland University
Ronald Nate, Brigham Young University, Idaho
Michael Nelson, Texas A&M University
Rebecca Neumann, University of Wisconsin—Milwaukee
Charles Newton, Houston Community College Southwest
Melinda Nish, Salt Lake Community College
Lee Nordgren, Indiana University at Bloomington
William C. O'Connor, Western Montana College–University of Montana
Fola Odebunmi, Cypress College
Charles Okeke, College of Southern Nevada
Sanjay Paul, Elizabethtown College
Ken Peterson, Furman University
Tim Petry, North Dakota State University
Charles Pflanz, Scottsdale Community College
Jonathon Phillips, North Carolina State University
Paul Poast, Ohio State University
Greg Pratt, Mesa Community College
Fernando Quijano, Dickinson State University
Ratha Ramoo, Diablo Valley College
Karen Reid, University of Wisconsin, Parkside
Mary Rigdon, University of Texas, Austin
Helen Roberts, University of Illinois, Chicago
Greg Rose, Sacramento City College
Barbara Ross, Kapi'olani Community College

Jeffrey Rous, University of North Texas
June Roux, Salem Community College
Udayan Roy, Long Island University
Mark Rush, University of Florida
Joseph Santos, South Dakota State University
Roland Santos, Lakeland Community College
Ted Scheinman, Mount Hood Community College
Jerry Schwartz, Broward Community College
Gautam Sethi, Bard College
Margaret Anne Shannon, Georgia Southern University
Virginia Shingleton, Valparaiso University
Steven S. Shwiff, Texas A & M—Commerce
Charles Sicotte, Rock Valley College
Martin Spechler, Indiana University
John Stiver, University of Connecticut
Terry Sutton, Southeast Missouri State University
Donna Thompson, Brookdale Community College
James Thorson, Southern Connecticut State University
Marc Tomljanovich, Colgate University
Cynthia Royal Tori, Valdosta State University
Ngoc-Bich Tran, San Jacinto College South
Nora Underwood, University of California, Davis
Christian Weber, Seattle University
Ethel Weeks, Nassau Community College
Jack Wegman, Santa Rosa Junior College
Jason White, Northwest Missouri State University
Benjamin Widner, Colorado State University
Barbara Wiens-Tuers, Pennsylvania State University, Altoona
William Wood, James Madison University
Ben Young, University of Missouri, Kansas City
Michael Youngblood, Rock Valley College
Bassam Yousif, Indiana State University
Inske Zandvliet, Brookhaven College
Joachim Zietz, Middle Tennessee State University
Armand Zottola, Central Connecticut State University

Foundations of Microeconomics: Flexibility Chart

Core Principles	Policy Applications	Optional

Core Principles

1. Getting Started

2. The U.S. and Global Economies
Not just a descriptive chapter. Defines the factors of production and introduces the circular flow model.

3. The Economic Problem
Carefully paced and complete first look at the fundamental economic problem. Includes explanation of efficiency and comparative advantage.

4. Demand and Supply
Carefully paced and complete explanation of this core topic.

5. Elasticities of Demand and Supply
A gentle explanation of elasticity with the emphasis on understanding and interpreting elasticity.

6. Efficiency and Fairness of Markets
A chapter that provides a description of the alternative methods of allocating resources and an explanation of the efficiency and fairness of market outcomes. The chapter unifies the micro chapters, and enables a wide range of policy applications to be studied early in the course.

12. Production and Cost

13. Perfect Competition

14. Monopoly

15. Monopolistic Competition

16. Oligopoly

Policy Applications

These chapters are similar to the corresponding chapters in *Foundations of Macroeconomics* and *Foundations of Microeconomics*, but are not identical and are an introduction specifically to both microeconomics and macroeconomics.

7. Government Influences on Markets
Explains the effects of price ceilings, price floors, and production quotas.

8. Taxes
Explains the incidence of taxes and discusses efficiency and equity issues. Chapters 3 through 6 are prerequisites.

9. Externalities
Describes full range of externalities, explains the Coase theorem, and the use of taxes, subsidies, and market solutions. Chapters 3 through 8 are prerequisites.

10. Public Goods and Common Resources
Describes the four types of goods and explains the free-rider problem and the problem of the commons. Chapters 3 through 8 are prerequisites.

Some or all of these chapters may be omitted. Chapter 12 is the foundation of the group and cannot be omitted if any of the others are to be covered. Chapters 15 and 16 build on both 13 and 14.

17. Regulation and Antitrust Law

19. Inequality and Poverty
Explains the sources of inequality and its trends and evaluates alternative redistribution methods.

Optional

1. Appendix: Making and Using Graphs
Good for students with a fear of graphs.

11. Consumer Choice and Demand
This optional chapter may be covered at any point after Chapter 3. Explains both marginal utility theory and (in an appendix) indifference curves.

18. Demand and Supply in Factor Markets
Enables you to cover all the factor market issues in a single chapter.

20. International Trade
Extensive discussion of gains from trade and costs of protection. Can be covered any time after Chapter 3 (with care).

21. International Finance
Application of demand and supply to foreign exchange market. Can be covered any time after Chapter 4 (with care).

Four Alternative Micro Sequences

Traditional	Public Policy Emphasis	Business Emphasis (shorter)	Policy Emphasis (shorter)
1. Getting Started	1. Getting Started	1. Getting Started	1. Getting Started
2. The U.S. and Global Economies	2. The U.S. and Global Economies	2. The U.S. and Global Economies	2. The U.S. and Global Economies
3. The Economic Problem	3. The Economic Problem	3. The Economic Problem	3. The Economic Problem
4. Demand and Supply	4. Demand and Supply	4. Demand and Supply	4. Demand and Supply
5. Elasticities of Demand and Supply	5. Elasticities of Demand and Supply	5. Elasticities of Demand and Supply	5. Elasticities of Demand and Supply
6. Efficiency and Fairness of Markets	6. Efficiency and Fairness of Markets	6. Efficiency and Fairness of Markets	6. Efficiency and Fairness of Markets
7. Government Influences on Markets	7. Government Influences on Markets	7. Government Influences on Markets	7. Government Influences on Markets
11. Consumer Choice and Demand	8. Taxes	12. Production and Cost	8. Taxes
12. Production and Cost	9. Externalities	13. Perfect Competition	9. Externalities
13. Perfect Competition	10. Public Goods and Common Resources	14. Monopoly	10. Public Goods and Common Resources
14. Monopoly	12. Production and Cost	15. Monopolistic Competition	18. Demand and Supply in Factor Markets
15. Monopolistic Competition	13. Perfect Competition	16. Oligopoly	19. Inequality and Poverty
16. Oligopoly	14. Monopoly	17. Regulation and Antitrust Law	20. International Trade
17. Regulation and Antitrust Law	17. Regulation and Antitrust Law	18. Demand and Supply in Factor Markets	
18. Demand and Supply in Factor Markets	18. Demand and Supply in Factor Markets		
19. Inequality and Poverty	19. Inequality and Poverty		
20. International Trade	20. International Trade		

Getting Started

CHAPTER 1

CHAPTER CHECKLIST

When you have completed your study of this chapter,
you will be able to

1 Define economics and explain the kinds of questions that economists try to answer.

2 Explain the core ideas that define the economic way of thinking.

Natasha was earning $90,000 a year at Palm, the maker of hand-held PCs, when the firm sent her to train some of its workers in India. On her return to California, Natasha was laid off—replaced, she suspects, by one of the Indians she had trained. You probably think that it is totally unfair for Natasha to have to compete for a job with workers in poor countries who make only a few dollars a day. Yet because Palm is careful to control its costs, you can buy one of its hand-held PCs for $99. Should we pay more for our PCs so that Natasha can keep her job? Or should Natasha find another job?

Forbes magazine says that there are 691 billionaires in the world. Close to half of them live in the United States. At the top of the pile is Bill Gates, a co-founder of Microsoft, with $50 billion. At the other end of the scale are the 1 billion people who try to scrape by on a dollar a day or less. Isn't there way too much inequality in the world today?

Your economics course will help you to answer questions like the ones we've just asked. And it will help you to understand the powerful forces that shape our world and provide insights that will guide you in your everyday life and work.

1.1 DEFINITION AND QUESTIONS

All economic questions and problems arise because human wants exceed the resources available to satisfy them. We want good health and long lives. We want spacious and comfortable homes. We want a huge range of sports and recreational equipment from running shoes to jet skis. We want the time to enjoy our favorite sports, video games, novels, music, and movies; to travel to exotic places; and just to hang out with friends.

■ Scarcity

Scarcity
The condition that arises because wants exceed the ability of resources to satisfy them.

Our inability to satisfy all our wants is called **scarcity**. The ability of each of us to satisfy our wants is limited by the time we have, the incomes we earn, and the prices we pay for the things we buy. These limits mean that everyone has unsatisfied wants. The ability of all of us as a society to satisfy our wants is limited by the productive resources that exist. These resources include the gifts of nature, our labor and ingenuity, and tools and equipment that we have made.

Everyone, poor and rich alike, faces scarcity. A child wants a $1.00 can of soda and two 50¢ packs of gum but has only $1.00 in his pocket. He faces scarcity. A millionaire wants to spend the weekend playing golf and spend the same weekend at the office attending a business strategy meeting. She faces scarcity. The U.S. government wants to increase defense spending and cut taxes. It faces scarcity. An entire society wants improved health care, an Internet connection in every classroom, an ambitious space exploration program, clean lakes and rivers, and so on. Society faces scarcity.

Faced with scarcity, we must make choices. We must choose among the available alternatives. The child must choose the soda or the gum. The millionaire must choose the golf game or the meeting. The government must choose defense or tax cuts. And society must choose among health care, computers, space exploration, the environment, and so on. Even parrots face scarcity!

Not only do I want a cracker—we all want a cracker!

© The New Yorker Collection 1985
Frank Modell from cartoonbank.com. All Rights Reserved.

■ Economics Defined

Economics is the social science that studies the choices that individuals, businesses, governments, and entire societies make as they cope with *scarcity* and the *incentives* that influence and reconcile those choices.

The subject is extremely broad and touches all aspects of our lives. To get beyond this definition of economics, you need to understand the kinds of questions that economists try to answer and the way they think and go about seeking those answers.

We begin with some key economic questions. Although the scope of economics is broad and the range of questions that economists address is equally broad, two big questions provide a useful summary of the scope of economics:

- How do choices end up determining *what, how,* and *for whom* goods and services get produced?
- When do choices made in the pursuit of *self-interest* also promote the *social interest*?

■ What, How, and For Whom?

Goods and services are the objects and actions that people value and produce to satisfy human wants. Goods are objects that satisfy wants. Running shoes and ketchup are examples. Services are actions that satisfy wants. Haircuts and rock concerts are examples. We produce a dazzling array of goods and services that range from necessities such as food, houses, and health care to leisure items such as DVD players and roller coaster rides.

What?

What determines the quantities of corn we grow, homes we build, and DVD players we produce? Sixty years ago, 25 percent of Americans worked on a farm. That number has shrunk to less than 3 percent today. Over the same period, the number of people who produce goods—in mining, construction, and manufacturing—has also shrunk, from 30 percent to 20 percent. The decrease in farming and the production of goods is matched by an increase in the production of services. How will these quantities change in the future as ongoing changes in technology make an ever-wider array of goods and services available to us?

How?

How are goods and services produced? In a vineyard in France, basket-carrying workers pick the annual grape crop by hand. In a vineyard in California, a huge machine and a few workers do the same job that a hundred grape pickers in France do. Look around you and you will see many examples of this phenomenon—the same job being done in different ways. In some supermarkets, checkout clerks key in prices. In others, they use a laser scanner. One farmer keeps track of his livestock feeding schedules and inventories by using paper-and-pencil records, while another uses a personal computer. GM hires workers to weld auto bodies in some of its plants and uses robots to do the job in others.

Why do we use machines in some cases and people in others? Do mechanization and technological change destroy more jobs than they create? Do they make us better off or worse off?

Economics
The social science that studies the choices that we make as we cope with *scarcity* and the *incentives* that influence and reconcile our choices.

Goods and services
The objects (goods) and the actions (services) that people value and produce to satisfy human wants.

In a California vineyard a machine and a few workers do the same job as a hundred grape pickers in France.

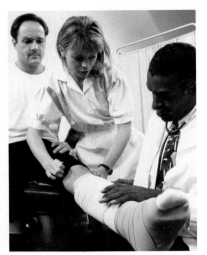

A doctor gets more of the goods and services produced than a nurse or a medical assistant gets.

For Whom?

For whom are goods and services produced? The answer to this question depends on the incomes that people earn and the prices they pay for the goods and services they buy. At given prices, a person who has a high income is able to buy more goods and services than a person who has a low income. Doctors earn much higher incomes than do nurses and medical assistants. So doctors get more of the goods and services produced than nurses and medical assistants get.

You probably know about many other persistent differences in incomes. Men, on the average, earn more than women. Whites, on the average, earn more than minorities. College graduates, on the average, earn more than high school graduates. Americans, on the average, earn more than Europeans, who in turn earn more, on the average, than Asians and Africans. But there are some significant exceptions. The people of Japan and Hong Kong now earn an average income similar to that of Americans. And there is a lot of income inequality throughout the world.

What determines the incomes we earn? Why do doctors earn larger incomes than nurses? Why do white male college graduates earn more than minority female high school graduates? Why do Americans earn more, on the average, than Africans?

Economics explains how the choices that individuals, businesses, and governments make and the interactions of those choices end up determining *what*, *how*, and *for whom* goods and services get produced. In answering these questions, we have a deeper agenda in mind. We're not interesting in just knowing how many DVD players get produced, how they get produced, and who gets to enjoy them. We ultimately want to know the answer to the second big economic question that we'll now explore.

■ When Is the Pursuit of Self-Interest in the Social Interest?

Every day, you and 296 million other Americans, along with 6.1 billion people in the rest of the world, make economic choices that result in *"what," "how,"* and *"for whom"* goods and services get produced.

Are the goods and services produced, and the quantities in which they are produced, the right ones? Do the scarce resources get used in the best possible way? Do the goods and services that we produce go to the people who benefit most from them?

Self-Interest and the Social Interest

Self-interest
The choices that are best for the individual who makes them.

Social interest
The choices that are best for society as a whole.

Choices that are the best for the individual who makes them are choices made in the pursuit of **self-interest**. Choices that are the best for society as a whole are said to be in the **social interest**. The social interest has two dimensions: *efficiency* and *equity*. We'll explore these concepts in later chapters. For now, think of efficiency as being achieved by baking the biggest possible pie. And think of equity as being achieved by sharing the pie in the fairest possible way.

You know that your own choices are the best ones for you—or at least you *think* they're the best at the time that you make them. You use your time and other resources in the way that makes most sense to you. But you don't think much about how your choices affect other people. You order a home delivery pizza because you're hungry and want to eat. You don't order it thinking that the delivery person or the cook needs an income. You make choices that are in your self-interest—choices that you think are best for you.

When you act on your economic decisions, you come into contact with thousands of other people who produce and deliver the goods and services that you decide to buy or who buy the things that you sell. These people have made their own decisions—what to produce and how to produce it, whom to hire or whom to work for, and so on.

Like you, everyone else makes choices that they think are best for them. When the pizza delivery person shows up at your home, he's not doing you a favor. He's earning his income and hoping for a good tip.

Could it be possible that when each one of us makes choices that are in our own best interest—our self-interest—it turns out that these choices are also the best for society as a whole—in the social interest?

Much of the rest of this book helps you to learn what economists know about this question and its answer. To help you start thinking about the question, we're going to illustrate it with eight topics that generate heated discussion in today's world. You're already at least a little bit familiar with each one of them. They are

- Globalization and international outsourcing
- The new economy
- Disappearing tropical rainforests
- Water shortages
- Global warming
- Natural disasters
- Unemployment
- A Social Security time bomb

Globalization and International Outsourcing

Globalization and international outsourcing—the expansion of international trade and the production of components and services by firms in other countries—has been going on for centuries. But during the 1990s, its pace accelerated as advances in microchips, satellites, and fiber-optic cables lowered the cost of communication. A phone call, a video-conference, or a face-to-face meeting involving people who live 10,000 miles apart has become an everyday and easily affordable event.

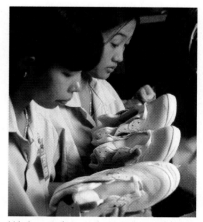

Workers in Asia make our shoes.

This explosion of communication has globalized production decisions. When Nike produces more sports shoes, people in China, Indonesia, or Malaysia get more work. When Steven Spielberg wants an animation sequence for a new movie, programmers in New Zealand write the code. And when China Airlines wants a new airplane, Americans who work for Boeing build it.

The number of jobs in manufacturing and routine services is shrinking in the United States and Europe and expanding in India, China, and other Asian economies. And production is growing more rapidly in Asia than in the United States and Europe. China is already the world's second largest economy, and if the current trends continue, it will become the largest economy during the 2020s.

But globalization is leaving some people behind. The nations of Africa and parts of South America are not sharing in the prosperity that globalization is bringing to other parts of the world.

Is globalization in the social interest, or does it benefit some at the expense of others? The owners of multinational firms clearly benefit from lower production costs. So do the consumers of low-cost imported goods and services. But don't displaced American workers lose? And doesn't even the worker in Malaysia who sews your new running shoes for a few cents an hour also lose?

The New Economy

The 1980s and 1990s were years of extraordinary economic change that have been called the *Information Revolution*. This name suggests a parallel with the *Industrial Revolution* of the years around 1800 and the *Agricultural Revolution* of 12,000 years ago.

The computer chip has transformed our lives.

The changes that occurred during the last 25 years were based on one major technology: the microprocessor or computer chip. Moore's law predicted that the number of transistors that could be placed on one integrated chip would double every 18 months. This prediction turned out to be remarkably accurate.

The spin-offs from faster and cheaper computing have been widespread. Telecommunications became much faster and cheaper, music and movie recording became more realistic and cheaper, millions of routine tasks that previously required human decision and action were automated. You encounter these automated tasks every day when you check out at the supermarket, use an ATM, or call a government department or large business. All the new products and processes and the low-cost computing power that made them possible were produced by people who made choices in the pursuit of self-interest. They did not result from any grand design or government plan.

When Gordon Moore set up Intel and started making chips, no one had told him to do so, and he wasn't thinking how much easier it would be for you to turn in your essay on time if you had a faster PC. When Bill Gates quit Harvard to set up Microsoft, he wasn't trying to create the best operating system and improve people's computing experience. Moore and Gates and thousands of other entrepreneurs were in hot pursuit of the big payoffs that many of them achieved. Yet their actions did make many other people better off. They did advance the social interest.

But could more have been done? Were resources used in the best possible way during the information revolution? Did Intel make the best possible chips and sell them in the right quantities for the right prices? Or was the quality of the chips too low and the price too high? And what about Microsoft? Did Bill Gates have to be paid almost $50 billion to produce the successive generations of Windows and Word? Were these programs developed in the social interest?

Disappearing Tropical Rainforests

Tropical rainforests in South America, Africa, and Asia support the lives of 30 million species of plants, animals, and insects—approaching 50 percent of all species on the planet. The Amazon rainforest alone converts about 1 trillion pounds of carbon dioxide into oxygen each year. These rainforests also provide us with the ingredients for many goods including soaps, mouthwashes, shampoos, food preservatives, rubber, nuts, and fruits.

Logging is destroying the world's rainforests.

Yet tropical rainforests cover less than two percent of the earth's surface and are heading for extinction. Logging, cattle ranching, mining, oil extraction, hydroelectric dams, and subsistence farming are destroying the equivalent to two football fields every second, or an area larger than New York City every day. At the current rate of destruction, almost all the tropical rainforest ecosystems will be gone by 2030.

Each one of us makes economic choices that are in our self-interest to consume products, some of which are destroying our rainforests. Are our choices damaging the social interest? And if they are, what can be done to change the incentives we face and change our behavior?

Water Shortages

The world is awash with water—it is our most abundant resource. But 97 percent of it is seawater. Another 2 percent is frozen in glaciers and ice. The 1 percent of the earth's water that is available for human consumption would be sufficient if only it were in the right places. Finland, Canada, and a few other places have more water than they can use, but Australia, Africa, and California (and many other places) could use much more water than they can get.

Some people pay less for water than others. California farmers, for example, pay less than California households. Some of the highest prices for water are faced by people in the poorest countries who must either buy from a water dealer's truck or carry water in buckets over many miles.

In the United States, water is provided by public enterprises. In the United Kingdom, private companies deliver the water.

In India and Bangladesh, plenty of rain falls, but it falls during a short wet season and the rest of the year is dry. Dams could help to reduce the shortage in the dry season but too few have been built in those countries.

Are we managing our water resources properly? Are the decisions that each of us makes in our self-interest to use, conserve, and transport water also in the social interest?

Water is abundant but clean water is scarce.

Global Warming

The earth is getting hotter. Since the late nineteenth century, its surface temperature has increased about 1 degree Fahrenheit, and close to a half of that increase occurred over the past 25 years. While these changes are small, particularly when viewed against the temperature fluctuations associated with Ice Ages, they are large enough to have a lot of people worried.

Most climate scientists believe that the current warming has come at least in part from human economic activity—from self-interested choices—and that, if left unchecked, the warming will bring large future economic costs.

As part of an attempt to slow global warming, an international meeting in Japan in 1997 led to the Kyoto Protocol, an agreement that seeks legally binding emissions cuts for the industrialized nations. But the Protocol does not impose limits on the poorer developing nations. Almost the entire world signed onto Kyoto. But the United States and Australia refused to do so. They argue that the agreement does too little to address the global warming problem and that their own independent efforts will make a more effective contribution.

Human activity is raising the earth's temperature.

Are the choices that each of us makes to use energy damaging the social interest? What needs to be done to make our choices serve the social interest? Would the United States signing onto the Kyoto Protocol serve the social interest? What other measures must be introduced?

Natural Disasters

When Hurricane Katrina hit New Orleans on August 29, 2005, a thousand people died, tens of thousands lost everything they owned, and hundreds of thousands were forced from their homes. Much of the city was flooded and polluted, and posed a health risk for those who remained. Looting erupted as desperate people sought food and medicine and as others seized an opportunity to profit from tragedy and the temporary absence of law and order. Beyond the human tragedies, crude oil production and gasoline refining took a hit and one of the nation's busiest ports was silenced.

Katrina highlighted the tension between self-interest and the social interest.

But Katrina didn't only unleash devastation and disaster for the people of New Orleans. It also unleashed an economic response. The prices of oil and gasoline increased, which encouraged more careful use of these now less plentiful resources. The price of plywood needed to repair damaged homes jumped, which brought forth a greater quantity of this now more valued item.

Millions of individual Americans contributed money and thousands who work for organizations such as the Red Cross and the Salvation Army contributed time, energy, and effort to bring shelter, food, and comfort to the displaced. Governments also acted, but more slowly. Gradually levees were restored, streets were pumped dry, and the city slowly started to return to life.

The events that played out following Katrina provide a powerful illustration of the tension between self-interest and the social interest and raise questions about the ability of markets and governments to cope with major disasters.

Without government enforced laws, self-interest can be carried too far and damage the social interest. But can government do more? What is the best balance between government and private provision of services and aid to people struck down by natural disaster? And do price hikes that clearly serve the self-interest of producers and hurt the self-interest of consumers further the social interest?

Unemployment

During the 1930s, in a period called the *Great Depression*, more than 20 percent of the labor force was unemployed. One of the triumphs of economics is that we have developed policies that can stabilize the economy and avoid depressions. Yet even today, when only 5 percent of Americans are unemployed, more than 40 percent of African-American teenagers are unemployed. Why can't everyone who wants a job find one? If economic choices arise from scarcity, why are resources left unused?

During the 1930s, the longest lines were for jobs.

People get jobs because other people think they can earn a profit by hiring them. And people accept jobs when they think the pay and other conditions are good enough. So the number of people with jobs is determined by the self-interest of employers and workers. But is the number of jobs also in the social interest?

A Social Security Time Bomb

Every single day since September 30, 2004, the U.S. government has run a budget deficit of $2.21 billion, which means that the government's debt has increased each day by that amount. On March 2, 2005, the day these words were written, your personal share of the outstanding government debt was $26,094.

Also, during 2004, Americans bought goods and services from the rest of the world in excess of what foreigners bought from the United States to the tune of $600 billion. To pay for these goods and services, Americans borrowed from the rest of the world.

These large deficits are just the beginning of an even bigger problem. From about 2019 onwards, the retirement and health-care benefits to which older Americans are entitled are going to cost increasingly more than the current Social Security taxes can pay for. With no changes in taxes or benefit rates, the deficit and debt will swell ever higher.

A social security time bomb is ticking as benefits grow faster than contributions.

Deficits and the debts they create cannot persist indefinitely, and debts must somehow be repaid. They will most likely be repaid by you, not by your parents. When we make our voter choices and our choices to buy from or sell to the rest of the world, we pursue our self-interest. Do our choices damage the social interest?

CHECKPOINT 1.1

1 **Define economics and explain the kinds of questions that economists try to answer.**

Practice Problems 1.1

1. Economics studies choices that arise from one fact. What is that fact?
2. Provide three examples of wants in the United States today that are especially pressing but not satisfied.
3. Which of the following headlines deals with *what, how,* and *for whom* questions?
   a. With more research, we will cure cancer.
   b. A good education is the right of every child.
   c. The government must trim its budget deficit.
4. Explain how the following headlines concern self-interest and social interest:
   a. Whole Foods, a U.S. supermarket, is opening in Britain and Starbucks is everywhere in China.
   b. Cigarette packs must carry a health warning.

Exercises 1.1

1. Every day, we make many choices. Why can't we avoid having to make choices?
2. Look at today's newspaper and find an example of a want that is not satisfied.
3. Check the local media for headlines that ask two of the *what, how,* and *for whom* questions.
4. Which of the following headlines deals with *what, how,* and *for whom* questions?
   a. Major league baseball's turf keepers earn about $85,000, umpires earn about $350,000, and players make millions a year.
   b. Many full-service gas stations are switching to self-serve.
   c. Retail trends analysts make as much as $300,000 a year, while retail salespeople make less than $10 an hour.
5. Explain how the following headlines concern self-interest and social interest:
   a. President George W. Bush powers his Texas ranch with solar electricity.
   b. Today's upper-class traveler goes on safari in southern Africa or stays at eco-resorts that cost $1,000 a night but do not have electricity.

Solutions to Practice Problems 1.1

1. The fact is scarcity—human wants exceed the resources available.
2. Security from international terrorism, cleaner air in our cities, better public schools. (You can perhaps think of some more.)
3a. More research is a *how* question, and a cure for cancer is a *what* question.
3b. Good education is a *what* question, and every child is a *for whom* question.
3c. Whether the government cuts expenditures or raises taxes, it is a *for whom* question and a *what* question.
4a. Decisions made by Whole Foods and Starbucks are in their self-interest.
4b. The health warning concerns the social interest, but the person who heeds it makes a decision in self-interest.

1.2 THE ECONOMIC WAY OF THINKING

The definition of economics and the kinds of questions that economists try to answer give you a flavor of the scope of economics. But they don't tell you how economists *think* about these questions and go about seeking answers to them. You're now going to see how economists approach their work.

We'll break this task into three parts. First, we'll explain the core ideas that economists constantly and repeatedly use to frame their view of the world. These ideas will soon have you thinking like an economist. Second, we'll explain the distinction between the micro and macro views of the economic world. Finally, we'll look at economics both as a social science and as a policy tool that governments, businesses, and *you* can use.

■ Core Economic Ideas

Five core ideas summarize the economic approach or economic way of thinking about the choices that must be made to cope with scarcity:

- People make *rational choices* by comparing costs and benefits.
- *Cost* is what you *must* give up to get something.
- *Benefit* is what you gain when you get something and is measured by what you *are willing to* give up to get it.
- A rational choice is made on the *margin.*
- Choices respond to *incentives.*

■ Rational Choice

The most basic idea of economics is that in making choices, people act rationally. A **rational choice** is one that uses the available resources to best achieve the objective of the person making the choice.

Rational choice
A choice that uses the available resources to best achieve the objective of the person making the choice.

Only the wants and preferences of the person making a choice are relevant to determine its rationality. For example, you might like chocolate ice cream more than vanilla ice cream, but your friend prefers vanilla. So it is rational for you to choose chocolate and for your friend to choose vanilla.

A rational choice might turn out not to have been the best choice after the event. A farmer might decide to plant wheat rather than soybeans. Then, when the crop comes to market, the price of soybeans might be much higher than the price of wheat. The farmer's choice was rational when it was made, but subsequent events made it less profitable than the alternative choice.

The idea of rational choice provides an answer to the first question: What goods and services will get produced and in what quantities? The answer is: Those that people rationally choose to buy!

But how do people choose rationally? Why have most people chosen to buy Microsoft's Windows operating system rather than another? Why do more people today choose to drink bottled water and sports energy drinks than did in the past? Why has the U.S. government chosen to fund the building of an interstate highway system and not an interstate high-speed railroad system?

We make rational choices by comparing *costs* and *benefits.* But economists think about costs and benefits in a special and revealing way. Let's look at the economic concepts of cost and benefit.

■ Cost: What You *Must* Give Up

Whatever you choose to do, you could have done something else instead. You could have done lots of things other than what you actually did. But one of these other things is the *best* alternative given up. The best thing that you must give up to get something is the **opportunity cost** of the thing that you get. The thing that you could have chosen—the highest-valued alternative forgone—is the opportunity cost of the thing that you did choose.

We use the term *opportunity cost* to emphasize that when we make a choice in the face of scarcity, we give up an opportunity to do something else. You can quit school right now, or you can remain in school. Suppose that if you quit school, the best job you can get is at Kinko's, where you can earn $10,000 during the year. The opportunity cost of remaining in school includes the things that you could have bought with this $10,000. The opportunity cost also includes the value of the leisure time that you must forgo to study.

Opportunity cost of the thing you get is *only* the alternative forgone. It does not include all the expenditures that you make. For example, your expenditure on tuition is part of the opportunity cost of being in school. But your meal plan and rent are not. Whether you're in school or working, you must eat and have somewhere to live. So the cost of your school meal plan and your rent are *not* part of the opportunity cost of being in school.

Also, past expenditures that cannot be reversed are not part of opportunity cost. Suppose you've paid your term's tuition and it is nonrefundable. If you now contemplate quitting school, the paid tuition is irrelevant. It is called a sunk cost. A **sunk cost** is a previously incurred and irreversible cost. Whether you remain in school or quit school, the tuition that you've paid is not part of the opportunity cost of remaining in school.

■ Benefit: Gain Measured by What You *Are Willing to* Give Up

The **benefit** of something is the gain or pleasure that it brings. Benefit is how a person *feels* about something. For example, you might be anxious to get *Tekken 5*, a recently released video game. It will bring you a large benefit. And you might have almost no interest in a Yo Yo Ma CD of Vivaldi's cello concertos. It will bring you a small benefit.

Opportunity cost
The opportunity cost of something is the best thing you *must* give up to get it.

Sunk cost
A previously incurred and irreversible cost.

Benefit
The benefit of something is the gain or pleasure that it brings.

For these students, the opportunity cost of being in school is worth bearing.

For the full-time fast-food worker, the opportunity cost of remaining in school is too high.

Economists measure the benefit of something by what a person *is willing to* give up to get it. You can buy CDs or magazines. The magazines that you are willing to give up to get a CD measure the benefit that you get from a CD.

■ On the Margin

Margin means "border" or "edge." So you can think of a choice on the margin as one that adjusts the borders or edges of a plan to determine the best course of action. Making a choice on the **margin** means comparing *all* the relevant alternatives systematically and incrementally.

For example, you must choose how to divide the next hour between studying and e-mailing your friends. To make this choice, you must evaluate the costs and benefits of the alternative possible allocations of your next hour. You choose on the margin by considering whether you will be better off or worse off if you spend an extra few minutes studying or an extra few minutes e-mailing.

The margin might involve a small change, as it does when you're deciding how to divide an hour between studying and e-mailing friends. Or it might involve a large change, as it does, for example, when you're deciding whether to remain in school for another year. Attending school for part of the year is no better (and might be worse) than not attending at all. So you likely will want to commit the entire year to school or to something else. But you still choose on the margin. It is just that the marginal change is now a change for one year rather than a change for a few minutes.

Marginal Cost

The opportunity cost of a one-unit increase in an activity is called **marginal cost**. Marginal cost is what you *must* give up to get *one more* unit of something. Think about your marginal cost of going to the movies for a third time in a week. Your marginal cost is what you must give up to see that one additional movie. It is *not* what you give up to see all three movies. The reason is that you've already given up something for two movies, so you don't count this cost as resulting from the decision to see the third movie.

The marginal cost of any activity increases as you do more of it. You know that going to the movies decreases your study time and lowers your grade. Suppose that seeing a second movie in a week lowers your grade by five percentage points. Seeing a third movie will lower your grade by more than five percentage points. Your marginal cost of moviegoing is increasing.

Marginal Benefit

The benefit of a one-unit increase in an activity is called **marginal benefit**. Marginal benefit is what you gain when you get *one more* unit of something. But the marginal benefit of something *is measured by* what you *are willing to* give up to get that one additional unit.

A fundamental feature of marginal benefit is that it diminishes. Think about your marginal benefit from movies. If you've been studying hard and haven't seen a movie this week, your marginal benefit from seeing your next movie is large. But if you've been on a movie binge this week, you now want a break and your marginal benefit is small.

Because the marginal benefit of a movie decreases as you see more movies, you are willing to give up less to see one more movie. For example, you know that going to the movies decreases your study time and lowers your grade. You pay

---

Margin
A choice on the margin is a choice that is made by comparing *all* the relevant alternatives systematically and incrementally.

Marginal cost
The opportunity cost that arises from a one-unit increase in an activity. The marginal cost of something is what you *must* give up to get *one additional* unit of it.

Marginal benefit
The benefit that arises from a one-unit increase in an activity. The marginal benefit of something is *measured* by what you are *willing to* give up to get *one additional* unit of it.

for seeing a movie with a lower grade. You might be willing to give up ten percentage points to see your first movie in a week. But you won't be willing to take such a big hit on your grade to see a second movie in a week. Your willingness to pay to see a movie is decreasing.

Making a Rational Choice

So will you go to the movies for that third time in a week? If the marginal cost is less than the marginal benefit, your rational choice will be to see the third movie. If the marginal cost exceeds the marginal benefit, your rational choice will be to spend the evening studying. We make a rational choice and use our scarce resources in the way that makes us as well off as possible when we take those actions for which marginal benefit exceeds or equals marginal cost.

■ Responding to Incentives

The choices we make depend on the incentives we face. An **incentive** is a reward or a penalty—a "carrot" or a "stick"—that encourages or discourages an action. We respond positively to "carrots" and negatively to "sticks." The carrots that we face are marginal benefits. The sticks are marginal costs. A change in marginal benefit or a change in marginal cost brings a change in the incentives that we face and leads us to change our actions.

Most students believe that the payoff from studying just before a test is greater than the payoff from studying a month before a test. In other words, as a test date approaches, the marginal benefit of studying increases and the incentive to study becomes stronger. For this reason, we observe an increase in study time and a decrease in leisure pursuits during the last few days before a test. And the more important the test, the greater is this effect.

A change in marginal cost changes incentives. For example, suppose that last week, you found your course work easy and scored 100 percent on your practice quizzes. The marginal cost of taking an evening off to enjoy a movie was low. Your grade on this week's test will not suffer, so you have a movie feast. But this week the going has gotten tough. You are just not getting it, and your practice test scores are low. If you take off even one evening, your grade on next week's test will suffer. The marginal cost of seeing a movie is higher this week than it was last week. So you decide to give the movies a miss.

A central idea of economics is that by observing changes in incentives, we can predict how choices will change.

Incentive
A reward or a penalty—a "carrot" or a "stick"—that encourages or discourages an action.

Changes in marginal benefit and marginal cost change the incentive to study or to enjoy a movie.

■ The Micro and Macro Views of the World

Just as doctors specialize in different branches of medicine, so economists specialize in different branches of economics. The major division of the subject is into two parts: microeconomics (or micro) and macroeconomics (or macro).

Microeconomics

Microeconomics is the study of the choices that individuals and businesses make and the way these choices interact and are influenced by governments. Some examples of microeconomic questions are: Will you buy a flat screen or traditional television? Will Sony sell more PlayStations if it cuts the price? Will a cut in the income tax rate encourage people to work longer hours? Will a hike in the gas tax lead to smaller automobiles? Are MP3 downloads killing CDs?

Macroeconomics

Macroeconomics is the study of the aggregate (or total) effects on the national economy and the global economy of the choices that individuals, businesses, and governments make. Some examples of macroeconomic questions are: Why did production and jobs expand so slowly in the United States in the early 2000s? Why are incomes growing much faster in China and India than in the United States? Why are production and incomes stagnating in Japan? Why are Americans borrowing more than $2 billion a day from the rest of the world?

Micro and Macro Dimensions

All the issues that we reviewed earlier in this chapter—globalization and international outsourcing, the new economy, disappearing tropical rainforests, water shortages, global warming, natural disasters, unemployment, and the Social Security time bomb— have a micro and a macro dimension.

The effect of globalization and international outsourcing on the textile industry is a micro topic; its effect on average incomes in the United States and other countries is a macro topic. The influence of the Internet and online commerce is a micro topic; its influence on economy-wide production and jobs is a macro topic. The disappearing tropical rainforests, water shortages, global warming, and natural disasters affect individual industries and products, which are micro topics, but also affect total production, incomes, and jobs, which are macro topics. Unemployment in a region or industry is a micro topic; the national unemployment rate is a macro topic. And finally, Social Security arrangements affect the distribution of income, a micro topic, and the stability of the entire economy, a macro topic.

Microeconomics
The study of the choices that individuals and businesses make and the way these choices interact and are influenced by governments.

Macroeconomics
The study of the aggregate (or total) effects on the national economy and the global economy of the choices that individuals, businesses, and governments make.

The distinction between microeconomics and macroeconomics is similar to the distinction between two views of a display of flags in an Olympic stadium. The micro view (left) is of a single participant and the actions he or she is taking. The macro view (right) is the patterns formed by the joint actions of all the people participating in the entire display.

■ Economics as Social Science

As social scientists, economists seek to discover how the economic world works. In pursuit of this goal, like all scientists, they distinguish between two types of statements:

- Positive statements
- Normative statements

Positive Statements

Positive statements are about what *is*. They say what is currently believed about the way the world operates. A positive statement might be right or wrong. But we can test a positive statement by checking it against the facts. "Our planet is warming because of the amount of coal that we're burning" is a positive statement. "A rise in the minimum wage will bring more teenage unemployment" is another positive statement. Each statement might be right or wrong, and it can be tested.

A central task of economists is to test positive statements about how the economic world works and to weed out those that are wrong. Economics first got off the ground in the late 1700s (see *Eye on the Past* on p. 17), so economics is a young subject compared with, for example, math and physics, and much remains to be discovered.

Normative Statements

Normative statements are statements about what *ought to be*. These statements depend on values and cannot be tested. The statement "We ought to cut back on our use of coal" is a normative statement. "The minimum wage should not be increased" is another normative statement. You may agree or disagree with either of these statements, but you can't test them. They express an opinion, but they don't assert a fact that can be checked. And they are not economics.

Unscrambling Cause and Effect

Economists are especially interested in positive statements about cause and effect. Are computers getting cheaper because people are buying them in greater quantities? Or are people buying computers in greater quantities because they are getting cheaper? Or is some third factor causing both the price of a computer to fall and the quantity of computers to increase? These are examples of positive statements that economists want to test. But doing so can be difficult.

The central idea that economists (and all scientists) use to unscramble cause and effect is *ceteris paribus*. **Ceteris paribus** is a Latin term (often abbreviated as *cet. par.*) that means "other things being equal" or "if all other relevant things remain the same." Ensuring that other things are equal is crucial in many activities, including athletic events, and all successful attempts to make scientific progress use this device. By changing one factor at a time and holding all the other relevant factors constant, we isolate the factor of interest and are able to investigate its effects in the clearest possible way.

In economics, we observe the outcomes of the simultaneous operation of many factors. Consequently, it is hard to sort out the effects of each individual factor and to compare the effects with what a model predicts. To cope with this problem, economists use natural experiments, statistical investigations, and economic experiments.

Ceteris paribus
Other things remaining the same (often abbreviated as *cet. par.*).

In track and field, other things are equal.

A natural experiment is a situation that arises in the ordinary course of economic life in which the one factor of interest is different and other things are equal (or similar). For example, Canada has higher unemployment benefits than the United States, but the people in the two nations are similar. So to study the effect of unemployment benefits on the unemployment rate, economists might compare the United States with Canada.

A statistical investigation looks for a **correlation**—a tendency for the values of two variables to move together (either in the same direction or in opposite directions) in a predictable and related way. For example, cigarette smoking and lung cancer are correlated. Sometimes a correlation shows a causal influence of one variable on the other. For example, smoking causes lung cancer. But sometimes the direction of causation is hard to determine.

An economic experiment puts people in a decision-making situation and varies the influence of one factor at a time to discover how they respond.

Correlation
The tendency for the values of two variables to move in a predictable and related way.

■ Economics as Policy Tool

Economics is useful. And you don't have to be an economist to think like one and to use the insights of economics as a policy tool. The subject provides a way of approaching problems in all aspects of our lives:

- Personal
- Business
- Government

Personal Economic Policy

Should you take out a student loan? Should you get a weekend job? Should you buy a used car or a new one? Should you rent an apartment or take out a loan and buy one? Should you pay off your credit card balance or make just the minimum payment? How should you allocate your time between study, working for a wage, caring for family members, and having fun? How should you allocate your time between studying economics and your other subjects? Should you quit school after getting a bachelor's degree or should you go for a masters or a professional qualification?

All these questions involve a marginal benefit and a marginal cost. And although some of the numbers might be hard to pin down, you will make more solid decisions if you approach these questions with the tools of economics.

Business Economic Policy

Should Sony make only flat panel televisions and stop making conventional ones? Should Texaco get more oil and gas from the Gulf of Mexico or from Alaska? Should Palm outsource its online customer services to India or run the operation from California? Should Miramax produce *Shrek 3*, a sequel to *Shrek 2*? Can Microsoft compete with Google in the search engine business? Can eBay compete with the surge of new Internet auction services? Is Manny Ramirez really worth $22,500,000 to the Boston Red Sox?

Like personal economic questions, these business questions involve the evaluation of a marginal benefit and a marginal cost. Some of the questions require a broader investigation of the interactions of individuals and firms. But again, by approaching these questions with the tools of economics and by hiring economists as advisers, businesses can make better decisions.

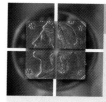

Adam Smith and the Birth of Economics as a Modern Social Science

Many people had written about economics before Adam Smith, but he made economics a social science.

Born in 1723 in Kirkcaldy, a small fishing town near Edinburgh, Scotland, Smith was the only child of the town's customs officer. Lured from his professorship (he was a full professor at 28) by a wealthy Scottish duke who gave him a pension of £300 a year—ten times the average income at that time—Smith devoted ten years to writing his masterpiece, *An Inquiry into the Nature and Causes of the Wealth of Nations,* published in 1776.

Why, Adam Smith asked in that book, are some nations wealthy while others are poor? He was pondering these questions at the height of the Industrial Revolution. During these years, new technologies were applied to the manufacture of textiles, iron, transportation, and agriculture.

Adam Smith answered his questions by emphasizing the role of the division of labor and free markets. To illustrate his argument, he used the example of a pin factory. He guessed that one person, using the hand tools available in the 1770s, might make 20 pins a day. Yet, he observed, by using those same hand tools but breaking the process into a number of individually small operations in which people specialize—by the division of labor—ten people could make a staggering 48,000 pins a day. One draws out the wire, another straightens it, a third cuts it, a fourth points it, a fifth grinds it. Three specialists make the head, and a fourth attaches it. Finally, the pin is polished and packaged.

But a large market is needed to support the division of labor: One factory employing ten workers would need to sell more than 15 million pins a year to stay in business!

Government Economic Policy

How can California balance its budget? Should the federal government cut taxes or raise them? How can the tax system be simplified? Should people be permitted to invest their Social Security money in stocks that they pick themselves? Should Medicaid and Medicare be extended to the entire population? Should there be a special tax to penalize corporations that send jobs overseas? Should cheap foreign imports of furniture and textiles be limited? Should the farms that grow tomatoes and sugar beets receive a subsidy? Should water be transported from Washington and Oregon to California?

These government policy questions call for decisions that involve the evaluation of a marginal benefit and a marginal cost and an investigation of the interactions of individuals and businesses. Yet again, by approaching these questions with the tools of economics, governments make better decisions.

Notice that all the policy questions we've just posed involve a blend of the positive and the normative. Economics can't help with the normative part—the objective. But for a given objective, economics provides a method of evaluating alternative solutions. That method is to evaluate the marginal benefits and marginal costs and to find the solution that brings the greatest available gain.

2 Explain the core ideas that define the economic way of thinking.

Practice Problems 1.2

1. Every week, Kate plays tennis for two hours, and her grade on each math test is 70 percent. Last week, after playing for two hours, Kate considered playing for another hour. She decided to play for another hour and cut her study time by one hour. But last week, her math grade fell to 60 percent.
   a. What was Kate's opportunity cost of the third hour of tennis?
   b. Given that Kate played the third hour, what can you conclude about her marginal benefit and marginal cost of the second hour of tennis?
   c. Was Kate's decision to play the third hour of tennis rational?
   d. Did Kate make her decision on the margin?
2. Check the local media and find an example of:
   a. A positive statement
   b. A normative statement

Exercises 1.2

1. Bill Gates gives away millions of dollars a year to universities, cancer research, a children's hospital, and the Seattle Symphony. Are his donations rational? In making these donations, might Bill Gates have responded to any incentive? Does he make his decision about his donations on the margin?

2. Tony is an engineering student, who is considering taking an extra course in history. What things might be part of his costs and benefits of the history course? Think of an incentive that might encourage him to take the course.

3. Check the local media and find three examples of:
   a. Macroeconomic issues and microeconomic issues
   b. Positive statements
   c. Normative statements
   d. Economics as a policy tool

Solutions to Practice Problems 1.2

1a. Kate's opportunity cost of the third hour of tennis was the ten-percentage point drop in her grade.
1b. The marginal benefit from the second hour of tennis must have exceeded the marginal cost of the second hour because Kate chose to play the third hour.
1c. If marginal benefit exceeded marginal cost, Kate's decision was rational.
1d. Kate made her decision on the margin because she considered the benefit and cost of one additional hour.

2a. "The Butterfly House must be kept near 80 degrees at all times, or butterflies won't fly." is a positive statement because it can be tested against the facts.
2b. "Flex-time, which allows employees to shift their work hours over a two-week period, will allow workers to better meet family needs." is a normative statement because it cannot be tested.

CHAPTER CHECKPOINT

Key Points

1 **Define economics and explain the kinds of questions that economists try to answer.**

- Economics is the social science that studies the choices that we make as we cope with scarcity and the incentives that influence and reconcile our choices.

- The first big question of economics is: How do the choices that people make end up determining *what, how,* and *for whom* goods and services get produced?

- The second big question is: When do choices made in the pursuit of *self-interest* also promote the *social interest*?

2 **Explain the core ideas that define the economic way of thinking.**

- Five core ideas define the economic way of thinking:
    1. People make *rational* choices by comparing costs and benefits.
    2. Cost is what you *must* give up to get something.
    3. Benefit is what you gain when you get something and is measured by what you *are willing to* give up to get it.
    4. A rational choice is made on the *margin*.
    5. Choices respond to *incentives*.

- Microeconomics is the study of individual choices and interactions, and macroeconomics is the study of the national economy and global economy.

- Economists try to understand how the economic world works by testing positive statements using natural experiments, statistical investigations, and economic experiments.

- Economics is a tool for personal, business, and government decisions.

Key Terms

Benefit, 11
Ceteris paribus, 15
Correlation, 16
Economics, 3
Goods and services, 3
Incentive, 13

Macroeconomics, 14
Margin, 12
Marginal benefit, 12
Marginal cost, 12
Microeconomics, 14
Opportunity cost, 11

Rational choice, 10
Scarcity, 2
Self-interest, 4
Social interest, 4
Sunk cost, 11

Exercises

1. Provide three examples of scarcity that illustrate why even the 691 billionaires in the world face scarcity.

2. Think about the following news items and label each as involving a *what, how,* or *for whom* question:
   a. Today, most stores use computers to keep their inventory records, whereas 20 years ago most stores used paper records.
   b. Health-care professionals and drug companies say that Medicaid drug rebates should be available to everyone in need.
   c. A doubling of the gas tax might lead to a better public transit system.

3. Arnold Schwartzenegger chose politics over making a movie such as a sequel to *Terminator 3*. In making his decision to run for governor of California, did he make his choice at the margin? Was his choice rational? Did he face an opportunity cost? If so, what might have been some of the components of his opportunity cost?

4. Pam, Pru, and Pat are deciding how they will celebrate the New Year. Pam prefers to go on a cruise, is happy to go to Hawaii, but does not want to go skiing. Pru prefers to go skiing, is happy to go to Hawaii, but does not want to go on a cruise. Pat prefers to go to Hawaii or to take a cruise but does not want to go skiing. Their decision is to go to Hawaii. Is this decision rational? What is the opportunity cost of the trip to Hawaii for each of them? What is the benefit that each gets?

5. Your school has decided to increase the intake of new students next year. What economic concepts would your school consider in reaching its decision? Would the school make its decision at the margin?

6. Provide examples of two monetary and two non-monetary incentives, a carrot and a stick of each, that have influenced major government decisions during the past few years.

7. Think about the following news items and label each as involving a microeconomic or a macroeconomic issue:
   a. An increase in the tax on cigarettes will decrease teenage smoking.
   b. It would be better if the United States spent more on cleaning up the environment and less on space exploration.
   c. An increase in the number of police on inner-city streets will reduce the crime rate.
   d. The Congress will consider raising the minimum wage.

8. Label each of the following news items as a positive or a normative statement:
   a. The poor pay too much for housing.
   b. The number of farms has decreased over the last 50 years.
   c. The population in rural areas has remained constant over the past decade.

9. Explain why economists use the *ceteris paribus* assumption.

10. Find in the media one example of economics being used as a tool by each of a person, a business, and a government to make a decision.

Critical Thinking

11. Andrew Whittaker Jr. of West Virginia got a surprise present on Christmas Day 2002 when he won the $314.9 million jackpot of the Powerball lottery. This jackpot was the biggest ever won by a single person in U.S. history.
    a. Do the people who buy lottery tickets face scarcity?
    b. Do the winners of big prizes face scarcity after receiving their winners' checks?
    c. Do you think lotteries have both microeconomic effects and macroeconomic effects or only microeconomic effects? Explain.
    d. How do you think lotteries change what and for whom goods and services are produced?
    e. Think about the statement "Lotteries create more problems than they solve and should be banned." Which part of this statement is positive and how might it be tested? Which part of this statement is normative?
    f. Do people face a marginal cost and a marginal benefit when they decide to buy a lottery ticket?
    g. Does a person who buys a lottery ticket make a rational choice?
    h. Do the people who buy lottery tickets respond to incentives?
    i. How do you think the size of the jackpot affects the number of lottery tickets sold? What role do incentives play in this response?

12. *Shrek 2* was the most successful movie of 2004, with box office receipts of more than $346 million. Creating a successful movie brings pleasure to millions, generates work for thousands, and makes a few people rich.
    a. What contribution does a movie like *Shrek 2* make to coping with scarcity?
    b. Does the decision to make a blockbuster movie mean that some other more desirable activities get fewer resources than they deserve?
    c. Was your answer to part **b** a positive or a normative answer? Explain.
    d. Who decides whether a movie is going to be a blockbuster?
    e. How do you think the creation of a blockbuster movie influences what, how, and for whom goods and services are produced?
    f. What do you think are some of the marginal costs and marginal benefits that the producer of a movie faces?
    g. Suppose that Mike Myers had been offered a bigger and better part in another movie and that to hire him for *Shrek 2*, the producer had to double Mike Myers' pay. What incentives would have changed? How might the changed incentives have changed the choices that people made?

13. Think about each of the following situations and explain how they affect incentives and might change the choices that people make.
    a. A hurricane hits Central Florida.
    b. The World Series begins tonight but a thunderstorm warning is in effect for the area in which the stadium is located.
    c. The price of a personal computer falls to $50.
    d. Political instability in the Middle East cuts world oil production and sends the price of gasoline to $4 a gallon.
    e. Your school builds a new parking garage that increases the number of parking places available but doubles the price of parking on campus.

Web Exercises

If you haven't already done so, take a few minutes to visit MyEconLab, sign in, and obtain your username and password. Browse the Web site and become familiar with its structure and content. You'll soon appreciate that MyEconLab is a very useful and powerful learning tool. For each chapter, you will find sample tests, a study plan based on your test results, interactive tutorials and graphics, e-text with animations of your textbook figures, and much more. You will also find the links you need to work the Web exercises.

Use the links on MyEconLab to work the following exercises.

14. Visit the Show Us the Jobs Web site, click on "Your state" and read the Jobs Crisis report. Now visit the Bureau of Labor Statistics (BLS) Web site and check the data on jobs in your state. How does the official jobs situation for your state as reported by the BLS compare with the Jobs Crisis report?

15. Visit the Campaign for Tobacco-Free Kids. Obtain data on changes in state tobacco taxes and changes in state tobacco consumption.
    a. Calculate the percentage change in tobacco taxes in each of the states for which you have data.
    b. Make a graph that plots the percentage change in the tobacco tax on the x-axis and the percentage change in state tobacco consumption on the y-axis.
    c. Describe the relationship between these two variables. (Look at pp. 23, 24, and 25 if you need help with making and interpreting your graph.)
    d. How would you expect a rise in the tobacco tax to influence the incentive for a young person to smoke cigarettes?
    e. Do the data that you've obtained confirm what you expected or were you surprised by the data? Explain your answer.
    f. What can you infer about cause and effect in the data on tobacco taxes and tobacco consumption?
    g. What is the main obstacle to drawing a strong conclusion about the effect of tobacco taxes on tobacco consumption?

16. Visit the *Statistical Abstract of the United States* and obtain data on the levels of average annual pay and the percentage of persons with a bachelor's degree in each of the states.
    a. Which state has the highest average pay and which has the lowest?
    b. Where in the ranking of average pay does your state stand?
    c. Which state has the highest percentage of people with a bachelor's degree and which has the lowest?
    d. Where in the ranking of people with a bachelor's degree does your state stand?
    e. What do you think these numbers tell us about what, how, or for whom goods and services are produced?
    f. What is the difficulty in using these numbers to determine whether education levels influence pay levels?

17. Visit the Inflation Calculator. Then make this choice: You can have $11 and pay the prices of 1805, or you can have $100 and pay the prices of 2005. Which do you prefer and why?

When you have completed your study of this appendix, you will be able to

1 Interpret a scatter diagram, a time-series graph, and a cross-section graph.

2 Interpret the graphs used in economic models.

3 Define and calculate slope.

4 Graph relationships among more than two variables.

■ Basic Idea

A graph represents a quantity as a distance and enables us to visualize the relationship between two variables. To make a graph, we set two lines called *axes* perpendicular to each other, like those in Figure A1.1. The vertical line is called the *y*-axis, and the horizontal line is called the *x*-axis. The common zero point is called the *origin*. In Figure A1.1, the *x*-axis measures temperature in degrees Fahrenheit. A movement to the right shows an increase in temperature, and a movement to the left shows a decrease in temperature. The *y*-axis represents ice cream consumption, measured in gallons per day. To make a graph, we need a value of the variable on the *x*-axis and a corresponding value of the variable on the *y*-axis. For example, if the temperature is 40°F, ice cream consumption is 5 gallons a day at point *A* in the graph. If the temperature is 80°F, ice cream consumption is 20 gallons a day at point *B* in the graph. Graphs like that in Figure A1.1 can be used to show any type of quantitative data on two variables.

■ FIGURE A1.1

Making a Graph

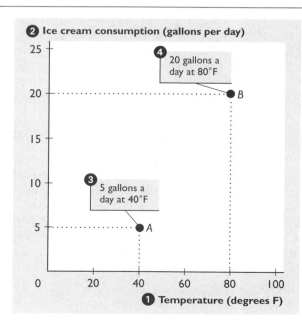

All graphs have axes that measure quantities as distances.

1 The horizontal axis (x-axis) measures temperature in degrees Fahrenheit. A movement to the right shows an increase in temperature.

2 The vertical axis (y-axis) measures ice cream consumption in gallons per day. A movement upward shows an increase in ice cream consumption.

3 Point A shows that 5 gallons of ice cream are consumed on a day when the temperature is 40°F.

4 Point B shows that 20 gallons of ice cream are consumed on a day when the temperature is 80°F.

23

■ Interpreting Data Graphs

Scatter diagram
A graph of the value of one variable against the value of another variable.

A **scatter diagram** is a graph of the value of one variable against the value of another variable. It is used to reveal whether a relationship exists between two variables and to describe the relationship. Figure A1.2 shows two examples.

Figure A1.2(a) shows the relationship between expenditure and income. Each point shows expenditure per person and income per person in the United States in a given year from 1995 to 2005. The points are "scattered" within the graph. The label on each point shows its year. The point marked 00 shows that in 2000, income per person was $25,500 and expenditure per person was $23,900. This scatter diagram reveals that as income increases, expenditure also increases.

Figure A1.2(b) shows the relationship between the number of minutes of international phone calls made from the United States and the average price per minute. This scatter diagram reveals that as the price per minute falls, the number of minutes called increases.

Time-series graph
A graph that measures time on the x-axis and the variable or variables in which we are interested on the y-axis.

A **time-series graph** measures time (for example, months or years) on the x-axis and the variable or variables in which we are interested on the y-axis. Figure A1.2(c) shows an example. In this graph, time (on the x-axis) is measured in years, which run from 1980 to 2005. The variable that we are interested in is the price of coffee, and it is measured on the y-axis.

A time-series graph conveys an enormous amount of information quickly and easily, as this example illustrates. It shows when the value is

1. High or low. When the line is a long way from the x-axis, the price is high, as it was in 1997. When the line is close to the x-axis, the price is low, as it was in 1993.

2. Rising or falling. When the line slopes upward, as in 1988, the price is rising. When the line slopes downward, as in 2001, the price is falling.

3. Rising or falling quickly or slowly. If the line is steep, then the price is rising or falling quickly. If the line is not steep, the price is rising or falling slowly. For example, the price rose quickly in 1988 and slowly in 1984. The price fell quickly in 2001 and slowly in 2003.

Trend
A general tendency for the value of a variable to rise or fall.

A time-series graph also reveals whether the variable has a trend. A **trend** is a general tendency for the value of a variable to rise or fall. You can see that the price of coffee had a general tendency to rise from 1982 to the late 1990s. That is, although the price rose and fell, it had a general tendency to rise.

With a time-series graph, we can compare different periods quickly. Figure A1.2(c) shows that the 1990s were different from the 1980s. The price of coffee fluctuated more violently in the 1990s than it did in the 1980s. This graph conveys a wealth of information, and it does so in much less space than we have used to describe only some of its features.

Cross-section graph
A graph that shows the values of an economic variable for different groups in a population at a point in time.

A **cross-section graph** shows the values of an economic variable for different groups in a population at a point in time. Figure A1.2(d) is an example of a cross-section graph. It shows the percentage of people who participated in selected sports activities in the United States. This graph uses bars rather than dots and lines, and the length of each bar indicates the participation rate. Figure A1.2(d) enables you to compare the participation rates in these ten sporting activities. And you can do so much more quickly and clearly than by looking at a list of numbers.

FIGURE A1.2

Data Graphs

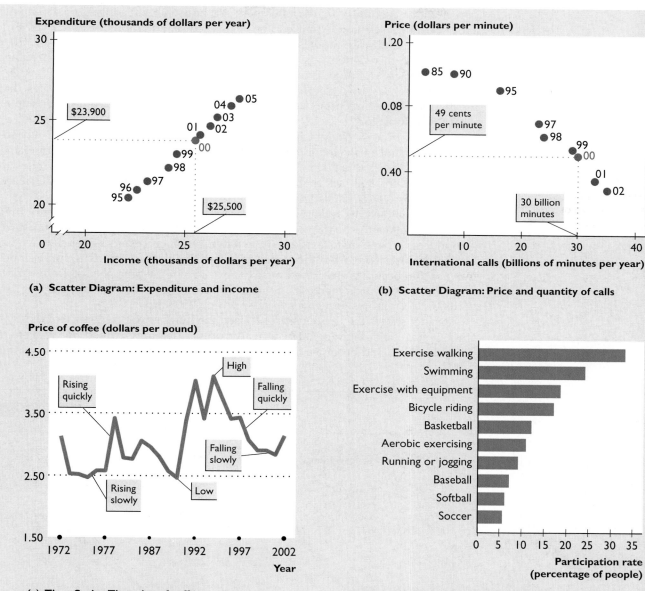

(a) Scatter Diagram: Expenditure and income

(b) Scatter Diagram: Price and quantity of calls

(c) Time Series: The price of coffee

(d) Cross Section: Participation in selected sports activities

A scatter diagram reveals the relationship between two variables. In part (a), as income increases, expenditure increases. In part (b), as the price per minute falls, the number of minutes called increases.

A time-series graph plots the value of a variable on the *y*-axis against time on the *x*-axis. Part (c) plots the price of coffee each

year from 1980 to 2005. The graph shows when the price of coffee was high and low, when it increased and decreased, and when it changed quickly and slowly.

A cross-section graph shows the value of a variable across the members of a population. Part (d) shows the participation rate in the United States in each of ten sporting activities.

■ Interpreting Graphs Used in Economic Models

We use graphs to show the relationships among the variables in an economic model. An *economic model* is a simplified description of the economy or of a component of the economy such as a business or a household. It consists of statements about economic behavior that can be expressed as equations or as curves in a graph. Economists use models to explore the effects of different policies or other influences on the economy in ways similar to those used to test model airplanes in wind tunnels and models of the climate.

Figure A1.3 shows graphs of the relationships between two variables that move in the same direction. Such a relationship is called a **positive relationship** or **direct relationship**.

Part (a) shows a straight-line relationship, which is called a **linear relationship**. The distance traveled in 5 hours increases as the speed increases. For example, point *A* shows that 200 miles are traveled in 5 hours at a speed of 40 miles an hour. And point *B* shows that the distance traveled increases to 300 miles if the speed increases to 60 miles an hour.

Part (b) shows the relationship between distance sprinted and recovery time (the time it takes the heart rate to return to its normal resting rate). An upward-sloping curved line that starts out quite flat but then becomes steeper as we move along the curve away from the origin describes this relationship. The curve slopes upward and becomes steeper because the extra recovery time needed from sprinting another 100 yards increases. It takes 5 minutes to recover from sprinting 100 yards but 15 minutes to recover from sprinting 200 yards.

Part (c) shows the relationship between the number of problems worked by a student and the amount of study time. An upward-sloping curved line that starts out quite steep and becomes flatter as we move away from the origin shows this

Positive relationship or direct relationship
A relationship between two variables that move in the same direction.

Linear relationship
A relationship that graphs as a straight line.

■ **FIGURE A1.3**
Positive (Direct) Relationships

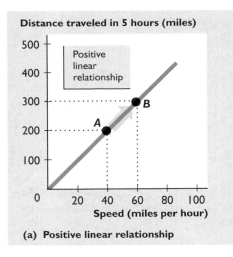

(a) **Positive linear relationship**

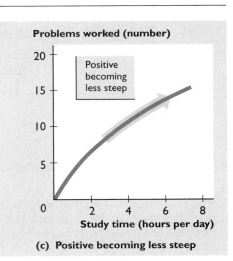

(b) **Positive becoming steeper**

(c) **Positive becoming less steep**

Part (a) shows that as speed increases, the distance traveled increases along a straight line.

Part (b) shows that as the distance sprinted increases, recovery time increases along a curve that becomes steeper.

Part (c) shows that as study time increases, the number of problems worked increases along a curve that becomes less steep.

relationship. Study time becomes less effective as you increase the hours worked and become more tired.

Figure A1.4 shows relationships between two variables that move in opposite directions. Such a relationship is called a **negative relationship** or **inverse relationship**.

Part (a) shows the relationship between the number of hours for playing squash and the number of hours for playing tennis when the total number of hours available is five. One extra hour spent playing tennis means one hour less playing squash and vice versa. This relationship is negative and linear.

Part (b) shows the relationship between the cost per mile traveled and the length of a journey. The longer the journey, the lower is the cost per mile. But as the journey length increases, the cost per mile decreases, and the fall in the cost gets smaller. This feature of the relationship is shown by the fact that the curve slopes downward, starting out steep at a short journey length and then becoming flatter as the journey length increases. This relationship arises because some of the costs such as auto insurance are fixed, and the fixed costs are spread over a longer journey.

Part (c) shows the relationship between the amount of leisure time and the number of problems worked by a student. Increasing leisure time produces an increasingly large reduction in the number of problems worked. This relationship is a negative one that starts out with a gentle slope at a small number of leisure hours and becomes steeper as the number of leisure hours increases. This relationship is a different view of the idea shown in Figure A1.3(c).

Many relationships in economic models have a maximum or a minimum. For example, firms try to make the largest possible profit and to produce at the lowest possible cost. Figure A1.5 shows relationships that have a maximum or a minimum.

Negative relationship or inverse relationship
A relationship between two variables that move in opposite directions.

■ **FIGURE A1.4**

Negative (Inverse) Relationships

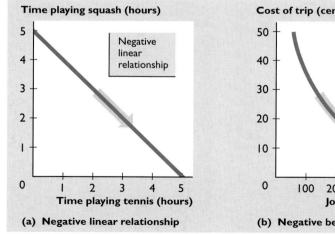

(a) Negative linear relationship

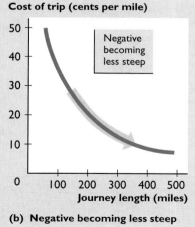

(b) Negative becoming less steep

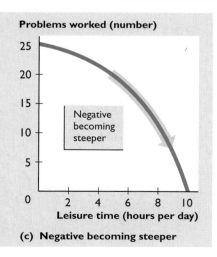

(c) Negative becoming steeper

Part (a) shows that as the time playing tennis increases, the time playing squash decreases along a straight line.

Part (b) shows that as the journey length increases, the cost of the trip falls along a curve that becomes less steep.

Part (c) shows that as leisure time increases, the number of problems worked decreases along a curve that becomes steeper.

■ **FIGURE A1.5**
Maximum and Minimum Points

In part (a), as the rainfall increases, the curve **1** slopes upward as the yield per acre rises, **2** is flat at point *A*, the maximum yield, and then **3** slopes downward as the yield per acre falls.

In part (b), as the speed increases, the curve **1** slopes downward as the cost per mile falls, **2** is flat at the minimum point *B*, and then **3** slopes upward as the cost per mile rises.

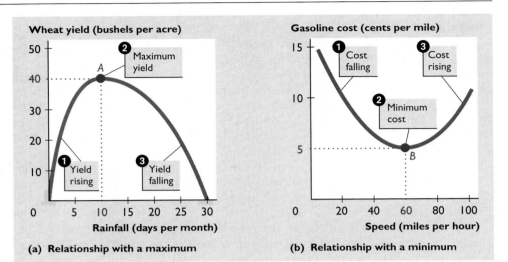

(a) Relationship with a maximum

(b) Relationship with a minimum

Part (a) shows the relationship that starts out sloping upward, reaches a maximum, and then slopes downward. Part (b) shows a relationship that begins sloping downward, falls to a minimum, and then slopes upward.

Finally, there are many situations in which, no matter what happens to the value of one variable, the other variable remains constant. Sometimes we want to show two variables that are unrelated in a graph. Figure A1.6 shows two graphs in which the variables are independent.

■ **FIGURE A1.6**
Variables That Are Unrelated

In part (a), as the price of bananas increases, the student's grade in economics remains at 75 percent. These variables are unrelated, and the curve is horizontal.

In part (b), the vineyards of France produce 3 billion gallons of wine no matter what the rainfall in California is. These variables are unrelated, and the curve is vertical.

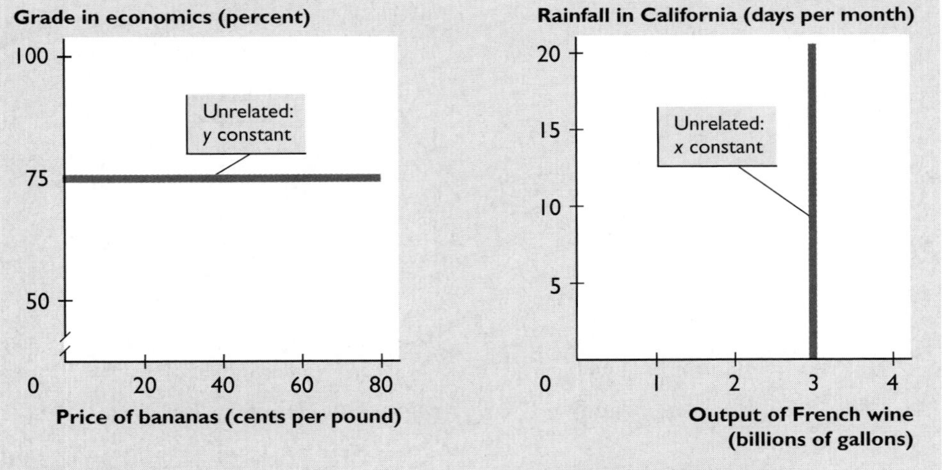

Grade in economics (percent)

Unrelated:
y constant

Price of bananas (cents per pound)

(a) Unrelated: y constant

Rainfall in California (days per month)

Unrelated:
x constant

**Output of French wine
(billions of gallons)**

(b) Unrelated: x constant

■ The Slope of a Relationship

We can measure the influence of one variable on another by the slope of the relationship. The **slope** of a relationship is the change in the value of the variable measured on the y-axis divided by the change in the value of the variable measured on the x-axis. We use the Greek letter Δ (delta) to represent "change in." So Δy means the change in the value of y, and Δx means the change in the value of x, and the slope of the relationship is

$$\Delta y \div \Delta x.$$

If a large change in y is associated with a small change in x, the slope is large and the curve is steep. If a small change in y is associated with a large change in x, the slope is small and the curve is flat.

Figure A1.7 shows you how to calculate slope. The slope of a straight line is the same regardless of where on the line you calculate it—the slope is constant. In part (a), when x increases from 2 to 6, y increases from 3 to 6. The change in x is 4—that is, Δx is 4. The change in y is 3—that is, Δy is 3. The slope of that line is 3/4. In part (b), when x increases from 2 to 6, y *decreases* from 6 to 3. The change in y is *minus* 3—that is, Δy is -3. The change in x is plus 4—that is, Δx is 4. The slope of the curve is $-3/4$.

In part (c), we calculate the slope at a point on a curve. To do so, place a ruler on the graph so that it touches point A and no other point on the curve, then draw a straight line along the edge of the ruler. The slope of this straight line is the slope of the curve at point A. This slope is 3/4.

Slope
The change in the value of the variable measured on the y-axis divided by the change in the value of the variable measured on the x-axis.

■ FIGURE A1.7
Calculating Slope

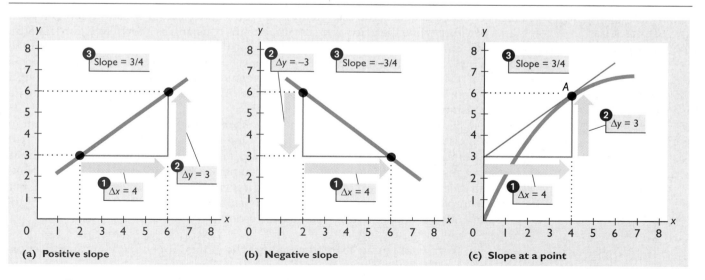

(a) Positive slope   **(b) Negative slope**   **(c) Slope at a point**

In part (a), ❶ when Δx is 4, ❷ Δy is 3, so ❸ the slope ($\Delta y \div \Delta x$) is 3/4.

In part (b), ❶ when Δx is 4, ❷ Δy is -3, so ❸ the slope ($\Delta y \div \Delta x$) is $-3/4$.

In part (c), the slope of the curve at point A equals the slope of the red line. ❶ When Δx is 4, ❷ Δy is 3, so ❸ the slope ($\Delta y \div \Delta x$) is 3/4.

■ Relationships Among More Than Two Variables

We have seen that we can graph the relationship between two variables as a point formed by the x and y values. But most of the relationships in economics involve relationships among many variables, not just two. For example, the amount of ice cream consumed depends on the price of ice cream and the temperature. If ice cream is expensive and the temperature is low, people eat much less ice cream than when ice cream is inexpensive and the temperature is high. For any given price of ice cream, the quantity consumed varies with the temperature; and for any given temperature, the quantity of ice cream consumed varies with its price.

Figure A1.8 shows a relationship among three variables. The table shows the number of gallons of ice cream consumed per day at various temperatures and ice cream prices. How can we graph these numbers?

To graph a relationship that involves more than two variables, we use the *ceteris paribus* assumption.

Ceteris Paribus

The Latin phrase *ceteris paribus* means "other things remaining the same." Every laboratory experiment is an attempt to create *ceteris paribus* and isolate the relationship of interest. We use the same method to make a graph.

Figure A1.8(a) shows an example. This graph shows what happens to the quantity of ice cream consumed when the price of ice cream varies while the temperature remains the same. The curve labeled 70°F shows the relationship between ice cream consumption and the price of ice cream if the temperature is 70°F. The numbers used to plot that curve are those in the first and fourth columns of the table in Figure A1.8. For example, if the temperature is 70°F, 10 gallons are consumed when the price is 60¢ a scoop and 18 gallons are consumed when the price is 30¢ a scoop. The curve labeled 90°F shows the relationship between consumption and the price when the temperature is 90°F.

We can also show the relationship between ice cream consumption and temperature while the price of ice cream remains constant, as shown in Figure A1.8(b). The curve labeled 60¢ shows how the consumption of ice cream varies with the temperature when the price of ice cream is 60¢ a scoop, and a second curve shows the relationship when the price of ice cream is 15¢ a scoop. For example, at 60¢ a scoop, 10 gallons are consumed when the temperature is 70°F and 20 gallons are consumed when the temperature is 90°F.

Figure A1.8(c) shows the combinations of temperature and price that result in a constant consumption of ice cream. One curve shows the combinations that result in 10 gallons a day being consumed, and the other shows the combinations that result in 7 gallons a day being consumed. A high price and a high temperature lead to the same consumption as a lower price and a lower temperature. For example, 10 gallons of ice cream are consumed at 90°F and 90¢ a scoop, at 70°F and 60¢ a scoop, and at 50°F and 45¢ a scoop.

With what you've learned about graphs in this Appendix, you can move forward with your study of economics. There are no graphs in this textbook that are more complicated than the ones you've studied here.

■ FIGURE A1.8

Graphing a Relationship Among Three Variables

Price (cents per scoop)	Ice cream consumption (gallons per day)			
	30°F	50°F	70°F	90°F
15	12	18	25	50
30	10	12	18	37
45	7	10	13	27
60	5	7	10	20
75	3	5	7	14
90	2	3	5	10
105	1	2	3	6

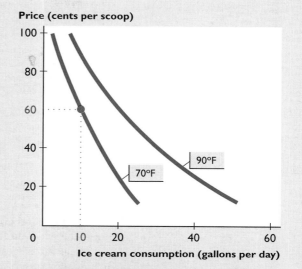

(a) Price and consumption at a given temperature

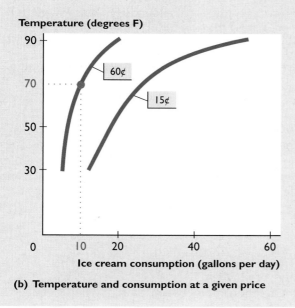

(b) Temperature and consumption at a given price

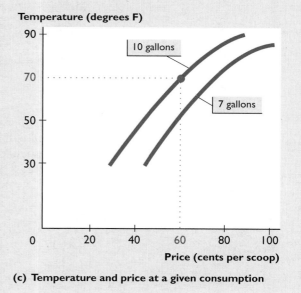

(c) Temperature and price at a given consumption

The table tells us how many gallons of ice cream are consumed each day at different prices and different temperatures. For example, if the price is 60¢ a scoop and the temperature is 70°F, 10 gallons of ice cream are consumed. This set of values is highlighted in the table and each part of the figure.

Part (a) shows the relationship between price and consumption when temperature is held constant. One curve holds temperature at 90°F, and the other at 70°F.

Part (b) shows the relationship between temperature and consumption when price is held constant. One curve holds the price at 60¢ a scoop, and the other at 15¢ a scoop.

Part (c) shows the relationship between temperature and price when consumption is held constant. One curve holds consumption at 10 gallons a day, and the other at 7 gallons a day.

Exercises

The spreadsheet provides data on the U.S. economy: Column A is the year; the other columns are actual and projected expenditures per person in dollars per year on recorded music (column B), Internet services (column C), and movies in theaters (column D). Use this spreadsheet to answer exercises 1, 2, 3, 4, and 5.

	A	B	C	D
1	1992	43	4	23
2	1993	47	5	24
3	1994	56	6	25
4	1995	57	11	25
5	1996	57	17	27
6	1997	55	26	29
7	1998	56	32	30
8	1999	58	37	31
9	2000	62	43	32
10	2001	66	48	33
11	2002	69	53	34
12	2003	73	57	36

1. Draw a scatter diagram to show the relationship between expenditure on recorded music and expenditure on Internet services. Describe the relationship.

2. Draw a scatter diagram to show the relationship between expenditure on Internet services and expenditure on movies in theaters. Describe the relationship.

3. Draw a scatter diagram to show the relationship between expenditure on recorded music and expenditure on movies in theaters. Describe the relationship.

4. Draw a time-series graph of expenditure on Internet services. Say in which year or years (a) expenditure was highest, (b) expenditure was lowest, (c) expenditure increased the most, and (d) expenditure increased the least. Also, say whether the data show a trend and describe its direction.

5. Draw a time-series graph of expenditure on recorded music. Say in which year or years (a) expenditure was highest, (b) expenditure was lowest, (c) expenditure increased the most, and (d) expenditure increased the least. Also, say whether the data show a trend and describe its direction.

6. Draw a graph to show the relationship between the two variables x and y:

x	0	1	2	3	4	5	6	7	8
y	0	1	4	9	16	25	36	49	64

    a. Is the relationship positive or negative?
    b. Calculate the slope of the relationship between x and y when x equals 2 and when x equals 4.
    c. How does the slope of the relationship change as the value of x increases?
    d. Think of some economic relationships that might be similar to this one.

7. Draw a graph to show the relationship between the two variables x and y:

x	0	1	2	3	4	5	6	7	8
y	60	49	39	30	22	15	9	4	0

    a. Is the relationship positive or negative?
    b. Calculate the slope of the relationship between x and y when x equals 2 and when x equals 4.
    c. How does the slope of the relationship change as the value of x increases?
    d. Think of some economic relationships that might be similar to this one.

Price (dollars per ride)	Balloon rides (number per day)		
	50°F	70°F	90°F
5	32	50	40
10	27	40	32
15	18	32	27
20	10	27	18

8. The table provides data on the price of a balloon ride, the temperature, and the number of rides a day. Draw graphs to show the relationship between:
    a. The price and the number of rides, holding the temperature constant.
    b. The number of rides and the temperature, holding the price constant.
    c. The temperature and the price, holding the number of rides constant.

The U.S. and Global Economies

CHAPTER CHECKLIST

**When you have completed your study of this chapter,
you will be able to**

1 Describe what, how, and for whom goods and services are produced in
the United States.

2 Use the circular flow model to provide a picture of how households
and firms interact.

3 Describe what, how, and for whom goods and services are produced in
the global economy.

Scott Clark delivers mail around Virginia and
earns more than he did at the job he lost when
Viasystems, Inc. closed its Richmond plant. But
Scott is working longer hours, and his benefits
have gone. Yet Scott is better off than many of
his friends. One of them, Raffael, now a guard in
an armored car, has taken a big pay cut.

Half a world away, Chown Chong Chin and
her husband have just got new jobs in a furniture factory in
the Chinese province of Dong Guan. By leaving their rural
life of farming and fishing, they have tripled their income.

Scott and Raffael are like many Americans who, in the
face of ongoing changes in technology and international
competition, are switching from manufacturing jobs to service jobs. And Chown Chong and her husband are like many
Chinese who are switching from farming to factory jobs.

This chapter puts these lives and *your life* in a broad perspective by looking at the patterns and changes in *what, how,*
and *for whom* goods and services are produced.

2.1 WHAT, HOW, AND FOR WHOM?

Walk around a shopping mall and pay close attention to the range of goods and services that are being offered for sale. Go inside some of the shops and look at the labels to see where various items are manufactured. The next time you travel on an interstate highway, look at the large trucks and pay attention to the names and products printed on their sides and the places in which the trucks are registered. Open the Yellow Pages and flip through a few sections. Notice the huge range of goods and services that businesses are offering.

You've just done a sampling of *what* goods and services are produced and consumed in the United States today.

■ What Do We Produce?

We can divide the vast array of goods and services that are produced into two large groups:

- Consumption goods and services
- Capital goods

Consumption goods and services are items that are bought by individuals and used to provide personal enjoyment and contribute to a person's quality of life. They include items such as housing, SUVs, popcorn and fruit juice, movies and chocolate bars, microwave ovens and inline skates, and dental and dry cleaning services. The key feature of a consumption good or service—and hence its name—is that it doesn't last long. It can be used just once and then it is gone.

Capital goods are goods that are bought by businesses to increase their productive resources or by governments to enhance the social infrastructure. They include items such as auto assembly lines, shopping malls, airplanes, and oil tankers. And capital goods include highways, water supply systems, and GPS satellites. The key feature of a capital good is that it is durable. It can be used many times and sometimes over a long period.

By far the largest part of what we produce today is services, not goods. Figure 2.1(a) shows the production of the largest six services and four goods. Health services are the largest item and represent 13 percent of the value of total production. Real estate services comes next at 12 percent. The main component of this item is the services of rental and owner-occupied housing. Education is the next largest item, followed by retail and wholesale trades.

The largest categories of goods—construction—accounts for less than 5 percent of the value of total production, and the next three—utilities, food, and chemicals—each accounts for 2 percent or less.

What we produce is changing, and *Eye on the Past* on p. 36 provides a big-picture view of the changes over the past 65 years. The major change is a shift from producing goods to providing services. This change has been the most dramatic in the way we consume our food. Figure 2.1(b) provides some data on this change. In 1930, Americans spent 24 percent of their income on food. Today, we spend 11 percent. And in 1930, Americans spent 13 percent of their food budget on meals away from home. Today, we spend 40 percent.

These changes in what we produce and the way we consume are driven by our rising incomes, which in turn arise from changes in *how* we produce.

Consumption goods and services
Goods and services that are bought by individuals and used to provide personal enjoyment and contribute to a person's quality of life.

Capital goods
Goods that are bought by businesses to increase their productive resources and by governments to enhance the social infrastructure.

▇ FIGURE 2.1
What We Produce

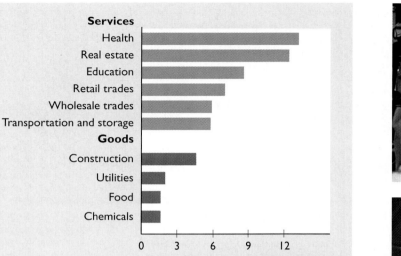

(a) Some of the details

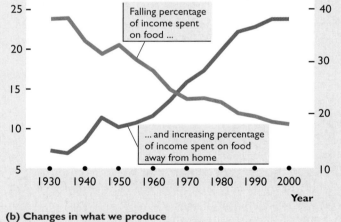

(b) Changes in what we produce

SOURCES OF DATA: Bureau of Economic Analysis and *Statistical Abstract of the United States,* 1999 and 2004–2005.

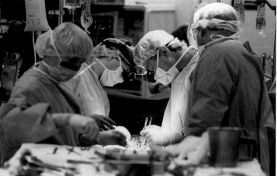

Health and real estate services, education, retail and wholesale trades, and transportation and storage are the largest six services produced. Construction, utilities, food, and chemicals are the largest categories of goods produced. Services production greatly exceeds goods production and is growing faster.

Americans spend a decreasing share of their total expenditure on food and other necessities and an increasing share on services such as meals away from home.

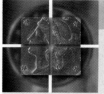

Changes in What We Produce

Sixty-five years ago, one American in four worked on a farm. That number has shrunk to one in thirty-five. The number of people who produce goods—in mining, construction, and manufacturing—has also shrunk, from one in three to one in five. In contrast, the number of people who produce services has expanded from one in two to almost four in five. These changes in employment reflect changes in what we produce—services.

The story of Scott Clark and his friend Raffael (in the chapter opener) is just one example of the effects of this ongoing expansion of service jobs and shrinking of manufacturing jobs.

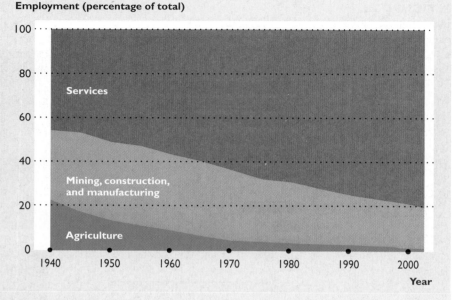

Employment (percentage of total)

SOURCE OF DATA: U.S. Census Bureau, *Statistical Abstract of the United States*, 1999 and 2004–2005.

This process is not new. You can see a similar trend over the past 60 years.

And that trend is likely to continue.

■ How Do We Produce?

Goods and services are produced by using productive resources. Economists call the productive resources **factors of production**. Factors of production are grouped into four categories:

- Land
- Labor
- Capital
- Entrepreneurship

Factors of production
The productive resources that are used to produce goods and services—land, labor, capital, and entrepreneurship.

Land

In economics, **land** includes all the "gifts of nature" that we use to produce goods and services. Land is what, in everyday language, we call *natural resources*. It includes land in the everyday sense, minerals, energy, water, air, and wild plants, animals, birds, and fish. Some of these resources are renewable, and some are non-renewable. The U.S. Geological Survey maintains a national inventory of the quantity and quality of natural resources and monitors changes to that inventory.

The United States covers almost 2 billion acres. About 45 percent of the land is forest, lakes, and national parks. In 2000, almost 50 percent of the land was used for agriculture and 5 percent was urban, but urban land use is growing and agricultural land use is shrinking.

Our land surface and water resources are renewable, and some of our mineral resources can be recycled. But many mineral resources can be used only once. They are nonrenewable resources. Of these, the United States has vast known reserves of coal but much smaller known reserves of oil and natural gas.

Land
The "gifts of nature," or *natural resources*, that we use to produce goods and services.

Labor

Labor is the work time and work effort that people devote to producing goods and services. It includes the physical and mental efforts of all the people who work on farms and construction sites and in factories, shops, and offices. The Census Bureau and Bureau of Labor Statistics measure the nation's labor force every month.

In the United States in May 2005, 148.9 million people had jobs or were available for work. Some worked full time, some worked part time, and some were unemployed but looking for an acceptable vacant job. The total amount of time worked during 2005 was about 240 billion hours.

The quantity of labor increases as the adult population increases. The quantity of labor also increases if a larger percentage of the population takes jobs. During the past 50 years, a larger proportion of women have taken paid work and this trend has increased the quantity of labor.

The quality of labor depends on how skilled people are. Economists use a special name for human skill: human capital. **Human capital** is the knowledge and skill that people obtain from education, on-the-job training, and work experience.

You are building your own human capital right now as you work on your economics course and other subjects. And your human capital will continue to grow when you get a full-time job and become better at it. Human capital improves the *quality* of labor.

Figure 2.2 shows that today 85 percent of the U.S. population has completed high school and 27 percent has a college or university degree.

Labor
The work time and work effort that people devote to producing goods and services.

Human capital
The knowledge and skill that people obtain from education, on-the-job training, and work experience.

■ FIGURE 2.2

Measures of Human Capital

myeconlab

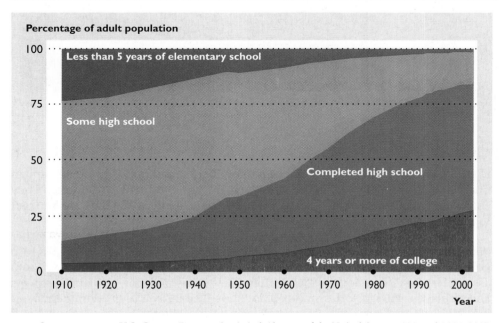

Percentage of adult population

Less than 5 years of elementary school

Some high school

Completed high school

4 years or more of college

Year

Human capital improves the quality of labor. And the level of education that people attain is a major influence on an economy's human capital.

In 2004, 27 percent of the U.S. population had 4 years or more of college education, up from 3 percent in 1910. An additional 58 percent had completed high school, up from 11 percent in 1910.

SOURCE OF DATA: U.S. Census Bureau, *Statistical Abstract of the United States,* 1999 and 2004–2005.

Changes in How We Produce in the New Economy

The new economy consists of the jobs and businesses that produce and use computers and equipment powered by computer chips. This new economy is highly visible in your daily life.

The pairs of images here remind you of two examples. In each pair, a new technology enables capital to replace labor.

The top pair of pictures illustrate the replacement of bank tellers (labor) with ATMs (capital). Although the ATM was invented almost 40 years ago, when it made its first appearance, it was located only inside banks and was not able to update customers' accounts. It is only in the last decade that ATMs have spread to corner stores and enable us to get cash and check our bank balance from almost anywhere in the world.

The bottom pair of pictures illustrate a more recent replacement of labor with capital. In the past few years, machines that enable passengers to do their own flight check-in and issue their own boarding pass have been springing up in our airports. For international flights, some of these machines now even check passport details.

The number of bank teller and airport check-in clerk jobs is shrinking. But these new technologies are creating a whole range of new jobs for people who make, program, install, and repair these machines.

Capital

In everyday language, we talk about money, stocks, and bonds as being capital. These items are *financial capital,* and they are not productive resources. They enable people to provide businesses with financial resources, but they are *not* used to produce goods and services. They are not capital.

Capital consists of the tools, instruments, machines, buildings, and other items that have been produced in the past and that businesses now use to produce goods and services. Capital includes hammers and screwdrivers, computers, auto assembly lines, office towers and warehouses, dams and power plants, airports and airplanes, shirt factories, and cookie shops. The Bureau of Economic Analysis in the U.S. Department of Commerce keeps track of the total value of capital and how it grows over time. In the United States today, it is around $35 trillion. The global value of capital is about $145 trillion.

Capital
Tools, instruments, machines, buildings, and other items that have been produced in the past and that businesses now use to produce goods and services.

Entrepreneurship

Entrepreneurship is the human resource that organizes labor, land, and capital. Entrepreneurs come up with new ideas about what and how to produce, make business decisions, and bear the risks that arise from these decisions.

The quantity of entrepreneurship is hard to describe or measure. At some periods, there appears to be a great deal of imaginative entrepreneurship around. People such as Sam Walton, who created Wal-Mart, one of the world's largest retailers; Bill Gates, who founded the Microsoft empire; and Michael Dell, who established Dell Computers, are examples of extraordinary entrepreneurial talent. But these highly visible entrepreneurs are just the tip of an iceberg that consists of hundreds of thousands of people who run businesses, large and small.

Entrepreneurship
The human resource that organizes labor, land, and capital.

■ For Whom Do We Produce?

Who gets the goods and services that are produced depends on the incomes that people earn and the goods and services that they choose to buy. A large income enables a person to buy large quantities of goods and services. A small income leaves a person with few options and small quantities of goods and services.

People earn their incomes by selling the services of the factors of production they own. **Rent** is paid for the use of land, **wages** are paid for the services of labor, **interest** is paid for the use of capital, and entrepreneurs receive a **profit** (or incur a **loss**) for running their businesses. What are the shares of these four factor incomes in the United States? Which factor receives the largest share?

Rent
Income paid for the use of land.

Wages
Income paid for the services of labor.

Interest
Income paid for the use of capital.

Profit (or loss)
Income earned by an entrepreneur for running a business.

■ **FIGURE 2.3**
For Whom?

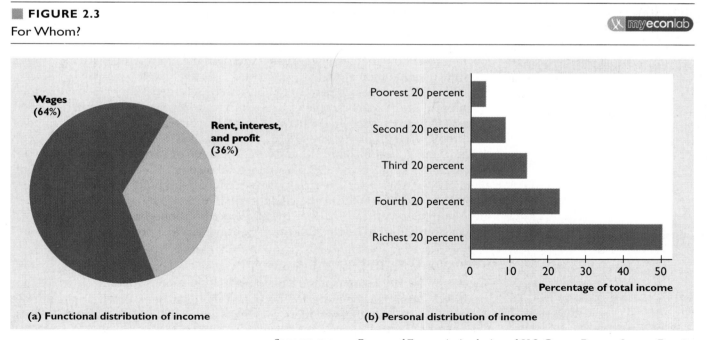

(a) Functional distribution of income

(b) Personal distribution of income

SOURCES OF DATA: Bureau of Economic Analysis and U.S. Census Bureau, *Income, Poverty, and Health Insurance in the United States: 2004,* Current Population Reports P60-229, 2005.

In 2005, wages (the income from labor) were 64 percent of total income. Rent, interest, and profit (the income from land, capital, and entrepreneurship) totaled the remaining 36 percent.

In 2004, the 20 percent of the population with the highest incomes received 50 percent of total income. The 20 percent with the lowest incomes received only 3.4 percent of total income.

Functional distribution of income
The distribution of income among the factors of production.

Functional Distribution of Income

The **functional distribution of income** is the distribution of income among the factors of production. Figure 2.3(a) shows that wages, the income from labor, were 64 percent of total income in 2005. The national accounts don't split the remaining income into rent, interest, and profit. Instead, they report the profits of corporations and of small businesses. These incomes are a mixture of rent, interest, and profit and were 36 percent of total income in 2005. These percentages remain remarkably constant over time.

The data in Figure 2.3(a) tell us how income is distributed among the factors of production. But the data don't tell us how income is distributed among individuals.

Personal Distribution of Income

You know of lots of people who earn very large incomes. Tiger Woods wins several million dollars a year in prize money and earns substantially more than this amount in endorsements. The average salary of major league baseball players in 2004 was almost $3 million, and some stars, such as Alex Rodriguez, Carlos Delgado, Derek Jeter, Barry Bonds, Pedro Martinez, Mo Vaughn, Shawn Green, and Mike Piazza earned more than $16 million. Manny Ramirez, the top earner in 2004, picked up a cool $22.5 million.

You know of even more people who earn very small incomes. Servers at McDonald's average around $6.50 an hour; checkout clerks, gas station attendants, and textile and leather workers earn less than $10 an hour.

Personal distribution of income
The distribution of income among households.

Figure 2.3(b) shows the **personal distribution of income**—the distribution of income among households. Households (individuals or people living together) are divided into five groups, each of which represents 20 percent of all households. If incomes were equal, each 20 percent group would earn 20 percent of total income. You know that incomes are unequal, and the figure provides a measure of just how unequal they are.

In 2004, the poorest 20 percent of households received only 3.4 percent of total income and the average income of this group was only $10,000 a year. The second poorest 20 percent received 8.7 percent of total income and the average income of this group was still pretty low at $26,000 a year. The middle 20 percent received 14.7 percent of total income and an average income of $44,000 a year. The second richest 20 percent received 23.2 percent of total income. The incomes in this group averaged $70,000 a year. The richest 20 percent of households received 50 percent of total income and on the average had incomes of $147,000 a year. On the basis of these numbers, you can see that the 20 percent of households with the highest incomes can afford to buy half of the goods and services produced.

Changing Distribution of Income

The distribution of income in the United States—for whom goods and services get produced—has been changing and becoming more unequal. People in the middle and lower part of the distribution, like Scott and Raffael in the chapter opener, have lost out on the average. And people at the top end of the distribution have gained. The rich have become richer. But it isn't the case, on the whole, that the poor have become poorer. They just haven't become richer as fast as the rich have. There is also a lot of movement across the income distribution as some people fall on hard times and others enjoy successes.

CHECKPOINT 2.1

1 Describe what, how, and for whom goods and services are produced in the United States.

Practice Problems 2.1

1. Name the two broad categories of goods and services that we use in economics and provide an example of each (different from those in the chapter).

2. Name the four factors of production and the incomes they earn.

3. Distinguish between the functional distribution of income and the personal distribution of income.

4. In the United States, which factor of production earned the largest share of income in 2005 and what percentage did it earn?

Exercises 2.1

1. What is the distinction between consumption goods and services and capital goods? Which one of them brings an increase in productive resources?

2. Describe how the quality of the U.S. labor force, as measured by the level of education, changed during the last few decades.

3. If everyone in the United States were to consume an equal quantity of goods and services, what percentage of total income would the poorest 20 percent of households have to receive from higher-income groups? What percentage would the second poorest 20 percent have to receive?

4. Compare the percentage of total U.S. income that labor earns with the percentage earned by all the other factors of production combined.

Solutions to Practice Problems 2.1

1. The two categories are consumption goods and services and capital goods. An example of a consumption good is a shirt. An example of a consumption service is a haircut. An example of a capital good is an oil rig.

2. The factors of production are land, labor, capital, and entrepreneurship. Land earns rent; labor earns wages; capital earns interest; and entrepreneurship earns profit or incurs a loss.

3. The functional distribution of income shows the percentage of total income received by each factor of production. The personal distribution of income shows the percentage of total income received by households.

4. Labor is the factor of production that earns the largest share of income in the United States. In 2005, labor earned 64 percent of total income.

2.2 THE CIRCULAR FLOWS

Circular flow model
A model of the economy that shows the circular flow of expenditures and incomes that result from decision-makers' choices and the way those choices interact to determine what, how, and for whom goods and services are produced.

Households
Individuals or groups of people living together.

Firms
The institutions that organize the production of goods and services.

We can organize the data you've just studied using the **circular flow model**—a model of the economy that shows the circular flow of expenditures and incomes that result from decision-makers' choices and the way those choices interact to determine what, how, and for whom goods and services are produced. Figure 2.4 shows the circular flow model.

■ Households and Firms

Households are individuals or groups of people living together. The 112 million households in the United States own the factors of production—land, labor, capital, and entrepreneurship—and choose the quantities of these resources to provide to firms. Households also choose the quantities of goods and services to buy.

Firms are the institutions that organize the production of goods and services. The 20 million firms in the United States choose the quantities of the factors of production to hire and the quantities of goods and services to produce.

■ Markets

Market
Any arrangement that brings buyers and sellers together and enables them to get information and do business with each other.

Households choose the quantities of the factors of production to provide to firms, and firms choose the quantities of the services of the factors of production to hire. Firms choose the quantities of goods and services to produce and households choose the quantities of goods and services to buy. How are these choices coordinated and made compatible? The answer is: by markets.

A **market** is any arrangement that brings buyers and sellers together and enables them to get information and do business with each other. An example is the market in which oil is bought and sold—the world oil market. The world oil market is not a place. It is the network of oil producers, oil users, wholesalers, and brokers who buy and sell oil. In the world oil market, decision makers do not meet physically. They make deals by telephone, fax, and the Internet.

Figure 2.4 identifies two types of markets: goods markets and factor markets. **Goods markets** are markets in which goods and services are bought and sold. **Factor markets** are markets in which factors of production are bought and sold.

Goods markets
Markets in which goods and services are bought and sold.

Factor markets
Markets in which factors of production are bought and sold.

■ Real Flows and Money Flows

When households choose the quantities of land, labor, capital, and entrepreneurship to offer in factor markets, they respond to the incomes they receive—rent for land, wages for labor, interest for capital, and profit for entrepreneurship. When firms choose the quantities of factors to hire, they respond to the rent, wages, interest, and profits they must pay to households.

Similarly, when firms choose the quantities of goods and services to produce and offer for sale in goods markets, they respond to the amounts that they receive from the expenditures that households make. And when households choose the quantities of goods and services to buy, they respond to the amounts they must pay to firms.

Figure 2.4 shows the flows that result from these choices made by households and firms. The flows shown in orange are *real flows:* the flows of factors of production that go from households through factor markets to firms and of the goods and services that go from firms through goods markets to households. The flows in the opposite direction are *money flows:* the flows of payments made in exchange for factors of production (shown in blue) and of expenditures on goods and services (shown in red).

Lying behind these real flows and money flows are millions of individual choices about what to consume, what to produce, and how to produce. These choices result in buying plans by households and selling plans by firms in goods markets. And the choices result in selling plans by households and buying plans by firms in factor markets. When these buying plans and selling plans are carried out, they determine the prices that people pay and the incomes they earn and so determine for whom goods and services are produced.

How do markets coordinate all these decisions?

Coordinating Decisions

Markets coordinate the decisions of millions of individuals and firms through price adjustments. To see how, think about your local markets for hamburgers and hot dogs. Suppose that some people who want to buy hamburgers are not able to

---

■ FIGURE 2.4
The Circular Flow Model

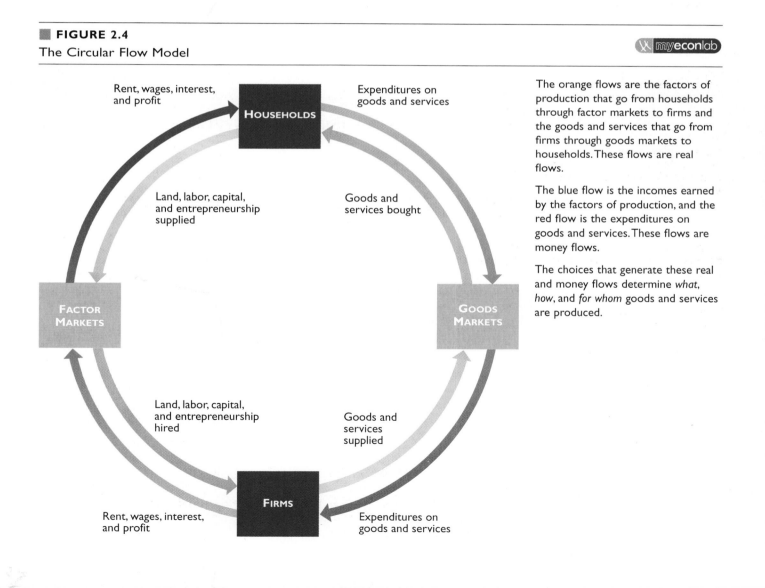

The orange flows are the factors of production that go from households through factor markets to firms and the goods and services that go from firms through goods markets to households. These flows are real flows.

The blue flow is the incomes earned by the factors of production, and the red flow is the expenditures on goods and services. These flows are money flows.

The choices that generate these real and money flows determine *what*, *how*, and *for whom* goods and services are produced.

do so because too few are being offered for sale. And suppose that some producers have unsold hot dogs on their hands because too few people want to buy them. To make the choices of buyers and sellers compatible, some buyers must scale back their appetites for hamburgers and accept hot dogs, or more hamburgers and fewer hot dogs must be offered for sale, or both must happen.

A rise in the price of a hamburger and a fall in the price of a hot dog achieve this outcome. Producers have an incentive to offer more hamburgers and fewer hot dogs for sale. And at least some people will be encouraged to change their lunch plans. Fewer people will buy hamburgers, and more will buy hot dogs.

Alternatively, suppose that more hamburgers and fewer hot dogs are available than people want to buy. Now, a fall in the price of a hamburger and a rise in the price of a hot dog solve the problem. Producers have an incentive to offer fewer hamburgers and more hot dogs for sale. And now people will buy more hamburgers and fewer hot dogs.

With the right prices, the plans of producers and consumers will be compatible. You'll learn in Chapter 4 just how markets achieve this coordination of the buying plans of households and the selling plans of firms.

CHECKPOINT 2.2

myeconlab

2   Use the circular flow model to provide a picture of how households and firms interact.

Practice Problem 2.2

1.   What are the real flows and money flows that run between households and firms in the circular flow model?

Exercises 2.2

1.   What are the choices made by households and firms that determine what, how, and for whom goods and services are produced? Where, in the circular flow model, do those choices appear?
2.   How do the choices that firms make about what to produce get coordinated with the choices that households make about what to buy?

Solution to Practice Problem 2.2

1.   The real flows are
   • The services of factors of production that go from households to firms through factor markets.
   • The goods and services that go from firms to households through goods markets.

   The money flows are
   • Factor incomes that go from firms to households through factor markets.
   • Expenditures that go from households to firms through goods markets.

2.3 THE GLOBAL ECONOMY

We're now going to look at *what, how,* and *for whom* goods and services get produced in the global economy. We'll begin with a brief overview of the people and countries that form the global economy.

■ The People

Visit the Web site of the U.S. Census Bureau and go to the population clocks to find out how many people there are today in both the United States and the entire world.

On the day these words were written, March 13, 2005, the U.S. clock recorded a population of 295,649,027. The world clock recorded a global population of 6,424,033,498. The U.S. clock ticks along showing a population increase of one person every 14 seconds. The world clock spins faster, adding 34 people in the same 14 seconds.

■ The Countries

The world's 6.42 billion (and rising) population lives in 175 countries, which the International Monetary Fund classifies into two broad groups of economies:

- Advanced economies
- Emerging market and developing economies

Advanced Economies

Advanced economies are the richest 29 countries (or areas). The United States, Japan, Italy, Germany, France, the United Kingdom, and Canada belong to this group. So do four new industrial Asian economies: Hong Kong, South Korea, Singapore, and Taiwan. The other advanced economies include Australia, New Zealand, and most of the rest of Western Europe. Almost 1 billion people (15 percent of the world's population) live in the advanced economies.

Emerging Market and Developing Economies

Emerging market economies are the 28 countries in Central and Eastern Europe and Asia that were, until the early 1990s, part of the Soviet Union or one of its satellites. Russia is the largest of these economies. Others include the Czech Republic, Hungary, Poland, Ukraine, and Mongolia.

Almost 500 million people live in these countries—only about half of the number in the advanced economies. But these countries are important because they are emerging (hence the name) from a system of state-owned production, central economic planning, and heavily regulated markets to a system of free enterprise and unregulated markets.

Developing economies are the 118 countries in Africa, Asia, the Middle East, Europe, and Central and South America that have not yet achieved high average incomes for their people. Average incomes in these economies vary a great deal, but in all cases, these average incomes are much lower than those in the advanced economies, and in some cases, they are extremely low. More than 5 billion people—almost four out of every five people—live in developing economies.

■ *What* in the Global Economy?

First, let's look at the big picture. Imagine that each year the global economy produces an enormous pie. In 2005, the pie was worth about $60 trillion! To give this number some meaning, if the pie were shared equally among the world's 6.5 billion people, each of us would get a slice worth a bit more than $9,000.

Where Is the Global Pie Baked?

Figure 2.5 shows us where in the world the pie is baked. The advanced economies produce 44 percent—18 percent in the United States and 26 percent in the other advanced economies. Another 16 percent comes from the emerging market economies. These economies, which produce 60 percent of the world's goods and services (by value) are home to only 23 percent of the world's population.

Most of the rest of the global pie comes from Asia. China produces 12 percent of the total, and the rest of the developing Asian economies produce 13 percent. The developing countries of Africa and the Middle East produce 8 percent and the Western Hemisphere—Mexico and South America—produces the rest.

The sizes of the slices in the global production pie are gradually changing. The U.S. share is shrinking, and China's share is expanding.

Unlike the slices of an apple pie, those of the global pie have different fillings. Some slices have more oil and other energy-generating goods, some have more food and other agricultural products, some have more clothing, some have more housing services, some have more autos, and so on.

■ FIGURE 2.5
What in the World Economy in 2005   ⓧ myeconlab

If we show the value of production in the world economy as a pie, the United States produces a slice that is 18 percent of the total. The other advanced economies produce 26 percent of the total. The next-biggest slice comes from the emerging market economies, with 16 percent of the total. This 60 percent of the world's production comes from 23 percent of the world's population.

Most of the rest of the global pie comes from Asia. China produces a 12 percent slice, and the rest of the developing Asian economies produce another 13 percent. The developing countries of Africa, the Middle East, and the Western Hemisphere produce the rest.

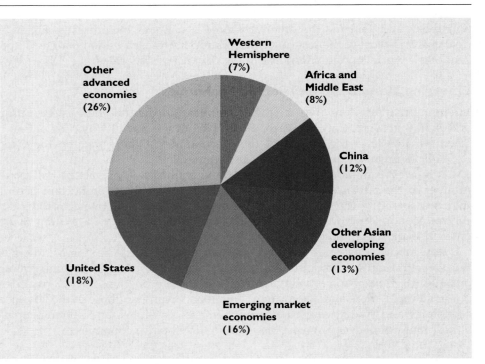

SOURCE OF DATA: International Monetary Fund, World Economic Outlook Database.

Let's take a quick look at some of these differences by looking at three broad groups:

- Energy
- Food
- Other goods and services

Energy

Land is the key resource for producing energy and the location of oil, natural gas, and coal determines the sources of the world's energy. These resources are distributed unevenly across the globe.

No one knows exactly how much oil, natural gas, and coal is available. But we know what are called the "proven reserves." These are the quantities that have been detected and that can be extracted and used with existing technologies at current costs. Beyond the proven reserves are other reserves that are known but will need a new and more costly technology to extract them. And beyond these reserves are those that are yet to be discovered. China is the largest underexplored region where it is suspected large additional reserves will be found.

You can see in Figure 2.6 why the United States takes a strong interest in the stability of the Middle East. Two thirds of the world's oil reserves and two fifths of the natural gas reserves are located in the Middle East, and most of them in just three countries: Saudi Arabia, Iraq, and Iran. North America, in contrast, has only 5 percent of the world's oil reserves and 4 percent of the natural gas reserves. But the world's known coal reserves are distributed more in North America's favor with a quarter of them in the United States. China also has large quantities of coal.

■ FIGURE 2.6

Energy Sources in the World Economy   myeconlab

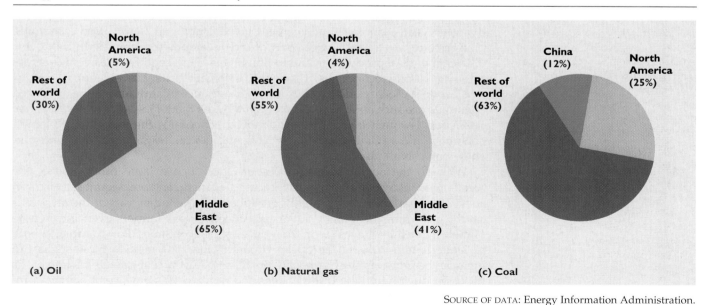

(a) Oil

North America (5%)
Rest of world (30%)
Middle East (65%)

(b) Natural gas

North America (4%)
Rest of world (55%)
Middle East (41%)

(c) Coal

China (12%)
North America (25%)
Rest of world (63%)

SOURCE OF DATA: Energy Information Administration.

Most of the world's proven oil reserves are in the Middle East (Saudi Arabia, Iraq, and Iran). North America has 5 percent of these reserves. The Middle East also has the largest share of natural gas reserves. North America has only 4 percent of these reserves. Coal is abundant in North America and in China.

How Long Will it Last?   We don't know how long our oil, natural gas, and coal will last. But we can calculate the number of years for which current proven reserves will last if they are used at the current rate. This number underestimates how long reserves will last because we will discover new sources and cheaper ways of extracting hard-to-reach reserves. And it overestimates how long reserves will last because the rate at which we're using these resources is increasing. But it provides a handy benchmark.

The world's oil reserves will last for about 40 years at the current rate of production. But this number has been *increasing!* We have been discovering more reserves than we've been using. The world's natural gas will last for about 60 years at the current rate of use, and coal will last for 200 years. So we're not going to run out of energy resources anytime soon. But we are going to run out one day. And oil will be the first to run dry.

What About the Wind and the Sun?   Why don't we make more use of the wind and the sun and less of oil, gas, and coal? Part of the answer is that we are doing just that. Worldwide, the use of wind and solar power to generate electricity is increasing at twice the rate of other methods. But even after two decades of faster growth, the wind and sun provide only a tiny 2 percent of the world's electricity, way behind oil, natural gas, and coal at 64 percent and nuclear at 17 percent. Hydroelectric generation makes up the rest.

Another part of the answer is that everything has a cost—an opportunity cost—and with the technologies currently available, the cost of generating electricity is lower with coal, oil, or natural gas than with windmills or solar cells.

Food

You saw earlier in this chapter that agriculture is a small part of the U.S. economy. It is also a small part of the production of the other advanced economies. Total agricultural production in the United States is 1.4 percent of total production. The percentage is a bit higher in the European Union and a bit lower in Japan and the other advanced Asian economies and averages 1.8 percent for all 29 advanced economies.

Agriculture is a much larger part of the developing economies. In India, it is 23 percent of total production, and in Brazil, it is 10 percent. On the average across all the developing economies, it is about 14 percent of total production.

Despite these large differences in the importance of agriculture, the advanced economies produce about one third of the world's food. How come? Because *total* production is much larger in the advanced economies than in the developing economies, and a small percentage of a big number can be greater than a large percentage of a small number!

Why do the advanced economies produce such a large proportion of the world's food? Part of the answer is that large, efficient, and well-equipped farms in the advanced economies are highly productive. But another part of the answer is that the governments of many advanced economies pay farmers to enable them to compete against lower-cost food from developing economies. For example, in both the United States and the European Union, farmers are paid to grow sugar. But sugar can be grown in the Caribbean, Brazil, and Australia at a small fraction of the cost of producing it in the United States and Europe. This practice of paying farmers in rich countries deprives farmers in poor countries of global markets and is an example of the conflict between the pursuit of self-interest and the social interest.

Other Goods and Services

If you were to visit a shopping mall in Canada, England, Australia, Japan, or any of the other advanced economies, you would wonder whether you had left the United States. Of course, you would see McDonald's golden arches. You would see them in any of the 119 countries in which one or more of McDonald's 30,000 restaurants are located. But you'd also see Starbucks, Burger King, Pizza Hut, Domino's Pizza, KFC, Kmart, Wal-Mart, Target, the United Colors of Benetton, Gap, Tommy Hilfiger, Tie Rack, the upscale Louis Vuitton and Burberry's, and a host of other familiar names.

McDonald's in Shanghai.

The similarities among the advanced economies goes beyond the view from the shopping mall. The structure of *what* is produced is similar in these economies. You've just seen that in all of them, agriculture is small. Manufacturing is also small and represents between a quarter and a third of the economy; and services are the major and fastest-growing part of the economy.

What is produced in the developing economies contrasts sharply with that of the advanced economies. Here, as you've just seen, agriculture remains a big part of the picture. But it is shrinking relative to the other parts of the economy. Manufacturing is the big story. Developing economies have relatively large and growing industries producing items such as textiles, footwear, sporting equipment, toys, electronic goods, furniture, steel, and even automobiles. The service industries in these economies are also important but not as large a proportion of the total economy as they are in the advanced economies.

The emerging market economies stand between the advanced and developing economies but most of them are closer to the advanced economies.

■ *How* in the Global Economy?

Goods and services are produced by entrepreneurs using land, labor, and capital. Each country or region has its own blend of these resources. But there are some interesting common patterns and crucial differences between the advanced and developing economies that we'll now examine.

Starbucks in Paris, France.

Human Capital Differences

The quality of labor depends on human capital. And differences in human capital in advanced and developing economies are enormous. The proportion of the population with a college or university degree is tiny in developing economies. Even the proportion of the population that has completed high school is small. And in the poorest of the developing economies, many children even miss out on basic primary education. They just don't go to school at all.

On-the-job training and experience are also much more extensive in the advanced economies than in the developing economies.

A component of human capital that we tend to take for granted is our physical ability and state of health. Again, there is a huge contrast between the advanced and developing economies.

Physical Capital Differences

The major feature of an advanced economy that differentiates it from a developing economy is the amount of capital available for producing goods and services. The differences begin with the basic transportation system. In the advanced

Beijing has a highway system to match that of any advanced country. But away from the major cities, many of China's roads are unpaved and driving on them is slow and sometimes hazardous.

economies, a well-developed highway system connects all the major cities and points of production. You can see this difference most vividly by opening a road atlas of North America and contrasting the U.S. interstate highway system with the sparse highways of Mexico. You would see a similar contrast if you flipped through a road atlas of Western Europe and Africa.

But it isn't the case that the developing economies have no highways. In fact, some of them have the newest and the best. But the new and best are usually inside and around the major cities. The smaller centers and rural areas of developing economies often have some of the worst roads in the world.

The contrast in vehicles is perhaps even greater than that in highways. In an advanced economy, you're unlikely to run across a horse-drawn wagon. But in a developing economy, animal power can still be found, and trucks are often old and unreliable.

The contrasts in the transportation system are matched by those on farms and in factories. In general, the more advanced the economy, the greater are the amount and sophistication of the capital equipment used in the production process. But again, the contrast is not all black and white. Some factories in India, China, and other parts of Asia use the very latest technologies. Furniture manufacture is an example. To make furniture of a quality that Americans are willing to buy, firms in Asia use machines like those in the furniture factories of South Carolina.

Again, it is the extensiveness of the use of modern capital-intensive technologies that distinguishes a developing economy from an advanced economy. All the factories in the advanced economies are capital intensive. But only some in the developing economies are.

The differences in human and physical capital between advanced and developing economies have a big effect on who gets the goods and services.

■ *For Whom* in the Global Economy?

Who gets the world's goods and services depends on the incomes that people earn. So how are incomes distributed across the world?

Personal Distribution of Income

You saw earlier (on pp. 39–40) that in the United States, the lowest-paid 20 percent of the population receives 3.4 percent of total income and the highest-paid 20 percent receives 50 percent of total income. The personal distribution of income in the world economy is much more unequal. According to World Bank data, the lowest-paid 20 percent of the world's population receives 2 percent of world income, and the highest-paid 20 percent receives about 70 percent of world income.

International Distribution

Much of the greater inequality at the global level arises from differences in average incomes among countries. Figure 2.7 shows some of these differences. It shows the dollar value of what people can afford each day on the average. You can see that in the United States, that number is $108 a day—an average person in the United States can buy goods and services that cost $108. This amount is around five times the world average. Canada has an average income close to 90 percent of that in the United States. Japan, Germany, France, Italy, the United Kingdom, and the other advanced economies have average incomes around two thirds that of the United States. Income levels fall off quickly as we move farther down the graph, with Africa achieving average incomes of only $6 a day.

FIGURE 2.7

For Whom in the Global Economy in 2005

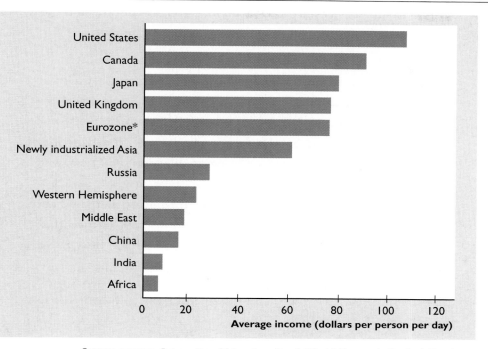

SOURCE OF DATA: International Monetary Fund, World Economic Outlook Database.

In 2005, the average income per day in the United States was $108. It was $90 in Canada and $80 in Japan. In advanced European economies such as the United Kingdom, it was about $75. The number falls off rapidly to about $27 in Russia, $14 in China, $8 in India, and $6 in Africa.

*The Eurozone is the countries of Europe that use the euro.

Changes in *For Whom* in the Global Economy

As people have lost well-paid manufacturing jobs and found lower-paid service jobs, inequality has increased in the United States and in most other advanced economies. In the developing economies, inequality is also increasing, but for a different reason. There, people who are willing to move, like Chown Chong and her husband, are enjoying rapidly rising incomes. But those who remain behind in the rural areas find their incomes either stagnating or falling.

A Happy Paradox and a Huge Challenge

Despite the increase in inequality inside most countries, inequality across the entire world has decreased during the past 20 years. And most important, according to Xavier Sala-i-Martin, an economics professor at Columbia University, extreme poverty has declined. Professor Sala-i-Martin estimates that between 1976 and 1998, the number of people who earn $1 a day or less fell by 235 million and the number who earn $2 a day or less fell by 450 million. This happy situation arises because in China and India, the two largest nations, incomes have increased rapidly and lifted millions from extreme poverty.

But between 1970 and 1998, the number of people in Africa who earn $1 a day or less increased by 175 million, and the number who earn $2 a day or less increased by 227 million. In 1960, 11 percent of the world's poor lived in Africa. In 1998, 66 percent did. Lifting Africa from poverty is one of today's biggest challenges.

The U.S. and Global Economies in YOUR Life

You've encountered a lot of facts and trends about what, how, and for whom goods and services are produced in the U.S. economy and the global economy. How can you use this information? In two ways:

1. As you think about your future career, you are now better informed about some of the key trends. You know that a job in a manufacturing business is likely to be tough. A job in a service business is more likely to lead to success. Health care, education, communication, and entertainment are all likely to expand in the future and be sources of increasing employment and rising wages.

2. As you think about the stand you will take on the political question of protecting U.S. jobs, you are better informed about the basic facts and trends. But you have not yet learned the crucial bit of economics that will help you decide how to vote. That comes in the next chapter. So stay tuned!

CHECKPOINT 2.3

myeconlab

3 **Describe what, how, and for whom goods and services are produced in the global economy.**

Practice Problem 2.3

1. Describe what, how, and for whom goods and services are produced in developing economies.

Exercise 2.3

1. Describe how inequality around the world has changed over the past few decades.

Solution to Practice Problem 2.3

1. In developing countries: agriculture is the largest percentage, manufacturing is an increasing percentage, and services are important but a small percentage of total production; most production does not use modern capital-intensive technologies, but some industries do; and people who are willing and can find jobs in factories experience increasing income, while those working in rural industries are left behind.

CHAPTER CHECKPOINT

Key Points

1 **Describe what, how, and for whom goods and services are produced in the United States.**

- Goods and services are divided into two broad groups: Consumption goods and services and capital goods.
- Goods and services are produced by using the four factors of production: land, labor, capital, and entrepreneurship.
- The incomes people earn (rent for land, wages for labor, interest for capital, and profit for entrepreneurship) determine who gets what is produced.

2 **Use the circular flow model to provide a picture of how households and firms interact.**

- The circular flow model shows the real flows of the services of the factors of production that flow from households to firms and the real flows of goods and services that flow from firms to households.
- The circular flow model also shows the corresponding money flows of incomes from firms to households and expenditures from households to firms.

3 **Describe what, how, and for whom goods and services are produced in the global economy.**

- Sixty percent of the world's production (by value) comes from the advanced industrial countries and the emerging market economies.
- Production in the advanced economies uses more capital (both machines and human). But some parts of the developing economies use the latest capital and technologies.
- The global distribution of income is more unequal than the U.S. distribution. Poverty has fallen in Asia but has increased in Africa.

Key Terms

Capital, 38
Capital goods, 34
Circular flow model, 42
Consumption goods and services, 34
Entrepreneurship, 39
Factor markets, 42
Factors of production, 36

Firms, 42
Functional distribution of income, 40
Goods markets, 42
Households, 42
Human capital, 37
Interest, 39
Labor, 37

Land, 36
Market, 42
Personal distribution of income, 40
Profit (or loss), 39
Rent, 39
Wages, 39

Exercises

1. Which of the following items are *not* consumption goods and services and why?
   a. A chocolate bar
   b. A ski lift
   c. A golf ball
   d. An interstate highway
   e. An airplane
   f. A stealth bomber

2. Which of the following items are *not* capital goods and why?
   a. An auto assembly line
   b. A shopping mall
   c. A golf ball
   d. An interstate highway
   e. An oil tanker
   f. A construction worker

3. Which of the following items are *not* factors of production and why?
   a. Vans used by a baker to deliver bread
   b. 1,000 shares of Amazon.com stock
   c. Undiscovered oil
   d. A garbage truck
   e. A pack of bubble gum
   f. The President of the United States

4. In the United Kingdom, the following are the percentages of total income received by each 20 percent of the population: 2, 7, 15, 25, and 51. Is inequality greater in the United Kingdom than it is in the United States?

5. On a graph of the circular flow model, label the flows in which the following items occur:
   a. Disney uses some capital owned by Donald Trump.
   b. Dell sells a computer to Nicole Kidman.
   c. McDonald's hires Jessica.
   d. FedEx rents some land from Warren Buffett.
   e. Kinko's pays you $100 for weekend work.
   f. You pay your apartment rent.
   g. A student earns interest on her savings at the Bank of America.
   h. General Electric pays dividends to its stockholders.
   i. Microsoft pays Bill Gates a profit.

6. Compare the scale of agricultural production in the advanced and developing economies. In which is the percentage higher? In which is the total amount produced greater? In which is the cost of production lower?

7. You've seen that the global distribution of income is unequal. Why do you think it is unequal?

8. Think about the trends in what and how goods and services are produced in the U.S. and global economies:
   a. Which jobs will grow fastest in the future? Explain your answer.
   b. What do you think will happen to the quality of labor over the next decade? Explain your answer.
   c. Do you think that at some future time, there will be no jobs in the United States and all the jobs will be in developing economies? Why or why not?

Critical Thinking

9. You saw in the chapter opener that Scott and Raffael, like many other Americans, lost their manufacturing jobs and found new service jobs. Why is the United States becoming a service-producing economy? You also saw that Chown Chong Chin and her husband, like many other Chinese, left their farm jobs to get manufacturing jobs. Why is China becoming a manufacturing economy?

   Reflecting on these trends, do you think that we should be concerned that most of our clothing, electronic goods, and other manufactured goods come from abroad? Organize your answer around the following four points:
   a. Who in the United States do you think benefits from the availability of cheap foreign-produced clothing, electronic goods, and other manufactured goods?
   b. Who in the United States do you think bears the cost of cheap foreign-produced goods?
   c. Who in the rest of the world do you think benefits from the United States buying foreign-produced goods?
   d. Who in the rest of the world do you think bears the cost of the United States buying cheap foreign-produced goods?

10. In the United States, urban areas use only a bit more than 100 million acres of the total 1,944 million acres of land. But urban use has increased by 35 million acres in just 20 years. In light of this change, do you think that we should be concerned that too much of our land is becoming urban? Organize your answer around the following five points:
    a. What type of land gets transferred to urban use?
    b. Who benefits from the transfer of an acre of farmland to an acre of suburban housing?
    c. Who bears the cost of the transfer of an acre of farmland to an acre of suburban housing?
    d. What steps could be taken to slow the transfer of farmland to urban use?
    e. Is there a case for not just slowing the transfer of farmland to urban use but either stopping it completely or even trying to reverse the trend?

11. "If the trends in schooling continue, at some point in the future, everyone will have a college degree and no one will be available to work as a janitor or garbage collector." Critically evaluate this statement.

12. "Income is unequally distributed, but because wages account for more than 70 percent of total income, any redistribution from the rich to the poor means taking from wage earners to give to others." What is wrong with the reasoning in this statement?

13. Average incomes are rising, but incomes are becoming more unequal in most countries. Which do you think is better and why: to live in an economy with a high average income but great inequality or in one with a low average and little inequality?

14. How can it be that the distribution of income has become more unequal within most countries, yet the global distribution of income has become more equal? What problems remain despite the lessening of inequality at the global level?

Web Exercises

Use the links on MyEconLab to work the following exercises.

15. Visit washingtonpost.com and read the article about Scott Clark, Raffael, and others in the Richmond area and visit News-Record.com and read the article about Chown Chong Chin and her husband.
    a. What opportunity costs have these people borne?
    b. What benefits have they received?
    c. Can you think of anything that the U.S. government could have done to improve the lives of Scott and Raffael?
    d. Can you think of anything that the Chinese government could do to improve the lives of Chown Chong Chin and her husband?

16. Review the special "20th Century Statistics" section of the 1999 *Statistical Abstract of the United States* and find the table that describes trends in the characteristics of housing and the items that people own.
    a. Describe the trend in the ownership of homes. Do more people own or rent their homes today than the proportions in 1940?
    b. Describe the trend in the ownership of mobile homes and trailers.
    c. Describe the trend in plumbing facilities.
    d. Describe the trend in vehicle ownership.
    e. Describe the trend in telephone ownership.
    f. Can you explain the trends that you've found?

17. Review the special "20th Century Statistics" section of the 1999 *Statistical Abstract of the United States* and find the table that describes trends in transportation.
    a. Describe the trend in air travel.
    b. Describe the trend in the price of air travel.
    c. Can you explain the trends that you've found?
    d. How might these trends be influenced by the events of September 11, 2001?

18. Review the special "20th Century Statistics" section of the 1999 *Statistical Abstract of the United States* and find the table that describes trends in transportation.
    a. Describe the trend in road travel.
    b. Can you explain the trend that you've found?
    c. How might this trend be influenced by the events of September 11, 2001?

19. Visit the regional income pages of the Bureau of Economic Analysis at the U.S. Department of Commerce.
    a. Obtain data on per capita personal income for the states as a percentage of U.S. per capita personal income.
    b. Which state has the highest per capita income and which has the lowest?
    c. Where in the ranking does your state stand?
    d. Can you think of reasons for the ranking that you've found?
    e. Does the ranking change much from year to year? Why or why not?

20. Visit the University of Michigan's Statistical Resources on the Web.
    a. Find data that interest you and that provide information about what, how, and for whom goods and services are produced.
    b. Find data that tell you about the scale and trends in international trade.

The Economic Problem

CHAPTER 3

CHAPTER CHECKLIST

When you have completed your study of this chapter,
you will be able to

1. Use the production possibilities frontier to illustrate the economic problem.

2. Calculate opportunity cost.

3. Define efficiency and describe an efficient use of resources.

4. Explain what makes production possibilities expand.

5. Explain how people gain from specialization and trade.

If you enjoy music, you probably have an iPod or are thinking about getting one. Apple sold around 10 million of them in 2003 and 2004, and they are an increasingly common sight on campus and in the gym. The transition from the Walkman of the 1980s to the Discman of the 1990s to the iPod of today is an example of technological change expanding our consumption possibilities and changing the opportunity costs we face. Though our choices expand, we continue to face scarcity.

In this chapter, you will study an economic model of scarcity, choice, and opportunity cost that helps us to understand the choices that people and societies make. You will also learn about the central idea of economics: *efficiency*. And you will see what makes our production possibilities expand and how we gain by specializing and trading with each other.

3.1 PRODUCTION POSSIBILITIES

Every working day in the mines, factories, shops, and offices and on the farms and construction sites across the United States, we produce a vast array of goods and services. In the United States in 2005, 240 billion hours of labor equipped with $35 trillion worth of capital produced $12 trillion worth of goods and services.

Although our production capability is enormous, it is limited by our available resources and by technology. At any given time, we have fixed quantities of the factors of production and a fixed state of technology. Because our wants exceed our resources, we must make choices. We must rank our wants and decide which wants to satisfy and which to leave unsatisfied. In using our scarce resources, we make rational choices. And to make a rational choice, we must determine the costs and benefits of the alternatives.

Your first task in this chapter is to learn about an economic model of scarcity, choice, and opportunity cost—a model called the production possibilities frontier.

■ Production Possibilities Frontier

Production possibilities frontier

The boundary between the combinations of goods and services that can be produced and the combinations that cannot be produced, given the available factors of production and the state of technology.

The **production possibilities frontier** is the boundary between the combinations of goods and services that can be produced and the combinations that cannot be produced, given the available factors of production—land, labor, capital, and entrepreneurship—and the state of technology.

Although we produce millions of different goods and services, we can visualize the limits to production most easily if we imagine a simpler world that produces just two goods.

Imagine an economy that produces only bottled water and CDs. All the land, labor, capital, and entrepreneurship available gets used to produce these two goods.

Land can be used either for the water wells and springs and bottling plants that are required to make bottles of water or for space on which to build CD factories. Labor can be trained to work as water bottlers or as CD makers. Capital can be used for tapping springs and making water filtration plants or for the computers and lasers that make CDs. And entrepreneurs can put their creative talents to managing water resources and bottling factories or to running electronics businesses that make CDs. In every case, the more resources that get used to produce bottled water, the fewer are left for producing CDs.

We can illustrate the production possibilities frontier by using either a table or a graph. The table in Figure 3.1 describes six production possibilities for bottled water and CDs. These possibilities are alternative combinations of the quantities of the two goods that can be produced using all the economy's resources.

One possibility, *A*, is to allocate no factors of production to making bottled water, so bottled water production is zero. In this case, all the factors of production are used to make CDs and they can produce 15 million CDs a year. Another possibility, *B*, is to allocate the resources to bottled water production that are sufficient to produce 1 million bottles a year. But the resources that are being used in water-bottling plants must be taken from CD factories. So the economy can now produce only 14 million CDs a year. Possibilities *C, D, E,* and *F* show other combinations of the quantities of these two goods that the economy can produce. Possibility *F* uses all the resources to produce 5 million bottles of water a year and allocates no resources to producing CDs.

The graph in Figure 3.1 illustrates the production possibilities frontier, *PPF*, for bottled water and CDs. It is a graph of the production possibilities in the table. The *x*-axis shows the production of bottled water, and the *y*-axis shows the production of CDs. Each point on the graph labeled *A* through *F* represents the possibility in the table identified by the same letter. For example, point *B* represents the production of 1 million bottles of water and 14 million CDs. These quantities also appear in the table as possibility *B*.

The *PPF* is a valuable tool for illustrating the effects of scarcity and its consequences. The *PPF* puts three features of production possibilities in sharp focus. They are the distinctions between

- Attainable and unattainable combinations
- Efficient and inefficient production
- Tradeoffs and free lunches

FIGURE 3.1

The Production Possibilities Frontier

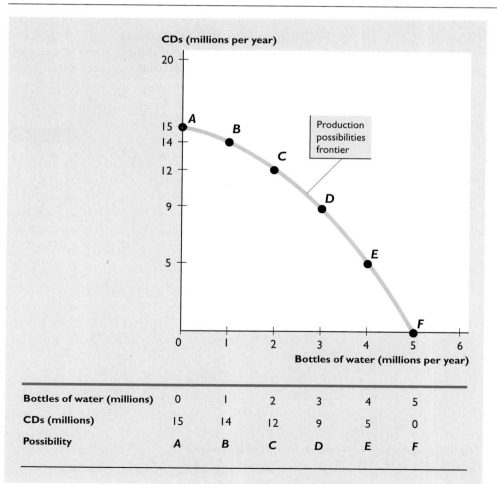

The table and the graph show the production possibilities frontier for bottled water and CDs.

Point *A* tells us that if the economy produces no bottled water, the maximum quantity of CDs it can produce is 15 million a year. Each point *A, B, C, D, E,* and *F* in the figure represents the possibility in the table identified by the same letter. The line passing through these points is the production possibilities frontier.

Bottles of water (millions)	0	1	2	3	4	5
CDs (millions)	15	14	12	9	5	0
Possibility	*A*	*B*	*C*	*D*	*E*	*F*

Attainable and Unattainable Combinations

Because the *PPF* shows the *limits* to production, it separates attainable combinations from unattainable ones. The economy can produce combinations of bottled water and CDs that are smaller than those on the *PPF,* and it can produce any of the combinations *on* the *PPF.* These combinations of bottled water and CDs are attainable. But it is impossible to produce combinations that are larger than those on the *PPF.* These combinations are unattainable.

Figure 3.2 emphasizes the attainable and unattainable combinations. Only the points on the *PPF* and inside it (in the orange area) are attainable. The combinations of bottled water and CDs beyond the *PPF* (in the white area), such as the combination at point G, are unattainable. These points illustrate combinations that cannot be produced with the current resources and technology. The *PPF* tells us that the economy can produce 4 million bottles of water and 5 million CDs at point *E or* 2 million bottles of water and 12 million CDs at point *C.* But the economy cannot produce 4 million bottles of water and 12 million CDs at point *G.*

Efficient and Inefficient Production

Production efficiency

A situation in which we cannot produce more of one good or service without producing less of something else.

Production is efficient when the economy is getting all that it can from its resources. More exactly, **production efficiency** occurs when it is not possible to produce more of one good or service without producing less of something else. For production to be efficient, there must be full employment—not just of labor but of all the available factors of production—and each resource must be assigned to the task that it performs comparatively better than other resources can.

▨ FIGURE 3.2

Attainable and Unattainable Combinations

The production possibilities frontier, *PPF,* separates attainable combinations from unattainable ones. The economy can produce at any point *inside* the *PPF* (the orange area) or *on* the frontier. Any point outside the production possibilities frontier such as point G is unattainable.

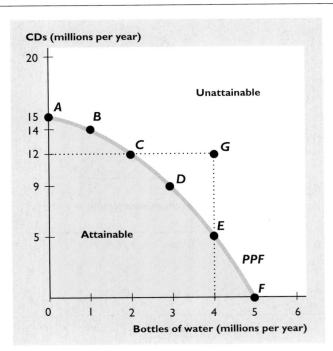

Figure 3.3 illustrates the distinction between efficient and inefficient production. With *inefficient* production, the economy might be at point *H*, where it produces 3 million bottles of water and 5 million CDs. With an *efficient* use of the economy's resources, it is possible to produce at a point on the *PPF* such as point *D* or *E*. At point *D*, there are more CDs and the same quantity of bottled water as at point *H*. And at point *E*, there are more bottles of water and the same quantity of CDs as at point *H*. At points *D* and *E*, production is efficient.

Tradeoffs and Free Lunches

A **tradeoff** is an exchange—giving up one thing to get something else. You trade off income for a better grade when you decide to cut back on the hours you spend on your weekend job and allocate the time to extra study. The Ford Motor Company faces a tradeoff when it cuts the production of trucks and uses the resources saved to produce more SUVs. The federal government faces a tradeoff when it cuts NASA's space exploration program and allocates more resources to homeland security. As a society, we face a tradeoff when we decide to cut down a forest and destroy the habitat of the spotted owl.

The production possibilities frontier illustrates the idea of a tradeoff. The *PPF* in Figure 3.3 shows how. If the economy produces at point *E* and people want to produce more CDs, they must forgo some bottled water. In the move from point *E* to point *D*, people trade off bottles of water for CDs.

Economists often express the central idea of economics—that choices involve tradeoffs—with the saying "There is no such thing as a free lunch." A **free lunch** is a gift—getting something without giving up something else. What does the

Tradeoff
An exchange—giving up one thing to get something else.

Free lunch
A gift—getting something without giving up something else.

■ FIGURE 3.3

Efficient and Inefficient Production, Tradeoffs, and Free Lunches

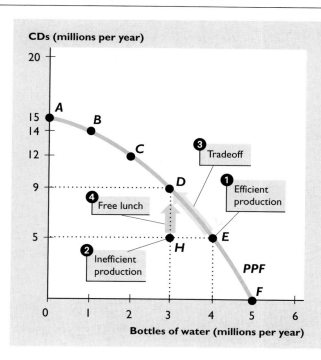

❶ When production occurs at a point on the *PPF*, such as point *E*, resources are used efficiently.

❷ When production occurs at a point inside the *PPF*, such as point *H*, resources are used inefficiently.

❸ When production is efficient—on the *PPF*—the economy faces a tradeoff. To move from point *E* to point *D* requires that some bottled water be given up for more CDs.

❹ When production is inefficient—inside the *PPF*—there is a free lunch. To move from point *H* to point *D* does not involve a tradeoff.

famous saying mean? Suppose some resources are not being used or are not being used efficiently. Isn't it then possible to avoid a tradeoff and get a free lunch?

The answer is yes. You can see why in Figure 3.3. If production is taking place *inside* the *PPF* at point *H*, then it is possible to move to point *D* and increase the production of CDs by using currently unused resources or by using resources in their most productive way. Nothing is forgone to increase production—there is a free lunch.

When production is efficient—at a point on the *PPF*—choosing to produce more of one good involves a tradeoff. But if production is inefficient—at a point inside the *PPF*—there is a free lunch. More of some goods and services can be produced without producing less of any others.

So "there is no such thing as a free lunch" means that when resources are used efficiently, every choice involves a tradeoff. Because economists view people as making rational choices, they expect that resources will be used efficiently. That is why they emphasize the tradeoff idea and deny the existence of free lunches. We might *sometimes* get a free lunch, but we *almost always* face tradeoffs.

REALITY CHECK

The *PPF* in YOUR Life

Think about your own production possibilities frontier. Two "goods" that concern you a great deal are your grade point average (GPA) and the amount of free time you have available to spend either working for an income or having fun.

The figure illustrates the *PPF* for a student who goes to class and studies for 48 hours each week and works or has fun (and sleeps) for the other 120 hours. The student is getting a GPA of 4.

■ How does *your PPF* compare with the one in the figure?

■ Show on this *PPF* what happens if you decide to go to a movie with friends instead of studying for your economics exam.

■ What is the tradeoff involved in your decision?

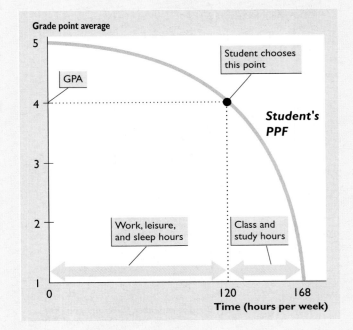

CHECKPOINT 3.1

1 Use the production possibilities frontier to illustrate the economic problem.

Practice Problem 3.1

1. Robinson Crusoe, a shipwrecked sailor, lived alone on a deserted island. His only resources were the land, which provided fish and fruit, and 8 hours a day of his labor, which he could allocate to catching fish or picking fruit. He varied the time spent on these two activities and kept a record of his production. Table 1 shows the numbers that Crusoe wrote in the sand.
   a. Use these numbers to make Crusoe's *PPF*.
   b. Which combinations (in pounds) are attainable and which are unattainable: (i) 10 fish and 30 fruit, (ii) 13 fish and 26 fruit, (iii) 16.5 fish and 21 fruit?
   c. Which combinations (in pounds) use all of Crusoe's 8 hours a day: (i) 15 fish and 21 fruit, (ii) 7 fish and 30 fruit, (iii) 18 fish and 0 fruit?
   d. Which combinations (in pounds) provide Crusoe with a free lunch and which confront him with a tradeoff when he increases fruit by 1: (i) 18 fish and 0 fruit, (ii) 15 fish and 15 fruit, (iii) 13 fish and 26 fruit?

TABLE 1

Hours	Fish (pounds)		Fruit (pounds)
0	0		0
1	4.0	or	8
2	7.5	or	15
3	10.5	or	21
4	13.0	or	26
5	15.0	or	30
6	16.5	or	33
7	17.5	or	35
8	18.0	or	36

Exercise 3.1

1. In the winter, Robinson Crusoe in practice problem 3.1 can work only 5 hours a day. Table 2 shows the quantities that Crusoe can produce in winter.
   a. Use these numbers to make Crusoe's *PPF* in winter.
   b. Which combinations (in pounds) are attainable and which are unattainable: (i) 7.5 fish and 11 fruit, (ii) 9 fish and 11 fruit, (iii) 5.5 fish and 14 fruit?
   c. Which combinations (in pounds) use all of Crusoe's 5 hours a day, which provide a free lunch, and which confront him with a tradeoff: (i) 10 fish and 0 fruit, (ii) 9 fish and 6 fruit, (iii) 3 fish and 16 fruit?

TABLE 2

Hours	Fish (pounds)		Fruit (pounds)
0	0		0
1	3.0	or	6
2	5.5	or	11
3	7.5	or	15
4	9.0	or	18
5	10.0	or	20

Solution to Practice Problem 3.1

1a. Table 3 sets out Crusoe's *PPF*. Crusoe can produce the fish and fruit that lie on his *PPF* if he uses a total of 8 hours a day. If he picks fruit for 8 hours, he picks 36 pounds and catches no fish (row *A*). If he picks fruit for 7 hours, he picks 35 pounds and has 1 hour for fishing in which he catches 4 pounds (row *B*). Check that you can construct the other rows of Table 3.

1b. (i) 10 fish and 30 fruit is attainable because Crusoe can produce 10.5 fish and 30 fruit (row *D* of Table 3). (ii) 13 fish and 26 fruit is attainable (row *E*). (iii) 16.5 fish and 21 fruit is unattainable because when Crusoe catches 16.5 fish he can pick only 15 fruit (row *G*).

1c. (i) 15 fish and 21 fruit uses all 8 hours—it is on his *PPF* (row *F*). (ii) 7 fish and 30 fruit does not use all 8 hours—it is inside his *PPF* (row *C*). (iii) 18 fish and 0 fruit uses all 8 hours—it is on his *PPF* (row *I*).

1d. (i) 18 fish and 0 fruit involves a tradeoff because it is on his *PPF*. (ii) 15 fish and 15 fruit provides a free lunch because it is inside his *PPF*. (iii) 13 fish and 26 fruit involves a tradeoff because it is on his *PPF*.

TABLE 3

Possibility	Fish (pounds)		Fruit (pounds)
A	0	and	36
B	4.0	and	35
C	7.5	and	33
D	10.5	and	30
E	13.0	and	26
F	15.0	and	21
G	16.5	and	15
H	17.5	and	8
I	18.0	and	0

3.2 OPPORTUNITY COST

You've seen that moving from one point to another on the *PPF* involves a trade-off. But what are the terms of the tradeoff? How much of one item must be forgone to obtain an additional unit of another item—a large amount or a small amount? The answer is given by opportunity cost—the best thing you must give up to get something (see p. 11). We can use the *PPF* to calculate opportunity cost.

■ The Opportunity Cost of a Bottle of Water

The opportunity cost of a bottle of water is the number of CDs forgone to get an additional bottle of water. It is calculated as the number of CDs forgone divided by the number of bottles of water gained.

Figure 3.4 illustrates the calculation. At point *A*, the quantities produced are zero water and 15 million CDs; and at point *B*, the quantities produced are 1 million bottles of water and 14 million CDs. To gain 1 million bottles of water by moving from point *A* to point *B*, 1 million CDs are forgone. So the opportunity cost of 1 bottle of water is 1 CD.

At point *C*, the quantities produced are 2 million bottles of water and 12 million CDs. To gain 1 million bottles of water by moving from point *B* to point *C*, 2 million CDs are forgone. So the opportunity cost of 1 bottle of water is 2 CDs.

If you repeat these calculations, moving from *C* to *D*, *D* to *E*, and *E* to *F*, you will obtain the opportunity costs shown in the table and the graph.

■ **FIGURE 3.4**

Calculating the Opportunity Cost of a Bottle of Water

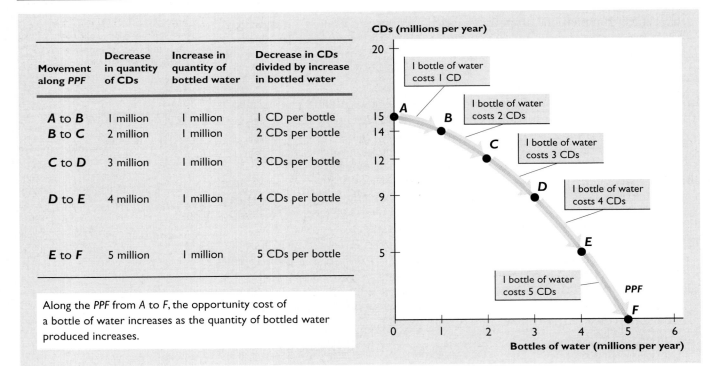

Movement along *PPF*	Decrease in quantity of CDs	Increase in quantity of bottled water	Decrease in CDs divided by increase in bottled water
A to *B*	1 million	1 million	1 CD per bottle
B to *C*	2 million	1 million	2 CDs per bottle
C to *D*	3 million	1 million	3 CDs per bottle
D to *E*	4 million	1 million	4 CDs per bottle
E to *F*	5 million	1 million	5 CDs per bottle

Along the *PPF* from *A* to *F*, the opportunity cost of a bottle of water increases as the quantity of bottled water produced increases.

■ Increasing Opportunity Cost

Look at the numbers that we've just calculated for the opportunity cost of a bottle of water and notice that they follow a striking pattern. The opportunity cost of water increases as the quantity of water produced increases. Figure 3.5 shows this increasing opportunity cost.

■ Slope of the *PPF* and Opportunity Cost

The magnitude of the *slope* of the *PPF* measures opportunity cost. And because the *PPF* in Figure 3.4 is bowed outward, its slope changes and gets steeper as the quantity of water produced increases.

When a small quantity of water is produced—between points *A* and *B*—the *PPF* has a gentle slope and the opportunity cost of a bottle of water is low. A given increase in the quantity of water costs a small decrease in the quantity of CDs. When a large quantity of water is produced—between points *E* and *F*—the *PPF* is steep and the opportunity cost of a bottle of water is high. A given increase in the quantity of water costs a large decrease in the quantity of CDs.

Note that if the *PPF* were linear, it would have a constant slope and the opportunity cost of a bottle of water would be constant. The same quantity of CDs would be forgone for each bottle of water.

Why is the *PPF* not linear? Why is it bowed outward? The reason is that resources are not equally productive in all activities. When a small quantity of water is produced, the people who work at Aqua Springs are the best at bottling

■ FIGURE 3.5
The Opportunity Cost of a Bottle of Water

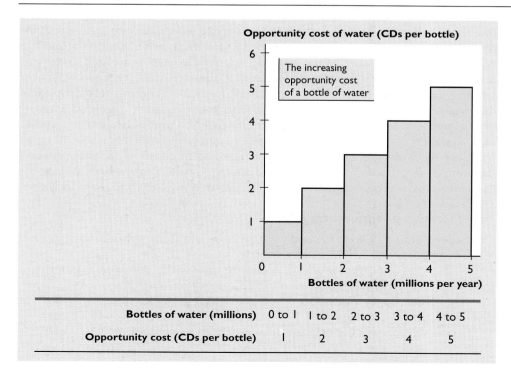

Because the *PPF* in Figure 3.4 is bowed outward, the opportunity cost of a bottle of water increases as the quantity of water produced increases.

Bottles of water (millions)	0 to 1	1 to 2	2 to 3	3 to 4	4 to 5
Opportunity cost (CDs per bottle)	1	2	3	4	5

water and the worst at making CDs. And some of the people who are working at Sony making CDs would be more productive at water bottling than they are at making CDs. In this situation, if workers move from Sony to Aqua Springs, a small quantity of CDs is forgone to get a given increase in the quantity of water.

But when a large quantity of water is produced, most people are working at Aqua Springs and the few people who work at Sony are the very best at making CDs and the worst at bottling water. In this situation, if workers move from Sony to Aqua Springs, a large quantity of CDs is forgone to get a given increase in the quantity of water.

■ Opportunity Cost Is a Ratio

You've seen that the opportunity cost of a bottle of water is the number of CDs forgone divided by the number of bottles of water gained—the *ratio* of CDs forgone to water gained.

Similarly, the opportunity cost of a CD is the number of bottles of water forgone divided by the number of CDs gained—the *ratio* of water forgone to CDs gained.

You saw that to gain 1 million bottles of water by moving along the *PPF* in Figure 3.4 from *C* to *D* costs 3 million CDs. So the opportunity cost of a bottle of water is 3 CDs.

By moving along the *PPF* in the opposite direction, from *D* to *C*, brings a gain of 3 million CDs at the cost of 1 million bottles of water. So the opportunity cost of a CD is 1/3 of a bottle of water.

Notice that the opportunity cost of a CD is equal to the inverse of the opportunity cost of a bottle of water. And just as in the case of water, the opportunity cost of a CD increases as the quantity of CDs produced increases.

■ Increasing Opportunity Costs Are Everywhere

Just about every activity that you can think of is one with an increasing opportunity cost. We allocate the most skillful farmers and the most fertile land to the production of food. And we allocate the best doctors and the least fertile land to the production of health-care services. If we shift fertile land and tractors away from farming to hospitals and ambulances and ask farmers to become hospital porters, the production of food drops drastically and the increase in the production of health-care services is small. The opportunity cost of a unit of health-care services rises. Similarly, if we shift our resources away from health care toward farming, we must use more doctors and nurses as farmers and more hospitals as hydroponic tomato factories. The decrease in the production of health-care services is large, but the increase in food production is small. The opportunity cost of a unit of food rises.

Your Increasing Opportunity Cost

Flip back to your *PPF* for time and GPA on p. 62 and think about its implications for your opportunity cost of a higher grade.

What is the opportunity cost of spending time with your friends in terms of the grade you might receive on your exam?

What is the opportunity cost of a higher grade in terms of the activities you give up to study?

Do you face increasing opportunity costs in these activities?

CHECKPOINT 3.2

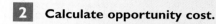

2 Calculate opportunity cost.

Practice Problem 3.2

1. Table 1 shows Robinson Crusoe's production possibilities.
   a. Use the data in Table 1 to make a table that shows Crusoe's opportunity cost of a pound of fish as he increases the time he spends fishing and decreases the time that he spends picking fruit.
   b. If Crusoe increases his production of fruit from 21 pounds to 26 pounds and decreases his production of fish from 15 pounds to 13 pounds, what is his opportunity cost of a pound of fruit? Explain your answer.
   c. If Crusoe is producing 10 pounds of fish and 20 pounds of fruit, what is his opportunity cost of a pound of fruit and a pound of fish? Explain your answer.

Exercise 3.2

1. Table 2 shows Robinson Crusoe's production possibilities in winter.
   a. Use the data in Table 2 to make a table that shows Crusoe's opportunity cost of a pound of fruit as he increases the time he spends picking fruit and decreases the time he spends fishing.
   b. If Crusoe currently catches 5.5 pounds of fish and picks 11 pounds of fruit a day, calculate his opportunity cost of a pound of fruit and of a pound of fish. Explain your answer.
   c. If Crusoe increases the amount of fish caught from 5.5 to 7.5 pounds and decreases the amount of fruit picked from 15 to 11 pounds, what is his opportunity cost of a pound of fish? Explain your answer.
   d. Does Crusoe's opportunity cost of a pound of fruit increase as he spends more time picking fruit? Explain why or why not.

Solution to Practice Problem 3.2

1a. Crusoe's opportunity cost of a pound of fish is the fruit given up divided by the gain in fish as he moves along his *PPF*, increasing the time he spends fishing and decreasing the time he spends picking fruit. For example, when Crusoe spends no time fishing, he produces the quantities in row *A* in Table 1. When he spends more time fishing and moves to row *B* in Table 1, the gain in fish is 4 pounds and the fruit given up is 1 pound. So the opportunity cost of a pound of fish is 1/4 of a pound of fruit. Check that you can derive the other rows of Table 3.

1b. The opportunity cost of a pound of fruit is 2/5 of a pound of fish. To gain 5 pounds of fruit, he forgoes 2 pounds of fish. The opportunity cost of a pound of fruit is the 2 pounds of fish forgone divided by 5 pounds of fruit gained. This opportunity cost is the inverse of the opportunity cost of a pound of fish (Table 3, move from *E* to *F*).

1c. If Crusoe is producing 10 pounds of fish and 20 pounds of fruit, his opportunity cost of fruit and of fish is zero because to gain a pound of fruit and a pound of fish, he doesn't have to give up anything. He is producing a combination inside his *PPF*.

TABLE 1

Possibility	Fish (pounds)	Fruit (pounds)
A	0	36
B	4.0	35
C	7.5	33
D	10.5	30
E	13.0	26
F	15.0	21
G	16.5	15
H	17.5	8
I	18.0	0

TABLE 2

Possibility	Fish (pounds)	Fruit (pounds)
A	0	20
B	3.0	18
C	5.5	15
D	7.5	11
E	9.0	6
F	10.0	0

TABLE 3

Move from	Gain in fish (pounds)	Fruit given up (pounds)	Opportunity cost of fish (pounds of fruit)
A to B	4.0	1	0.25
B to C	3.5	2	0.57
C to D	3.0	3	1.00
D to E	2.5	4	1.60
E to F	2.0	5	2.50
F to G	1.5	6	4.00
G to H	1.0	7	7.00
H to I	0.5	8	16.00

3.3 USING RESOURCES EFFICIENTLY

Environmentalists say that we should expand the use of clean solar technologies and burn less oil and coal. They also say that we should create clean mass transit systems and decrease our reliance on the automobile. Political leaders of all parties say that we should hire more teachers to reduce class size and improve education. Many also want to spend more on prescription drug plans for seniors and improve health care for the uninsured. Some political leaders want to enter into a new phase of defense spending and create an effective antimissile defense system. All of these policy proposals and the political debates that surround them are about allocative efficiency.

Economists use the idea of allocative efficiency in a broad way that cuts to the heart of these debates. **Allocative efficiency** occurs when the quantities of goods and services produced are those that people value most highly. To put it another way, resources are *allocated efficiently* when we cannot produce more of a good or service without giving up some of another good or service that people *value more highly.*

If people value a pollution-free environment more highly than they value cheap electric power, it is efficient to use high-cost clean technologies to produce electricity. In this case, limiting the use of coal and oil and expanding the use of solar energy sources would be efficient. If people value the flexibility of being able to choose when and where to travel more highly than they value low-cost, low-pollution, safe transportation, it is efficient to use high-cost, polluting, accident-prone automobiles.

So just what is the efficient energy policy: one that favors clean-energy technologies or one that burns oil and coal? What is the efficient method of urban transportation: one that uses a clean mass transit system or a system of freeways and private automobiles? And what are the efficient quantities of education, health care, and national defense?

These are questions that have enormous consequences for human welfare, and they are difficult questions. But you can see the essence of the answers by thinking about the simpler question: What is the efficient quantity of bottled water to produce? The answer to this question provides the principles that underlie the answers to all questions about how to use our scarce resources.

Allocative efficiency
A situation in which the quantities of goods and services produced are those that people value most highly—it is not possible to produce more of a good or service without giving up some of another good that people value more highly.

■ Two Conditions for Allocative Efficiency

Allocative efficiency is achieved when two conditions are met:

- Production efficiency—producing on the *PPF*
- Producing at the highest-valued point on the *PPF*

Production Efficiency—Producing On the *PPF*

You've seen that *production efficiency* is achieved when it is not possible to produce more of one good or service without producing less of something else. When production is efficient, the economy is *on* its *PPF*. If production occurs *inside* the *PPF*, production is *inefficient.* Either some resources are unemployed or some resources are not being used in their most productive way. Putting unemployed resources to work and reallocating misused resources to their most productive use enables more to be produced.

When resources are unemployed or misused, it is possible to produce more of a good without incurring an opportunity cost. So production is not efficient. Only when all resources are fully employed and the economy is operating on the *PPF* is it impossible to produce more of one good or service without producing less of another good or service.

Producing at the Highest-Valued Point on the *PPF*

Allocative efficiency is achieved when the combination of goods and services produced on the *PPF* are those that are valued most highly. All the combinations of goods and services on the *PPF* achieve *production efficiency*. Each of these combinations is such that, to produce more of one good, the quantity produced of another good must decrease. But only one of these combinations achieves *allocative efficiency*. That is, only one combination is the most highly valued.

To find this combination, we need some additional information that is not contained in the *PPF*. The *PPF*, remember, tells us what it is *possible* to produce and provides information about opportunity cost. The *PPF* does not tell us the *value* of what we produce. To determine the value, we use the concept of marginal benefit.

■ Marginal Benefit

You learned in Chapter 1 (pp. 12–13) that the *benefit* of something is the gain or pleasure that it brings. Benefit is how a person *feels* about something. We defined *marginal benefit* as the benefit that a person receives from consuming one more unit of a good or service.

You also learned in Chapter 1 that economists measure the benefit of something by what a person *is willing to* give up to get it. So a person's *marginal* benefit of a good or service is what that person *is willing to* give up to get *one more* unit of it.

It is a general principle that the more we have of any good or service, the smaller is our marginal benefit from it—the principle of decreasing marginal benefit. To understand the principle of decreasing marginal benefit, think about your own marginal benefit from bottled water. If bottled water is very hard to come by and you can buy only one or two bottles a year, you will be very pleased to get one more bottle. The marginal benefit of that bottle of water is high. In this situation, you are willing to give up quite a lot of some other good or service to get one more bottle of water. But if there is plenty of bottled water around and you have as much as you can drink, you will get almost no benefit from one more bottle. So you are willing to give up almost nothing for that bottle of water.

The principle of diminishing marginal benefit applies to all goods and services. You get a lot of pleasure from one slice of pizza. A second slice is fine, too, but not quite as satisfying as the first one. But eat three, four, five, six, and more slices, and each additional slice is less enjoyable than the previous one. You get diminishing marginal benefit from pizza. So the more pizza you have, the less of some other good or service you would be willing to give up to get one more slice.

Although marginal benefit expresses a person's *feeling* toward a good or service, it is nonetheless a real, objective phenomenon. It is as real as the physical limits to production that we express in the *PPF*. The *PPF* shows what is *feasible*. Marginal benefit is an expression of what is *desirable*. And we need a way of describing marginal benefit that is as concrete as the *PPF*.

Let's see how economists describe marginal benefit.

Marginal Benefit Schedule and Curve

We describe marginal benefit by using either a marginal benefit schedule or a marginal benefit curve. Figure 3.6 illustrates these concepts, and we continue to use the same two goods as before: bottled water and CDs. The marginal benefit from a bottle of water can be expressed as the number of CDs that a person is willing to forgo to get one more bottle. This amount decreases as the quantity of bottled water available increases.

Begin by looking at the table below the graph. In possibility *A*, 1 million bottles of water are available, and at that quantity, people are willing to give up 4.5 CDs for a bottle of water. As the quantity of bottled water available increases, the amount that people are willing to give up for an additional bottle falls—3.5 CDs per bottle when 2 million bottles are available in possibility *B*, 2.5 CDs per bottle when 3 million bottles are available in possibility *C*, and 1.5 CDs per bottle when 4 million bottles are available in possibility *D*.

The marginal benefit curve is a graph of the marginal benefit schedule. The points *A*, *B*, *C*, and *D* on the marginal benefit curve correspond to the possibilities *A*, *B*, *C*, and *D* of the marginal benefit schedule.

The marginal benefit from a bottle of water and the opportunity cost of a bottle of water that you studied on p. 64 are both measured in CDs per bottle. But they are *not* the same concept. The opportunity cost of a bottle of water is the quantity of CDs that people *must forgo* to get another bottle. The marginal benefit from a bottle of water is the quantity of CDs that people are *willing to forgo* to get another bottle.

■ **FIGURE 3.6**

Marginal Benefit of a Bottle of Water

The table and the graph show the marginal benefit of a bottle of water.

Point *A* tells us that if the quantity of water produced is 1 million bottles a year, the maximum quantity of CDs that people are willing to give up for an additional bottle of water is 4.5 CDs. Each point *A*, *B*, *C*, and *D* in the graph represents the possibility in the table identified by the same letter.

The line passing through these points is the marginal benefit curve. The marginal benefit of a bottle of water decreases as the quantity of bottled water available increases.

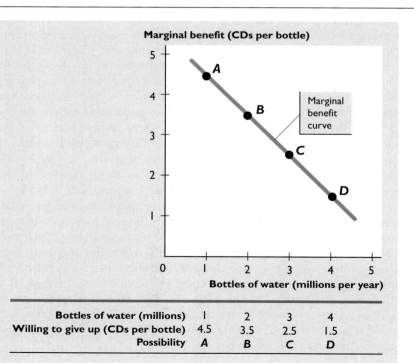

Bottles of water (millions)	1	2	3	4
Willing to give up (CDs per bottle)	4.5	3.5	2.5	1.5
Possibility	*A*	*B*	*C*	*D*

Marginal Cost

To achieve allocative efficiency, we must compare the marginal benefit of a bottle of water with its marginal cost. We defined *marginal cost* in Chapter 1 (p. 12) as the opportunity cost of producing one more unit of a good or service. You've seen how we can calculate opportunity cost as we move along the production possibilities frontier. We can calculate marginal cost in a similar way. The marginal cost of a bottle of water is the opportunity cost of one additional bottle—the quantity of CDs that must be given up to get one more bottle of water as we move along the *PPF*.

Figure 3.7 illustrates the marginal cost of a bottle of water based on the opportunity cost numbers that you've already calculated. The opportunity cost of the first 1 million bottles of water is 1 million CDs. So on the average over the range from zero to 1 million, 1 bottle of water costs 1 CD. Because this value is the average over a range, we graph it at the midpoint of the range—midway between zero and 1 million. The opportunity cost of the second 1 million bottles of water is 2 million CDs. So on the average over this range, 1 bottle of water costs 2 CDs. We graph this cost midway between 1 million and 2 million on the graph.

Figure 3.7 shows that the marginal cost curve of bottled water slopes upward. That is, as the quantity of bottled water produced increases, the marginal cost of bottled water increases. This increasing marginal cost occurs for the same reason the opportunity cost increases.

Let's use the concepts of marginal benefit and marginal cost to discover the efficient quantity of bottled water to produce.

FIGURE 3.7
Marginal Cost of a Bottle of Water

myeconlab

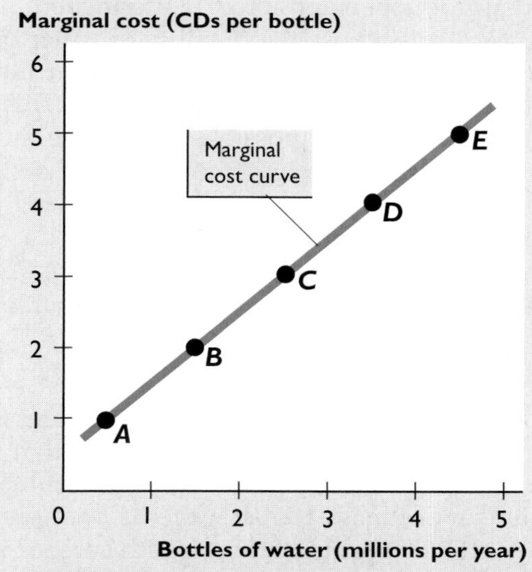

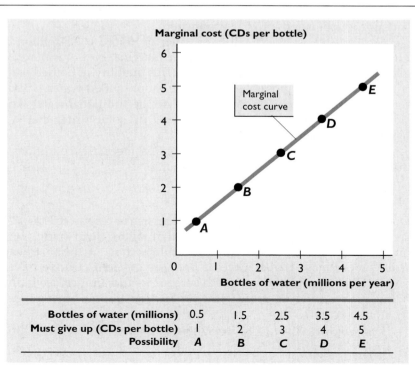

Bottles of water (millions)	0.5	1.5	2.5	3.5	4.5
Must give up (CDs per bottle)	1	2	3	4	5
Possibility	*A*	*B*	*C*	*D*	*E*

The table and the graph show the marginal cost of a bottle of water. Marginal cost is the opportunity cost of producing one more unit and is derived from the *PPF*.

Points *A, B, C, D,* and *E* in the graph represent the possibilities in the table. The marginal cost curve shows that the marginal cost of a bottle of water increases as the quantity of bottled water produced increases.

■ Efficient Use of Resources

Resource use is efficient when the goods and services that are produced are the ones that people value most highly. That is, when resources are allocated efficiently, it is not possible to produce more of any good without producing less of something else that is valued even more highly.

We can illustrate an efficient use of resources by continuing to use the example of bottled water and CDs. Figure 3.8(a) shows the production possibilities frontier (the same as in Figure 3.1 on p. 59). And Figure 3.8(b) shows the marginal cost (*MC*) and marginal benefit (*MB*) of a bottle of water.

Suppose that the quantity of water produced is 1.5 million bottles on the *PPF* in Figure 3.8(a). This quantity of water meets the condition for production efficiency because it is on the *PPF*. But does it meet the condition for allocative efficiency? To answer this question, we need to compare marginal benefit and marginal cost in Figure 3.8(b). At this quantity of water, the marginal benefit of water is 4 CDs per bottle, but the marginal cost of water is only 2 CDs per bottle. Because people value an additional bottle of water more highly than the cost to produce it, too little water is being produced (and too many CDs are being produced). Greater value can be obtained from the economy's resources by moving some of them out of CD production and into bottled water production.

Now suppose that the quantity of water produced is 3.5 million bottles on the *PPF* in Figure 3.8(a). Again, this point meets the condition for production efficiency because it is on the *PPF*. To check whether it meets the condition for allocative efficiency, we again need to compare marginal benefit and marginal cost. At this quantity of water, the marginal benefit of water is now 2 CDs per bottle, but the marginal cost of water is 4 CDs per bottle. Because people value an additional bottle of water less highly than the cost to produce it, too much water is being produced (and too few CDs are being produced). Greater value can now be obtained from the economy's resources by moving some of them out of bottled water production and into CD production.

Finally, suppose the quantity of water produced is 2.5 million bottles on the *PPF* in Figure 3.8(a). At this quantity, the marginal cost of water equals the marginal benefit. Both are 3 CDs per bottle. This quantity of bottled water (and CDs) is efficient. It is not possible to produce more bottled water without giving up some CDs that are valued more highly than the additional water. And it isn't possible to produce more CDs without giving up some water that is valued more highly than the additional CDs.

So 2.5 million bottles of water on the *PPF* meets the conditions for both production efficiency and allocative efficiency.

■ Efficiency in the U.S. Economy

Does the U.S. economy achieve an efficient use of resources? Do we have an efficient energy policy, or would a policy that favors clean-energy technologies be more efficient? Do we have an efficient method of urban transportation, or would more mass transit systems be more efficient? Do we have the efficient quantities of education and health care, or would an increase in the production of these items and a decrease in the production of some other goods and services be more efficient?

You will learn how to address these questions in Chapters 6 through 10.

FIGURE 3.8
The Efficient Quantity of Bottled Water

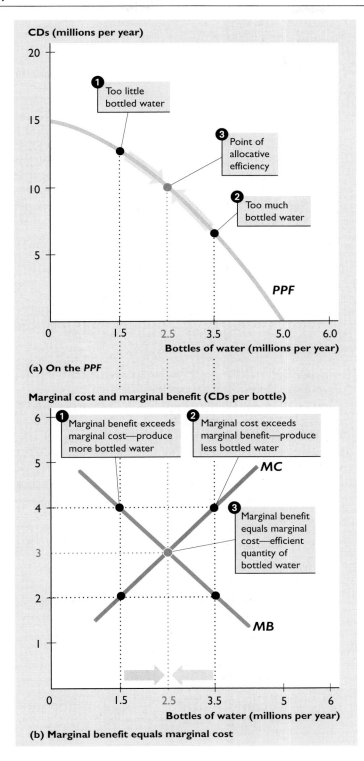

(a) On the PPF

(b) Marginal benefit equals marginal cost

Production efficiency occurs at all points on the *PPF*. But only one point meets the condition for allocative efficiency.

❶ When the quantity of water is 1.5 million bottles in part (a), too little bottled water is being produced because in part (b), the marginal benefit of water exceeds the marginal cost. It is efficient to produce more water.

❷ When the quantity of water is 3.5 million bottles in part (a), too much bottled water is being produced because in part (b), the marginal cost of water exceeds the marginal benefit. It is efficient to produce less water.

❸ When the quantity of water is 2.5 million bottles in part (a), the efficient quantity of bottled water is being produced because in part (b), the marginal cost of water equals the marginal benefit.

3 Define efficiency and describe an efficient use of resources.

Practice Problems 3.3

TABLE 1

Possibility	Bananas (bunches)	Coffee (pounds)
A	70	40
B	50	100
C	30	140
D	10	160

1. Table 1 shows a nation's production possibilities of bananas and coffee. Use the table to calculate the nation's marginal cost of a bunch of bananas. Draw the marginal cost curve.

2. Use the following data to draw the nation's marginal benefit curve for a bunch of bananas:
   a. When 20 bunches of bananas are available, people are willing to give up 3 pounds of coffee to get an additional bunch of bananas.
   b. When 40 bunches of bananas are available, people are willing to give up 2 pounds of coffee to get an additional bunch of bananas.
   c. When 60 bunches of bananas are available, people are willing to give up 1 pound of coffee to get an additional bunch of bananas.

3. Use the data in practice problems 1 and 2 to calculate the efficient use of the nation's resources.

Exercise 3.3

1. Use the *PPF* shown in Figure 1(a) and the marginal benefit curve shown in Figure 1(b) to find the efficient quantities of yogurt and ice cream.

Solutions to Practice Problems 3.3

FIGURE 1

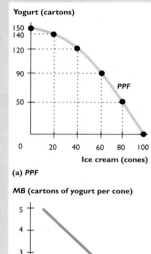

(a) *PPF*

(b) Marginal benefit

1. Figure 2 shows the marginal cost curve. When the quantity of bananas increases from 10 to 30 bunches, the quantity of coffee decreases from 160 to 140 pounds. The gain in bananas is 20 bunches, and the coffee given up is 20 pounds. So the opportunity cost of 1 bunch of bananas is 1 pound of coffee. In the figure, marginal cost is 1 pound of coffee at the midpoint between 10 and 30 bunches, which is 20 bunches of bananas. When the quantity of bananas increases from 30 to 50 bunches, coffee decreases from 140 to 100 pounds. The gain in bananas is 20 bunches, and the coffee given up is 40 pounds. So the opportunity cost of 1 bunch of bananas is 2 pounds of coffee. In the figure, marginal cost is 2 pounds of coffee at the midpoint between 30 and 50 bunches, which is 40 bunches of bananas.

2. Figure 2 shows the marginal benefit curve, which slopes downward because as more bananas are available, the marginal benefit from an additional bunch of bananas decreases.

3. The nation uses its resources efficiently when it produces 40 bunches of bananas and (approximately) 120 pounds of coffee. When the nation produces this combination, production is on the *PPF* (production efficiency), and it is the highest-valued combination because marginal benefit equals marginal cost (allocative efficiency).

FIGURE 2

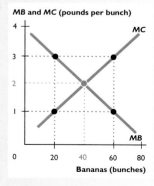

3.4 ECONOMIC GROWTH

Economic growth is the sustained expansion of production possibilities. Our economy grows when we develop better technologies for producing goods and services; improve the quality of labor by education, on-the-job training, and work experience; and get more machines to help us produce.

We can see how economic growth occurs by using the *PPF*. But to study economic growth, we must change the two goods. We need to look at the *PPF* for a consumption good and a capital good.

Figure 3.9 shows the *PPF* for bottled water—a consumption good—and water-bottling plants—a capital good. By using today's resources to produce bottling plants, the economy can expand its future production possibilities. The amount by which production possibilities expand depends on the quantity of capital—number of new bottling plants—produced. Producing no new plants (at point *L*) keeps the *PPF* in its original position. Decreasing the production of bottled water and producing 2 new bottling plants (at point *K*) increases production possibilities and shifts the *PPF* outward to the new *PPF*. The greater the production of new capital, the faster is the expansion of production possibilities.

But economic growth is not free. To make it happen, consumption must decrease. The move from *L* to *K* in Figure 3.9 means forgoing 2 million bottles of water now. The opportunity cost of producing more bottling plants is producing fewer bottles of water for consumption today.

Also, economic growth is no magic formula for abolishing scarcity. Economic growth shifts the *PPF* outward, but on the new *PPF*, we continue to face opportunity costs. To keep producing capital, current consumption must be less than its maximum possible level.

Economic growth
The sustained expansion of production possibilities.

■ FIGURE 3.9
Expanding Production Possibilities

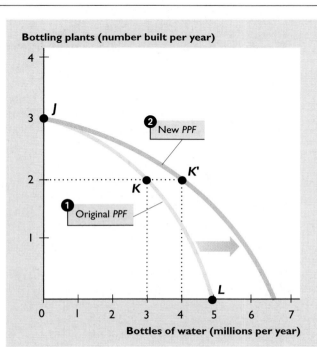

Bottling plants (number built per year)

Bottles of water (millions per year)

❶ If firms allocate no resources to producing water-bottling plants and produce 5 million bottles of water a year at point *L*, the *PPF* doesn't change.

❷ If firms decrease water production to 3 million bottles a year and produce 2 water-bottling plants, at point *K*, production possibilities will expand. After a year, the *PPF* shifts outward to the new *PPF* and production can move to point *K'*.

Hong Kong's Rapid Economic Growth

Hong Kong's production possibilities per person were 25 percent of those of the United States in 1960. By 2000, they had grown to become 80 percent of U.S. production possibilities. Hong Kong grew faster than the United States because it allocated more of its resources to accumulating capital and less to consumption than the United States did.

In 1960, the United States and Hong Kong produced at point A on their respective PPFs. In 2000, Hong Kong was at point B and the United States was at point C.

If Hong Kong continues to produce at a point such as B, it will grow more rapidly than the United States and its PPF will eventually move out beyond the U.S. PPF. But if Hong Kong produces at a point such as D, the pace of expansion of its PPF will slow.

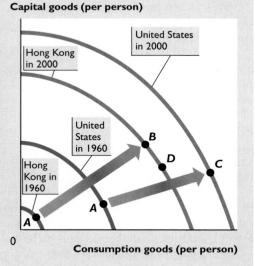

Capital goods (per person)

Hong Kong in 2000

United States in 2000

United States in 1960

Hong Kong in 1960

B

D

C

A

A

0

Consumption goods (per person)

CHECKPOINT 3.4

4 **Explain what makes production possibilities expand.**

Practice Problem 3.4

TABLE 1

Possibility	Education services (graduates)	Consumption goods (units)
A	1,000	0
B	750	1,000
C	500	2,000
D	0	3,000

1. Table 1 shows an economy that produces education services and consumption goods. If the economy currently produces 500 graduates a year and 2,000 units of consumption goods, what is the opportunity cost of economic growth?

Exercise 3.4

1. If the economy shown in Table 1 uses all its resources to produce consumption goods, at what rate will the economy grow? If the economy increases the number of graduates from 0 to 750, will the economy experience economic growth? Explain your answer.

Solution to Practice Problem 3.4

1. The opportunity cost of producing 500 graduates a year is 1,000 units (3,000 minus 2,000) of consumption goods forgone.

3.5 SPECIALIZATION AND TRADE

A person can produce several goods or can concentrate on producing one good and then trading some of that good for those produced by others. Concentrating on the production of only one good is called *specialization.* We are going to discover how people gain by specializing in the production of the good in which they have a *comparative advantage.*

■ Comparative Advantage

A person has a **comparative advantage** in an activity if that person can perform the activity at a lower opportunity cost than someone else. Let's explore the idea of comparative advantage by looking at two smoothie bars: one operated by Liz and the other operated by Joe.

Liz's Smoothie Bar

Liz produces smoothies and salads. In Liz's high-tech bar, she can turn out *either* a smoothie *or* a salad every 90 seconds. If she spends all her time making smoothies, she produces 40 an hour. If she spends all her time making salads, she also produces 40 an hour. If she splits her time equally between the two, she can produce 20 smoothies *and* 20 salads an hour. For each additional smoothie Liz produces, she must decrease her production of salads by one, and for each additional salad Liz produces, she must decrease her production of smoothies by one. So

> **Liz's opportunity cost of producing 1 smoothie is 1 salad,**

and

> **Liz's opportunity cost of producing 1 salad is 1 smoothie.**

Liz's customers buy smoothies and salads in equal quantities, so Liz splits her time equally between the items and produces 20 smoothies and 20 salads an hour.

Joe's Smoothie Bar

Joe also produces both smoothies and salads. But Joe's bar is smaller than Liz's. Also, Joe has only one blender, and it's a slow, old machine. Even if Joe uses all his resources to produce smoothies, he can produce only 6 an hour. But Joe is pretty good in the salad department, so if he uses all his resources to make salads, he can produce 30 an hour. Joe's ability to make smoothies and salads is the same regardless of how he splits an hour between the two tasks. He can make a salad in 2 minutes or a smoothie in 10 minutes. For each additional smoothie Joe produces, he must decrease his production of salads by 5. And for each additional salad Joe produces, he must decrease his production of smoothies by 1/5 of a smoothie. So

> **Joe's opportunity cost of producing 1 smoothie is 5 salads,**

and

> **Joe's opportunity cost of producing 1 salad is 1/5 of a smoothie.**

Joe's customers, like Liz's, buy smoothies and salads in equal quantities. So Joe spends 50 minutes of each hour making smoothies and 10 minutes of each hour making salads. With this division of his time, Joe produces 5 smoothies and 5 salads an hour.

Comparative advantage
The ability of a person to perform an activity or produce a good or service at a lower opportunity cost than someone else.

TABLE 3.1   LIZ'S PRODUCTION POSSIBILITIES

Item	Minutes to produce 1	Quantity per hour
Smoothies	1.5	40
Salads	1.5	40

TABLE 3.2   JOE'S PRODUCTION POSSIBILITIES

Item	Minutes to produce 1	Quantity per hour
Smoothies	10	6
Salads	2	30

Liz's Absolute Advantage

You can see from the numbers that describe the two smoothie bars that Liz is four times as productive as Joe—her 20 smoothies and 20 salads an hour are four times Joe's 5 smoothies and 5 salads. Liz has an **absolute advantage**—she is more productive than Joe in producing both smoothies and salads. But Liz has a comparative advantage in only one of the activities.

Liz's Comparative Advantage

In which of the two activities does Liz have a *comparative* advantage? Recall that comparative advantage is a situation in which one person's opportunity cost of producing a good is lower than another person's opportunity cost of producing that same good. Liz has a comparative advantage in producing smoothies. Her opportunity cost of a smoothie is 1 salad, whereas Joe's opportunity cost of a smoothie is 5 salads.

Joe's Comparative Advantage

If Liz has a comparative advantage in producing smoothies, Joe must have a comparative advantage in producing salads. His opportunity cost of a salad is 1/5 of a smoothie, while Liz's opportunity cost of a salad is 1 smoothie.

■ Achieving Gains from Trade

Liz and Joe run into each other one evening in a singles bar. After a few minutes of getting acquainted, Liz tells Joe about her amazingly profitable smoothie business that is selling 20 smoothies and 20 salads an hour. Her only problem, she tells Joe, is that she wishes she could produce more because potential customers leave when her lines get too long.

Joe isn't sure whether to risk spoiling his chances by telling Liz about his own struggling business. But he takes the risk. When he explains to Liz that he spends 50 minutes of every hour making 5 smoothies and 10 minutes making 5 salads, Liz's eyes pop. "Have I got a deal for you!" she exclaims.

Here's the deal that Liz sketches on a paper napkin. Joe stops making smoothies and allocates all his time to producing salads. And Liz increases her production of smoothies to 35 an hour and cuts her production of salads to 5 an hour—see Table 3.3(a). They then trade. Liz sells Joe 10 smoothies and Joe sells Liz 20 salads—the price of a smoothie is 2 salads—see Table 3.3(b).

After the trade, Joe has 10 salads—the 30 he produces minus the 20 he sells to Liz. And he has the 10 smoothies that he buys from Liz. So Joe doubles the quantities of smoothies and salads he can sell—see Table 3.3(c). Liz has 25 smoothies—the 35 she produces minus the 10 she sells to Joe. And she has 25 salads—the 5 she produces plus the 20 she buys from Joe—see Table 3.3(c). Both Liz and Joe gain 5 smoothies and 5 salads—see Table 3.3(d).

Liz draws a figure (Figure 3.10) to illustrate her suggestion. The red *PPF* is Joe's and the blue *PPF* is Liz's. They are each producing at the points marked *A*. Liz's proposal is that they each produce at the points marked *B*. They then trade—exchange—smoothies and salads at a price of 2 salads per smoothie, or 1/2 of a smoothie per salad. Liz gets salads for 1/2 a smoothie each, which is less than the 1 smoothie that it costs her to produce them. And Joe gets smoothies for 2 salads each, which is less than the 5 salads it costs him to produce them. Each moves to the points marked *C, outside* their respective *PPFs*.

Absolute advantage
When one person is more productive than another person in several or even all activities.

TABLE 3.3   LIZ AND JOE GAIN FROM TRADE

(a) Production	Liz	Joe
Smoothies	35	0
Salads	5	30

(b) Trade		
Smoothies	sell 10	buy 10
Salads	buy 20	sell 20

(c) After Trade		
Smoothies	25	10
Salads	25	10

(d) Gains from Trade		
Smoothies	+5	+5
Salads	+5	+5

FIGURE 3.10

The Gains from Specialization

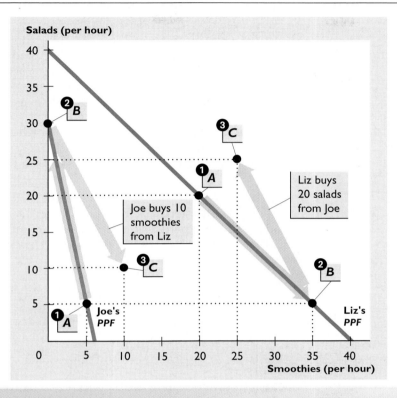

❶ Liz and Joe each produce at point A on their respective *PPFs*. Liz has a comparative advantage in smoothies, and Joe has a comparative advantage in salads.

❷ Joe specializes in salads and Liz increases her production of smoothies, so they each produce at point B on their respective *PPFs*.

❸ They exchange smoothies for salads at a price of 2 salads per smoothie. Each goes to C— a point outside their individual *PPFs*. They each gain 5 salads and 5 smoothies.

REALITY CHECK

Comparative Advantage in YOUR Life

What you have learned in this chapter has huge implications for the way you organize your life and for the position that you take on the political hot potato of global outsourcing.

1. Just as an economy expands its production possibilities by accumulating capital, so also you will expand your production possibilities by accumulating *human* capital.

2. By discovering *your* comparative advantage, you will be able to focus on producing the items that make you as well off as possible. Think hard about what *you* enjoy doing and that you do comparatively better than others.

3. Regardless of whether outsourcing is around the corner (like Liz and Joe) or around the globe (like the United States and India), both parties gain by exploiting their comparative advantage.

5 Explain how people gain from specialization and trade.

Practice Problem 3.5

TABLE 1   TONY'S PRODUCTION POSSIBILITIES

Snowboards (per week)		Skis (per week)
25	and	0
20	and	10
15	and	20
10	and	30
5	and	40
0	and	50

TABLE 2   PATTY'S PRODUCTION POSSIBILITIES

Snowboards (per week)		Skis (per week)
20	and	0
10	and	5
0	and	10

TABLE 3   SARA'S PRODUCTION POSSIBILITIES

Boards (per week)		Sails (per week)
15	and	0
12	and	2
9	and	4
6	and	6
3	and	8
0	and	10

TABLE 4   SID'S PRODUCTION POSSIBILITIES

Boards (per week)		Sails (per week)
40	and	0
32	and	12
24	and	24
16	and	36
8	and	48
0	and	60

1. Tony and Patty produce skis and snowboards. Tables 1 and 2 show their production possibilities per week. Each week, Tony produces 5 snowboards and 40 skis and Patty produces 10 snowboards and 5 skis.
   a. Calculate Tony's opportunity cost of a snowboard.
   b. Calculate Patty's opportunity cost of a snowboard.
   c. Who has a comparative advantage in producing snowboards?
   d. Who has a comparative advantage in producing skis?
   e. If they specialize and trade 1 snowboard for 1 ski, who will gain?

Exercise 3.5

1. Sara and Sid produce boards and sails for windsurfing. Tables 3 and 4 show their production possibilities per week. Each week, Sara produces 6 boards and 6 sails, and Sid produces 24 boards and 24 sails.
   a. Calculate Sara's opportunity cost of a board.
   b. Calculate Sid's opportunity cost of a board.
   c. Who has a comparative advantage in producing boards?
   d. Who has a comparative advantage in producing sails?
   e. Can Sara and Sid gain by changing their production and trading 1 board for 1 sail? Explain why or why not.

Solution to Practice Problem 3.5

1a. Tony's production possibilities show that to produce 5 more snowboards he must produce 10 fewer skis. So for Tony, the opportunity cost of producing a snowboard is 2 skis.

1b. Patty's production possibilities show that to produce 10 more snowboards, she must produce 5 fewer skis. So for Patty, the opportunity cost of producing a snowboard is 1/2 a ski.

1c. Patty has a comparative advantage in producing snowboards because her opportunity cost of producing a snowboard is less than Tony's.

1d. Tony has a comparative advantage in producing skis. For each ski produced, Tony gives up making 1/2 a snowboard. His opportunity cost of a ski is 1/2 a snowboard. For each ski that Patty produces, she must give up producing 2 snowboards. Her opportunity cost of a ski is 2 snowboards. So Tony's opportunity cost of a ski is lower than Patty's.

1e. Patty specializes in snowboards, and Tony specializes in skis. Patty produces 20 snowboards and Tony produces 50 skis. Before specializing, they produced 15 snowboards (10 by Patty and 5 by Tony) and 45 skis (40 by Tony and 5 by Patty). By specializing, they have increased their total output by 5 snowboards and 5 skis. They can share this gain by trading 1 ski for 1 snowboard. Patty can get skis from Tony for less than it costs her to produce them. Tony can buy snowboards from Patty for less than it cost him to produce them. Both Patty and Tony achieve gains from specialization and trade.

CHAPTER CHECKPOINT

Key Points

1 | **Use the production possibilities frontier to illustrate the economic problem.**

- The production possibilities frontier, *PPF*, describes the limits to what can be produced by fully and efficiently using all the available resources.
- Points inside and on the *PPF* are attainable. Points outside the *PPF* are unattainable.
- Production at any point on the *PPF* achieves production efficiency. Production at a point inside the *PPF* is inefficient.
- When production is efficient—on the *PPF*—people face a tradeoff. If production is at a point inside the *PPF*, there is a free lunch.

2 | **Calculate opportunity cost.**

- Along the *PPF*, the opportunity cost of X (the item on the x-axis) is the decrease in Y (the item on the y-axis) divided by the increase in X.
- The opportunity cost of Y is the inverse of the opportunity cost of X.
- The opportunity cost of producing a good increases as the quantity of the good produced increases.

3 | **Define efficiency and describe an efficient use of resources.**

- Resource use is efficient when there is production efficiency and allocative efficiency.
- Production efficiency occurs at *all* points *on* the *PPF*.
- Allocative efficiency occurs at the *one* point on the *PPF* at which marginal benefit equals marginal cost.

4 | **Explain what makes production possibilities expand.**

- Technological change and increases in capital and human capital expand production possibilities.
- The opportunity cost of economic growth is the decrease in current consumption.

5 | **Explain how people gain from specialization and trade.**

- A person has a comparative advantage in an activity if he or she can perform that activity at a lower opportunity cost than someone else.
- People gain by increasing the production of the item in which they have a comparative advantage and trading.

Key Terms

Absolute advantage, 78
Allocative efficiency, 68
Comparative advantage, 77

Economic growth, 75
Free lunch, 61
Production efficiency, 60

Production possibilities frontier, 58
Tradeoff, 61

TABLE 1

Corn (bushels per year)		Beef (pounds per year)
1,000	and	0
800	and	900
600	and	1,200
400	and	1,400
200	and	1,450
0	and	1,500

TABLE 2

Entertainment (units)		Good food (units)
100	and	0
80	and	30
60	and	50
40	and	60
20	and	65
0	and	67

TABLE 3

Movies (per week)	Marginal cost	Marginal benefit
	(CDs per movie)	
1	2	8
2	4	6
3	6	4
4	8	2
5	10	0

TABLE 4

Robot services (units per year)		Consumption goods (units per year)
0	and	2,000
1	and	1,900
2	and	1,700
3	and	1,400
4	and	1,000
5	and	500

Exercises

1. Table 1 shows the quantities of corn and beef that a farm can produce.
   a. Draw a graph of the farm's production possibilities frontier.
   b. Can the farm produce 500 bushels of corn and 500 pounds of beef a year?
   c. Can the farm produce 800 bushels of corn and 1,200 pounds of beef a year?
   d. What is the opportunity cost of the farm increasing beef production from 900 pounds to 1,200 pounds a year?
   e. If the farm produces 400 bushels of corn and 1,400 pounds of beef a year, is the farm using its resources efficiently? Explain your answer.

2. On Leisure Island, the only resources are 5 units of capital and 10 hours of labor a day. Table 2 shows the maximum quantities of entertainment and good food that Leisure Island can produce.
   a. Draw Leisure Island's production possibilities frontier.
   b. Is an output of 50 units of entertainment and 50 units of good food attainable? If so, is production efficient? What would be the opportunity cost of producing an additional unit of entertainment?
   c. Is an output of 40 units of entertainment and 60 units of good food attainable? If so, what would be the opportunity cost of producing an additional unit of entertainment? Do the people on Leisure Island face a tradeoff?
   d. What can you say about the opportunity cost of a unit of good food as the people on Leisure Island allocate more resources to producing good food?
   e. What is the marginal cost of a unit of entertainment when Leisure Island produces 60 units of entertainment and 50 units of good food?
   f. If the efficient quantity of entertainment is 40 units, what is the marginal benefit from entertainment?

3. Table 3 gives Taylor's marginal cost of and marginal benefit from a movie.
   a. If Taylor sees 2 movies a week, what must she give up to see a third movie?
   b. If Taylor sees 2 movies a week, what is she willing to give up to see a third movie?
   c. What is Taylor's efficient number of movies per week?

4. Tommy spends 5 hours per night playing chess online. He really enjoys playing chess, but over recent weeks, his economics grade has dropped. Tommy makes a rational decision to spend only 2 hours per night playing chess online. When Tommy spent 5 hours per night playing chess, did his marginal cost exceed his marginal benefit or did his marginal benefit exceed his marginal cost? Explain.

5. Table 4 shows the quantities of robots and consumption goods that the country Alpha can produce along its production possibilities frontier.
   a. If Alpha produces 2,000 units of consumption goods a year, will Alpha experience economic growth? Explain.
   b. If Alpha produces 1,100 units of consumption goods a year, will Alpha experience economic growth? Explain.
   c. If Alpha currently produces no robots and now decides to produce 1 robot a year, what is the cost of its economic growth?

6. People can now obtain music from Web sites such as iTunes and MP3.com.
   a. Have these Web sites changed the *PPF* for recorded music and other goods and services? If so, how has it changed?
   b. Is there still a tradeoff between recorded music and other goods and services, or is the opportunity cost of recorded music now zero?

7. AIDS has become an acute problem in Africa.
   a. How has the spread of AIDS influenced the *PPF* of the economies of Africa?
   b. Has the spread of AIDS increased the opportunity cost of some goods and services? Has it decreased the opportunity cost of anything?

8. A farm grows wheat and produces pigs. The marginal cost of producing each of these products increases as more of it is produced.
   a. Make a graph that illustrates the farm's *PPF.*
   b. The farm adopts a new technology, which allows the farm to use fewer resources to fatten pigs. Use your graph to illustrate the impact of the new technology on the farm's *PPF.*
   c. With the farm using the new technology in part **b**, has the opportunity cost of producing a ton of wheat changed? If so, how? If not, why not?

9. Explain how each of the following items might change the U.S. production possibilities frontier. In each case, is an opportunity cost incurred? If so, what is it? If not, why not?
   a. The government of California spends more on education.
   b. CNN hires more reporters to cover breaking news stories from around the world.
   c. Google announces a new intelligent search engine.
   d. A severe frost wipes out the Florida citrus crop.
   e. Wild brushfires sweep through large parts of California and Arizona.

10. Table 5 sets out Tom's production possibilities and Table 6 sets out Tessa's production possibilities. Tom allocates all his resources and produces 2 bats and 20 balls an hour. Tessa allocates all her resources and produces 2 bats and 40 balls an hour.
    a. Calculate Tom's opportunity cost of a ball.
    b. Calculate Tessa's opportunity cost of a ball.
    c. Who has a comparative advantage in producing balls?
    d. Who has a comparative advantage in producing bats?
    e. If Tom or Tessa specialized in producing the good in which he or she has a comparative advantage and they traded 1 bat for 15 balls, who would gain from the specialization and trade and why?

11. Mexico has 100 million workers, and each worker can produce 3 cars a year or 3 tons of steel a year. Canada has 25 million workers, and each worker in Canada can produce 10 cars a year or 6 tons of steel a year. Suppose that each country produces only cars and steel.
    a. Draw a graph of Canada's production possibilities frontier.
    b. Draw a graph of Mexico's production possibilities frontier.
    c. Calculate the opportunity cost of producing 1 ton of steel in each country.
    d. Calculate the opportunity cost of producing 1 car in each country.
    e. Does either country have an absolute advantage? If so, which one and why?
    f. In which country is the marginal cost of producing a car lower?

TABLE 5

Bats (per hour)		Balls (per hour)
0	and	40
1	and	30
2	and	20
3	and	10
4	and	0

TABLE 6

Bats (per hour)		Balls (per hour)
0	and	80
1	and	60
2	and	40
3	and	20
4	and	0

Critical Thinking

12. Think about the production of music and the effects of the technological changes that first brought the Walkman, then the Discman, and then the iPod.
    a. How might you go about finding the opportunity cost of listening to an hour of music using each of the technologies?
    b. How do you think each new technology changed the opportunity cost of listening to an hour of recorded music?
    c. Do you think any of the new technologies had an absolute advantage over its predecessor?
    d. Do you think any of the new technologies had a comparative advantage over its predecessor?

13. You have chosen to bear the opportunity cost of remaining in school to obtain a degree. Explain, using the concepts of rational choice, marginal cost, and marginal benefit:
    a. Why have you made this choice?
    b. Why did Bill Gates quit school before completing his degree?
    c. Why do so many people quit school at the end of grade 12?
    d. What can the government do to encourage more people to attend college?

14. The Kyoto agreement requires countries to achieve greenhouse gas reduction targets over the next ten years. The Canadian government has signed the Kyoto agreement, but the U.S. government will not sign it.
    a. As the Canadian government allocates more resources over the next ten years to reducing pollution, how will the Canadian *PPF* change?
    b. Do you think that Canadian economic growth will change by more than U.S. economic growth changes? Or will growth in neither country be affected? Explain your answer.
    c. Do you think that Canada will gain or lose some of its comparative advantage relative to the United States? Explain your answer.

Web Exercises

Use the links on MyEconLab to work the following exercises.

15. Visit the U.S. Census Bureau population clocks.
    a. What is the estimated population of the United States?
    b. What is the estimated population of the world?
    c. How fast is the U.S. population increasing? (Use the second timer on your computer clock to determine the pace of increase.)
    d. How fast is the world population increasing?
    e. What do the population increases that you've found imply about the U.S. *PPF* and the world *PPF*? Which is moving faster?

16. Review the article "Chicago School Tradeoff" on the New Republic Web site.
    a. What does the article report about opinion in the United States about outsourcing?
    b. How would you reconcile the reported views of people as producers and consumers?
    c. On the basis of what you have learned in this chapter, write a brief note that explains why you agree or disagree with the position taken by the author.

Demand and Supply

CHAPTER 4

CHAPTER CHECKLIST

When you have completed your study of this chapter,
you will be able to

1 Distinguish between quantity demanded and demand and explain what determines demand.

2 Distinguish between quantity supplied and supply and explain what determines supply.

3 Explain how demand and supply determine price and quantity in a market and explain the effects of changes in demand and supply.

When gasoline prices are rising, many people blame greedy oil companies. But aren't the oil companies always greedy? Weren't they greedy when prices were low and stable? It isn't difficult to see that greedy oil companies are not the source of high or rising gas prices.

To explain rising prices, we need to point to some factor that has changed. And we need to understand the forces at work. Those forces are demand and supply. Economists use the demand and supply model to explain how markets work. Greed—or self-interest as economists prefer to call it—lies at the core of the model. The demand and supply model explains how the self-interested decisions of buyers and sellers end up being compatible and how they determine market prices. And it explains how those prices in turn influence what, how, and for whom goods and services get produced.

COMPETITIVE MARKETS

When you need a new pair of running shoes, want a bagel and a latte, or need to fly home for Thanksgiving, you must find a place where people sell those items or offer those services. The place in which you find them is a *market*.

You learned in Chapter 2 that a market is any arrangement that brings buyers and sellers together. A market has two sides: buyers (demanders) and sellers (suppliers). There are markets for *goods* such as apples and hiking boots, for *services* such as haircuts and tennis lessons, for *resources* such as computer programmers and tractors, and for other manufactured *inputs* such as memory chips and auto parts. There are also markets for money such as Japanese yen and for financial securities such as Yahoo! stock. Only imagination limits what can be traded in markets.

Some markets are physical places where buyers and sellers meet and where an auctioneer or a broker helps to determine the prices. Examples of this type of market are the New York Stock Exchange; wholesale fish, meat, and produce markets; and used car auctions.

Some markets are groups of people spread around the world who never meet and know little about each other but are connected through the Internet or by telephone. Examples of this type of market are the e-commerce markets, currency markets, and Internet auctions such as eBay.

But most markets are unorganized collections of buyers and sellers. You do most of your trading in this type of market. An example is the market for basketball shoes. The buyers in this $3-billion-a-year market are the 45 million Americans who play basketball (or who want to make a fashion statement) and are looking for a new pair of shoes. The sellers are the tens of thousands of retail sports equipment and footwear stores. Each buyer can visit several different stores, and each seller knows that the buyer has a choice of stores.

Markets vary in the intensity of competition that buyers and sellers face. In this chapter, we're going to study a *competitive market* that has so many buyers and so many sellers that no single buyer or seller can influence the price.

Markets for running shoes . . .

coffee and bagel . . .

and airline travel.

4.1 DEMAND

First, we'll study the behavior of buyers in a competitive market. The **quantity demanded** of any good, service, or resource is the amount that people are willing and able to buy during a specified period at a specified price. For example, when spring water costs $1 a bottle, you decide to buy 2 bottles a day. The 2 bottles a day is your quantity demanded of spring water.

The quantity demanded is measured as an amount *per unit of time*. For example, your quantity demanded of water is 2 bottles *per day*. We could express this quantity as 14 bottles per week or some other number per month or per year. But without a time dimension, a particular number of bottles has no meaning.

Many things influence buying plans, and one of them is price. We look first at the relationship between quantity demanded and price. To study this relationship, we keep all other influences on buying plans the same and we ask: How, other things remaining the same, does the quantity demanded of a good change as its price varies? The law of demand provides the answer.

■ The Law of Demand

The **law of demand** states

> **Other things remaining the same, if the price of a good rises, the quantity demanded of that good decreases; and if the price of a good falls, the quantity demanded of that good increases.**

So the law of demand states that when all else remains the same, if the price of a Palm Pilot falls, people will buy more Palm Pilots; or if the price of a baseball ticket rises, people will buy fewer baseball tickets.

Why does the quantity demanded increase if the price falls, all other things remaining the same?

The answer is that, faced with a limited budget, people always have an incentive to find the best deals they can. If the price of one item falls and the prices of all other items remain the same, the item with the lower price is a better deal than it was before. So people buy more of this item. Suppose, for example, that the price of bottled water fell from $1 a bottle to 25 cents a bottle while the price of Gatorade remained at $1 a bottle. Wouldn't some people switch from Gatorade to water? By doing so, they save 75 cents a bottle, which they can spend on other things they previously couldn't afford.

Think about the things that you buy and ask yourself: Which of these items does *not* obey the law of demand? If the price of a new textbook were lower, other things remaining the same (including the price of a used textbook), would you buy more new textbooks? Then think about all the things that you do not now buy but would if you could afford them. How cheap would a PC have to be for you to buy *both* a desktop and a laptop? There is a price that is low enough to entice you!

■ Demand Schedule and Demand Curve

Demand is the relationship between the quantity demanded and the price of a good when all other influences on buying plans remain the same. The quantity demanded is *one* quantity at *one* price. *Demand* is a *list of quantities at different prices* illustrated by a demand schedule and a demand curve.

Quantity demanded
The amount of any good, service, or resource that people are willing and able to buy during a specified period at a specified price.

Demand
The relationship between the quantity demanded and the price of a good when all other influences on buying plans remain the same.

Demand schedule

A list of the quantities demanded at each different price when all the other influences on buying plans remain the same.

Demand curve

A graph of the relationship between the quantity demanded of a good and its price when all the other influences on buying plans remain the same.

A **demand schedule** is a list of the quantities demanded at each different price when *all the other influences on buying plans remain the same*. The table in Figure 4.1 is one person's (Tina's) demand schedule for bottled water. It tells us that if the price of water is $2.00 a bottle, Tina buys no water. Her quantity demanded is 0 bottles a day. If the price of water is $1.50 a bottle, her quantity demanded is 1 bottle a day. Tina's quantity demanded increases to 2 bottles a day at a price of $1.00 a bottle and to 3 bottles a day at a price of 50 cents a bottle.

A **demand curve** is a graph of the relationship between the quantity demanded of a good and its price when all the other influences on buying plans remain the same. The points on the demand curve labeled A through D represent the rows A through D of the demand schedule. For example, point B on the graph represents row B of the demand schedule and shows that the quantity demanded is 1 bottle a day when the price is $1.50 a bottle. Point C on the demand curve represents row C of the demand schedule and shows that the quantity demanded is 2 bottles a day when the price is $1.00 a bottle.

The downward slope of the demand curve illustrates the law of demand. Along the demand curve, when the price of the good *falls*, the quantity demanded *increases*. For example, in Figure 4.1, when the price of a bottle of water falls from $1.00 to 50 cents, the quantity demanded increases from 2 bottles a day to 3 bottles a day. And when the price *rises*, the quantity demanded *decreases*. For example, when the price rises from $1.00 to $1.50 a bottle, the quantity demanded decreases from 2 bottles a day to 1 bottle a day.

▓ FIGURE 4.1
Demand Schedule and Demand Curve

Ⓧ **myeconlab**

The table shows a demand schedule that lists the quantity of water demanded at each price if all other influences on buying plans remain the same. At a price of $1.50 a bottle, the quantity demanded is 1 bottle a day.

The demand curve shows the relationship between the quantity demanded and price, everything else remaining the same. The downward-sloping demand curve illustrates the law of demand. When the price falls, the quantity demanded increases; and when the price rises, the quantity demanded decreases.

	Price (dollars per bottle)	Quantity demanded (bottles per day)
A	2.00	0
B	1.50	1
C	1.00	2
D	0.50	3

■ Individual Demand and Market Demand

The demand schedule and the demand curve that you've just studied are for one person. To study a market, we must determine the market demand.

Market demand is the sum of the demands of all the buyers in a market. To find the market demand, imagine a market in which there are only two buyers: Tina and Tim. The table in Figure 4.2 shows three demand schedules: Tina's, Tim's, and the market demand schedule. Tina's demand schedule is the same as before. It shows the quantity of water demanded by Tina at each different price. Tim's demand schedule tells us the quantity of water demanded by Tim at each price. To find the quantity of water demanded in the market, we sum the quantities demanded by Tina and Tim. For example, at a price of $1.00 a bottle, the quantity demanded by Tina is 2 bottles a day, the quantity demanded by Tim is 1 bottle a day, and so the quantity demanded in the market is 3 bottles a day.

Tina's demand curve in part (a) and Tim's demand curve in part (b) are graphs of the two individual demand schedules. The market demand curve in part (c) is a graph of the market demand schedule. At a given price, the quantity demanded on the market demand curve equals the horizontal sum of the quantities demanded on the individual demand curves.

Market demand
The sum of the demands of all the buyers in the market.

■ FIGURE 4.2
Individual Demand and Market Demand

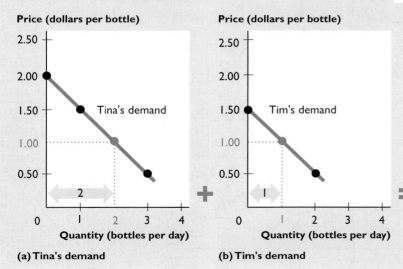

Price (dollars per bottle)	Quantity demanded (bottles per day)		
	Tina	Tim	Market
2.00	0	0	0
1.50	1	0	1
1.00	2 +	1 =	3
0.50	3	2	5

The market demand schedule is the sum of the individual demand schedules, and the market demand curve is the horizontal sum of the individual demand curves.

At a price of $1 a bottle, the quantity demanded by Tina is 2 bottles a day and the quantity demanded by Tim is 1 bottle a day, so the total quantity demanded in the market is 3 bottles a day.

(a) Tina's demand   **(b) Tim's demand**   **(c) Market demand**

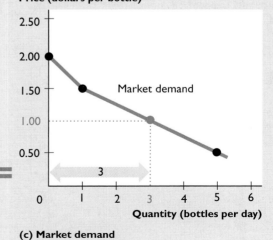

■ Changes in Demand

The demand curve shows how the quantity demanded changes when the price of the good changes but *all other influences on buying plans remain the same*. When any of these other influences on buying plans change, there is a **change in demand**, which means that there is a new demand schedule and new demand curve. *The demand curve shifts.*

Demand can either increase or decrease and Figure 4.3 illustrates the two cases. Initially, the demand curve is D_0. When demand decreases, the demand curve shifts leftward to D_1. On demand curve D_1, the quantity demanded at each price is smaller. And when demand increases, the demand curve shifts rightward to D_2. On demand curve D_2, the quantity demanded at each price is greater.

The main influences on buying plans that change demand are

- Prices of related goods
- Income
- Expectations
- Number of buyers
- Preferences

Prices of Related Goods

Every good has substitutes. A **substitute** for a good is another good that can be consumed in its place. Chocolate cake is a substitute for cheesecake, and bottled water is a substitute for Gatorade.

Many goods have complements. A **complement** of a good is another good that is consumed with it. Wrist guards are a complement of in-line skates, and bottled water is a complement of fitness center services.

Change in demand
A change in the quantity that people plan to buy when any influence on buying plans other than the price of the good changes.

Substitute
A good that can be consumed in place of another good.

Complement
A good that is consumed with another good.

■ **FIGURE 4.3**
Changes in Demand

A change in any influence on buying plans, other than a change in the price of the good itself, changes demand and shifts the demand curve.

❶ When demand decreases, the demand curve shifts leftward from D_0 to D_1.

❷ When demand increases, the demand curve shifts rightward from D_0 to D_2.

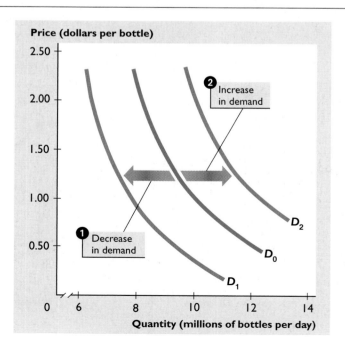

A Change in the Price of a Substitute The demand for a good *increases* if the price of one of its substitutes *rises;* and the demand for a good *decreases* if the price of one of its substitutes *falls*. That is, the demand for a good and the price of one of its substitutes move in the *same direction*. For example, the demand for cheesecake increases when the price of chocolate cake rises.

A Change in the Price of a Complement The demand for a good *decreases* if the price of one of its complements *rises;* and the demand for a good *increases* if the price of one of its complements *falls*. That is, the demand for a good and the price of one of its complements move in *opposite directions*. For example, the demand for wrist guards decreases when the price of in-line skates rises.

Income

Faced with scarcity, people try to get the most out of their income. And when income increases, options expand. With a higher income, you might buy more of the things you're already buying or some things that you couldn't afford before. You might even stop buying some things and switch to something else.

A good is a **normal good** if a rise in income brings an increase in demand and a fall in income brings a decrease in demand. For example, if you buy more bottled water when your income increases, then bottled water is a normal good. Most goods are normal goods (hence the name).

A good is an **inferior good** if a rise in income brings a *decrease* in demand and a fall in income brings an *increase* in demand. For example, if when your income increases, you buy fewer plastic milk crates and more bookcases, then a plastic milk crate is an inferior good.

Normal good
A good for which demand increases when income increases and demand decreases when income decreases.

Inferior good
A good for which demand decreases when income increases and demand increases when income decreases.

Expectations

Expected future income and prices influence demand. For example, you are offered a well-paid summer job, so you go to Cancun during spring break. Your demand for vacation travel has increased. Or if you expect the price of ramen noodles to rise next week, you buy a big enough stockpile of it now to get you through the rest of the school year. Your demand for ramen noodles today has increased.

Number of Buyers

The greater the number of buyers in a market, the larger is demand. For example, the demand for parking spaces, movies, bottled water, or just about anything is greater in New York City than it is in Boise, Idaho.

Preferences

Tastes or *preferences,* as economists call them, influence demand. When preferences change, the demand for one item increases and the demand for another item (or items) decreases. For example, preferences have changed as people have become better informed about the health hazards of tobacco. This change in preferences has decreased the demand for cigarettes and has increased the demand for nicotine patches.

Preferences also change when new goods become available. For example, the development of MP3 technology has decreased the demand for CDs and has increased the demand for Internet service and MP3 players.

■ Change in Quantity Demanded Versus Change in Demand

The influences on buyers' plans you've just considered bring a *change in demand*. These are all the influences on buying plans *except for the price of the good*. To avoid confusion, when *the price of the good changes* and all other influences on buying plans remain the same, we say there has been a **change in the quantity demanded**.

The distinction between a change in demand and a change in the quantity demanded is crucial for figuring out how a market responds to the forces that hit it. Figure 4.4 illustrates and summarizes the distinction:

Change in the quantity demanded
A change in the quantity of a good that people plan to buy that results from a change in the price of the good with all other influences on buying plans remaining the same.

- If the price of bottled water *rises* when everything else remains the same, the quantity demanded of bottled water *decreases* and there is a *movement up* along the demand curve D_0. If the price *falls* when everything else remains the same, the quantity demanded *increases* and there is a *movement down* along the demand curve D_0.
- If some influence on buyers' plans other than the price of bottled water changes, there is a change in demand. When the demand for bottled water *decreases*, the demand curve *shifts leftward* to D_1. When the demand for bottled water *increases*, the demand curve *shifts rightward* to D_2.

When you are thinking about the influences on demand, try to get into the habit of asking: Does this influence change the quantity demanded or does it change demand? The test is: Did the price of the good change or did some other influence change? If the price changed, then quantity demanded changed. If some other influence changed and the price remained constant, then demand changed.

■ FIGURE 4.4
Change in Quantity Demanded Versus Change in Demand

❶ **A decrease in the quantity demanded**
If the price of a good rises, *cet. par.*, the quantity demanded decreases. There is a movement up along the demand curve D_0.

❷ **A decrease in demand**
Demand decreases and the demand curve shifts leftward (from D_0 to D_1) if

- The price of a substitute falls.
- The price of a complement rises.
- The price of the good is expected to fall or income is expected to fall in the future.
- Income decreases.*
- The number of buyers decreases.

* Bottled water is a normal good.

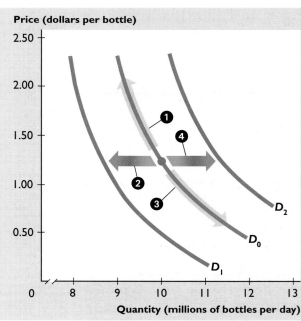

❸ **An increase in the quantity demanded**
If the price of a good falls, *cet. par.*, the quantity demanded increases. There is a movement down along the demand curve D_0.

❹ **An increase in demand**
Demand increases and the demand curve shifts rightward (from D_0 to D_2) if

- The price of a substitute rises.
- The price of a complement falls.
- The price of the good is expected to rise or income is expected to rise in the future.
- Income increases.*
- The number of buyers increases.

CHECKPOINT 4.1

1 **Distinguish between quantity demanded and demand and explain what determines demand.**

Practice Problem 4.1

1. In the market for cell phones, several events occur, one at a time. Explain the influence of each event on the quantity demanded of cell phones and on the demand for cell phones. Use a graph to illustrate the effects of each event. Does any event (or events) illustrate the law of demand? The events are
   a. The price of a cell phone falls.
   b. The price of a call made from a cell phone falls.
   c. After a public outcry against the ringing of cell phones, cities and towns ban cell phones from public places.
   d. Incomes increase.
   e. Rumor has it that the price of a cell phone will rise next month.
   f. With the introduction of camera phones, cell phones are more popular.

Exercise 4.1

1. In the market for Caribbean cruises, several events occur, one at a time. Explain the influence of each event on the quantity demanded of Caribbean cruises and the demand for Caribbean cruises. Use a graph to illustrate the effects of each event. Does any event illustrate the law of demand? The events are
   a. Caribbean cruises become more popular.
   b. The price of a Caribbean cruise rises.
   c. The price of a cruise to Asia falls.
   d. Celebrity Cruises launches its new "students only" Caribbean cruises.
   e. People expect the price of a Caribbean cruise to fall next season.
   f. Cruise companies increase the number of leading rock artists for their onboard entertainment.

Solution to Practice Problem 4.1

1a. A fall in the price of a cell phone increases the quantity demanded of cell phones, shown by a movement down along the demand curve for cell phones (Figure 1) and is an example of the law of demand in action.

1b. A call made from a cell phone is a complement of a cell phone. So when the price of a call from a cell phone falls, the demand for cell phones increases. The demand curve shifts rightward (Figure 2).

1c. The ban on using cell phones in public places changes preferences and decreases the demand for cell phones. The demand curve shifts leftward (Figure 2).

1d. A cell phone is (likely) a normal good. So when income increases, the demand for cell phones increases. The demand curve for cell phones shifts rightward (Figure 2).

1e. A rise in the expected price of a cell phone increases the demand for cell phones now. The demand curve for cell phones shifts rightward (Figure 2).

1f. An increase in the number of buyers increases the demand for cell phones. The demand curve shifts rightward (Figure 2).

FIGURE 1

Price

Quantity demanded increases

D

0   Quantity

FIGURE 2

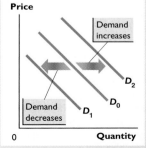

Price

Demand increases

D_2

D_0

Demand decreases

D_1

0   Quantity

4.2 SUPPLY

A market has two sides. On one side are the buyers, or demanders, that we've just studied. On the other side of the market are the sellers, or suppliers. We now study the forces that determine suppliers' plans.

Quantity supplied
The amount of any good, service, or resource that people are willing and able to sell during a specified period at a specified price.

The **quantity supplied** of a good, service, or resource is the amount that people are willing and able to sell during a specified period at a specified price. For example, when the price of spring water is $1.50 a bottle, a spring owner decides to sell 2,000 bottles a day. The 2,000 bottles a day is the quantity supplied of spring water by this individual producer. (As in the case of demand, the quantity supplied is measured as an amount *per unit of time*.)

Many things influence selling plans, and one of them is the price. We look first at the relationship between quantity supplied of a good and its price. To study this relationship, we keep all other influences on selling plans the same. And we ask: How, other things remaining the same, does the quantity supplied of a good change as its price varies? The law of supply provides the answer.

■ The Law of Supply

The **law of supply** states

> **Other things remaining the same, if the price of a good rises, the quantity supplied of that good increases; and if the price of a good falls, the quantity supplied of that good decreases.**

So the law of supply states that when all else remains the same, if the price of bottled water rises, spring owners will offer more water for sale; if the price of a CD falls, Sony Corp. will offer fewer CDs for sale.

Why, other things remaining the same, does the quantity supplied increase if the price rises and decrease if the price falls? Part of the answer lies in the principle of increasing opportunity cost (see p. 66). Because factors of production are not equally productive in all activities, as more of a good is produced, the opportunity cost of producing it increases. A higher price provides the incentive to bear the higher opportunity cost of increased production. Another part of the answer is that for a given cost, the higher price brings a larger profit, so sellers have greater incentive to increase production.

Think about the resources that you own and can offer for sale to others and ask yourself: Which of these items does *not* obey the law of supply? If the wage rate for summer jobs increased, would you have an incentive to work longer hours and bear the higher opportunity cost of forgone leisure? If the bank offered a higher interest rate on deposits, would you have an incentive to save more and bear the higher opportunity cost of forgone consumption? If the used book dealer offered a higher price for last year's textbooks, would you have an incentive to sell that handy math text and bear the higher opportunity cost of visiting the library when you needed to check a formula?

■ Supply Schedule and Supply Curve

Supply
The relationship between the quantity supplied and the price of a good when all other influences on selling plans remain the same.

Supply is the relationship between the quantity supplied and the price of a good when all other influences on selling plans remain the same. The quantity supplied is *one* quantity at *one* price. *Supply* is a *list of quantities at different prices* illustrated by a supply schedule and a supply curve.

A **supply schedule** lists the quantities supplied at each different price when all the other influences on selling plans remain the same. The table in Figure 4.5 is one firm's (Agua's) supply schedule for bottled water. It tells us that if the price of water is 50 cents a bottle, Agua plans to sell no water. Its quantity supplied is 0 bottles a day. If the price of water is $1.00 a bottle, Agua's quantity supplied is 1,000 bottles a day. Agua's quantity supplied increases to 2,000 bottles a day at a price of $1.50 a bottle and to 3,000 bottles a day at a price of $2.00 a bottle.

A **supply curve** is a graph of the relationship between the quantity supplied of a good and its price when all the other influences on selling plans remain the same. The points on the supply curve labeled *A* through *D* represent the rows *A* through *D* of the supply schedule. For example, point *C* on the supply curve represents row *C* of the supply schedule and shows that the quantity supplied is 1,000 bottles a day when the price is $1.00 a bottle. Point *B* on the supply curve represents row *B* of the supply schedule and shows that the quantity supplied is 2,000 bottles a day when the price is $1.50 a bottle.

The upward slope of the supply curve illustrates the law of supply. Along the supply curve, when the price of the good *rises*, the quantity supplied *increases*. For example, in Figure 4.5, when the price of a bottle of water rises from $1.50 to $2.00, the quantity supplied increases from 2,000 bottles a day to 3,000 bottles a day. And when the price *falls*, the quantity supplied *decreases*. For example, when the price falls from $1.50 to $1.00 a bottle, the quantity supplied decreases from 2,000 bottles a day to 1,000 bottles a day.

Supply schedule
A list of the quantities supplied at each different price when all the other influences on selling plans remain the same.

Supply curve
A graph of the relationship between the quantity supplied of a good and its price when all the other influences on selling plans remain the same.

FIGURE 4.5

Supply Schedule and Supply Curve

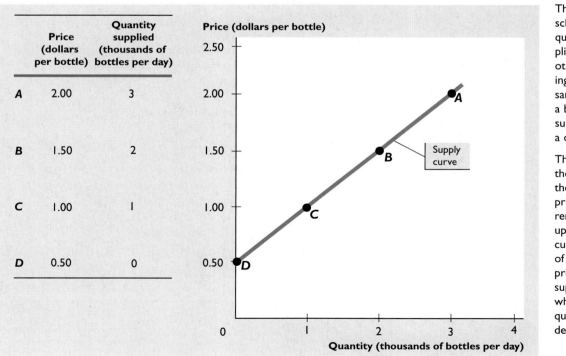

	Price (dollars per bottle)	Quantity supplied (thousands of bottles per day)
A	2.00	3
B	1.50	2
C	1.00	1
D	0.50	0

The table shows a supply schedule that lists the quantity of water supplied at each price if all other influences on selling plans remain the same. At a price of $1.50 a bottle, the quantity supplied is 2,000 bottles a day.

The supply curve shows the relationship between the quantity supplied and price, everything else remaining the same. The upward-sloping supply curve illustrates the law of supply. When the price rises, the quantity supplied increases; and when the price falls, the quantity supplied decreases.

■ Individual Supply and Market Supply

The supply schedule and the supply curve that you've just studied are for one seller. To study a market, we must determine the market supply.

Market supply is the sum of the supplies of all the sellers in the market. To find the market supply of water, imagine a market in which there are only two sellers: Agua and Prima. The table in Figure 4.6 shows three supply schedules: Agua's, Prima's, and the market supply schedule. Agua's supply schedule is the same as before. Prima's supply schedule tells us the quantity of water that Prima plans to sell at each price. To find the quantity of water supplied in the market, we sum the quantities supplied by Agua and Prima. For example, at a price of $1.00 a bottle, the quantity supplied by Agua is 1,000 bottles a day, the quantity supplied by Prima is 2,000 bottles a day, and the quantity supplied in the market is 3,000 bottles a day.

Agua's supply curve in part (a) and Prima's supply curve in part (b) are graphs of the two individual supply schedules. The market supply curve in part (c) is a graph of the market supply schedule. At a given price, the quantity supplied on the market supply curve equals the horizontal sum of the quantities supplied on the individual supply curves.

Market supply
The sum of the supplies of all the sellers in the market.

FIGURE 4.6
Individual Supply and Market Supply

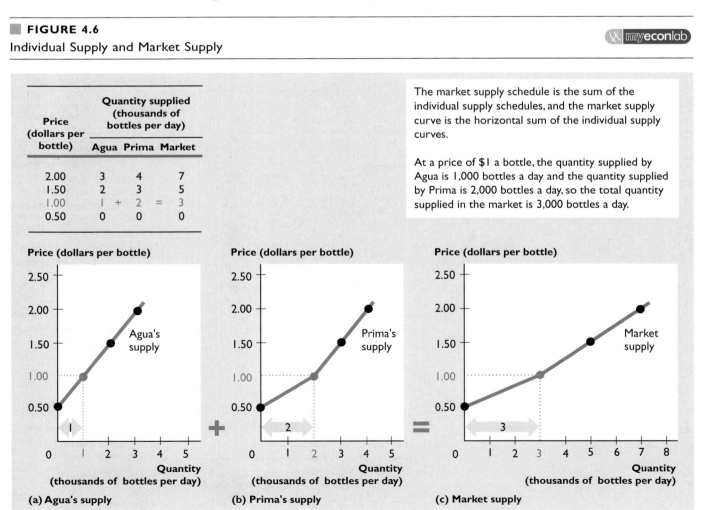

The market supply schedule is the sum of the individual supply schedules, and the market supply curve is the horizontal sum of the individual supply curves.

At a price of $1 a bottle, the quantity supplied by Agua is 1,000 bottles a day and the quantity supplied by Prima is 2,000 bottles a day, so the total quantity supplied in the market is 3,000 bottles a day.

	Quantity supplied (thousands of bottles per day)		
Price (dollars per bottle)	Agua	Prima	Market
2.00	3	4	7
1.50	2	3	5
1.00	1 +	2 =	3
0.50	0	0	0

(a) Agua's supply

(b) Prima's supply

(c) Market supply

■ Changes in Supply

The supply curve shows how the quantity supplied changes when the price of the good changes but *all other influences on selling plans remain the same.* When any of these other influences on selling plans change, there is a **change in supply**, which means that there is a new supply schedule and new supply curve. *The supply curve shifts.*

Supply can either increase or decrease, and Figure 4.7 illustrates the two cases. Initially, the supply curve is S_0. When supply decreases, the supply curve shifts leftward to S_1. On supply curve S_1, the quantity supplied at each price is smaller. And when supply increases, the supply curve shifts rightward to S_2. On supply curve S_2, the quantity supplied at each price is greater.

The main influences on selling plans that change supply are

- Prices of related goods
- Prices of resources and other inputs
- Expectations
- Number of sellers
- Productivity

Change in supply
A change in the quantity that suppliers plan to sell when any influence on selling plans other than the price of the good changes.

Prices of Related Goods

Related goods are either substitutes *in production* or complements *in production.* A **substitute in production** for a good is another good that can be produced in its place. Button-fly jeans are substitutes in production for cargo pants in a clothing factory.

A **complement in production** of a good is another good that is produced along with it. Cream is a complement in production of skim milk in a dairy.

Substitute in production
A good that can be produced in place of another good.

Complement in production
A good that is produced along with another good.

■ FIGURE 4.7
Changes in Supply

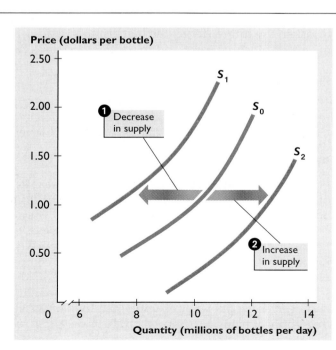

Price (dollars per bottle)

Quantity (millions of bottles per day)

A change in any influence on selling plans other than a change in the price of the good itself changes supply and shifts the supply curve.

❶ When supply decreases, the supply curve shifts leftward from S_0 to S_1.

❷ When supply increases, the supply curve shifts rightward from S_0 to S_2.

A Change in the Price of a Substitute in Production The supply of a good *decreases* if the price of one of its substitutes in production *rises;* and the supply of a good *increases* if the price of one of its substitutes in production *falls.* That is, the supply of a good and the price of one of its substitutes in production move in *opposite directions.* For example, a clothing factory can produce cargo pants or button-fly jeans, so these goods are substitutes in production. When the price of button-fly jeans rises, the clothing factory switches production from cargo pants to button-fly jeans, so the supply of cargo pants decreases.

A Change in the Price of a Complement in Production The supply of a good *increases* if the price of one of its complements in production *rises;* and the supply of a good *decreases* if the price of one of its complements in production *falls.* That is, the supply of a good and the price of one of its complements in production move in the *same direction.* For example, when a dairy produces skim milk, it also produces cream, so these goods are complements in production. When the price of skim milk rises, the dairy produces more skim milk, so the supply of cream increases.

Prices of Resources and Other Inputs

Supply changes when the price of a resource or other input used to produce the good changes. The reason is that resource and input prices influence the cost of production. And the more it costs to produce a good, the smaller is the quantity supplied of that good at each price (other things remaining the same). For example, if the wage rate of bottling-plant workers rises, it costs more to produce a bottle of water. So the supply of bottled water decreases.

Expectations

Expectations about future prices influence supply. For example, a severe frost that wipes out Florida's citrus crop doesn't change the production of orange juice today. But it will decrease production later in the year when the current crop would normally have been harvested. So people expect the price of orange juice to rise in the future. To get the higher future price, some firms will increase their inventory of frozen juice, and this action decreases the supply of juice today.

Number of Sellers

The greater the number of sellers in a market, the larger is the supply. For example, many new sellers have developed springs and water-bottling plants in the United States, and the supply of bottled water has increased.

Productivity

Productivity is output per unit of input. An increase in productivity lowers the cost of producing the good and increases its supply. A decrease in productivity has the opposite effect and decreases supply.

Technological change and the increased use of capital increase productivity. For example, advances in electronic technology have lowered the cost of producing a computer and increased the supply of computers. Technological change brings new goods such as the iPod, the supply of which was previously zero.

Natural events such as severe weather and earthquakes decrease productivity and decrease supply. For example, the Indian Ocean tsunami of 2004 decreased the supply of many agricultural products, fish, and seafood in many areas of Asia.

■ Change in Quantity Supplied Versus Change in Supply

The influences on sellers' plans you've just considered bring a *change in supply*. These are all the influences on sellers' plans *except the price of the good*. To avoid confusion, when the *price of the good changes* and all other influences on selling plans remain the same, we say there has been a **change in the quantity supplied**.

The distinction between a change in supply and a change in the quantity supplied is crucial for figuring out how a market responds to the forces that hit it. Figure 4.8 illustrates and summarizes the distinction:

- If the price of bottled water *falls* when other things remain the same, the quantity supplied of bottled water *decreases* and there is a *movement down* along the supply curve S_0. If the price *rises* when other things remain the same, the quantity supplied *increases* and there is a *movement up* along the supply curve S_0.
- If any influence on water bottlers' plans other than the price of bottled water changes, there is a change in the supply of bottled water. When the supply of bottled water *decreases*, the supply curve *shifts leftward* to S_1. When the supply of bottled water *increases*, the supply curve *shifts rightward* to S_2.

When you are thinking about the influences on supply, get into the habit of asking: Does this influence change the quantity supplied or does it change supply? The test is: Did the price change or did some other influence change? If the price of the good changed, then quantity supplied changed. If some other influence changed and the price of the good remained constant, then supply changed.

Change in the quantity supplied
A change in the quantity of a good that suppliers plan to sell that results from a change in the price of the good.

■ FIGURE 4.8
Change in Quantity Supplied Versus Change in Supply

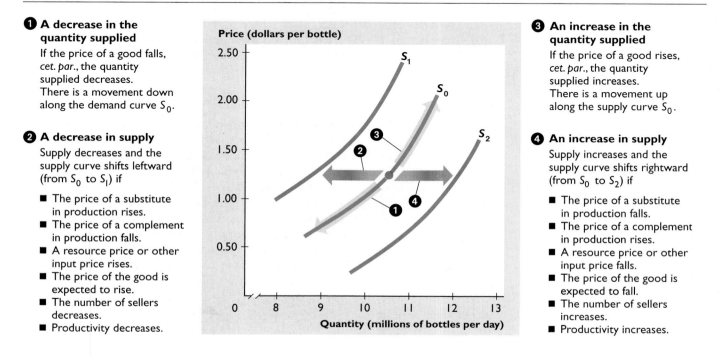

❶ A decrease in the quantity supplied

If the price of a good falls, *cet. par.*, the quantity supplied decreases. There is a movement down along the demand curve S_0.

❷ A decrease in supply

Supply decreases and the supply curve shifts leftward (from S_0 to S_1) if

- The price of a substitute in production rises.
- The price of a complement in production falls.
- A resource price or other input price rises.
- The price of the good is expected to rise.
- The number of sellers decreases.
- Productivity decreases.

❸ An increase in the quantity supplied

If the price of a good rises, *cet. par.*, the quantity supplied increases. There is a movement up along the supply curve S_0.

❹ An increase in supply

Supply increases and the supply curve shifts rightward (from S_0 to S_2) if

- The price of a substitute in production falls.
- The price of a complement in production rises.
- A resource price or other input price falls.
- The price of the good is expected to fall.
- The number of sellers increases.
- Productivity increases.

2 **Distinguish between quantity supplied and supply and explain what determines supply.**

Practice Problem 4.2

1. Timber beams are made from logs, and in the process of making beams, the mill produces sawdust, which is made into pressed wood. In the market for timber beams, several events occur one at a time. Explain the influence of each event on the quantity supplied of timber beams and the supply of timber beams. Use a graph to illustrate the effects of each event. Does any event (or events) illustrate the law of supply? These events are
    a. The wage rate of sawmill workers rises.
    b. The price of sawdust rises.
    c. The price of a timber beam rises.
    d. The price of a timber beam is expected to rise next year.
    e. Environmentalists convince Congress to introduce a new law that reduces the amount of forest that can be cut for timber products.
    f. A new technology lowers the cost of producing timber beams.

Exercise 4.2

1. In the market for DVDs, several events occur one at a time. Explain the influence of each event on the quantity supplied of DVDs and the supply of DVDs. Use a graph to illustrate the effects of each event. Does any event (or events) illustrate the law of supply? These events are
    a. The price of a CD falls.
    b. A new robot technology lowers the cost of producing DVDs.
    c. The price of a DVD falls.
    d. The price of a DVD is expected to rise next year.
    e. The wage rate paid to DVD factory workers increases.

FIGURE 1

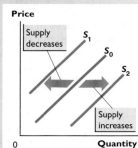

FIGURE 2

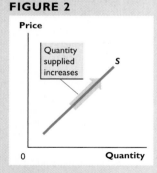

Solution to Practice Problem 4.2

1a. A rise in the wage rate of sawmill workers decreases the supply of timber beams. The supply curve of timber beams shifts leftward (Figure 1).
1b. Sawdust and timber beams are complements in production. A rise in the price of sawdust increases the supply of timber beams. The supply curve of timber beams shifts rightward (Figure 1).
1c. A rise in the price of a timber beam increases the quantity supplied of timber beams, which is shown as a movement up along the supply curve of timber beams and is an example of the law of supply in action (Figure 2).
1d. The expected rise in the price of a timber beam decreases the supply of timber beams now. The supply curve of timber beams shifts leftward (Figure 1).
1e. The new law decreases the supply of timber beams. The supply curve of timber beams shifts leftward (Figure 1).
1f. The new technology increases the supply of timber beams and shifts the supply curve rightward (Figure 1).

4.3 MARKET EQUILIBRIUM

In everyday language, "equilibrium" means "opposing forces are in balance." Demand and supply are opposing forces. And **market equilibrium** occurs when the quantity demanded equals the quantity supplied—when buyers' and sellers' plans are in balance. At the **equilibrium price**, the quantity demanded equals the quantity supplied. The **equilibrium quantity** is the quantity bought and sold at the equilibrium price.

In the market for bottled water in Figure 4.9, equilibrium occurs where the demand curve and the supply curve intersect. The equilibrium price is $1.00 a bottle, and the equilibrium quantity is 10 million bottles a day.

■ Price: A Market's Automatic Regulator

When equilibrium is disturbed, market forces restore it. The **law of market forces** states

When there is a shortage, the price rises; and when there is a surplus, the price falls.

A **shortage** or **excess demand** is a situation in which the quantity demanded exceeds the quantity supplied. If there is a shortage, buyers must pay a higher price to get more; and sellers are pleased to take the higher price. So the price rises. But a rising price is exactly what is needed to restore equilibrium because a shortage arises when the price is below the equilibrium price.

A **surplus** or **excess supply** is a situation in which the quantity supplied exceeds the quantity demanded. If there is a surplus, suppliers must cut the price to sell more; and buyers are pleased to take the lower price. So the price falls. But

Market equilibrium
When the quantity demanded equals the quantity supplied—buyers' and sellers' plans are in balance.

Equilibrium price
The price at which the quantity demanded equals the quantity supplied.

Equilibrium quantity
The quantity bought and sold at the equilibrium price.

Shortage or excess demand
A situation in which the quantity demanded exceeds the quantity supplied.

Surplus or excess supply
A situation in which the quantity supplied exceeds the quantity demanded.

▒ FIGURE 4.9
Equilibrium Price and Equilibrium Quantity

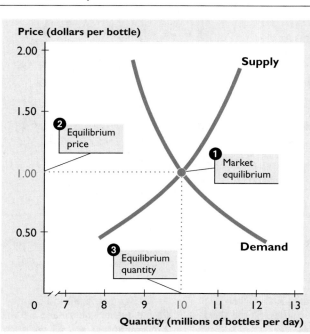

❶ Market equilibrium occurs at the intersection of the demand curve and the supply curve.

❷ The equilibrium price is $1.00 a bottle.

❸ At the equilibrium price, the quantity demanded and the quantity supplied are 10 million bottles a day, which is the equilibrium quantity.

a falling price is exactly what the market needs to restore equilibrium because a surplus arises when the the price is above the equilibrium price.

In Figure 4.10(a), at 75 cents a bottle, there is a shortage: The price rises, the quantity demanded decreases, the quantity supplied increases, and the shortage is eliminated at $1.00 a bottle. In Figure 4.10(b), at $1.50 a bottle, there is a surplus: The price falls, the quantity demanded increases, the quantity supplied decreases, and the surplus is eliminated at $1.00 a bottle.

■ Predicting Price Changes: Three Questions

Because price adjustments eliminate shortages and surpluses, markets are normally in equilibrium. And when an event disturbs an equilibrium, a new equilibrium soon emerges. So to explain and predict changes in prices and quantities, we need to consider only changes in the *equilibrium* price and the *equilibrium* quantity. We can work out the effects of an event on a market by answering three questions:

1. Does the event influence demand or supply?
2. Does the event *increase* or *decrease* demand or supply—shift the demand curve or the supply curve *rightward* or *leftward*?
3. What are the new *equilibrium* price and *equilibrium* quantity and how have they changed?

■ FIGURE 4.10
The Forces That Achieve Equilibrium   myeconlab

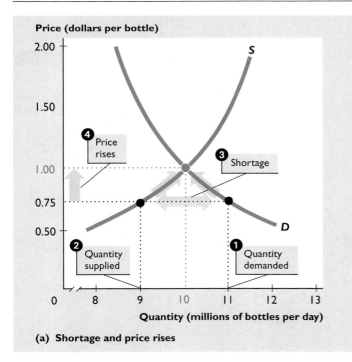

(a) Shortage and price rises

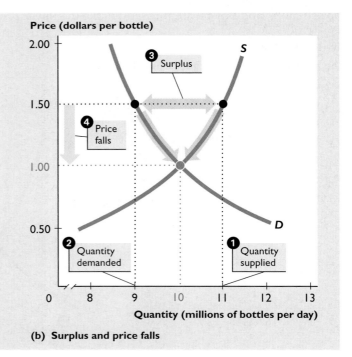

(b) Surplus and price falls

At 75 cents a bottle, ❶ the quantity demanded is 11 million bottles, ❷ the quantity supplied is 9 million bottles, ❸ the shortage is 2 million bottles, and ❹ the price rises.

At $1.50 a bottle, ❶ the quantity supplied is 11 million bottles, ❷ the quantity demanded is 9 million bottles, ❸ the surplus is 2 million bottles, and ❹ the price falls.

■ Effects of Changes in Demand

Let's practice answering the three questions by working out the effects of an event in the market for bottled water: A new study says that tap water is unsafe.

1. With tap water unsafe, the demand for bottled water changes.
2. The demand for bottled water *increases*, and the demand curve *shifts right-ward*. Figure 4.11(a) shows the shift from D_0 to D_1.
3. There is now a *shortage* at $1.00 a bottle. The *price rises* to $1.50 a bottle, and the quantity increases to 11 million bottles.

Note that there is *no change in supply*. But the rise in price brings an *increase in the quantity supplied*—a movement along the supply curve.

Let's work out what happens if a new zero-calorie sports drink is invented.

1. The new drink is a substitute for bottled water, so the demand for bottled water changes.
2. The demand for bottled water *decreases*, and the demand curve *shifts left-ward*. Figure 4.11(b) shows the shift from D_0 to D_2.
3. There is now a *surplus* at $1.00 a bottle. The price *falls* to 75 cents a bottle, and the quantity decreases to 9 million bottles.

Note again that there is *no change in supply*. But the fall in price brings a *decrease in the quantity supplied*—a movement along the supply curve.

■ FIGURE 4.11
The Effects of a Change in Demand

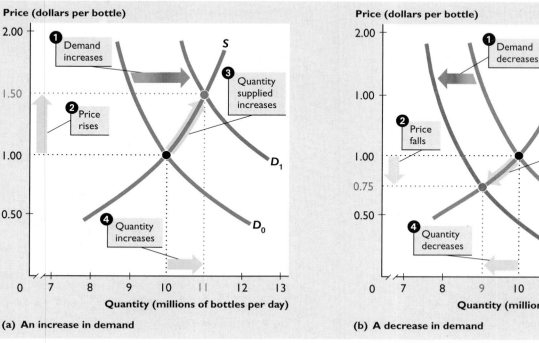
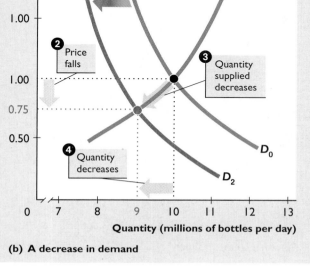

(a) An increase in demand

(b) A decrease in demand

❶ An increase in demand shifts the demand curve rightward to D_1 and creates a shortage. ❷ The price rises, ❸ the quantity supplied increases, and ❹ the equilibrium quantity increases.

❶ A decrease in demand shifts the demand curve leftward to D_2 and creates a surplus. ❷ The price falls, ❸ the quantity supplied decreases, and ❹ the equilibrium quantity decreases.

■ Effects of Changes in Supply

You can get more practice working out the effects of another event in the market for bottled water: European water bottlers buy springs and open new plants in the United States.

1. With more suppliers of bottled water, the supply changes.
2. The supply of bottled water *increases*, and the supply curve *shifts rightward*. Figure 4.12(a) shows the shift from S_0 to S_1.
3. There is now a *surplus* at $1.00 a bottle. The *price falls* to 75 cents a bottle, and the quantity increases to 11 million bottles.

Note that there is *no change in demand*. But the fall in price brings an *increase in the quantity demanded*—a movement along the demand curve.

What happens if a drought dries up some springs?

1. The drought changes the supply of water.
2. With fewer springs, the supply of bottled water *decreases*, and the supply curve *shifts leftward*. Figure 4.12(b) shows the shift from S_0 to S_2.
3. There is now a *shortage* at $1.00 a bottle. The *price rises* to $1.50 a bottle, and the quantity decreases to 9 million bottles.

Again, there is *no change in demand*. But the rise in price brings a *decrease in the quantity demanded*—a movement along the demand curve.

FIGURE 4.12
The Effects of a Change in Supply

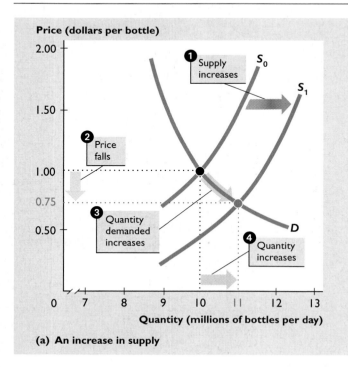

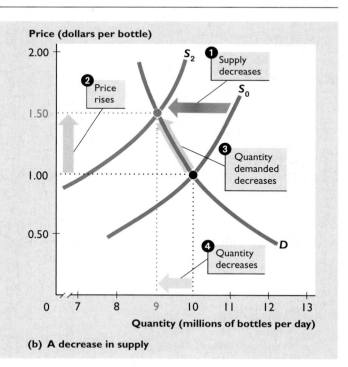

(a) An increase in supply

(b) A decrease in supply

❶ An increase in supply shifts the supply curve rightward to S_1 and creates a surplus. ❷ The price falls, ❸ the quantity demanded increases, and ❹ the equilibrium quantity increases.

❶ A decrease in supply shifts the supply curve leftward to S_2 and creates a shortage. ❷ The price rises, ❸ the quantity demanded decreases, and ❹ the equilibrium quantity decreases.

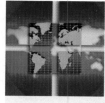
A Change in the Demand for Roses

Colombia and Ecuador grow most of the world's roses. On the average, the quantity of roses sold worldwide is around 6 million bunches a month. And the average price that consumers pay is around $40 a bunch.

But one month, February, is not a normal month. Each year, in February, the quantity of roses bought increases to four times that of any other month. The reason: Valentine's Day. And on Valentine's Day, the price of a bunch of roses doubles.

The demand-supply model explains these facts. The figure shows the supply curve of roses and two demand curves. The blue demand curve is the demand for roses in a normal month. This demand curve intersects the supply curve at an equilibrium price of $40 a bunch and an equilibrium quantity of 6 million bunches.

In February, the demand curve shifts rightward to the red curve. The equilibrium price rises to $80 a bunch and the equilibrium quantity increases to 24 million bunches.

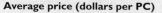

Price (dollars per bunch)

- 120
- 80 — February equilibrium — S
- 40 — Normal equilibrium — D_0 — D_{Feb}
- 0 — 6 — 24 — 36

Quantity (millions of bunches per month)

A Change in the Supply of PCs

You can buy a pretty neat notebook computer for around $700 and a desktop machine for as little as $350. Just a few years ago, you would have paid double these price and have got much less computing power for your money.

Why has the price of a PC fallen so dramatically?

Higher incomes have probably brought an increase in the demand for PCs (not shown in the figure). If this were the only influence on the market, the price would have risen.

Events that have increased the supply of PCs have brought the lower prices. Ongoing advances in technology have lowered the costs of computer chips, hard drives, and, most of all, monitors—both conventional ones and flat panel displays.

With an increase in supply, the supply curve has shifted rightward. At the old prices, there would be a surplus, so the price has fallen.

The lower price has brought an increase in the quantity of PCs demanded—a movement along the demand curve.

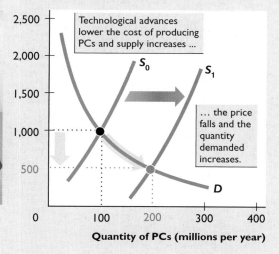

Average price (dollars per PC)

Technological advances lower the cost of producing PCs and supply increases ...

- 2,500
- 2,000 — S_0 — S_1
- 1,500
- 1,000 — ... the price falls and the quantity demanded increases.
- 500
- 0 — 100 — 200 — 300 — 400 — D

Quantity of PCs (millions per year)

■ Changes in Both Demand and Supply

When events occur that change *both* demand and supply, you can find the resulting change in the equilibrium price and equilibrium quantity by combining the cases you've just studied. Table 4.1 summarizes all the possible cases.

Increase in Both Demand and Supply

An increase in demand or an increase in supply increases the equilibrium quantity. So when demand and supply increase together, the quantity increases. But the price rises when demand increases and falls when supply increases. So when demand and supply increase together, we can't say what happens to the price unless we know the magnitudes of the changes. If demand increases by more than supply increases, the price rises. But if supply increases by more than demand increases, the price falls.

Decrease in Both Demand and Supply

A decrease in demand or a decrease in supply decreases the equilibrium quantity. So when demand and supply decrease together, the quantity decreases. But the price falls when demand decreases and rises when supply decreases. So when demand and supply decrease together, we can't say what happens to the price unless we know the magnitudes of the changes. If demand decreases by more than supply decreases, the price falls. But if supply decreases by more than demand decreases, the price rises.

Increase in Demand and Decrease in Supply

An increase in demand or a decrease in supply raises the equilibrium price, so combined, these changes raise the price. But an increase in demand increases the quantity, and a decrease in supply decreases the quantity. So when these changes occur together, we can't say what happens to the quantity unless we know the magnitudes of the changes. If demand increases by more than supply decreases, the quantity increases. But if supply decreases by more than demand increases, the quantity decreases.

Decrease in Demand and Increase in Supply

A decrease in demand or an increase in supply lowers the equilibrium price, so combined, these changes lower the price. But a decrease in demand decreases the quantity, and an increase in supply increases the quantity. So when these changes occur together, we can't say what happens to the quantity unless we know the magnitudes of the changes. If demand decreases by more than supply increases, the quantity decreases. But if supply increases by more than demand decreases, the quantity increases.

Table 4.1 lists all these effects. You can confirm them by revisiting Figures 4.11 and 4.12. Even better, by drawing your own demand-supply graphs, you can generate all these results. For the cases in which Table 4.1 lists "can't say" what happens to price or quantity, make some examples that go in each direction.

■ TABLE 4.1

How Price and Quantity Change When Demand or Supply Changes

Case	Change in demand	Change in supply	Effect on price	Effect on quantity	Illustrated in Figure
1.	Increase	None	Rise	Increase	4.11(a)
2.	Decrease	None	Fall	Decrease	4.11(b)
3.	None	Increase	Fall	Increase	4.12(a)
4.	None	Decrease	Rise	Decrease	4.12(b)
5.	Increase	Increase	Can't say	Increase	4.11(a) & 4.12(a)
6.	Decrease	Decrease	Can't say	Decrease	4.11(b) & 4.12(b)
7.	Increase	Decrease	Rise	Can't say	4.11(a) & 4.12(b)
8.	Decrease	Increase	Fall	Can't say	4.11(b) & 4.12(a)

REALITY CHECK

Demand and Supply in YOUR Life

The demand and supply model is going to be a big part of the rest of your life!

First, you will use it again and again during the rest of your economics course. The demand and supply model is one of your major tools. So having a firm grasp of this topic will bring an immediate practical payoff.

But second, and much more important, by understanding the laws of demand and supply and being aware of how prices adjust to balance these two opposing forces, you will have a much better appreciation of how *your* economic world works.

Every time you hear someone complaining about a price hike and blaming it on someone's greed, think about the law of market forces and the demand curve and the supply curve that intersect to determine that price.

As you shop for your favorite clothing, the latest music, and food items, try to describe the supply and demand influences on the prices of these goods and services.

3   **Explain how demand and supply determine price and quantity in a market and explain the effects of changes in demand and supply.**

Practice Problem 4.3

1. Table 1 shows the demand and supply schedules for milk.
   a. What is the equilibrium price and equilibrium quantity of milk?
   b. Describe the situation in the milk market if the price were $1.75 a carton and explain how the market reaches its new equilibrium.
   c. A drought decreases the quantity supplied by 45 cartons a day at each price. What is the new equilibrium and how does the market adjust to it?
   d. Milk becomes more popular and better feeds increase the quantity of milk. How do these events influence demand and supply? If there is no drought, do they create a shortage or a surplus at the equilibrium price in part **a**? Describe how the equilibrium price and equilibrium quantity change.

TABLE 1

Price (dollars per carton)	Quantity demanded	Quantity supplied
	(cartons per day)	
1.00	200	110
1.25	175	130
1.50	150	150
1.75	125	170
2.00	100	190

TABLE 2

Price (dollars per roll)	Quantity demanded	Quantity supplied
	(rolls per week)	
2.00	3,000	1,000
3.00	2,500	1,500
4.00	2,000	2,000
5.00	1,500	2,500
6.00	1,000	3,000

Exercise 4.3

1. Table 2 shows the demand and supply schedules for rolls of film.
   a. What is the market equilibrium?
   b. If the price of film is $3 a roll, describe the situation in the film market. Explain how market equilibrium is restored.
   c. A rise in income increases the quantity demanded by 1,000 rolls a week at each price. Explain how the film market adjusts to its new equilibrium.
   d. The number of film production lines increases, and at the same time, people switch to digital cameras. How do these events influence demand and supply? Do they create a shortage or a surplus at the equilibrium price in part **a**? Describe how the price and quantity change.

Solution to Practice Problem 4.3

1a. Equilibrium price is $1.50 a carton; equilibrium quantity is 150 cartons a day.

1b. At $1.75 a carton, the quantity demanded (125 cartons) is less than the quantity supplied (170 cartons), so there is a surplus of 45 cartons a day. The price begins to fall, and as it does, the quantity demanded increases, the quantity supplied decreases, and the surplus decreases. The price will fall until the surplus is eliminated. The price falls to a $1.50 a carton.

1c. The supply curve shifts leftward by 45 cartons a day. At $1.50 a carton, the quantity demanded (150 cartons) exceeds the quantity supplied (105 cartons), so there is a shortage of milk. The price begins to rise, and as it does, the quantity demanded decreases, the quantity supplied increases, and the shortage decreases. The price will rise until the shortage is eliminated. The new equilibrium occurs at $1.75 a carton and 125 cartons a day (Figure 1).

1d. When milk becomes more popular, demand increases. With better feeds, supply increases. If supply increases by more than demand, there will be a surplus at $1.50 a carton. The price falls, and the quantity increases. (Figure 2 illustrates.) If demand increases by more than supply, there will be a shortage at $1.50 a carton. The price rises, and the quantity increases. But if demand and supply increase by the same amount, there is no shortage or surplus and the price remains at $1.50 a carton. The quantity increases.

FIGURE 1

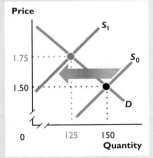

FIGURE 2

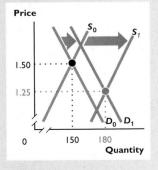

CHAPTER CHECKPOINT

Key Points

1 **Distinguish between quantity demanded and demand and explain what determines demand.**

- Other things remaining the same, the quantity demanded increases as the price falls and decreases as the price rises—the law of demand.
- The demand for a good is influenced by the prices of related goods, income, expectations about future income and prices, the number of buyers, and preferences. A change in any of these influences changes the demand for the good.

2 **Distinguish between quantity supplied and supply and explain what determines supply.**

- Other things remaining the same, the quantity supplied increases as the price rises and decreases as the price falls—the law of supply.
- The supply of a good is influenced by the prices of related goods, prices of resources and other inputs, expectations about future prices, the number of sellers, and productivity. A change in any of these influences changes the supply of the good.

3 **Explain how demand and supply determine price and quantity in a market and explain the effects of changes in demand and supply.**

- The law of market forces brings market equilibrium—the equilibrium price and equilibrium quantity at which buyers and sellers trade.
- The price adjusts to maintain market equilibrium—to keep the quantity demanded equal to the quantity supplied. A surplus brings a fall in the price to restore market equilibrium; a shortage brings a rise in the price to restore market equilibrium.
- Market equilibrium responds to changes in demand and supply. An increase in demand increases both the price and the quantity; a decrease in demand decreases both the price and the quantity. An increase in supply increases the quantity but decreases the price; and a decrease in supply decreases the quantity but increases the price.

Key Terms

Change in demand, 90
Change in the quantity demanded, 92
Change in the quantity supplied, 99
Change in supply, 97
Complement, 90
Complement in production, 97
Demand, 87
Demand curve, 88
Demand schedule, 88
Equilibrium price, 101

Equilibrium quantity, 101
Inferior good, 91
Law of demand, 87
Law of market forces, 101
Law of supply, 94
Market demand, 89
Market equilibrium, 101
Market supply, 96
Normal good, 91
Quantity demanded, 87

Quantity supplied, 94
Shortage or excess demand, 101
Substitute, 90
Substitute in production, 97
Supply, 94
Supply curve, 95
Supply schedule, 95
Surplus or excess supply, 101

Exercises

1. Explain how each of the following events changes the demand for or supply of air travel.
    a. Airfares tumble, while long-distance bus fares don't change.
    b. The price of jet fuel rises.
    c. Airlines reduce the number of flights each day.
    d. People expect airfares to increase next summer.
    e. As the winter turns very cold in New York, many people decide to take a midwinter break in Florida.
    f. With deep snow in the Rockies, many people flock to the ski slopes.
    g. The price of train travel falls.
    h. The price of a pound of air cargo increases.

2. Explain how each of the following events changes the demand for or supply of jeans.
    a. A new technology becomes available that cuts the time it takes to manufacture a pair of jeans by 50 percent.
    b. The price of the cloth (denim) used to make jeans falls.
    c. Jeans go out of fashion.
    d. The price of a pair of jeans falls.
    e. The wage rate paid to garment workers increases.
    f. Most baseball clubs start to sell their own brand of jeans.
    g. The price of a denim skirt doubles.
    h. People's income increase.

3. Use the laws of demand and supply to explain whether the following statements are true or false. In your explanation, distinguish between a change in demand and a change in the quantity demanded and between a change in supply and a change in the quantity supplied.
    a. The United States does not allow oranges from Brazil (the world's largest producer of oranges) to enter the United States. If Brazilian oranges were sold in the United States, oranges and orange juice would be cheaper.
    b. If soccer becomes more popular in the United States and basketball becomes less popular, the price of a pair of basketball shoes will rise.
    c. It is more expensive to ski in Aspen in the winter than in the spring.
    d. If the price of frozen yogurt falls, the quantity of ice cream consumed will decrease and the price of ice cream will rise.

4. What is the effect on the equilibrium price and quantity of orange juice of the following events if they occur one at a time?
    a. The price of apple juice decreases.
    b. The price of apple juice decreases, and the wage rate paid to orange grove workers increases.
    c. Orange juice becomes more popular, and a cheaper machine for picking oranges is used.
    d. Joggers switch from bottled water to orange juice.

5. Gasoline producers invent a new fuel that is cheaper and cleaner than gasoline. All new cars use the new fuel. Use a demand-supply graph to explain the effect of this new fuel on
    a. The price of gasoline and the quantity of gasoline bought.
    b. The price of a used car.

6. Table 1 shows the demand and supply schedules for mouse pads.
   a. What is the market equilibrium?
   b. If the price of a mouse pad is $7.00, describe the situation in the market. Explain how market equilibrium is restored.
   c. Explain what happens to the market equilibrium and how the market adjusts to its new equilibrium if a fall in the price of a computer changes the quantity demanded of mouse pads by 20 a week at each price.
   d. Explain what happens to the market equilibrium in part **a** if new voice-recognition software becomes popular and at the same time the cost of producing a mouse pad falls. Set out the three-step process of analysis and draw a graph to illustrate the adjustment process. Describe the change in the price and quantity of mouse pads.

TABLE I

Price (dollars per pad)	Quantity demanded	Quantity supplied
	(mouse pads per week)	
3.00	160	120
4.00	150	130
5.00	140	140
6.00	130	150
7.00	120	160
8.00	110	170

7. "As more people buy computers, the demand for Internet service will increase and the price of an Internet service will decrease. The decrease in the price of an Internet service will decrease the supply of Internet services." Is this statement true or false? Explain your answer.

8. Oil prices in March 2005 were 32 percent higher than in 2004. The price of oil was $56 a barrel. Explain how each of the following events might have led to this large increase in the price of oil. Use a demand-supply graph to illustrate your answers.
   a. A very cold winter in the United States and Europe in the first three months of 2005.
   b. OPEC was expected to increase its production in March but the increase was very small.
   c. Supply disruptions in the Middle East.
   d. Oil traders expect the price of oil to move to $60 a barrel.
   e. Rapid growth in the use of petroleum in China.

9. During 2004, orange growers in Florida experienced three hurricanes. As a result, the amount of oranges harvested in Florida was expected to be smaller than usual.
   a. Draw a demand-supply graph to show the equilibrium in the U.S. orange market in a normal year.
   b. Use your graph to illustrate the effect of the smaller harvests in Florida, given that orange growers in other states experienced normal growing conditions.
   c. How do you think the price of oranges and the quantity bought and sold changed in early 2005?
   d. What do you predict happened to the price of frozen orange juice in early 2005?

10. The world price of coffee fell during the early 2000s, but in 2005, the price increased.
    a. Draw a demand-supply graph to show the equilibrium in the world coffee market in 2000.
    b. During the early 2000s, countries such as Vietnam started to produce coffee and coffee shops such as Starbucks started to spring up across Europe and Asia. Explain how these events have changed the demand for and supply of coffee.
    c. Why do you think the price of coffee fell in the early 2000s and then rose?

Critical Thinking

11. The *Wall Street Journal* reports that the five major recording companies think that music downloads are too cheap at 99 cents per song. They would like to see a price between $1.25 and $2.99 per song.
    a. What determines the price of a music download?
    b. What role does self-interest—of both the recording companies and the people who download songs—play in the market for music downloads?
    c. What do you predict would happen in the market for music downloads if the major recording companies tried to hike the price to $2.99 a song?

12. In 1995, 90 salmon farms operated in British Columbia. In 1995, the Canadian government banned the creation of any new salmon farms because the farms create pollution and might introduce disease into the wild salmon population. In September 2002, the Canadian government lifted this ban. The Heart and Stroke Foundation tells us that "salmon is one of the healthiest foods we can eat. There's no shortage of it. We're eating three times as much of it as we did just a few years ago."
    a. What do you predict happened to the price of farm-raised salmon and the quantity of farm-raised salmon grown from 1996 through 2001?
    b. What effect do you think the lifting of the ban will have on the price of farm-raised salmon and the quantity of farm-raised salmon bought?
    c. If disease breaks out in the salmon farms of British Columbia, describe what effects it will have on the market for wild Pacific salmon.

Web Exercises

Use the links on MyEconLab to work the following exercises.

13. Obtain information about the history of the price of crude oil.
    a. What are the major changes that have occurred in the market for crude oil?
    b. On what three occasions did the price of oil rise by the largest amounts?
    c. What events occurred to trigger the price hikes that you've just described?
    d. Did the events that you've just described change the demand for crude oil, the supply, both, or neither? Explain your answer.
    e. Use the law of market forces and demand-supply graphs to explain the changes in the price and quantity of crude oil on the three occasions that you identified in part **b**.
    f. How do you think the price of crude oil influences the markets for coal and natural gas?
    g. How do you think the advances in technology that increased fuel efficiency in automobiles, airplanes, and home heating furnaces have influenced the world market for crude oil?

14. Visit eBay.
    a. What is eBay? Describe how eBay works.
    b. Do you think the prices of the items traded on eBay are determined by demand and supply or in some other way? Explain your answer.

Elasticities of Demand and Supply

CHAPTER 5

CHAPTER CHECKLIST

When you have completed your study of this chapter, you will be able to

1 Define, explain the factors that influence, and calculate the price elasticity of demand.

2 Define, explain the factors that influence, and calculate the price elasticity of supply.

3 Define and explain the factors that influence the cross elasticity of demand and the income elasticity of demand.

What do you do when the price of gasoline rises? If you're like most people, you keep filling your tank, groan a bit, and cut back on something less essential so that you can afford to spend more on gas. But don't some people find that the higher price puts an automobile out of reach and forces them to ride the bus? Also, rising incomes, especially in China and other parts of Asia, are increasing the demand for oil, which is bringing higher fuel prices. Are you going to keep buying the same quantity of gasoline when the price hits $3 a gallon, $5, $10?

To answer questions such as these, we need to know how responsive buying plans and selling plans are to a change in prices. You're now going to discover a powerful tool for describing demand and supply and predicting the magnitudes of price and quantity changes when either demand or supply changes. That tool is *elasticity*—the elasticity of demand and the elasticity of supply.

5.1 THE PRICE ELASTICITY OF DEMAND

A decrease in supply of gasoline brings a large rise in its price and a small decrease in the quantity that people buy. The reason is that buying plans for gasoline are not very responsive to a change in price. But an increase in the supply of airline services brings a small decrease in its price and a large increase in the quantity of air travel. In the case of air travel, buying plans are highly sensitive to a change in price. By knowing how sensitive or responsive buying plans are to price changes, we can predict how a given change in supply will change price and quantity.

But we often want to go further and predict by how much a price will change when some event occurs in a market. To make more precise predictions about the magnitudes of price and quantity changes, we need to know quite a lot more about a demand curve than the fact that it slopes downward. We need to know how responsive the quantity demanded is to price. Elasticity provides this information.

Price elasticity of demand
A measure of the responsiveness of the quantity demanded of a good to a change in its price when all other influences on buyers' plans remain the same.

The **price elasticity of demand** is a measure of the responsiveness of the quantity demanded of a good* to a change in its price when all other influences on buyers' plans remain the same.

To determine the price elasticity of demand, we compare the percentage change in the quantity demanded with the percentage change in price. But we calculate percentage changes in a special way.

■ Percentage Change in Price

Suppose that Starbucks raises the price of a latte from $3 to $5 a cup. What is the percentage change in price? The change in price is the new price minus the initial price. And the percentage change is calculated as the change in price divided by the initial price, all multiplied by 100. The formula for the percentage change is

$$\text{Percentage change in price} = \left(\frac{\text{New price} - \text{Initial price}}{\text{Initial price}} \right) \times 100.$$

In this example, the initial price is $3 and the new price is $5, so

$$\text{Percentage change in price} = \left(\frac{\$5 - \$3}{\$3} \right) \times 100 = \left(\frac{\$2}{\$3} \right) \times 100 = 66.67 \text{ percent.}$$

Now suppose that Starbucks cuts the price of a latte from $5 to $3 a cup. What now is the percentage change in price? The initial price is now $5 and the new price is $3, so the percentage change in price is calculated as

$$\text{Percentage change in price} = \left(\frac{\$3 - \$5}{\$5} \right) \times 100 = \left(\frac{-\$2}{\$5} \right) \times 100 = -40 \text{ percent.}$$

The same price change, $2, over the same interval, $3 to $5, is a different percentage change depending on whether the price rises or falls.

Because elasticity compares the percentage change in the quantity demanded with the percentage change in price, we need a measure of percentage change that does not depend on the direction of the price change. The measure that economists use is called the *midpoint method*.

_____

*What you learn in this chapter also applies to services and factors of production.

The Midpoint Method

To calculate the percentage change in price using the midpoint method, we divide the change in the price by the *average price*—the *average* of the new price and the initial price—and then multiply by 100. The average price is at the midpoint between the initial and the new price, hence the name *midpoint method*.

The formula for the percentage change using the midpoint method is

$$\text{Percentage change in price} = \left(\frac{\text{New price} - \text{Initial price}}{(\text{New price} + \text{Initial price}) \div 2} \right) \times 100.$$

In this formula, the numerator, (New price − Initial price), is the same as before. The denominator, (New price + Initial price) ÷ 2, is the average of the new price and the initial price.

To calculate the percentage change in the price of a Starbucks latte using the midpoint method, put $5 for new price and $3 for initial price in the formula:

$$\text{Percentage change in price} = \left(\frac{\$5 - \$3}{(\$5 + \$3) \div 2} \right) \times 100 = \left(\frac{\$2}{\$8 \div 2} \right) \times 100$$

$$= \left(\frac{\$2}{\$4} \right) \times 100 = 50 \text{ percent.}$$

Because the average price is the same regardless of whether the price rises or falls, the percentage change in price calculated by the midpoint method is the same for a price rise and a price fall. In this example, it is 50 percent.

■ Percentage Change in Quantity Demanded

Suppose that when the price of a latte rises from $3 to $5 a cup, the quantity demanded decreases from 15 cups to 5 cups an hour. The percentage change in the quantity demanded using the midpoint method is

$$\text{Percentage change in quantity} = \left(\frac{\text{New quantity} - \text{Initial quantity}}{(\text{New quantity} + \text{Initial quantity}) \div 2} \right) \times 100$$

$$= \left(\frac{5 - 15}{(5 + 15) \div 2} \right) \times 100 = \left(\frac{-10}{20 \div 2} \right) \times 100$$

$$= \left(\frac{-10}{10} \right) \times 100 = -100 \text{ percent.}$$

When the price of a good *rises*, the quantity demanded of it *decreases*—a *positive* change in price brings a *negative* change in the quantity demanded. Similarly, when the price of a good *falls*, the quantity demanded of it *increases*—this time a *negative* change in price brings a *positive* change in the quantity demanded.

To compare the percentage change in the price and the percentage change in the quantity demanded, we use the absolute values or magnitudes of the percentage changes and we ignore the minus sign.

■ Elastic and Inelastic Demand

To determine the responsiveness of the quantity of Starbucks latte demanded to its price, we need to compare the two percentage changes we've just calculated. The percentage change in quantity is 100 and the percentage change in price is 50, so the percentage change in quantity demanded is twice the percentage change in price. If we collected data on the prices and quantities of a number of goods and services (and we were careful to check that other things had remained the same), we could calculate lots of percentage changes. Our calculations would fall into three groups: The percentage change in the quantity demanded might exceed the percentage change in price, equal the percentage change in price, or be less than the percentage change in price. These three possibilities give three cases for the price elasticity of demand:

- Demand is **elastic** if the percentage change in the quantity demanded exceeds the percentage change in price.
- Demand is **unit elastic** if the percentage change in the quantity demanded equals the percentage change in price.
- Demand is **inelastic** if the percentage change in the quantity demanded is less than the percentage change in price.

Figure 5.1 shows the different types of demand curves that illustrate the range of possible price elasticities of demand. Part (a) shows an extreme case of an elastic demand called a **perfectly elastic demand**—an almost zero percentage change in the price brings a very large percentage change in the quantity demanded. Consumers are willing to buy any quantity of the good at a given price but none at a higher price. Part (b) shows an elastic demand—the percentage change in the quantity demanded exceeds the percentage change in price. Part (c) shows a unit elastic demand—the percentage change in the quantity demanded equals the percentage change in price. Part (d) shows an inelastic demand—the percentage change in the quantity demanded is less than the percentage change in price. Finally, part (e) shows an extreme case of an inelastic demand called a **perfectly inelastic demand**—the percentage change in the quantity demanded is zero for any percentage change in price.

■ Influences on the Price Elasticity of Demand

What makes the demand for some things elastic and the demand for others inelastic? The influences on the price elasticity of demand fall into two groups:

- Availability of substitutes
- Proportion of income spent

Availability of Substitutes

The demand for a good is elastic if a substitute for it is easy to find. Soft drink containers can be made of either aluminum or plastic and it doesn't matter which, so the demand for aluminum is elastic.

The demand for a good is inelastic if a substitute for it is hard to find. Oil has poor substitutes (imagine a coal-fueled car), so the demand for oil is inelastic.

Three main factors influence the ability to find a substitute for a good: whether the good is a luxury or a necessity, how narrowly it is defined, and the amount of time available to find a substitute for it.

Elastic demand
When the percentage change in the quantity demanded exceeds the percentage change in price.

Unit elastic demand
When the percentage change in the quantity demanded equals the percentage change in price.

Inelastic demand
When the percentage change in the quantity demanded is less than the percentage change in price.

Perfectly elastic demand
When the quantity demanded changes by a very large percentage in response to an almost zero percentage change in price.

Perfectly inelastic demand
When the quantity demanded remains constant as the price changes.

FIGURE 5.1
The Range of Price Elasticities of Demand

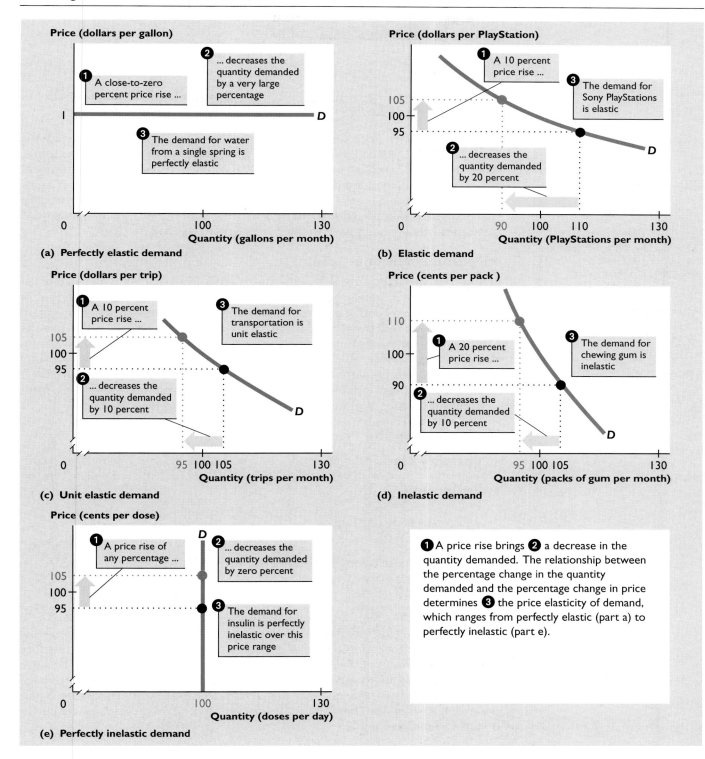

(a) Perfectly elastic demand

(b) Elastic demand

(c) Unit elastic demand

(d) Inelastic demand

(e) Perfectly inelastic demand

❶ A price rise brings ❷ a decrease in the quantity demanded. The relationship between the percentage change in the quantity demanded and the percentage change in price determines ❸ the price elasticity of demand, which ranges from perfectly elastic (part a) to perfectly inelastic (part e).

Luxury Versus Necessity   We call goods such as food and housing *necessities* and goods such as exotic vacations *luxuries*. A necessity has poor substitutes—you must eat—so the demand for a necessity is inelastic. A luxury has many substitutes—you don't absolutely have to go to Galapagos this summer—so the demand for a luxury is elastic.

Narrowness of Definition   The demand for a narrowly defined good is elastic. For example, the demand for a Starbucks latte is elastic because a New World latte is a good substitute for it. The demand for a broadly defined good is inelastic. For example, the demand for coffee is inelastic because tea is a poor substitute for it.

Time Elapsed Since Price Change   The longer the time that has elapsed since the price of a good changed, the more elastic is demand for the good. For example, when the price of gasoline increased steeply during the 1970s and 1980s, the quantity of gasoline demanded didn't change much because many people owned gas-guzzling automobiles—the demand for gasoline was inelastic. But eventually, fuel-efficient cars replaced gas guzzlers and the quantity of gasoline demanded decreased—the demand for gasoline became more elastic.

Proportion of Income Spent

A price rise, like a decrease in income, means that people cannot afford to buy the same quantities of goods and services as before. The greater the proportion of income spent on a good, the greater is the impact of a rise in its price on the quantity of that good that people can afford to buy and the more elastic is the demand for the good. For example, toothpaste takes a tiny proportion of your budget and housing takes a large proportion. If the price of toothpaste doubles, you buy almost as much toothpaste as before. Your demand for toothpaste is inelastic. If your apartment rent doubles, you shriek and look for more roommates. Your demand for housing is more elastic than is your demand for toothpaste.

■ Computing the Price Elasticity of Demand

To determine whether the demand for a good is elastic, unit elastic, or inelastic, we compute a numerical value for the price elasticity of demand by using the following formula:

$$\text{Price elasticity of demand} = \frac{\text{Percentage change in quantity demanded}}{\text{Percentage change in price}}.$$

- If the price elasticity of demand is greater than 1, demand is elastic.
- If the price elasticity of demand equals 1, demand is unit elastic.
- If the price elasticity of demand is less than 1, demand is inelastic.

Figure 5.2 illustrates and summarizes the calculation for the Starbucks latte example. Initially, the price is $3 a cup and 15 cups an hour are demanded—the initial point in the figure. Then the price rises to $5 a cup and the quantity demanded decreases to 5 cups an hour—the new point in the figure. The price rises by $2 a cup and the average (midpoint) price is $4 a cup, so the percentage change in price is 50. The quantity demanded decreases by 10 cups an hour and the average (midpoint) quantity is 10 cups an hour, so the percentage change in quantity demanded is 100.

FIGURE 5.2
Price Elasticity of Demand Calculation

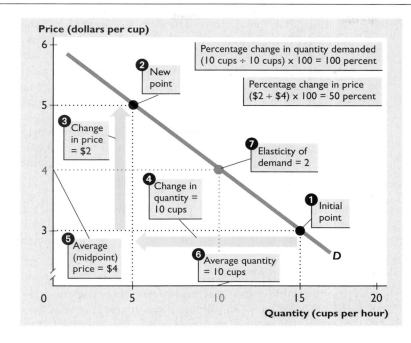

Using the above formula, you can see that the price elasticity of demand for a Starbucks latte is

1. At the initial point, the price is $3 a cup and the quantity demanded is 15 cups an hour.

2. At the new point, the price is $5 a cup and the quantity demanded is 5 cups an hour.

3. The change in price is $2 a cup, and 4. the change in the quantity demanded is 10 cups an hour.

5. The average price is $4 a cup, and the 6. average quantity demanded is 10 cups an hour.

The percentage change in quantity demanded is 100, the percentage change in price is 50, and 7. the price elasticity of demand is 2.

Using the above formula, you can see that the price elasticity of demand for a Starbucks latte is

$$\text{Price elasticity of demand} = \frac{100 \text{ percent}}{50 \text{ percent}} = 2.$$

The price elasticity of demand is 2 at the midpoint between the initial price and the new price on the demand curve. Over this price range, the demand for a Starbucks latte is elastic.

■ Interpreting the Price Elasticity of Demand Number

The number we've just calculated for a Starbucks latte is only an example. We don't have real data on the price and quantity. But suppose we did have real data and we discovered that the price elasticity of demand for a Starbucks latte is 2. What does this number tell us?

It tells us three main things:

1. The demand for Starbucks latte is elastic. Being elastic, the good has plenty of convenient substitutes (such as other brands of latte) and takes only a small proportion of buyers' incomes.

2. Starbucks must be careful not to charge too high a price for its latte. Pushing the price up brings in more revenue per cup but wipes out a lot of potential business.

3. The flip side of the second point: Even a slightly lower price could end up bringing in a lot more revenue.

■ Elasticity Along a Linear Demand Curve

Slope measures responsiveness. But elasticity is *not* the same as *slope*. You can see the distinction most clearly by looking at the price elasticity of demand along a linear (straight-line) demand curve. The slope is constant, but the elasticity varies. Figure 5.3 shows the same demand curve for a Starbucks latte as that in Figure 5.2 but with the axes extended to show lower prices and larger quantities demanded.

Let's calculate the elasticity of demand at point *A*. If the price rises from $3 to $5 a cup, the quantity demanded decreases from 15 to 5 cups an hour. The average price is $4 a cup, and the average quantity is 10 cups—point *A*. The elasticity of demand at point *A* is 2, and demand is elastic.

Let's calculate the elasticity of demand at point *C*. If the price falls from $3 to $1 a cup, the quantity demanded increases from 15 to 25 cups an hour. The average price is $2 a cup, and the average quantity is 20 cups—point *C*. The elasticity of demand at point *C* is 0.5, and demand is inelastic.

Finally, let's calculate the elasticity of demand at point *B*, which is the midpoint of the demand curve. If the price rises from $2 to $4 a cup, the quantity demanded decreases from 20 to 10 cups an hour. The average price is $3 a cup, and the average quantity is 15 cups—point *B*. The elasticity of demand at point *B* is 1, and demand is unit elastic.

Along a linear demand curve,

- Demand is unit elastic at the midpoint of the curve.
- Demand is elastic at all points above the midpoint of the curve.
- Demand is inelastic at all points below the midpoint of the curve.

■ FIGURE 5.3
Elasticity Along a Linear Demand Curve

On a linear demand curve, the slope is constant but the elasticity decreases as the price falls and the quantity demanded increases.

❶ At point *A*, demand is elastic.

❷ At point *B*, which is the midpoint of the demand curve, demand is unit elastic.

❸ At point *C*, demand is inelastic.

Demand is elastic at all points above the midpoint of the demand curve and inelastic at all points below the midpoint of the demand curve.

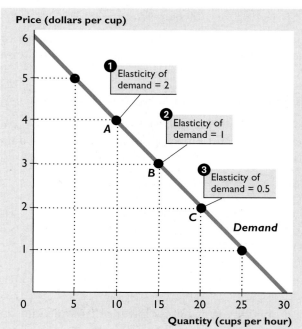

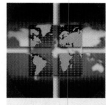

Price Elasticities of Demand

A rich American student is casual about her food. It costs only a few dollars a day, and she's going to have her burger, even at double the price. But a poor Tanzanian boy takes his food with deadly seriousness. He has a tough time getting, preparing, and even defending his food. A rise in the price of food means that he must cut back and eat even less.

The figure shows the percentage of income spent on food and the price elasticity of demand for food in ten countries. The larger the proportion of income spent on food, the larger is the price elasticity of demand for food.

As the low-income countries become richer, the proportion of income they spend on food will decrease and their demand for food will become more inelastic. Consequently, the world's demand for food will become more inelastic.

Harvests fluctuate and bring fluctuations in the price of food. And as the world demand for food becomes more and more inelastic, the fluctuations in the prices of food items will become larger.

The table shows a few real-world price elasticities of demand. The numbers in the table range from 1.52 for metals to 0.12 for food. Metals have good substitutes, such as plastics, while food has virtually no substitutes. As we move down the list of items, they have fewer good substitutes and are more likely to be regarded as necessities.

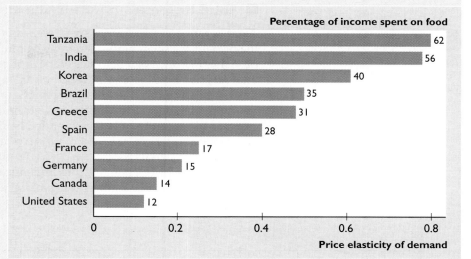

Percentage of income spent on food

Country	Price elasticity of demand	% income
Tanzania		62
India		56
Korea		40
Brazil		35
Greece		31
Spain		28
France		17
Germany		15
Canada		14
United States		12

Price elasticity of demand (horizontal axis 0 to 0.8)

Some Price Elasticities of Demand

Good or Service	Elasticity
Elastic Demand	
Metals	1.52
Electrical engineering products	1.39
Mechanical engineering products	1.30
Furniture	1.26
Motor vehicles	1.14
Instrument engineering products	1.10
Professional services	1.09
Transportation services	1.03
Inelastic Demand	
Gas, electricity, and water	0.92
Oil	0.91
Chemicals	0.89
Beverages (all types)	0.78
Clothing	0.64
Tobacco	0.61
Banking and insurance services	0.56
Housing services	0.55
Agricultural and fish products	0.42
Books, magazines, and newspapers	0.34
Food	0.12

SOURCES OF DATA: See p. C-1.

■ Total Revenue and the Price Elasticity of Demand

Total revenue
The amount spent on a good and received by its seller and equals the price of the good multiplied by the quantity sold.

Total revenue is the amount spent on a good and received by its sellers and equals the price of the good multiplied by the quantity of the good sold. For example, suppose that the price of a Starbucks latte is $3 and that 15 cups an hour are sold. Then total revenue is $3 a cup multiplied by 15 cups an hour, which equals $45 an hour.

We can use the demand curve for Starbucks latte to illustrate total revenue. Figure 5.4(a) shows the total revenue from the sale of latte when the price is $3 a cup and the quantity of latte demanded is 15 cups an hour. Total revenue is shown by the blue rectangle, the area of which equals $3, its height, multiplied by 15, its length, which equals $45.

When the price changes, total revenue can change in the same direction, the opposite direction, or remain constant. Which of these outcomes occurs depends

---

FIGURE 5.4

Total Revenue and the Price Elasticity of Demand

Total revenue equals price multiplied by quantity. In part (a), when the price is $3 a cup, the quantity demanded is 15 cups an hour and total revenue equals $45 an hour. When the price rises to $5 a cup, the quantity demanded decreases to 5 cups an hour and total revenue decreases to $25 an hour. Demand is elastic.

In part (b), when the price is $50 a book, the quantity demanded is 5 million books a year and total revenue equals $250 million a year. When the price rises to $75 a book, the quantity demanded decreases to 4 million books a year and total revenue increases to $300 million a year. Demand is inelastic.

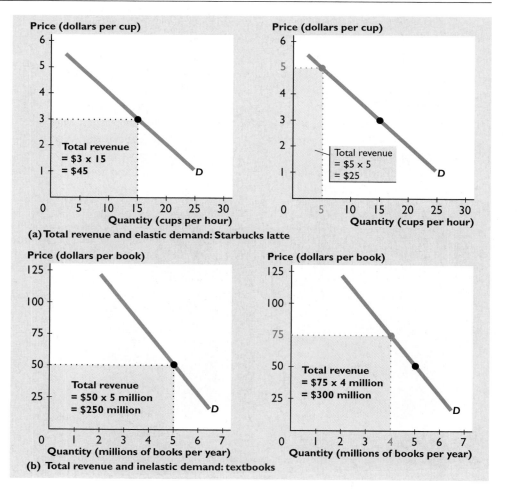

(a) Total revenue and elastic demand: Starbucks latte

(b) Total revenue and inelastic demand: textbooks

on the price elasticity of demand. By observing the change in total revenue that results from a price change (other things remaining the same), we can estimate the price elasticity of demand. This method of estimating the price elasticity of demand is called the **total revenue test**.

If demand is elastic, a given percentage rise in price brings a larger percentage decrease in the quantity demanded, so total revenue—price multiplied by quantity—decreases. Figure 5.4(a) shows this outcome. When the price of a latte is $3, the quantity demanded is 15 an hour and total revenue is $45 ($3 × 15). If the price of a latte rises to $5, the quantity demanded decreases to 5 an hour and total revenue *decreases* to $25 ($5 × 5).

If demand is inelastic, a given percentage rise in price brings a smaller percentage decrease in the quantity demanded, so total revenue increases. Figure 5.4(b) shows this outcome. When the price of a textbook is $50, the quantity demanded is 5 million a year and total revenue is $250 million ($50 × 5 million). If the price of a textbook rises to $75, the quantity demanded decreases to 4 million a year and total revenue *increases* to $300 million ($75 × 4 million).

The relationship between the price elasticity of demand and total revenue is

- If price and total revenue change in opposite directions, demand is elastic.
- If a price change leaves total revenue unchanged, demand is unit elastic.
- If price and total revenue change in the same direction, demand is inelastic.

Total revenue test
A method of estimating the price elasticity of demand by observing the change in total revenue that results from a price change (with all other influences on the quantity sold remaining unchanged).

REALITY CHECK

Elasticity in YOUR Life

Pay close attention the next time the price of something you buy rises. Did you spend more, the same, or less on this item?

Your expenditure on a good is its price multiplied by the quantity that you buy. So expenditure for the buyer is like total revenue for the seller. When the price of a good changes, the change in *your* expenditure on it depends on *your* elasticity of demand. When the price of a good *rises*, your demand for that good is

- ■ Elastic if your expenditure on it decreases.

- ■ Unit elastic if your expenditure on it remains constant.

- ■ Inelastic if your expenditure on it increases.

Think about why your demand for a good is elastic or inelastic by checking back to the list of influences on the price elasticity of demand on p. 116.

■ Applications of the Price Elasticity of Demand

Does a frost in Florida bring a massive or a modest rise in the price of oranges? And does a smaller orange crop mean bad news or good news for orange growers? Knowledge of the price elasticity of demand for oranges enables us to answer these questions.

Orange Prices and Total Revenue

Economists have estimated the price elasticity of demand for agricultural products to be about 0.4—an inelastic demand. If this number applies to the demand for oranges, then

$$\text{Price elasticity of demand} = 0.4 = \frac{\text{Percentage change in quantity demanded}}{\text{Percentage change in price}}.$$

If supply changes and demand doesn't, the percentage change in the quantity demanded equals the percentage change in the equilibrium quantity. So if a frost in Florida decreases the orange harvest and decreases the equilibrium quantity of oranges by 1 percent, the price of oranges will rise by 2.5 percent. The percentage change in the quantity demanded (1 percent) divided by the percentage change in price (2.5 percent) equals the price elasticity of demand (0.4).

So the answer to the first question is that when the frost strikes, the price of oranges will rise by a larger percentage than the percentage decrease in the quantity of oranges. But what happens to the total revenue of the orange growers?

The answer is again provided by knowledge of the price elasticity of demand. Because the price rises by a larger percentage than the percentage decrease in quantity, total revenue increases. A frost is bad news for consumers and those growers who lose their crops but good news for growers who escape the frost.

A Florida frost is bad news for buyers of orange juice and for growers who lose their crops but good news for growers who escape the frost.

Addiction and Elasticity

We can gain important insights that might help to design potentially effective policies for dealing with addiction to drugs, whether legal (such as tobacco and alcohol) or illegal (such as crack cocaine or heroin). Nonusers' demand for addictive substances is elastic. A moderately higher price leads to a substantially smaller number of people trying a drug and so exposing themselves to the possibility of becoming addicted to it. But the existing users' demand for addictive substances is inelastic. Even a substantial price rise brings only a modest decrease in the quantity demanded.

These facts about the price elasticity of demand mean that high taxes on cigarettes and alcohol limit the number of young people who become habitual users of these products, but high taxes have only a modest effect on the quantities consumed by established users.

Similarly, effective policing of imports of an illegal drug that limits its supply leads to a large price rise and a substantial decrease in the number of new users but only a small decrease in the quantity consumed by addicts. Expenditure on the drug by addicts increases. Further, because many drug addicts finance their purchases with crime, the amount of theft and burglary increases.

Cracking down on imports of illegal drugs limits supply, which leads to a large price increase. But it also increases the expenditure on drugs by addicts and increases the amount of crime that finances addiction.

Because the price elasticity of demand for drugs is low for addicts, any successful policy to decrease drug use will be one that focuses on the demand for drugs and attempts to change preferences through rehabilitation programs.

CHECKPOINT 5.1

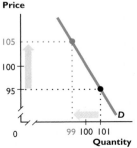

1 Define, explain the factors that influence, and calculate the price elasticity of demand.

Practice Problem 5.1

1. A 10 percent increase in the price of a good has led to a 2 percent decrease in the quantity demanded of that good.
   a. How would you describe the demand for this good?
   b. Are substitutes for this good easy to find or does it have poor substitutes?
   c. Is this good more likely to be a necessity or a luxury? Why?
   d. Is the good more likely to be narrowly or broadly defined? Why?
   e. Calculate the price elasticity of demand for this good.
   f. Explain how the total revenue from the sale of the good has changed.
   g. This good might be which of the following goods: orange juice, bread, toothpaste, theater tickets, clothing, blue jeans, Super Bowl tickets? Why?

Exercise 5.1

1. The price of Internet service rises from $24 to $26 a month, and the quantity demanded decreases from 204 million to 196 million subscribers.
   a. Calculate the percentage change in the price of Internet service.
   b. Calculate the percentage change in the quantity demanded of Internet services.
   c. Is the demand for Internet services elastic or inelastic?
   d. Would the demand for AOL service be more elastic or less elastic than the demand for Internet service? Why?
   e. Calculate the price elasticity of demand for Internet service.
   f. What is the change in the total revenue of Internet service providers?
   g. Explain why the concept of price elasticity of demand is useful.
   h. If the demand curve for Internet service is a straight line, is the price at which the demand for Internet service is unit elastic above or below $25 a month? Why?

Solution to Practice Problem 5.1

1a. Figure 1 illustrates a 10 percent increase in the price of a good that has led to a 2 percent decrease in the quantity demanded of it. The percentage change in the quantity demanded is less than the percentage change in the price, so the demand for the good is inelastic.

1b. Because the good has an inelastic demand, it usually has poor substitutes.

1c. Because the good has an inelastic demand, it is likely to be a necessity.

1d. Because the good has an inelastic demand, it is likely to be broadly defined.

1e. Price elasticity of demand equals the percentage change in the quantity demanded divided by the percentage change in price, which is 2 ÷ 10 or 0.2.

1f. When demand is inelastic, a price rise increases total revenue.

1g. The good might be a necessity (bread), have poor substitutes (toothpaste), or be broadly defined (clothing).

FIGURE 1

Price

105

100

95

0   99 100 101

Quantity

D

5.2 THE PRICE ELASTICITY OF SUPPLY

You know that when demand increases, the equilibrium price rises and the equilibrium quantity increases. But does the price rise by a large amount and the quantity increase by a little? Or does the price barely rise and the quantity increase by a large amount? To answer this question, we need to know the price elasticity of supply.

The **price elasticity of supply** is a measure of the responsiveness of the quantity supplied of a good to a change in its price when all other influences on sellers' plans remain the same. We determine the price elasticity of supply by comparing the percentage change in the quantity supplied with the percentage change in price.

■ Elastic and Inelastic Supply

Supply might be

- Elastic
- Unit elastic
- Inelastic

Figure 5.5 illustrates the range of supply elasticities. Figure 5.5(a) shows the extreme case of a **perfectly elastic supply**—an almost zero percentage change in price brings a very large percentage change in the quantity supplied. Figure 5.5(b) shows an **elastic supply**—the percentage change in the quantity supplied exceeds the percentage change in price. Figure 5.5(c) shows a **unit elastic supply**—the percentage change in the quantity supplied equals the percentage change in price. Figure 5.5(d) shows an **inelastic supply**—the percentage change in the quantity supplied is less than the percentage change in price. And Figure 5.5(e) shows the extreme case of a **perfectly inelastic supply**—the percentage change in the quantity supplied is zero when the price changes.

■ Influences on the Price Elasticity of Supply

What makes the supply of some things elastic and the supply of others inelastic? The two main influences on the price elasticity of supply are

- Production possibilities
- Storage possibilities

Production Possibilities

Some goods can be produced at a constant (or very gently rising) opportunity cost. These goods have an elastic supply. The silicon in your computer chips is an example of such a good. Silicon is extracted from sand at a tiny and almost constant opportunity cost. So the supply of silicon is perfectly elastic.

Some goods can be produced in only a fixed quantity. These goods have a perfectly inelastic supply. A beachfront home in Santa Monica can be built only on a unique beachfront lot. So the supply of these homes is perfectly inelastic.

Hotel rooms in New York City can't easily be used as office accommodation and office space cannot easily be converted into hotel rooms, so the supply of hotel rooms in New York City is inelastic. Paper and printing presses can be used to produce textbooks or magazines, and the supplies of these goods are elastic.

Price elasticity of supply
A measure of the responsiveness of the quantity supplied of a good to a change in its price when all other influences on sellers' plans remain the same.

Perfectly elastic supply
When the quantity supplied changes by a very large percentage in response to an almost zero percentage change in price.

Elastic supply
When the percentage change in the quantity supplied exceeds the percentage change in price.

Unit elastic supply
When the percentage change in the quantity supplied equals the percentage change in price.

Inelastic supply
When the percentage change in the quantity supplied is less than the percentage change in price.

Perfectly inelastic supply
When the quantity supplied remains the same as the price changes.

FIGURE 5.5
The Range of Price Elasticities of Supply

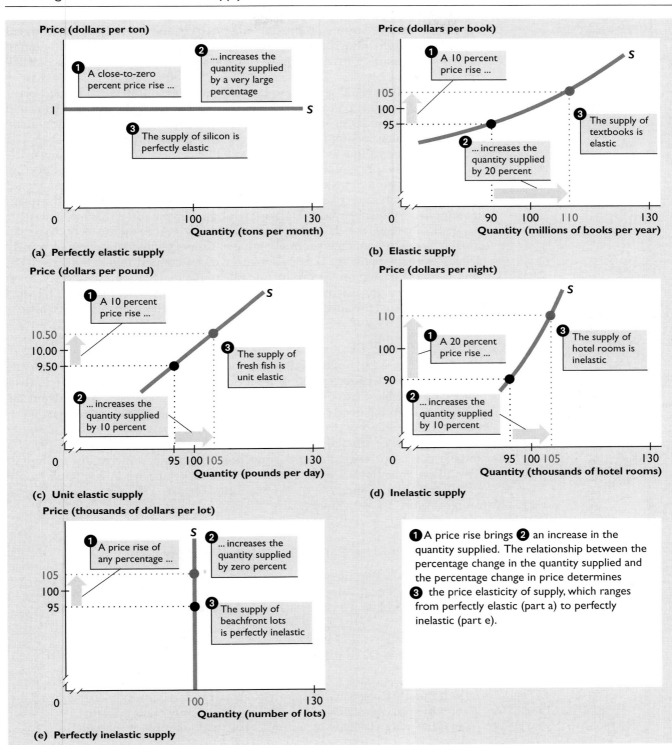

(a) Perfectly elastic supply

Price (dollars per ton)

❶ A close-to-zero percent price rise ...

❷ ... increases the quantity supplied by a very large percentage

❸ The supply of silicon is perfectly elastic

Quantity (tons per month)

(b) Elastic supply

Price (dollars per book)

❶ A 10 percent price rise ...

❷ ... increases the quantity supplied by 20 percent

❸ The supply of textbooks is elastic

Quantity (millions of books per year)

(c) Unit elastic supply

Price (dollars per pound)

❶ A 10 percent price rise ...

❷ ... increases the quantity supplied by 10 percent

❸ The supply of fresh fish is unit elastic

Quantity (pounds per day)

(d) Inelastic supply

Price (dollars per night)

❶ A 20 percent price rise ...

❷ ... increases the quantity supplied by 10 percent

❸ The supply of hotel rooms is inelastic

Quantity (thousands of hotel rooms)

(e) Perfectly inelastic supply

Price (thousands of dollars per lot)

❶ A price rise of any percentage ...

❷ ... increases the quantity supplied by zero percent

❸ The supply of beachfront lots is perfectly inelastic

Quantity (number of lots)

❶ A price rise brings ❷ an increase in the quantity supplied. The relationship between the percentage change in the quantity supplied and the percentage change in price determines ❸ the price elasticity of supply, which ranges from perfectly elastic (part a) to perfectly inelastic (part e).

Time Elapsed Since Price Change   As time passes after a price change, it becomes easier to change production plans and supply becomes more elastic. For some items—fruits and vegetables are examples—it is difficult or perhaps impossible to change the quantity supplied immediately after a price change. These goods have a perfectly inelastic supply on the day of a price change. The quantities supplied depend on crop-planting decisions that were made earlier. In the case of oranges, for example, planting decisions have to be made many years in advance of the crop being available.

Many manufactured goods also have an inelastic supply if production plans have had only a short period in which to change. For example, before it launched the PlayStation 2 in 2000, Sony made a forecast of demand, set a price, and made a production plan to supply the United States with the quantity that it believed people would be willing to buy. It turned out that demand outstripped Sony's earlier forecast. The price of a PlayStation 2 increased on eBay, an Internet auction market, to bring market equilibrium. At the high price that emerged, Sony would have liked to ship more PlayStations. But it could do nothing to increase the quantity supplied in the near term. The supply of the PlayStation 2 was inelastic.

As time passes, the elasticity of supply increases. After all the technologically possible ways of adjusting production have been exploited, supply is extremely elastic—perhaps perfectly elastic—for most manufactured items. By early 2001, Sony was able to step up the production rate of the PlayStation 2 and the price on eBay fell to the price at which Sony initially planned to sell the product. Over this longer time frame, the supply of the PlayStation 2 had become perfectly elastic.

Storage Possibilities

The elasticity of supply of a good that cannot be stored (for example, a perishable item such as fresh strawberries) or a service depends only on production possibilities. But the elasticity of supply of a good that can be stored depends on the decision to keep the good in storage or offer it for sale. A small price change can make a big difference to this decision, so the supply of a storable good is highly elastic. The cost of storage is the main influence on the elasticity of supply of a storable good. For example, rose growers in Colombia, anticipating a surge in demand on Valentine's Day in February, hold back supplies in late January and early February and increase their inventories of roses. They then release roses from inventory for Valentine's Day.

■ Computing the Price Elasticity of Supply

To determine whether the supply of a good is elastic, unit elastic, or inelastic, we compute a numerical value for the price elasticity of supply in a way similar to that used to calculate the price elasticity of demand. We use the formula:

$$\text{Price elasticity of supply} = \frac{\text{Percentage change in quantity supplied}}{\text{Percentage change in price}}$$

- If the price elasticity of supply is greater than 1, supply is elastic.
- If the price elasticity of supply equals 1, supply is unit elastic.
- If the price elasticity of supply is less than 1, supply is inelastic.

Let's calculate the price elasticity of supply of roses. We'll use the numbers that you saw in Chapter 4 on p. 105. Figure 5.6 illustrates and summarizes the calculation. In a normal month, the price of roses is $40 a bunch and 6 million bunches are supplied—the initial point in the figure. In February, the price rises to $80 a bunch and the quantity supplied increases to 24 million bunches—the new point in the figure. The price increases by $40 a bunch and the average, or midpoint, price is $60 a bunch, so the percentage change in the price is 66.67 percent. The quantity supplied increases by 18 million bunches and the average, or midpoint, quantity is 15 million bunches, so the percentage change in the quantity supplied is 120 percent.

Using the above formula, you can see that the price elasticity of supply of roses is

$$\text{Price elasticity of supply} = \frac{120 \text{ percent}}{66.67 \text{ percent}} = 1.8.$$

The price elasticity of supply is 1.8 at the midpoint between the initial point and the new point on the supply curve. In this example, over this price range, the supply of roses is elastic.

FIGURE 5.6

Price Elasticity of Supply Calculation

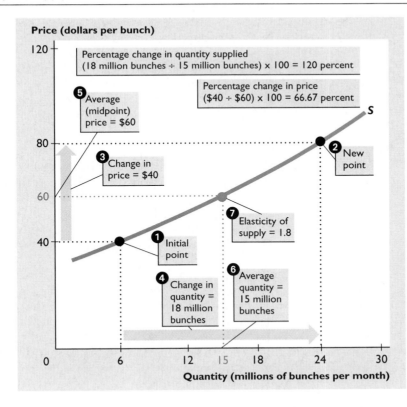

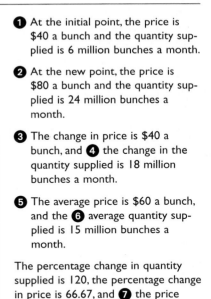

❶ At the initial point, the price is $40 a bunch and the quantity supplied is 6 million bunches a month.

❷ At the new point, the price is $80 a bunch and the quantity supplied is 24 million bunches a month.

❸ The change in price is $40 a bunch, and ❹ the change in the quantity supplied is 18 million bunches a month.

❺ The average price is $60 a bunch, and the ❻ average quantity supplied is 15 million bunches a month.

The percentage change in quantity supplied is 120, the percentage change in price is 66.67, and ❼ the price elasticity of supply is 1.8.

2 **Define, explain the factors that influence, and calculate the price elasticity of supply.**

Practice Problem 5.2

1. You are told that a 10 percent increase in the price of a good has led to a 1 percent increase in the quantity supplied of the good after one month. Use this information to answer the following questions.
   a. How would you describe the supply of this good?
   b. What can you say about the production possibilities of this good?
   c. Calculate the price elasticity of supply.
   d. If after one year, the quantity supplied has increased by 25 percent, describe how the supply has changed over the year.
   e. Calculate the elasticity of supply after one year.

Exercise 5.2

1. In 2002, the price of asparagus crashed from $45 a crate to $15 a crate. A typical Californian asparagus farmer would have supplied 2,000 crates a day at $45 a crate but at $15 a crate would plow the crop into the ground and supply nothing.
   a. How would you describe the Californian supply of asparagus?
   b. How do you think production possibilities and storage possibilities influence the price elasticity of supply of asparagus?
   c. Calculate the price elasticity of supply of Californian asparagus.
   d. If the price of asparagus remains at $15 a crate, do you think the elasticity of supply will change over the coming years? Explain your answer.
2. Use the data on the prices and quantities of roses in the *Eye on the Global Economy* on p. 105 to calculate the price elasticity of supply of roses.

Solution to Practice Problem 5.2

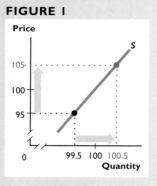

FIGURE I

1a. Figure 1 illustrates a 10 percent increase in the price of a good that has led to a 1 percent increase in the quantity supplied of it. The percentage change in the quantity supplied is less than the percentage change in the price of the good, so the supply of the good is inelastic.
1b. Because the quantity supplied increases by such a small percentage after one month, the factors of production that are used to produce this good are more likely to be unique or rare.
1c. The elasticity of supply equals the percentage change in the quantity supplied divided by the percentage change in the price, which is 1 ÷ 10 or 0.1.
1d. The supply of the good has become more elastic over the year since the price rise because other producers will have gradually started producing the good.
1e. The elasticity of supply equals the percentage change in the quantity supplied divided by the percentage change in the price. After one year, the elasticity of supply is 25 ÷ 10, which equals 2.5.

5.3 CROSS ELASTICITY AND INCOME ELASTICITY

Domino's Pizza in Chula Vista has a problem. Burger King has just cut its prices. Domino's manager, Pat, knows that pizzas and burgers are substitutes. He also knows that when the price of a substitute for pizza falls, the demand for pizza decreases. But by how much will the quantity of pizza bought decrease if Pat maintains his current price?

Pat also knows that pizza and soda are complements. He knows that if the price of a complement of pizza falls, the demand for pizza increases. So he wonders whether he might keep his customers by cutting the price he charges for soda. But he wants to know by how much he must cut the price of soda to keep selling the same quantity of pizza with cheaper burgers all around him.

To answer these questions, Pat needs to calculate the cross elasticity of demand. Let's examine this elasticity measure.

■ Cross Elasticity of Demand

The **cross elasticity of demand** is a measure of the responsiveness of the demand for a good to a change in the price of a substitute or complement when other things remain the same. It is calculated by using the formula:

$$\text{Cross elasticity of demand} = \frac{\text{Percentage change in quantity demanded of a good}}{\text{Percentage change in price of one of its substitutes or complements}}.$$

Cross elasticity of demand
A measure of the responsiveness of the demand for a good to a change in the price of a substitute or complement when other things remain the same.

Suppose that when the price of a burger falls by 10 percent, the quantity of pizza demanded decreases by 5 percent. The cross elasticity of demand for pizza with respect to the price of a burger is

$$\text{Cross elasticity of demand} = \frac{-5 \text{ percent}}{-10 \text{ percent}} = 0.5.$$

The cross elasticity of demand for a substitute is positive. A *fall* in the price of a substitute brings a *decrease* in the quantity demanded of the good. The quantity demanded of a good and the price of one of its substitutes change in the same direction.

Suppose that when the price of soda falls by 10 percent, the quantity of pizza demanded increases by 2 percent.* The cross elasticity of demand for pizza with respect to the price of soda is

$$\text{Cross elasticity of demand} = \frac{+2 \text{ percent}}{-10 \text{ percent}} = -0.2.$$

The cross elasticity of demand for a complement is negative. A *fall* in the price of a complement brings an *increase* in the quantity demanded of the good. The quantity demanded of a good and the price of one of its complements change in opposite directions.

---

*As before, these percentage changes are calculated by using the midpoint method.

FIGURE 5.7
Cross Elasticity of Demand

❶ A burger is a *substitute* for pizza. When the price of a burger falls, the demand curve for pizza shifts leftward from D_0 to D_1. At the fixed price of pizza, the quantity demanded of pizza decreases. The cross elasticity of the demand for pizza with respect to the price of a burger is *positive*.

❷ Soda is a *complement* of pizza. When the price of soda falls, the demand curve for pizza shifts rightward from D_0 to D_2. At the fixed price of pizza, the quantity demanded of pizza increases. The cross elasticity of the demand for pizza with respect to the price of soda is *negative*.

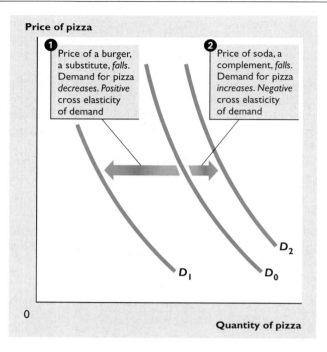

Price of pizza

❶ Price of a burger, a substitute, *falls*. Demand for pizza *decreases*. Positive cross elasticity of demand

❷ Price of soda, a complement, *falls*. Demand for pizza *increases*. Negative cross elasticity of demand

D_1 D_0 D_2

0   Quantity of pizza

Figure 5.7 illustrates these two cross elasticities of demand for pizza. When the price of a burger falls, the demand for pizza decreases and the demand curve for pizza shifts leftward from D_0 to D_1. When the price of soda falls, the demand for pizza increases and the demand curve for pizza shifts rightward from D_0 to D_2. The magnitude of the cross elasticity determines how far the demand curve shifts.

■ Income Elasticity of Demand

The U.S. and global economies are expanding, and people are enjoying rising incomes. This increasing prosperity brings an increasing demand for most types of goods. But by how much will the demand for different items increase? Will the demand for some items increase so rapidly that we spend an increasing percentage of our incomes on them? And will the demand for some items decrease?

Income elasticity of demand
A measure of the responsiveness of the demand for a good to a change in income when other things remain the same.

The answer depends on the income elasticity of demand. The **income elasticity of demand** is a measure of the responsiveness of the demand for a good to a change in income when other things remain the same. It is calculated by using the following formula:

$$\text{Income elasticity of demand} = \frac{\text{Percentage change in quantity demanded}}{\text{Percentage change in income}}.$$

The income elasticity of demand falls into three ranges:

- Greater than 1 (normal good, income elastic)
- Between zero and 1 (normal good, income inelastic)
- Less than zero (inferior good)

As our incomes increase: items that have an income elastic demand take an increasing share of income; items that have an income inelastic demand take a decreasing share of income; and items that have a negative income elasticity of demand take an absolutely smaller amount of income.

You can make some strong predictions about how the world will change over the coming years by knowing the income elasticities of demand of different goods and services. *Eye on the Global Economy* (below) provides a sampling of numbers.

These estimated income elasticities of demand tell us that we can expect air travel—both domestic and international—to become hugely more important; watching movies, having meals in restaurants, and even our haircuts and automobiles will take an increasing share of our incomes. Not shown in the table below, health care and education are two other prominent items the demand for which is income elastic. As our incomes grow, we can expect education and health care to take increasing shares of our incomes.

We'll be spending a decreasing percentage on clothing, phone calls, and food. The income elasticity of demand for food is less than one even for the poorest people. So we can predict a continuation of the trends of the past—shrinking agriculture and manufacturing and expanding services.

EYE ON THE GLOBAL ECONOMY

Income Elasticities of Demand

In the United States, necessities such as food and clothing are income inelastic; luxuries such as airline and foreign travel are income elastic.

The *level* of income has a big effect on income elasticities of demand. Using data for ten countries, the figure shows that the lower the income level, the more income elastic is the demand for food.

Some Income Elasticities of Demand

Good or Service	Elasticity
Income Elastic	
Airline travel	5.82
Movies	3.41
Foreign travel	3.08
Electricity	1.94
Restaurant meals	1.61
Local buses and trains	1.38
Haircuts	1.36
Cars	1.07
Income Inelastic	
Tobacco	0.86
Alcoholic beverages	0.62
Furniture	0.53
Clothing	0.51
Newspapers	0.38
Telephone	0.32
Food	0.14

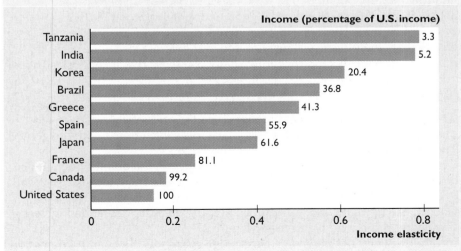

Income (percentage of U.S. income)

Tanzania	3.3
India	5.2
Korea	20.4
Brazil	36.8
Greece	41.3
Spain	55.9
Japan	61.6
France	81.1
Canada	99.2
United States	100

Income elasticity

SOURCES OF DATA: See page C-1.

3 **Define and explain the factors that influence the cross elasticity of demand and the income elasticity of demand.**

Practice Problems 5.3

1. If the quantity demanded of good *A* increases by 5 percent when the price of good *B* rises by 10 percent and other things remain the same,
   a. Are goods *A* and *B* complements or substitutes? Why?
   b. Describe how the demand for good *A* changes.
   c. Calculate the cross elasticity of demand.

2. If, when income rises by 5 percent and other things remain the same, the quantity demanded of good *C* increases by 1 percent,
   a. Is good *C* a normal good or an inferior good? Why?
   b. Describe how the demand for good *C* changes.
   c. Calculate the income elasticity of demand for good *C*.

Exercises 5.3

1. If, when the price of a pizza falls from $9 to $7 and other things remain the same, the quantity demanded of pizza increases from 100 to 200 an hour, the quantity demanded of burgers decreases from 200 to 100 an hour, and the quantity demanded of cola increases from 150 to 250 cans an hour,
   a. Are cola and pizza substitutes or complements? Why?
   b. Calculate the cross elasticity of demand for cola with respect to pizza.
   c. Are burgers and pizza substitutes or complements? Why?
   d. Calculate the cross elasticity of demand for burgers with respect to pizza.
   e. Of what use are these two cross elasticities of demand to the owner of a business that sells burgers and cola?

2. When incomes in Miami rise by 10 percent and other things remain the same, the quantity demanded of frozen fish cakes decreases by 5 percent and the quantity demanded of fresh fish increases by 15 percent.
   a. Are frozen fish cakes a normal good or an inferior good? Why?
   b. Calculate the income elasticity of demand for frozen fish cakes.
   c. Calculate the income elasticity of demand for fresh fish.
   d. How could a fish shop owner in Miami use these two income elasticities?

FIGURE I

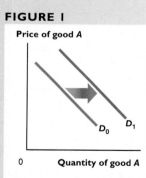

Price of good *A*

D_0 D_1

0   Quantity of good *A*

FIGURE 2

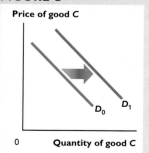

Price of good *C*

D_0 D_1

0   Quantity of good *C*

Solutions to Practice Problems 5.3

1a. Goods *A* and *B* are substitutes because when the price of good *B* rises, the quantity demanded of good *A* increases. People switch from good *B* to good *A*.
1b. The demand for good *A* increases (Figure 1).
1c. Cross elasticity of demand = Percentage change in the quantity demanded of good *A* ÷ Percentage increase in the price of good *B*, which is 5 ÷ 10 or 0.5.
2a. Good *C* is a normal good; as income rises, the quantity demanded increases.
2b. The demand for good *C* increases (Figure 2).
2c. Income elasticity of demand = Percentage change in the quantity demanded of good *C* ÷ Percentage increase in income, which is 1 ÷ 5 or 0.2.

CHAPTER CHECKPOINT

Key Points

1 **Define, explain the factors that influence, and calculate the price elasticity of demand.**

- The demand for a good is elastic if when its price changes, the percentage change in the quantity demanded exceeds the percentage change in price.
- The demand for a good is inelastic if when its price changes, the percentage change in the quantity demanded is less than the percentage change in price.
- The price elasticity of demand for a good depends on how easy it is to find substitutes for the good and on the proportion of income spent on it.
- Price elasticity of demand equals the percentage change in the quantity demanded divided by the percentage change in price.
- If demand is elastic, a rise in price leads to a decrease in total revenue. If demand is unit elastic, a rise in price leaves total revenue unchanged. And if demand is inelastic, a rise in price leads to an increase in total revenue.

2 **Define, explain the factors that influence, and calculate the price elasticity of supply.**

- The supply of a good is elastic if when its price changes, the percentage change in the quantity supplied exceeds the percentage change in price.
- The supply of a good is inelastic if when its price changes, the percentage change in the quantity supplied is less than the percentage change in price.
- The main influences on the price elasticity of supply are the flexibility of production possibilities and storage possibilities.

3 **Define and explain the factors that influence the cross elasticity of demand and the income elasticity of demand.**

- Cross elasticity of demand shows how the demand for a good changes when the price of one of its substitutes or complements changes.
- Cross elasticity is positive for substitutes and negative for complements.
- Income elasticity of demand shows how the demand for a good changes when income changes. For a normal good, the income elasticity of demand is positive. For an inferior good, the income elasticity of demand is negative.

Key Terms

Cross elasticity of demand, 131
Elastic demand, 116
Elastic supply, 126
Income elasticity of demand, 132
Inelastic demand, 116
Inelastic supply, 126

Perfectly elastic demand, 116
Perfectly elastic supply, 126
Perfectly inelastic demand, 116
Perfectly inelastic supply, 126
Price elasticity of demand, 114
Price elasticity of supply, 126

Total revenue, 122
Total revenue test, 123
Unit elastic demand, 116
Unit elastic supply, 126

Exercises

1. One winter recently, the price of home heating oil increased by 20 percent and the quantity demanded decreased by 2 percent, and with no change in the price of wool sweaters, the quantity demanded of wool sweaters increased by 10 percent.
    a. How would you describe the demand for home heating oil?
    b. Is home heating oil more likely to be a necessity or a luxury good? Why?
    c. How did the total revenue from the sale of home heating oil change? Why?
    d. Calculate the cross elasticity of demand of wool sweaters with respect to the price of home heating oil.
    e. Are home heating oil and wool sweaters substitutes or complements? Why?

FIGURE I

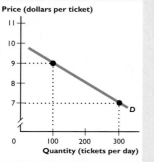

2. Figure 1 shows the demand for movie tickets.
    a. Is the demand for movie tickets elastic or inelastic over the price range $7 to $9 a ticket?
    b. If the price falls from $9 to $7 a ticket, will total revenue from the sale of movie tickets rise or fall? Explain.
    c. Calculate the price elasticity of demand for movie tickets.

3. The price elasticity of demand for Pete's chocolate chip cookies is 1.5. Pete wants to increase his total revenue. Would you recommend that Pete raise his price or lower his price of cookies? Explain your answer.

4. When heavy rain ruined the banana crop in Central America, the price of bananas rose from $1 a pound to $2 a pound. Banana sellers sold fewer bananas, but their total revenue remained unchanged.
    a. By how much did the quantity of bananas demanded change?
    b. Is the demand for bananas from Central America elastic or inelastic?

5. The price elasticity of demand for plane rides is 0.5. The price elasticity of demand for train rides is 0.2. The cross elasticity of demand for train rides with respect to the price of a plane ride is 0.4.
    a. If the price of a plane ride rises by 10 percent, what is the percentage change in the quantity demanded of plane rides?
    b. If the price of a plane ride rises by 10 percent, what is the percentage change in the quantity demanded of train rides?
    c. If the price of a train ride rises by 10 percent, what is the percentage change in the quantity demanded of train rides?
    d. When the price of a plane ride rises by 10 percent, what is the percentage change in the price of a train ride that will lead to no change in the quantity demanded of train rides?
    e. In part **d**, there is a movement along the demand curve for which ride and a shift of the demand curve for which ride?

6. When incomes increased by 10 percent, the quantity demanded of memberships in athletic clubs increased by 15 percent, the quantity of spring water demanded increased by 5 percent, and the quantity of sports drinks demanded decreased by 2 percent.
    a. Describe the demand for memberships in athletic clubs.
    b. Describe the demand for spring water.

    c. Describe the demand for sports drinks.

    d. The demand for which good is income elastic? Which is income inelastic?

    e. Which of the three goods are normal goods? Is any good an inferior good?

7. In Pioneer Ville, the price elasticity of demand for bus rides is 0.5, the income elasticity of demand for bus rides is −0.1, and the cross elasticity of demand for bus rides with respect to gasoline is 0.2.

    a. Is the demand for bus rides elastic or inelastic with respect to the price of a bus ride? Why?

    b. Would an increase in bus fares increase the bus company's total revenue? Explain your answer.

    c. Describe the relationship between bus rides and gasoline. Explain.

    d. If the price of gasoline increases by 10 percent with no change in the price of a bus ride, how will the number of bus rides change?

    e. If incomes in Pioneer Ville increase by 5 percent with no change in the price of a bus ride, how will the number of bus rides change?

    f. In Pioneer Ville, is a bus ride a normal good or an inferior good? Why?

    g. In Pioneer Ville, are bus rides and gasoline substitutes or complements? Why?

8. The income elasticity of demand for haircuts is 1.5, and the income elasticity of demand for food is 1.4. You take a weekend job, and the income you have to spend on food and haircuts doubles. If the prices of food and haircuts remain the same, will you double your expenditure on haircuts and double your expenditure on food? Explain why or why not.

9. Drought in many wheat-growing areas in 2002 cut the quantity of wheat grown by 2 percent. The price elasticity of demand for wheat is 0.5.

    a. By how much will the price of wheat rise?

    b. If pasta makers estimate that the change in the price of wheat in part **a** will increase the price of pasta by 25 percent and decrease the quantity demanded of pasta by 8 percent, what is the pasta makers' estimate of the price elasticity of demand for pasta?

    c. If pasta sauce makers estimate that, with the changes in part **b**, the quantity of pasta sauce demanded will decrease by 5 percent, what is the pasta sauce makers' estimate of the cross elasticity of demand for pasta sauce with respect to the price of pasta?

10. If textbooks became more expensive but no other prices changed and your income remained the same, do you think you would spend more, less, or the same as you now spend on textbooks? What does your answer tell you about *your* price elasticity of demand for textbooks?

Critical Thinking

11. How might the owners of the Houston Galleria shopping mall use the concept of cross elasticity of demand to determine the best combination of stores to operate in the Galleria?

12. "In a market in which demand is price inelastic, producers can gouge consumers and the government must set high standards of conduct for producers to ensure that consumers gets a fair deal." Do you agree or disagree with each part of this statement? Explain how you might go about testing the parts of the statement that are positive and lay bare the normative parts.

13. The Organization of the Petroleum Exporting Countries (OPEC) produces about 40 percent of the world's output of crude oil. OPEC knows that it can raise the world price of oil by cutting the total production of its member countries. OPEC also knows that the demand for crude oil is inelastic.
    a. Explain to the OPEC ministers, who are not economists, why it is not possible to conclude from these facts that OPEC's total revenue would increase if it were to cut its production.
    b. Does the elasticity of non-OPEC supply have any influence on how the price of crude oil changes when OPEC cuts production? Again, explain your answer in simple language that the OPEC ministers can understand.

14. Ron Gettelfinger, president of the United Auto Workers (UAW), wants your help. He has noticed that when he negotiates a pay increase for UAW members, the number of jobs available for them doesn't change at first, but then, over the next year or so, the number of jobs decreases. He has noticed that on the average, after a year, for every 1 percent rise in the wage rate, the number of jobs decreases by 1.5 percent.
    a. Describe the demand for UAW members' labor services.
    b. Calculate the price elasticity of demand for UAW members' labor services.
    c. How does the total wage bill of the employers of UAW members change immediately after a pay increase? Why?
    d. How does the total wage bill of the employers of UAW members change a year after a pay increase? Why?
    e. Can you think of any ways in which the UAW can make the demand for its members' labor services less elastic?
    f. Can you think of any ways in which the employers of UAW members can make the demand for labor services more elastic?

Web Exercises

Use the links on MyEconLab to work the following exercises.

15. Visit the Web site of the government of Canada and review the study of the price elasticity of demand for air travel.
    a. What are the six categories of air travel that the study used and why do you think it is necessary to break this service into several parts?
    b. Which category of air travel has the most inelastic demand? Why?
    c. Which category of air travel has the most elastic demand? Why?
    d. If the price of air travel falls, how will total expenditure on air travel change for each of the six categories in the study?
    e. How do you think an airline can use the information about the different price elasticities of demand? Hint: Think about the total revenue test.

16. Visit the Web sites of 3M and McDonald's. Think about the range of items each firm produces.
    a. Which firm do you think produces goods that have elastic demands? Why?
    b. If the demand for burgers is inelastic, does that mean that McDonald's can keep raising the price of a burger? Why or why not?
    c. If the demand for Post-it Notes is elastic, does that mean that 3M can be relied upon to keep the price of Post-it Notes low? Why or why not?

Efficiency and Fairness of Markets

CHAPTER CHECKLIST

When you have completed your study of this chapter,
you will be able to

1 Describe alternative methods of allocating scarce resources.

2 Distinguish between value and price and define consumer surplus.

3 Distinguish between cost and price and define producer surplus.

4 Evaluate the efficiency of the alternative methods of allocating scarce resources.

5 Explain the main ideas about fairness and evaluate the fairness of competitive markets and other allocation methods.

Markets make a lot of people unhappy! Unhappy because hard work doesn't always translate into a living wage. In the U.S. job markets, for example, around 12 million workers earn a wage of less than $6 an hour. Unhappy because where disaster strikes, price hikes seem to follow. A hurricane in Florida, a frost in Brazil, a tsunami in Asia—all send the prices of essential items sky high.

Do these examples show that markets are inefficient and unfair? Or are the outcomes just the result of markets making the best of it: allocating scarce resources efficiently and fairly in the social interest? These are the questions that we study in this chapter.

But if markets do a bad job, what are the alternatives? Can scarce resources be allocated more efficiently and fairly by means other than markets? We begin by reviewing alternative methods of allocating scarce resources.

6.1 RESOURCE ALLOCATION METHODS

The goal of this chapter is to evaluate the ability of markets to allocate resources in the social interest. The social interest has two dimensions: efficiency and fairness. So we must investigate whether the market is efficient and fair.

Because resources are scarce, they must be allocated somehow among their competing uses. But trading in markets isn't the only method. And to know whether the market does a good job, we need to compare it with its alternatives. So what are the alternatives?

Resources might be allocated by using any or some combination of the following methods:

- Market price
- Command
- Majority rule
- Contest
- First-come, first-served
- Sharing equally
- Lottery
- Personal characteristics
- Force

Let's see how each method works and look at an example of each.

■ Market Price

When a market price allocates a scarce resource, the people who get the resource are those who are willing and able to pay the market price. People who don't value the resource as highly as the market price leave it for others to buy and use.

Most of the scarce resources that you supply get allocated by market price. For example, you sell your labor services in a market. And you buy most of what you consume in markets.

Two kinds of people decide not to pay the market price: those who can afford to pay but choose not to buy and those who are too poor and simply can't afford to pay.

For many goods and services, distinguishing between those who choose not to buy and those who can't afford to pay doesn't matter. But for a few items, it does matter. For example, poor people can't afford to pay school fees and doctor's fees. The inability of poor people to buy items that most people consider to be essential is not handled well by the market price method and is usually dealt with by one of the other allocation methods.

But for most goods and services, the market turns out to do a good job. We'll examine just how good a job it does later in this chapter.

■ Command

Command system
A system that allocates resources by the order of someone in authority.

A **command system** allocates resources by the order (command) of someone in authority. Many resources get allocated by command. In the U.S. economy, the command system is used extensively inside firms and government bureaus. For example, if you have a job, most likely someone tells you what to do. Your labor time is allocated to specific tasks by a command.

Sometimes, a command system allocates the resources of an entire economy.

The former Soviet Union is an example. North Korea and Cuba are the only remaining command economies.

A command system works well in organizations in which the lines of authority and responsibility are clear and it is easy to monitor the activities being performed. But a command system works badly when applied to an entire economy. The range of activities to be monitored is just too large, and it is easy for people to fool those in authority. The system works so badly in North Korea that it fails even to deliver an adequate supply of food.

■ Majority Rule

Majority rule allocates resources in the way that a majority of voters choose. Societies use majority rule for some of their biggest decisions. For example, majority rule decides the tax rates that end up allocating scarce resources between private use and public use. And majority rule decides how tax dollars are allocated among competing uses such as national defense and health care for the aged.

Having 200 million people vote on every line in a nation's budget would be extremely costly. So instead of direct majority rule, the United States (and most other countries) use the system of representative government. Majority rule determines who will represent the people. And majority rule among the representatives decides the detailed allocation of scarce resources.

Majority rule works well when the decisions being made affect large numbers of people and self-interest must be suppressed to use resources most effectively.

■ Contest

A contest allocates resources to a winner (or a group of winners). The most obvious contests are sporting events. Serena Williams and Lindsay Davenport do battle on a tennis court, and the winner gets twice as much as the loser.

But contests are much more general than those in a sports arena, though we don't call them contests in ordinary speech. For example, Bill Gates won a big contest to provide the world's personal computer operating system, and Halle Berry won a type of contest to rise to the top of the movie-acting business.

Contests do a good job when the efforts of the "players" are hard to monitor and reward directly. By dangling the opportunity to win a big prize, people are motivated to work hard and try to become the "winner." Only a few people end up with a big prize, but many people work harder in the process of trying to win. So total production is much greater than it would be without the contest.

■ First-Come, First-Served

A first-come, first-served method allocates resources to those who are first in line. Most national parks allocate campsites in this way. Many casual restaurants won't accept reservations. They use first-come, first-served to allocate their scarce tables. The most visible example of first-come, first-served is the freeway. This scarce transportation resource gets allocated to the first to arrive at the on-ramp. If too many vehicles enter the freeway, the speed slows and people, in effect, wait in line for a bit of the "freeway" to become free!

First-come, first-served works best when, as in the above examples, a scarce resource can serve just one user at a time in a sequence. By serving the user who arrives first, this method minimizes the time spent waiting in line for the resource to become free.

■ Sharing Equally

When a resource is shared equally, everyone gets the same amount of it. You perhaps use this method to share dessert at a restaurant. People sometimes jointly own a vacation apartment and share its use equally.

To make equal shares work, people must be in agreement about its use and must make an arrangement to implement it. Sharing equally can work for small groups who share a set of common goals and ideals.

■ Lottery

Lotteries allocate resources to those who pick the winning number, draw the lucky cards, or come up lucky on some other gaming system. State lotteries and casinos reallocate millions of dollars worth of goods and services every year.

But lotteries are far more widespread than state jackpots and roulette wheels in casinos. They are used in a wide variety of situations to allocate scarce resources. The Federal Aviation Administration, for example, uses a lottery to allocate landing slots to airlines at New York City's LaGuardia airport.

Lotteries work well when there is no effective way to distinguish among potential users of a scarce resource.

■ Personal Characteristics

When resources are allocated on the basis of personal characteristics, people with the "right" characteristics get the resources. Some of the resources that matter most to you are allocated in this way. The people you like are the ones you spend the most time with. You try to avoid having to spend time with people you don't like. People choose marriage partners on the basis of personal characteristics. These uses of personal characteristics to allocate resources are regarded as completely natural and acceptable.

But this method also gets used in unacceptable ways. Allocating the best jobs to white, Anglo-Saxon males and discriminating against minorities and women is an example.

■ Force

Force plays a crucial role, for both good and ill, in allocating scarce resources. Let's start with the ill.

War, the use of military force by one nation against another, has played an enormous role historically in allocating resources. The economic supremacy of European settlers in the Americas and Australia owes much to the use of this method.

Theft, the taking of the property of others without their consent, also plays a large role. Both large-scale organized crime and small-scale petty crime collectively allocate billions of dollars worth of resources annually. A large amount of theft today is conducted by using sophisticated electronic methods that move resources from banks and thousands of innocent people.

But force plays a crucial positive role in allocating resources. It provides an effective method for the state to transfer wealth from the rich to the poor and the legal framework in which voluntary exchange in markets takes place.

Most income and wealth redistribution in modern societies occurs through a taxation and benefits system that is enforced by the power of the state. We vote for taxes and benefits—a majority vote allocation—but we use the power of the state to ensure that everyone complies with the rules and pays their allotted share.

A legal system is the foundation on which our market economy functions. Without courts to enforce contracts, it would not be possible to do business. But the courts could not enforce contracts without the ability to apply force if necessary. The state provides the ultimate force that enables the courts to do their work.

More broadly, the force of the state is essential to uphold the principle of the *rule of law*. This principle is the bedrock of civilized economic (and social and political) life. With the rule of law upheld, people can go about their daily economic lives with the assurance that their property will be protected—that they can sue for violations of their property (and be sued if they violate the property of others).

Free from the burden of protecting their property and confident in the knowledge that those with whom they trade will honor their agreements, people can get on with focusing on the activity at which they have a comparative advantage and trading for mutual gain.

In the next sections of this chapter, we're going to see how a market achieves an efficient use of resources, examine obstacles to efficiency, and see how sometimes, an alternative method might improve on the market. After looking at efficiency, we'll turn our attention to the more difficult issue of fairness.

CHECKPOINT 6.1

myeconlab

1 **Describe alternative methods of allocating scarce resources.**

Practice Problem 6.1

1. Which method is used to allocate the following scarce resources?
   a. Campus parking space between student areas and faculty areas
   b. A spot in a restricted student parking area
   c. Textbooks
   d. Host city for the Olympic Games

Exercise 6.1

1. Which method is used to allocate the following scarce resources?
   a. Airline tickets on the eve of Thanksgiving
   b. Goods at department stores in the January sales
   c. Presidency of the Students' Union
   d. The first serve in the final at the U.S. Open

Solution to Practice Problem 6.1

1a. A command system
1b. First-come, first served
1c. Market price (supplemented perhaps by sharing)
1d. Contest

6.2 VALUE, PRICE, AND CONSUMER SURPLUS

To investigate whether a market is efficient, we need to understand the connection between demand and marginal benefit and between supply and marginal cost.

■ Demand and Marginal Benefit

In everyday life, when we talk about "getting value for money," we're distinguishing between *value* and *price*. Value is what we get, and price is what we pay. In economics, the everyday idea of value is *marginal benefit*, which we measure as the maximum price that people are willing to pay for another unit of the good or service. The demand curve tells us this price. In Figure 6.1(a), the demand curve shows the quantity demanded at a given price—when the price is $10 a pizza, the quantity demanded is 10,000 pizzas a day. In Figure 6.1(b), the demand curve shows the maximum price that people are willing to pay when there is a given quantity—when 10,000 pizzas a day are available, the most that people are willing to pay for the 10,000th pizza is $10. The marginal benefit from the 10,000th pizza is $10.

A demand curve is a marginal benefit curve. The demand curve for pizza tells us the dollars' worth of other goods and services that people are willing to forgo to consume one more pizza.

Demand, Willingness to Pay, and Marginal Benefit

myeconlab

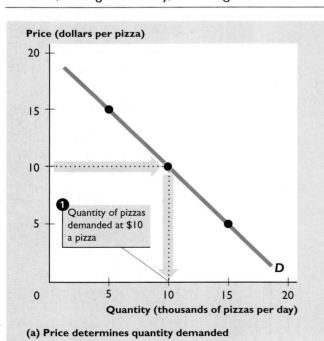

(a) Price determines quantity demanded

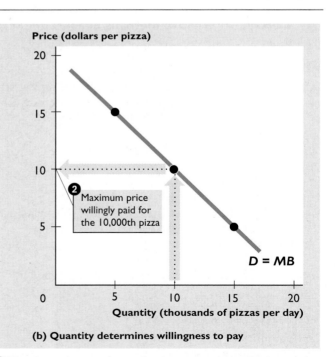

(b) Quantity determines willingness to pay

❶ The demand curve for pizza, *D*, shows the quantity of pizza demanded at each price, other things remaining the same. At $10 a pizza, the quantity demanded is 10,000 pizzas a day.

❷ The demand curve shows the maximum price willingly paid if there is a given quantity. If 10,000 pizzas are available, the maximum price willingly paid for the 10,000th pizza is $10.

■ Consumer Surplus

We don't always have to pay as much as we're willing to pay. When people buy something for less than it is worth to them, they receive a consumer surplus. **Consumer surplus** is the marginal benefit from a good minus the price paid for it, summed over the quantity consumed.

Figure 6.2 illustrates consumer surplus. Lisa's demand curve for pizza tells us the quantity of pizza she plans to buy at each price and her marginal benefit from pizza at each quantity. If the price of pizza is $1.00 a slice, Lisa buys 20 slices a week. She spends $20 on pizza, which is shown by the area of the blue rectangle.

To calculate Lisa's consumer surplus, we must find her consumer surplus on each slice and add these consumer surpluses together. For the 20th slice, her marginal benefit equals $1 and she pays $1, so her consumer surplus on this slice is zero. For the 10th slice (highlighted in the figure), her marginal benefit is $1.50. So on this slice, she receives a consumer surplus of $1.50 minus $1.00, which is 50¢. For the first slice, Lisa's marginal benefit is almost $2, so on this slice, she receives a consumer surplus of almost $1.

Lisa's consumer surplus—the sum of the consumer surpluses on the 20 slices she buys—is $10 a week, which is shown by the area of the green triangle. (The base of the triangle is 20 slices a week and its height is $1, so its area is 20 × $1 ÷ 2 = $10.)

Lisa's *total benefit* is the amount she pays, $20 (blue rectangle), plus her consumer surplus, $10 (green triangle), and is $30. Because Lisa must pay $20 for the pizza she consumes, her net benefit is equal to her total benefit minus what she pays. Consumer surplus is the net benefit to the consumer.

> **Consumer surplus**
> The marginal benefit from a good or service minus the price paid for it, summed over the quantity consumed.

■ FIGURE 6.2
A Consumer's Demand and Consumer Surplus

myeconlab

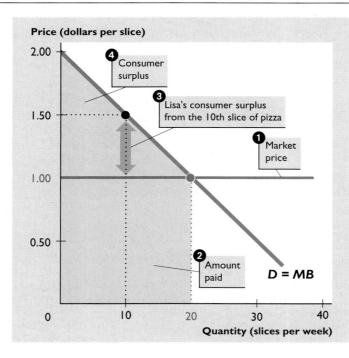

❶ The market price of pizza is $1.00 a slice.

❷ At the market price, Lisa buys 20 slices a week and spends $20 on pizza—the blue rectangle.

❸ Lisa's demand curve tells us that she is willing to pay $1.50 for the 10th slice, so she receives a consumer surplus of 50¢ on the 10th slice.

❹ Lisa's consumer surplus from the 20 slices she buys is $10—the area of the green triangle. Lisa's total benefit from pizza is the $20 she pays for it plus the $10 consumer surplus she receives, or $30.

2 **Distinguish between value and price and define consumer surplus.**

Practice Problem 6.2

FIGURE 1

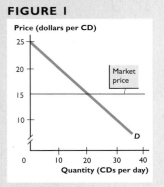

1. Figure 1 shows the demand curve for CDs and the market price of a CD. Use the figure to answer the following questions.
   a. What is the value of the 10th CD?
   b. What is the willingness to pay for the 20th CD?
   c. What is the consumer surplus on the 10th CD?
   d. What are the quantity of CDs bought and the consumer surplus?
   e. What is the amount paid for the CDs in part **d**?
   f. What is the total benefit from the CDs bought in part **d**?
   g. If the price rises to $20, what is the change in consumer surplus?

Exercise 6.2

FIGURE 2

1. Figure 2 shows the demand curve for ice cream cones and the market price of an ice cream cone. Use the figure to answer the following questions.
   a. What is the value of the 15th cone?
   b. What is the willingness to pay for the 5th cone?
   c. What is the consumer surplus on the 5th cone?
   d. What are the quantity of ice cream cones bought and consumer surplus?
   e. What is the total expenditure on ice cream cones?
   f. What is the total benefit from ice cream cones?
   g. If demand doubles, what is the change in consumer surplus?

Solution to Practice Problem 6.2

FIGURE 3

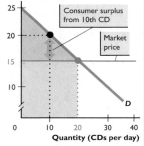

1a. The value of the 10th CD is the marginal benefit from the 10th CD. Value is equal to the maximum price that someone is willing to pay for the 10th CD, which is $20 (Figure 3).

1b. The willingness to pay for the 20th CD is the maximum price that someone is willing to pay for the 20th CD, which is $15 (Figure 3).

1c. The consumer surplus on the 10th CD is its marginal benefit minus the price of a CD, which is $20 − $15 = $5 (the green arrow in Figure 3).

1d. The quantity of CDs bought is 20 a day, and the consumer surplus is ($25 − $15) × 20 ÷ 2 = $100 (the green triangle in Figure 3).

FIGURE 4

1e. The amount paid for CDs is price multiplied by quantity bought, which is $15 × 20 = $300 (the blue rectangle in Figure 3).

1f. The total benefit from CDs is the amount paid for CDs plus the consumer surplus from CDs, which is $300 + $100 = $400.

1g. If the price rises to $20, the quantity of CDs bought decreases to 10 a day. The consumer surplus from CDs decreases to ($25 − $20) × 10 ÷ 2 = $25 (the small green triangle in Figure 4).

6.3 COST, PRICE, AND PRODUCER SURPLUS

What you are now going to learn about cost, price, and producer surplus parallels what you've learned about value, price, and consumer surplus.

■ Supply and Marginal Cost

Just as buyers distinguish between *value* and *price*, so sellers distinguish between *cost* and *price*. Cost is what a seller must give up to produce the good, and price is what a seller receives when the good is sold. The cost of producing one more unit of a good or service is its *marginal cost*. It is just worth producing one more unit of a good or service if the price for which it can be sold equals marginal cost. But the supply curve tells us this price. In Figure 6.3(a), the supply curve shows the quantity supplied at a given price—when the price of a pizza is $10, the quantity supplied is 10,000 pizzas a day. In Figure 6.3(b), the supply curve shows the minimum price that producers must receive to supply a given quantity—to supply 10,000 pizzas a day, producers must be able to get at least $10 for the 10,000th pizza. The marginal cost of the 10,000th pizza is $10. So:

> **A supply curve is a marginal cost curve. The supply curve of pizza tells us the dollars' worth of other goods and services that people must forgo if firms produce one more pizza.**

■ **FIGURE 6.3**

Supply, Minimum Supply Price, and Marginal Cost

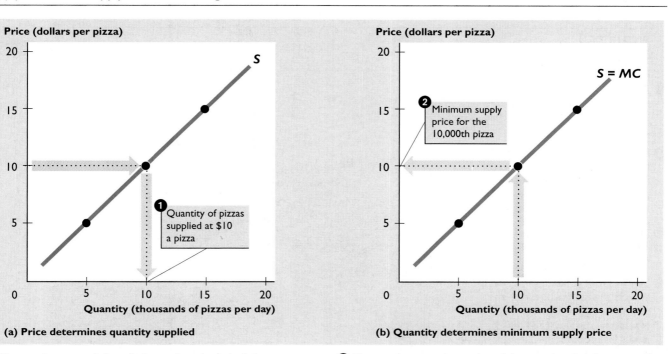

(a) Price determines quantity supplied

(b) Quantity determines minimum supply price

❶ The supply curve of pizza, S, shows the quantity of pizza supplied at each price, other things remaining the same. At $10 a pizza, the quantity supplied is 10,000 pizzas a day.

❷ The supply curve shows the minimum price that firms must be offered to supply a given quantity. The minimum supply price for the 10,000th pizza is $10.

■ Producer Surplus

Producer surplus
The price of a good minus the marginal cost of producing it, summed over the quantity produced.

When the price exceeds marginal cost, the firm obtains a producer surplus. **Producer surplus** is the price of a good minus the marginal cost of producing it, summed over the quantity produced.

Figure 6.4 illustrates producer surplus. Max can produce pizza or bake bread. The more pizza he bakes, the less bread he can bake. His marginal cost (opportunity cost) of pizza is the value of the bread he must forgo. The marginal cost of pizza increases as Max produces more pizza.

Max's supply curve of pizza tells us the quantity of pizza that Max plans to sell at each price and his marginal cost of producing at each quantity. If the price of a pizza is $10, Max produces 100 pizzas a day. Max's total revenue is $1,000 a day ($10 × 100 = $1,000).

To calculate Max's producer surplus, we must find the producer surplus on each pizza and add these producer surpluses together. The marginal cost of the 100th pizza is $10 and equals the $10 Max can sell it for, so his producer surplus on this pizza is zero. For the 50th pizza (highlighted in the figure), his marginal cost is $6. So on this pizza, he receives a producer surplus of $10 minus $6, which is $4. For the first pizza produced, Max's marginal cost is a bit more than $2, so on this pizza, he receives a producer surplus of almost $8.

Max's producer surplus—the sum of the producer surpluses on the 100 pizzas he sells—is $400 a day, which is shown by the blue triangle. (The base of the triangle is 100 pizzas a day and its height is $8, so its area is 100 × $8 ÷ 2 = $400.)

The red area shows Max's cost of producing 100 pizzas a day, which is $600. This amount equals Max's total revenue of $1,000 a day minus his producer surplus of $400 a day.

■ FIGURE 6.4
A Producer's Supply and Producer Surplus

❶ The market price of a pizza is $10. At this price, Max sells 100 pizzas a day and receives a total revenue of $1,000 a day.

❷ Max's supply curve shows that the minimum that he must be offered for the 50th pizza a day is $6, so he receives a producer surplus of $4 on the 50th pizza.

❸ Max's producer surplus from the 100 pizzas he sells is $400 a day— the area of the blue triangle.

❹ Max's cost of producing 100 pizzas a day is the red area beneath the marginal cost curve. It equals Max's total revenue of $1,000 minus his producer surplus of $400 and is $600 a day.

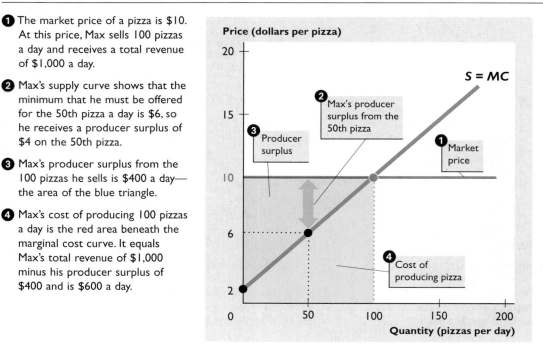

CHECKPOINT 6.3

3 **Distinguish between cost and price and define producer surplus.**

Practice Problem 6.3

1. Figure 1 shows the supply curve of CDs and the market price of a CD. Use the figure to answer the following questions.
   a. What is the marginal cost of the 10th CD?
   b. What is the minimum supply price of the 20th CD?
   c. What is the producer surplus on the 10th CD?
   d. What are the quantity of CDs sold and producer surplus?
   e. What is the total revenue from the CDs sold in part **d**?
   f. What is the cost of producing the CDs sold in part **d**?
   g. If the price falls to $10, what is producer surplus?

Exercise 6.3

1. Figure 2 shows the supply curve of ice cream cones and the market price of an ice cream cone. Use the figure to answer the following questions.
   a. What is the opportunity cost of the 15th cone?
   b. What is the minimum supply price of the 5th cone?
   c. What is the producer surplus on the 5th cone?
   d. What are the quantity of ice cream cones sold and producer surplus?
   e. What is the total revenue from ice cream cones?
   f. What is the total cost of producing ice cream cones?
   g. If the price falls to $2.00 a cone, what is the change in producer surplus?

Solution to Practice Problem 6.3

1a. The marginal cost of the 10th CD is equal to the minimum supply price for the 10th CD, which is $10 (Figure 3).

1b. The minimum supply price of the 20th CD is the marginal cost of the 20th CD, which is $15 (Figure 3).

1c. The producer surplus on the 10th CD is its market price minus its marginal cost, which is $15 − $10 = $5 (the blue arrow in Figure 3).

1d. The quantity sold is 20 a day. Producer surplus = ($15 − $5) × 20 ÷ 2 = $100 (blue triangle in Figure 3).

1e. The total revenue is price multiplied by quantity sold. Total revenue is $15 × 20 = $300.

1f. The cost of producing CDs equals total revenue minus producer surplus, which is $300 − $100 = $200 (the red area in Figure 3).

1g. The quantity sold decreases to 10 a day. The producer surplus decreases to ($10 − $5) × 10 ÷ 2 = $25 (the small blue triangle in Figure 4).

FIGURE 1

Price (dollars per CD)

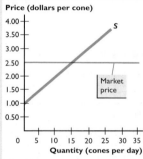

FIGURE 2

Price (dollars per cone)

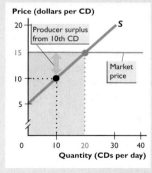

FIGURE 3

Price (dollars per CD)

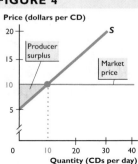

FIGURE 4

Price (dollars per CD)

6.4 ARE MARKETS EFFICIENT?

Figure 6.5 shows the market for pizza. The demand curve is *D*, the supply curve is *S*, the equilibrium price is $10 a pizza, and the equilibrium quantity is 10,000 pizzas a day. The market forces that you studied in Chapter 4 (pp. 101–102) pull the pizza market to its equilibrium and coordinate the plans of buyers and sellers. But does this competitive equilibrium deliver the efficient quantity of pizza?

If the equilibrium is efficient, it does more than coordinate plans. It coordinates them in the best possible way. Resources are used to produce the quantity of pizza that people value most highly. It is not possible to produce more pizza without giving up some of another good or service that is valued more highly. And if a smaller quantity of pizza is produced, resources are used to produce some other good that is not valued as highly as the pizza that is forgone.

■ Marginal Benefit Equals Marginal Cost

To check whether the equilibrium in Figure 6.5 is efficient, recall the interpretation of the demand curve as a marginal benefit curve and the supply curve as a marginal cost curve. The demand curve tells us the marginal benefit from pizza. The supply curve tells us the marginal cost of pizza. So where the demand curve and the supply curve intersect, marginal benefit equals marginal cost.

■ **FIGURE 6.5**

An Efficient Market for Pizza

❶ Market equilibrium occurs at a price of $10 a pizza and a quantity of 10,000 pizzas a day.

❷ The supply curve is also the marginal cost curve.

❸ The demand curve is also the marginal benefit curve.

Because at the market equilibrium, marginal benefit equals marginal cost, the ❹ efficient quantity of pizza is produced. The sum of the ❺ consumer surplus and ❻ producer surplus is maximized.

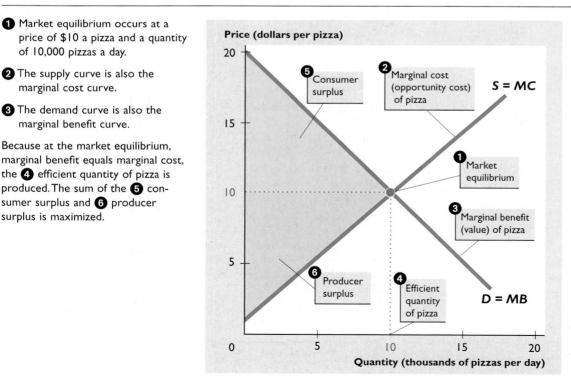

But this condition—marginal benefit equals marginal cost—is the condition that delivers an efficient use of resources. It allocates resources to the activities that create the greatest possible value. So a competitive equilibrium is efficient.

■ Total Surplus Is Maximized

Another way of checking that the equilibrium is efficient is to look at the total surplus that it generates. **Total surplus** is the sum of producer surplus and consumer surplus. A price above the equilibrium might increase producer surplus, but it would decrease consumer surplus by more. And a price below the equilibrium price might increase consumer surplus, but it would decrease producer surplus by more. The competitive equilibrium price maximizes total surplus.

Total surplus
The sum of producer surplus and consumer surplus.

In Figure 6.5, if production is less than 10,000 pizzas a day, someone is willing to buy a pizza for more than it costs to produce. So buyers and sellers gain if production increases. If production exceeds 10,000 pizzas a day, it costs more to produce a pizza than anyone is willing to pay for it. So buyers and sellers gain if production decreases. Only when 10,000 pizzas a day are produced is there no unexploited gain from changing the quantity of pizza produced, and total surplus is maximized.

Buyers and sellers each attempt to do the best they can for themselves—they pursue their self-interest. No one plans for an efficient outcome for society as a whole. No one worries about the social interest. Buyers seek the lowest possible price, and sellers seek the highest possible price. But as buyers and sellers pursue their self-interest, this astonishing outcome occurs: The social interest is served.

■ The Invisible Hand

Writing in his *Wealth of Nations* in 1776, Adam Smith was the first to suggest that competitive markets send resources to the uses in which they have the highest value. Smith believed that each participant in a competitive market is "led by an invisible hand to promote an end [the efficient use of resources] which was no part of his intention."

You can see the effects of the invisible hand at work every day. Your campus bookstore is stuffed with texts at the start of each term. It has the quantities that it predicts students will buy. The coffee shop has the variety and quantities of drinks and snacks that people plan to buy. Your local clothing shop has the sweatpants and socks and other items that you plan to buy. Truckloads of textbooks, coffee and cookies, and sweatpants and socks roll along our highways and bring these items to where you and your friends want to buy them. Firms that don't know you anticipate your wants and work hard to help you satisfy them.

No government organizes all this production, and no government auditor monitors producers to ensure that they serve the public interest. The allocation of scarce resources is not planned. It happens because prices adjust to make buying plans and selling plans compatible. And it happens in a way that sends resources to the uses in which they have the highest value.

Adam Smith explained why all this amazing activity occurs. "It is not from the benevolence of the butcher, the brewer, or the baker that we expect our dinner," he wrote, "but from their regard to their own interest."

Publishing companies, coffee growers, garment manufacturers, and a host of other producers are led by their regard for their own interest to serve *your* interest.

The Invisible Hand and e-Commerce

You can see the influence of the invisible hand at work in the cartoon and in today's information economy.

The cold drinks vendor has both cold drinks and shade. He has an opportunity cost and a minimum supply price of each item. The park bench reader has a marginal benefit from a cold drink and from shade. The transaction that occurs tells us that the reader's marginal benefit from shade exceeds the vendor's marginal cost but the vendor's marginal cost of a cold drink exceeds the reader's marginal benefit. The transaction creates consumer surplus and producer surplus. The vendor obtains a producer surplus from selling the shade for more than its opportunity cost, and the reader obtains a consumer surplus from buying the shade for less than its marginal benefit. In the third frame of the cartoon, both the consumer and the producer are better off than they were in the first frame. The umbrella has moved to its highest-valued use.

The market economy relentlessly performs the activity illustrated in the cartoon to achieve an efficient allocation of resources. And rarely has the market been working as hard as it is today. Think about a few of the changes that are taking place in our economy and notice how the market is guiding resources toward their efficient use.

New technologies have cut the cost of producing computers. As these advances have occurred, the supply of computers has increased and the price of a computer has fallen. Lower prices have encouraged an increase in the quantity demanded of this now less costly tool. The marginal benefit from computers is brought to equality with their marginal cost.

During the past few years, hundreds of Web sites have been established that are dedicated to facilitating trading in all types of goods, services, and factors of production. One of these sites is Freeshop.com (http://www.freeshop.com/), which organizes access to hundreds of other sites that among them offer more than 1,000 "free and trial offers."

Another notable online market maker is the electronic auction site eBay (http://www.ebay.com/), where you can offer to buy or sell any of a huge variety of items.

These e-commerce innovations are increasing consumer surplus, increasing producer surplus, and achieving yet greater allocative efficiency.

■ Underproduction and Overproduction

Inefficiency can occur because either too little of an item is produced—underproduction—or too much is produced—overproduction.

Underproduction

In Figure 6.6(a), the quantity of pizza produced is 5,000 a day. At this quantity, consumers are willing to pay $15 for a pizza that costs only $6 to produce. The quantity produced is inefficient—there is underproduction.

A **deadweight loss**, which is the decrease in total surplus that results from an inefficient underproduction or overproduction, measures the scale of the inefficiency. The gray triangle in Figure 6.6(a) shows the deadweight loss.

Deadweight loss
The decrease in total surplus that results from an inefficient underproduction or overproduction.

Overproduction

In Figure 6.6(b), the quantity of pizza produced is 15,000 a day. At this quantity, consumers are willing to pay only $5 for a pizza that costs $14 to produce. By producing the 15,000th pizza, $9 is lost. Again, the gray triangle shows the deadweight loss. The total surplus is smaller than its maximum by the amount of deadweight loss. The deadweight loss is borne by the entire society. It is not a loss for the consumers and a gain for the producer. It is a *social* loss.

■ FIGURE 6.6
Underproduction and Overproduction

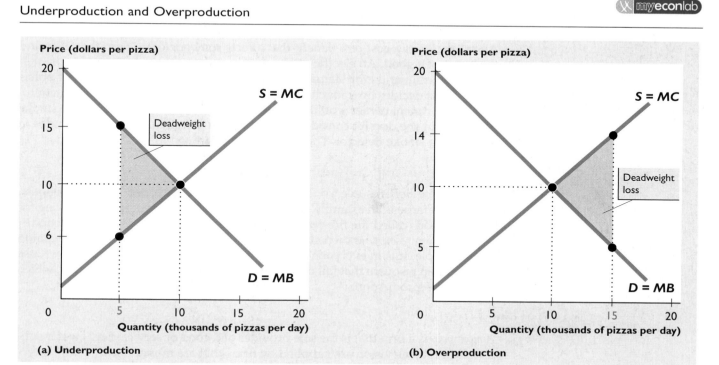

(a) Underproduction

If pizza production is restricted to 5,000 a day, a deadweight loss (the gray triangle) arises. Total surplus is reduced by the amount of the deadweight loss triangle. Underproduction is inefficient.

(b) Overproduction

If production increases to 15,000, a deadweight loss arises. Total surplus is reduced by the amount of the deadweight loss triangle. Overproduction is inefficient.

■ Obstacles to Efficiency

The obstacles to efficiency that bring underproduction or overproduction are

- Price and quantity regulations
- Taxes and subsidies
- Externalities
- Public goods and common resources
- Monopoly
- High transactions costs

Price and Quantity Regulations

Price regulations that put a cap on the rent a landlord is permitted to charge and laws that require employers to pay a minimum wage sometimes block the price adjustments that balance the quantity demanded and the quantity supplied and lead to underproduction. *Quantity regulations* that limit the amount that a farm is permitted to produce also lead to underproduction.

Taxes and Subsidies

Taxes increase the prices paid by buyers and lower the prices received by sellers. So taxes decrease the quantity produced and lead to underproduction. *Subsidies,* which are payments by the government to producers, decrease the prices paid by buyers and increase the prices received by sellers. So subsidies increase the quantity produced and lead to overproduction.

Externalities

An *externality* is a cost or a benefit that affects someone other than the seller and the buyer of a good. An electric utility creates an *external cost* by burning coal that brings acid rain and crop damage. The utility doesn't consider the cost of pollution when it decides how much power to produce. The result is overproduction.

An apartment owner would provide an *external benefit* if she installed a smoke detector. But she doesn't consider her neighbor's marginal benefit and decides to not install a smoke detector. There is underproduction.

Public Goods and Common Resources

A *public good* benefits everyone and no one can be excluded from its benefits. National defense is an example. It is in everyone's self-interest to avoid paying for a public good (called the *free-rider problem*), which leads to its underproduction.

A *common resource* is owned by no one but used by everyone. Atlantic salmon is an example. It is in everyone's self-interest to ignore the costs of their own use of a common resource that fall on others (called the *tragedy of the commons*), which leads to overproduction.

Monopoly

A *monopoly* is a firm that is the sole provider of a good or service. Local water supply and cable television are supplied by firms that are monopolies.

The self-interest of a monopoly is to maximize its profit. And because the monopoly has no competitors, it can set the price to achieve its self-interested goal. To achieve its goal, a monopoly produces too little and charges too high a price. It leads to underproduction.

High Transactions Costs

Stroll around a shopping mall and observe the retail markets in which you participate. You'll see that these markets employ enormous quantities of scarce labor and capital resources. It is costly to operate any market. Economists call the opportunity costs of making trades in a market **transactions costs**.

To use market prices as the allocators of scarce resources, its must be worth bearing the opportunity cost of establishing a market. Some markets are just too costly to operate. For example, when you want to play tennis on your local "free" court, you don't pay a market price for your slot on the court. You hang around until the court becomes vacant, and you "pay" with your waiting time.

When transactions costs are high, the market might underproduce.

Transactions costs
The opportunity costs of making trades in a market.

■ Alternatives to the Market

When a market is inefficient, can one of the alternative non-market methods that we described at the beginning of this chapter do a better job? Sometimes it can.

Table 6.1 summarizes the sources of market inefficiency and the possible remedies. Often, majority rule might be used, but majority rule has its own shortcomings. A group that pursues the self-interest of its members can become the majority. For example, price and quantity regulations that create deadweight loss are almost always the result of a self-interested group becoming the majority and imposing costs on the minority. Also, with majority rule, votes must be translated into actions by bureaucrats who have their own agendas.

Managers in firms issue commands and avoid the transactions costs that they would incur if they went to a market every time they needed a job done. First-come, first-served saves a lot of hassle in waiting lines. These lines could have markets in which people trade their place in the line—but someone would have to enforce the agreements. Can you imagine the hassle at a busy ATM if you had to buy your spot at the head of the line?

There is no one mechanism for allocating resources efficiently. But supplemented by majority rule, bypassed inside firms by command systems, and by occasionally using first-come, first-served, markets do an amazingly good job.

■ TABLE 6.1

Market Inefficiencies and Some Possible Remedies

Reason for inefficiency of market	Possible improvement over market
1. Price and quantity regulations	Remove regulation by majority rule
2. Taxes and subsidies	Minimize deadweight loss by majority rule
3. Externalities	Minimize deadweight loss by majority rule
4. Public goods	Allocate by majority rule
5. Common resources	Allocate by majority rule
6. Monopoly	Regulate by majority rule
7. High transactions costs	Command or first-come, first-served

4 **Evaluate the efficiency of the alternative methods of allocating scarce resources.**

Practice Problem 6.4

FIGURE 1

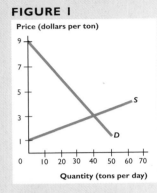

Price (dollars per ton)

Quantity (tons per day)

1. Figure 1 shows the market for paper.
   a. What are the equilibrium price and the equilibrium quantity of paper?
   b. In market equilibrium, what is consumer surplus?
   c. In market equilibrium, what is producer surplus?
   d. Is the market for paper efficient? Why or why not?
   e. If a news magazine lobbying group persuaded the government to pass a new law that requires producers to sell 50 tons of paper a day, would the market for paper be efficient? Why or why not?
   f. Shade the deadweight loss in part **e** on the figure.
   g. If an environmental lobbying group persuaded the government to pass a new law that limits the quantity of paper that producers sell to 20 tons a day, would the market for paper be efficient? Why or why not?
   h. In part **g**, what would be the deadweight loss?

Exercise 6.4

FIGURE 2

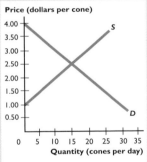

Price (dollars per cone)

Quantity (cones per day)

1. Figure 2 shows the market for ice cream cones.
   a. What are the equilibrium price and quantity of ice cream cones?
   b. In market equilibrium, what is consumer surplus?
   c. In market equilibrium, what is producer surplus?
   d. Is the market for ice cream cones efficient? Why or why not?
   e. If the government limits the quantity that producers can sell to 10 cones a day, would the market for ice cream cones be efficient? Explain.
   f. In part **e**, what would be the deadweight loss?
   g. If the government passed a law requiring producers to sell 20 ice cream cones a day, would the market for ice cream cones be efficient? Explain.
   h. In part **g**, what would be the deadweight loss?

Solution to Practice Problem 6.4

FIGURE 3

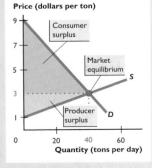

Price (dollars per ton)

Quantity (tons per day)

1a. Market equilibrium is 40 tons a day at a price of $3 a ton (Figure 3).

1b. Consumer surplus = ($9 − $3) × 40 ÷ 2 = $120 (the green triangle in Figure 3).

1c. Producer surplus = ($3 − $1) × 40 ÷ 2 = $40 (the blue triangle in Figure 3).

FIGURE 4

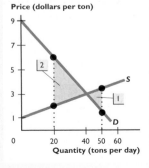

Price (dollars per ton)

Quantity (tons per day)

1d. The market is efficient because marginal benefit equals marginal cost and the sum of consumer surplus and producer surplus is a maximum.

1e. This market is inefficient because marginal cost exceeds marginal benefit.

1f. Deadweight loss is the gray triangle 1 in Figure 4.

1g. This market is now inefficient because marginal benefit exceeds marginal cost.

1h. Deadweight loss is the gray triangle 2 in Figure 4.

6.5 ARE MARKETS FAIR?

Is an efficient allocation of resources fair? Does the competitive market provide people with fair incomes for their work? And do people always pay a fair price for the things they buy? Do we need the government to step into some competitive markets to prevent the price from rising too high or falling too low?

When a natural disaster strikes, such as a severe winter storm or a hurricane, the prices of many essential items jump. The reason the prices jump is that some people have a greater demand and a greater willingness to pay while at the same time, the items are in limited supply. So the higher prices achieve an efficient allocation of scarce resources. News reports of these price hikes almost never talk about efficiency. Instead, they complain about unfairness. In Florida, there are even laws that prevent large price increases once a hurricane watch is in effect, and the state has set up an Anti-Gouging Hot Line.

Similarly, when low-skilled people work for a wage that is below what most would regard as a living wage, the media and politicians talk of employers taking unfair advantage of their workers.

How do we decide whether something is fair or unfair? You know when *you* think something is unfair. But how do you know? What are the *principles* of fairness?

Economists have a clear definition of efficiency: making the economic pie as large as possible and baking it at the lowest possible cost. But economists do not have a similarly clear definition of fairness—of what are fair shares of the economic pie for all the people who make it. A big reason for the lack of clarity is that ideas about fairness are not exclusively economic ideas. They also involve the study of ethics.

Think of economic life as a game—a serious game. A game has an outcome or result, and it has rules. All the players face the same rules, but they don't all get the same score. The equality of the rules and inequality of outcomes lies at the heart of discussions about fairness in economics. Two broad and generally conflicting approaches to fairness are

- It's not fair if the *result* isn't fair.
- It's not fair if the *rules* aren't fair.

■ It's Not Fair If the *Result* Isn't Fair

The earliest efforts to establish a principle of fairness were based on the view that the result is what matters. And the general idea was that it is unfair if people's incomes are too unequal. It is unfair that bank presidents earn millions of dollars a year while bank tellers earn only thousands of dollars a year. It is unfair that a store owner enjoys a larger profit and her customers pay higher prices in the aftermath of a winter storm.

But what is "too unequal"? Is it fair for some people to receive twice as much as others but not ten times as much or a hundred times as much? Or is all that matters that the poorest people shouldn't be "too poor"?

There was a lot of excitement during the nineteenth century when economists thought they had made an incredible discovery that answered these questions. And the answer was that *any* inequality is too much! Further, inequality brings inefficiency! This idea turns out to be wrong, but there is a lesson in the reason that it is wrong. So this idea is worth a closer look.

Utilitarianism

The nineteenth century idea that only equality brings efficiency is an extreme version of utilitarianism. **Utilitarianism** is a principle that states that we should strive to achieve "the greatest happiness for the greatest number." The people who developed this idea were known as utilitarians. They included two of the most eminent thinkers: Jeremy Bentham and John Stuart Mill.

Some utilitarians argued that to achieve "the greatest happiness for the greatest number," income must be transferred from the rich to the poor up to the point of complete equality—to the point at which there are no rich and no poor.

They reasoned in the following way: First, everyone has the same basic wants and is similar in the capacity to enjoy life. In the technical language of economics that you've now learned to use, everyone has the same marginal benefit schedule or curve. Second, the greater a person's income, the smaller is the marginal benefit of a dollar's worth of goods and services. The millionth dollar spent by a rich person brings a smaller marginal benefit to that person than the marginal benefit of the thousandth dollar spent by a poorer person. So by transferring a dollar from the millionaire to the poorer person, more is gained than is lost, and the two people added together are better off.

But the same is true for every dollar transferred until there is no poor or rich person. Only when everyone's share of the economic pie is the same as everyone else's are we sharing resources in the most efficient way and bringing the greatest attainable total benefit. So complete equality is not only the fair outcome but also the only efficient outcome. It maximizes the value of society's scarce resources.

The Big Tradeoff

One big problem with the utilitarian idea of complete equality is that it ignores the costs of making income transfers. Recognizing the costs of making income transfers leads to what is called the **big tradeoff**—a tradeoff between efficiency and fairness.

The big tradeoff is based on the following facts. Income can be transferred from people with high incomes to people with low incomes only by taxing high incomes. Taxing people's income from employment discourages work. It results in the quantity of labor being less than the efficient quantity. Taxing people's income from capital discourages saving. It results in the quantity of capital being less than the efficient quantity. With smaller quantities of both labor and capital, the quantity of goods and services produced is less than the efficient quantity. The economic pie shrinks.

Income redistribution creates a tradeoff between the size of the economic pie and the equality with which it is shared. The greater the scale of income redistribution through income taxes, the greater is the inefficiency—the smaller is the pie.

There is a second source of inefficiency: A dollar taken from a rich person does not end up as a dollar in the hands of a poorer person. Some of the dollar is spent on administration of the tax and transfer system. The cost of tax-collecting agencies, such as the IRS, and welfare-administering agencies, such as the Health Care Financing Administration, which administers Medicaid and Medicare, must be paid with some of the taxes collected. Also, taxpayers hire accountants, auditors, and lawyers to help them ensure that they pay the correct amount of tax. These activities use skilled labor and capital resources that could otherwise be used to produce other goods and services that people value.

You can see that when all these costs are taken into account, transferring a dollar from a rich person does not give a dollar to a poor person. It is even possible that with high taxes, those with low incomes end up being worse off. Suppose, for example, that highly taxed entrepreneurs decide to work less hard and shut down some of their businesses. Low-income workers get fired and must seek other, perhaps even lower-paid, work.

Because of the big tradeoff, those who say that fairness is equality propose a modified version of utilitarianism.

Make the Poorest as Well Off as Possible

Harvard philosopher John Rawls proposed a modified version of utilitarianism in a classic book, *A Theory of Justice,* published in 1971. Rawls said that, taking all the costs of income transfers into account, the fair distribution of the economic pie is the one that makes the poorest person as well off as possible. The incomes of rich people should be taxed and transferred to the poor. But the taxes must not be so high that they shrink the economic pie by so much that the poorest person ends up with a smaller piece. A bigger share of a smaller pie can be a smaller piece than a smaller share of a bigger pie. The goal is to make the piece enjoyed by the poorest person as big as possible. But this piece will not be an equal share.

The "fair results" ideas require a change in the results after the game is over. Some economists say that these changes are themselves unfair, and they propose a different way of thinking about fairness.

■ It's Not Fair If the *Rules* Aren't Fair

The idea that it's not fair if the rules aren't fair translates into *equality of opportunity*. Another Harvard philosopher, Robert Nozick, made this idea of fairness concrete in a book entitled *Anarchy, State, and Utopia,* published in 1974.

Equality of opportunity can arise only if two rules are followed:

* The state enforces laws that establish and protect private property.
* Private property may be transferred from one person to another only by voluntary exchange with everyone free to engage in such exchange.

The first rule says that everything that is valuable—all scarce resources and goods—must be owned by individuals and that the state must ensure that theft is prevented. The second rule says that the only legitimate way a person can acquire something is to buy it in exchange for something else that the person owns. If these rules are followed, regardless of what the result is, then the outcome is fair. It doesn't matter how unequally the economic pie is shared, provided that it is baked by people each one of whom voluntarily provides services in exchange for the share of the pie that is offered in compensation.

To see why the first rule is required for equality of opportunity, suppose that it is violated and that some resources are not owned. They are common property. Then everyone is free to participate in a grab to use them. The strongest will prevail. But when the strongest prevails, the strongest effectively *owns* the resources in question and can prevent others from enjoying them. The strong have greater opportunities than the weak. There is no equality of opportunity.

To see why the second rule is required for equality of opportunity, suppose that it is violated and we do not insist on voluntary exchange for transferring ownership of resources from one person to another. The alternative to voluntary exchange is *involuntary* transfer. In simple language, the alternative is theft.

Again, only the strong get what they want. The weak end up with only the resources and goods that the strong don't want.

In contrast, in Nozick's two rules, everyone—strong and weak—is treated in a similar way. Everyone is free to use their resources and human skills to create things that are valued by themselves and others and to exchange the fruits of their efforts with each other. This is the only set of arrangements that provides equality of opportunity.

No Big Tradeoff

In Nozick's view of fairness, there is no big tradeoff. If private property rights are enforced and if voluntary exchange takes place in a competitive market, then resources will be allocated efficiently. And the resulting distribution of income and wealth will be fair.

Involuntary transfers of income from the rich to the poor violate the principle of equality of opportunity. These transfers not only decrease the size of the economic pie by damaging incentives to work and save, but also unfairly restrict the opportunities of the current rich to enjoy the fruits of their efforts and restrict the opportunities of the current poor to become rich.

Let's illustrate Nozick's efficient and fair economy by thinking about what happens following a natural disaster.

A Price Hike in a Natural Disaster

Suppose that an earthquake breaks the pipes that deliver drinking water to a city and, in a competitive market for bottled water, the price jumps from $1 to $8. The marginal cost and marginal benefit of water is $8 a bottle.

The people who are willing and able to pay $8 get all the water that they want. And the people who are either unwilling or unable to pay $8 a bottle get no water. The people with water to sell make a gain, and the people who must buy water or go without water incur a loss. Because marginal benefit equals marginal cost, the water is being used *efficiently* and, says Nozick, it is also fair. You can see that water use is efficient. But it is less obvious that it is fair—that it provides equality of opportunity.

To see why the market provides equality of opportunity, suppose that the State directs the bottled water sellers to keep the price at $1 a bottle and to provide everyone with an equal share of the available water. Nothing has happened to change the equilibrium price of a bottle of water, so it remains at $8. Some of the people are willing to pay $8 to get more water. And at that price, some are willing to sell their "fair" share, which they bought for $1 a bottle. If voluntary exchange is permitted, people who value water at less than $8 a bottle will sell and people who are willing and able to pay $8 a bottle will buy. The water will be consumed by the same people as previously.

But there will now be a difference. The gainers are now the buyers for $1 a bottle. Some gain a consumer surplus from the share of water they get for $1 because they were willing to pay more. And some gain a producer surplus because they become sellers of water.

So different people gain in the two situations. But there is equality of opportunity only in the first situation. In the second situation, everyone except the shopowners is free to sell water at the market price. This arrangement discriminates against the water shopowners.

A Compromise

Most people, and probably most economists, have sympathy with the Nozick view but think it too extreme. They see a role for taxes and government income support schemes to transfer some income from the rich to the poor. Such transfers could be considered voluntary in the sense that they are decided by majority voting, and even those who vote against such transfers voluntarily participate in the political process.

Once we agree that using the tax system to make transfers from the rich to the poor is fair, we need to determine just what we mean by a fair tax. We'll look at this big question when we study the tax system in Chapter 8.

REALITY CHECK

Efficiency and Fairness in YOUR Life

You live in the national economy, your state economy, your regional economy, and your own household economy. The many decisions you must make affect efficiency and fairness at all these levels. But here, we'll focus on your own household economy.

Make a spreadsheet and on it identify all the factors of production that your household owns. Count all the person-hours available and any capital. Show how these resources are allocated.

By what methods are your household's scarce resources allocated? Identify those allocated by market price; by command; by first-come, first-served; and by equal shares. Are any resources allocated by majority vote?

Now the tough part: Are these resources allocated efficiently— meaning do the allocations maximize the household pie? To answer this question, think about how you can check whether marginal benefit equals marginal cost for each of your household's activities.

And now an even tougher question: Are the household's resources allocated fairly? To answer this question, think about how you can check whether there is equality of opportunity.

5 Explain the main ideas about fairness and evaluate the fairness of competitive markets and other allocation methods.

Practice Problem 6.5

1. A winter storm cuts the power supply and isolates a small town in the mountains. The people rush to buy candles from the town store, which is the only source of candles. The store owner decides to ration the candles to one per family but to keep the price of a candle unchanged.
   a. Who gets to use the candles?
   b. Who receives the consumer surplus on candles?
   c. Who receives the producer surplus on candles?
   d. Is the outcome efficient?
   e. Is the outcome fair according to the utilitarian principle?
   f. Is there equality of opportunity?

Exercise 6.5

1. An earthquake destroys the homes of a quarter of a city's population. People who are lucky enough to own one of the remaining homes offer rooms for rent at the highest amount that people are willing to pay.
   a. Who gets to occupy the available rooms?
   b. Who receives the consumer surplus on rooms?
   c. Who receives the producer surplus on rooms?
   d. Is the outcome efficient?
   e. Is this outcome fair or unfair?
   f. By what principle of fairness is the outcome fair or unfair?

Solution to Practice Problem 6.5

1a. The people who buy candles from the town store are not necessarily the people who use the candles. A buyer from the town store can sell a candle and will do so if he or she can get a price that exceeds his or her marginal benefit. The people who value the candles most—who are willing to pay the most—will use the candles.

1b. Only the people who are willing to pay the most for candles receive the consumer surplus on candles.

1c. The town store owner receives the same producer surplus as normal. People who sell the candles they buy from the store receive additional producer surplus.

1d. The outcome is efficient because the people who value the candles most use them.

1e. The outcome is unfair according to the utilitarian principle because candles are shared unequally.

1f. There is equality of opportunity because only voluntary exchanges occur.

CHAPTER CHECKPOINT

Key Points

1 Describe alternative methods of allocating scarce resources.

- Market price is one method of allocating scarce resources.
- Other methods are by command; majority rule; contest; first-come, first-served; sharing equally; lottery; personal characteristics; and force.
- All of the alternative methods are used and have benefits and costs.

2 Distinguish between value and price and define consumer surplus.

- Marginal benefit is measured by the maximum price that consumers are willing to pay for another unit of a good or service.
- A demand curve is a marginal benefit curve.
- Value is what people are *willing to* pay; price is what people *must* pay.
- Consumer surplus equals marginal benefit minus price, summed over the quantity consumed.

3 Distinguish between cost and price and define producer surplus.

- Marginal cost is measured by the minimum price producers must be offered to increase production by one unit.
- A supply curve is a marginal cost curve.
- Opportunity cost is what producers must pay; price is what producers receive.
- Producer surplus equals price minus marginal cost, summed over the quantity produced.

4 Evaluate the efficiency of the alternative methods of allocating scarce resources.

- In a competitive equilibrium, marginal benefit equals marginal cost and resource allocation is efficient.
- Price and quantity regulations, taxes, subsidies, externalities, public goods, common resources, monopoly, and high transactions costs lead to either underproduction or overproduction and create a deadweight loss.

5 Explain the main ideas about fairness and evaluate the fairness of competitive markets and other allocation methods.

- Ideas about fairness divide into two groups: fair *results* and fair *rules*.
- Fair results require income transfers from the rich to the poor.
- Fair rules require property rights and voluntary exchange.

Key Terms

Big tradeoff, 158	Deadweight loss, 153	Transactions costs, 155
Command system, 140	Producer surplus, 148	Utilitarianism, 158
Consumer surplus, 145	Total surplus, 151	

Exercises

TABLE I

Price (dollars per sandwich)	Quantity demanded	Quantity supplied
	(sandwiches per hour)	
0	400	0
1	350	50
2	300	100
3	250	150
4	200	200
5	150	250
6	100	300
7	50	350
8	0	400

1. Table 1 shows the demand and supply schedules for sandwiches. Use the table to answer the following questions:
    a. What is the price of a sandwich and what is the consumer surplus?
    b. What is the producer surplus?
    c. What is the efficient quantity of sandwiches?
    d. If the quantity demanded of sandwiches decreases by 100 per hour at each price, what is the price of a sandwich and what is the change in total surplus?
    e. If the quantity supplied of sandwiches decreases by 100 per hour at each price, what is the price of a sandwich and what is the change in total surplus?

2. Table 1 shows the demand and supply schedules for sandwiches. Use the table to answer the following questions:
    a. If Sandwiches To Go, Inc. buys all the sandwich producers and cuts production to 100 sandwiches an hour, what is the deadweight loss that is created?
    b. If in part **a**, Sandwiches To Go, Inc. rations sandwiches to two per person, is this distribution of sandwiches fair? By what principle of fairness would the distribution be unfair?

TABLE 2

Price (dollars per bag)	Quantity demanded before flood	Quantity demanded during flood	Quantity supplied
	(thousands of bags)		
0	40	70	0
1	35	65	5
2	30	60	10
3	25	55	15
4	20	50	20
5	15	45	25
6	10	40	30
7	5	35	35
8	0	30	40

3. Table 2 shows the demand and supply schedules for sandbags before and during a major flood. Use the table to answer the following questions:
    a. What happens to consumer surplus and producer surplus during the flood?
    b. Is the allocation of resources efficient (i) before the flood and (ii) during the flood?
    c. If, during the flood, the government allocated the available sandbags and gave all families an equal quantity of them, what would be the allocation method and how would consumer surplus, producer surplus, and the price of a sandbag change?
    d. Is the outcome described in part **c** more efficient than it would be if the government took no action? Explain.
    e. Is the outcome described in part **c** fairer than it would be if the government took no action? Explain.

4. In California, farmers pay a lower price for water than do city residents.
    a. What is this method of allocation of water resources?
    b. Is this allocation of water efficient? Explain why or why not.
    c. Is this use of water fair? Why or why not?

5. In California, farmers pay a lower price for water than do city residents. If farmers were charged the same price as city residents pay,
    a. Explain how the price of agricultural produce, the quantity of produce grown, consumer surplus, and producer surplus would change.
    b. What now is the method for allocating resources?
    c. Would the allocation of water now be more efficient? Why or why not?
    d. Would the use of water be fairer? Why or why not?

6. At the Metropolitan Museum of Art in New York, the regular admission price is $15 and the student price is $7.

   a. Is this arrangement efficient? Is it fair? Explain.

   b. When the museum puts on a special exhibition, the prices don't change but long lines develop. Would it be more efficient to increase the price that students pay? Explain why or why not.

   c. In part **c**, would the higher price for students be fairer? Explain why or why not.

7. Dan operates a one-person barbershop, and Zoe runs a large hairdressing salon. Table 3 shows the quantities of haircuts supplied by Dan and Zoe at various prices per haircut. Use the table to answer the following questions.

   a. If the price of a haircut is $15, who makes the larger producer surplus?

   b. If the price of a haircut is $10, who makes the larger producer surplus?

   c. Are both outcomes in parts **a** and **b** fair according to the utilitarian view of fairness? Explain why or why not.

   d. Are both outcomes in parts **a** and **b** fair according to John Rawls's view of fairness? Explain why or why not.

   e. Are both outcomes in parts **a** and **b** fair according to Robert Nozick's view of fairness? Explain why or why not.

TABLE 3

Price (dollars per haircut)	Quantity supplied Dan	Zoe
	(haircuts per day)	
0	0	0
5	0	0
10	2	0
15	4	40
20	6	60
25	8	80
30	10	100

Critical Thinking

8. The winner of the men's tennis singles at the U.S. Open is paid much more than the runner-up, but it takes two to have a singles final. Is this compensation arrangement efficient? Is it fair? Explain why it might illustrate the big tradeoff.

9. In tennis, men play the best of five sets and women play the best of three sets, but the winner of the men's tennis singles at the U.S. Open is paid the same as the winner of the women's singles. In contrast, in golf, men and women play the same number of holes and rounds, but the winners of men's golf tournaments are paid much more than the winners of women's golf tournaments. Are these compensation arrangements efficient? Are they fair? Explain.

10. Is it fair that Roger Federer wins so many tennis championships? Suppose the following rule were adopted: After three wins in a season, a professional tennis player is not permitted to compete for the rest of the season. Would this rule be fair? Explain why or why not.

11. Two roommates, Ratna and Sara, decide to cut their expenditure by buying one copy of the required math textbook and sharing it.

   a. What allocation methods do you think they would consider as feasible?

   b. What allocation method do you think would be more efficient?

   c. Will the allocation method you selected in part **b** be fair? Explain why or why not.

   d. In the last week of the semester, as the final exam approaches, how do you think the agreed allocation method would work out?

12. Poor countries that join the World Trade Organization (the WTO) must agree to prevent the illegal production of generic drugs that violate the patents of multinational drug companies and the illegal copying of music CDs, software, and textbooks that violate copyrights.

   a. Do you think that it is efficient or inefficient if people in poor countries create cheap copies of drugs, music, software, and textbooks? Explain.

using the concepts of marginal benefit, marginal cost, total surplus, and deadweight loss.

b. Do you think that it is fair or unfair if people in poor countries create cheap copies of drugs, music, software, and textbooks? Which concept of fairness do you think is relevant for deciding this issue? Why?

c. Would it be efficient or inefficient, fair or unfair, to impose a large fine on a poor country that failed to prevent the illegal production of generic drugs or the illegal copying of music CDs, software, and textbooks? Use the concepts of marginal benefit, marginal cost, total surplus, and deadweight loss to explain your answer.

d. In part c, would it be fair or unfair to impose a large fine? Explain.

myeconlab

Web Exercises

Use the links on MyEconLab to work the following exercises.

13. Download and review the report "LaGuardia Airport: Can the Airport and the Community Co-exist?" by Congressman Joseph Crowley.
   a. What are the resource allocation problems at LaGuardia airport?
   b. How does the Federal Aviation Administration allocate landing slots at LaGuardia?
   c. Is the method of allocating landing slots efficient? Is it fair?
   d. Design a method of allocating landing slots at LaGuardia that is efficient.
   e. Design a method of allocating landing slots at LaGuardia that is fair.
   f. Do your allocation methods present a tradeoff between efficiency and fairness? If so, explain why. If not, explain why not.

14. Visit the Web site of the Hoover Institution and read the essay "Price Controls on Gasoline? Bad Idea" by David R. Henderson.
   a. How would price controls on gasoline influence the quantity of gasoline? Would it lead to overproduction or underproduction?
   b. How would price controls on gasoline influence the marginal cost, marginal benefit, producer surplus, consumer surplus, and deadweight loss in the market for gasoline?
   c. Would price controls on gasoline be fair or unfair? Which concept of fairness is relevant to make your decision?

15. Visit the Web site of the Goldwater Institute and read the report "Light Rail: Inefficient, Ineffective and Unfair."
   a. What are the scarce resources involved in the discussion of a light rail system for the Phoenix area?
   b. What methods of resource allocation are discussed in the report?
   c. Why does the report conclude that a light rail system would be inefficient? Can you figure out where the deadweight loss is?
   d. Why does the report conclude that a light rail system would be unfair? Who would win? Who would lose? Whose opportunities would be restricted unfairly? Who would gain an unfair advantage on others?
   e. How would you design an efficient and fair solution to the transportation problems of the Phoenix area?

Government Influences on Markets

CHAPTER CHECKLIST

When you have completed your study of this chapter, you will be able to

1 Explain how a price ceiling works and show how a rent ceiling creates a housing shortage, inefficiency, and unfairness.

2 Explain how a price floor works and show how the minimum wage creates unemployment, inefficiency, and unfairness.

3 Explain how a price support in the market for an agricultural product creates a surplus, inefficiency, and unfairness.

Joe Calabrese likes high gasoline prices! Joe is the general manager of Cleveland's transit system and the high price of gas in 2005 brought a surge in the number of people riding his buses. But with the price of oil heading ever upward, how can the consumer be protected? Can the President wave a magic pen and sign an order that caps the price of oil?

Yoram lives in rental housing in Seattle. His rent is rising by 8 percent a year, but his wages are almost stagnant. Could the city impose rent controls to help people like Yoram? And could it provide more direct help by imposing a minimum wage law to keep Yoram's wage rising?

Jerry Henningfeld says his 900 acre farm in Wauconda, Illinois, isn't making him rich, and he is hoping prices will rise. Running a farm is like being a Cubs fan, he says: There's always next year! How can governments help Jerry and other farmers by keeping the prices of farm products high?

7.1 PRICE CEILINGS

Price ceiling or price cap
A government regulation that places an *upper* limit on the price at which a particular good, service, or factor of production may be traded.

A **price ceiling** (also called a **price cap**) is a government regulation that places an *upper* limit on the price at which a particular good, service, or factor of production may be traded. Trading at a higher price is illegal.

A price ceiling has been used in several markets. But the one that looms largest in everyone's budget is the housing market. The price of housing is the rent that people pay for a house or apartment. Demand and supply in the housing market determine the rent and the quantity of housing available.

Figure 7.1 illustrates the apartment rental market in Biloxi, Mississippi. The rent is $550 a month, and 4,000 apartments are rented.

Suppose that Biloxi apartment rents have increased by $100 a month in the past two years and that a Citizens' Action Group asks the mayor to roll rents back.

■ A Rent Ceiling

Rent ceiling
A regulation that makes it illegal to charge more than a specified rent for housing.

Responding to the demand, the mayor imposes a **rent ceiling**—a regulation that makes it illegal to charge more than a specified rent for housing.

The effect of a rent ceiling depends on whether it is imposed at a level above or below the equilibrium rent. In Figure 7.1, if the rent ceiling is set *above* $550 a month, nothing would change because people are already paying $550 a month.

But a rent ceiling that is set *below* the equilibrium rent has powerful effects on the market. The reason is that it attempts to prevent the rent from rising high enough to regulate the quantities demanded and supplied. The law and the market are in conflict, and one (or both) of them must yield.

■ FIGURE 7.1
A Housing Market

The figure shows the demand curve, *D*, and the supply curve, *S*, for rental housing.

❶ The market is in equilibrium when the quantity demanded equals the quantity supplied.

❷ The equilibrium price (rent) is $550 a month.

❸ The equilibrium quantity is 4,000 units of housing.

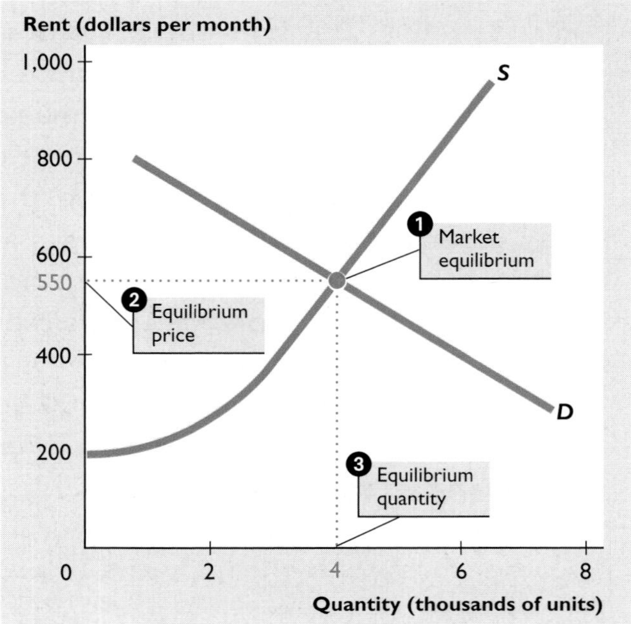

Figure 7.2 shows one effect of a rent ceiling that is set below the equilibrium rent. The rent ceiling is $400 a month. We've shaded the area *above* the rent ceiling because any rent in this region is illegal. At a rent of $400 a month, the quantity of housing supplied is 3,000 units and the quantity demanded is 6,000 units. So there is a shortage of 3,000 units of housing.

The first effect, then, of a rent ceiling is a housing shortage. People are seeking a larger amount of housing than builders and the owners of existing buildings have an incentive to make available.

But the story does not end here. The 3,000 units of housing that owners are willing to make available must somehow be allocated among people who are seeking 6,000 units. How is this allocation achieved? When a rent ceiling creates a housing shortage, two developments occur:

- A black market
- Increased search activity

A Black Market

A **black market** is an illegal market that operates alongside a government-regulated market. A rent ceiling sometimes creates a black market in housing as frustrated renters and landlords try to find ways of raising the rent above the legally imposed ceiling. Landlords want higher rents because they know that renters are willing to pay more for the existing quantity of housing. Renters are willing to pay more to jump to the head of the queue.

Because raising the rent is illegal, landlords and renters use creative tricks to get around the law. One of these tricks is for a new tenant to pay a high price for

Black market
An illegal market that operates alongside a government-regulated market.

FIGURE 7.2

A Rent Ceiling Creates a Shortage

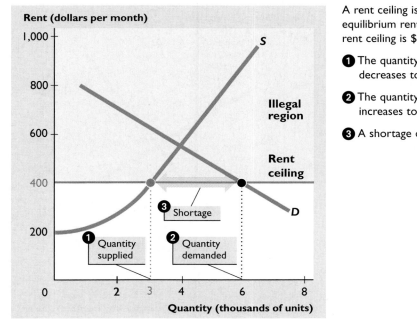

A rent ceiling is imposed below the equilibrium rent. In this example, the rent ceiling is $400 a month.

❶ The quantity of housing supplied decreases to 3,000 units.

❷ The quantity of housing demanded increases to 6,000 units.

❸ A shortage of 3,000 units arises.

worthless fittings—perhaps paying $2,000 for threadbare drapes. Another is for the tenant to pay a high price for new locks and keys—called "key money."

Figure 7.3 shows how high the black market rent might go in Biloxi. With strict enforcement of the rent ceiling, the quantity of housing available is 3,000 units. But at this quantity, renters are willing to offer as much as $625 a month— the amount determined on the demand curve.

So a small number of landlords illegally offer housing for rents up to $625 a month. The black market rent might be at any level between the rent ceiling of $400 and the maximum that a renter is willing to pay of $625.

Increased Search Activity

Search activity
The time spent looking for someone with whom to do business.

The time spent looking for someone with whom to do business is called **search activity**. We spend some time in search activity almost every time we buy something. You want the latest CD, and you know four stores that stock it. But which store has the best deal? You spend a few minutes on the telephone or Internet finding out. In some markets, we spend a lot of time searching. An example is the used car market. People spend a lot of time checking out alternative dealers and cars.

But when a price ceiling creates a shortage of housing, search activity *increases*. In a rent-controlled housing market, frustrated would-be renters scan the newspapers, not only for housing ads but also for death notices! Any information about newly available housing is useful. And they race to be first on the scene when news of a possible apartment breaks.

The *opportunity cost* of a good is equal to its price *plus* the value of the search time spent finding the good. So the opportunity cost of housing is equal to the rent plus the value of the search time spent looking for an apartment. Search activity

---

■ FIGURE 7.3

A Rent Ceiling Creates a Black Market and Housing Search

With a rent ceiling of $400 a month,

❶ 3,000 units of housing are available.

❷ Someone is willing to pay $625 a month for the 3,000th unit of housing.

❸ Black market rents might be as high as $625 a month and resources get used up in costly search activity.

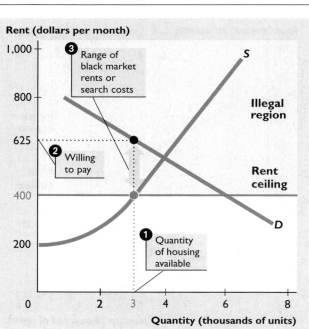

is costly. It uses time and other resources, such as telephones, automobiles, and gasoline that could have been used in other productive ways. In Figure 7.3, to find accommodation at $400 a month, someone who is willing to pay a rent of $625 a month would be willing to spend on search activity an amount that is equivalent to adding $225 a month to the rent. For a one-year lease, this amount is enormous.

A rent ceiling controls the rent portion of the cost of housing but not the search cost. So when the search cost is added to the rent, some people end up paying a higher opportunity cost for housing than they would if there were no rent ceiling.

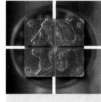

EYE ON THE PAST

An Earthquake and a Rent Ceiling: A Tale of Two Eras in One City

Let's transport ourselves to San Francisco in April 1906, as the city is suffering from a massive earthquake and fire.

You can sense the enormity of San Francisco's problems from a headline in the *New York Times* on April 20, 1906, describing the first days of the crisis:

Army of Homeless Fleeing from Devastated City
200,000 Without Shelter and Facing Famine

The commander of federal troops in charge of the emergency described the magnitude of the problem:

Not a hotel of note or importance was left standing. The great apartment houses had vanished ... two-hundred-and-twenty-five thousand people were ... homeless.[1]

In a single day, more than half the people in a city of 400,000 had lost their homes. Temporary shelters and camps alleviated some of the problem, but the apartment buildings and houses left standing had to accommodate 40 percent more people than they had before the earthquake.

The *San Francisco Chronicle* was not published for more than a month after the earthquake. When it reappeared on May 24, 1906, the city's housing shortage—what would seem to be a major news item that would still be of grave importance—was not even mentioned. Milton Friedman and George Stigler describe the situation:

There is not a single mention of a housing shortage! The classified advertisements listed sixty-four offers of flats and houses for rent, and nineteen of houses for sale, against five advertisements of flats or houses wanted. Then and there-

after a considerable number of all types of accommodation ... were offered for rent.[2]

How did San Francisco cope with such a devastating decrease in the supply of housing? The answer is that a free market brought a rise in the rent and an increase in the intensity of use of the buildings that remained. People rented out rooms that they had previously used themselves. The high rents were an incentive for owners to rebuild as quickly as possible.

At the end of World War II (in 1945), the population of San Francisco grew by 30 percent. At the same time, a large-scale building program increased the number of houses and apartments by 20 percent. So each dwelling unit had to accommodate 10 percent more people. San Francisco had a housing "problem" about a quarter of the magnitude of that following the 1906 earthquake. Yet in 1946, the city's housing shortage was a huge political problem. Newspaper advertisements seeking apartments outnumbered those offering apartments by more than seven to one. Why? San Francisco had rent ceilings in 1946. It had a free housing market in 1906.

[1] Milton Friedman and George J. Stigler, "Roofs or Ceilings? The Current Housing Problem," in *Popular Essays on Current Problems*, Vol. I, No. 2 (New York: Foundation for Economic Education, 1946), 3–159.

[2] Friedman and Stigler, p. 3.

■ Are Rent Ceilings Efficient?

A housing market with no rent ceiling determines the rent at which the quantity demanded equals the quantity supplied. In this situation, scarce housing resources are allocated efficiently because the marginal cost of housing equals the marginal benefit. Figure 7.4(a) shows this efficient outcome in the Biloxi apartment rental market. In this efficient market, total surplus—the sum of *consumer surplus* (the green area) and *producer surplus* (the blue area)—is maximized at the equilibrium rent and quantity of housing (see Chapter 6, p. 151).

Figure 7.4(b) shows that with a rent ceiling, the outcome is inefficient. Marginal benefit exceeds marginal cost. Producer surplus and consumer surplus shrink, and a deadweight loss (the gray area) arises. This loss is borne by the people who can't find housing and by landlords who can't offer housing at the lower rent ceiling.

But the total loss exceeds the deadweight loss. Resources get used in costly search activity and in evading the law in the black market. The value of these resources might be as large as the red rectangle. There is yet a further loss: the cost of enforcing the rent ceiling law. This loss, which is borne by taxpayers, is not visible in the figure.

■ FIGURE 7.4
The Inefficiency of a Rent Ceiling

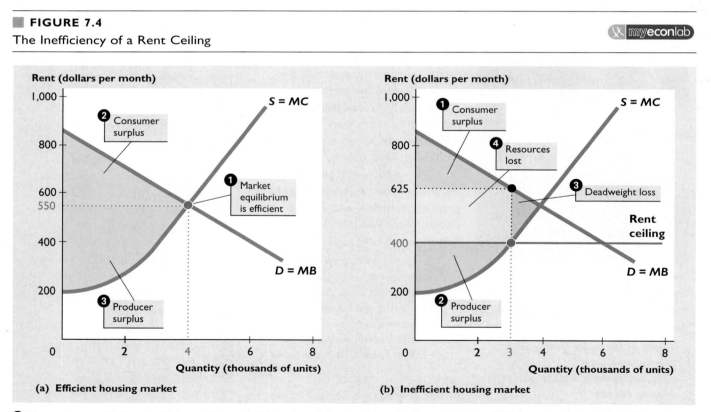

(a) Efficient housing market

(b) Inefficient housing market

❶ The market equilibrium is efficient with marginal benefit equal to marginal cost. Total surplus, the sum of ❷ consumer surplus (green area) and ❸ producer surplus (blue area), is maximized.

A rent ceiling is inefficient. ❶ Consumer surplus and ❷ producer surplus shrink, a ❸ deadweight loss arises, and ❹ resources are lost in search activity and evading the rent ceiling law.

Although a rent ceiling causes inefficiency, not everyone loses. The people who live in apartments at the rent ceiling get an increase in consumer surplus, and landlords who charge a black market rent get an increase in producer surplus.

The costs of a rent ceiling that we've just considered are only the initial costs. With the rent below the market rent, landlords have no incentive to maintain their buildings in a good state of repair. So over time, the quality and quantity of housing supplied *decrease* and the loss arising from a rent ceiling increases.

The size of the loss from a rent ceiling depends on the elasticities of supply and demand. If supply is inelastic, a rent ceiling brings a small decrease in the quantity of housing supplied. And if demand is inelastic, a rent ceiling brings a small increase in the quantity of housing demanded. So the more inelastic the supply or the demand, the smaller is the shortage of housing and the smaller is the deadweight loss.

With rent ceilings, landlords have no incentive to maintain buildings, and the quality and quantity of housing supplied decrease.

■ Are Rent Ceilings Fair?

We've seen that rent ceilings prevent scarce resources from being allocated efficiently—resources do not flow to their highest-valued use. But don't they ensure that scarce housing resources are allocated more fairly?

You learned in Chapter 6 (pp. 153–157) that fairness is a complex idea about which there are two broad views: fair *results* versus fair *rules*. Rent controls violate the fair rules view of fairness because they block voluntary exchange. But do they deliver a fair result? Do rent ceilings ensure that scarce housing goes to the poor people whose need is greatest?

Blocking rent adjustments that bring the quantity of housing demanded into equality with the quantity supplied doesn't end scarcity. So when the law prevents the rent from adjusting and blocks the price mechanism from allocating scarce housing, some other allocation mechanism must be used. If that mechanism were one that provided the housing to the poorest, then the allocation might be regarded as fair.

But the mechanisms that get used do not usually achieve such an outcome. First-come, first-served is one allocation mechanism. Discrimination based on race, ethnicity, or sex is another. Discrimination against young newcomers and in favor of old established families is yet another. None of these mechanisms delivers a fair outcome.

Rent ceilings in New York City provide examples of these mechanisms at work. The main beneficiaries of rent ceilings in New York City are families that have lived in the city for a long time—including some rich and famous ones. These families enjoy low rents while newcomers pay high rents for hard-to-find apartments.

■ If Rent Ceilings Are So Bad, Why Do We Have Them?

The economic case against rent ceilings is now widely accepted, so *new* rent ceiling laws are rare. But when governments try to repeal rent control laws, as the New York City government did in 1999, current renters lobby politicians to maintain the ceilings. Also, people who are prevented from finding housing would be happy if they got lucky and managed to find a rent-controlled apartment. So there is plenty of political support for rent ceilings.

Apartment owners who oppose rent ceilings are a minority, so their views are not a powerful influence on politicians. Because more people support rent ceilings than oppose them, politicians are sometimes willing to support them too.

1 **Explain how a price ceiling works and show how a rent ceiling creates a housing shortage, inefficiency, and unfairness.**

Practice Problem 7.1

FIGURE 1

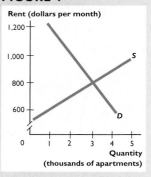

1. Figure 1 shows the rental market for apartments in Corsicana, Texas.
   a. What is the rent in this suburb and how many apartments are rented?
   b. If the city government imposes a rent ceiling of $900 a month, what is the rent and how many apartments are rented?
   c. If the city government imposes a rent ceiling of $600 a month, what is the rent and how many apartments are rented?
   d. With a strictly enforced rent ceiling of $600 a month, is the housing market efficient? Explain why or why not.
   e. If the city strictly enforces the rent ceiling of $600 a month, is the housing market fair? Explain why or why not.
   f. If a black market develops in part **d**, how high could the black market rent be? Explain your answer.

Exercise 7.1

FIGURE 2

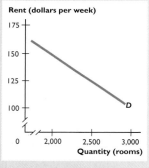

1. Figure 2 shows the demand for on-campus student housing at the University of Idaho, in Moscow, Idaho. The college has 2,000 rooms for rent.
   a. What is the equilibrium rent and how many rooms are rented?
   b. If the college sets a rent ceiling on on-campus housing of $125 a week, how would you describe the on-campus housing market? Would the allocation of housing be efficient? Would it be fair?
   c. If the rent ceiling of $125 a week were strictly enforced and there were no black market, who would gain and who would lose?
   d. If a black market developed as a result of the $125 a week rent ceiling, what range of rents would be offered for a room? Would the allocation of housing be efficient? Would it be fair? Explain.

Solution to Practice Problem 7.1

FIGURE 3

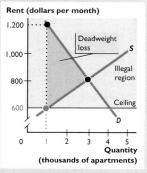

1a. The equilibrium rent is $800 a month, and 3,000 apartments are rented.

1b. A rent ceiling of $900 a month is above the equilibrium rent, so the outcome is the market equilibrium rent of $800 a month with 3,000 apartments rented.

1c. With the rent ceiling at $600 a month, the number of apartments rented is 1,000 and the rent is $600 a month (Figure 3).

1d. The housing market is not efficient. With 1,000 apartments rented, marginal benefit exceeds marginal cost and a deadweight loss arises (Figure 3).

1e. The rent ceiling makes the allocation of housing less fair in both views of fairness: It blocks voluntary transactions, and it does not provide more housing to those in most need.

1f. In a black market, some people are willing to rent an apartment for more than the rent ceiling. The highest rent that someone would offer is $1,200 a month. This rent equals someone's willingness to pay for the 1,000th apartment (Figure 3).

7.2 PRICE FLOORS

A **price floor** is a government regulation that places a *lower* limit on the price at which a particular good, service, or factor of production may be traded. Trading at a lower price is illegal.

Price floors are used in many markets. But the one that looms largest is the labor market. The price of labor is the wage rate that people earn. Demand and supply in the labor market determine the wage rate and the quantity of labor employed.

Figure 7.5 illustrates the market for fast-food servers in Yuma, Arizona. In this market, the demand for labor curve is *D*. On this demand curve, at a wage rate of $10 an hour, the quantity of fast-food servers demanded is zero. If A&W, Burger King, Taco Bell, McDonald's, Wendy's, and the other fast-food places had to pay servers $10 an hour, they wouldn't hire any. They would replace servers with vending machines! But at wage rates below $10 an hour, they would hire servers. At a wage rate of $5 an hour, firms would hire 5,000 servers.

On the supply side of the market, no one is willing to work for $2 an hour. To attract servers, firms must pay more than $2 an hour.

Equilibrium in this market occurs at a wage rate of $5 an hour with 5,000 people employed as servers.

Suppose that the government thinks that no one should have to work for a wage rate as low as $5 an hour and decides that it wants to increase the wage rate. Can the government improve conditions for these workers by passing a minimum wage law? Let's find out.

Price floor
A government regulation that places a *lower* limit on the price at which a particular good, service, or factor of production may be traded.

FIGURE 7.5
A Market for Fast-Food Servers

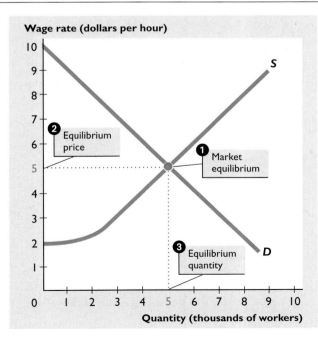

The figure shows the demand curve, *D*, and the supply curve, *S*, for fast-food servers.

❶ The market is in equilibrium when the quantity demanded equals the quantity supplied.

❷ The equilibrium price (wage rate) is $5 an hour.

❸ The equilibrium quantity is 5,000 servers.

■ The Minimum Wage

Minimum wage law
A government regulation that makes hiring labor for less than a specified wage illegal.

A **minimum wage law** is a government regulation that makes hiring labor for less than a specified wage illegal. Firms are free to pay a wage rate that exceeds the minimum wage but may not pay less than the minimum. A minimum wage is an example of a price floor.

The effect of a price floor depends on whether it is set below or above the equilibrium price. In Figure 7.5, the equilibrium wage rate is $5 an hour, and at this wage rate, firms hire 5,000 workers. If the government introduced a minimum wage below $5 an hour, nothing would change. The reason is that firms are already paying $5 an hour, and because this wage exceeds the minimum wage, the wage rate paid doesn't change. Firms continue to hire 5,000 workers.

But the aim of a minimum wage is to boost the incomes of low-wage earners. So in the markets for the lowest-paid labor, the minimum wage will exceed the equilibrium wage.

Suppose that the government introduces a minimum wage of $7 an hour. Figure 7.6 shows the effects of this law. Wage rates below $7 an hour are illegal, so we've shaded the illegal region *below* the minimum wage. Firms and workers are no longer permitted to operate at the equilibrium point in this market because it is in the illegal region. Market forces and political forces are in conflict.

The government can set a minimum wage. But it can't tell employers how many workers to hire. If firms must pay $7 an hour for labor, they will hire only 3,000 workers. At the equilibrium wage rate of $5 an hour, firms hired 5,000 workers. So when the minimum wage is introduced, firms fire 2,000 workers.

■ **FIGURE 7.6**

A Minimum Wage Creates Unemployment

A minimum wage is introduced above the equilibrium wage rate. In this example, the minimum wage rate is $7 an hour.

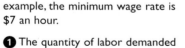

❶ The quantity of labor demanded decreases to 3,000 workers.

❷ The quantity of labor supplied increases to 7,000 people.

❸ 4,000 people are unemployed.

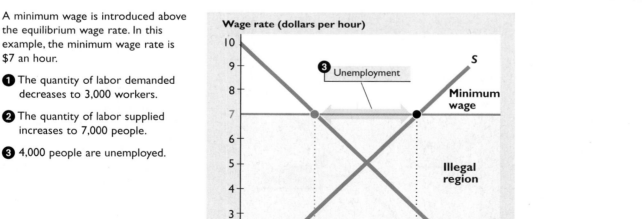

But at a wage rate of $7 an hour, another 2,000 people who didn't want to work for $5 an hour now try to find work as servers. So at $7 an hour, the quantity supplied is 7,000 people. With 2,000 workers fired and another 2,000 looking for work at the higher wage rate, 4,000 people who would like to work as servers are unemployed.

The 3,000 jobs available must somehow be allocated among the 7,000 people who are available for and willing to work. How is this allocation achieved? The answer is by increased job-search activity and illegal hiring.

Increased Job-Search Activity

People spend a great deal of time and resources finding a good job. But with a minimum wage, more people are looking for jobs than the number of jobs available. Frustrated unemployed people spend time and other resources searching for hard-to-find jobs. In Figure 7.7, to find a job at $7 an hour, someone who is willing to work for $3 an hour would be willing to spend on job-search activity an amount that is equivalent to subtracting $4 an hour from the wage rate. For a job that might last a year or more, this amount is large.

Illegal Hiring

With more people looking for work than the number of jobs available, some firms and workers might agree to do business at an illegal wage rate below the minimum wage in a black market.

■ FIGURE 7.7

A Minimum Wage Increases Job Search

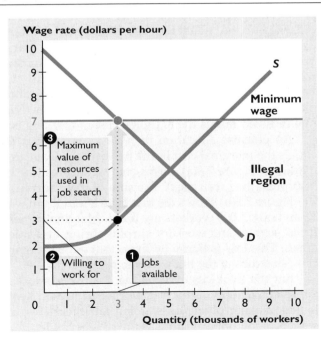

The minimum wage rate is set at $7 an hour:

❶ 3,000 jobs are available.

❷ The lowest wage rate for which someone is willing to work is $3 an hour.

❸ Illegal wage rates might range from just below the legal minimum of $7 an hour to the lowest wage rate that someone is willing to accept: $3 an hour.

The maximum that people are willing to spend on job search is an amount equivalent to subtracting $4 an hour—the $7 they would receive if they found a job minus the $3 they are willing to work for—from the wage rate.

The Federal Minimum Wage

The federal government's *Fair Labor Standards Act* sets the minimum wage, which was last changed in 1997, when it was raised to $5.15 an hour.

The minimum wage creates unemployment. But how much unemployment does it create? Until recently, most economists believed that a 10 percent increase in the minimum wage decreased teenage employment by between 1 and 3 percent.

David Card of the University of California at Berkeley and Alan Krueger of Princeton University have challenged this view. They claim that following a rise in the minimum wage in California, New Jersey, and Texas, the *employment* rate of low-income workers *increased*. They suggest three reasons why a rise in the wage rate might increase employment:
(1) Workers become more conscientious and productive.
(2) Workers are less likely to quit, so costly labor turnover is reduced.
(3) Managers make a firm's operations more efficient.

Most economists are skeptical about these ideas. They say that if higher wages make workers more productive and reduce labor turnover, firms will freely pay workers a higher wage. And they argue that there are other explanations for the employment increase that Card and Krueger found.

Daniel Hamermesh of the University of Texas at Austin says that they got the timing wrong. Firms *anticipated* the minimum wage rise and so cut employment *before* it occurred. Looking at employment changes *after* the minimum wage increased missed its main effect. Finis Welch of Texas A&M University and Kevin Murphy of the University of Chicago say that the employment effects that Card and Krueger found are caused by regional differences in economic growth, not changes in the minimum wage.

Also, looking only at employment misses the supply-side effect of the minimum wage. It brings an increase in the number of people who drop out of high school to look for work.

■ Is the Minimum Wage Efficient?

The efficient allocation of a factor of production is similar to that of a good or service, which you studied in Chapter 6. The demand for labor tells us about the marginal benefit of labor to the firms that hire it. Firms benefit because the labor they hire produces the goods or services that they sell. Firms are willing to pay a wage rate equal to the benefit they receive from an additional hour of labor. So in Figure 7.8(a), the demand curve for labor tells us the marginal benefit that the firms in Yuma receive from hiring fast-food servers. The marginal benefit minus the wage rate is a surplus for the firms.

The supply of labor tells us about the marginal cost of working. To work, people must forgo leisure or working in the home, activities that they value. The wage rate received minus the marginal cost of working is a surplus for workers.

An efficient allocation of labor occurs when the marginal benefit to firms equals the marginal cost borne by workers. Such an allocation occurs in the labor market in Figure 7.8(a). Firms enjoy a surplus (the blue area), and workers enjoy a surplus (the green area). The sum of these surpluses is maximized.

Figure 7.8(b) shows the loss from a minimum wage. With a minimum wage of $7 an hour, 3,000 workers are hired. Marginal benefit exceeds marginal cost. The firms' surplus and workers' surplus shrink, and a deadweight loss (the gray area) arises. This loss is borne by firms that cut back employment and by people who can't find jobs at the higher wage rate.

But the total loss exceeds the deadweight loss. Resources get used in costly job-search activity as each unemployed person keeps looking for a job—writing letters, making phone calls, going for interviews, and so on. The value of these resources might be as large as the red rectangle.

FIGURE 7.8

The Inefficiency of the Minimum Wage

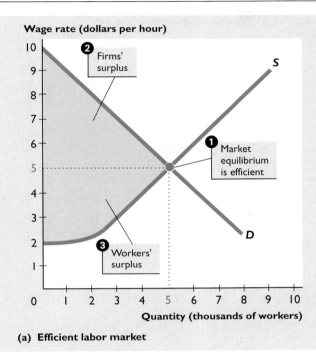

(a) Efficient labor market

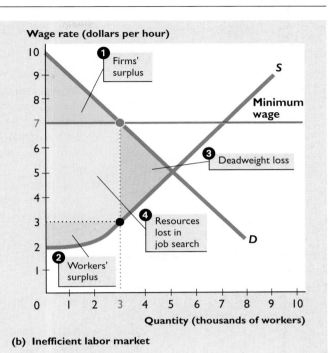

(b) Inefficient labor market

❶ The market equilibrium is efficient with marginal benefit equal to marginal cost. The sum of ❷ the firms' surplus (blue area) and ❸ workers' surplus (green area) is maximized.

A minimum wage is inefficient. ❶ The firms' surplus and ❷ workers' surplus shrink, a ❸ deadweight loss arises, and ❹ resources are lost in job search.

◼ Is the Minimum Wage Fair?

The minimum wage is unfair on both views of fairness: It delivers an unfair *result* and imposes unfair *rules.* The *result* is unfair because only those people who find jobs benefit. The unemployed end up worse off than they would be with no minimum wage. And those who get jobs are probably not the least well off. When the wage rate doesn't allocate jobs, discrimination, another source of unfairness, increases. The minimum wage imposes unfair *rules* because it blocks voluntary exchange. Firms are willing to hire more labor and people are willing to work more. But they are not permitted by the minimum wage law to do so.

◼ If the Minimum Wage Is So Bad, Why Do We Have It?

Although the minimum wage is inefficient, not everyone loses from it. The people who find jobs at the minimum wage rate are better off. Other supporters of the minimum wage believe that the elasticities of demand and supply in the labor market are low, so not much unemployment results. Labor unions support the minimum wage because it puts upward pressure on all wage rates, including those of union workers. Nonunion labor is a substitute for union labor, so when the minimum wage rises, the demand for union labor increases.

Pizza delivery people gain from the minimum wage.

2 Explain how a price floor works and show how the minimum wage creates unemployment, inefficiency, and unfairness.

Practice Problem 7.2

1. Figure 1 shows the market for tomato pickers in southern California.
   a. What is the equilibrium wage rate of tomato pickers and what is the equilibrium quantity of tomato pickers employed?
   b. Is the market for tomato pickers efficient?
   c. If California introduces a minimum wage for tomato pickers of $4 an hour, how many tomato pickers are employed and how many are unemployed?
   d. If California introduces a minimum wage for tomato pickers of $8 an hour, how many tomato pickers are employed and how many are unemployed?
   e. Is the minimum wage of $8 an hour efficient? Is it fair?
   f. Who gains and who loses from the minimum wage of $8 an hour?

FIGURE 1

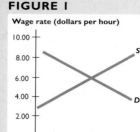

Wage rate (dollars per hour)

Exercise 7.2

1. Figure 2 shows a market for private math tutors in College Station organized by the Students' Union.
   a. What is the wage rate that math tutors earn and how many are employed?
   b. If the Students' Union sets the minimum wage for private math tutors at $15 an hour, how many tutors are unemployed?
   c. If the Students' Union sets the minimum wage for private tutors at $8 an hour, how many tutors are unemployed?
   d. Is a minimum wage of $8 an hour efficient? Is it fair?
   e. Is a minimum wage of $15 an hour efficient? Is it fair?
   f. If a black market gets going, what wage rate might some tutors earn?

FIGURE 2

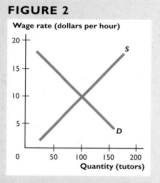

Wage rate (dollars per hour)

Solution to Practice Problem 7.2

1a. The equilibrium wage rate is $6 an hour, and 4,000 pickers are employed.
1b. The market for tomato pickers is efficient because the marginal benefit to tomato growers equals the marginal cost borne by the pickers.
1c. The minimum wage of $4 an hour is below the equilibrium wage rate, so 4,000 tomato pickers are employed and none are unemployed.
1d. The minimum wage of $8 an hour is above the equilibrium wage rate, so 3,000 pickers are employed (determined by the demand for tomato pickers) and 5,000 people would like to work as pickers for $8 an hour (determined by the supply curve), so 2,000 are unemployed (Figure 3).
1e. The minimum wage of $8 an hour is not efficient because it creates a deadweight loss—the marginal benefit to growers (on the demand curve) exceeds the marginal cost to pickers (on the supply curve). An additional loss arises as unemployed tomato pickers search for jobs. The minimum wage is unfair on both views of fairness.
1f. Tomato pickers who find work at $8 an hour gain. Tomato growers and unemployed pickers lose.

FIGURE 3

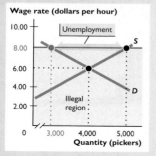

Wage rate (dollars per hour)

7.3 PRICE SUPPORTS IN AGRICULTURE

"The nation has got to eat," declared President George W. Bush when he asked Congress to spend $170 billion to support U.S. farmers. The United States is not alone among the advanced economies in spending billions of dollars each year on farm support. Governments in all the advanced economies do it, and none more than those of the European Union and Japan.

■ How Governments Intervene in Markets for Farm Products

The methods that governments use to support farms vary, but they almost always involve three elements:

- Isolate the domestic market from global competition
- Introduce a price floor
- Pay the farms a subsidy

Isolate Domestic Market

A government can't regulate a market price without first isolating the domestic market from global competition. If the cost of production in the rest of the world is lower than that in the domestic economy and if foreign producers are free to sell in the domestic market, the forces of demand and supply drive the price down and swamp any efforts by the government to influence the price.

To isolate the domestic market, the government restricts imports from the rest of the world.

Introduce a Price Floor

A price floor in an agricultural market is called a **price support**, because the floor is maintained by a government guarantee to buy any surplus output at that price. You saw that a price floor in the labor market—a minimum wage—creates a surplus of labor that shows up as unemployment. A price support in an agricultural market also generates a surplus. At the support price, the quantity supplied exceeds the quantity demanded. What happens to the surplus makes the effects of a price support different from those of a minimum wage. The government buys the surplus.

Price support
A price floor in an agricultural market maintained by a government guarantee to buy any surplus output at that price.

Subsidy

A **subsidy** is a payment by the government to a producer to cover part of the cost of production. When the government buys the surplus produced by farmers, it provides them with a subsidy. Without the subsidy, farmers could not cover their costs because they would not be able to sell the surplus.

Let's see how a price support works.

Subsidy
A payment by the government to a producer to cover part of the cost of production.

■ Price Support: An Illustration

To see the effects of a price support, we'll look at the market for sugar beets. Both the United States and the European Union have price supports for sugar beets.

Figure 7.9 shows the market. This market is isolated from rest-of-world influences. The demand curve, D, tells us the quantities demanded at each price in the domestic economy only. And the supply curve, S, tells us the quantities supplied at each price by domestic farmers.

Free Market Reference Point

With no price support, the equilibrium price is $25 a ton and the equilibrium quantity is 25 million tons a year. The market is efficient only if the price in the rest of the world is also $25 a ton. If the price in the rest of the world is less than $25 a ton, it is efficient for the domestic farmers to produce less and for some sugar beets to be imported at the lower price (and lower opportunity cost) available in the rest of the world. But if the price in the rest of the world exceeds $25 a ton, it is efficient for domestic farmers to increase production and export some of it.

Price Support and Subsidy

Suppose the government introduces a price support at $35 a ton. To make the price support work, the government agrees to pay farmers $35 for every ton of sugar beets they produce and can't sell on the market.

The farmers produce the quantity shown by the market supply curve. At a price of $35 a ton, the quantity supplied is 30 million tons a year, so production increases to this amount.

Domestic users of sugar beets cut back their purchases. At $35 a ton, the quantity demanded is 20 million tons a year, and purchases decrease to this amount.

Because farmers produce a greater quantity than domestic users are willing to buy, something must be done with the surplus. If the farmers just dumped the surplus on the market, you can see what would happen. The price would fall to that at which consumers are willing to pay for the quantity produced.

To make the price support work, the government buys the surplus. In this example, the government buys 10 million tons for $35 a ton and provides a subsidy to the farmers of $350 million.

■ FIGURE 7.9

The Domestic Market for Sugar Beets

The market for sugar beets is isolated from global competition.

❶ With no intervention, the competitive equilibrium price is $25 a ton and the equilibrium quantity is 25 million tons a year.

❷ The government intervenes in this market and sets a support price at $35 a ton.

❸ The quantity produced increases to 30 million tons a year.

❹ The quantity bought by domestic users decreases to 20 million tons a year.

❺ The government buys the surplus of 10 million tons a year and pays the farmers a subsidy.

❻ A deadweight loss arises.

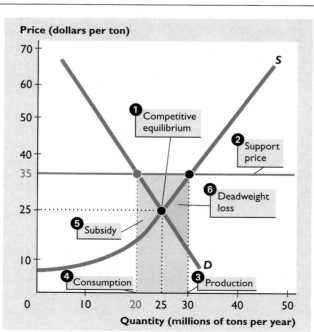

The price support increases farmers' total revenue. Without a subsidy, farmers would receive a total revenue of $625 billion ($25 a ton multiplied by 25 million tons). With a subsidy, they receive a total revenue of $1,050 billion ($35 a ton multiplied by 30 million tons).

The price support is inefficient because it creates a deadweight loss. Marginal cost exceeds marginal benefit. Farmers gain but buyers, who are also the taxpayers who end up paying the subsidy, lose. And buyers' losses exceed the farmers' gains by the amount of the deadweight loss.

Effects on the Rest of the World

The rest of the world receives a double-whammy from price supports. First, import restrictions in advanced economies deny developing economies access to the food markets of the advanced economies. The result is lower prices and smaller farm production in the developing economies.

Second, the surplus produced in the advanced economies gets sold in the rest of the world. So the price and the quantity produced in the rest of the world are depressed even further.

So the subsidies to U.S. farmers are paid not only by U.S. taxpayers and consumers but also by poor farmers in the developing economies.

REALITY CHECK

Price Ceilings and Price Floors in YOUR Life

Price ceilings and price floors play a role in *your* life in two ways:

1. They affect some of the markets in which you trade, and
2. They require you to take a stand as a voter.

The zero price you pay for using a freeway is a type of price ceiling. The next time you're stuck in traffic and moving at a crawl, think about how a free market in road use would allow you to zip along.

Think about your own (or a friend's) labor market experiences. Have you wanted a job and been willing and available to work, but unable to get hired? Would you have taken a job for a slightly lower wage if one had been available?

Develop your own considered view on price supports in agricultural markets. Do you think they are efficient? Do you think they are fair? Do you support them or oppose them?

3 **Explain how a price support in the market for an agricultural product creates a surplus, inefficiency, and unfairness.**

Practice Problem 7.3

FIGURE 1

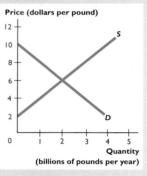

1. Figure 1 shows the market for tomatoes.
   a. What are the equilibrium price and quantity of tomatoes?
   b. Is the market for tomatoes efficient?
   c. If the government introduces a price support for tomatoes at $8 per pound, what is the quantity of tomatoes produced and what is the surplus?
   d. If the government introduces a price support for tomatoes at $8 per pound, what is the subsidy received by tomato farmers?
   e. Is the price support efficient?
   f. Who gains and who loses from the price support and what is the deadweight loss?
   g. Could the price support be regarded as being fair?

Exercise 7.3

FIGURE 2

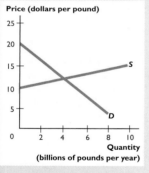

1. Figure 2 shows the market for peanuts.
   a. What are the equilibrium price and quantity of peanuts?
   b. Is the market for peanuts efficient?
   c. If the government introduces a price support for peanuts at $15 per pound, what is the quantity of peanuts produced and what is the surplus?
   d. If the government introduces a price support for peanuts at $15 per pound, what is the subsidy paid to peanut farmers?
   e. Is the price support efficient?
   f. Who gains and who loses from the price support and what is the deadweight loss?
   g. Does the peanut price support redistribute more than the tomato price support in the practice problem? Explain.

Solution to Practice Problem 7.3

FIGURE 3

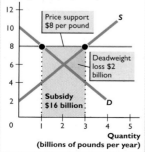

1a. The equilibrium price is $6 a pound, and the equilibrium quantity is 2 billion pounds a year.

1b. The market for tomatoes is efficient—marginal benefit equals marginal cost.

1c. At a support price of $8 a pound, 3 billion pounds are produced and 1 billion pounds are demanded, so there is a surplus of 2 billion pounds (Figure 3).

1d. At a support price of $8 a pound, the subsidy is $8 per pound on 2 billion pounds, which is $16 billion (Figure 3).

1e. The price support is not efficient because it creates a deadweight loss—the marginal benefit (on the demand curve) is less than the marginal cost (on the supply curve).

1f. Consumers/taxpayers lose. They pay more for tomatoes and pay taxes to fund the subsidy. Farmers gain. The deadweight loss is $2 billion (the gray triangle.)

1g. The outcome is unfair on both views of fairness unless farmers are poorer than the consumers, in which case it might be fair to boost farmer's incomes.

CHAPTER CHECKPOINT

Key Points

1 **Explain how a price ceiling works and show how a rent ceiling creates a housing shortage, inefficiency, and unfairness.**

- A price ceiling set above the equilibrium price has no effects.
- A price ceiling set below the equilibrium price creates a shortage, increased search activity, and a black market.
- A price ceiling is inefficient and unfair.
- A rent ceiling is an example of a price ceiling.

2 **Explain how a price floor works and show how the minimum wage creates unemployment, inefficiency, and unfairness.**

- A price floor set below the equilibrium price has no effects.
- A price floor set above the equilibrium price creates a surplus, increased search activity, and illegal trading.
- A price floor is inefficient and unfair.
- A minimum wage is an example of a price floor.

3 **Explain how a price support in the market for an agricultural product creates a surplus, inefficiency, and unfairness.**

- A price support increases the quantity produced, decreases the quantity consumed, and creates a surplus.
- To maintain the support price, the government buys the surplus and subsidizes the producer.
- A price support benefits the producer but costs the consumer/taxpayer more than the producer gains—it creates a deadweight loss.
- A price support is inefficient and is usually unfair.

Key Terms

Black market, 169
Minimum wage law, 176
Price cap, 168

Price ceiling, 168
Price floor, 175
Price support, 181

Rent ceiling, 168
Search activity, 170
Subsidy, 181

TABLE 1

Rent (dollars per month)	Quantity demanded	Quantity supplied
	(rooms)	
500	2,500	2,000
550	2,250	2,000
600	2,000	2,000
650	1,750	2,000
700	1,500	2,000
750	1,250	2,000

Exercises

1. Table 1 shows the demand and supply schedules for on-campus housing.
   a. What are the equilibrium rent and number of rooms?
   b. If the college puts a rent ceiling on rooms of $650 a month, what is the rent and how many rooms are rented?
   c. If the college puts a rent ceiling on rooms of $550 a month, what is the rent and how many rooms are rented?
   d. If the college strictly enforces the rent ceiling of $550 a month, is the on-campus housing market efficient? Explain why or why not.
   e. If a black market develops, how high could the black market rent be? Explain.
   f. If a black market develops, is the housing market fair? Explain your answer.

2. During the 1996 Olympic Games, many residents of Atlanta left the city and rented out their homes. Despite the increase in the quantity of housing available, rents soared. If at the time of the 1996 Olympic Games, the city of Atlanta had imposed a rent ceiling, describe how the housing market would have functioned.

3. Concerned about the political fallout from rising gas prices, the government decides to impose a price ceiling on gasoline of $2.00 a gallon.
   a. Explain how the market for gasoline would react to this price ceiling if
      (i) The oil-producing nations increased production and drove the equilibrium price of gasoline to $1.50 a gallon.
      (ii) A global shortage of oil sent the equilibrium price of gasoline to $2.50 a gallon.
   b. Which of the situations in part a would result in an efficient use of resources? Explain.

4. Suppose the government introduced a ceiling on the fees that lawyers are permitted to charge.
   a. Explain the effects of such a ceiling on
      (i) The amount of work done by lawyers.
      (ii) The consumer surplus of people who hire lawyers.
      (iii) The producer surplus of law firms.
   b. Would this fee ceiling result in an efficient use of resources? Why or why not?

TABLE 2

Wage rate (dollars per hour)	Quantity demanded	Quantity supplied
	(student workers)	
5.00	600	300
5.50	500	350
6.00	400	400
6.50	300	450
7.00	200	500
7.50	100	550

5. Table 2 shows the demand and supply schedules for student workers at on-campus venues.
   a. What is the equilibrium wage rate of student workers and what is the equilibrium number of students employed?
   b. Is the market for student workers at on-campus venues efficient?
   c. If the college introduces a minimum wage of $5.50 an hour, how many students are employed at on-campus venues and how many are unemployed?
   d. If the college introduces a minimum wage of $6.50 an hour, how many students are employed at on-campus venues and how many are unemployed?
   e. Is the minimum wage of $6.50 an hour efficient? Is it fair?
   f. Who gains and who loses from the minimum wage of $6.50 an hour?

6. Bakers earn $15 an hour, gas pump attendants earn $6 an hour, and copy shop workers earn $7 an hour. If the government introduces a minimum wage of $7 an hour, explain how the markets for bakers, gas pump attendants, and copy shop workers will respond initially to the minimum wage.

7. The equilibrium price of beef falls to $2 a pound, a price at which cattle ranchers can't survive. To help the struggling ranchers, the government declares that it is illegal to buy beef for less than $5 a pound. But the government does not offer to buy the surplus and subsidize the ranchers. Instead, it appoints a large number of observers to keep a close watch on the beef market and ensure that the law is observed to the letter. Black market traders are effectively eliminated.
   a. Describe the situation in the beef market.
   b. Explain why the cattle ranchers want the government to abandon the price floor.

8. In exercise 7, the equilibrium price of beef falls to $2 a pound—a price at which cattle ranchers can't survive. Now the government introduces a price support and subsidy.
   a. Describe the situation in the beef market after the introduction of the price support and subsidy.
   b. Would you expect the cattle ranchers to be happier with this arrangement than they would be with a price floor and no subsidy? Explain.

9. Table 3 shows the demand and supply schedules for mushrooms.
   a. What are the equilibrium price and quantity of mushrooms?
   b. Is the market for mushrooms efficient?
   c. If the government introduces a price support for mushrooms of $4 per pound, what is the quantity of mushrooms produced and what is the surplus of mushrooms?
   d. Is there a deadweight loss from a price support of $4 a pound?
   e. If the government introduces a price support for mushrooms of $6 per pound, what is the quantity of mushrooms produced and what is the surplus?
   f. Is the price support of $6 a pound efficient?
   g. Who gains from a price support set at $6 a pound?
   h. Who loses from a price support set at $6 a pound?
   i. What is the deadweight loss if the price support is set at $6 a pound?

TABLE 3

Price (dollars per pound)	Quantity demanded	Quantity supplied
	(pounds per week)	
1.00	5,000	2,000
2.00	4,500	2,500
3.00	4,000	3,000
4.00	3,500	3,500
5.00	3,000	4,000
6.00	2,500	4,500

10. Table 4 shows the domestic demand and supply schedules of oranges.
    a. With no imported oranges, what are the equilibrium price and quantity of oranges?
    b. If the government introduces a price support of $250 per ton, what is the quantity of oranges produced and what is the surplus of oranges?
    c. What is the deadweight loss created by the price support and what is the subsidy the government must pay domestic producers?
    d. Is the domestic market for oranges fair?
    e. If the government sells the surplus of oranges on the world market for oranges, what changes will occur in the world market for oranges?

TABLE 4

Price (dollars per ton)	Quantity demanded	Quantity supplied
	(tons per year)	
50	16	10
100	15	11
150	14	12
200	13	13
250	12	14
300	11	15
350	10	16

Critical Thinking

11. The New York City Rent Guidelines Board is mandated to establish rent adjustments for the nearly one million apartments and houses that are subject to the city's Rent Stabilization Law. The board holds public hearings to consider testimony from owners, tenants, advocacy groups, and housing industry experts. Write a brief report to the New York City Rent Guidelines Board that explains why it is not possible to improve on permitting the market forces of supply and demand to determine rents at the levels that make the quantity demanded and quantity supplied equal.

TABLE 5

Year	Minimum wage (dollars per hour)	Unemployment rate (16 years and older)	Unemployment rate (aged 16 to 19)
1995	4.45	5.6	17.1
1996	4.75	5.3	16.2
1997	5.15	5.0	16.8
1998	5.15	4.5	15.0
1999	5.15	4.3	13.9
2000	5.15	4.0	11.9
2001	5.15	4.6	14.4

12. Table 5 provides data on the minimum wage in the United States from 1995 to 2001. The table also provides data on the unemployment rate of all persons over 16 and of those aged 16 to 19. On the political campaign trail, a Republican presents these data and says that they support the view that the minimum wage causes unemployment among young people. A Democrat presents these same data and says they show that the minimum wage has no effect on the unemployment rate of any age groups.
    a. What claims can be made and cannot be made about the effects of the minimum wage on the unemployment rate?
    b. Do these data provide any evidence that bears on the issue? Explain why they do or do not help to resolve the issue.

13. A hurricane has destroyed most of the homes and cut off the drinking water, gas, and electricity in a city. Under these conditions, the mayor decides to impose rent ceilings and price ceilings on water, gas, and electricity.
    a. Predict the consequences of the mayor's decision in both the short run and the long run.
    b. Explain who will gain, who will lose, and whether you think the deadweight loss from the price regulations is worth bearing.

14. "Market prices might be fine in a rich country, but in a poor African nation where there are shortages of most items, without government control of prices everything would be too expensive." Do you agree or disagree with this statement? Use the concepts of efficiency and fairness to explain why.

Web Exercises

Use the links on MyEconLab to work the following exercises.

15. Visit the Web site of the Harvard Living Wage Campaign.
    a. What is the campaign for a living wage?
    b. How would you distinguish the minimum wage from a living wage?
    c. If the Living Wage Campaign succeeds in getting wages increased above their equilibrium levels, what do you predict its effect will be?
    d. Would a living wage above the equilibrium wage be efficient?
    e. Who would gain and who would lose from a living wage above the equilibrium wage?
    f. Would a living wage above the equilibrium wage be fair?

16. Visit British Sugar to find information about the sugar market in Europe.
    a. Why do European nations subsidize the production of sugar?
    b. How do European sugar subsidies influence the price of sugar that consumers pay?
    c. How do European sugar subsidies influence the global sugar market?

CHAPTER 8

Taxes

CHAPTER CHECKLIST

**When you have completed your study of this chapter,
you will be able to**

1 Explain how taxes change prices and quantities, are shared by buyers
and sellers, and create inefficiency.

2 Explain how income taxes and Social Security taxes change wage
rates and employment, are shared by employers and workers, and
create inefficiency.

3 Review ideas about the fairness of the tax system.

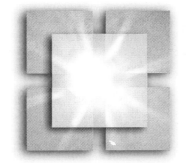

Jody is excited to be starting her new job at the
Bank of Alabama. She is now earning $47,000 a
year—more than $900 a week. She views her
first payslip with excitement—followed by dismay. Her $900 a week has become $660! She
stares at the numbers: Medicare $12.75, Federal
tax $102, Social Security $55, Alabama state tax
$30, Jefferson County tax $4.50, Birmingham
city tax $9—a tax bill of $213. Parking and other deductions
take another $27.

And when Jody spends her $660, she gets whacked with
a 4 percent sales tax and a 16 cent a gallon gas tax. She's
glad her good habits let her avoid Alabama's smoke and
drink taxes!

What are the effects of the taxes that governments
impose? Who bears the burden of these taxes? How do
taxes affect the efficiency of markets? Can Congress target
taxes at businesses so that workers pay less tax? Is the tax
system fair? This chapter answers these questions.

8.1 TAXES ON BUYERS AND SELLERS

Almost every time you buy something—a late-night order of chow mein, a plane ticket, a tank of gasoline—you pay a tax. On some items, you pay a sales tax that is added to the advertised price. On other items, you pay an excise tax—often at a high rate like the tax on gasoline—that is included in the advertised price.

But do you really pay these taxes? When a tax is added to the advertised price, isn't it obvious that *you* pay the tax? Isn't the price higher than it otherwise would be by an amount equal to the tax?

And what about a tax that is buried in the price, such as that on gasoline. Who pays that tax? Does the seller just pass on the full amount of the tax to you, the buyer? Or does the seller pay the tax by taking a lower price and leaving the price you pay unchanged?

To answer these questions, let's suppose that TIFS, the Tax Illegal File Sharing lobby, has persuaded the government to collect a $10 tax on every new MP3 player and use the tax revenue to compensate artists. But an argument is raging between those who claim that the buyer benefits and should pay the tax and those who claim that the seller profits and should pay the tax.

■ Tax Incidence

Tax incidence

The division of the burden of a tax between the buyer and the seller.

Tax incidence is the division of the burden of a tax between the buyer and the seller. We're going to find the incidence of a $10 tax on MP3 players with two different taxes: a tax on the buyer and a tax on the seller.

Figure 8.1 shows the market for MP3 players. With no tax, the equilibrium price is $100 and the equilibrium quantity is 5,000 players a week.

When a good is taxed, it has two prices: a price that excludes the tax and a price that includes the tax. Buyers respond only to the price that includes the tax, because that is the price they pay. Sellers respond only to the price that excludes the tax, because that is the price they receive. The tax is like a wedge between these two prices.

Figure 8.1(a) shows what happens if the government taxes the buyer. The tax doesn't change the buyer's willingness and ability to pay. But it changes how the amount paid is split between the seller and the government. The demand curve, *D*, tells us the *total* amount that buyers are willing and able to pay. And the red curve *D* − *tax* tells us what the buyers are willing to pay to the sellers, given that they must pay $10 to the government on each item bought. The red curve, *D* − *tax*, lies $10 below the blue demand curve.

Equilibrium occurs where the red *D* − *tax* curve intersects the supply curve, *S*. The buyer pays the equilibrium net-of-tax price $95 plus the $10 tax: $105. The seller receives the net-of-tax price $95. The government collects a tax revenue of $10 a player on 2,000 players, or $20,000 (shown by the purple rectangle).

Figure 8.1(b) shows what happens if the government taxes the seller. The tax acts like an increase in the suppliers' cost, so supply decreases and the supply curve shifts to the red curve labeled *S* + *tax*. This curve tells us what sellers are willing to accept, given that they must pay the government $10 on each item sold. The red curve, *S* + *tax*, lies $10 above the supply curve.

Equilibrium occurs where the red *S* + *tax* curve intersects the demand curve, *D*. The buyer pays the equilibrium market price $105. The seller receives the net-of-tax price $95. The government collects a tax revenue of $20,000.

FIGURE 8.1

A Tax on MP3 Players

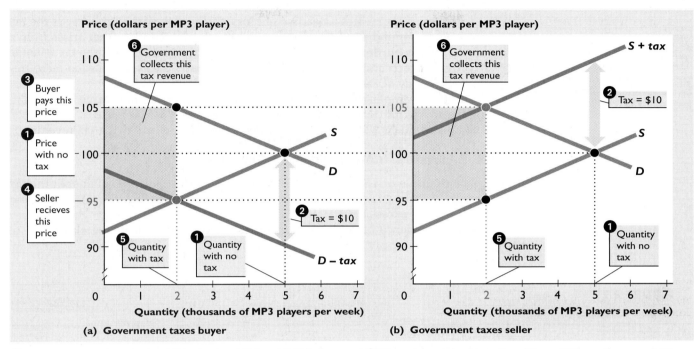

(a) Government taxes buyer

(b) Government taxes seller

❶ With no tax, the price of an MP3 player is $100 and 5,000 players a week are bought. ❷ A $10 tax on buyers of MP3 players shifts the demand curve to *D − tax* in part (a). A $10 tax on sellers of MP3 players shifts the supply curve to *S + tax* in part (b). ❸ The price paid by buyers rises to $105—an increase of $5.

❹ The price received by sellers falls to $95—a decrease of $5. ❺ The quantity decreases to 2,000 players a week. ❻ The government collects tax revenue of $20,000 a week—the purple rectangle. The burden of the tax is split equally between the buyer and the seller—each pays $5 per player.

You can now see that the argument about making the buyer pay or the seller pay is futile. The buyer pays the same price, the seller receives the same price, and the government receives the same tax revenue on the same quantity regardless of whether the government taxes the buyer or the seller.

In this example, the buyer and the seller share the burden of the tax equally. But in most cases, the burden will be shared unequally and might even fall entirely on one side of the market. We'll explore what determines the incidence of a tax below. But first, let's see how a tax creates inefficiency.

Taxes and Efficiency

You've seen that resources are used efficiently when marginal benefit equals marginal cost. You've also seen that a tax places a wedge between the buyer's price and the seller's price. But the buyer's price equals the marginal benefit and the seller's price equals marginal cost. So a tax puts a wedge between marginal benefit and marginal cost. The equilibrium quantity is less than the efficient quantity, and a deadweight loss arises..

Figure 8.2 shows the inefficiency of a tax. We'll assume that the government taxes the seller. In part (a), with no tax, marginal benefit equals marginal cost and

Excess burden
The amount by which the burden of a tax exceeds the tax revenue received by the government—the deadweight loss from a tax.

the market is efficient. In part (b), with a tax, marginal benefit exceeds marginal cost. Consumer surplus and producer surplus shrink. Part of each surplus goes to the government as tax revenue—the purple area—and part of each surplus becomes a deadweight loss—the gray area.

Because a tax creates a deadweight loss, the burden of the tax exceeds the tax revenue. To remind us of this fact, we call the deadweight loss that arises from a tax the **excess burden** of the tax. But because the government uses the tax revenue to provide goods and services that people value, only the excess burden measures the inefficiency of the tax.

In this example, the excess burden is large. You can see how large by calculating the area of the deadweight loss triangle. This area is $15,000 ($10 × 3,000 ÷ 2). The tax revenue is $20,000, so the excess burden is 75 percent of the tax revenue.

■ Incidence, Inefficiency, and Elasticity

In the example of a $10 tax on MP3 players, the buyer and the seller split the tax equally and the excess burden is large. What determines how the tax is split and the size of its excess burden?

The incidence of a tax and its excess burden depend on the elasticities of demand and supply in the following ways:

■ FIGURE 8.2
Taxes and Efficiency

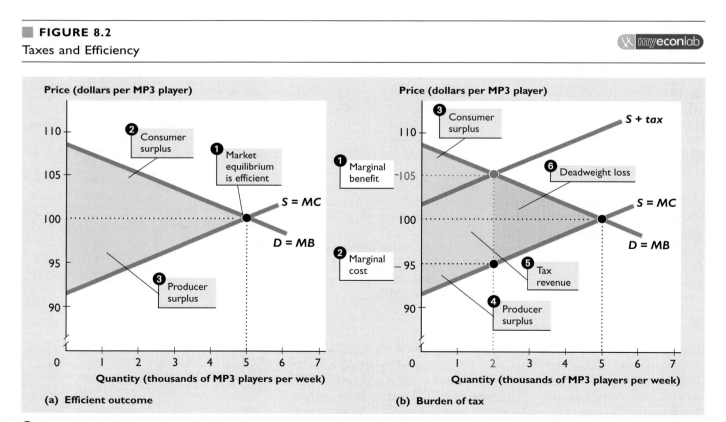

(a) Efficient outcome

(b) Burden of tax

❶ The market is efficient with marginal benefit equal to marginal cost. Total surplus—the sum of ❷ consumer surplus (green area) and ❸ producer surplus (blue area)—is at its maximum possible level.

A $10 tax drives a wedge between ❶ marginal benefit and ❷ marginal cost. ❸ Consumer surplus and ❹ producer surplus shrink by the amount of the ❺ tax revenue plus the ❻ deadweight loss. The deadweight loss is the excess burden of the tax.

- For a given elasticity of supply, the buyer pays a larger share of the tax the more inelastic is the demand for the good.
- For a given elasticity of demand, the seller pays a larger share of the tax the more inelastic is the supply of the good.
- The more inelastic is demand *or* supply, the smaller is the excess burden.

■ Incidence, Inefficiency, and the Elasticity of Demand

To see how the division of a tax between the buyer and the seller and the size of the excess burden depend on the elasticity of demand, we'll look at two extremes.

Perfectly Inelastic Demand: Buyer Pays and Efficient

Figure 8.3(a) shows the market for insulin, a vital daily medication of diabetics. Demand is perfectly inelastic at 100,000 doses a week, as shown by the vertical demand curve. With no tax, the price is $2 a dose. A 20¢ a dose tax raises the price to $2.20, but the quantity does not change. The tax leaves the price received by the seller unchanged but raises the price paid by the buyer by the entire tax. The outcome is efficient (there is no deadweight loss) because marginal benefit equals marginal cost.

Perfectly Elastic Demand: Seller Pays and Inefficient

Figure 8.3(b) shows the market for pink marker pens. Demand is perfectly elastic at $1 a pen, as shown by the horizontal demand curve. If pink pens are less expensive than other pens, everyone uses pink. If pink pens are more expensive than other pens, no one uses a pink pen. With no tax, the price of a pink pen is $1 and the quantity is 4,000 pens a week. A 10¢ a pen tax leaves the price at $1 a pen, but the quantity decreases to 1,000 a week. The price paid by the buyer is unchanged and the seller pays the entire tax. The outcome is inefficient because marginal benefit exceeds marginal cost and a deadweight loss arises.

■ **FIGURE 8.3**

Incidence, Inefficiency, and the Elasticity of Demand

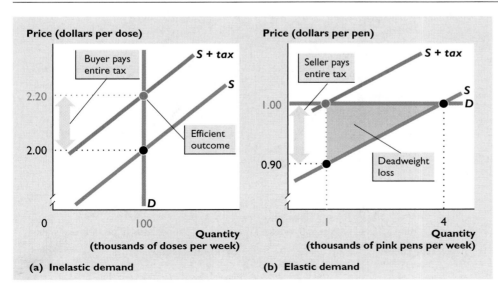

(a) Inelastic demand

(b) Elastic demand

In part (a), the demand for insulin is perfectly inelastic. A tax of 20¢ a dose raises the price by 20¢, and the buyer pays all the tax. But marginal benefit still equals marginal cost, so the outcome is efficient.

In part (b), the demand for pink marker pens is perfectly elastic. A tax of 10¢ a pen lowers the price received by the seller by 10¢, and the seller pays all the tax. Marginal benefit exceeds marginal cost, so the outcome is inefficient. The deadweight loss is the excess burden of the tax and measures its inefficiency.

■ Incidence, Inefficiency, and the Elasticity of Supply

To see how the division of a tax between the buyer and the seller depends on the elasticity of supply, we'll again look at two extremes.

Perfectly Inelastic Supply: Seller Pays and Efficient

Figure 8.4(a) shows the market for spring water that flows at a constant rate that can't be controlled. Supply is perfectly inelastic at 100,000 bottles a week, as shown by the vertical supply curve. With no tax, the price is 50¢ a bottle and the 100,000 bottles that flow from the spring are bought. A tax of 5¢ a bottle leaves the quantity unchanged at 100,000 bottles a week. But buyers are willing to buy the 100,000 bottles only if the price is 50¢ a bottle. So the price remains at 50¢ a bottle. The tax lowers the price received by the seller by 5¢ a bottle. The seller pays the entire tax.

But marginal benefit equals marginal cost, so there is no deadweight loss and the outcome is efficient.

Perfectly Elastic Supply: Buyer Pays and Inefficient

Figure 8.4(b) shows the market for sand from which computer-chip makers extract silicon. Supply of this sand is perfectly elastic at a price of 10¢ a pound as shown by the horizontal supply curve. With no tax, the price is 10¢ a pound and 5,000 pounds a week are bought. A 1¢ a pound sand tax raises the price to 11¢, and the quantity decreases to 3,000 pounds a week. The buyer pays the entire tax.

Marginal benefit exceeds marginal cost, so a deadweight loss arises and the outcome is inefficient.

■ FIGURE 8.4
Incidence, Inefficiency, and the Elasticity of Supply

In part (a), the supply of a bottle of spring water is perfectly inelastic. A tax of 5¢ a bottle lowers the price received by the seller by 5¢ a bottle, and the seller pays all the tax. Marginal benefit equals marginal cost, so the outcome is efficient.

In part (b), the supply of sand is perfectly elastic. A tax of 1¢ a pound increases the price by 1¢ a pound, and the buyer pays all the tax. Marginal benefit exceeds marginal cost, so the outcome is inefficient. The deadweight loss is the excess burden of the tax and measures its inefficiency.

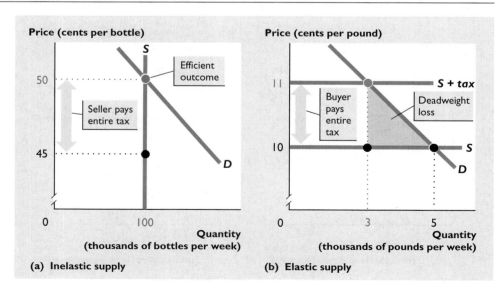

(a) Inelastic supply

(b) Elastic supply

CHECKPOINT 8.1

1 **Explain how taxes change prices and quantities, are shared by buyers and sellers, and create inefficiency.**

Practice Problem 8.1

1. Figure 1 shows the market for softballs in which softballs are not taxed. Now softballs are taxed at 60 cents a ball.
   a. If buyers are taxed, what price do buyers pay?
   b. If sellers are taxed, what price do sellers receive?
   c. How many softballs are bought and sold?
   d. What is the tax revenue from sales of softballs?
   e. What is the excess burden of the tax on softballs?
   f. Which is more inelastic: the demand for or supply of softballs? Why?

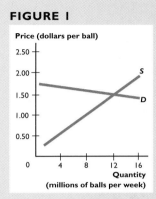

FIGURE 1

Exercises 8.1

1. With the increased popularity of cell phones, the government introduces a tax of $20 a cell phone and a tax of 10¢ a call on a cell phone. Suppose that the supply of cell phones is elastic, the demand for cell phones is inelastic, the supply of calls is perfectly elastic, and the demand for calls is elastic.
   a. Who pays more of the tax on a phone, the buyer or the seller?
   b. Who pays more of the tax on a call, the buyer or the seller?
   c. Would the taxes reduce the number of cell phones bought?
   d. Would the taxes reduce the number of calls made from cell phones?
   e. Which tax would raise more revenue for the government? Why?
   f. Which tax do you think would have the greater excess burden? Why?

2. The supply of apartments in New York City is inelastic, and the demand for apartments is elastic. The city introduces a tax on apartment rentals.
   a. Explain why landlords would pay more of the tax than renters.
   b. Explain why the government would collect a large revenue from this tax.

Solution to Practice Problem 8.1

1a. With a 60¢ tax on buyers, the demand curve shifts downward by 60¢. Buyers pay $1.60 a softball (Figure 2).

1b. With a 60¢ tax on sellers, the supply curve shifts upward by 60¢. Sellers receive $1.00 a softball (Figure 3).

1c. 8 million softballs a week (Figure 2 or 3).

1d. The tax revenue is $0.60 × 8 million, which is $4.8 million a week (the purple rectangle in Figure 2 or 3).

1e. The excess burden of the tax is $1.2 million. Excess burden equals the deadweight loss, illustrated by the gray triangle in Figure 2 or 3, which is (4 million balls × 60¢ a ball) ÷ 2 or $1.2 million.

1f. Supply is more inelastic because the seller pays the larger share of the tax.

FIGURE 2

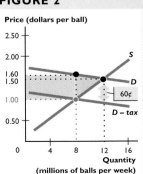

FIGURE 3

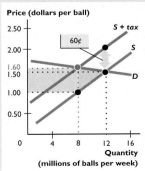

8.2 INCOME TAX AND SOCIAL SECURITY TAX

Income taxes are paid on personal incomes and corporate profits. In 2004, personal income taxes raised more than $1 trillion for the federal government and another $300 billion for state and local governments. Corporation income taxes raised $250 billion for the federal government and $40 billion for the state governments. We'll look first at the effects of personal income taxes, then at corporation income taxes, and finally at Social Security taxes.

■ The Personal Income Tax

Taxable income

Total income minus a personal exemption and a standard exemption (or other allowable deductions).

The amount of income tax that a person pays depends on her or his **taxable income**, which equals total income minus a *personal exemption* and a *standard deduction* (or other allowable deductions). For the federal income tax in 2004, the personal exemption was $3,100 and the standard deduction was $4,850 for a single person. So for a single person, taxable income equals total income minus $7,950.

The tax rate depends on the income level, and Figure 8.5 shows how the tax rate for a single person increases with income. The percentages in the table are

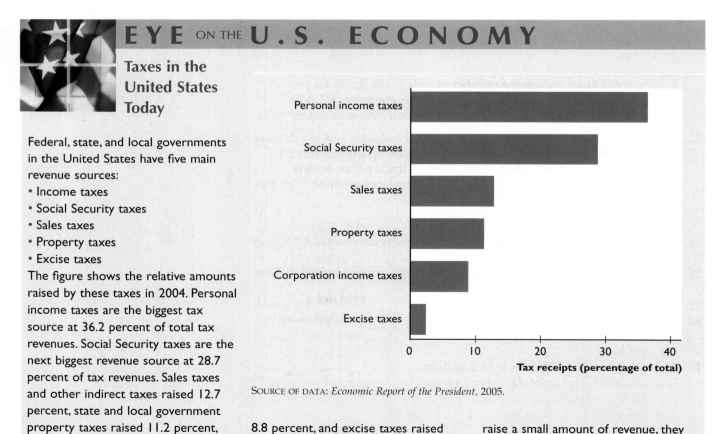

EYE ON THE U.S. ECONOMY

Taxes in the United States Today

Federal, state, and local governments in the United States have five main revenue sources:

• Income taxes
• Social Security taxes
• Sales taxes
• Property taxes
• Excise taxes

The figure shows the relative amounts raised by these taxes in 2004. Personal income taxes are the biggest tax source at 36.2 percent of total tax revenues. Social Security taxes are the next biggest revenue source at 28.7 percent of tax revenues. Sales taxes and other indirect taxes raised 12.7 percent, state and local government property taxes raised 11.2 percent, income taxes on corporations raised

SOURCE OF DATA: *Economic Report of the President*, 2005.

8.8 percent, and excise taxes raised 2.3 percent. Although excise taxes

raise a small amount of revenue, they have big effects on some markets.

◼ FIGURE 8.5

Marginal Tax Rates and Average Tax Rates

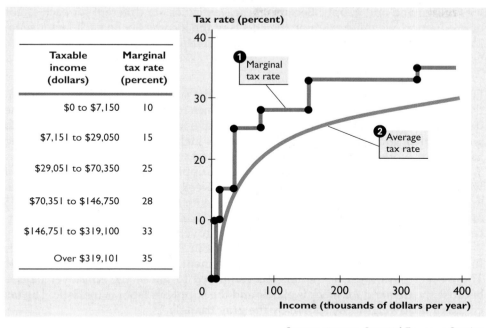

Taxable income (dollars)	Marginal tax rate (percent)
$0 to $7,150	10
$7,151 to $29,050	15
$29,051 to $70,350	25
$70,351 to $146,750	28
$146,751 to $319,100	33
Over $319,101	35

❶ The marginal tax rate increases with income. The table provides the data for 2004.

❷ The average tax rate increases with income, but the average rate is less than the marginal rate.

SOURCE OF DATA: Internal Revenue Service.

marginal tax rates. A **marginal tax rate** is the percentage of an additional dollar of income that is paid in tax. For example, if taxable income increases from $7,149 to $7,150, the tax paid on the additional dollar is 10 cents and the marginal tax rate is 10 percent. If taxable income increases from $319,100 to $319,101, the tax paid on the additional dollar is 35 cents and the marginal tax rate is 35 percent.

The **average tax rate** is the percentage of income that is paid in tax. The average tax rate is less than the marginal tax rate. For example, suppose a single person earns $50,000 in a year. Tax paid is zero on the first $7,950 plus $715 (10 percent) on the next $7,150 plus $3,285 (15 percent) on the next $21,900 plus $3,250 on the remaining $13,000. Total taxes equal $7,250, which is 14.5 percent of $50,000. The average tax rate is 14.5 percent.

If the average tax rate increases as income increases, the tax is a **progressive tax**. The personal income tax is a progressive tax. To see this feature of the income tax, calculate another average tax rate for someone whose income is $100,000 a year. Tax paid is zero on the first $7,950 plus $715 (10 percent) on the next $7,150 plus $3,285 (15 percent) on the next $21,900 plus $10,325 on the next $41,300 plus $6,076 on the remaining $21,700. Total taxes equal $20,401, which is 20.4 percent of $100,000. The average tax rate is 20.4 percent.

A progressive tax contrasts with a **proportional tax**, which has the same average tax rate at all income levels, and a **regressive tax**, which has a decreasing average tax rate as income increases.

Marginal tax rate
The percentage of an additional dollar of income that is paid in tax.

Average tax rate
The percentage of income that is paid in tax.

Progressive tax
A tax whose average rate increases as income increases.

Proportional tax
A tax whose average rate is constant at all income levels.

Regressive tax
A tax whose average rate decreases as income increases.

■ The Effects of the Income Tax

The income tax is a tax on sellers—the sellers of the services of labor, capital, and land. You know that the incidence and inefficiency of a tax depend on the elasticities of demand and supply. Because these elasticities are different for each factor of production, we must examine the effects of the income tax on each factor separately. Let's look first at the effects of the tax on labor income.

Tax on Labor Income

Figure 8.6 shows the demand curve, *LD*, and the supply curve, *LS*, in a competitive labor market. Firms can substitute machines for labor in many tasks, so the demand for labor is elastic. But most people have few good options other than to work for their income, so the supply of labor is inelastic. In this example, with no income tax, workers would earn $19 an hour and work 40 hours a week.

With a 20 percent income tax, the labor supply curve shifts to *LS + tax*. If workers are willing to supply the 40th hour a week for $19 with no tax, then with a 20 percent tax, they are willing to supply the 40th hour only if the wage is $23.75 an hour. That is, they want to get the $19 they received before plus $4.75 (20 percent of $23.75) that they now must pay to the government.

The equilibrium wage rate rises to $20 an hour, but the after-tax wage rate falls to $16 an hour—the tax is $4 an hour. Employment decreases to 35 hours a week. The worker pays most of the tax—$3 compared to the $1 the employer pays—because the demand for labor is elastic and the supply of labor is inelastic. The tax creates a deadweight loss shown by the gray triangle.

▨ FIGURE 8.6

A Tax on Labor Income

(X) myeconlab

With no income tax, workers would earn $19 an hour and work 40 hours a week.

❶ Workers face a 20 percent marginal income tax rate. The income tax decreases the supply of labor, raises the wage rate, and lowers the after-tax wage rate. Because the demand for labor is elastic and the supply of labor is inelastic, the tax ❷ paid by the employer is less than that ❸ paid by the worker. The quantity of labor employed is less than the efficient quantity, so ❹ a deadweight loss arises.

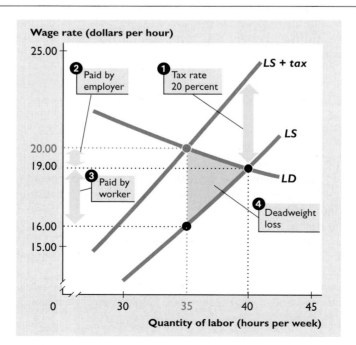

Tax on Capital Income

Capital income—interest on bonds and bank deposits and dividends on stocks—is taxed at the same rate as other sources of income. But dividends on stocks get taxed twice because corporations also pay a tax on the profits that are paid out as dividends. In his 2003 economic stimulus package, President Bush proposed the abolition of this double taxation of dividends.

Figure 8.7 shows the demand curve, *KD*, and the supply curve, *KS*, in a competitive capital market. Because firms can substitute machines for labor in many tasks, the demand for capital is elastic. Capital is internationally mobile, and its supply is highly elastic. In this example, firms can obtain all the capital they wish at an interest rate of 6 percent a year, so the supply of capital is perfectly elastic. With no income tax, firms use $40 billion worth of capital.

With a 40 percent tax on capital income, the supply curve shifts to *KS* + *tax*. Lenders want to receive an additional 4 percent interest to pay their capital income tax and are not willing to lend for less than 10 percent a year.

With the capital income tax, the quantity of capital decreases to $20 billion and the interest rate rises to 10 percent a year. Firms pay the entire capital income tax, and lenders receive the same after-tax interest rate as they receive in the absence of a capital income tax. The tax creates a deadweight loss shown by the gray triangle.

Tax on the Income from Land and Other Unique Resources

Each plot of land and reserve of mineral or other natural resource is unique, so its supply is perfectly inelastic. A fixed amount of the resource is supplied regardless of the rent offered for its use.

FIGURE 8.7
A Tax on Capital Income

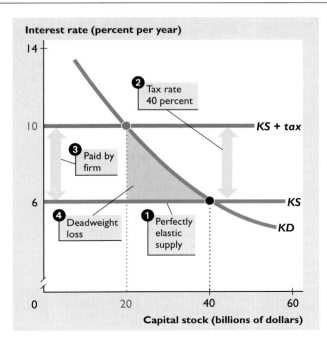

❶ The supply of capital is highly elastic (here perfectly elastic). With no tax on capital income, the interest rate is 6 percent a year and firms use $40 billion of capital.

With a ❷ 40 percent tax on income from capital, the supply curve becomes *KS* + *tax*. The interest rate rises to 10 percent a year, and ❸ firms pay the entire tax. The quantity of capital used is less than the efficient quantity, so ❹ a deadweight loss arises.

President Bush's Tax Cuts

In 2003, President Bush proposed a number of tax cuts to stimulate production and employment. The table lists the five major proposals and the size of the tax cut they would bring in 2003 and over the ten years to 2013.

Magnitude of Cuts

As a percentage of total personal income taxes, the proposed tax cut is large. In 2003 alone, total personal income tax payments fell from $1,006 billion to $908 billion, a cut of 9.7 percent.

But as a percentage of total personal income, the tax cut looks much more modest. In 2003, total personal income was about $9,400 billion. So a tax cut of $98 billion was only 1 percent of total personal income.

The average annual tax cut planned was $67 billion (one tenth of the ten-year total of $670 billion). This tax cut is 6.7 percent of the 2003 level of total personal income taxes and less than 1 percent of 2003 total personal income.

Who stands to benefit from these tax cuts? Will the tax cuts contribute to the efficiency of the economy? And are they fair?

Incidence of Tax Cuts

You can figure out who will benefit from the tax cuts—the incidence of the tax cuts—from what you've learned in this chapter.

Lower taxes on labor income will mainly benefit workers because the elasticity of demand for labor is much greater than the elasticity of supply of labor.

Lower taxes on capital income that result from the exclusion of dividends will have little effect on the after-tax income of savers. Because the supply of capital is highly elastic, the cost of capital to firms will fall and the quantity of capital will increase. Output and employment will also increase.

Efficiency of Tax Cuts

You can figure out how the tax cuts contribute to economic efficiency from what you've learned in this chapter.

Lower taxes on labor income will increase employment, but not by much because the supply of labor is inelastic. With the limited effect on employment, the deadweight loss from the labor income tax will decrease, but not by much.

Lower taxes on capital income will have a potentially large effect on efficiency. Because both the demand for capital and the supply of capital are elastic, a small tax cut brings a large increase in the quantity of capital and a large decrease in the deadweight loss from the tax on capital income.

Fairness of Tax Cuts

Whether the tax cuts are fair is controversial and depends on the criterion of fairness used. According to the U.S. Treasury, people who earn $200,000 a year or more will get 40 percent of the tax cuts and people who earn $30,000 a year or less will get less than 3 percent of the tax cuts.

But those with a high income pay most of the taxes, so it is not surprising that they benefit most from lower taxes.

If the tax cuts are expressed as percentages of taxes currently paid, the lower income groups benefit most. People with incomes of $30,000 a year or less get a tax cut of 17 percent, while people with incomes of $200,000 a year or more get a tax cut of 11 percent.

President Bush's Tax Cuts	2003	2003–2013
	Billions of dollars	
Accelerate income tax cuts	28	64
Exclude dividends from personal income tax	20	364
Accelerate reduction of marriage tax penalty	19	58
Accelerate child tax-credit increase	16	91
Accelerate expansion of 10 percent income tax bracket	5	48
Other measures	10	45
Total	98	670

SOURCE OF DATA: U.S. Treasury.

Figure 8.8(a) illustrates a tax on land income. In this example, a fixed 250 billion acres is supplied regardless of the rent. The equilibrium quantity of land is determined purely by supply and the equilibrium rent is determined by the demand for land. In this example, the equilibrium rent is $1,000 an acre.

When a 40 percent tax is imposed on rent income, landowners pay all of the tax. Their after-tax income falls to $600 an acre. This tax is efficient because the equilibrium quantity of land used is the same with the tax as without it. The tax generates no deadweight loss (excess burden) and is ideal from the perspective of efficiency.

The principle that applies to a tax on income from land also applies to the income from any unique resource that has a perfectly inelastic supply. Another example of such a resource is the talent of an outstanding movie star or television personality.

Figure 8.8(b) illustrates this case. Suppose that Barbara Walters is willing to do 24 big television interviews a year. Her supply of interview services is perfectly inelastic at that quantity. The networks compete for her services, and the demand curve reflects their willingness to pay for them. The equilibrium price is $250,000 per interview or $6 million a year. If Barbara Walters pays a 40 percent tax on this income, she receives an after-tax income of $150,000 per interview or $3.6 million a year. Barbara Walters pays the entire tax. The price paid by the networks is unaffected by this tax, and Barbara Walters performs the same number of interviews with the tax as without it. This tax creates no deadweight loss (excess burden).

■ FIGURE 8.8

A Tax on Land and Other Unique Resource Income

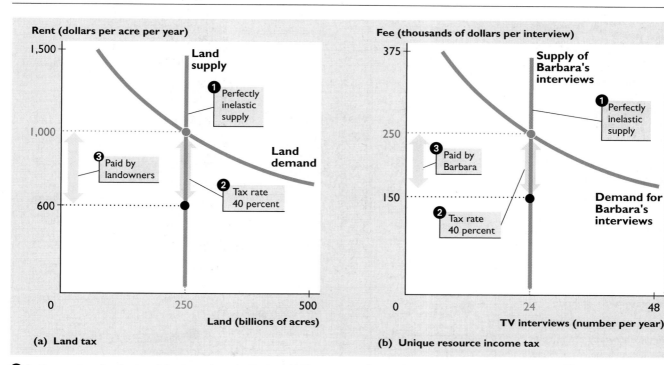

(a) Land tax

(b) Unique resource income tax

❶ In the markets for land and for interviews by Barbara Walters, supply is highly inelastic (here perfectly inelastic). With a ❷ 40 percent tax on income from these resources, the supply curve and the market price remain unchanged, and ❸ landowners and Barbara Walters pay the entire tax. The quantity of the resource used is unchanged and the tax is efficient.

■ The Social Security Tax

Social Security is never far from the headlines. And as the population gets older and more and more people begin to receive Social Security benefits, the cry to "fix Social Security" can only keep getting louder. The fundamental problem of ever-growing outlays must somehow be addressed.

One possible solution to the Social Security problem in the United States is to change the entitlements and cut the outlays. But this possibility is not popular and probably will not be the solution that is chosen. The other possibility is to increase the Social Security tax.

Currently, the law says that Social Security taxes fall equally on workers and employers. But does this outcome actually occur? If Congress decides to increase the Social Security tax, can Congress target employers and shield workers?

The Social Security tax is just like the other taxes you've studied in this chapter. Its incidence depends on the elasticities of demand and supply in the labor market and not on the wishes of Congress. Let's confirm this assertion by looking at two distinct arrangements: First, the tax is imposed only on workers, and second, the tax is imposed only on employers.

A Social Security Tax on Workers

Figure 8.9 shows the effects of a Social Security tax when the law says that workers must pay the entire tax. Without any taxes, the wage rate is $6 an hour and 4,000 people are employed. Now suppose that the government introduces a 20 percent Social Security tax on workers. If 4,000 people were willing to work for $6 an hour, this quantity of labor will now be supplied only if people can earn $6 an

FIGURE 8.9
A Social Security Tax on Workers

With no taxes, 4,000 people are employed at a wage rate of $6 an hour.

❶ A Social Security tax on workers of 20 percent shifts the supply curve to *LS + tax*.

❷ The wage rate rises to $6.25 an hour, an increase of 25¢ an hour.

❸ The quantity of labor employed decreases to 3,000 workers.

❹ Workers receive $5 an hour—a decrease of $1 an hour.

❺ The government collects tax revenue shown by the purple rectangle.

Workers pay most of the tax because the supply of labor is more inelastic than the demand for labor.

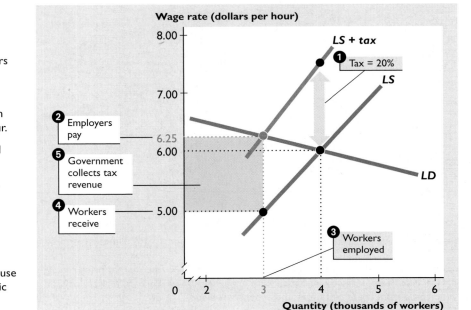

hour *after tax*. With a tax rate of 20 percent, the pre-tax wage rate will need to be $7.50 an hour to deliver an after-tax wage rate of $6 an hour. (Check that 20 percent of $7.50 is $1.50, so the wage rate after tax is $6.) The supply of labor curve shifts to the curve labeled *LS + tax*—a decrease in the supply of labor.

The wage rate rises to $6.25 an hour, and 3,000 workers are employed. With a wage rate of $6.25 an hour, employees *receive* that amount minus a 20 percent tax, which is $5 an hour. (Check that $1.25 equals 20 percent, or one fifth, of $6.25.)

So when the government puts a Social Security tax on workers, employers pay 25 cents and workers pay $1. This division of the burden of the tax arises because the demand for labor is more elastic than the supply of labor.

A Social Security Tax on Employers

Figure 8.10 shows the effects of a Social Security tax on employers. As before, with no taxes, the equilibrium wage rate is $6 an hour and 4,000 people are employed. With a $1.25 an hour tax, firms are no longer willing to hire 4,000 people at a $6 an hour wage rate. Because they must pay $1.25 an hour to the government, they will hire 4,000 people at a wage rate of $6 minus $1.25, which is $4.75 an hour.

The demand for labor decreases, and the demand curve shifts to *LD − tax*. The wage rate falls to $5 an hour, and 3,000 workers are employed. The total cost of labor to the firm is $6.25 an hour—the $5 an hour wage plus the $1.25 an hour tax.

The tax on employers delivers the same outcome as the tax on workers. Workers receive the same take-home wage, and firms pay the same total wage. Congress cannot decide who pays the Social Security tax. When the laws of Congress come into conflict with the laws of economics, economics wins. Congress can't repeal the laws of supply and demand!

■ FIGURE 8.10

A Social Security Tax on Employers

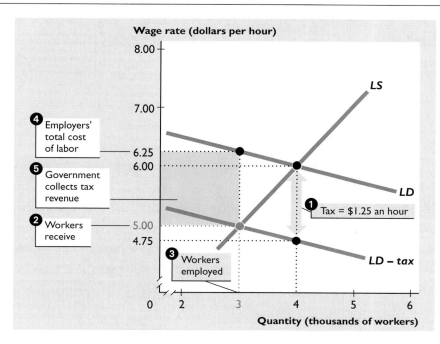

With no taxes, 4,000 people are employed at a wage rate of $6 an hour.

❶ A tax on employers of $1.25 an hour shifts the demand curve leftward to *LD − tax*.

❷ The wage rate falls to $5 an hour, a decrease of $1 an hour.

❸ The quantity of labor employed decreases to 3,000 workers.

❹ Employers' total cost of labor rises to $6.25 an hour—the wage rate of $5 an hour plus the $1.25 an hour tax.

❺ The government collects tax revenue shown by the purple rectangle.

The Origins and History of the U.S. Income Tax

Tax rate (percent)

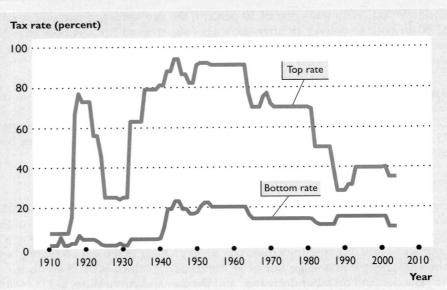

Top rate

Bottom rate

SOURCE OF DATA: Congressional Joint Committee on Taxation.

1861	First federal income tax—3 percent on all incomes above $800 a year.
1872	Income tax was repealed. (Tariffs on imports provided government revenue.)
1895	Income tax reestablished, but the Supreme Court ruled it unconstitutional.
1913	The 16th Amendment to the Constitution made the federal income tax legal.
1913–2004	Tax rates fluctuated, but the bottom rate remained around 15 percent and the top rate was gradually lowered.

REALITY CHECK

Taxes in YOUR Life

The Tax Foundation has calculated "Tax Freedom Day"—the date by when an average U.S. citizen has worked long enough to pay a year's tax bill. In 2004, that day was April 17. The 107 days Americans must work to pay taxes break down this way:

> 38 days to pay personal income taxes
>
> 30 days to pay Social Security taxes
>
> 16 days to pay sales and excise taxes
>
> 11 days to pay property taxes
>
> 9 days to pay corporate income taxes
>
> 3 days for all other taxes

Work out your own "Tax Freedom Day" by recording the taxes you pay in a year. Express this number as a percentage of your annual income and then find the number of days (as a percentage of 365) that this amount of tax represents. If you think taxes are high in the United States, think again. "Tax Freedom Day" in Sweden is July 18!

CHECKPOINT 8.2

myeconlab

2 Explain how income taxes and Social Security taxes change wage rates and employment, are shared by employers and workers, and create inefficiency.

Practice Problems 8.2

1. Florida levies the following taxes: a 5.5 percent corporate income tax, a 6 percent sales tax, taxes of 4 cents a gallon on gasoline, 33.9 cents a pack on cigarettes, $0.48 a gallon on beer and $2.25 a gallon on wine, and property taxes that vary across the counties and range from 1.4 percent to 2.0 percent of property values. Classify Florida's taxes into progressive, proportional, and regressive taxes.

2. Explain why Tiger Woods pays his own Social Security tax and the PGA (the Professional Golf Association) pays none of it.

3. Which tax is more inefficient: a tax on land rent or a tax on capital income? Explain.

Exercise 8.2

1. California taxes personal incomes, and in 2004, there were six tax brackets that ranged from 1.0 percent on a taxable income of $6,146 to 9.3 percent on taxable incomes above $40,345. California has an 8.84 percent corporate income tax. California has a 7.25 percent sales tax. Other taxes are 18 cents a gallon on gasoline, 87 cents a pack on cigarettes, and $0.20 per gallon on beer and wine. Property taxes vary across the counties and range from 1 percent to 2 percent of property values.
    a. Classify California's taxes into progressive, proportional, and regressive taxes.
    b. Which of California's taxes creates the biggest excess burden? Explain.

Solutions to Practice Problems 8.2

1. If counties with the higher rates are those with high property values, then Florida's property taxes are progressive. The corporate income tax does not vary with income, so this tax is a proportional tax. Saving increases with income, so expenditure as a fraction of income decreases as income increases. So the sales tax, gasoline tax, cigarette tax, and beer tax are regressive taxes.

2. Tiger Woods pays his Social Security tax and the PGA pays none of it because the supply of Tiger Woods' services is (most likely) perfectly inelastic. The elasticities of demand and supply determine who pays the tax.

3. A tax on capital income is more inefficient than a tax on land rent. A tax on capital income has the larger effect on the quantities of factors of production employed than does a tax on land rent because the supply of land is perfectly inelastic while the supply of capital is highly (and perhaps perfectly) elastic. The larger the deadweight loss created by the tax (the excess burden of the tax), the more inefficient is the tax.

8.3 FAIRNESS AND THE BIG TRADEOFF

We've examined the incidence and the efficiency of different types of taxes. These topics have occupied most of this chapter because they are the issues about taxes that economics can address. But when political leaders debate tax issues, it is fairness, not just incidence and efficiency, that gets the most attention. Democrats complain that Republican tax cuts are unfair because they give the benefits of lower taxes to the rich. Republicans counter that because the rich pay most of the taxes, it is fair that they get most of the tax cuts. No easy answers are available to the questions about the fairness of taxes. And economists have proposed two conflicting principles of fairness to apply to a tax system:

- The benefits principle
- The ability-to-pay principle

■ The Benefits Principle

Benefits principle
The proposition that people should pay taxes equal to the benefits they receive from public goods and services.

The **benefits principle** is the proposition that people should pay taxes equal to the benefits they receive from public goods and services. This arrangement is fair because it means that those who benefit most pay the most. It makes tax payments and the consumption of government-provided services similar to private consumption expenditures. If taxes are based on the benefits principle, the people who enjoy the largest benefits pay the most for them.

To implement the benefits principle, it would be necessary to have an objective method of measuring each individual's marginal benefit from government-provided goods. In the absence of such a method, the principle can be used to justify a wide range of different taxes.

For example, the benefits principle can justify high fuel taxes to pay for public highways. Here, the argument would be that those who value the highways most use them most and so should pay most of the cost of providing them. Similarly, the benefits principle can justify high taxes on alcoholic beverages and tobacco products. Here, the argument would be that those who drink and smoke the most place the largest burden on public health-care services and so should pay the greater part of the cost of those services.

The benefits principle can also be used to justify a progressive income tax. Here, the argument would be that the rich receive a disproportionately large share of the benefit from law and order and from living in a secure environment, so they should pay the largest share of providing these services.

■ The Ability-to-Pay Principle

Ability-to-pay principle
The proposition that people should pay taxes according to how easily they can bear the burden.

The **ability-to-pay principle** is the proposition that people should pay taxes according to how easily they can bear the burden. A rich person can more easily bear the burden of providing public goods than a poor person can, so the rich should pay higher taxes than the poor. The ability-to-pay principle involves comparing people along two dimensions: horizontally and vertically.

Horizontal Equity

Horizontal equity
The requirement that taxpayers with the same ability to pay should pay the same taxes.

If taxes are based on ability to pay, taxpayers with the same ability to pay should pay the same taxes, a situation called **horizontal equity**. While horizontal equity is easy to agree with in principle, it is difficult to implement in practice. If two people are identical in every respect, horizontal equity is easy to apply. But how do we compare people who are similar but not identical? The greatest difficulty arises in working out differences in ability to pay that arise from the state of a person's health and from a person's family responsibilities. The U.S. income tax has many special deductions and other rules that aim to achieve horizontal equity.

Vertical Equity

If horizontal comparisons are difficult, vertical comparisons are impossible. **Vertical equity** is the requirement that taxpayers with a greater ability to pay bear a greater share of the taxes. This proposition easily translates into the requirement that people with higher incomes should pay higher taxes. But it provides no help in determining how steeply taxes should increase as income increases. Should taxes be proportional to income? Should they be regressive? Should they be progressive? All of these arrangements have higher-income people paying higher taxes, so they all satisfy the basic idea of vertical equity. But most people have strong views that include the extent to which the rich should pay more.

You've seen that the U.S. tax code uses progressive income taxes—average tax rates that increase with income. Progressive taxes are justified as fair on the basis of the principle of vertical equity. But their use to achieve vertical equity produces a problem for the attainment of horizontal equity. The problem shows up most clearly in the U.S. tax code in its treatment of single people and married couples.

Vertical equity
The requirement that taxpayers with a greater ability to pay bear a greater share of the taxes.

■ The Marriage Tax Problem

Should a married couple (or two people living together) be treated as two individual taxpayers or as a single taxpayer? Until some changes were introduced in 2003, the U.S. tax code treated a married couple is a single taxpayer. This arrangement means that when a man and a woman get married, they stop paying income tax as two individuals and instead pay as one individual. To see the marriage tax problem, suppose the tax code (simpler than that in the United States) is as follows: no deductions or exemptions, incomes up to $20,000 a year bear no tax, and incomes in excess of $20,000 are taxed at 10 percent.

Now think about Al and Judy, two struggling young journalists, each of whom earns $20,000 a year and who get married. As single people, they paid no tax. Married, their income is $40,000, so they pay $2,000 a year in tax (10 percent of $20,000). Their marriage tax is $2,000 a year. (This example is *much* more severe than the marriage tax in the United States, but it serves to highlight the source of the problem.)

A married couple or two individuals?

We could make a simple change to the tax law to overcome this problem for Al and Judy: Tax married couples as two single persons. That is what is done in most countries and what some economists say should be done in the United States. If we make this change in the tax law, Al and Judy pay no tax after their marriage just as before. We've solved the marriage tax problem.

Before we conclude that this small change to the tax code would clean up a source of unfairness, let's think about its effect on Denise and Frank. Frank is a painter whose work just doesn't sell. He has no income. Denise is a successful artist whose work is in steady demand and earns her $40,000 a year. As two single artists, Frank pays no tax and Denise pays $2,000 a year (10 percent of $20,000). If they marry, under the arrangement that taxes a married couple as a single taxpayer, they still pay $2,000 in tax.

Now compare Frank and Denise with Al and Judy. If we tax married couples as a single taxpayer, both couples earn $40,000 a year and both pay income tax of $2,000 a year. But if we tax them as single persons, Frank and Denise pay $2,000 a year and Al and Judy pay nothing. So which is fair?

Horizontal equity requires Frank and Denise to be treated like Al and Judy. Taxing them as couples rather than as individuals achieves this outcome. But it taxes marriage, which seems unfair.

This problem arises from the progressive tax. It would not arise if taxes were proportional. Because horizontal equity conflicts with progressive taxes, some people say that only proportional taxes are fair.

■ The Big Tradeoff

Questions about the fairness of taxes conflict with efficiency questions and create the *big tradeoff* that you met in Chapter 6. The taxes that generate the greatest deadweight loss are those on the income from capital. But most capital is owned by a relatively small number of people who have the greatest ability to pay taxes. So there is a conflict between efficiency and fairness. We want a tax system that is efficient, in the sense that it raises the revenue that the government needs to provide public goods and services, but we want a tax system that shares the burden of providing these goods and services fairly. Our tax system is an evolving compromise that juggles these two goals.

CHECKPOINT 8.3   (X) myeconlab

3   **Review ideas about the fairness of the tax system.**

Practice Problem 8.3

1. In Hong Kong, the marginal income tax rates range from 2 percent to 20 percent. Does Hong Kong place greater weight on the ability-to-pay principle than does the United States? Does Hong Kong place a greater weight on efficiency and a smaller weight on fairness than does the United States?

Exercise 8.3

1. In Canada, the marginal income tax rates range from 22 percent to 40 percent. Does Canada place greater weight on the ability-to-pay principle than does the United States? Does Canada place a greater weight on efficiency and a smaller weight on fairness than does the United States?

Solution to Practice Problem 8.3

1. Income tax rates are lower in Hong Kong than in the United States, so Hong Kong places less weight on the ability-to-pay principle than does the United States. With income tax rates in Hong Kong lower than in the United States, Hong Kong places a greater weight on efficiency and a smaller weight on fairness than does the United States.

CHAPTER CHECKPOINT

Key Points

1 **Explain how taxes change prices and quantities, are shared by buyers and sellers, and create inefficiency.**

- A tax on buyers has the same effect as a tax on sellers. It increases the price paid by the buyer and lowers the price received by the seller.
- A tax creates inefficiency by driving a wedge between marginal benefit and marginal cost and creating a deadweight loss.
- The less elastic the demand or the more elastic the supply, the greater is the price increase and the larger is the share of the tax paid by the buyer.
- If demand is perfectly elastic or supply is perfectly inelastic, the seller pays all the tax. And if demand is perfectly inelastic or supply is perfectly elastic, the buyer pays all the tax.
- If demand or supply is perfectly inelastic, the tax creates no deadweight loss and is efficient.

2 **Explain how income taxes and Social Security taxes change wage rates and employment, are shared by employers and workers, and create inefficiency.**

- Taxes can be progressive (the average tax rate rises with income), proportional (the average tax rate is constant), or regressive (the average tax rate falls with income).
- The U.S. income tax is progressive.
- The shares of the income tax paid by firms and households depend on the elasticity of demand and the elasticity of supply of the factors of production.
- The elasticities of demand and supply, not Congress, determine who pays the income tax and who pays the Social Security tax.
- The more elastic is either the demand or supply of a factor of production, the greater is the excess burden of an income tax.

3 **Review ideas about the fairness of the tax system.**

- The two main principles of fairness of taxes—the benefits principle and the ability-to-pay principle—do not deliver universally accepted standards of fairness, and vertical equity and horizontal equity can come into conflict.

Key Terms

Ability-to-pay principle, 206
Average tax rate, 197
Benefits principle, 206
Excess burden, 192

Horizontal equity, 206
Marginal tax rate, 197
Progressive tax, 197
Proportional tax, 197

Regressive tax, 197
Taxable income, 196
Tax incidence, 190
Vertical equity, 207

Ⓧ myeconlab

Exercises

1. In Florida, sunscreen and sunglasses are vital items. If the tax on sellers of these items is doubled from 5.5 percent to 11 percent, who will pay most of the tax increase: buyers or sellers? Will the tax increase halve the quantity of sunscreen and sunglasses bought?

2. Table 1 illustrates the market for Internet service. Use a demand-supply graph to answer the following questions.
   a. What is the market price of an Internet service?
   b. If the government taxes Internet service $15 a month, what price would the buyer of an Internet service pay?
   c. What price would the seller of the Internet service receive?
   d. Does the buyer or the seller pay more of the tax?
   e. What is the tax revenue collected by the government?
   f. What is the excess burden of the tax?

TABLE 1

Price (dollars per month)	Quantity demanded	Quantity supplied
	(units per month)	
0	30	0
10	25	10
20	20	20
30	15	30
40	10	40
50	5	50
60	0	60

3. The supply of luxury boats is perfectly elastic, and the demand for luxury boats is unit elastic. The government decides to tax luxury boats 20 percent. Before the tax is introduced, the price of a luxury boat is $1 million and 240 luxury boats a week are bought.
   a. What is the price that buyers of a luxury boat pay after the tax is imposed?
   b. How is the tax split between buyers and sellers?
   c. How much tax revenue will the government raise?
   d. Show in a graph the excess burden of this tax.
   e. Is this tax efficient? Explain your answer.
   f. Is this tax fair? Explain your answer.

4. Table 2 shows the demand schedule and the supply schedule of toothpaste. If the government decides to tax toothpaste $1.50 a tube:
   a. What price do buyers pay for toothpaste?
   b. What price do sellers receive?
   c. How much tax revenue does the government collect?
   d. What is the excess burden of the tax?

TABLE 2

Price (dollars per tube)	Quantity demanded	Quantity supplied
	(thousands of tubes per week)	
0.00	11	6.5
0.50	10	7.0
1.00	9	7.5
1.50	8	8.0
2.00	7	8.5
2.50	6	9.0
3.00	5	9.5
3.50	4	10.0
4.00	3	10.5
4.50	2	11.0
5.00	1	11.5

5. In exercise 4, suppose that when the government taxes toothpaste $1.50 a tube, all toothpaste manufacturers announce that to counteract the government's outrageous action, they will cut the price they charge by $1 a tube.
   a. Are the toothpaste manufacturers making a generous move to support oral hygiene or just seeking credit for market forces that are outside their control? Explain your answer using an appropriate graph.
   b. If the price charged by toothpaste makers fell by less than $1 a tube, would there be a shortage or a surplus of toothpaste? Explain your answer using an appropriate graph.

6. To encourage inner-city youths to spend more time playing sports, the government introduces a super income tax of 10 percent on professional basketball players and plans to use the revenue to improve inner-city sports facilities.
   a. Will the super income tax raise much revenue for the government?
   b. Who will pay most of the tax: the players or the team owners?
   c. Will the tax create a large or a small excess burden?

7. In an attempt to raise more revenue, the government decides to increase the tax on buyers of coffee.
    a. What will determine how much more Starbucks charges for a coffee?
    b. How will the quantity of coffee bought in coffee shops change?
    c. Will the government raise much revenue from the coffee tax?

8. Concerned about the political fallout from rising gas prices, the government decides to cut the tax on gasoline. Explain how the market for gasoline would react to this tax cut if
    a. The oil-producing nations increased production and drove the equilibrium price of gasoline down.
    b. A global shortage of oil sent the equilibrium price of gasoline up.

9. In 2002, New York State raised the cigarette tax by 39 cents to $1.50 a pack. Then New York City raised the tax from 8 cents to $1.50 a pack. These taxes raised the price of cigarettes to about $7.50 a pack—the highest in the nation.
    a. How will the $3 tax increase change the price buyers pay and the price sellers receive?
    b. Who will pay more of the tax increase? Buyers or sellers?
    c. Will these tax increases change the revenue collected by the government and the city? If so, will revenue increase or decrease? Explain why.
    d. How will these taxes change consumer surplus and producer surplus?
    e. Which of these tax hikes will have more excess burden?
    f. Everyone who buys cigarettes pays the $3 tax a pack. Is this tax a progressive, regressive, or proportional tax? Explain.

10. Larry earns $25,000 and pays $2,500 in tax, while Suzy earns $50,000 and pays $15,000 in tax. If Larry's income increases by $100, his tax increases by $12, but if Suzy's income increases by $100, her tax increases by $35.
    a. Calculate Larry's average tax rate and marginal tax rate.
    b. Calculate Suzy's average tax rate and marginal tax rate.
    c. Is the income tax fair? Explain.

11. Bakers earn $10 an hour, gas pump attendants earn $6 an hour, and copy shop workers earn $7 an hour.
    a. If the government introduces an income tax of $1 an hour, explain how the markets for bakers, gas pump attendants, and copy shop workers will respond.
    b. Calculate the marginal tax rates for bakers, gas pump attendants, and copy shop workers.
    c. Is this tax progressive, regressive, or proportional?

12. Figure 1 illustrates the labor market in a country that does not tax labor income.
    a. How many workers are employed and what is the wage rate they earn?
    b. If the government introduces a social security tax on workers of $2 per worker, what are the number of workers employed, the wage rate paid by employers, the wage rate received by workers, the number of workers no longer employed, and the tax revenue collected by the government?
    c. If the government splits the social security tax equally between workers and employers, what now are your answers to part **b**?
    d. Is the social security tax in part **b** or **c** fairer? Explain.

FIGURE 1

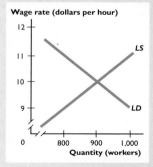

Critical Thinking

14. The government of the U.S. Virgin Islands seeks your help to evaluate two tax schemes. In scheme A, food is not taxed, luxury goods are taxed 10 percent, and all other goods are taxed at 5 percent. In scheme B, there is a flat 3 percent tax on all goods and services. The government asks you to explain what research must be undertaken and what features of the markets for food, luxury goods, and other goods will influence how the prices and quantities of food, luxury goods, and all other goods will differ under the two schemes.

15. In exercise 14, which tax would be more efficient if both schemes generated the same amount of tax revenue? The government asks you to explain what research must be undertaken and what features of the markets for food, luxury goods, and other goods will influence the excess burden of the taxes under the two schemes.

16. A study by Citizens for Tax Justice and the Children's Defense Fund says that the richest 1 percent of Americans will receive 50 percent of the benefit of the tax cuts that Congress enacted in 2001. Debate this assessment. What assumptions about the elasticities of demand and supply for high-wage labor and capital might be consistent with this assessment? What other facts about demand and supply and market outcomes would you need to know? If the assessment is correct, is such an outcome likely to be efficient? Is such an outcome fair on any of the standard principles of fairness?

Web Exercises

Use the links on MyEconLab to work the following exercises.

17. Obtain data on the sales tax rates in each state.
    a. Which states have the highest sales tax rate and which states have the lowest?
    b. Compare the sales taxes in your state with those in the neighboring states. Of these states, which do you think has the biggest excess burden of these taxes?
    c. Compare California with the nearby states of Nevada and Washington. In which state do you think consumer surplus and producer surplus (per person) is greatest? Why?

18. Learn about the poll tax introduced in Great Britain during the 1980s.
    a. What is a poll tax? Is a poll tax a progressive, regressive, or proportional tax?
    b. How do you think the effects of a poll tax differ from those of a sales tax?
    c. Why do you think a poll tax generates anger and rioting?
    d. Despite its problems, do you think a poll tax is efficient? Explain why.

19. Visit *Slate* and read the article by Steven Landsburg entitled "Bush's Tax Cuts Are Unfair..."
    a. To whom are the Bush tax cuts unfair?
    b. Do you agree with Steven Landsburg? Explain why or why not.

Externalities

CHAPTER CHECKLIST

When you have completed your study of this chapter,
you will be able to

1 Explain why negative externalities lead to inefficient overproduction and how property rights, pollution charges, and taxes can achieve a more efficient outcome.

2 Explain why positive externalities lead to inefficient underproduction and how public provision, subsidies, vouchers, and patents can achieve a more efficient outcome.

Paul J. Evanson is Chairman, President, and Chief Executive Officer of Allegheny Electric, a power utility that operates the Fort Martin Power Station in Maidsville, West Virginia. Mr. Evanson is a good man and a respected, accomplished, well-paid manager. But Fort Martin is the dirtiest coal-fired power plant in the United States. How can governments create incentives—sticks or carrots—that align the self-interest of Mr. Evanson, his stockholders, and his customers with the social interest?

Rob Goldston is director of the Princeton Plasma Physics Laboratory, a group of physicists, engineers, and technicians who are trying to make fusion energy a reality. Fusion would provide abundant low-cost energy with no air pollution. If this scientific breakthrough can be achieved everyone on the planet will enjoy enormous benefits. How can governments provide the incentives to ensure that the scale of research that brings advances in technology is in the social interest?

These are the questions that we study in this chapter.

EXTERNALITIES IN OUR DAILY LIVES

Externality
A cost or a benefit that arises from production that falls on someone other than the producer or a cost or benefit that arises from consumption that falls on someone other than the consumer.

Negative externality
A production or consumption activity that creates an external cost.

Positive externality
A production or consumption activity that creates an external benefit.

An **externality** is a cost or a benefit that arises from production that falls on someone other than the producer or a cost or a benefit that arises from consumption that falls on someone other than the consumer. Before we embark on the two main tasks of this chapter, we're going to review the range of externalities, classify them, and give some everyday examples.

First, an externality can arise from either a production activity or a consumption activity. Second, it can be either a **negative externality**, which imposes an external cost, or a **positive externality**, which provides an external benefit. So there are four types of externalities:

- Negative production externalities
- Positive production externalities
- Negative consumption externalities
- Positive consumption externalities

■ Negative Production Externalities

When the U.S. Open tennis tournament is being played at Flushing Meadows, players, spectators, and television viewers around the world share a negative production externality that many New Yorkers experience every day: the noise of airplanes taking off from LaGuardia Airport. Aircraft noise imposes a large cost on millions of people who live under the flight paths to airports in every major city.

Logging and the clearing of forests are sources of another negative production externality. These activities destroy the habitat of wildlife and influence the amount of carbon dioxide in the atmosphere, which has a long-term effect on temperature. So these external costs are borne by everyone and by future generations.

Pollution, which we examine in more detail in the next section, is a major example of this type of externality.

■ Positive Production Externalities

To produce orange blossom honey, Honey Run Honey of Chico, California, locates beehives next to an orange orchard. The honeybees collect pollen and nectar from the orange blossoms to make the honey. At the same time, they transfer pollen

Negative production externality.

Positive production externality.

between the blossoms, which helps to fertilize the blossoms. Two positive production externalities are present in this example. Honey Run Honey gets a positive production externality from the owner of the orange orchard; and the orange grower gets a positive production externality from Honey Run.

■ Negative Consumption Externalities

Negative consumption externalities are a source of irritation for most of us. Smoking tobacco in a confined space creates fumes that many people find unpleasant and that pose a health risk. So smoking in restaurants and on airplanes generates a negative externality. To avoid this negative externality, many restaurants and all airlines ban smoking. But while a smoking ban avoids a negative consumption externality for most people, it imposes a negative external cost on smokers who would prefer to enjoy the consumption of tobacco while dining or taking a plane trip.

Noisy parties and outdoor rock concerts are other examples of negative consumption externalities. They are also examples of the fact that a simple ban on an activity is not a solution. Banning noisy parties avoids the external cost on sleep-seeking neighbors, but it results in the sleepers imposing an external cost on the fun-seeking partygoers.

Permitting dandelions to grow in lawns, not picking up leaves in the fall, allowing a dog to bark loudly or to foul a neighbor's lawn, and letting a cell phone ring in class are other examples of negative consumption externalities.

■ Positive Consumption Externalities

When you get a flu vaccination, you lower your risk of being infected. If you avoid the flu, your neighbor, who didn't get vaccinated, has a better chance of remaining healthy. Flu vaccinations generate positive consumption externalities.

When the owner of a historic building restores it, everyone who sees the building gets pleasure from it. Similarly, when someone erects a spectacular home—such as those built by Frank Lloyd Wright during the 1920s and 1930s—or other exciting building—such as the Chrysler and Empire State Buildings in New York or the Wrigley Building in Chicago—an external consumption benefit flows to everyone who has an opportunity to view it.

Education, which we examine in more detail in this chapter, is a major example of this type of externality.

Negative consumption externality.   *Positive consumption externality.*

9.1 NEGATIVE EXTERNALITIES: POLLUTION

You've just seen that pollution is an example of a negative externality. Both production and consumption activities create pollution. But here, we'll focus on pollution as a negative production externality. When a chemical factory dumps waste into a river, the people who live by the river and use it for fishing and boating bear the cost of the pollution. The chemical factory does not consider the cost of pollution when it decides the quantity of chemicals to produce. The factory's supply curve is based on its own costs, not on the costs that it inflicts on others. You're going to discover that when external costs are present, we produce more output than the efficient quantity and we get more pollution than the efficient quantity.

Pollution and other environmental problems are not new. Preindustrial towns and cities in Europe had severe sewage disposal problems that created cholera epidemics and plagues that killed millions. Nor is the desire to find solutions to environmental problems new. The development in the fourteenth century of a pure water supply and the hygienic disposal of garbage and sewage are examples of early contributions to improving the quality of the environment.

Popular discussions about pollution and the environment often pay little attention to economics. They focus on physical aspects of the environment, not on costs and benefits. A common assumption is that activities that damage the environment are normally wrong and must cease. In contrast, an economic study of the environment emphasizes costs and benefits. Economists talk about the efficient amount of pollution or environmental damage. This emphasis on costs and benefits does not mean that economists, as citizens, don't have the same goals as others and value a healthy environment. Nor does it mean that economists have the right answers and everyone else has the wrong ones. Rather, economics provides a set of tools and principles that help to clarify the issues.

The starting point for an economic analysis of the environment is the distinction between private costs and social costs.

■ Private Costs and Social Costs

A *private cost* of production is a cost that is borne by the producer of a good or service. *Marginal cost* is the cost of producing an *additional unit* of a good or service. So **marginal private cost** (*MC*) is the cost of producing an additional unit of a good or service that is borne by the producer of that good or service.

You've seen that an *external cost* is a cost of producing a good or service that is *not* borne by the producer but borne by other people. A **marginal external cost** is the cost of producing an additional unit of a good or service that falls on people other than the producer.

Marginal social cost (*MSC*) is the marginal cost incurred by the entire society—by the producer and by everyone else on whom the cost falls—and is the sum of marginal private cost and marginal external cost. That is,

$$MSC = MC + \text{Marginal external cost.}$$

We express costs in dollars. But we must always remember that a cost is an opportunity cost—the best thing we give up to get something. A marginal external cost is what someone other than the producer of a good or service must give up when the producer makes one more unit of the item. Something real that people value, such as a clean river or clean air, is given up.

Marginal private cost
The cost of producing an additional unit of a good or service that is borne by the producer of that good or service.

Marginal external cost
The cost of producing an additional unit of a good or service that falls on people other than the producer.

Marginal social cost
The marginal cost incurred by the entire society—by the producer and by everyone else on whom the cost falls. It is the sum of marginal private cost and marginal external cost.

Valuing an External Cost

Economists use market prices to put a dollar value on the cost of pollution. For example, suppose that there are two similar rivers, one polluted and the other clean. Five hundred identical homes are built along the side of each river. The homes on the clean river rent for $2,500 a month, and those on the polluted river rent for $1,500 a month. If the pollution is the only detectable difference between the two rivers and the two locations, the rent decrease of $1,000 per month is the cost of the pollution. For the 500 homes, the external cost is $500,000 a month.

External Cost and Output

Figure 9.1 shows an example of the relationship between output and cost in a chemical industry that pollutes. The marginal cost curve, *MC*, describes the private marginal cost borne by the firms that produce the chemical. Marginal cost increases as the quantity of the chemical produced increases. If the firms dump waste into a river, they impose an external cost that increases with the amount of the chemical produced. The marginal social cost curve, *MSC*, is the sum of marginal private cost and marginal external cost. For example, when firms produce 4,000 tons of chemical a month, marginal private cost is $100 a ton, marginal external cost is $125 a ton, and marginal social cost is $225 a ton.

In Figure 9.1, as the quantity of the chemical produced increases, the amount of pollution increases and the external cost of pollution increases. The quantity of the chemical produced and the pollution created depend on how the market for the chemical operates. First, we'll see what happens when the industry is free to pollute.

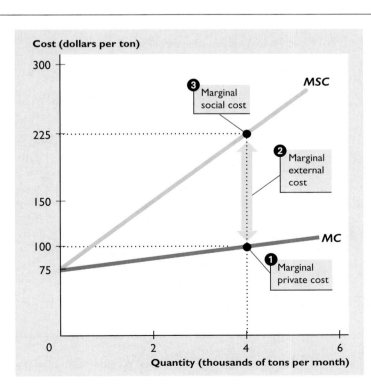

The *MC* curve shows the private marginal cost borne by the factories that produce a chemical. The *MSC* curve shows the sum of marginal private cost and marginal external cost.

When the quantity of chemical produced is 4,000 tons a month, ❶ marginal private cost is $100 a ton, ❷ marginal external cost is $125 a ton, and ❸ marginal social cost is $225 a ton.

■ Production and Pollution: How Much?

When an industry is unregulated, the amount of pollution it creates depends on the market equilibrium price and quantity of the good produced. Figure 9.2 illustrates the outcome in the market for a pollution-creating chemical.

The demand curve for the chemical is *D*. This curve also measures the marginal benefit, *MB*, to the buyers of the chemical (see Chapter 6, p. 144). The supply curve is *S*. This curve also measures the marginal private cost, *MC*, of the producers (see Chapter 6, p. 147). The supply curve is the marginal private cost curve because when firms make their production and supply decisions, they consider only the costs that they will bear. Market equilibrium occurs at a price of $100 a ton and a quantity of 4,000 tons of chemical a month.

This equilibrium is inefficient. You learned in Chapter 6 that the allocation of resources is efficient when marginal benefit equals marginal cost. But we must count all the costs—private and external—when we compare marginal benefit and marginal cost. So with an external cost, the allocation is efficient when marginal benefit equals marginal *social* cost. This outcome occurs when the quantity of the chemical produced is 2,000 tons a month. The market equilibrium *overproduces* by 2,000 tons a month and creates a deadweight loss, the gray triangle.

How can the people who live by the polluted river get the chemical factories to decrease their output of the chemical and create less pollution? If some method can be found to achieve this outcome, everyone—the owners of the factories and the residents of the riverside homes—can gain. Let's explore some solutions.

■ **FIGURE 9.2**

Inefficiency with an External Cost

The market supply curve is the marginal private cost curve, *S* = *MC*. The demand curve is the marginal benefit curve, *D* = *MB*. The marginal social cost curve is *MSC*.

❶ Market equilibrium at a price of $100 a ton and 4,000 tons of chemical a month is inefficient because ❷ marginal social cost exceeds ❸ marginal benefit.

❹ The efficient quantity of chemical is 2,000 tons a month where marginal benefit equals marginal social cost.

❺ The gray triangle shows the deadweight loss created by the pollution externality.

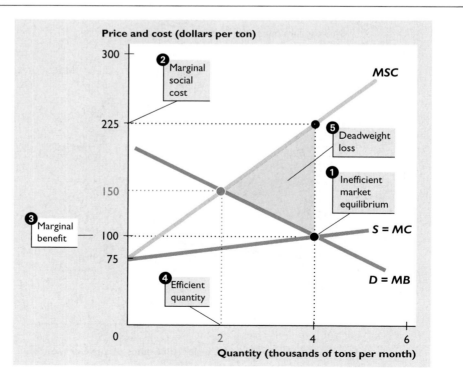

■ Property Rights

Sometimes it is possible to reduce the inefficiency arising from an externality by establishing a property right where one does not currently exist. **Property rights** are legally established titles to the ownership, use, and disposal of factors of production and goods and services that are enforceable in the courts.

Suppose that the chemical factories own the river and the 500 homes alongside it. The rent that people are willing to pay depends on the amount of pollution. Using the earlier example, people are willing to pay $2,500 a month to live alongside a pollution-free river but only $1,500 a month to live with the pollution created by 4,000 tons of chemical a month. If the factories produce this quantity, they lose $1,000 a month for each home and a total of $500,000 a month.

The chemical factories are now confronted with the cost of their pollution decision. They might still decide to pollute, but if they do, they face the opportunity cost of their actions—forgone rent from the people who live by the river.

Figure 9.3 illustrates the outcome. With property rights in place, the marginal cost curve in Figure 9.2 no longer measures all the factories' costs of producing the chemical. It excludes the pollution cost that they must now bear. The former *MSC* curve now becomes the marginal private cost curve *MC*. The market supply curve is based on all the marginal costs and is the curve labeled $S = MC$.

Market equilibrium now occurs at a price of $150 a ton and a quantity of 2,000 tons a month. This outcome is efficient. The factories still produce some pollution, but it is the efficient quantity.

Property rights
Legally established titles to the ownership, use, and disposal of factors of production and goods and services that are enforceable in the courts.

■ FIGURE 9.3
Property Rights Achieve an Efficient Outcome

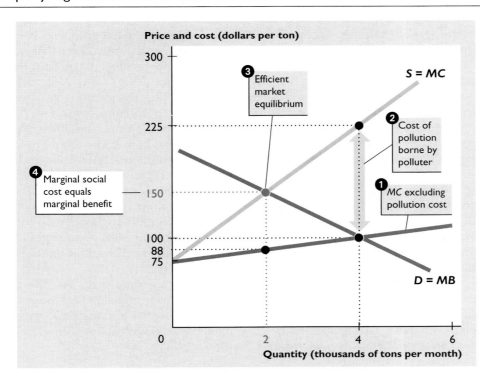

① With property rights, the marginal cost curve that excludes the cost of pollution shows only part of the producers' marginal cost.

The marginal private cost curve includes ② the cost of pollution, so the supply curve is $S = MC$.

③ Market equilibrium is at a price of $150 a ton and a quantity of 2,000 tons of chemical a month and is efficient because ④ marginal social cost equals marginal benefit.

■ The Coase Theorem

Does it matter how property rights are assigned? Does it matter whether the polluter or the victim of the pollution owns the resource that might be polluted? Until 1960, everyone—including economists who had thought long and hard about the problem—thought that it did matter. But in 1960, Ronald Coase had a remarkable insight, now called the Coase theorem.

Coase theorem
The proposition that if property rights exist, only a small number of parties are involved, and transactions costs are low, then private transactions are efficient and the outcome is not affected by who is assigned the property right.

The **Coase theorem** is the proposition that if property rights exist, only a small number of parties are involved, and transactions costs are low, then private transactions are efficient. There are no externalities because the transacting parties take all the costs and benefits into account. Furthermore, it doesn't matter who has the property rights.

Application of the Coase Theorem

Let's apply the Coase theorem to the polluted river. In the example that we've just studied, the factories own both the river and the homes. Suppose that instead, the residents own both their homes and the river. Now the factories must pay a fee to the homeowners for the right to dump their waste. The greater the quantity of waste dumped into the river, the more the factories must pay. So again, the factories face the opportunity cost of the pollution they create. The quantity of chemical produced and the amount of waste dumped are the same, whoever owns the homes and the river. If the factories own them, they bear the cost of pollution because they receive a lower income from home rents. And if the residents own the homes and the river, the factories bear the cost of pollution because they must pay a fee to the homeowners. In both cases, the factories bear the cost of their pollution and dump the efficient amount of waste into the river.

Transactions costs
The opportunity costs of conducting a transaction.

The Coase solution works only when transactions costs are low. **Transactions costs** are the opportunity costs of conducting a transaction. For example, when you buy a house, you incur a series of transactions costs. You might pay a real estate agent to help you find the best place and a financial planner to help you get the best loan, and you pay a lawyer to run checks that assure you that the seller owns the property and that after you've paid for it, the ownership has been properly transferred to you.

In the example of the homes alongside a river, the transactions costs that are incurred by a small number of chemical factories and a few homeowners might be low enough to enable them to negotiate the deals that produce an efficient outcome. But in many situations, transactions costs are so high that it would be inefficient to incur them. In these situations, the Coase solution is not available.

Suppose, for example, that everyone owns the airspace above their homes up to, say, 10 miles. If someone pollutes your airspace, you can charge a fee. But to collect the fee, you must identify who is polluting your airspace and persuade them to pay you. Imagine the cost to you and the 50 million people who live in your part of the United States (and perhaps in Canada or Mexico) of negotiating and enforcing agreements with the several thousand factories that emit sulfur dioxide and create acid rain that falls on your property!

In this situation, we use public choices through governments to cope with externalities. But the transactions costs that prevent us from using the Coase solution are opportunity costs, and governments can't wave a magician's wand to eliminate them. So attempts by the government to deal with externalities offer no easy solution. Let's look at some of these attempts.

■ Government Actions in the Face of External Costs

The three main methods that governments use to cope with externalities are

- Emission charges
- Marketable permits
- Taxes

Emission Charges

Emission charges confront a polluter with the external cost of pollution and provide an incentive to seek new technologies that are less polluting. In the United States, the Environmental Protection Agency (EPA) sets emission charges, which are, in effect, a price per unit of pollution. The more pollution a firm creates, the more it pays in emission charges. This method of dealing with environmental externalities has been used only modestly in the United States, but it is common in Europe. For example, in France, Germany, and the Netherlands, water polluters pay a waste disposal charge.

To work out the emission charge that achieves efficiency, the regulator must determine the marginal external cost of pollution at different levels of output and levy a charge on polluters that equals that cost. The polluter then incurs a marginal cost that includes both private and external costs. But to achieve the efficient outcome, the regulator needs a lot of information about the polluting industry that, in practice, is not available.

Another way of overcoming excess pollution is to issue firms with pollution quotas that they can buy and sell—with marketable permits. Let's look at this alternative.

Marketable Permits

An alternative to an emission charge is to assign each polluter an emission limit. Provided that the marginal benefit and marginal cost are assessed correctly, the same efficient outcome can be achieved with emission limits as with emission charges. But in the case of emission limits, a cap must be set for each polluter.

Marketable permits are a clever way of overcoming the need for the regulator to know every firm's marginal cost schedule. The government issues an emissions permit to each firm, and firms can buy and sell these permits. Firms with a low marginal cost of reducing pollution sell permits and firms with a high marginal cost of reducing pollution buy permits. The market in permits determines the price at which firms trade permits. And firms buy or sell permits until their marginal cost of pollution equals the market price.

The 1990 Clear Air Act and the 1994 Regional Clean Air Incentives Market (RECLAIM) in the Los Angeles basin successfully use this method of dealing with pollution. The method provides an even stronger incentive than do emission charges to find technologies that pollute less because the price of a permit to pollute rises as the demand for permits increases.

Taxes

The government can use taxes as an incentive for producers to cut back on an activity that creates an external cost. By setting the tax rate equal to the marginal external cost, firms can be made to behave in the same way as they would if they bore the cost of the externality directly.

Pollution Trends

Air quality in the United States is getting better. Lead has been almost eliminated, and sulfur dioxide, carbon monoxide, and suspended particulates have been reduced substantially. But nitrogen dioxide and ozone have persisted at close to their 1975 levels.

The earth's average temperature has increased over the past 100 years, and most of the increase occurred before 1940. No one knows why this temperature increase has occurred, but some scientists believe the cause to be carbon dioxide emissions from road transportation and electric utilities, methane created by cows and other livestock, nitrous oxide emissions of electric utilities and from fertilizers, and chlorofluorocarbons (CFCs) from refrigeration equipment and (in the past) aerosols.

The ozone layer in the earth's atmosphere protects us from cancer-causing ultraviolet rays from the sun. A hole in the ozone layer over Antarctica is getting bigger. How our industrial activity influences the ozone layer is not well understood, but some scientists think that CFCs are one source of ozone layer depletion.

The largest sources of water pollution are the dumping of industrial waste and treated sewage in lakes and rivers and the runoff from fertilizers. A more dramatic source is the accidental spilling of crude oil into the oceans such as the *Exxon Valdez* spill in Alaska in 1989 and an even larger spill from the *Prestige* off Spain in 2002. The most frightening is the dumping of nuclear waste into the ocean by the former Soviet Union.

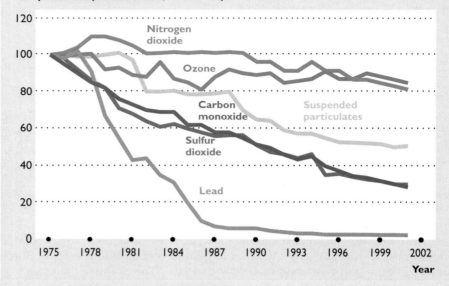

Air pollutants (index number, 1975 = 100)

SOURCE OF DATA: Environmental Protection Agency, *National Air Quality: 2001 Status and Trends,* 2002.

Land pollution arises from dumping toxic waste products. Ordinary household garbage does not pose a pollution problem unless dumped garbage seeps into the water supply. This possibility increases as less suitable landfill sites are used. It is estimated that 80 percent of existing landfills in the United States will be full by 2010.

Some densely populated regions (such as New York and New Jersey) and densely populated countries (such as Japan and the Netherlands), where land costs are high, are seeking less costly alternatives to landfill, such as recycling and incineration. Recycling is an apparently attractive alternative, but it requires an investment in new technologies to be effective. Incineration is a high-cost alternative to landfill, and it produces air pollution. These alternatives become efficient only when the cost of using landfills is high, as it is in densely populated regions and countries.

Effects of Government Actions

To see how government actions can change market outcomes in the face of externalities, let's return to the example of the chemical factories and houses alongside the river.

Assume that the government has assessed the marginal external cost of pollution accurately and imposes a tax on the chemical factories that exactly equals this external cost.

Figure 9.4 illustrates the effects of this pollution tax. The demand curve and marginal benefit curve $D = MB$ and the firms' marginal cost curve MC are the same as those in Figure 9.2. The pollution tax equals the marginal external cost of the pollution. We add this tax to marginal cost to find the market supply curve. This curve is the one labeled $S = MC + tax = MSC$. This curve is the market supply curve because it tells us the quantity of chemical supplied at each price given the firms' marginal cost and the pollution tax they must pay. This curve is also the marginal social cost curve because the pollution tax has been set equal to the marginal external cost.

Demand and supply now determine the market equilibrium price at $150 a ton and the equilibrium quantity at 2,000 tons of chemical a month. At this scale of chemical production, the marginal social cost is $150 a ton and the marginal benefit is $150 a ton, so the outcome is efficient. The firms incur a marginal cost of $88 a ton and pay a tax of $62 a ton. The government collects tax revenue of $124,000 a month.

▧ FIGURE 9.4

A Pollution Tax

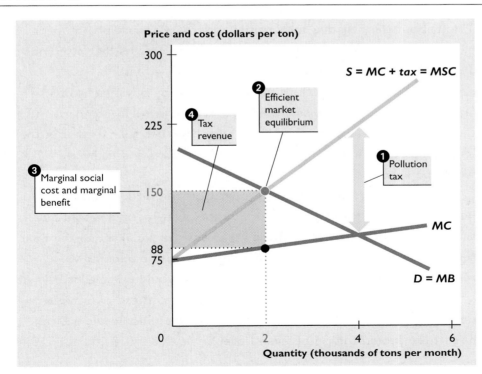

❶ A pollution tax is imposed that is equal to the marginal external cost of pollution. The supply curve becomes the marginal private cost curve, MC, plus the tax—the curve labeled $S = MC + tax$.

Because the pollution tax equals the marginal external cost, the supply curve is also the marginal social cost curve MSC.

❷ Market equilibrium is at a price of $150 a ton and a quantity of 2,000 tons a month and is efficient because ❸ marginal social cost equals marginal benefit.

❹ The government collects tax revenue shown by the purple rectangle.

E Y E ON THE G L O B A L   E C O N O M Y

A Carbon Fuel Tax?

The gasoline tax in the United Kingdom and in most other countries is much higher than that in the United States. Why don't we have a higher gas tax to encourage a large reduction in emissions?

Part of the reason is that many people don't accept the scientific evidence that emissions produce global warming. Climatologists are uncertain about how carbon emissions translate into atmospheric concentrations. And economists are uncertain about how a temperature increase translates into economic costs and benefits.

Another factor weighing against a large change in fuel use is that the costs are certain and would be borne now, while the benefits, if any, would come many years in the future.

A final factor working against a large change in fuel use is the international pattern and trend. Today, carbon pollution comes in equal doses from industrial and developing economies. But by 2050, three quarters of carbon pollution will come from the developing economies (if the trends persist).

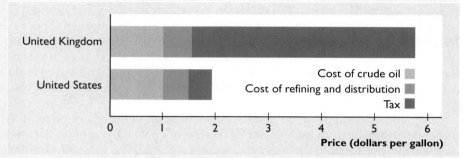

SOURCES OF DATA: Energy Information Administration and Automobile Association.

REALITY CHECK

Externalities in YOUR Life

Think about the negative and positive externalities that play a huge part in *your* life. And think about the sticks and carrots that attempt to align your self-interest with the social interest.

You respond to the stick of the gasoline tax by buying a little bit less gas than you otherwise would. This stick is small in comparison to that in most other countries. With a bigger gas tax, such as that in the United Kingdom, for example, traffic on our roads and highways would be lighter.

You are responding to the huge carrot of subsidized tuition by being in school. Faced with full-cost tuition, many people would quit school. Without subsidized college education (as you'll see in the next section), fewer people would have a degree and the benefits we all receive from living in a well-educated society would be smaller.

Think about your attitude as a citizen-voter to these two externalities. Have our politicians set the right incentives? Should the gas tax be higher? Should tuition be even lower?

CHECKPOINT 9.1

1 **Explain why negative externalities lead to inefficient overproduction and how property rights, pollution charges, and taxes can achieve a more efficient outcome.**

Practice Problem 9.1

1. Figure 1 illustrates the unregulated market for pesticide. When the factories produce pesticide, they also create waste, which they dump into a lake on the outskirts of the town. If the marginal external cost of the dumped waste is equal to the marginal private cost of producing the pesticide, then the marginal social cost of producing the pesticide is double the marginal private cost.
   a. What is the quantity of pesticide produced if no one owns the lake?
   b. What is the efficient quantity of pesticide?
   c. If the residents of the town own the lake, what is the quantity of pesticide produced and how much do the pesticide factories pay to residents of the town?
   d. If the pesticide factories own the lake, how much pesticide is produced?
   e. Suppose that no one owns the lake but that the government levies a pollution tax. What is the tax per ton of pesticide that will achieve the efficient outcome?

FIGURE 1

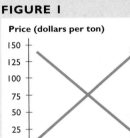

Exercise 9.1

1. Suppose that, in practice problem 9.1, the marginal external cost increases to twice the marginal private cost, so the marginal social cost of producing the pesticide is three times the marginal private cost. With no property rights, the government issues enough marketable permits to the town's residents to enable the factory to produce the efficient output of pesticide.
   a. How much pesticide gets produced?
   b. What is the price of a permit?
   c. How, if at all, would the outcome change if the government allocated the permits to the factories instead of to the town's residents?

Solution to Practice Problem 9.1

1a. The quantity of pesticide produced is 30 tons a week (Figure 2).
1b. The efficient quantity of pesticide is 20 tons a week. At the efficient quantity, the marginal benefit to the factories equals the marginal social cost, which is the sum of the marginal private cost and the marginal external cost. When the factories produce 20 tons a week, the marginal social cost is $100 a ton and the marginal benefit is $100 a ton.
1c. The quantity of pesticide produced is the efficient quantity, 20 tons a week, and the factories pay the townspeople the marginal external cost of $50 a ton.
1d. The factories produce the efficient quantity: 20 tons a week.
1e. A tax of $50 a ton will achieve the efficient quantity of pesticide produced.

FIGURE 2

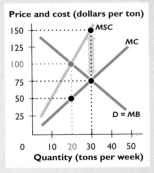

9.2 POSITIVE EXTERNALITIES: KNOWLEDGE

Knowledge comes from education and research. To study the economics of knowledge, we must distinguish between private benefits and social benefits.

■ Private Benefits and Social Benefits

A *private benefit* is a benefit that the consumer of a good or service receives. So **marginal private benefit** (*MB*) is the benefit from an additional unit of a good or service that the consumer of that good or service receives.

An *external benefit* is a benefit from a good or service that someone other than the consumer receives. A **marginal external benefit** is the benefit from an additional unit of a good or service that people other than the consumer enjoy.

Marginal social benefit (*MSB*) is the marginal benefit enjoyed by society—by the consumers of a good or service (marginal private benefit) and by others who benefit from it (the marginal external benefit). That is,

$$MSB = MB + \text{Marginal external benefit.}$$

Figure 9.5 shows an example of the relationship between marginal private benefit, marginal external benefit, and marginal social benefit. The marginal benefit curve, *MB*, describes the marginal private benefit—such as expanded job opportunities and higher incomes—enjoyed by college graduates. Marginal private benefit decreases as the quantity of education increases.

Marginal private benefit
The benefit from an additional unit of a good or service that the consumer of that good or service receives.

Marginal external benefit
The benefit from an additional unit of a good or service that people other than the consumer of the good or service enjoy.

Marginal social benefit
The marginal benefit enjoyed by society—by the consumers of a good or service and by everyone else who benefit from it. It is the sum of marginal private benefit and marginal external benefit.

■ FIGURE 9.5
An External Benefit

The *MB* curve shows the marginal private benefit enjoyed by the people who receive a college education. The *MSB* curve shows the sum of marginal private benefit and marginal external benefit.

When 15 million students attend college, ❶ marginal private benefit is $10,000 per student, ❷ marginal external benefit is $15,000 per student, and ❸ marginal social benefit is $25,000 per student.

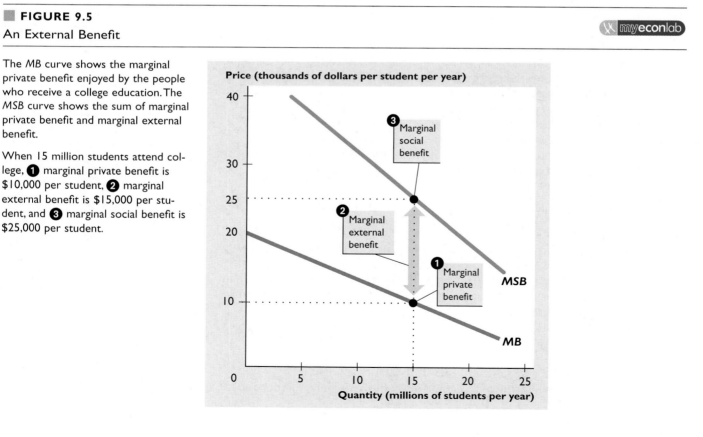

But college graduates generate external benefits. On the average, college graduates communicate more effectively with others and tend to be better citizens. Their crime rates are lower, and they are more tolerant of the views of others. And a society with a large number of college graduates can support activities such as high-quality music, theater, and other organized social activities.

In the example in Figure 9.5, the marginal external benefit is $15,000 per student per year when 15 million students enroll in college. The marginal social benefit curve, *MSB*, is the sum of marginal private benefit and marginal external benefit. For example, when 15 million students a year enroll in college, the marginal private benefit is $10,000 per student and the marginal external benefit is $15,000 per student, so the marginal social benefit is $25,000 per student.

When people make decisions about how much schooling to undertake, they ignore its external benefits and consider only its private benefits. The result is that if education were provided by private schools that charged full-cost tuition, we would produce too few college graduates.

Figure 9.6 illustrates the underproduction if the government left education to the private market. The supply curve is the marginal cost curve of the private schools, *S* = *MC*. The demand curve is the marginal private benefit curve, *D* = *MB*. Market equilibrium is at a tuition of $15,000 per student per year and 7.5 million students per year. At this equilibrium, marginal social benefit is $38,000 per student, which exceeds marginal cost by $23,000. Too few students enroll in college. The efficient number is 15 million, where marginal social benefit equals marginal cost. The gray triangle shows the deadweight loss created by the underproduction.

■ FIGURE 9.6

Inefficiency with an External Benefit

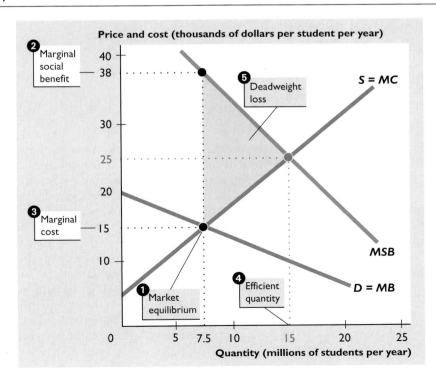

The market demand curve is the marginal private benefit curve, *D* = *MB*. The supply curve is the marginal cost curve, *S* = *MC*.

❶ Market equilibrium is at a tuition of $15,000 a year and 7.5 million students and is inefficient because ❷ marginal social benefit exceeds ❸ marginal cost.

❹ The marginal social benefit curve is *MSB*, so the efficient number of students is 15 million a year.

❺ The gray triangle shows the deadweight loss created because too few students enroll in college.

Underproduction similar to that in Figure 9.6 would occur at other levels of education—grade school and high school—if an unregulated market produced it. When children learn basic reading, writing, and number skills, they receive the private benefit of increased earning power. But even these basic skills bring the external benefit of developing better citizens.

External benefits also arise from research that leads to the discovery of new knowledge. When Isaac Newton worked out the formulas for calculating the rate of response of one variable to another—calculus—everyone was free to use his method. When a spreadsheet program called VisiCalc was invented, Lotus Corporation and Microsoft were free to copy the basic idea and create 1-2-3 and Excel. When the first shopping mall was built and found to be a successful way of arranging retailing, everyone was free to copy the idea, and malls spread like mushrooms.

Once someone has discovered how to do something, others can copy the basic idea. They do have to work to copy an idea, so they face an opportunity cost. But they do not usually have to pay the person who made the discovery to use it. When people make decisions about how much research to undertake, they ignore its external benefits and consider only its private benefits.

When people make decisions about the quantity of education or the amount of research to undertake, they balance the marginal private cost against the marginal private benefit. They ignore the external benefit. As a result, if we left education and research to unregulated market forces, we would get too little of these activities.

To get closer to producing the efficient quantity of a good or service that generates an external benefit, we make public choices, through governments, to modify the market outcome.

■ Government Actions in the Face of External Benefits

Four devices that governments can use to achieve a more efficient allocation of resources in the presence of external benefits, such as those that arise from education and research, are

- Public provision
- Private subsidies
- Vouchers
- Patents and copyrights

Public Provision

Public provision is the production of a good or service by a public authority that receives most of its revenue from the government. Education services produced by the public universities, colleges, and schools are examples of public provision.

Figure 9.7(a) shows how public provision might overcome the underproduction that arises in Figure 9.6. Public provision cannot lower the cost of production, so marginal cost is the same as before. Marginal private benefit and marginal external benefit are also the same as before.

The efficient quantity occurs where marginal social benefit equals marginal cost. In Figure 9.7(a), this quantity is 15 million students per year. Tuition is set to ensure that the efficient number of students enrolls. That is, tuition is set at the level that equals the marginal private benefit at the efficient quantity. In Figure 9.7(a), tuition is $10,000 a year. The rest of the cost of the public university is borne by the taxpayers and, in this example, is $15,000 per student per year.

Public provision
The production of a good or service by a public authority that receives most of its revenue from the government.

Private Subsidies

A **subsidy** is a payment by the government to a producer to cover part of the costs of production. By giving producers a subsidy, the government can induce private decision makers to consider external benefits when they make their choices.

Figure 9.7(b) shows how a subsidy to private colleges works. In the absence of a subsidy, the marginal cost curve is the market supply curve of private college education, $S = MC$. The marginal benefit is the demand curve, $D = MB$. In this example, the government provides a subsidy to colleges of $15,000 per student per year. We must subtract the subsidy from the marginal cost of education to find the colleges' supply curve. That curve is $S = MC - subsidy$ in the figure. The equilibrium tuition (market price) is $10,000 a year, and the equilibrium quantity is 15 million students. To educate 15 million students, colleges incur a marginal cost of $25,000 a year. The marginal social benefit is also $25,000 a year. So with marginal cost equal to marginal social benefit, the subsidy has achieved an efficient outcome. The tuition and the subsidy just cover the colleges' marginal cost.

Whether a public school operating on government-provided funds or a private school receiving a subsidy does a better job is a difficult question to resolve.

Subsidy
A payment by the government to a producer to cover part of the costs of production.

FIGURE 9.7

Public Provision or Private Subsidy to Achieve an Efficient Outcome

(a) Public provision

(b) Private subsidy

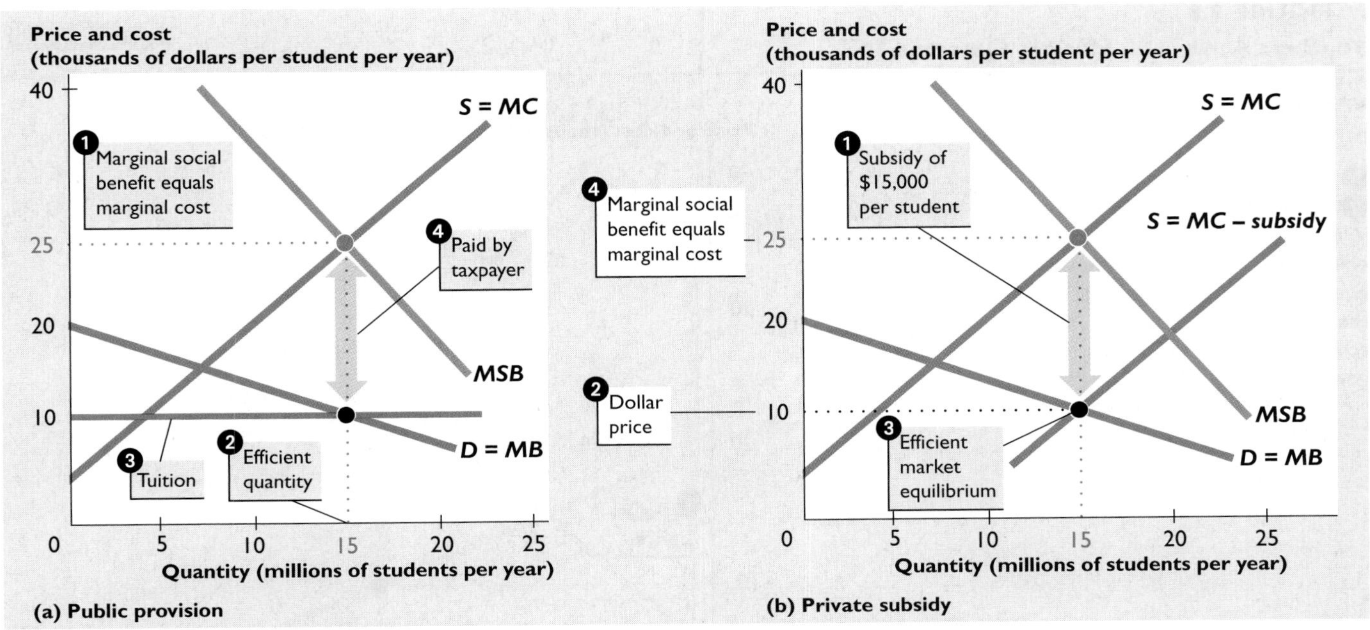

❶ Marginal social benefit equals marginal cost with 15 million students enrolled in college, the ❷ efficient quantity.

❸ Tuition is set at $10,000 per year, and ❹ the taxpayers cover the remaining $15,000 of marginal cost per student.

With a ❶ subsidy of $15,000 per student, the supply curve is $S = MC - subsidy$. ❷ The equilibrium price is $10,000, and ❸ the market equilibrium is efficient with 15 million students enrolled in college. ❹ Marginal social benefit equals marginal cost.

It turns on the efficiency of alternative mechanisms for monitoring school performance and on the strength of the incentives that school boards and private school operators have to deliver a high-quality service.

Vouchers

Voucher

A token that the government provides to households that can be used to buy specified goods or services.

A **voucher** is a token that the government provides to households, which they can use to buy specified goods or services. Food stamps that the U.S. Department of Agriculture provides under a federal Food Stamp Program are examples of vouchers. The vouchers (stamps) can be spent only on food and are designed to improve the diet and health of extremely poor families.

School vouchers have been advocated as a means of improving the quality of education and have been used in Cleveland and Milwaukee, though a proposition to introduce school vouchers in Michigan was defeated in the 2000 election.

A school voucher allows parents to choose the school their children will attend and to use the voucher to pay part of the cost. The school cashes the vouchers to pay its bills. A voucher could be provided to a college student in a similar way, and although technically not a voucher, a federal Pell Grant has a similar effect.

Because vouchers can be spent only on a specified item, they increase the willingness to pay for that item and so increase the demand for it. Figure 9.8 shows how a voucher system works. The government provides vouchers worth $15,000 per student per year. Parents (or students) use these vouchers to supplement the dollars they pay for college education. The market equilibrium occurs at a price of

---

FIGURE 9.8

Vouchers Achieve an Efficient Outcome

Ⓧ myeconlab

With vouchers, buyers are willing to pay *MB* plus the value of the voucher.

❶ With a voucher worth **$15,000,**
❷ the market equilibrium is efficient. With 15 million students enrolled in college, ❸ marginal social benefit equals marginal cost. The tuition, ❹ the dollar price, is $10,000 and the school collects $15,000 from the government.

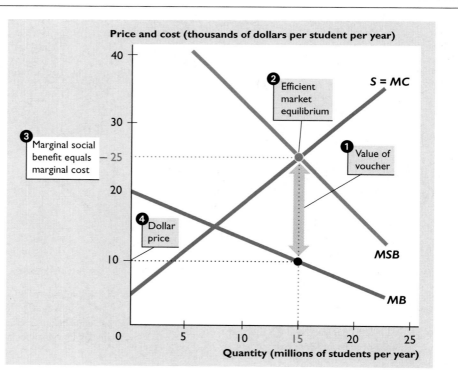

$25,000 per student per year and 15 million students attend college. Each student pays $10,000 tuition, and schools collect an additional $15,000 per student from the voucher.

If the government estimates the value of the external benefit correctly and makes the value of the voucher equal the marginal external benefit, the outcome from the voucher scheme is efficient. Marginal cost equals marginal social benefit, and the deadweight loss is eliminated.

Vouchers are similar to subsidies, but they provide the consumer rather than the producer with the financial resources. Advocates of vouchers say that they offer a more efficient outcome than subsidies do because the consumer can monitor school performance more effectively than the government can.

Patents and Copyrights

Every inventor benefits from previous inventions. Some inventions are so fundamental that they benefit many subsequent inventors. Some examples are calculus, invented by Newton and Leibniz, and the structure of DNA discovered by Crick and Watson. *Basic research* is the activity that leads to the development of these fundamental tools.

Research and development efforts build on the fruits of basic research to refine and improve on earlier advances. For example, each advance in knowledge about how to design and manufacture a processor chip for a PC has brought ever-larger increments in performance and productivity. Similarly, each advance in knowledge about how to design and build an airplane has brought ever larger increments in performance: Orville and Wilbur Wright's "Flyer 1" was a one-seat plane that could hop a farmer's field. The Lockheed Constellation could fly 120 passengers from New York to London, with two refueling stops, not much space, and a lot of noise and vibration. The latest Boeing 747 can carry 450 people nonstop from Los Angeles to Sydney or New York to Tokyo (flights of 7,500 miles that take 14 hours). Examples of the cumulative fruits of research and development efforts such as these can be found in fields as diverse as agriculture, biogenetics, communications, entertainment, medicine, and publishing.

Because discoveries build on previous discoveries, research generates external benefits. So it is necessary to use public policies to ensure that those who develop new ideas have incentives to encourage an efficient level of effort. The main way of providing the right incentives uses the central idea of the Coase theorem and assigns property rights—called **intellectual property rights**—to creators. The legal device for establishing intellectual property rights is the patent or copyright. A **patent** or **copyright** is a government-sanctioned exclusive right granted to the inventor of a good, service, or productive process to produce, use, and sell the invention for a given number of years. A patent enables the developer of a new idea to prevent others from benefiting freely from an invention for a limited number of years. But to obtain the protection of the law, an inventor must make knowledge of the invention public.

Although patents encourage invention and innovation, they do so at an economic cost. While a patent is in place, its holder has a monopoly. And monopoly is another source of inefficiency (which is explained in Chapter 14). But without patents, the effort to develop new goods, services, or processes is diminished and the flow of new inventions is slowed. So the efficient outcome is a compromise that balances the benefits of more inventions against the cost of temporary monopoly in newly invented activities.

Intellectual property rights
The property rights of the creators of knowledge and other discoveries.

Patent or copyright
A government-sanctioned exclusive right granted to the inventor of a good, service, or productive process to produce, use, and sell the invention for a given number of years.

2 **Explain why positive externalities lead to inefficient underproduction and how public provision, subsidies, vouchers, and patents can achieve a more efficient outcome.**

Practice Problem 9.2

FIGURE I

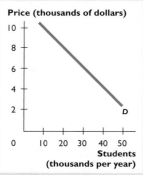

1. Figure 1 shows the marginal private benefit from college education. The marginal cost of a college education is a constant $6,000 a year. The marginal external benefit from a college education is $4,000 per student per year.
   a. If colleges are private and government has no involvement in college education, how many people will undertake a college education and what will be the tuition?
   b. What is the efficient number of students?
   c. If the government decides to provide public colleges, what tuition will these colleges charge to achieve the efficient number of students? How much will taxpayers have to pay?
   d. If the government decides to subsidize private colleges, what subsidy will achieve the efficient number of college students?
   e. If the government offers vouchers to those who enroll at a college and no subsidy, what is the value of the voucher that will achieve the efficient number of students?

FIGURE 2

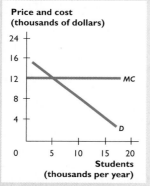

Exercise 9.2

1. Figure 2 shows the marginal private benefit from a law degree and the marginal cost of obtaining a law degree. The marginal external benefit is $8,000 per law graduate per year.
   a. If colleges are private and the government is not involved in educating lawyers, how many people enroll in law school and what is the tuition?
   b. What is the efficient number of law students?
   c. If the government decides to provide public law schools, what tuition will the public schools charge to achieve the efficient number of students?
   d. If the government decides to subsidize private law schools, what subsidy will achieve the efficient number of students?
   e. If the government offers vouchers to law students, what is the value of the voucher that will achieve the efficient number of students?

FIGURE 3

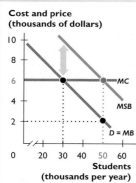

Solution to Practice Problem 9.2

1a. The tuition will be $6,000 a year, and 30,000 students will enroll—the intersection of the *MB* and *MC* curves (Figure 3).
1b. The efficient number of students is 50,000 a year—the intersection of the *MSB* and *MC* curves (Figure 3).
1c. To enroll 50,000 students, public colleges would charge $2,000 per student and taxpayers would pay $4,000 per student (Figure 3).
1d. The subsidy would be $4,000 per student, which is equal to the marginal external benefit.
1e. The value of the voucher will be $4,000. Enrollment will be 50,000 if the tuition is $2,000. But the private college tuition is $6,000, so to get 50,000 students to enroll, the value of the voucher will have to be $4,000.

CHAPTER CHECKPOINT

Key Points

1 Explain why negative externalities lead to inefficient overproduction and how property rights, pollution charges, and taxes can achieve a more efficient outcome.

- External costs are costs of production that fall on people other than the producer of a good or service. Marginal social cost equals marginal private cost plus marginal external cost.
- Producers take account only of marginal private cost and produce more than the efficient quantity when there is a marginal external cost.
- Sometimes it is possible to overcome a negative externality by assigning a property right.
- When property rights cannot be assigned, governments might overcome a negative externality by using emission charges, marketable permits, or taxes.

2 Explain why positive externalities lead to inefficient underproduction and how public provision, subsidies, vouchers, and patents can achieve a more efficient outcome.

- External benefits are benefits that are received by people other than the consumer of a good or service. Marginal social benefit equals marginal private benefit plus marginal external benefit.
- External benefits from education arise because better-educated people are better citizens, commit fewer crimes, and support social activities.
- External benefits from research arise because once someone has worked out a basic idea, others can copy.
- Vouchers or subsidies to private schools or the provision of public education below cost can achieve a more efficient provision of education.
- Patents and copyrights create intellectual property rights and an incentive to innovate. But they do so by creating a temporary monopoly, the cost of which must be balanced against the benefit of more inventive activity.

Key Terms

Coase theorem, 220
Copyright, 231
Externality, 214
Intellectual property rights, 231
Marginal external benefit, 226
Marginal external cost, 216

Marginal private benefit, 226
Marginal private cost, 216
Marginal social benefit, 226
Marginal social cost, 216
Negative externality, 214
Patent, 231

Positive externality, 214
Property rights, 219
Public provision, 228
Subsidy, 229
Transactions costs, 220
Voucher, 230

myeconlab

TABLE 1

Pollution cut (percentage)	Property taxes willingly paid (dollars per day)	Total cost of pollution cut (dollars per day)
0	0	0
10	150	10
20	285	25
30	405	45
40	510	70
50	600	100
60	675	135
70	735	175
80	780	220
90	810	270

TABLE 2

Students (millions per year)	Marginal private benefit (dollars per student per year)
1	5,000
2	3,000
3	2,000
4	1,500
5	1,200
6	1,000
7	800
8	500

Exercises

1. A city borders on a polluting steel mill. Table 1 shows the cost of cutting the pollution and the property taxes that people are willing to pay at different levels of pollution. Assume that the property taxes willingly paid measure the total benefit from cleaner air that results from the percentage cut in pollution.
   a. With no pollution control, how much pollution will there be?
   b. What is the efficient percentage decrease in pollution?
   c. If the city owns the steel mill, how much pollution will there be?
   d. If the city is a company town owned by the steel mill, how much pollution will there be?

2. Tom and Larry are working on a project that requires them to spend a day together. Tom likes to smoke, and his marginal benefit from one cigar a day is $20. The price of a cigar is $2. Larry dislikes cigar smoke, and his marginal benefit from a smoke-free environment is $25 a day. What is the outcome if
   a. They meet at Tom's home?
   b. They meet at Larry's home?

3. If in exercise 2, Tom's marginal benefit from one cigar a day is $25 and Larry's marginal benefit from a smoke-free environment is $20 a day, what is the outcome if they:
   a. Meet at Tom's home?
   b. Meet at Larry's home?

4. The marginal cost of educating a college student is $5,000 a year. Table 2 shows the marginal private benefit schedule from a college education. The marginal external benefit for college education is $2,000 per student per year.
   a. With no public colleges and no government involvement in college education, how many students will enroll and what is the tuition?
   b. If the government subsidizes private colleges and sets the subsidy so that the efficient number of students will enroll in college, what is the subsidy per student? How many students will enroll?
   c. If the government offers vouchers to students (but no subsidy to private colleges) and values the vouchers so that the efficient number of students will enroll in college, what is the value of the voucher? How many students will enroll?

5. For many people, distance education has cut the cost of a college education. If in exercise 4, an Internet course cuts the cost to $3,500 a year and increases the marginal external benefit to $3,000 per student per year, what now are your answers to exercise 4?

6. Suppose that researchers could not obtain patents for their discoveries.
   a. What do you think would happen to the pace of technological change?
   b. Would consumers' or producers' interests be damaged by a lack of patent protection?
   c. Would anyone gain?

7. Suppose that popular singers could not obtain copyrights for their recordings.
   a. What do you think would happen to the quantity and quality of recorded music?
   b. Would consumers be better off because they could buy cheaper CDs? Explain why or why not.

Critical Thinking

8. The Kyoto Protocol on greenhouse gas emissions was adopted at the United Nations Framework Convention on Climate Change in 1997. The major provision of the protocol is a set of national targets, with dates, for the reduction of greenhouse gas emissions. Countries with large amounts of emissions (of which the United States is one) have the most severe targets. The United States has steadfastly refused to ratify the Kyoto Protocol, but the European Union has ratified it.
   a. Why might the United States be reluctant to ratify the Kyoto Protocol?
   b. Why do you think the European Union was willing to ratify it?
   c. In light of the principles you've learned in this chapter, what types of data would you need to collect if you were to determine whether the emission target for the United States laid out in the Kyoto Protocol is efficient?
   d. What is your own view on whether the United States should ratify the Kyoto Protocol and why?

9. The price of gasoline in Europe is much higher than that in the United States, and the reason is that the gas tax is much higher in Europe than in the United States.
   a. What is the range of externalities that arise from automobiles?
   b. In light of the principles you've learned in this chapter, what is the case *for* increasing the gas tax in the United States to the European level?
   c. In light of the principles you've learned in this chapter, what is the case *against* increasing the gas tax in the United States to the European level?
   d. What is your view on whether the United States should raise the gas tax to the European level and why?

10. The debate over school vouchers often creates more heat than light.
    a. Why do you think that school vouchers are controversial?
    b. In light of the principles you've learned in this chapter, what is the case *for* replacing the existing school funding arrangements with vouchers?
    c. In light of the principles you've learned in this chapter, what is the case *against* replacing the existing school funding arrangements with vouchers?

11. It has been estimated that developing new technologies and figuring out how to use them account for more than half of economic growth—the expansion of production possibilities. In light of this fact:
    a. Do you think that the government should subsidize research and development?
    b. Do you think that the government should subsidize basic research?
    c. Do you think it would be a good idea to award prizes to firms for the successful development of a new technology?
    d. Do you think that firms should be given tax breaks for the successful development of a new technology?
    e. Do you think the patent laws should be strengthened so that the inventor of a new technology can be protected from competition for longer than is currently the case?
    f. Provide your own ranking of the alternatives in parts **a** through **e** along with the further alternative of leaving research and development to unregulated market forces. Explain your ranking, being explicit about your assumptions about the efficiency of each approach.

Web Exercises

Use the links on MyEconLab to work the following exercises.

12. Visit the EPA "Search Your Community" page. Enter your zip code in the box provided and press the "Submit" button.
    a. Obtain information about a negative production externality in your neighborhood.
    b. Explain which, if any, of the tools reviewed in this chapter the government is using to address this externality.
    c. Explain how the government's action will work or why you think it will not work. Use the concepts of marginal private cost, marginal external cost, marginal social cost, and efficiency in your explanation.
    d. If you think the current measures for dealing with this externality are not working or are not working well enough, what do you think needs to be done? Again, use the concepts of marginal private cost, marginal external cost, marginal social cost, and efficiency in your analysis.

13. Visit the EPA "Ground Water and Drinking Water" page.
    a. What types of externalities arise in the production of safe drinking water?
    b. Review and summarize the elements of the cost-benefit analysis that the EPA is undertaking on this issue.
    c. What do you think are the main outstanding issues to be resolved in ensuring the provision of safe drinking water in the United States? Use the concepts of marginal private cost, marginal external cost, marginal social cost, and efficiency in your analysis.

14. Visit the *Cape Cod Times* and read the article about wind farms off the New England coast.
    a. What types of externalities arise in the production of electricity using wind technologies?
    b. Comparing the externalities from wind technologies with those from burning coal and oil, which do you think are the more widespread and affect more people?
    c. How do you think the external costs of using wind technologies should be dealt with? Compare all the alternative methods suggested by the range of solutions considered in this chapter.
    d. Can you think of reasons why, despite the lower external costs, a campaign against the use of wind technology might be more successful than a campaign against the use of coal or oil?

15. Learn about the destruction of the habitat of the northern spotted owl.
    a. What production activity is creating problems for the northern spotted owl?
    b. What type of externalities arise from this production activity?
    c. How would you set about designing a method for dealing with this externality?

16. Visit the Global Policy site and read about the idea of introducing a carbon tax. Explain how a carbon tax might work. How would a carbon tax change the choices of Allegheny Electric and its customers? Who would bear the costs of the tax and who would enjoy the benefits?

Public Goods and Common Resources

Zanab has just finished loading her MP3 player with a bunch of tunes that she got from her friend Saacha. She doesn't know how Saacha gets so many great tunes, but he's always got the latest and shares them freely. But Zanab is worried. What if Saacha gets his files illegally and is sharing them with lots of people? That's not only illegal—it deprives artists and recording companies of incomes, and it might even dry up the supply of new tunes! Zanab is worrying about a "free-rider problem."

Tammy McCorkle loves her job as a Ranger Supervisor at the South Mountain Recreation Area on the Appalachian Trail. But Tammy is concerned about the state of the Annapolis Rock, a spot that towers above Cumberland Valley and offers breathtaking views. The repeated erection of tents and the incessant trampling of feet have left the rock totally devoid of plant life. And past camp fires and trash litter the cliffs. Tammy is worrying about a "tragedy of the commons."

You will study these two problems in this chapter.

10.1 CLASSIFYING GOODS AND RESOURCES

What's the difference between the services provided by the city police department and those provided by Brinks, a private security firm that loads ATMs for banks? What's the difference between fish in the Pacific Ocean and fish produced by East Point Seafood Company, a Seattle fish farm? What's the difference between a live Kelly Clarkson concert and a concert on network television? You will have several answers for these questions based on differences in your perceived quality of the items. But if we ignore such differences, a general answer is the same for each question: Each pair differs in the extent to which people can be *excluded* from consuming them and in the extent to which one person's consumption *rivals* the consumption of others.

■ Excludable

Excludable
A good, service, or resource is excludable if it is possible to prevent someone from enjoying its benefits.

A good, service, or resource is **excludable** if it is possible to prevent someone from enjoying its benefits. Brinks's security services, East Point Seafood's fish, and Kelly Clarkson concerts are examples. You must pay to consume them.

A good, service, or resource is **nonexcludable** if it is impossible (or extremely costly) to prevent someone from benefiting from it. The services of the city police department, fish in the Pacific Ocean, and a concert on network television are examples. When a police cruiser slows the traffic on a highway to the speed limit, it lowers the risk of an accident to all the road users. It can't exclude some road users from the lower risk. Anyone with a boat can try to catch the fish in the ocean. And anyone with a TV can watch a network broadcast.

Nonexcludable
A good, service, or resource is nonexcludable if it is impossible to prevent someone from benefiting from it.

■ Rival

Rival
A good, service, or resource is rival if its use by one person decreases the quantity available to someone else.

A good, service, or resource is **rival** if its use by one person decreases the quantity available for someone else. Brinks might work for two banks, but one truck can't deliver cash to two banks at the same time. A fish, whether in the ocean or on a fish farm, can be consumed only once. And one seat at a concert can hold only one person at a time. These items are rival.

A good, service, or resource is **nonrival** if its use by one person does not decrease the quantity available for someone else. The services of the city police department and a concert on network television are nonrival. The arrival of one more person in a neighborhood doesn't lower the level of police protection enjoyed by the community. And when one additional person switches on the TV, no other viewer is affected.

Nonrival
A good, service, or resource is nonrival if its use by one person does not decrease the quantity available to someone else.

■ A Fourfold Classification

Figure 10.1 classifies goods, services, and resources into four types using the two criteria that we've just considered.

Private Goods

Private good
A good or service that can be consumed by only one person at a time and only by the person who has bought it or owns it.

A good or service that is both rival and excludable (top left of Figure 10.1) is a **private good**: It can be consumed by only one person at a time and only by the person who has bought it or owns it. A can of Coke is an example of a private good. Only one person enjoys the benefits of a single can of Coke, and everyone except the person who bought the can is excluded from consuming it. The fish on East Point Seafood's farm are another example of a private good.

Public Goods

A good or service that is both nonrival and nonexcludable (bottom right of Figure 10.1) is a **public good**: It can be consumed simultaneously by everyone, and no one can be excluded from enjoying its benefits. A flood-control levee is an example of a public good. Everyone who lives in a protected flood plain enjoys the benefits, and no one can be excluded from receiving those benefits. The system of law and order provided by the courts and the body of laws is another example.

Public good
A good or service that can be consumed simultaneously by everyone and from which no one can be excluded.

Common Resources

A resource that is rival and nonexcludable (top right of Figure 10.1) is a **common resource**: A unit of it can be used only once, but no one can be prevented from using what is available. Ocean fish and the earth's atmosphere are examples of common resources. Ocean fish are rival because a fish taken by one person is not available for anyone else, and they are nonexcludable because it is difficult to prevent people from catching them. The earth's atmosphere is rival because oxygen used by one person is not available for anyone else, and it is nonexcludable because we can't prevent people from breathing!

Common resource
A resource that can be used only once, but no one can be prevented from using what is available.

Natural Monopolies

A good that is nonrival but excludable (bottom left of Figure 10.1) is a good produced by a *natural monopoly*. We define natural monopoly in Chapter 14, p. 346. A natural monopoly is a firm that can produce at a lower cost than two or more firms can. Examples are the Internet, cable television, and a bridge or tunnel. One more user doesn't decrease the enjoyment of the other users, and people can be excluded with user codes, scramblers, and tollgates.

▉ FIGURE 10.1
Fourfold Classification of Goods

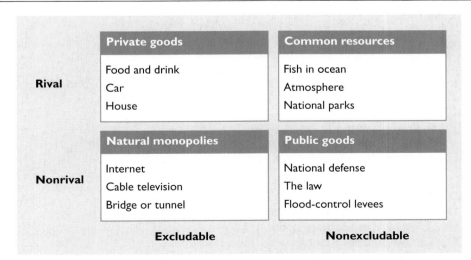

	Private goods	**Common resources**
Rival	Food and drink Car House	Fish in ocean Atmosphere National parks
	Natural monopolies	**Public goods**
Nonrival	Internet Cable television Bridge or tunnel	National defense The law Flood-control levees
	Excludable	**Nonexcludable**

Goods that are rival and excludable are private goods (top left).

Goods that are nonrival and nonexcludable are public goods (bottom right).

Goods and resources that are rival but nonexcludable are common resources (top right).

Goods that are nonrival but excludable are goods produced by a natural monopoly (bottom left).

SOURCE OF DATA: Adapted from and inspired by E. S. Savas, *Privatizing the Public Sector*, Chatham House Publishers, Inc., Chatham, NJ, 1982, p. 34.

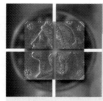
Is a Lighthouse a Public Good?

One of the great classical economists, John Stuart Mill, used the lighthouse as an example of a public good. And economists used Mill's example for two centuries, until it was challenged in 1974 by Ronald Coase (see p. 220). Coase discovered that before the nineteenth century, lighthouses in England were built and operated by private companies that earned profits by charging tolls on ships docking at nearby ports. A ship that refused to pay the lighthouse toll was excluded from using the port. So even the ser-

vices of a lighthouse, when it is near a port, are excludable! Such a lighthouse is an example of a natural monopoly, not a public good.

(see p. 220)

CHECKPOINT 10.1

ⓧ myeconlab

1   Distinguish among private goods, public goods, and common resources.

Practice Problem 10.1

1. Classify each of the following as a public good, a private good, or a common resource:
   a. Fire protection
   b. A Big Mac
   c. The Mississippi River

Exercise 10.1

1. Classify each of the following as a public good, a private good, or a common resource:
   a. The Grand Canyon
   b. Street lighting in urban areas
   c. Flood control in the Mississippi watershed
   d. A CD

Solution to Practice Problem 10.1

1a. Fire protection is a public good.
1b. A Big Mac is a private good.
1c. The Mississippi River is a common resource.

10.2 PUBLIC GOODS AND THE FREE-RIDER PROBLEM

Why does the U.S. government provide our national defense and district court system? Why do the state governments provide flood-control levees? Why do our city governments provide fire and police services? Why don't we buy our national defense from North Pole Protection, Inc., a private firm that competes for our dollars in the marketplace in the same way that McDonald's does? Why don't private engineering firms provide levees? Why don't we buy our policing and fire services from Brinks and other private firms? The answer is that all of these goods are public goods—goods that are nonexcludable and nonrival—and such goods create a free-rider problem.

■ The Free-Rider Problem

A **free rider** is a person who enjoys the benefits of a good or service without paying for it. Because everyone consumes the same quantity of a public good and no one can be excluded from enjoying its benefits, no one has an incentive to pay for it. Everyone has an incentive to free ride. The free-rider problem is that the private market, left on its own, would provide too small a quantity of a public good. To produce the efficient quantity, government action is required.

To see how a private market would provide too little of a public good and how government might provide the efficient quantity, we need to consider the marginal benefit and the marginal cost of a public good. The marginal benefit of a public good is a bit different from that of a private good, so we'll begin on the benefit side of the calculation.

Free rider
A person who enjoys the benefits of a good or service without paying for it.

Some public goods.

■ The Marginal Benefit of a Public Good

To learn about the marginal benefit of a public good, think about a concrete example. Lisa and Max share a common parking area that has no security lighting. Both of them would like some lights. But how many lights? What is the value or benefit of just one light, of adding a second, and perhaps of adding a third light? To answer this question, we must somehow combine the value of lights to both Lisa and Max and find the marginal benefit of different quantities of lights—the marginal benefit curve of lights.

For a private good, the marginal benefit curve is the market demand curve. But everyone pays the same market price for a private good and each person chooses the quantity they wish to buy at that price. In contrast, for a public good, everyone must consume the same quantity. But each person puts a different private value on that quantity. So how are we to find the equivalent of the demand curve for a public good? Figure 10.2 answers this question and illustrates the calculation of marginal benefit and the marginal benefit curve.

Lisa and Max know their own marginal benefit from different levels of security lighting. The tables in parts (a) and (b) of Figure 10.2 show these marginal benefits. The curves MB_L and MB_M are Lisa's and Max's marginal benefit curves. Each person's marginal benefit from a public good diminishes as the quantity of the good increases—just as it does for a private good. For Lisa, the marginal benefit from the first light is $80, and from the second it is $60. By the time 5 lights are installed, Lisa's marginal benefit is zero. For Max, the marginal benefit from the first light is $50, and from the second it is $40. By the time 5 lights are installed, Max perceives only $10 worth of marginal benefit.

The table in part (c) of Figure 10.2 shows the marginal benefit for the entire economy. We obtain this curve by summing the individual marginal benefits at each quantity. For example, with 3 lights, the marginal benefit is $70 ($40 for Lisa plus $30 for Max) and with 4 lights, the marginal benefit is $40 ($20 for Lisa plus $20 for Max). The curve MB is the marginal benefit curve.

Because we find the marginal benefit of a public good by summing the marginal benefits of all individuals at each *quantity*—we find the marginal benefit curve by summing the individual marginal benefit curves *vertically*. In contrast, to obtain the MB curve for a private good—which is also the market demand curve—we sum the quantities demanded by all individuals at each *price*—we sum the individual demand curves *horizontally* (see Chapter 4, p. 89).

Notice that the marginal benefit curve for a public good is both a marginal private benefit curve and marginal social benefit curve. A public good doesn't have external benefits (see Chapter 9, p. 226). Everyone consumes a public good in equal quantities, and everyone benefits from it. So the marginal benefit curve includes all the benefits. We could call it the marginal social benefit curve.

The principle that we've learned in this example of security lights for Lisa and Max applies to the marginal benefit of a public good such as national defense in our economy with its 290 million people. The marginal benefit of national defense is the sum of the marginal benefits of all 290 million people.

■ The Marginal Cost of a Public Good

The marginal cost of a public good is determined in exactly the same way as that of a private good. The principle of *increasing marginal cost* that you learned in Chapter 3 and Chapter 6 applies to the marginal cost of a public good. So the marginal cost curve of a public good slopes upward.

FIGURE 10.2

Marginal Benefit of a Public Good

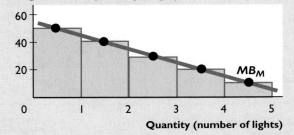

(a) Lisa's marginal benefit

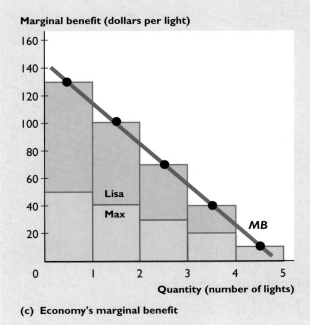

(b) Max's marginal benefit

(c) Economy's marginal benefit

The marginal benefit curves for a public good are MB_L for Lisa and MB_M for Max. The marginal benefit of the public good for the economy is the sum of the marginal benefits of all individuals at each quantity. The marginal benefit curve for the economy is MB.

Quantity of lights	0	1	2	3	4	5
Lisa's MB (dollars per light)		80	60	40	20	0

Quantity of lights	0	1	2	3	4	5
Max's MB (dollars per light)		50	40	30	20	10

Quantity of lights	0	1	2	3	4	5
Lisa's MB (dollars per light)		80	60	40	20	0
Max's MB (dollars per light)		50	40	30	20	10
Economy's MB (dollars per light)		130	100	70	40	10

■ The Efficient Quantity of a Public Good

To determine the efficient quantity, we use exactly the same principles that you first learned in Chapter 6 and that you've used repeatedly in Chapters 7 and 8. We find the quantity at which marginal benefit equals marginal cost.

Figure 10.3 shows the marginal benefit curve *MB* and marginal cost curve *MC* of surveillance satellites that provide national defense services. The *MB* curve is based on the same principle that determines the marginal benefit of the two-person (Lisa and Max) economy for security lights. If marginal benefit exceeds marginal cost, resources can be used more efficiently by increasing the quantity produced. If marginal cost exceeds marginal benefit, resources can be used more efficiently by decreasing the quantity produced. And if marginal benefit equals marginal cost, resources are being used efficiently. In this example, marginal benefit equals marginal cost with 200 satellites.

■ Private Provision: Underproduction

Could a private firm—say, North Pole Protection, Inc.—deliver the efficient quantity of satellites? Most likely, it couldn't because no one would have an incentive to buy his or her share of the satellite system. Everyone would reason as follows: "The number of satellites provided by North Pole Protection, Inc., is not affected by my decision to pay my share or not. But my own private consumption will be greater if I free ride and do not pay my share of the cost of the satellite system. If I do not pay, I enjoy the same level of security and I can buy more private goods. I will spend my money on private goods and free ride on the public good." Such reasoning is the free-rider problem. If everyone reasons the same way, North Pole Protection, Inc., has no revenue and so provides no satellites.

■ **FIGURE 10.3**

The Efficient Quantity and Private Underproduction of a Public Good   (X) myeconlab

❶ With fewer than 200 satellites, marginal benefit *MB* exceeds marginal cost *MC*. An increase in the quantity will make resource use more efficient.

❷ With more than 200 satellites, marginal cost exceeds marginal benefit. A decrease in the quantity will make resource use more efficient.

❸ With 200 satellites, marginal benefit *MB* equals marginal cost *MC*. Resource use is efficient.

❹ The efficient quantity is 200 satellites.

❺ Private provision leads to underproduction—in the extreme, to zero production.

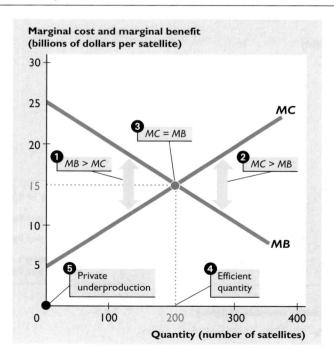

Public Provision: Efficient Production

The political process might be efficient or inefficient. We look first at an efficient outcome. There are two political parties, the Hawks and the Doves, which agree on all issues except for the quantity of defense satellites. The Hawks want 300 satellites, and the Doves want 100 satellites. But both parties want to get elected, so they run a voter survey and discover the marginal benefit curve of Figure 10.4. They also consult with satellite producers to establish the marginal cost schedule. The parties then do a "what-if" analysis. If the Hawks propose 300 satellites and the Doves propose 100 satellites, the voters will be equally unhappy with both parties. Compared to the efficient quantity, the Doves want an underprovision of 100 satellites and the Hawks want an overprovision of 100 satellites. The dead-weight losses are equal. So the election would be too close to call.

Contemplating this outcome, the Hawks realize that they are too hawkish to get elected. They figure that if they scale back to 250 satellites, they will win the election if the Doves propose 100 satellites. The Doves reason in a similar way and figure that if they increase the number of satellites to 150, they can win the election if the Hawks propose 300 satellites. But each party knows how the other is reasoning. And they each realize that they must provide 200 satellites, or they will lose the election. So they both propose 200 satellites. The voters are indifferent between the parties, and each party receives 50 percent of the vote.

FIGURE 10.4
An Efficient Political Outcome

(a) Parties' preferences

(b) Political outcome

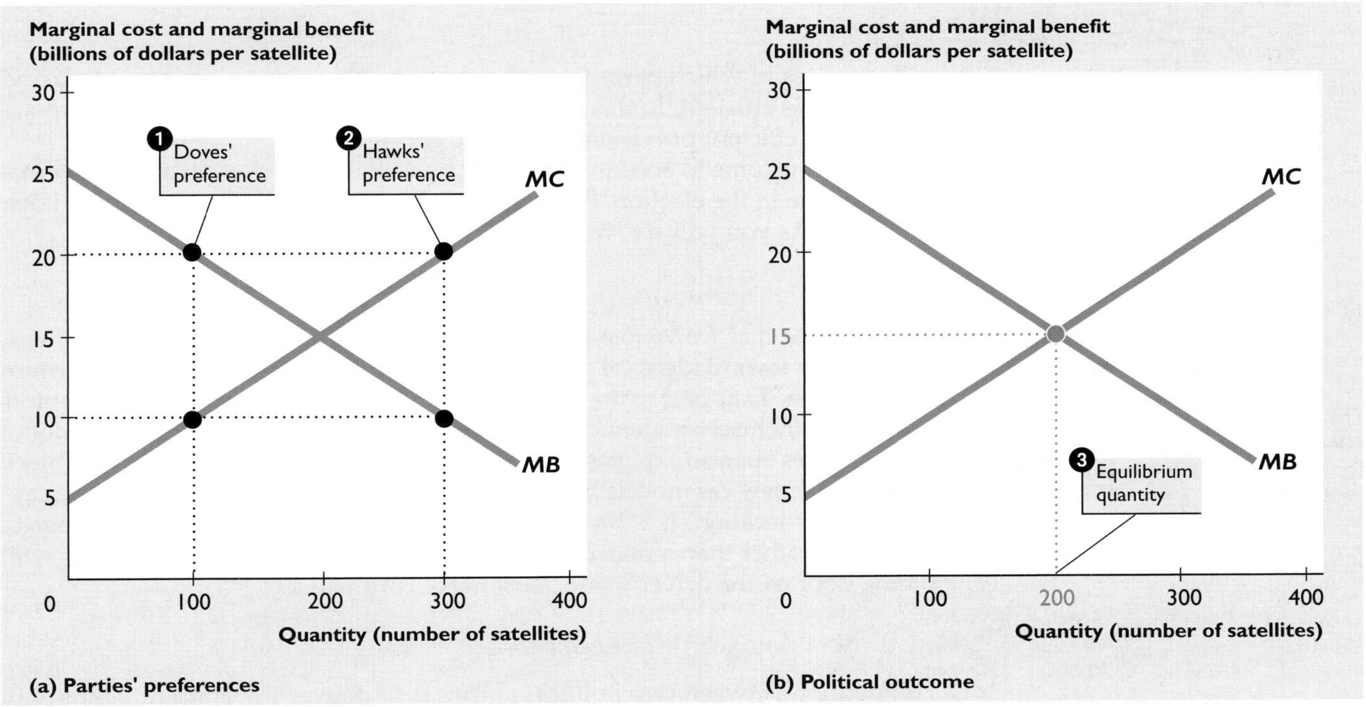

1 The Doves would like to provide 100 satellites. **2** The Hawks would like to provide 300 satellites.

3 The political outcome is 200 satellites because unless each party proposes 200 satellites, the other party can beat it in an election.

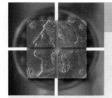
Defense Spending

Following the terrorist attacks of September 11, 2001, defense spending increased yet again. But the increase was much smaller than those of the 1960s and 1980s.

The marginal benefit of national defense changes as global events change the demands placed on the military.

During the Vietnam War, U.S. defense spending increased to more than 9 percent of total income. During the early 1970s, successive administrations pursued dialog with China and arms reduction agreements with the Soviet Union and U.S. defense spending as a percentage of total income decreased.

During the early 1980s, the Reagan administration increased the pressure on the Soviet Union and increased defense spending.

The end of the Cold War brought further defense spending cuts during the 1990s.

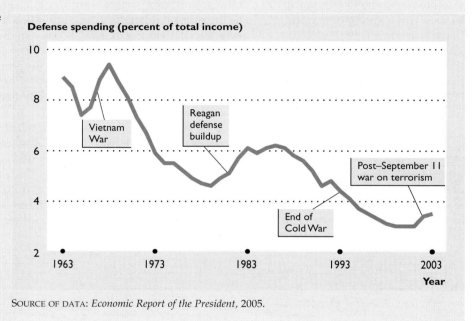

Defense spending (percent of total income)

SOURCE OF DATA: *Economic Report of the President*, 2005.

Regardless of which party wins the election, 200 satellites are provided. And this quantity is efficient. In this example, competition in the political marketplace results in the efficient provision of a public good.

For this outcome to occur, voters must be well informed, evaluate the alternatives, and vote in the election. Political parties must be well informed about voter preferences. As you will see, we can't expect to achieve this outcome.

The Principle of Minimum Differentiation

Principle of minimum differentiation
The tendency for competitors to make themselves identical to appeal to the maximum number of clients or voters.

In the example that we've just studied, the two parties propose identical policies. This tendency toward identical policies is an example of the **principle of minimum differentiation**: To appeal to the maximum number of clients or voters, competitors tend to make themselves identical. This principle not only describes the behavior of political parties but also explains why fast-food restaurants cluster in the same block and even why new car models have similar features. If McDonald's opens a restaurant in a new location, it is more likely that Burger King will open next door to McDonald's rather than a mile down the road. If Chrysler designs a new van with a sliding door on the driver's side, most likely Ford will too.

■ Public Provision: Overproduction

If competition between two political parties is to deliver the efficient quantity of satellites, the Defense Department—the Pentagon—must cooperate and help to achieve this outcome.

Objective of Bureaucrats

A bureau head wants to maximize her or his department's budget. A bigger budget brings greater status and power. So the Pentagon's objective is to maximize the defense budget.

Figure 10.5 shows the outcome if the Pentagon is successful in the pursuit of its goal. The Pentagon might try to persuade the politicians that 200 satellites cost more than the originally budgeted amount; or the Pentagon might press its position more strongly and argue for more than 200 satellites. In Figure 10.5, the Pentagon persuades the politicians to go for 300 satellites.

Why don't the politicians block the Pentagon? Won't overproducing satellites cost future votes? It will if voters are well informed and know what is best for them. But voters might not be well informed. And well-informed interest groups might enable the Pentagon to achieve its objective and overcome the objections of the politicians.

Rational Ignorance

Rational choice balances marginal benefit and marginal cost. An implication of rational choice is that it is rational for a voter to be ignorant about an issue unless that issue has a perceptible effect on the voter's well-being. **Rational ignorance** is the decision not to acquire information because the marginal cost of doing so exceeds the marginal benefit. For example, each voter in the United States knows that he or she can make virtually no difference to the defense policy of the U.S. government. Each voter also knows that it would take an enormous amount of

Rational ignorance
The decision not to acquire information because the marginal cost of doing so exceeds the marginal benefit.

FIGURE 10.5

Inefficient Bureaucratic Overproduction

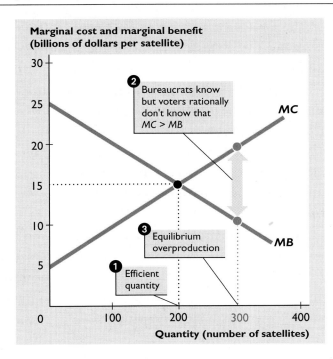

❶ The efficient quantity is 200 satellites with marginal benefit *MB* equal to marginal cost *MC*.

❷ Bureaucrats are well-informed and voters are rationally ignorant, so bureaucrats are able to increase production (and their budget) to a level at which marginal cost *MC* exceeds marginal benefit *MB*.

❸ With 300 satellites, marginal cost exceeds marginal benefit. Inefficient overproduction occurs.

time and effort to become even moderately well informed about alternative defense technologies. So voters remain relatively uninformed about the technicalities of defense issues. (Although we are using defense policy as an example, the same principle applies to all aspects of government economic activity.)

All voters benefit from national defense. But not all voters produce national defense—only a small number work in the defense industry. Voters who own or work for firms that produce satellites have a direct personal interest in defense because it affects their incomes. These voters have an incentive to become well informed about defense issues and to lobby politicians to further their own interests. In collaboration with the defense bureaucracy, these voters exert a larger influence on public policy than do the relatively uninformed voters who only benefit from this public good.

Why Government Is Large

Now that you know how the quantity of a public good is determined, you can explain part of the reason why government is large: inefficient overproduction of public goods. Once a bureaucracy gets established, its goal of budget maximization combined with voters' rational ignorance explains why the government takes a large proportion of total income.

REALITY CHECK

A Free-Rider Problem in YOUR Life

We've studied a free-rider problem for which public provision is a solution. But what about Zanab's free-rider problem (and possibly yours) that arises from sharing music files?

The legal right to copy an MP3 file is restricted by the copyright laws. But these files are nonrival because they can be illegally copied and shared at the click of a mouse.

An MP3 file isn't as nonexcludable as national defense, but it is costly to exclude anyone who wants to copy a file. So MP3 files create a free-rider problem.

Should we try to solve this problem by having the government provide our pop, jazz, rock, and classical music? Not a good idea! Can you imagine Donald Rumsfeld telling Alicia Keys what her next record will be?

The government could make everyone who buys an MP3 player pay a tax and use the revenue to compensate artists and recording companies. But the best solution is for the government to uphold property rights so that recording companies can pursue illegal file sharers and hit them with large penalties.

CHECKPOINT 10.2

2 Explain the free-rider problem and how public provision might help to overcome that problem.

Practice Problems 10.2

1. For each of the following goods, explain whether there is a free-rider problem. If there is no such problem, how is it avoided?
   a. Fire protection
   b. July 4th fireworks display
   c. Interstate 80 in rural Wyoming

2. Table 1 provides information about a mosquito control program.
   a. What quantity of spraying would a private mosquito control program provide?
   b. What is the efficient quantity of spraying?
   c. In a single-issue election on the quantity of spraying, what quantity would the winner of the election provide?

TABLE 1

Quantity (square miles sprayed per day)	Marginal cost (dollars per day)	Marginal benefit (dollars per day)
0	0	0
1	1,000	5,000
2	2,000	4,000
3	3,000	3,000
4	4,000	2,000
5	5,000	1,000

Exercises 10.2

1. For each of the following goods, explain whether there is a free-rider problem. If there is no such problem, how is it avoided?
   a. The Grand Canyon
   b. Street lighting in urban areas
   c. Flood control in the Mississippi watershed
   d. The beach at Santa Monica

2. Table 2 provides information about fire protection in Amarillo, Texas.
   a. What quantity of fire protection would a private company provide?
   b. What is the efficient quantity of fire protection?
   c. In a single-issue election on the quantity of fire protection, what quantity would the winner of the election provide?

TABLE 2

Quantity (number of fire stations)	Marginal cost (cents per $100 of property per year)	Marginal benefit (cents per $100 of property per year)
0	0	0
1	2.08	60.00
2	3.04	30.00
3	4.00	10.00
4	4.06	4.06
5	5.12	3.00

Solutions to Practice Problems 10.2

1a. Fire protection is a public good.
1b. July 4th fireworks display is a public good.
   In parts **a** and **b**, the free-rider problem is avoided by public provision and financing through taxes.
1c. Interstate 80 in rural Wyoming is a public good. The public good creates a free-rider problem that is avoided because governments collect various taxes via the tax on gas and the vehicle registration fee.

2a. A private mosquito control program would provide zero spraying because the free-rider problem would prevail.
2b. The efficient quantity is 3 square miles a day—the quantity at which the marginal benefit equals the marginal cost.
2c. The winner will provide the efficient quantity: 3 square miles sprayed a day.

10.3 COMMON RESOURCES

Atlantic Ocean cod stocks have been declining since the 1950s, and some marine biologists fear that this species is in danger of becoming extinct in some regions. The whale population of the South Pacific has been declining also, and some groups are lobbying to establish a whale sanctuary in the waters around Australia and New Zealand to regenerate the population. Since the start of the Industrial Revolution in 1750, the concentration of carbon dioxide in the atmosphere has steadily increased. It is estimated that it is about 30 percent higher today than it was in 1750.

These situations involve common property, and the problem that we have identified is called the "tragedy of the commons."

■ The Tragedy of the Commons

Tragedy of the commons
The absence of incentives to prevent the overuse and depletion of a commonly owned resource.

The **tragedy of the commons** is the absence of incentives to prevent the overuse and depletion of a commonly owned resource. If no one owns a resource, no one considers the effects of her or his use of the resource on others. To appreciate the tragedy of the commons, we'll look at a concrete example: fishing for cod in the North Atlantic Ocean.

Figure 10.6 illustrates the relationship between the number of boats and the sustainable quantity of fish caught. As the number of boats increases from zero to 5,000, the sustainable catch increases to a maximum of 250,000 tons a month. As the number of boats increases above 5,000, the sustainable catch begins to

---

■ FIGURE 10.6

Sustainable Production of Fish

As the number of boats increases, the quantity of fish caught increases, but only up to some maximum sustainable catch. Beyond that level, more boats mean a diminished stock of fish and a smaller sustainable catch.

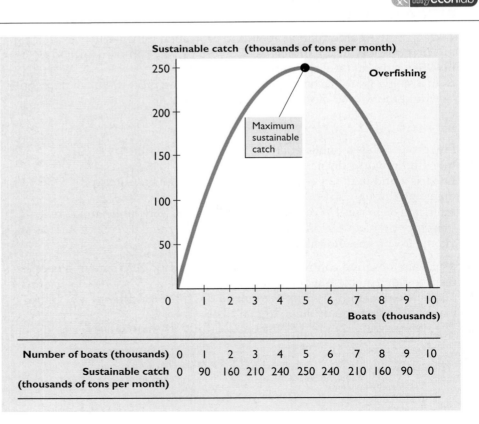

Number of boats (thousands)	0	1	2	3	4	5	6	7	8	9	10
Sustainable catch (thousands of tons per month)	0	90	160	210	240	250	240	210	160	90	0

decrease. By the time 10,000 boats are fishing, the fish stock is depleted to the point at which no fish are available. In the region above 5,000 boats, there is overfishing. Overfishing arises if the number of boats increases to the point at which the fish stock begins to decrease so the remaining fish are harder to find and catch.

Why would overfishing occur? Why isn't the maximum number of boats that take to the sea 5,000, the number that maximizes the sustainable catch? To answer this question, we need to look at the marginal cost and marginal benefit to an individual fisher: marginal private benefit.

Suppose that the marginal cost of a fishing boat is the equivalent of 20 tons of fish per month. That is, if a fishing boat can catch at least 20 tons a month, the boat owner earns a producer surplus and is willing to go fishing. Figure 10.7 shows the marginal cost curve labeled *MC*.

The marginal private benefit is the quantity of fish that one boat can catch in a month. This quantity depends on the number of boats being used. To calculate it, we divide the total catch by the number of boats. The table in Figure 10.7 shows this calculation. One boat catches 100 tons a month. With 1,000 boats, the total catch is 90,000 tons and the catch per boat is 90 tons. With 2,000 boats, the total catch is 160,000 tons and the catch per boat is 80 tons. As more boats take to the ocean, the catch per boat decreases. By the time there are 8,000 boats, each boat is catching just 20 tons a month. Figure 10.7 shows the marginal private benefit curve, *MPB*.

You can see in Figure 10.7 that with fewer than 8,000 boats, each boat catches more fish than it costs to catch them. Because boat owners can gain from fishing, the number of boats increases to 8,000 and there is an overfishing equilibrium.

FIGURE 10.7
Why Overfishing Occurs

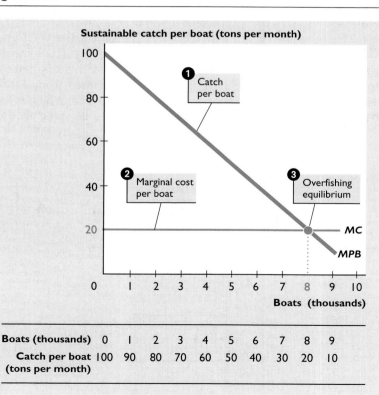

❶ The catch per boat (total catch divided by number of boats) decreases as the number of boats increases. The catch per boat is the marginal private benefit, *MPB*, of a boat.

❷ The marginal cost of a boat is equivalent to 20 tons of fish a month, shown by the curve *MC*.

❸ The equilibrium quantity of boats is 8,000, which means there is an overfishing equilibrium.

Boats (thousands)	0	1	2	3	4	5	6	7	8	9
Catch per boat (tons per month)	100	90	80	70	60	50	40	30	20	10

■ The Efficient Use of the Commons

The quantity of fish caught by each boat decreases as additional boats are introduced. But when individual boat owners are deciding whether to fish, they ignore this decrease. Only the marginal *private* benefit is considered. The result is an *inefficient* overuse of the resource. What is the efficient use of the resource? To answer this question, we need to know the marginal *social* benefit of a boat.

Marginal Social Benefit

The marginal social benefit of a boat is the increase in the total fish catch that results from an additional boat, not the catch per boat. Table 10.1 summarizes the calculation of marginal social benefit. The marginal social benefit is the change in the total catch divided by the change in the number of boats. For example, in rows *C* and *D* of the table, when the number of boats increases by 1,000, the catch increases by 50,000 tons, so the increase in the catch per boat equals 50 tons. In the table, we place this amount midway between the two rows because it is the marginal social benefit at 2,500 boats, midway between the two levels that we used to calculate it. The other numbers in the table are calculated in a similar way.

Figure 10.8 shows marginal social benefit as the *MSB* curve and the marginal private benefit curve, *MPB*. Notice that at any given number of boats, marginal social benefit is less than marginal private benefit. Each boat benefits privately from the average catch, but the addition of one more boat *decreases* the catch of every boat, and this decrease must be subtracted from the catch of the additional boat to determine the social benefit from the additional boat.

Efficient Use

Figure 10.8 also shows the marginal cost curve, *MC*, and the efficient use of the resource. Resource use is efficient when marginal social benefit equals marginal cost. This outcome occurs with 4,000 boats, each catching 60 tons of fish a month. You can see in Table 10.1 that when the number of boats increases from 3,000 to 4,000 (3,500 being the midpoint), marginal social benefit is 30 tons, which exceeds marginal cost. When the number of boats increases from 4,000 to 5,000 (4,500 being the midpoint), marginal social benefit is 10 tons, which is less than marginal cost. At 4,000 boats, marginal social benefit is 20 tons, which equals marginal cost.

■ TABLE 10.1

Marginal Social Benefit of a Common Resource

The marginal social benefit of a fishing boat is the change in total benefit that results from an additional boat. For example, when the number of boats increases from 1,000 to 2,000 (row *B* to row *C*), the total catch increases from 90,000 to 160,000 tons a month, an increase of 70,000 tons a month, so the marginal social benefit of one boat is 70 tons of fish.

	Boats (thousands)	Total catch (thousands of tons)	Marginal social benefit (tons per boat)
A	0	0	
			90
B	1	90	
			70
C	2	160	
			50
D	3	210	
			30
E	4	240	
			10
F	5	250	

FIGURE 10.8
Efficient Use of a Common Resource

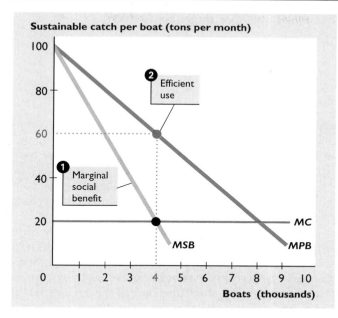

Sustainable catch per boat (tons per month)

❶ The marginal *social* benefit, *MSB*, of a boat (increase in total catch divided by increase in number of boats) decreases as the number of boats increases. For any quantity of boats, the marginal social benefit of a boat is *less* than the marginal private benefit, *MPB*.

❷ The efficient quantity of boats is 4,000, and the sustainable catch is 60 tons per boat.

EYE ON THE PAST

The Commons of England's Middle Ages

The term "the tragedy of the commons" comes from fourteenth century England, where areas of rough grassland surrounded villages. The commons were open to all and were used for grazing cows and sheep owned by the villagers.

Because the commons were open to all, no one had an incentive to ensure that the land was not overgrazed. The result was an overgrazing situation similar to that of overfishing in some of today's oceans.

During the sixteenth century, when the price of wool increased, England became a wool exporter to the world.

Sheep farming became profitable, and sheep owners needed better control of the land they used. So the commons were gradually enclosed and privatized. Overgrazing ended, and land use became more efficient.

■ Achieving an Efficient Outcome

Defining the conditions under which a common resource is used efficiently is easier than bringing those conditions about. To use a common resource efficiently, three main methods might be used:

- Property rights
- Quotas
- Individual transferable quotas (ITQs)

Property Rights

A common resource that no one owns and that anyone is free to use contrasts with *private property,* which is a resource that *someone* owns and has an incentive to use in the way that maximizes its value. One way of overcoming the tragedy of the commons is to remove the commons and make it private property. By assigning private property rights, each owner faces the same conditions as society faces. The *MSB* curve of Figure 10.8 becomes the marginal *private* benefit curve, and the use of the resource is efficient.

The private property solution to the tragedy of the commons *is* available in some cases—see *Eye on the Past* on p. 253. A modern example is the airwaves that we use to carry our cell phone messages. The right to use this space—called the frequency spectrum—has been auctioned by governments to the highest bidders, and the owner of a particular part of the spectrum is the only one who is permitted to use it (or license someone else to use it).

But this solution is not always available. It would be difficult, for example, to assign private property rights to the oceans. It would not be impossible, but the cost of enforcing private property rights over thousands of square miles of ocean would be high. And it would be even harder to assign and protect private property rights to the atmosphere. When private property rights are too costly to assign and enforce, some form of government intervention is used, and quotas are the simplest.

Quotas

A *quota* is an upper limit to the quantity of a good that may legally be produced in a specified period. If a quota is set below the efficient output level, it drives a wedge between marginal benefit and marginal cost and is inefficient. But in the case of the use of common property, the market is inefficient because it is overproducing. So a quota that limits production can bring a move toward a more efficient outcome.

Figure 10.9(a) shows a quota that achieves an efficient use of a common resource. A quota is set for total production at the quantity at which marginal social benefit equals marginal cost. Here, that quantity is what 4,000 boats can produce. Individual boat owners are assigned their own share of the total permitted catch. If everyone sticks to the assigned quota, the outcome is efficient.

But everyone has an incentive to cheat on the assigned quota. The reason is that marginal private benefit exceeds marginal cost. So by catching more than the allocated quota, each boat owner gets a higher income. If everyone breaks the quota, overproduction returns and the tragedy of the commons remains. A simple quota can work only if the production of each person can be monitored. Where producers are hard to monitor, the quota breaks down.

Individual Transferable Quotas

Where producers are hard to monitor, a more sophisticated quota system can be used. An **individual transferable quota (ITQ)** is a production limit that is assigned to an individual, who is free to transfer the quota to someone else. A market in ITQs emerges, and ITQs are transferred at their market price.

Figure 10.9(b) shows how ITQs work. In the market for ITQs, the price is the highest price that an ITQ is worth. If the number of ITQs issued equals the efficient production level, that price will equal the amount shown in the figure. This price equals the marginal private benefit at the quota quantity minus the private marginal cost of using a boat. The price rises to this level because people who don't have a quota would be willing to pay this amount to acquire the right to fish. And people who do own a quota could sell it for this price, so to not sell it is to incur an opportunity cost. The result is that the marginal cost, which now includes the cost of the ITQ, rises from MC_0 to MC_1. The equilibrium is efficient.

ITQs have been used extensively by New Zealand and Australia to conserve fish stocks in the South Pacific Ocean, and they have a good record. People still have an incentive to cheat and produce more than the amount for which they have a quota. But such cheating is rare because the ITQs are well policed from the air.

> **Individual transferable quota (ITQ)**
> A production limit that is assigned to an individual, who is free to transfer the quota to someone else.

FIGURE 10.9
Two Ways of Coping with the Tragedy of the Commons

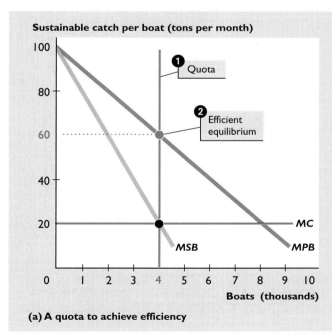

(a) A quota to achieve efficiency

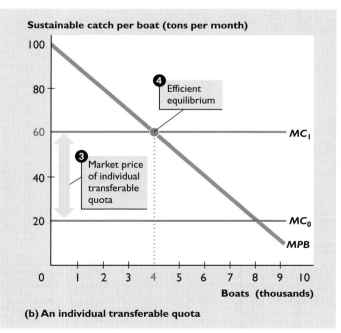

(b) An individual transferable quota

1 A quota is set at the efficient quantity, which makes the number of boats equal to the quantity at which marginal social benefit, *MSB*, equals marginal cost, *MC*. **2** If the quota is not broken, the outcome is efficient.

ITQs are issued on a scale that keeps output at the efficient level and **3** the market price of an ITQ equals the marginal private benefit minus marginal cost. **4** The outcome is efficient.

3 **Explain the tragedy of the commons and review the possible solutions to that problem.**

Practice Problem 10.3

TABLE 1

Number of cows	Milk output (gallons per day)
100	300
200	500
300	600
400	600
500	500
600	300
700	0

1. In an English village in 1375, cows graze on common pasture and can produce milk in the amounts shown in Table 1. The marginal private cost of a cow is zero.
   a. What is the marginal private benefit at each quantity of cows?
   b. What is the equilibrium number of cows?
   c. What is the marginal social benefit at each quantity of cows?
   d. What are the efficient number of cows and quantity of milk to produce?
   e. If the common pasture were converted to private land and fenced off, how many cows would the landowner keep?
   f. If ITQs were issued for the efficient quantity of milk production, what would be the market price of an ITQ?

Exercise 10.3

TABLE 2

Number of wells	Oil output (gallons per day)
0	0
2	12
4	22
6	30
8	36
10	40
12	42
14	42

1. An oil reserve runs under plots of land owned by seven people. Each person has the right to sink a well on her or his land and take oil from the reserve. The amount of oil that is produced depends on the number of wells sunk and is shown in Table 2. The marginal private cost of a well is 4 gallons a day.
   a. What is the marginal private benefit at each quantity of wells?
   b. What are the equilibrium number of wells and quantity of oil produced?
   c. What is the marginal social benefit at each quantity of wells?
   d. What are the efficient number of wells and quantity of oil to produce?
   e. If the common reserve were owned by only one person, how many wells would be sunk and how much oil would be produced?
   f. How much would someone offer the seven owners to rent the rights to all the oil in the common reserve? (Use gallons of oil as the units.)

Solution to Practice Problem 10.3

TABLE 3

Number of cows	Milk output (gallons per day)	MSB (gallons per cow)	MPB (gallons per cow)
0	0		—
		3	
100	300		3.0
		2	
200	500		2.5
		1	
300	600		2.0
		0	
400	600		1.5
		−1	
500	500		1.0
		−2	
600	300		0.5
		−3	
700	0		0

1a. Table 3 shows the marginal private benefit per cow.
1b. The equilibrium number of cows is 700, and no milk is produced.
1c. Table 3 shows the marginal social benefit at each quantity of cows.
1d. The efficient number of cows is the number at which marginal social benefit is zero and equals marginal cost. This number of cows is 350 (midway between 300 and 400 cows in the table). The efficient quantity of milk is the milk output of 350 cows, which is 600 gallons a day.
1e. If the common pasture were converted to private land and fenced off, the landowner would keep 350 cows because the milk output is maximized at this number of cows.
1f. The market price of an ITQ would be 1.75 gallons of milk (midway between 2.0 and 1.5 gallons per cow in the table). This price is the marginal private benefit at the efficient quantity minus marginal cost, which is zero.

CHAPTER CHECKPOINT

Key Points

1 **Distinguish among private goods, public goods, and common resources.**

- A private good is a good or service that is rival and excludable.
- A public good is a good or service that is nonrival and nonexcludable.
- A common resource is a resource that is rival but nonexcludable.

2 **Explain the free-rider problem and how public provision might help to overcome that problem.**

- A public good creates a free-rider problem—no one has a private incentive to pay her or his share of the cost of providing a public good.
- The efficient level of provision of a public good is that at which marginal benefit equals marginal cost.
- Competition between political parties, each of which tries to appeal to the maximum number of voters, can lead to the efficient scale of provision of a public good and to both parties proposing the same policies—the principle of minimum differentiation.
- Bureaucrats try to maximize their budgets, and if voters are rationally ignorant, they might vote to support taxes that provide public goods in quantities that exceed the efficient quantity.

3 **Explain the tragedy of the commons and review the possible solutions to that problem.**

- Common resources create the tragedy of the commons—no one has a private incentive to conserve the resource and use it at an efficient rate.
- A common resource is used to the point at which the marginal private benefit equals the marginal cost.
- The efficient use of a common resource is the point at which marginal social benefit equals marginal cost.
- A common resource might be used efficiently by creating a private property right, setting a quota, or issuing individual transferable quotas.

Key Terms

Common resource, 239
Excludable, 238
Free rider, 241
Individual transferable
    quota (ITQ), 255

Nonexcludable, 238
Nonrival, 238
Principle of minimum
    differentiation, 246
Private good, 238

Public good, 239
Rational ignorance, 247
Rival, 238
Tragedy of the commons, 250

(X myeconlab)

Exercises

1. Classify each of the following items as a private good, a public good, or a common resource. With each public good, is there a free-rider problem? If not, how is the free-rider problem avoided? With each common resource, is there a tragedy of the commons? If not, how is the tragedy of the commons avoided?
   a. New Year's Eve celebrations in Times Square, New York
   b. The Santa Monica freeway on a Friday afternoon
   c. A sewer system
   d. The railway network
   e. A skateboard
   f. Niagara Falls

2. Make a list with three examples that are different from those in Figure 10.1 and different from those in exercise 1 of a private good, a public good, and a common resource.
   a. Which of the items you've listed are likely to leave people with a smaller quantity than they are willing to buy?
   b. Which of the items you've listed are likely to make people concerned that the quantity exceeds what they would like to buy?
   c. Which of the items you've listed are unlikely to be either in short supply or too abundant?

3. Figure 1 shows the marginal benefit and marginal cost of a waste disposal system in a city of 1 million people.
   a. What is the efficient capacity of the waste disposal system?
   b. How much would each person have to pay in taxes if the city installed the efficient capacity?
   c. If voters are well informed about the costs and benefits of the waste disposal system, what capacity will voters choose in a referendum?
   d. If voters are rationally ignorant, will bureaucrats install the efficient capacity? Explain your answer.

4. Table 1 shows the value of cod caught in the Atlantic Ocean by European and North American fishing boats. It also shows the value that concerned citizens of Europe and North America place on the Atlantic cod stock. The marginal cost of operating a cod fishing boat is $70,000 a month.
   a. What is the marginal private benefit of each fishing boat?
   b. What is the marginal social cost of each fishing boat?
   c. With no regulation of cod fishing, what is the equilibrium number of boats and the approximate value of cod caught?
   d. Is the equilibrium in part c an overfishing outcome?
   e. What is the marginal social benefit of each fishing boat?
   f. What is the efficient number of boats?
   g. What is the efficient value of cod to catch?
   h. Do you think that the concerned citizens of Europe and North America and the fishing industry will agree about how much cod should be caught?
   i. If the United States, Canada, and the European Union issued ITQs to fishing boats to limit the cod catch to the efficient quantity, what would be the price of an ITQ?

FIGURE 1

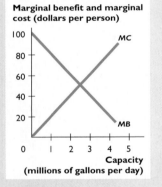

Marginal benefit and marginal cost (dollars per person)

TABLE 1

Number of fishing boats	Value of cod caught (thousands of dollars per month)	Value placed on cod stock by concerned citizens (thousands of dollars per month)
0	0	10,000
10	2,000	9,000
20	3,500	8,000
30	4,500	7,000
40	4,800	6,000
50	5,000	5,000
60	4,800	4,000
70	4,200	3,000
80	2,400	2,000

Critical Thinking

5. If hikers and others were required to pay a fee to use the Appalachian Trail, would the use of this common resource be more efficient? Would it be even more efficient if the most popular spots such as Annapolis Rock had more highly priced access? Why do you think we don't see more market solutions to the tragedy of the commons?

6. "Creating private property rights to the ocean and its fish, even if only through transferable quotas, is immoral." Do you think that relying on the morality and public spirit of the fishing industry is a potentially effective way of avoiding overfishing? Provide reasons.

7. Although the scientific evidence is not firm, most people agree that global warming is a real phenomenon and that the increase in carbon dioxide that has resulted from burning coal and oil is a significant contributor to the average temperature of the atmosphere. If we could measure the marginal social cost of global warming and the marginal social benefit of controlling it, how could we use those measurements to achieve an efficient use of our common atmospheric resources? What special problems arise, if any, from the fact that there is no global central authority but, instead, 200 or so independent nations?

8. "The tragedy of the commons is a problem only because people don't think about the consequences of their actions. If people were educated to see the damage they do to the environment, there would be no problem." Do you think education is a potentially viable solution to the tragedy of the commons? Provide reasons.

9. To produce the efficient quantity of a public good, we need to know the marginal cost of producing it and its marginal benefit.
    a. Do you think that we could get a better measure of marginal benefit if people were offered the opportunity to vote for each public good as a single issue rather than, as now, for an entire package of public goods?
    b. What would be some of the negative consequences of voting for each public good as a single issue?

10. Almost every day, you read about or hear complaints that the government isn't doing enough to address a perceived problem. And almost always, the issue comes down to spending more tax revenue on a particular public good. It might be medical research, cheap drugs for the poor or aged, a better-equipped military, better public schools and universities, and so on.
    a. On the basis of what you've learned about public goods, why do you think people complain in these ways?
    b. Is the volume of lobbying a sign that the political system delivers too little? Or does it deliver too much despite the complaining?

11. Can you think of any public goods that are provided privately with people paying for them voluntarily? How is the free-rider problem solved in this case? Could the solution be applied more widely? Why or why not?

Web Exercises

Use the links on MyEconLab to work the following exercises.

12. Visit Mark Skousen and read his essay on the private provision of public goods.
    a. Are the examples that he uses actually public goods?
    b. Could you use his proposed solution for national defense? Why or why not?
    c. Could you use his proposed solution for the court system? Why or why not?

13. Review the key points in the Kyoto Protocol on global warming.
    a. What are the common resources that the Kyoto Protocol seeks to conserve?
    b. What special difficulties lie in the path of conserving these resources?
    c. Can you think of an international solution to the problem of global warming?

14. Review Chapter 1 of Bjorn Lomborg's book *The Skeptical Environmentalist*.
    a. Summarize Lomborg's views and contrast them with the views that led to the Kyoto Protocol.
    b. If Lomborg is correct, does that mean that the environment can be left to the market?
    c. Can you think of an international solution to the problem of global warming?

15. Review the discussion of the case for private jails.
    a. What is the case for private rather than public jails?
    b. How does a private jail overcome the free-rider problem?
    c. Are there any general lessons to be learned from private jails?

16. Find information about the top defense contractors—the firms that supply the U.S. military with its equipment.
    a. Why do private firms produce the equipment that provides national defense, a public good?
    b. What is the difference between a private defense contractor and a private jail?
    c. Think about and comment on the distinction between the public production of a public good and the public consumption of a public good.

17. Find information about the budget of the U.S. government.
    a. How much of what the U.S. government spends is on public goods?
    b. How much of what the U.S. government spends is just redistributing income from one group to another? Is redistribution a public good? Explain why or why not.

18. Find information about spending by the U.S. government and by governments in other major countries.
    a. Does the U.S. government spend a greater, smaller, or about the same percentage of income as most other countries?
    b. What might your answer to part **a** suggest about the marginal benefit and marginal cost of public goods in the countries for which you have data?
    c. What other possible reasons can you think of for international differences in government spending on public goods?

Consumer Choice and Demand

CHAPTER CHECKLIST

When you have completed your study of this chapter, you will be able to

1 Calculate and graph a budget line that shows the limits to a person's consumption possibilities.

2 Explain marginal utility theory and use it to derive a consumer's demand curve.

3 Use marginal utility theory to explain the paradox of value: why water is vital but cheap while diamonds are relatively useless but expensive.

As Amy settled into her back-of-the-plane seat, she was surprised by the familiar face of the person sitting next to her. "Excuse me sir," she said, "but you look awfully like Steve Forbes." "I hope I do," came the reply. "I *am* Steve Forbes.

Steve Forbes, owner of *Forbes Magazine*, said to be worth around half a billion dollars, owner of an island in Fiji, a Boeing 727, and a chateau in France, sometimes travels coach!

You're not likely to run into Tiger Woods at the back of a plane. Like most top golfers, Tiger does most of his traveling in his private jet.

Why can Steve Forbes sometimes be seen traveling coach and Tiger Woods never? What determines the way in which people choose to spend their income—whether a large amount or a small one?

This chapter explains a model of consumer choice that helps us to understand and even predict the choices that people make.

11.1 CONSUMPTION POSSIBILITIES

We begin our study of consumption choices by learning about the limits to what a person can afford to buy. Your consumption choices are limited by your income and by the prices that you must pay. We summarize these influences on buying plans in a budget line.

■ The Budget Line

Budget line
A line that describes the limits to consumption possibilities and that depends on a consumer's budget and the prices of goods and services.

A **budget line** describes the limits to consumption possibilities. Tina has already committed most of her income to renting an apartment, buying textbooks, paying her campus meal plan, and saving a few dollars each month. Having made these decisions, Tina has a remaining budget of $4 a day, which she spends on two goods: bottled water and chewing gum. The price of water is $1 a bottle, and the price of gum is 50¢ a pack. If Tina spends all of her available budget, she reaches the limits of her consumption of bottled water and gum.

Figure 11.1 illustrates Tina's budget line. Rows *A* through *E* in the table show five possible ways of spending $4 on these two goods. If Tina spends all of her $4 on gum, she can buy 8 packs a day. In this case, she has nothing available to spend on bottled water. Row *A* shows this possibility. At the other extreme, if Tina spends her entire $4 on bottled water, she can buy 4 bottles a day and no gum. Row *E* shows this possibility. Rows *B*, *C*, and *D* show three other possible combinations that Tina can afford.

■ FIGURE 11.1
Consumption Possibilities

Tina's budget line shows the boundary between what she can and cannot afford. The rows of the table list Tina's affordable combinations of bottled water and chewing gum when her budget is $4 a day, the price of water is $1 a bottle, and the price of chewing gum is 50¢ a pack. For example, row *A* tells us that Tina exhausts her $4 budget when she buys 8 packs of gum and no water.

The figure graphs Tina's budget line. Points *A* through *E* on the graph represent the rows of the table.

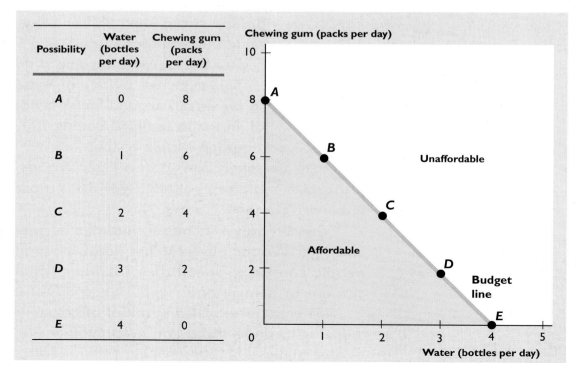

Possibility	Water (bottles per day)	Chewing gum (packs per day)
A	0	8
B	1	6
C	2	4
D	3	2
E	4	0

Points *A* through *E* in the figure graph the possibilities in the table. The line passing through these points is Tina's budget line, which marks the boundary between what she can and cannot afford. She can afford any combination on the budget line and inside it (in the orange area). She cannot afford any combination outside the budget line (in the white area).

The budget line in Figure 11.1 is similar to the *production possibilities frontier*, or *PPF*, in Chapter 3 (pp. 58–59). Both curves show a limit to what is feasible. But the *PPF* is a technological limit that changes only when technology changes. The budget line depends on the consumer's budget and on prices, so it changes when the budget or prices change.

■ A Change in the Budget

Figure 11.2 shows the effect of a change in Tina's budget on her consumption possibilities. When Tina's budget increases, her consumption possibilities expand, and her budget line shifts outward. When her budget decreases, her consumption possibilities shrink and her budget line shifts inward.

On the initial budget line (the same as in Figure 11.1), Tina's budget is $4. On a day on which Tina loses her purse with $2 in it, she has only $2 to spend. Her new budget line in Figure 11.2 shows how much she can consume with a budget of $2. She can buy any of the combinations on the $2 budget line.

On a day on which Tina sells an old CD for $2, she has $6 available and her budget line shifts rightward. She can now buy any of the combinations on the $6 budget line.

■ **FIGURE 11.2**

Changes in a Consumer's Budget

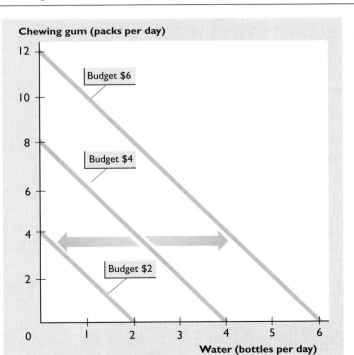

A decrease in the budget shifts the budget line leftward, and an increase in the budget shifts the budget line rightward.

■ Changes in Prices

If the price of one good rises when the prices of other goods and the budget remain the same, consumption possibilities shrink. If the price of one good falls when the prices of other goods and the budget remain the same, consumption possibilities expand. To see these changes in consumption possibilities, let's see what happens to Tina's budget line when the price of a bottle of water changes.

A Fall in the Price of Water

Figure 11.3 shows the effect on Tina's budget line of a fall in the price of a bottle of water from $1 to 50¢ when the price of gum and her budget remain unchanged. If Tina spends all her budget on bottled water, she can now afford 8 bottles a day. Her consumption possibilities have expanded. But because the price of gum is unchanged, if she spends all her budget on gum, she can still afford only 8 packs of gum a day. Her budget line has rotated outward.

A Rise in the Price of Water

Figure 11.4 shows the effect on Tina's budget line of a rise in the price of a bottle of water from $1 to $2 when the price of gum and her budget remain unchanged. If Tina spends all of her budget on bottled water, she can now afford only 2 bottles a day. Tina's consumption possibilities have shrunk. But again, because the price of gum is unchanged, if Tina spends all her budget on gum, she can still afford 8 packs of gum a day. Her budget line has rotated inward.

■ FIGURE 11.3

A Fall in the Price of Water

When the price of water falls from $1 a bottle to 50¢ a bottle, the budget line rotates outward and becomes less steep.

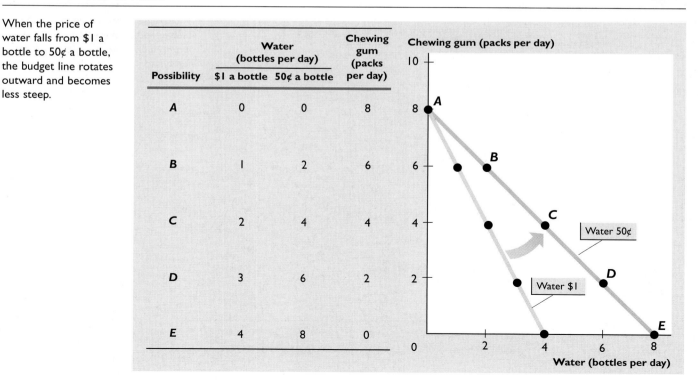

Possibility	Water (bottles per day) $1 a bottle	Water (bottles per day) 50¢ a bottle	Chewing gum (packs per day)
A	0	0	8
B	1	2	6
C	2	4	4
D	3	6	2
E	4	8	0

■ Prices and the Slope of the Budget Line

Notice that when the price of bottled water changes and the price of gum remains unchanged, the slope of the budget line changes. In Figure 11.3, when the price of bottled water falls, the budget line becomes less steep. In Figure 11.4, when the price of a bottle of water rises, the budget line becomes steeper.

Recall that "slope equals rise over run." The rise is an *increase* in the quantity of gum, and the run is a *decrease* in the quantity of bottled water. The slope of the budget line is negative, which means that there is a tradeoff between the two goods. Along the budget line, consuming more of one good implies consuming less of the other good. The slope of the budget line is an *opportunity cost*. It tells us what the consumer must give up to get one more unit of a good.

Let's calculate the slopes of the three budget lines in Figures 11.3 and 11.4:

- When the price of water is $1 a bottle, the slope of the budget line is 8 packs of gum divided by 4 bottles of water, which equals 2 packs of gum per bottle.
- When the price of water is 50¢ a bottle, the slope of the budget line is 8 packs of gum divided by 8 bottles water, which equals 1 pack of gum per bottle.
- When the price of water is $2 a bottle, the slope of the budget line is 8 packs of gum divided by 2 bottles of water, which equals 4 packs of gum per bottle.

A Rise in the Price of Water

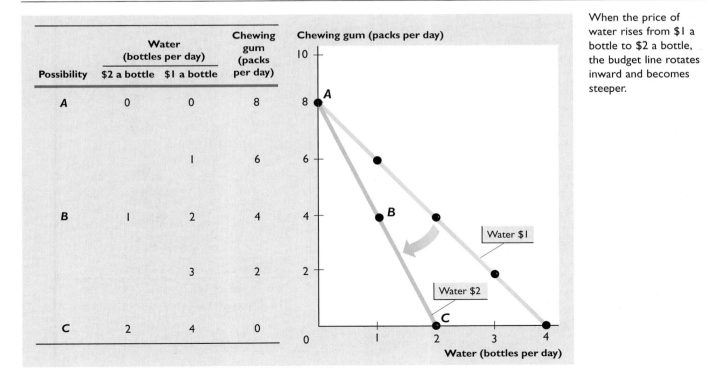

When the price of water rises from $1 a bottle to $2 a bottle, the budget line rotates inward and becomes steeper.

Possibility	Water (bottles per day) $2 a bottle	Water (bottles per day) $1 a bottle	Chewing gum (packs per day)
A	0	0	8
		1	6
B	1	2	4
		3	2
C	2	4	0

Think about what these slopes mean as opportunity costs. When the price of water is $1 a bottle and the price of gum is 50¢ a pack, it costs 2 packs of gum to buy a bottle of water. When the price of water is 50¢ a bottle and the price of gum is 50¢ a pack, it costs 1 pack of gum to buy a bottle of water. And when the price of water is $2 a bottle and the price of gum is 50¢ a pack, it costs 4 packs of gum to buy a bottle of water.

Relative price

The price of one good in terms of another good—an opportunity cost. It equals the price of one good divided by the price of another good.

Another name for an opportunity cost is a relative price. A **relative price** is the price of one good in terms of another good. If the price of gum is 50¢ a pack and the price of water is $1 a bottle, the relative price of water is 2 packs of gum per bottle. It is calculated as the price of water divided by the price of gum ($1 a bottle ÷ 50¢ a pack = 2 packs per bottle).

When the price of the good plotted on the *x*-axis falls, other things remaining the same, the budget line becomes less steep, and the opportunity cost and relative price of the good on the *x*-axis fall.

EYE ON THE U.S. ECONOMY

Relative Prices on the Move

Over a number of years, relative prices change a great deal. Some of the most dramatic changes occur in high-technology products such as computers. But many other relative prices change, and many fall.

The figure shows the price changes between 1995 and 2005 of 16 items that featured in most student's budgets.

Gasoline and college books and supplies have had some of the largest relative price increases.

The price of a personal computer has fallen by 90 percent. Other large relative price declines have been in coffee and long-distance phone calls. But bananas, electricity, and a host of other items have relatively lower prices today than they did 10 years ago.

These changes in relative prices change people's consumption possibilities and change the choices that they make. Lower prices provide an incentive to buy greater quantities, and higher prices provide an incentive to find substitutes and buy smaller quantities.

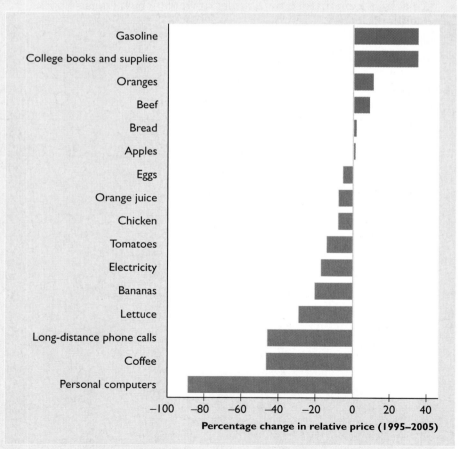

Percentage change in relative price (1995–2005)

Source of data: Bureau of Labor Statistics.

CHECKPOINT 11.1

1 **Calculate and graph a budget line that shows the limits to a person's consumption possibilities.**

Practice Problem 11.1

1. Jerry's burger and magazine budget is $12 a week. The price of a burger is $2, and the price of a magazine is $4.
   a. List the combinations of burgers and magazines that Jerry can afford.
   b. Draw a graph of Jerry's budget line with the quantity of burgers plotted on the x-axis.
   c. What is the relative price of a magazine? Explain your answer.
   d. Describe how the budget line in part **b** changes if, other things remaining the same, the following changes occur one at a time:
      • The price of a magazine falls.
      • Jerry's budget for burgers and magazines increases.

Exercise 11.1

1. Jenny's burger and salad budget is $36 a week. The price of a burger is $3, and the price of a salad is $2.
   a. List the combinations of burgers and salads that Jenny can afford.
   b. Draw a graph of Jenny's budget line with the quantity of burgers plotted on the x-axis.
   c. Describe how Jenny's budget line in part **b** changes if, other things remaining the same, the following changes occur one at a time:
      • The price of a burger falls.
      • Jenny's burger and salad budget decreases.
   d. How does the relative price of a salad change if the price of a burger halves? Explain your answer.

FIGURE 1

Solution to Practice Problem 11.1

1a. Jerry can afford the combinations that cost the $12 in his budget: 3 magazines and no burgers; 2 magazines and 2 burgers; 1 magazine and 4 burgers; no magazines and 6 burgers.

1b. The budget line is a straight line from 3 magazines on the y-axis to 6 burgers on the x-axis (Figure 1).

1c. The relative price of a magazine is the number of burgers that Jerry must forgo to get 1 magazine, which equals the price of a magazine divided by the price of a burger, or 2 burgers per magazine.

1d. With a lower price of a magazine, the number of magazines that Jerry can buy with $12 increases. The budget line rotates outward (Figure 2). With a bigger budget, Jerry can buy more of both magazines and burgers. The budget line shifts outward (Figure 3).

FIGURE 2

FIGURE 3

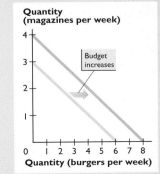

11.2 MARGINAL UTILITY THEORY

The budget line tells us about consumption *possibilities*, but it doesn't tell us a person's consumption *choice*. The quantities of goods and services that people choose depend on consumption possibilities and *preferences*. Economists use the concept of utility* to describe preferences. You are going to learn how economists use the concept of utility to explain the quantities that people choose to buy and predict how those quantities change when prices change. You will see how economists derive a consumer's demand curve from utility-maximizing choices.

■ Utility

Utility

The benefit or satisfaction that a person gets from the consumption of a good or service.

The benefit or satisfaction that a person gets from the consumption of a good or service is called **utility**. In everyday language, "utility" means "usefulness." In economics, it is an index of how much a person wants something. Utility is a bit like temperature. It is a useful but abstract concept measured in arbitrary units.

Temperature: An Analogy

You know when you feel hot, and you know when you feel cold. But you can't *observe* temperature itself. It is an abstract concept. You can observe water turning to steam if it is hot enough or turning to ice if it is cold enough. And you can use a thermometer to predict when such changes will occur.

The scale on the thermometer is what we call temperature. But the units in which we measure temperature are arbitrary. For example, we can accurately predict that when a Celsius thermometer shows a temperature of 0, water will turn to ice. But the units of measurement do not matter because this same event also occurs when a Fahrenheit thermometer shows a temperature of 32. Similarly, when a Celsius thermometer shows a temperature of 100, water will boil. But this same event also occurs when a Fahrenheit thermometer shows a temperature of 212.

The concept of utility helps us to make predictions about consumption choices in much the same way that the concept of temperature helps us to make predictions about physical phenomena. But marginal utility theory is not as precise as the theory that enables us to predict when water will turn to ice or steam. The main reason is that people's preferences sometimes change.

Let's now see how we can use the concept of utility to describe preferences.

■ Total Utility

Total utility

The total benefit that a person gets from the consumption of a good or service. Total utility generally increases as the quantity consumed of a good increases.

Total utility is the total benefit that a person gets from the consumption of a good or service. Total utility depends on the quantity of the good consumed—more consumption generally gives more total utility. Table 11.1 shows Tina's total utility from bottled water and chewing gum. If she consumes no bottled water and no gum, she gets no utility. If she consumes 1 bottle of water a day, she gets 15 units of utility. If she consumes 1 pack of gum a day, it provides her with 32 units of utility. As Tina increases the quantity of bottled water and packs of gum she consumes, her total utility from each increases.

---

*Economists also use an alternative method of describing preferences called *indifference curves*, which are described in the optional appendix to this chapter.

Tina's total utility numbers tell us that she gets a lot of pleasure from chewing gum. The first pack a day gives her more than twice the utility that her first bottle of water provides. But by the time Tina has consumed 7 packs of gum in a day, the 8th pack gives her no more utility. An 8th bottle of water, on the other hand, does increase her total utility.

■ Marginal Utility

Marginal utility is the change in total utility that results from a one-unit increase in the quantity of a good consumed. Table 11.1 shows the calculation of Tina's marginal utility from bottled water and chewing gum. Let's find Tina's marginal utility from a 3rd bottle of water a day (highlighted in the table). Her total utility from 3 bottles is 36 units, and her total utility from 2 bottles is 27 units. So for Tina, the marginal utility from drinking a 3rd bottle of water each day is

Marginal utility of 3rd bottle = 36 units − 27 units = 9 units.

In the table, marginal utility appears midway between the quantities because the *change* in consumption produces the *marginal* utility. The table displays the marginal utility for each quantity of water and gum consumed.

Notice that Tina's marginal utility decreases as her consumption of water and gum increases. For example, her marginal utility from bottled water decreases from 15 units for the first bottle to 12 units from the second and 9 units from the third. Similarly, her marginal utility from chewing gum decreases from 32 units for the first pack to 16 units for the second and 8 units for the third. We call this decrease in marginal utility as the quantity of a good consumed increases the principle of **diminishing marginal utility**.

To see why marginal utility diminishes, think about the following situations: In one, you've been studying all day and have had nothing to drink. Someone offers you a bottle of water. The marginal utility you get from that water is large.

Marginal utility
The change in total utility that results from a one-unit increase in the quantity of a good consumed.

Diminishing marginal utility
The general tendency for marginal utility to decrease as the quantity of a good consumed increases.

■ **TABLE 11.1**

Tina's Total Utility and Marginal Utility

Bottled water			Chewing gum		
Quantity (bottles per day)	Total utility	Marginal utility	Quantity (packs per day)	Total utility	Marginal utility
0	0		0	0	
		15			32
1	15		1	32	
		12			16
2	27		2	48	
		9			8
3	36		3	56	
		6			6
4	42		4	62	
		5			4
5	47		5	66	
		4			2
6	51		6	68	
		3			1
7	54		7	69	
		2			0
8	56		8	69	

The table shows Tina's total utility and marginal utility for bottled water and chewing gum. Marginal utility is the change in total utility when the quantity consumed increases by one unit. When Tina's consumption of bottled water increases from 2 bottles a day to 3 bottles per day, her total utility from bottled water increases from 27 units to 36 units. So Tina's marginal utility of the 3rd bottle a day is 9 units. Total utility increases and marginal utility diminishes as the quantity consumed increases.

With Tina's numbers, it provides 15 units of utility. In the second situation, you've been on a bottled water binge. You've drunk 7 bottles during the day. Now someone offers you another bottle of water, and you say thanks very much and sip it slowly. You enjoy the 8th bottle of the day, but the marginal utility from the 8th bottle is only 2 units.

Similarly, suppose you've been unable to buy a pack of gum for more than a day. A friend offers you a pack. Relief! You chew and receive 32 units of utility. On another day, you've chewed until your jaws ache and have gone through 7 packs. You're offered an 8th, and this time you say thanks very much but I'll pass on that one. You know that the 8th pack of gum would bring you no marginal utility.

For Tina, the marginal utility of gum diminishes more rapidly than does the marginal utility of bottled water.

We can illustrate the features of a consumer's preferences that we've just described with a total utility curve and a marginal utility curve. Figure 11.5 shows Tina's total utility and marginal utility from bottled water. You can see the principle of diminishing marginal utility in this figure. Part (a) shows us that as Tina drinks more bottled water, her total utility from it increases. It also shows that total utility increases at a decreasing rate. You can see diminishing marginal utility in part (a) because the step increases in utility get smaller as the quantity of water consumed increases.

Part (b) graphs Tina's marginal utility. The steps in part (a) are placed side by side in part (b). We've enlarged the scale of the *y*-axis in part (b) to emphasize the diminishing marginal utility. The curve that passes through the midpoints of the bars in part (b) is Tina's marginal utility curve.

The numbers in Table 11.1 and the graphs in Figure 11.5 describe Tina's preferences and, along with her budget line, enable us to predict the choices that she makes. That is our next task.

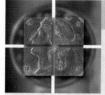

EYE ON THE PAST

Jeremy Bentham, William Stanley Jevons, and the Birth of Utility

The concept of utility was revolutionary when Jeremy Bentham (1748–1832) proposed it in the early 1800s. He used the idea to advance his then radical support for free education, free medical care, and social security. It took another fifty years before William Stanley Jevons (1835–1882) developed the concept of *marginal* utility and used it to pre-

dict people's consumption choices. Jevons's main claim to fame in his own day was his suggestion—wrong

as it turned out—that sunspots cause business cycles. But his lasting legacy is the marginal utility theory.

Jeremy Bentham

William Stanley Jevons

■ FIGURE 11.5
Total Utility and Marginal Utility

myeconlab

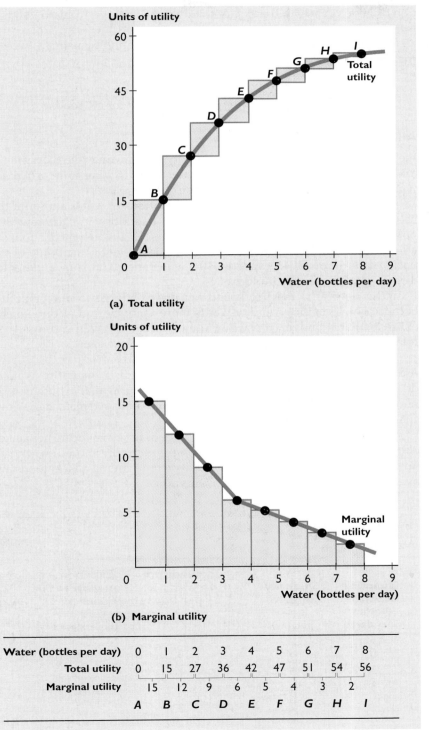

(a) Total utility

(b) Marginal utility

Part (a) graphs Tina's total utility from bottled water. It also shows as a bar the extra total utility she gains from each additional bottle of water—her marginal utility—as the steps along the total utility curve.

Part (b) shows how Tina's marginal utility from bottled water diminishes by placing the bars shown in part (a) side by side as a series of declining steps.

Water (bottles per day)	0	1	2	3	4	5	6	7	8
Total utility	0	15	27	36	42	47	51	54	56
Marginal utility		15	12	9	6	5	4	3	2
	A	B	C	D	E	F	G	H	I

■ Maximizing Total Utility

The consumer's goal is to allocate the available budget in the way that maximizes total utility. The consumer achieves this goal by choosing the affordable combination of goods at which the *sum* of the utilities obtained from all goods consumed is as large as possible.

Utility-maximizing rule
The rule that leads to the greatest total utility from all the goods and services consumed. The rule is
1. Allocate the entire available budget.
2. Make the marginal utility per dollar equal for all goods.

We can find a consumer's best budget allocation by using a two-step **utility-maximizing rule**:

1. Allocate the entire available budget.
2. Make the marginal utility per dollar equal for all goods.

Allocate the Available Budget

We're going to see how the two-step utility-maximizing rule works for Tina as she allocates $4 a day between bottled water and chewing gum when the price of water is $1 a bottle and the price of gum is 50¢ a pack.

The first step is to establish the combinations of water and gum that cost $4. Table 11.2 shows these combinations. The quantities in each row describe one point that is on Tina's budget line (in Figure 11.1), which means that she can just afford to buy each combination. For example, if she buys 1 bottle of water and 6 packs of gum (row *B*), she spends $1 on water and $3 on gum, and her total expenditure equals her entire budget of $4.

Why does Tina need to spend her entire budget to maximize utility? It is because she faces scarcity. She wants more than she can afford, so she uses the entire available budget. If she had some budget left over, she could increase her total utility by buying more of either good.

A Side Note on Saving and Other Goods   Spending the entire available budget doesn't necessarily mean not saving anything. The available budget is the amount remaining after choosing how much to save and, in Tina's case, how much to spend on some other goods.

The principles that explain Tina's choice of how to allocate her currently available budget between water and chewing gum apply more broadly and explain how a consumer allocates her or his total income among all the goods and services available and saving for future consumption.

■ **TABLE 11.2**

Tina's Affordable Combinations of Water and Gum   ⓧ myeconlab

The rows of the table show Tina's affordable combinations of water and gum when she has $4 to spend on these two items, the price of water is $1 a bottle, and the price of gum is 50¢ a pack. Each combination *A* through *E* is a point on Tina's budget line in Figure 11.1.

	Quantity of water (bottles per day)	Quantity of gum (packs per day)	Expenditure on water at $1 per bottle	Expenditure on gum at 50¢ per pack	Total expenditure
			(dollars per day)		
A	0	8	0	4	4
B	1	6	1	3	4
C	2	4	2	2	4
D	3	2	3	1	4
E	4	0	4	0	4

Equalize the Marginal Utility Per Dollar

The second step to finding a consumer's best budget allocation is to establish the affordable combination that makes the marginal utility per dollar equal for both goods. The **marginal utility per dollar** is the marginal utility from a good relative to the price of the good.

Marginal utility per dollar
The marginal utility from a good relative to the price paid for the good.

Calculating the Marginal Utility per Dollar To calculate the marginal utility per dollar, we divide the marginal utility from a good by the price of the good. For example, if Tina buys 1 pack of gum a day, her marginal utility from the 1 pack is 32 units. The price of a pack of gum is 50¢, so the marginal utility per dollar from gum is 32 units divided by 50¢, which equals 64 units of utility per dollar. If Tina buys 1 bottle of water a day, her marginal utility from the 1 bottle of water is 15 units. The price of a bottle of water is $1, so Tina's marginal utility per dollar from bottled water is 15 units divided by $1, which equals 15 units of utility per dollar.

Why Equal Marginal Utility per Dollar Maximizes Total Utility Suppose that Tina can get more utility by shifting a dollar of expenditure from water to gum. What do you know about the marginal utility per dollar from water and gum? You know that the gain in utility from the extra gum must be greater than the loss of utility from the smaller quantity of water. So the marginal utility per dollar from gum must have been greater than the marginal utility per dollar from water. The top balance scale in Figure 11.6 illustrates this situation.

But as Tina buys more gum, the marginal utility from gum decreases and so does the marginal utility per dollar from gum. And as she buys less water, the marginal utility per dollar from water increases.

When the marginal utility per dollar from gum is equal to the marginal utility per dollar from water, Tina cannot get more utility by shifting a dollar from one good to the other. If Tina did buy more gum, the gain in utility from more gum would be less than the loss in utility from less water. The bottom balance scale in Figure 11.6 illustrates this situation.

■ **FIGURE 11.6**

Utility-Maximizing Balancing Act

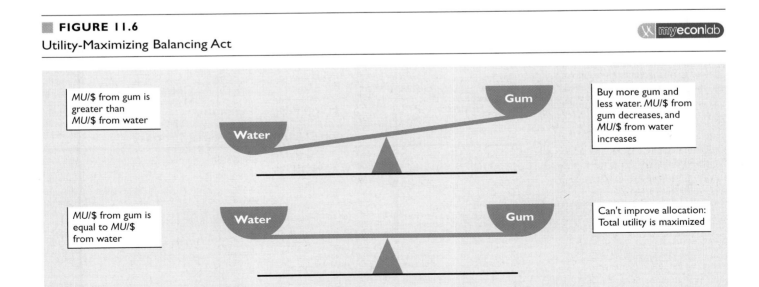

Finding Tina's Utility-Maximizing Choice To find Tina's utility-maximizing choice, we need to calculate the marginal utility per dollar for only the affordable combinations that exhaust her budget. Other combinations are irrelevant. Either they are not affordable or they waste some of the budget.

Table 11.3 shows Tina's marginal utilities per dollar from water and gum for all the affordable combinations that exhaust her budget.

Begin by checking that you can calculate the marginal utilities per dollar. Let's do a sample calculation on row *D*. In this row of the table, Tina buys 3 bottles of water and 2 packs of gum. Her marginal utility from water is 9 units, and because the price of water is $1 a bottle, her marginal utility per dollar from water is 9 divided by $1, which is 9 units per dollar. Her marginal utility from gum is 16 units and because the price of gum is 50¢ a pack, her marginal utility per dollar from gum is 16 divided by 50¢, which is 32 units per dollar.

You can see in the table that the combination that equalizes the marginal utilities per dollar is 2 bottles of water and 4 packs of gum—in row *C*.

Suppose that Tina were to move from row *C* to row *D* and buy 3 bottles of water and only 2 packs of gum. You can see that with this allocation of her budget, Tina's marginal utility per dollar from water is 9 units of utility per dollar and her marginal utility per dollar from gum is 32 units per dollar.

Making this move, Tina would gain 9 units per dollar from the extra water and she would lose 12 units per dollar from the forgone gum. Tina would be worse off with this combination.

Now suppose that Tina were to move from row *C* to row *B* and buy 1 bottle of water and 6 packs of gum. You can see that with this allocation of her budget, Tina's marginal utility per dollar from water is 15 units per dollar and her marginal utility per dollar from gum is 4 units per dollar.

Making this move, Tina would gain 4 units per dollar from the extra gum but she would lose 12 units per dollar from the forgone water. Again, Tina would be worse off with this combination.

Tina can do no better than to buy 2 bottles of water and 4 packs of gum.

■ **TABLE 11.3**   ⓧ myeconlab

Tina's Marginal Utilities per Dollar: Water $1 a Bottle and Gum 50¢ a Pack

The rows of the table show Tina's marginal utility per dollar from water and gum for the affordable combinations when her budget is $4, the price of water is $1 a bottle, and the price of gum is 50¢ a pack. By equalizing the marginal utilities per dollar from water and gum, Tina maximizes her total utility. Her utility-maximizing choice is to buy 2 bottles of water and 4 packs of gum.

	Bottled water			Chewing gum		
	Quantity (bottles per day)	Marginal utility	Marginal utility per dollar	Quantity (packs per day)	Marginal utility	Marginal utility per dollar
A	0			8	0	0
				7	1	2
B	1	15	15	6	2	4
				5	4	8
C	2	12	12	4	6	12
				3	8	16
D	3	9	9	2	16	32
				1	32	64
E	4	6	6	0		

■ Finding an Individual Demand Curve

We can use marginal utility theory to find a person's demand schedule and demand curve. In fact, we've just found one entry in Tina's demand schedule and one point on her demand curve for bottled water: When the price of bottled water is $1 and other things remain the same (the price of gum is 50¢ and her budget is $4 a day), the quantity of water that Tina buys is 2 bottles a day (row *C* in Table 11.3).

Let's find a second entry in Tina's demand schedule and point on her demand curve for water—the quantity of water that Tina buys when the price of water falls to 50¢ a bottle and other things remain the same.

You know right away that Tina will buy more bottled water. Why? With the fall in the price of water, the marginal utility per dollar from water increases and must now exceed the marginal utility per dollar from gum. Also, with a lower price of water, Tina can afford to buy more water each day.

If Tina continued to consume 2 bottles of water and 4 packs of gum when the price of water halved, her marginal utility per dollar from bottled water would double to 24 units per dollar, which is twice the marginal utility per dollar from gum. Also, Tina would be spending only $3, so she would have another $1 available. Suppose that she spent the spare $1 on bottled water. She would then be consuming 4 bottles of water a day.

Table 11.4 shows some of Tina's new affordable combinations and the marginal utility per dollar from each good. Row *E* shows that when Tina spends all her $4 and consumes 4 bottles of water and 4 packs of gum a day, her marginal utility per dollar from bottled water is 12 and her marginal utility per dollar from gum is 12. So this combination is Tina's new choice.

You've now found a second entry in Tina's demand schedule and point on her demand curve for bottled water: When the price of bottled water is 50¢ (other things remaining the same), Tina buys 4 bottles of water a day.

In this example, Tina increases the quantity of water consumed and does not change her consumption of gum. This outcome is special to this numerical example and doesn't usually happen.

Figure 11.7 shows Tina's demand curve that we've just derived.

■ TABLE 11.4

Tina's Marginal Utilities per Dollar: Water 50¢ a Bottle and Gum 50¢ a Pack

	Bottled water			Chewing gum		
	Quantity (bottles per day)	Marginal utility	Marginal utility per dollar	Quantity (packs per day)	Marginal utility	Marginal utility per dollar
D	3	9	18	5	4	8
E	4	6	12	4	6	12
F	5	5	10	3	8	16

The rows of the table show Tina's marginal utility per dollar from water and gum for the affordable combinations when her budget is $4, the price of water is 50¢ a bottle, and the price of gum is 50¢ a pack. By equalizing the marginal utilities per dollar from water and gum, Tina maximizes her total utility. Her utility-maximizing choice is to buy 4 bottles of water and 4 packs of gum.

Tina's Demand for Bottled Water

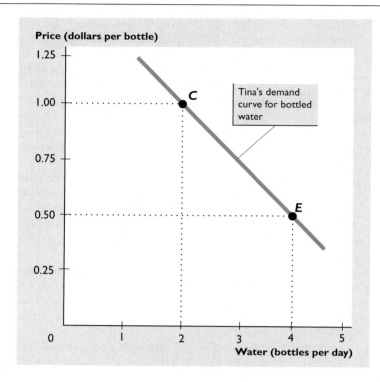

When the price of water is $1 a bottle (and her budget is $4 and the price of a pack of gum is 50¢), Tina buys 2 bottles of water and 4 packs of gum a day. She is at point C on her demand curve for water.

When the price of water falls to 50¢ a bottle and other things remain the same, Tina buys 4 bottles of water and 4 packs of gum a day and moves to point E on her demand curve for bottled water.

■ The Power of Marginal Analysis

The method that we've used to find Tina's utility-maximizing choice of bottled water and gum is an example of the power of marginal analysis. By comparing the marginal gain from having more of one good with the marginal loss from having less of another good, Tina gets the maximum attainable utility.

More generally, if the marginal gain from an action exceeds the marginal loss, take the action. You have met this principle before, and you will meet it time and again in your study of economics. Soon, you will find yourself using it when you make your own choices, especially when you must make a big decision.

■ Units of Utility

In calculating Tina's utility-maximizing choice, we didn't use the concept of *total* utility. All our calculations use *marginal utility* and *price*. By making the marginal utility per dollar from each good equal, we know that Tina maximizes her total utility.

This way of viewing maximum utility is important: It means that the units in which utility is measured do not matter. We could double or halve all the numbers measuring utility or multiply them by any other positive number. None of these changes in the units used to measure utility makes any difference to the outcome. Just as changing from degrees Celsius to degrees Fahrenheit doesn't affect a prediction about the freezing point of water, so changing the units of utility doesn't affect our prediction about the consumption choice that maximizes total utility.

CHECKPOINT 11.2

2 Explain marginal utility theory and use it to derive a consumer's demand curve.

Practice Problem 11.2

1. Table 1 shows Jerry's total utility from burgers and magazines.
   a. Calculate Jerry's marginal utility from the second burger in the week.
   b. If the price of a burger is $2, calculate the marginal utility per dollar from burgers when Jerry buys 2 burgers a week.
   c. Calculate Jerry's marginal utility from the second magazine in the week.
   d. If the price of a magazine is $4, calculate the marginal utility per dollar from magazines when Jerry buys 2 magazines.
   e. When the price of a burger is $2, the price of a magazine is $4, and Jerry has $12 a week to spend, Jerry buys 2 burgers and 2 magazines. Does he maximize his total utility? Explain your answer.

TABLE 1

Burgers		Magazines	
Quantity per week	Total utility	Quantity per week	Total utility
0	0	0	0
1	14	1	100
2	24	2	120
3	32	3	134
4	38	4	144

Exercise 11.2

1. Table 2 shows Wanda's total utility for juice and pasta. The price of a can of juice is $1, the price of a dish of pasta is $4, and Wanda has $11 a week to spend on these two items.
   a. Calculate Wanda's marginal utility from the third dish of pasta a week.
   b. Calculate the marginal utility per dollar from pasta when Wanda has 3 dishes of pasta a week.
   c. Calculate Wanda's marginal utility from the fourth can of juice in a week.
   d. Calculate the marginal utility per dollar from juice when Wanda buys 2 cans of juice a week.
   e. If Wanda buys 2 cans of juice and 2 dishes of pasta a week, is she maximizing her total utility? If Wanda is not maximizing her total utility, explain how she would adjust her consumption choice to do so.

TABLE 2

Juice		Pasta	
Cans per week	Total utility	Dishes per week	Total utility
0	0	0	0
1	22	1	64
2	40	2	120
3	54	3	168
4	60	4	208
5	62	5	240
6	62	6	264

Solution to Practice Problem 11.2

1a. The marginal utility from the second burger equals the total utility from 2 burgers minus the total utility from 1 burger, which is 24 − 14 or 10 units.

1b. When Jerry buys 2 burgers, the marginal utility per dollar from burgers equals the marginal utility of the second burger (10) divided by the price of a burger ($2), which equals 5.

1c. The marginal utility from the second magazine equals the total utility from 2 magazines minus the total utility from 1 magazine, which is 120 − 100 or 20 units.

1d. When Jerry buys 2 magazines, the marginal utility per dollar from magazines equals the marginal utility of the second magazine (20) divided by the price of a magazine ($4), which equals 5.

1e. When a burger costs $2 and a magazine costs $4, Jerry buys 2 burgers and 2 magazines. Jerry has $12 to spend, so he spends his entire budget. The marginal utility per dollar from burgers (5, answer **b**) equals the marginal utility per dollar from magazines (5, answer **d**), so Jerry maximizes his total utility.

11.3 EFFICIENCY, PRICE, AND VALUE

Marginal utility theory helps us to deepen our understanding of the concept of efficiency and to see more clearly the distinction between *value* and *price*. Let's see how.

■ Consumer Efficiency

When Tina allocates her limited budget to maximize total utility, she is using her resources efficiently. Any other allocation of her budget would leave her able to attain a higher level of total utility.

But when Tina has allocated her budget to maximize total utility, she is *on* her demand curve for each good. A demand curve describes the quantity demanded at each price *when total utility is maximized*. When we studied efficiency in Chapter 6, we learned that a demand curve is also a willingness-to-pay curve. It tells us a consumer's *marginal benefit*—the benefit from consuming an additional unit of a good. You can now give the idea of marginal benefit a deeper meaning.

> **Marginal benefit is the maximum price a consumer is willing to pay for an extra unit of a good or service when total utility is maximized.**

■ The Paradox of Value

For centuries, philosophers were puzzled by the paradox of value. Water is more valuable than a diamond because water is essential to life itself. Yet water is much cheaper than a diamond. Why? Adam Smith tried to solve this paradox, but it was not until marginal utility theory had been developed that anyone could give a satisfactory answer.

You can solve this puzzle by distinguishing between *total* utility and *marginal* utility. Total utility tells us about relative value; marginal utility tells us about relative price. The total utility from water is enormous. But remember, the more we consume of something, the smaller is its marginal utility. We use so much water that its marginal utility—the benefit we get from one more glass of water—diminishes to a small value. Diamonds, on the other hand, have a small total utility relative to water, but because we buy few diamonds, they have a large marginal utility. When a household has maximized its total utility, it has allocated its budget so that the marginal utility per dollar is equal for all goods. Diamonds have a high price and a high marginal utility. Water has a low price and a low marginal utility. When the high marginal utility of diamonds is divided by the high price of a diamond, the result is a marginal utility per dollar that equals the low marginal utility of water divided by the low price of water. The marginal utility per dollar is the same for diamonds as for water.

Consumer Surplus

Consumer surplus measures value in excess of the amount paid. In Figure 11.8, the demand for and supply of water in part (a) determine the price of water P_W and the quantity of water consumed Q_W. The demand for and supply of diamonds in part (b) determine the price of a diamond P_D and the quantity of diamonds Q_D. Water is cheap but provides a large consumer surplus, while diamonds are expensive but provide a small consumer surplus.

FIGURE 11.8
The Paradox of Value

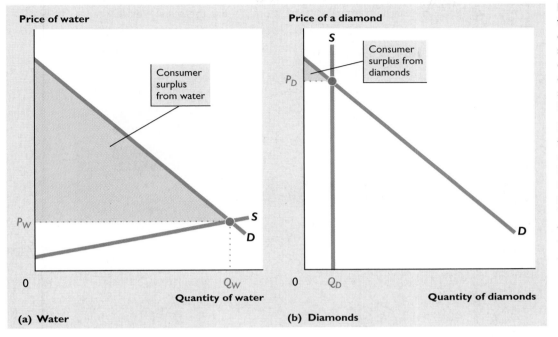

(a) Water

(b) Diamonds

Part (a) shows the demand for water, D, and the supply of water, S. Demand and supply determine the price of water at P_W and the quantity at Q_W. The consumer surplus from water is the large green triangle.

Part (b) shows the demand for diamonds, D, and the supply of diamonds. S. Demand and supply determine the price of a diamond at P_D and the quantity at Q_D. The consumer surplus from diamonds is the small green triangle.

Water is valuable—has a large consumer surplus—but cheap. Diamonds are less valuable than water—have a smaller consumer surplus—but are expensive.

CHECKPOINT 11.3

3   **Use marginal utility theory to explain the paradox of value: why water is vital but cheap while diamonds are relatively useless but expensive.**

Practice Problem 11.3

1.   In a year, Tony rents 500 videos at $3 each and buys 10,000 gallons of tap water, for which he pays $50. Tony is maximizing total utility. If Tony's marginal utility from water is 0.5 unit per gallon, what is his marginal utility from a video rental? Which good is the more valuable to Tony: water or videos? Why?

Exercise 11.3

1.   Which good is more valuable to you: water or your economics text?

Solution to Practice Problem 11.3

1.   Marginal utility of a video rental ÷ $3 = Marginal utility of a gallon of water ÷ 0.5¢. So the marginal utility of a video rental is 600 times the marginal utility of a gallon of water, which is 600 × 0.5 or 300 units. Most likely, the total utility from water is larger, so Tony values water more than videos.

Maximizing Utility in Beverage Markets

The figure shows how the quantities of bottled water, soda, and beer consumed in the United States changed during the 1990s. You can understand these changes by using marginal utility theory.

To maximize total utility, people make the marginal utility per dollar equal for all goods. So people buy bottled water, soda, and beer in quantities that make the marginal utilities per dollar from them equal.

The price of bottled water fell as more firms entered the market and increased supply. The price of soda also fell.

The true price of beer, or opportunity cost of beer, increased. The money price of beer didn't change much, but improved policing and stiffer penalties for drunk driving increased the cost of drinking beer.

These changes in what people drink are the responses to changes in prices and the attempt to make the marginal utilities per dollar equal for them.

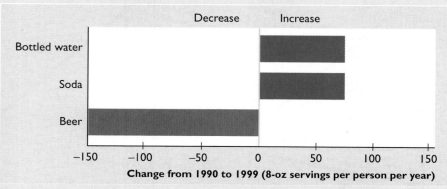

SOURCE OF DATA: *Detroit News.*

REALITY CHECK

Marginal Utility in YOUR Life

You're probably thinking that this marginal utility stuff is pretty unreal! You know that you don't go around the mall with a marginal utility calculator in hand. You just buy what you can afford and want, and that's all there is to it.

Well, marginal utility theory isn't about *how* people make their choices. It's about *what* choices people make. It's a tool that enables economists to explain people's choices.

You see lots of examples of people juggling their purchases to equalize marginal utilities per dollar. The next time you're in a supermarket, note the items that someone had second thoughts about and stuffed into the magazine rack by the checkout. When the crunch came to pay, the marginal utility per dollar was just not high enough.

You'll even find yourself actually using marginal utility to make your own decisions. It clarifies the options, and it helps to make the value of the alternatives explicit.

CHAPTER CHECKPOINT

Key Points

1 **Calculate and graph a budget line that shows the limits to a person's consumption possibilities.**

- Consumption possibilities and preferences determine consumption choices.
- Consumption possibilities are constrained by the budget and prices. Some combinations of goods are affordable, and some are not affordable.
- The budget line is the boundary between what a person can and cannot afford with a given budget and given prices.
- The slope of the budget line determines the relative price of the good measured on the x-axis in terms of the good measured on the y-axis.
- A change in one price changes the slope of the budget line. A change in the budget shifts the budget line but does not change its slope.

2 **Explain marginal utility theory and use it to derive a consumer's demand curve.**

- Total utility is maximized when the entire budget is spent and marginal utility per dollar is equal for all goods.
- If the marginal utility per dollar from good A exceeds that on good B, total utility increases if the quantity purchased of good A increases and the quantity purchased of good B decreases.
- Marginal utility theory implies the law of demand. That is, other things remaining the same, the higher the price of a good, the smaller is the quantity demanded of that good.

3 **Use marginal utility theory to explain the paradox of value: why water is vital but cheap while diamonds are relatively useless but expensive.**

- When consumers maximize total utility, they use resources efficiently.
- Marginal utility theory resolves the paradox of value.
- When we talk loosely about value, we are thinking of *total* utility or consumer surplus. But price is related to *marginal* utility.
- Water, which we consume in large amounts, has a high total utility and a large consumer surplus but a low price and low marginal utility.
- Diamonds, which we consume in small amounts, have a low total utility and a small consumer surplus but a high price and a high marginal utility.

Key Terms

Budget line, 262
Diminishing marginal utility, 269
Marginal utility, 269

Marginal utility per dollar, 273
Relative price, 266
Total utility, 268

Utility, 268
Utility-maximizing rule, 272

myeconlab

Exercises

1. Amy has $12 a week to spend on coffee and soda. The price of coffee is $2 a cup, and the price of soda is $1 a can.
   a. Make a table that shows Amy's budget line.
   b. Draw a graph of Amy's budget line.
   c. Can Amy afford to buy 7 cans of soda and 2 cups of coffee a week?
   d. Can Amy afford to buy 7 cups of coffee and 2 cans of soda a week?
   e. What is the relative price of a cup of coffee?
   f. What is the relative price of a can of soda?

2. Amy, in exercise 1, has $12 a week to spend on coffee and soda and the price of soda remains at $1 a can but the price of coffee rises to $3 a cup.
   a. Make a table that shows Amy's new consumption possibilities.
   b. Draw Amy's new budget line on the graph that you made to answer exercise 1b.
   c. If Amy buys 6 cans of soda, what is the maximum number of cups of coffee she can buy in a month?
   d. What now is the relative price of coffee?
   e. Has the relative price of soda changed? If so, has it increased or decreased?

3. Table 1 shows Ben's utility from orange juice.
   a. Calculate the values of A, B, C, and D.
   b. Why, given these numbers, would Ben ever want to buy more than one carton of orange juice a day?
   c. Why, given these numbers, would Ben ever want to buy no orange juice?
   d. Does the principle of diminishing marginal utility apply to Ben's consumption of orange juice? How do you know?

4. Use the numbers in Table 11.1 on p. 269 to make graphs of Tina's total utility and marginal utility from chewing gum.
   a. Compare Tina's marginal utility from chewing gum with that from bottled water. Which diminishes more rapidly?
   b. The price of gum is 25¢ a pack and the price of water is 50¢ a bottle. If Tina is spending all her budget by consuming 4 packs of gum and 4 bottles of water, is she maximizing total utility?
   c. If in the situation described in part b, Tina is not maximizing total utility, can she increase her total utility by consuming more water or more gum? Explain your answer.

5. Tina is maximizing her utility. If her budget increases, will she buy more bottled water or more chewing gum? Why? (Hint: Use her marginal utility for bottled water and chewing gum in Table 11.1 on p. 269.)

6. Tina is maximizing her utility. If her budget increases and at the same time, the price of a bottle of water rises, what can you say about how Tina's consumption of bottled water and chewing gum will change? (Hint: Use her marginal utility for bottled water and chewing gum in Table 11.1 on p. 269.)

7. Table 2 shows Martha's total utility from cake and pasta.
   a. Calculate Martha's total utility when she buys 3 cakes and 2 dishes of pasta a week.

TABLE 1

Orange juice (cartons per day)	Total utility	Marginal utility
0	0	
		7
1	7	
		5
2	A	
		B
3	15	
		2
4	C	
		D
5	18	

b. Calculate Martha's marginal utility from the third cake in a week.

c. If the price of a cake is $4, calculate the marginal utility per dollar from cake when Martha buys 3 cakes a week.

d. Calculate Martha's marginal utility from the second dish of pasta in a week.

e. If the price of pasta is $8 a dish, calculate the marginal utility per dollar from pasta when Martha buys 2 dishes a week.

f. When the price of a cake is $4, the price of pasta is $8 a dish, and Martha has $24 a week to spend, she buys 2 cakes and 2 dishes of pasta. Does she maximize her total utility? Explain your answer.

8. Use the information in Table 2 to answer the following questions:
   a. When the price of a cake is $4, Martha has $24 to spend, and the price of pasta falls from $8 to $4 a dish, what quantities of cake and pasta does Martha buy?
   b. What are two points on Martha's demand curve for pasta?
   c. Is Martha's demand for pasta elastic or inelastic?
   d. When the price of a cake is $4, the price of pasta is $8 a dish, and Martha's available income increases to $40 a week, what quantities of cake and pasta does Martha buy?

9. Tim buys 2 pizzas and sees 1 movie a week when he has $16 to spend, a movie ticket is $8, and the price of a pizza is $4.
   a. What is the relative price of a movie ticket?
   b. If the price of a movie ticket falls to $4,
      i. How will Tim's consumption possibilities change? Explain.
      ii. Will Tim change what he buys with his $16? Explain your answer.
      iii. How will Tim's consumption of pizza change?

10. Every day, Josie buys 2 cups of coffee and 1 sandwich for lunch. The price of a cup of coffee is $2 and the price of a sandwich is $5. Josie's choice of lunch maximizes her total utility, and she spends only $9 on lunch.
   a. Compare Josie's marginal utility from coffee with her marginal utility from the sandwich.
   b. Is Josie's allocation of her $9 efficient? Explain.

11. Adrienne loves riding her horse every weekend. She pays $500 a month to the stable to care for her horse, but she tells a friend that she thinks she's getting a real bargain and would willingly pay twice the price for the great service she gets from the stable and the fun she gets every weekend. Adrienne's only other significant expense is her apartment rent, which is $1,000 a month. Unlike the stable, she doesn't think the deal she gets from her landlord is all that good, and she is on the verge of looking for something better for the same price.
   a. From which does Adrienne get the greater marginal utility: her horse or her apartment?
   b. From which does Adrienne get the greater total utility: her horse or her apartment?
   c. How does Adrienne's consumption of horse-riding and housing explain the paradox of value?

TABLE 2

Cake		Pasta	
Quantity per week	Total utility	Dishes per week	Total utility
0	0	0	0
1	10	1	20
2	18	2	36
3	25	3	48
4	31	4	56
5	36	5	60
6	40	6	60

Critical Thinking

12. Some students buy a college meal plan, and some pay for each meal as they consume it.
    a. Why would a student decide to buy a meal plan rather than pay for each meal as it is consumed? Explain using marginal utility theory.
    b. What does marginal utility theory predict about the demand for lunches by the two groups?
    c. Who gets the greater marginal utility from lunch: someone who buys a meal plan or someone who pays for each lunch as it is consumed?
    d. Suppose the price of a lunch increases and all other relevant factors remain unchanged. What does marginal utility theory predict will happen to the quantity of lunches demanded by each group?

13. In a bid to attract new customers to public transportation, the Maryland Transit Authority had a free-ride day.
    a. Why would some people who don't normally use public transportation use it on a free-ride day?
    b. Why would some people who don't normally use public transportation still not use it on a free-ride day? (Hint: Think about the opportunity cost of a trip.)
    c. What does marginal utility theory predict about the demand for public transportation on the day after the free-ride day? Do you think the theory is correct?

14. Why do you think the percentage of income spent on food has decreased while the percentage of income spent on cars has increased during the past 50 years? Use the marginal utility theory to explain these trends.

Web Exercises

Use the links on MyEconLab to work the following exercises.

15. Visit the Maryland Transit Authority Web site and get information about fares and passes.
    a. Show the effects of the different ticket options on the consumer's consumption possibilities.
    b. How would a person decide whether to pay for each trip, to buy a day pass, or to buy a pass for a longer period? Use marginal utility theory to answer this question.
    c. How do you think the number of riders would change if the price of a single trip fell and the price of a day pass increased?

16. Work this exercise with a friend or in a group. Visit Dick's Sporting Goods.
    a. Imagine that each of you has been given a $500 voucher to spend only at Dick's Sporting Goods. Select the items that maximize your total utility.
    b. Compare the choices that each member of your group has made and use the ideas of marginal utility theory to explain the differences.
    c. How would your choices have changed if your voucher had been worth $1,000 and all the prices were doubled? Explain with reference to your budget line.

17. Visit Shopper.com. Look up the prices at the different stores listed on the Web site of an iPod that excites you. If you were going to buy this item, from which store would you buy it and why? Explain your answer using the ideas of marginal utility theory.

You are going to discover a neat idea—that of drawing a map of a person's preferences. A preference map is based on the intuitively appealing assumption that people can sort all the possible combinations of goods into three groups: preferred, not preferred, and indifferent. To make this idea concrete, let's ask Tina to tell us how she ranks combinations of bottled water and chewing gum.

■ An Indifference Curve

Figure A11.1(a) shows part of Tina's answer. She tells us that she currently consumes 2 bottles of water and 4 packs of gum a day at point C. She then lists all the combinations of bottled water and chewing gum that she says are as acceptable to her as her current consumption. When we plot these combinations of water and gum, we get the green curve. This curve is the key element in a map of preferences and is called an indifference curve.

An **indifference curve** is a line that shows combinations of goods among which a consumer is *indifferent*. The indifference curve in Figure A11.1(a) tells us that Tina is just as happy to consume 2 bottles of water and 4 packs of gum a day at point C as to consume the combination of water and gum at any other point along the indifference curve. Tina also says that she prefers all the combinations of bottled water and gum above the indifference curve—the yellow area—to those on the indifference curve. These combinations contain more water, more gum, or more of both. She also prefers any combination on the indifference curve to any

Indifference curve
A line that shows combinations of goods among which a consumer is *indifferent*.

■ **FIGURE A11.1**

A Preference Map

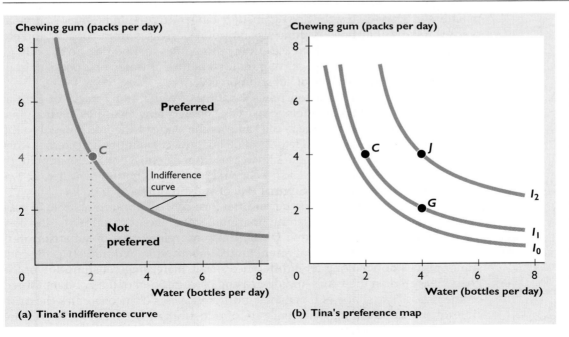

(a) Tina's indifference curve

(b) Tina's preference map

In part (a), Tina consumes 2 bottles of water and 4 packs of chewing gum a day at point C. She is indifferent between all the points on the green indifference curve. She prefers any point above the indifference curve (yellow area) to any point on it, and she prefers any point on the indifference curve to any point below it (gray area).

Part (b) shows three indifference curves of Tina's preference map. She prefers point J to point C or G, so she prefers any point on I_2 to any point on I_1.

combination in the gray area below the indifference curve. These combinations contain less water, less gum, or less of both.

The indifference curve in Figure A11.1(a) is just one of a whole family of such curves. This indifference curve appears again in Figure A11.1(b) labeled I_1. The curves labeled I_0 and I_2 are two other indifference curves. Tina prefers any point on indifference curve I_2, such as point J, to any point on indifference curve I_1, such as points C or G. She prefers any point on I_1 to any point on I_0. We refer to I_2 as being a higher indifference curve than I_1 and to I_1 as being higher than I_0.

A preference map is a series of indifference curves that resemble the contour lines on a map. By looking at the shape of the contour lines on a map, we can draw conclusions about the terrain. Similarly, by looking at the shape of the indifference curves, we can draw conclusions about a person's preferences.

■ Marginal Rate of Substitution

Marginal rate of substitution
The rate at which a person will give up good y (the good measured on the y-axis) to get more of good x (the good measured on the x-axis) and at the same time remain on the same indifference curve.

The concept of the marginal rate of substitution is the key to "reading" a preference map. The **marginal rate of substitution** (*MRS*) is the rate at which a person will give up good y (the good measured on the y-axis) to get more of good x (the good measured on the x-axis) and at the same time remain indifferent (remain on the same indifference curve). The marginal rate of substitution is measured by the magnitude of the slope of an indifference curve.

If the indifference curve is *steep*, the marginal rate of substitution is *high*. The person is willing to give up a large quantity of good y to get a small quantity of good x while remaining indifferent. But if the indifference curve is *flat*, the marginal rate of substitution is *low*. The person is willing to give up only a small amount of good y to get a large amount of good x to remain indifferent.

Figure A11.2 shows you how to calculate the marginal rate of substitution. Suppose that Tina consumes 2 bottles of water and 4 packs of gum at point C on indifference curve I_1. We calculate her marginal rate of substitution by measuring the magnitude of the slope of the indifference curve at point C. To measure this magnitude, place a straight line against, or tangent to, the indifference curve at point C. Along that line, as gum consumption decreases from 8 packs to zero packs, water consumption increases from zero bottles to 4 bottles. So at point C, Tina is willing to give up 8 packs of gum for 4 bottles of water, or 2 packs of gum per bottle. Her marginal rate of substitution is 2.

Now suppose that Tina consumes 4 bottles of water and 2 packs of gum at point G. The slope of the indifference curve at point G now measures her marginal rate of substitution. That slope is the same as the slope of the line tangent to the indifference curve at point G. Here, as chewing gum consumption decreases from 4 packs to zero, water consumption increases from zero to 8 bottles. So at point G, Tina is willing to give up 4 packs of chewing gum for 8 bottles of water, or 1/2 pack of gum per bottle. Her marginal rate of substitution is 1/2.

Diminishing marginal rate of substitution
The general tendency for the marginal rate of substitution to decrease as the consumer moves down along the indifference curve, increasing consumption of the good measured on the x-axis and decreasing consumption of the good measured on the y-axis.

As Tina moves down along her indifference curve, her marginal rate of substitution diminishes. Diminishing marginal rate of substitution is the key assumption of consumer theory. **Diminishing marginal rate of substitution** is the general tendency for the marginal rate of substitution to diminish as the consumer moves down along an indifference curve, increasing consumption of the good measured on the x-axis and decreasing consumption of the good measured on the y-axis. The shape of a person's indifference curves incorporates the principle of the diminishing marginal rate of substitution because the curves are bowed toward the origin.

■ **FIGURE A11.2**
The Marginal Rate of Substitution

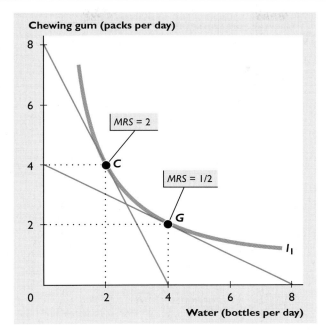

The magnitude of the slope of an indifference curve is called the marginal rate of substitution (*MRS*).

The red line at point *C* tells us that Tina is willing to give up 8 packs of gum to consume 4 bottles of water. Her marginal rate of substitution at point *C* is 8 divided by 4, which equals 2.

The red line at point *G* tells us that Tina is willing to give up 4 packs of gum to get 8 bottles of water. Her marginal rate of substitution at point *G* is 4 divided by 8, which equals 1/2.

■ Consumer Equilibrium

The consumer's goal is to buy the affordable quantities of goods that make the consumer as well off as possible. The indifference curves describe the consumer's preferences, and they tell us that the higher the indifference curve, the better off is the consumer. So the consumer's goal can be restated as being to allocate his or her budget in such a way as to get onto the highest attainable indifference curve.

The consumer's budget and the prices of the goods limit the consumer's choices. The budget line illustrated in Figure 11.1 (p. 262) summarizes the limits on the consumer's choice. We combine the indifference curves of Figure A11.1(b) with the budget line of Figure 11.1 to work out the consumer's choice and find the consumer equilibrium.

Figure A11.3 shows Tina's budget line from Figure 11.1 and her indifference curves from Figure A11.1(b). Tina's best affordable point is 2 bottles of water and 4 packs of gum—at point *C*. Here, Tina

- Is on her budget line
- Is on her highest attainable indifference curve
- Has a marginal rate of substitution between water and gum equal to the relative price of water and gum.

For every point inside the budget line, such as point *L*, there are points *on* the budget line that Tina prefers. For example, she prefers any point on the budget line between *F* and *H* to point *L*. So she chooses a point on the budget line.

FIGURE A11.3

Consumer Equilibrium

Tina's best affordable point is C. At that point, she is on her budget line and also on the highest attainable indifference curve.

At a point such as H, Tina is willing to give up more bottled water in exchange for chewing gum than she has to. She can move to point L, which is just as good as point H, and have some unspent budget. She can spend that budget and move to C, a point that she prefers to point L.

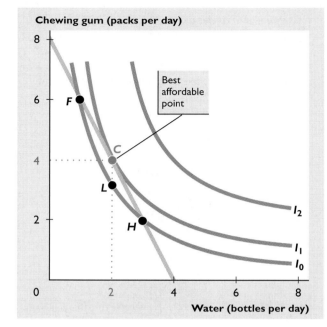

Every point on the budget line lies on an indifference curve. For example, point H lies on the indifference curve I_0. At point H, Tina's marginal rate of substitution (the magnitude of the slope of the indifference curve I_0) is less than the relative price (the magnitude of the slope of the budget line). Tina is willing to give up more bottled water in exchange for chewing gum than the budget line says she must. So she moves along her budget line from H toward C. As she does so, she passes through a number of indifference curves (not shown in the figure) located between indifference curves I_0 and I_1. All of these indifference curves are higher than I_0, so Tina prefers any point on them to point H. But when Tina gets to point C, she is on the highest attainable indifference curve. If she keeps moving along the budget line, she starts to encounter indifference curves that are lower than I_1. So Tina chooses point C—her best affordable point.

At the chosen point, the marginal rate of substitution (the magnitude of the slope of the indifference curve) equals the relative price (the magnitude of the slope of the budget line).

We can now use this model of consumer choice to predict the effect of a change in the price of water on the quantity of water demanded. That is, we can use this model to generate the demand curve for bottled water.

■ Deriving the Demand Curve

To derive Tina's demand curve for bottled water, we change the price of water, shift the budget line, and work out the new best affordable point. Figure A11.4(a) shows the change in the budget line and the change in consumer equilibrium when the price of water falls from $1 a bottle to 50¢ a bottle.

Initially, when the price of water is $1 a bottle, Tina consumes at point C in part (a). When the price of a bottle of water falls from $1 to 50¢, her budget line rotates outward and she can now get onto a higher indifference curve. Her best affordable point is now point K. Tina increases the quantity of water she buys from 2 to 4 bottles a day. She continues to buy 4 packs of gum a day.

Figure A11.4(b) shows Tina's demand curve for bottled water. When the price of water is $1 a bottle, she buys 2 bottles a day, at point A. When the price of water falls to 50¢ a bottle, she buys 4 bottles a day, at point B. Tina's demand curve traces out her best affordable quantity of water as the price of a bottle of water varies.

▪ FIGURE A11.4

Deriving Tina's Demand Curve

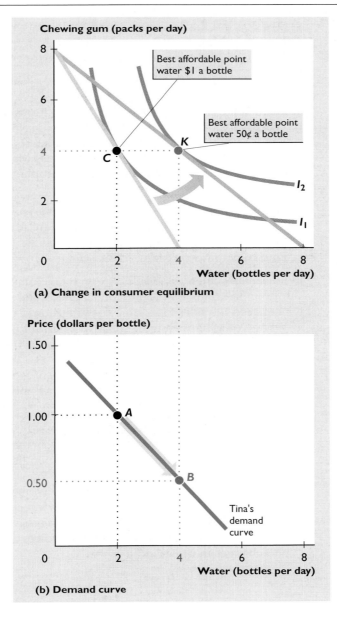

(a) Change in consumer equilibrium

(b) Demand curve

In part (a), Tina initially consumes at point C. When the price of water falls from $1 to 50¢ a bottle, she consumes at point K.

In part (b), when the price of water falls from $1 to 50¢ a bottle, Tina moves along her demand curve for bottled water from point A to point B.

Exercises

FIGURE 1

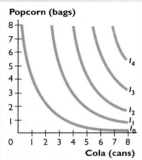

1. Sara has a budget of $12 a week. Popcorn costs $3 a bag, and cola costs $3 a can. Figure 1 illustrates Sara's preferences.
   a. What is the relative price of cola in terms of popcorn?
   b. What is the opportunity cost of a can of cola?
   c. Draw a graph of Sara's budget line with cola on the *x*-axis.
   d. What are the quantities of popcorn and cola that Sara buys?
   e. What is Sara's marginal rate of substitution of popcorn for cola at the point at which she consumes?

2. Suppose that in the situation described in exercise 1, the price of cola falls to $1.50 a can and the price of popcorn and Sara's budget remain constant.
   a. Find the new quantities of cola and popcorn that Sara buys.
   b. Find two points on Sara's demand curve for cola.

FIGURE 2

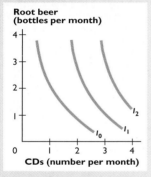

3. Marc has a budget of $20 a month. Root beer costs $5 a bottle, and CDs cost $10 each. Figure 2 illustrates his preferences.
   a. What is the relative price of root beer in terms of CDs?
   b. What is the opportunity cost of a bottle of root beer?
   c. Draw a graph of Marc's budget line with CDs on the *x*-axis.
   d. What quantities of root beer and CDs does Marc buy?
   e. Calculate Marc's marginal rate of substitution of CDs for root beer at the point at which he consumes.

4. Now suppose that in the situation described in exercise 3, the price of a CD falls to $5 and the price of root beer and Marc's budget remain constant.
   a. Find the new quantities of root beer and CDs that Marc buys.
   b. Find two points on Marc's demand curve for CDs.

5. In most states, there is no sales tax on food. Some people say that a consumption tax, a tax that is paid on all goods and services, would be better. If we replaced the sales tax with a consumption tax,
   a. What would happen to the relative price of food and haircuts?
   b. What would happen to the budget line showing the quantities of food and haircuts you can afford to buy?
   c. How would you change your purchases of food and haircuts?
   d. Which type of tax is best for the consumer and why?

6. Jim spends all his income on apartment rent, food, clothing, and vacations. He gets a pay raise from $3,000 a month to $4,000 a month. At the same time, airfares and other vacation-related costs increase by 50 percent.
   a. How do you think Jim will change his spending pattern as a result of the changes in his income and prices?
   b. Can you say whether Jim is better off or worse off in his new situation?
   c. If all prices rise by 50 percent, how does Jim change his purchases? Can you now say whether he is better off or worse off?
   d. Show in a graph the changes in Jim's choices that the change in income and changes in prices induce.

Production and Cost

CHAPTER CHECKLIST

When you have completed your study of this chapter, you will be able to

1 Explain how economists measure a firm's cost of production and profit.

2 Explain the relationship between a firm's output and labor employed in the short run.

3 Explain the relationship between a firm's output and costs in the short run.

4 Derive and explain a firm's long-run average cost curve.

Samantha is beaming. Her business plan impressed the bank, she got the loan she needed, and Sam's Smoothies has just ended its first year of operations on a high. But Samantha made some tough decisions to keep her business efficient and profitable. She was careful to hire exactly the amount of labor she needed and operate the right number of blenders and other equipment.

In this chapter, you're going to see the principles that guided Samantha to make decisions that minimized her production cost.

You will use what you learn in this chapter again and again in the three chapters that follow, so it is very important that you thoroughly understand the content of this chapter before moving forward to Chapter 13.

12.1 ECONOMIC COST AND PROFIT

The 20 million firms in the United States differ in size and in what they produce. But they all perform the same basic economic function: They hire factors of production and organize them to produce and sell goods and services. To understand the behavior of a firm, we need to know its goals.

■ The Firm's Goal

If you asked a group of entrepreneurs what they are trying to achieve, you would get many different answers. Some would talk about making a high-quality product, others about business growth, others about market share, and others about job satisfaction of the work force. All of these goals might be pursued, but they are not the fundamental goal. They are a means to a deeper goal.

The firm's goal is to *maximize profit.* A firm that does not seek to maximize profit is either eliminated or bought by firms that *do* seek to achieve that goal. To calculate a firm's profit, we must determine its total revenue and total cost. Economists have a special way of defining and measuring cost and profit, which we'll explain and illustrate by looking at Sam's Smoothies, a firm that is owned and operated by Samantha.

■ Accounting Cost and Profit

In 2004, Sam's Smoothies' total revenue from the sale of smoothies was $150,000. The firm paid $20,000 for fruit, yogurt, and honey; $22,000 in wages for the labor it hired; and $3,000 in interest to the bank. These expenses totaled $45,000.

Sam's accountant said that the depreciation of the firm's blenders, refrigerators, and shop during 2004 was $10,000. Depreciation is the fall in the value of the firm's capital, and accountants calculate it by using the Internal Revenue Service's rules, which are based on standards set by the Financial Accounting Standards Board. So the accountant reported Sam's Smoothies' total cost for 2004 as $55,000 and the firm's profit as $95,000—$150,000 of total revenue minus $55,000 of total costs.

Sam's accountant measures cost and profit to ensure that the firm pays the correct amount of income tax and to show the bank how Sam's has used its bank loan. Economists have a different purpose: to predict the decisions that a firm makes to maximize its profit. These decisions respond to *opportunity cost* and *economic profit*.

■ Opportunity Cost

To produce its output, a firm employs factors of production: land, labor, capital, and entrepreneurship. Another firm could have used these same resources to produce other goods or services. In Chapter 3 (pp. 64–66), resources can be used to produce either bottled water or CDs, so the opportunity cost of producing a bottle of water is the number of CDs forgone. Pilots who fly passengers for United Airlines can't at the same time fly freight for FedEx. Construction workers who are building an office high-rise can't simultaneously build apartments. A communications satellite operating at peak capacity can carry television signals or e-mail messages but not both at the same time. A journalist writing for the *New York Times* can't at the same time create Web news reports for CNN. And Samantha can't simultaneously run her smoothies business and a flower shop.

The highest-valued alternative forgone is the opportunity cost of a firm's production. From the viewpoint of the firm, this opportunity cost is the amount that the firm must pay the owners of the factors of production it employs to attract them from their best alternative use. So a firm's opportunity cost of production is the cost of the factors of production it employs.

To determine these costs, let's return to Sam's and look at the opportunity cost of producing smoothies.

Explicit Costs and Implicit Costs

The amount that a firm pays to attract resources from their best alternative use is either an explicit cost or an implicit cost. A cost paid in money is an **explicit cost**. Because the amount spent could have been spent on something else, an explicit cost is an opportunity cost. The wages that Samantha pays labor, the interest she pays the bank, and her expenditure on fruit, yogurt, and honey are explicit costs.

A firm incurs an **implicit cost** when it uses a factor of production but does not make a direct money payment for its use. The two categories of implicit cost are economic depreciation and the cost of the resources of the firm's owner.

Economic depreciation is the opportunity cost of the firm using capital that it owns. It is measured as the change in the *market value* of capital—the market price of the capital at the beginning of a period minus its market price at the end of a period. Suppose that Samantha could have sold her blenders, refrigerators, and shop on December 31, 2003, for $250,000. If she can sell the same capital on December 31, 2004, for $246,000, her economic depreciation during 2004 is $4,000. This is the opportunity cost of using her capital during 2004, not the $10,000 depreciation calculated by Sam's accountant.

Interest is another cost of capital. When the firm's owner provides the funds used to buy capital, the opportunity cost of those funds is the interest income forgone by not using them in the best alternative way. If Sam loaned her firm funds that could have earned her $1,000 in interest, this amount is an implicit cost of producing smoothies.

When a firm's owner supplies labor, the opportunity cost of the owner's time spent working for the firm is the wage income forgone by not working in the best alternative job. For example, instead of working at her next best job that pays $34,000 a year, Sam supplies labor to her smoothies business. This implicit cost of $34,000 is part of the opportunity cost of producing smoothies.

Finally, a firm's owner often supplies entrepreneurship, the factor of production that organizes the business and bears the risk of running it. The return to entrepreneurship is **normal profit**. Normal profit is part of a firm's opportunity cost because it is the cost of a forgone alternative—running another firm. Instead of running Sam's Smoothies, Sam could earn $16,000 a year running a flower shop. This amount is an implicit cost of production at Sam's Smoothies.

■ Economic Profit

A firm's **economic profit** equals total revenue minus total cost. Total revenue is the amount received from the sale of the product. It is the price of the output multiplied by the quantity sold. Total cost is the sum of the explicit costs and implicit costs and is the opportunity cost of production.

Explicit cost
A cost paid in money.

Implicit cost
An opportunity cost incurred by a firm when it uses a factor of production for which it does not make a direct money payment.

Economic depreciation
An opportunity cost of a firm using capital that it owns—measured as the change in the *market value* of capital over a given period.

Normal profit
The return to entrepreneurship. Normal profit is part of a firm's opportunity cost because it is the cost of not running another firm.

Economic profit
A firm's total revenue minus total cost.

■ TABLE 12.1
Economic Accounting

Item		
Total Revenue		**$150,000**
Explicit Costs		
Cost of fruit, yogurt, and honey	$20,000	
Wages	$22,000	
Interest	$3,000	
Implicit Costs		
Samantha's forgone wages	$34,000	
Samantha's forgone interest	$1,000	
Economic depreciation	$4,000	
Normal profit	$16,000	
Opportunity Cost		**$100,000**
Economic Profit		**$50,000**

Because one of the firm's implicit costs is *normal profit*, the return to the entrepreneur equals normal profit plus economic profit. If a firm incurs an economic loss, the entrepreneur receives less than normal profit.

Table 12.1 summarizes the economic cost concepts, and Figure 12.1 compares the economic view and the accounting view of cost and profit. The total revenue received by Sam's Smoothies is $150,000; the opportunity cost of the resources that Sam uses is $100,000; and Sam's economic profit is $50,000.

■ FIGURE 12.1
Two Views of Cost and Profit

Economists measure economic profit as total revenue minus opportunity cost. Opportunity cost includes explicit costs and implicit costs. Normal profit is an implicit cost. Accountants measure profit as total revenue minus explicit costs—costs paid in money—and depreciation.

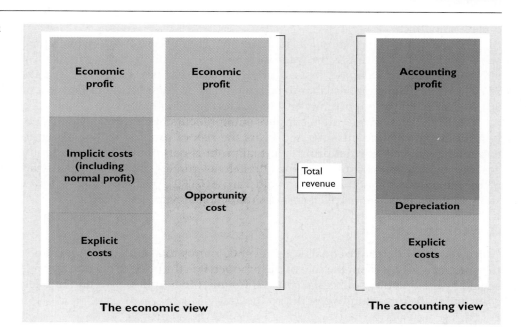

The economic view   The accounting view

CHECKPOINT 12.1

1 Explain how economists measure a firm's cost of production and profit.

Practice Problem 12.1

1. Lee is a computer programmer who earned $35,000 in 2003. But Lee loves water sports, and in 2004, he opened a body board manufacturing business. At the end of the first year of operation, he submitted the following information to his accountant:

   i. He stopped renting out his cottage for $3,500 a year and used it as his factory. The market value of the cottage increased from $70,000 to $71,000.
   ii. He spent $50,000 on materials, phone, utilities, etc.
   iii. He leased machines for $10,000 a year.
   iv. He paid $15,000 in wages.
   v. He used $10,000 from his savings account, which earns 5 percent a year interest.
   vi. He borrowed $40,000 at 10 percent a year from the bank.
   vii. He sold $160,000 worth of body boards.
   viii. Normal profit is $25,000 a year.

   a. Calculate Lee's explicit costs and implicit costs.
   b. Calculate Lee's economic profit.
   c. Lee's accountant recorded the depreciation on Lee's cottage during 2004 as $7,000. What did the accountant say Lee's profit or loss was?

Exercise 12.1

1. In 2003, Toni taught music and earned $20,000. She also earned $4,000 by renting out her basement. On January 1, 2004, she quit teaching, stopped renting out her basement, and began to use it as the office for her new Web site design business. She took $2,000 from her savings account to buy a computer. During 2004, she paid $1,500 for the lease of a Web server and $1,750 for high-speed Internet service. She received a total revenue from Web site designing of $45,000 and earned interest at 5 percent a year on her savings account balance. Normal profit is $55,000 a year. At the end of 2004, Toni could have sold her computer for $500.
   a. Calculate Toni's explicit costs and implicit costs in 2004.
   b. Calculate Toni's economic profit in 2004.

Solution to Practice Problem 12.1

1a. Explicit costs are costs paid with money: items (ii), (iii), (iv), and (vi). Explicit costs are $50,000 + $10,000 + $15,000 + $4,000, or $79,000. Implicit costs are the wages forgone and items (i), (v), and (viii) minus the increase in the market value of the cottage. That is, implicit costs are $35,000 + $3,500 + $500 + $25,000 − $1,000, or $63,000.

1b. Economic profit equals total revenue minus total cost. Total cost is the sum of explicit costs plus implicit costs: $79,000 + $63,000, or $142,000. So Lee's economic profit is $160,000 − $142,000, or $18,000.

1c. The accountant measures Lee's profit as total revenue minus explicit costs minus depreciation: $160,000 − $79,000 − $7,000, or $74,000.

SHORT RUN AND LONG RUN

The main goal of this chapter is to explore the influences on a firm's cost. The key influence on cost is the quantity of output that the firm produces per period. The greater the output rate, the higher is the total cost of production. But the effect of a change in production on cost depends on how soon the firm wants to act. A firm that plans to change its output rate tomorrow has fewer options than does a firm that plans ahead and intends to change its production six months from now.

To study the relationship between a firm's output decision and its costs, we distinguish between two decision time frames:

- The short run
- The long run

The Short Run: Fixed Plant

Short run

The time frame in which the quantities of some resources are fixed. In the short run, a firm can usually change the quantity of labor it uses but not its technology and quantity of capital.

The **short run** is the time frame in which the quantities of some resources are fixed. For most firms, the fixed resources are the firm's technology and capital—its equipment and buildings. The management organization is also fixed in the short run. The fixed resources that a firm uses are its *fixed factors of production* and the resources that it can vary are its *variable factors of production*. The collection of fixed resources is the firm's *plant*. So in the short run, a firm's plant is fixed.

Sam's Smoothies' plant is its blenders, refrigerators, and shop. Sam's cannot change these inputs in the short run. An electric power utility can't change the number of generators it uses in the short run. An airport can't change the number of runways, terminal buildings, and traffic control facilities in the short run.

To increase output in the short run, a firm must increase the quantity of variable factors it uses. Labor is usually the variable factor of production. To produce more smoothies, Sam must hire more labor. Similarly, to increase the production of electricity, a utility must hire more engineers and run its generators for longer hours. To increase the volume of traffic it handles, an airport must hire more check-in clerks, cargo handlers, and air-traffic controllers.

Short-run decisions are easily reversed. A firm can increase or decrease output in the short run by increasing or decreasing the number of labor hours it hires.

The Long Run: Variable Plant

Long run

The time frame in which the quantities of *all* resources can be varied.

The **long run** is the time frame in which the quantities of *all* resources can be varied. That is, the long run is a period in which the firm can change its *plant*.

To increase output in the long run, a firm can increase the size of its plant. Sam's Smoothies can install more blenders and refrigerators and increase the size of its shop. An electric power utility can install more generators. And an airport can build more runways, terminals, and traffic-control facilities.

Long-run decisions are *not* easily reversed. Once a firm buys a new plant, its resale value is usually much less than the amount the firm paid for it. The difference between the cost of the plant and its resale value is a *sunk cost*. A sunk cost is irrelevant to the firm's decisions (see Chapter 1, p. 14). The only costs that influence the firm's decisions are the short-run cost of changing its labor inputs and the long-run cost of changing its plant.

We're going to study costs in the short run and the long run. We begin with the short run and describe the limits to the firm's production possibilities.

12.2 SHORT-RUN PRODUCTION

To increase the output of a fixed plant, a firm must increase the quantity of labor it employs. We describe the relationship between output and the quantity of labor employed by using three related concepts:

- Total product
- Marginal product
- Average product

■ Total Product

Total product (*TP*) is the total quantity of a good produced in a given period. Total product is an output *rate*—the number of units produced per unit of time (for example, per hour, day, or week). Total product increases as the quantity of labor employed increases, and we illustrate this relationship as a total product schedule and total product curve like those in Figure 12.2. The total product schedule (the table below the graph) lists the maximum quantities of smoothies per hour that Sam can produce with her existing plant at each quantity of labor. Points *A* through *H* on the *TP* curve correspond to the columns in the table.

Total product
The total quantity of a good produced in a given period.

■ **FIGURE 12.2**
Total Product Schedule and Total Product Curve

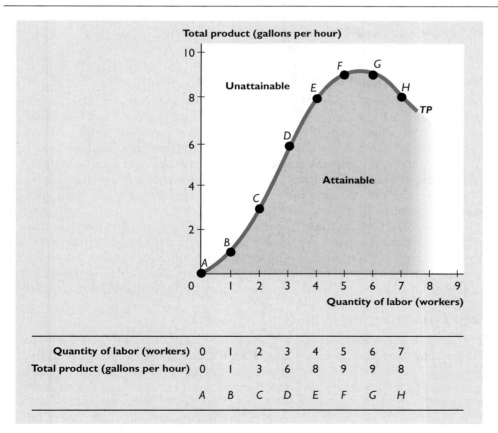

Quantity of labor (workers)	0	1	2	3	4	5	6	7
Total product (gallons per hour)	0	1	3	6	8	9	9	8
	A	*B*	*C*	*D*	*E*	*F*	*G*	*H*

The total product schedule shows how the quantity of smoothies that Sam's can produce changes as the quantity of labor employed changes. In column *C*, Sam's employs 2 workers and can produce 3 gallons of smoothies an hour.

The total product curve, *TP*, graphs the data in the table. Points *A* through *H* on the curve correspond to the columns of the table. The total product curve separates attainable outputs from unattainable outputs. Points below the *TP* curve are inefficient. Points on the *TP* curve are efficient.

Like the *production possibilities frontier* (see Chapter 3, p. 58), the total product curve separates attainable outputs from unattainable outputs. All the points that lie above the curve are unattainable. Points that lie below the curve, in the orange area, are attainable. But they are inefficient: They use more labor than is necessary to produce a given output. Only the points *on* the total product curve are efficient.

■ Marginal Product

Marginal product
The change in total product that results from a one-unit increase in the quantity of labor employed.

Marginal product (*MP*) is the change in total product that results from a one-unit increase in the quantity of labor employed. It tells us the contribution to total product of adding one additional worker. When the quantity of labor increases by more (or less) than one worker, we calculate marginal product as

Marginal product = Change in total product ÷ Change in quantity of labor.

Figure 12.3 shows Sam's Smoothies' marginal product curve, *MP*, and its relationship with the total product curve. You can see that as the quantity of labor increases from 1 to 3 workers, marginal product increases. But as yet more workers are employed, marginal product decreases. When the seventh worker is employed, marginal product is negative.

Notice that the steeper the slope of the total product curve in part (a), the greater is marginal product in part (b). And when the total product curve turns downward in part (a), marginal product is negative in part (b).

The total product curve and marginal product curve in Figure 12.3 incorporate a feature that is shared by all production processes in firms as different as the Ford Motor Company, Jim's Barber Shop, and Sam's Smoothies:

- Increasing marginal returns initially
- Decreasing marginal returns eventually

Increasing Marginal Returns

Increasing marginal returns
When the marginal product of an additional worker exceeds the marginal product of the previous worker.

Increasing marginal returns occur when the marginal product of an additional worker exceeds the marginal product of the previous worker. Increasing marginal returns occur when a small number of workers are employed and arise from increased specialization and division of labor in the production process.

For example, if Samantha employs just one worker, that person must learn all the aspects of making smoothies: running the blender, cleaning it, fixing breakdowns, buying and checking the fruit, and serving the customers. That one person must perform all these tasks.

If Samantha hires a second person, the two workers can specialize in different parts of the production process. As a result, two workers can produce more than twice as much as one worker. The marginal product of the second worker is greater than the marginal product of the first worker. Marginal returns are increasing. Most production processes experience increasing marginal returns initially.

Decreasing Marginal Returns

Decreasing marginal returns
When the marginal product of an additional worker is less than the marginal product of the previous worker.

All production processes eventually reach a point of *decreasing* marginal returns. **Decreasing marginal returns** occur when the marginal product of an additional worker is less than the marginal product of the previous worker. Decreasing marginal returns arise from the fact that more and more workers use the same equipment and work space. As more workers are employed, there is less and less that is productive for the additional worker to do. For example, if Samantha hires a

■ FIGURE 12.3

Total Product and Marginal Product

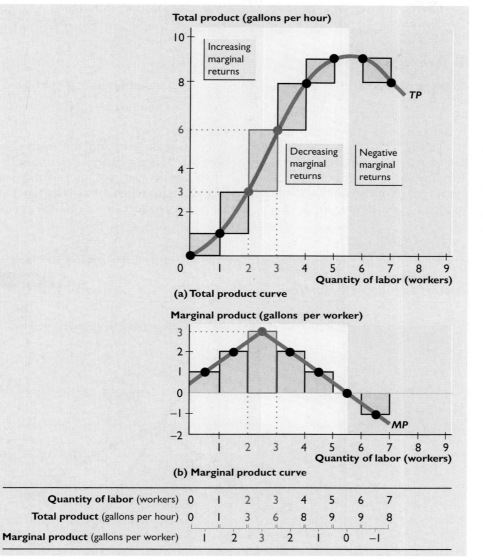

(a) Total product curve

(b) Marginal product curve

Quantity of labor (workers)	0	1	2	3	4	5	6	7
Total product (gallons per hour)	0	1	3	6	8	9	9	8
Marginal product (gallons per worker)		1	2	3	2	1	0	−1

The table calculates marginal product, and the orange bars illustrate it. When labor increases from 2 to 3 workers, total product increases from 3 gallons to 6 gallons an hour. So marginal product is the orange bar whose height is 3 gallons (in both parts of the figure).

In part (b), marginal product is graphed midway between the labor inputs to emphasize that it is the result of *changing* inputs. Marginal product increases to a maximum (when 3 workers are employed in this example) and then declines— diminishing marginal product.

fourth worker, output increases but not by as much as it did when she hired the third worker. In this case, three workers exhaust all the possible gains from specialization and the division of labor. By hiring a fourth worker, Sam's produces more smoothies per hour, but the equipment is being operated closer to its limits. Sometimes the fourth worker has nothing to do because the machines are running without the need for further attention.

Hiring yet more workers continues to increase output but by successively smaller amounts until Samantha hires the sixth worker, at which point total product stops rising. Add a seventh worker, and the workplace is so congested that the workers get in each other's way and total product falls.

Decreasing marginal returns are so pervasive that they qualify for the status of a law: the **law of decreasing returns**, which states that

> **As a firm uses more of a variable input, with a given quantity of fixed inputs, the marginal product of the variable input eventually decreases.**

■ Average Product

Average product
Total product divided by the quantity of an input. The average product of labor is total product divided by the quantity of labor employed.

Average product (*AP*) is the total product per worker employed. It is calculated as

$$\text{Average product} = \text{Total product} \div \text{Quantity of labor.}$$

Another name for average product is *productivity*.

Figure 12.4 shows the average product of labor, *AP*, and the relationship between average product and marginal product. Average product increases from 1 to 3 workers (its maximum value) but then decreases as yet more workers are employed. Notice also that average product is largest when average product and marginal product are equal. That is, the marginal product curve cuts the average

---

■ FIGURE 12.4

Average Product and Marginal Product

The table calculates average product. For example, when the quantity of labor is 3 workers, total product is 6 gallons an hour, so average product is 6 gallons ÷ 3 workers = 2 gallons a worker.

The average product curve is *AP*. When marginal product exceeds average product, average product is increasing. When marginal product is less than average product, average product is decreasing.

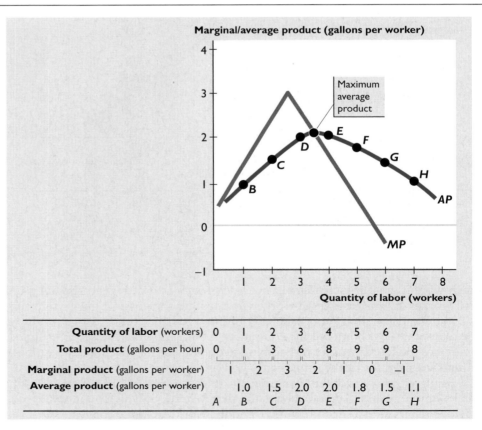

Quantity of labor (workers)	0	1		2		3		4		5		6		7
Total product (gallons per hour)	0	1		3		6		8		9		9		8
Marginal product (gallons per worker)			1		2		3		2		1		0		−1
Average product (gallons per worker)		1.0		1.5		2.0		2.0		1.8		1.5		1.1
	A	*B*		*C*		*D*		*E*		*F*		*G*		*H*

product curve at the point of maximum average product. For employment levels at which marginal product exceeds average product, the average product curve slopes upward and average product increases as more labor is employed. For employment levels at which marginal product is less than average product, the average product curve slopes downward and average product decreases as more labor is employed.

The relationship between average product and marginal product is a general feature of the relationship between the average value and the marginal value of any variable. Let's look at a familiar example.

Marginal and Average Values in YOUR Life

Jen, a part-time student, takes one course each semester over five semesters. In the first semester, she takes calculus and her grade is a C (2). This grade is her marginal grade. It is also her average grade—her GPA.

In the next semester, Jen takes French and gets a B (3)—her new marginal grade. Because her marginal grade exceeds her average grade, the marginal grade pulls her average up. Her GPA rises to 2.5.

In the third semester, Jen takes economics and gets an A (4). Again her marginal grade exceeds her average, so the marginal grade pulls her average up. Jen's GPA is now 3—the average of 2, 3, and 4.

In the fourth semester, she takes history and gets a B (3). Now her marginal grade equals her average, so her average doesn't change. It remains at 3.

In the fifth semester, Jen takes English and gets a C (2). Because her marginal grade, 2, is below her average of 3, the marginal grade pulls the average down. Her GPA falls.

This everyday relationship between average and marginal grades is similar to the relationship between average and marginal product.

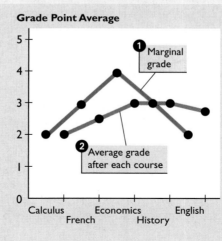

2   Explain the relationship between a firm's output and labor employed in the short run.

Practice Problem 12.2

1. Tom leases a farmer's field and grows pineapples. Tom hires students to pick and pack the pineapples. Table 1 sets out Tom's total product schedule.
   a. Calculate the marginal product of the third student.
   b. Calculate the average product of three students.
   c. Over what numbers of students does marginal product increase?
   d. When marginal product increases, compare average product and marginal product.

Exercise 12.2

1. Lizzie hires students in the summer to paint houses. Table 2 sets out her total product schedule.
   a. Calculate the marginal product of the fourth student.
   b. Calculate the average product of four students.
   c. Over what numbers of students does marginal product decrease?
   d. When marginal product decreases, compare average product and marginal product.

Solution to Practice Problem 12.2

1a. Marginal product of the third student is the change in total product that results from hiring the third student. When Tom hires 2 students, total product is 220 pineapples a day. When Tom hires 3 students, total product is 300 pineapples a day. Marginal product of the third student is the total product of 3 students minus the total product of 2 students, which is 300 pineapples − 220 pineapples a day, or 80 pineapples a day.

1b. Average product equals total product divided by the number of students. When Tom hires 3 students, total product is 300 pineapples a day, so average product is 300 pineapples a day ÷ 3 students, which equals 100 pineapples a day.

1c. Marginal product of the first student is 100 pineapples a day, that of the second student is 120 pineapples a day, and that of the third student is 80 pineapples a day. So marginal product increases when Tom hires the first and second students.

1d. When Tom hires 1 student, marginal product is 100 pineapples per student and average product is 100 pineapples per student. When Tom hires 2 students, marginal product is 120 pineapples per student and average product is 110 pineapples per student. That is, when Tom hires the second student, marginal product exceeds average product.

TABLE 1

Labor (students)	Total product (pineapples per day)
0	0
1	100
2	220
3	300
4	360
5	400
6	420
7	430

TABLE 2

Labor (students)	Total product (houses painted per week)
0	0
1	2
2	5
3	9
4	12
5	14
6	15

12.3 SHORT-RUN COST

To produce more output (total product) in the short run, a firm must employ more labor, which means that it must increase its costs. We describe the relationship between output and cost using three cost concepts:

- Total cost
- Marginal cost
- Average cost

■ Total Cost

A firm's **total cost** (*TC*) is the cost of all the factors of production used by the firm. Total cost divides into two parts: total fixed cost and total variable cost. **Total fixed cost** (*TFC*) is the cost of a firm's fixed factors of production: land, capital, and entrepreneurship. Because in the short run, the quantities of these inputs don't change as output changes, total fixed cost doesn't change as output changes. **Total variable cost** (*TVC*) is the cost of a firm's variable factor of production—labor. To change its output in the short run, a firm must change the quantity of labor it employs, so total variable cost changes as output changes.

Total cost is the sum of total fixed cost and total variable cost. That is,

$$TC = TFC + TVC.$$

Table 12.2 shows Sam's Smoothies' total costs. Sam's fixed costs are $10 an hour regardless of whether it operates or not—*TFC* is $10 an hour. To produce smoothies, Samantha hires labor, which costs $6 an hour. *TVC*, which increases as output increases, equals the number of workers per hour multiplied by $6. For example, to produce 6 gallons an hour, Samantha hires 3 workers, so *TVC* is $18 an hour. *TC* is the sum of *TFC* and *TVC*. So to produce 6 gallons an hour, *TC* is $28. Check the calculation in each row and note that to produce some quantities— 2 gallons an hour, for example—Sam hires a worker for only part of the hour.

Total cost
The cost of all the factors of production used by a firm.

Total fixed cost
The cost of the firm's fixed factors of production—the cost of land, capital, and entrepreneurship.

Total variable cost
The cost of the firm's variable factor of production—the cost of labor.

■ TABLE 12.2
Sam's Smoothies' Total Costs

Labor (workers per hour)	Output (gallons per hour)	Total fixed cost	Total variable cost	Total cost
			(dollars per hour)	
0	0	10	0.00	10.00
1.00	1	10	6.00	16.00
1.60	2	10	9.60	19.60
2.00	3	10	12.00	22.00
2.35	4	10	14.10	24.10
2.70	5	10	16.20	26.20
3.00	6	10	18.00	28.00
3.40	7	10	20.40	30.40
4.00	8	10	24.00	34.00
5.00	9	10	30.00	40.00

Figure 12.5 illustrates Sam's total cost curves. The green total fixed cost curve (*TFC*) is horizontal because total fixed cost does not change when output changes. It is a constant at $10 an hour. The purple total variable cost curve (*TVC*) and the blue total cost curve (*TC*) both slope upward because variable cost increases as output increases. The arrows highlight total fixed cost as the vertical distance between the *TVC* and *TC* curve.

Let's now look at Sam's Smoothies' marginal cost.

■ Marginal Cost

In Figure 12.5, total variable cost and total cost increase at a decreasing rate at small levels of output and then begin to increase at an increasing rate as output increases. To understand these patterns in the changes in total cost, we need to use the concept of *marginal cost*.

Marginal cost
The change in total cost that results from a one-unit increase in output.

A firm's **marginal cost** is the change in total cost the results from a one-unit increase in output. Table 12.3 calculates the marginal cost for Sam's Smoothies. When, for example, output increases from 5 gallons to 6 gallons an hour, total cost increases from $26.20 to $28. So the marginal cost of this gallon of smoothie is $1.80 ($28 − $26.20).

Marginal cost tells us how total cost changes as output changes. The final cost concept tells us what it costs, on the average, to produce a unit of output. Let's now look at Sam's average costs.

■ **FIGURE 12.5**

Total Cost Curves at Sam's Smoothies

Total fixed cost (*TFC*) is constant—it graphs as a horizontal line—and total variable cost (*TVC*) increases as output increases. Total cost (*TC*) also increases as output increases. The vertical distance between the total cost curve and the total variable cost curve is total fixed cost, as illustrated by the two arrows.

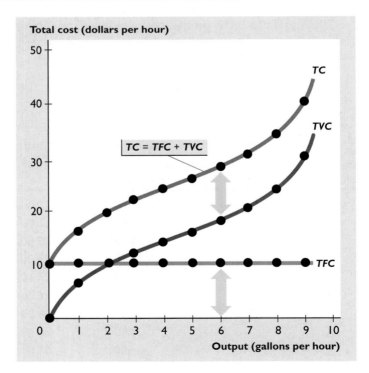

■ Average Cost

There are three average cost concepts:

- Average fixed cost
- Average variable cost
- Average total cost

Average fixed cost (*AFC*) is total fixed cost per unit of output. **Average variable cost** (*AVC*) is total variable cost per unit of output. **Average total cost** (*ATC*) is total cost per unit of output. The average cost concepts are calculated from the total cost concepts as follows:

$$TC = TFC + TVC.$$

Divide each total cost term by the quantity produced, *Q*, to give

$$\frac{TC}{Q} = \frac{TFC}{Q} + \frac{TVC}{Q}$$

or

$$ATC = AFC + AVC.$$

Table 12.3 shows these average costs. For example, when output is 3 gallons an hour, average fixed cost is ($10 ÷ 3), which equals $3.33; average variable cost is ($12 ÷ 3), which equals $4.00; and average total cost is ($22 ÷ 3), which equals $7.33. Note that average total cost ($7.33) equals average fixed cost ($3.33) plus average variable cost ($4.00).

Average fixed cost
Total fixed cost per unit of output.

Average variable cost
Total variable cost per unit of output.

Average total cost
Total cost per unit of output, which equals average fixed cost plus average variable cost.

■ **TABLE 12.3**

Sam's Smoothies' Marginal Cost and Average Cost

Output (gallons per hour)	Total cost (dollars per hour)	Marginal cost (dollars per gallon)	Average fixed cost	Average variable cost	Average total cost
				(dollars per gallon)	
0	10.00		–	–	–
		6.00			
1	16.00		10.00	6.00	16.00
		3.60			
2	19.60		5.00	4.80	9.80
		2.40			
3	22.00		3.33	4.00	7.33
		2.10			
4	24.10		2.50	3.53	6.03
		2.10			
5	26.20		2.00	3.24	5.24
		1.80			
6	28.00		1.67	3.00	4.67
		2.40			
7	30.40		1.43	2.91	4.34
		3.60			
8	34.00		1.25	3.00	4.25
		6.00			
9	40.00		1.11	3.33	4.44

Figure 12.6 graphs the marginal cost and average cost data in Table 12.3. The red marginal cost curve (MC) is U-shaped because of the way in which marginal product changes. Recall that when Samantha hires a second or a third worker, marginal product increases and output increases to 6 gallons an hour (Figure 12.3 on p. 299). Over this output range, marginal cost decreases as output increases. When Samantha hires a fourth or more workers, marginal product decreases but output increases up to 9 gallons an hour (Figure 12.3). Over this output range, marginal cost increases as output increases.

The green average fixed cost curve (AFC) slopes downward. As output increases, the same constant total fixed cost is spread over a larger output. The blue average total cost curve (ATC) and the purple average variable cost curve (AVC) are U-shaped. The vertical distance between the average total cost and average variable cost curves is equal to average fixed cost—as indicated by the two arrows. That distance shrinks as output increases because average fixed cost decreases with increasing output.

The marginal cost curve intersects the average variable cost curve and the average total cost curve at their minimum points. That is, when marginal cost is less than average cost, average cost is decreasing; and when marginal cost exceeds average cost, average cost is increasing. This relationship holds for both the ATC curve and the AVC curve and is another example of the relationship you saw in Figure 12.4 for average product and marginal product.

▪ FIGURE 12.6

Average Cost Curves and Marginal Cost Curve at Sam's Smoothies ⓧ myeconlab

Average fixed cost (AFC) decreases as output increases. The average total cost curve (ATC) and average variable cost curve (AVC) are U-shaped. The vertical distance between these two curves is equal to average fixed cost, as illustrated by the two arrows.

Marginal cost is the change in total cost when output increases by one unit. The marginal cost curve (MC) is U-shaped and intersects the average variable cost curve and the average total cost curve at their minimum points.

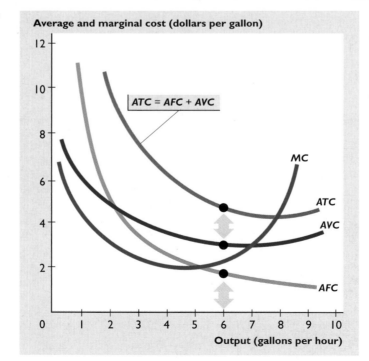

■ Why the Average Total Cost Curve Is U-Shaped

Average total cost, *ATC*, is the sum of average fixed cost, *AFC*, and average variable cost, *AVC*. So the shape of the *ATC* curve combines the shapes of the *AFC* and *AVC* curves. The U-shape of the average total cost curve arises from the influence of two opposing forces:

- Spreading total fixed cost over a larger output
- Decreasing marginal returns

When output increases, the firm spreads its total fixed costs over a larger output and its average fixed cost decreases—its average fixed cost curve slopes downward.

Decreasing marginal returns means that as output increases, ever larger amounts of labor are needed to produce an additional unit of output. So average variable cost eventually increases, and the *AVC* curve eventually slopes upward.

The shape of the average total cost curve combines these two effects. Initially, as output increases, both average fixed cost and average variable cost decrease, so average total cost decreases and the *ATC* curve slopes downward. But as output increases further and decreasing marginal returns set in, average variable cost begins to increase. Eventually, average variable cost increases more quickly than average fixed cost decreases, so average total cost increases and the *ATC* curve slopes upward.

All the short-run cost concepts that you've met are summarized in Table 12.4.

■ TABLE 12.4
A Compact Glossary of Costs

Term	Symbol	Definition	Equation
Fixed cost		The cost of a fixed factor of production that is independent of the quantity produced	
Variable cost		The cost of a variable factor of production that varies with the quantity produced	
Total fixed cost	TFC	Cost of the fixed factors of production	
Total variable cost	TVC	Cost of the variable factor of production	
Total cost	TC	Cost of all factors of production	$TC = TFC + TVC$
Marginal cost	MC	Change in total cost resulting from a one-unit increase in output (Q)	$MC = \Delta TC \div \Delta Q^*$
Average fixed cost	AFC	Total fixed cost per unit of output	$AFC = TFC \div Q$
Average variable cost	AVC	Total variable cost per unit of output	$AVC = TVC \div Q$
Average total cost	ATC	Total cost per unit of output	$ATC = AFC + AVC$

*In this equation, the Greek letter delta (Δ) stands for "change in."

■ Cost Curves and Product Curves

A firm's cost curves and product curves are linked, and Figure 12.7 shows how. The top figure shows the average product curve and the marginal product curve. The bottom figure shows the average variable cost curve and the marginal cost curve.

The figure highlights the links between the product and cost curves. At low levels of employment and output, as the firm hires more labor, marginal product and average product rise and output increases faster than costs. So marginal cost and average variable cost fall. Then, at the point of maximum marginal product, marginal cost is a minimum. As the firm hires more labor, marginal product decreases and marginal cost increases. But average product continues to rise, and average variable cost continues to fall. Then, at the point of maximum average product, average variable cost is a minimum. As the firm hires even more labor, average product decreases and average variable cost increases.

■ Shifts in the Cost Curves

The position of a firm's short-run cost curves in Figures 12.5 and 12.6 depend on two factors:

- Technology
- Prices of factors of production

Technology

A technological change that increases productivity shifts the total product curve upward. It also shifts the marginal product curve and the average product curve upward. With a better technology, the same inputs can produce more output, so an advance in technology lowers the average and marginal costs and shifts the short-run cost curves downward.

For example, advances in robotic technology have increased productivity in the automobile industry. As a result, the product curves of DaimlerChrysler, Ford, and GM have shifted upward, and their average and marginal cost curves have shifted downward. But the relationships between their product curves and cost curves have not changed. The curves are still linked, as in Figure 12.7.

Often a technological advance results in a firm using more capital, a fixed input, and less labor, a variable input. For example, today telephone companies use computers to connect long-distance calls instead of the human operators they used in the 1980s. When a telephone company makes this change, total variable cost decreases and total cost decreases, but total fixed cost increases. This change in the mix of fixed cost and variable cost means that at small output levels, average total cost might increase, but at large output levels, average total cost decreases.

Prices of Factors of Production

An increase in the price of a factor of production increases costs and shifts the cost curves. But how the curves shift depends on which resource price changes. An increase in rent or some other component of *fixed* cost shifts the fixed cost curves (*TFC* and *AFC*) upward and shifts the total cost curve (*TC*) upward but leaves the variable cost curves (*AVC* and *TVC*) and the marginal cost curve (*MC*) unchanged.

FIGURE 12.7
Product Curves and Cost Curves

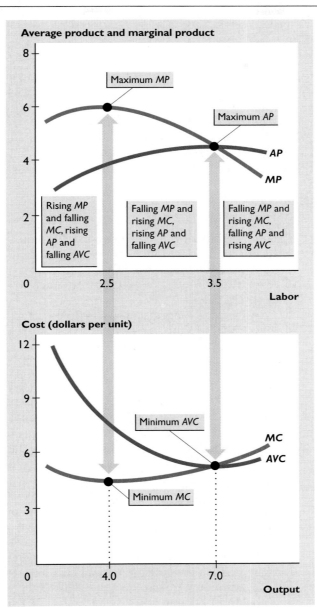

A firm's marginal cost curve is linked to its marginal product curve. If marginal product rises, marginal cost falls. If marginal product is a maximum, marginal cost is a minimum. If marginal product diminishes, marginal cost rises.

A firm's average variable cost curve is linked to its average product curve. If average product rises, average variable cost falls. If average product is a maximum, average variable cost is a minimum. If average product diminishes, average variable cost rises.

An increase in wage rates or some other component of *variable* cost shifts the variable cost curves (*TVC* and *AVC*) and the marginal cost curve (*MC*) upward but leaves the fixed cost curves (*AFC* and *TFC*) unchanged. So, for example, if the interest expense paid by a trucking company increases, the fixed cost of transportation services increases, but if the wage rate paid to truck drivers increases, the variable cost and marginal cost of transportation services increase.

3   **Explain the relationship between a firm's output and costs in the short run.**

Practice Problem 12.3

1. Tom leases a farmer's field for $120 a day and grows pineapples. Tom pays students $100 a day to pick and pack the pineapples. Tom leases capital at $80 a day. Table 1 gives the daily output.
   a. Construct the total cost schedule.
   b. Construct the average total cost schedule.
   c. Construct the marginal cost schedule.
   d. At what output is Tom's average total cost a minimum?

TABLE 1

Labor (students)	Output (pineapples per day)
0	0
1	100
2	220
3	300
4	360
5	400
6	420
7	430

Exercise 12.3

1. Lizzie hires students at $50 a day to paint houses. She leases equipment that costs her $100 a day. Table 2 shows her total product schedule.
   a. Construct the total variable cost and total cost schedules.
   b. Construct the average fixed cost, average variable cost, and average total cost schedules.
   c. Construct the marginal cost schedule.
   d. Check that the gap between total cost and total variable cost is the same at all outputs. Explain why.

TABLE 2

Labor (students)	Output (pineapples per day)
0	0
1	2
2	5
3	9
4	12
5	14
6	15

Solution to Practice Problem 12.3

1a. Total cost is the sum of total fixed cost and total variable cost. Tom leases the farmer's field for $120 a day and leases capital for $80 a day, so Tom's total fixed cost is $200 a day. Total variable cost is the wages of the students. For example, when Tom hires 3 students, the total variable cost is $300 a day. So when Tom hires 3 students, total cost is $500 a day. The *TC* column of Table 3 shows the total cost schedule.

1b. Average total cost is the total cost divided by total product. For example, when Tom hires 3 students, they pick and pack 300 pineapples a day, and Tom's total cost is $500 a day. Average total cost is $1.67 a pineapple. The *ATC* column of Table 3 shows the average total cost schedule.

1c. Marginal cost is the increase in total cost that results from picking and packing one additional pineapple a day. The total cost (from Table 3) of picking and packing 100 pineapples a day is $300. The total cost of picking and packing 220 pineapples a day is $400. The increase in the number of pineapples is 120, and the increase in total cost is $100. So the marginal cost is the increase in total cost divided by the increase in the number of pineapples. Marginal cost equals $100 ÷ 120 pineapples, which is $0.83 a pineapple. The *MC* column of Table 3 shows the marginal cost schedule.

1d. At the minimum of average total cost, average total cost equals marginal cost. Minimum average total cost is $1.67 a pineapple at 330 pineapples a day—midpoint between 300 and 360 pineapples.

TABLE 3

Labor	TP	TC	MC	ATC
0	0	200		–
			1.00	
1	100	300		3.00
			0.83	
2	220	400		1.82
			1.25	
3	300	500		1.67
			1.67	
4	360	600		1.67
			2.50	
5	400	700		1.75
			5.00	
6	420	800		1.90
			10.00	
7	430	900		2.09

12.4 LONG-RUN COST

In the long run, a firm can vary both the quantity of labor and the quantity of capital. A small firm, such as Sam's Smoothies, can increase its plant size by moving into a larger building and installing more machines. A big firm such as General Motors can decrease its plant size by closing down some production lines.

We are now going to see how costs vary in the long run when a firm varies its plant—the quantity of capital it uses—along with the quantity of labor it uses.

The first thing that happens is that the distinction between fixed cost and variable cost disappears. All costs are variable in the long run.

■ Plant Size and Cost

When a firm changes its plant size, its cost of producing a given output changes. In Table 12.3 and Figure 12.6, the lowest average total cost that Samantha can achieve is $4.25 a gallon, which occurs when she produces 8 gallons of smoothie an hour. Samantha wonders what would happen to her average total cost if she increased the size of her plant by renting a bigger building and installing a larger number of blenders and refrigerators. Will the average total cost of producing a gallon of smoothie fall, rise, or remain the same?

Each of these three outcomes is possible, and they arise because when a firm changes the size of its plant, it might experience

- Economies of scale
- Diseconomies of scale
- Constant returns to scale

Economies of Scale

If when a firm increases its plant size and labor employed by the same percentage, its output increases by a larger percentage, the firm's average total cost decreases. The firm experiences **economies of scale**. The main source of economies of scale is greater specialization of both labor and capital.

Economies of scale
A condition in which, when a firm increases its plant size and labor employed by the same percentage, its output increases by a larger percentage and its average total cost decreases.

Specialization of Labor   If GM produced 100 cars a week, each production line worker would have to perform many different tasks. But if GM produces 10,000 cars a week, each worker can specialize in a small number of tasks and become highly proficient at them. The result is that the average product of labor increases and the average total cost of producing a car falls.

Specialization also occurs off the production line. For example, a small firm usually does not have a specialist sales manager, personnel manager, and production manager. One person covers all these activities. But when a firm is large enough, specialists perform these activities. Average product increases, and the average total cost falls.

Specialization of Capital   At a small output rate, firms often must employ general-purpose machines and tools. For example, with an output of a few gallons an hour, Sam's Smoothies uses regular blenders like the one in your kitchen. But if Sam's produces hundreds of gallons an hour, it uses custom blenders that fill, empty, and clean themselves. The result is that the output rate is larger and the average total cost of producing a gallon of smoothie is lower.

Diseconomies of scale
A condition in which, when a firm increases its plant size and labor employed by the same percentage, its output increases by a smaller percentage and its average total cost increases.

Diseconomies of Scale

If when a firm increases its plant size and labor employed by the same percentage, output increases by a smaller percentage, the firm's average total cost increases. The firm experiences **diseconomies of scale**. Diseconomies of scale arise from the difficulty of coordinating and controlling a large enterprise. The larger the firm, the greater is the cost of communicating both up and down the management hierarchy and among managers. Eventually, management complexity brings rising average cost. Diseconomies of scale occur in all production processes but in some perhaps only at a very large output rate.

Constant Returns to Scale

Constant returns to scale
A condition in which, when a firm increases its plant size and labor employed by the same percentage, its output increases by the same percentage and its average total cost remains constant.

If when a firm increases its plant size and labor employed by the same percentage, output increases by that same percentage, the firm's average total cost remains constant. The firm experiences **constant returns to scale**. Constant returns to scale occur when a firm is able to replicate its existing production facility including its management system. For example, General Motors might double its production of Cavaliers by doubling its production facility for those cars. It can build an identical production line and hire an identical number of workers. With the two identical production lines, GM produces exactly twice as many cars. The average cost of producing a Cavalier is identical in the two plants. So when production increases, average total cost remains constant.

■ The Long-Run Average Cost Curve

Long-run average cost curve
A curve that shows the lowest average cost at which it is possible to produce each output when the firm has had sufficient time to change both its plant size and labor employed.

The **long-run average cost curve** shows the lowest average cost at which it is possible to produce each output when the firm has had sufficient time to change both its plant size and its labor force.

Figure 12.8 shows Sam's Smoothies' long-run average cost curve $LRAC$. This long-run average cost curve is derived from the short-run average total cost curves for different possible plant sizes.

With its current small plant, Sam's Smoothies operates on the average total cost curve ATC_1 in Figure 12.8. The other three average total cost curves are for successively bigger plants. In this example, for outputs up to 5 gallons an hour, the existing plant with average total cost curve ATC_1 produces smoothies at the lowest attainable average cost. For outputs between 5 and 10 gallons an hour, average total cost is lowest on ATC_2. For outputs between 10 and 15 gallons an hour, average total cost is lowest on ATC_3. And for outputs in excess of 15 gallons an hour, average total cost is lowest on ATC_4.

The segment of each of the four average total cost curves for which that plant has the lowest average total cost is highlighted in dark blue in Figure 12.8. The scallop-shaped curve made up of these four segments is Sam's Smoothies' long-run average cost curve.

Economies and Diseconomies of Scale

When economies of scale are present, the $LRAC$ curve slopes downward. The $LRAC$ curve in Figure 12.8 shows that Sam's Smoothies experiences economies of scale for output rates up to 9 gallons an hour. At output rates between 9 and 12 gallons an hour, the firm experiences constant returns to scale. And at output rates that exceed 12 gallons an hour, the firm experiences diseconomies of scale.

■ FIGURE 12.8
Long-run Average Cost Curve

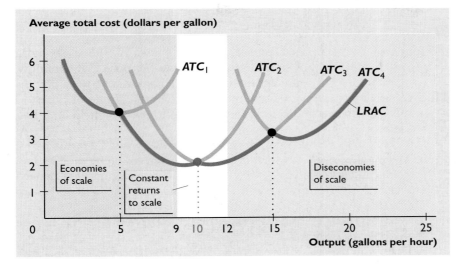

In the long run, Samantha can vary both capital and labor inputs. The long-run average cost curve traces the lowest attainable average total cost of producing each output.

Sam's experiences economies of scale as output increases to 9 gallons an hour, constant returns to scale for outputs between 9 gallons and 12 gallons an hour, and diseconomics of scale for outputs that exceed 12 gallons an hour.

EYE ON THE U.S. ECONOMY

The ATM and the Cost of Getting Cash

Most banks use automated teller machines—ATMs—to dispense cash. But small credit unions don't have ATMs. Instead, they employ tellers.

Gemini Consulting of Morristown, New Jersey, estimates that the average total cost of a transaction is $1.07 for a teller and 27¢ for an ATM. Given these numbers, why don't small credit unions install ATMs and lay off their tellers?

The answer is scale. At a small number of transactions per month, it costs less to use a teller than an ATM. In the figure, the average total cost curve for transactions done with a teller is ATC_T. The average total cost

curve for transactions done with an ATM is ATC_A. You can see that if the number of transactions is Q a month, the average total cost per transaction is the same for both methods. For a bank that does more than Q transac-

tions per month, the least-cost method is the ATM. For a credit union that does fewer than Q transactions a month, its least-cost method is the teller. More technology is not always more efficient.

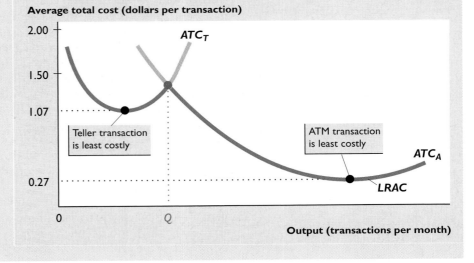

4 Derive and explain a firm's long-run average cost curve.

Practice Problem 12.4

1. Tom grows pineapples. He leases a farmer's field for $120 a day and capital for $80 a day. He hires students at $100 a day. Suppose that Tom now leases two fields for $240 a day and twice as much capital for $160 a day. Tom discovers that his output is the numbers in the third column of Table 1. The numbers in the second column are his output with one field and the original amount of capital.
   a. Find Tom's average total cost curve schedule when he farms two fields.
   b. Make a graph of Tom's average total cost curves using one field and two fields, and show on the graph Tom's long-run average cost curve.
   c. Over what output range will Tom operate with one field and at what output rate will he operate with two fields?
   d. What happens to Tom's average total cost curve if he farms two fields and doubles his capital?
   e. Does Tom experience economies of scale or diseconomies of scale?

TABLE I

Labor (students per day)	Output with I field	Output with 2 fields
	(pineapples per day)	
0	0	0
1	100	220
2	220	460
3	300	620
4	360	740
5	400	820
6	420	860
7	430	880

Exercise 12.4

1. Lizzie hires students at $50 a day to paint houses. She leases equipment that costs her $100 a day. Suppose that Lizzie doubles the number of students she hires and doubles the amount of equipment that she leases. If Lizzie experiences diseconomies of scale,
   a. Explain what has happened to her average total cost curve.
   b. Explain what might be the source of those diseconomies of scale.

Solution to Practice Problem 12.4

1a. Total cost is fixed cost of $400 a day plus $100 a day for each student hired. Average total cost is the total cost divided by output. The "ATC (2 fields)" column of Table 2 shows Tom's average total cost schedule.

TABLE 2

TP (I field)	ATC (I field)	TP (2 fields)	ATC (2 fields)
100	3.00	220	2.27
220	1.82	460	1.30
300	1.67	620	1.13
360	1.67	740	1.08
400	1.75	820	1.10
420	1.90	860	1.16
430	2.09	880	1.25

1b. Figure 1 shows Tom's average total cost curves using one field as ATC_1. This curve graphs the data on ATC and TP in Table 3 on p. 310. Using two fields, the average total cost curve is ATC_2. Tom's long-run average cost curve is the lower segments of these two ATC curves, highlighted in Figure 1.

FIGURE I

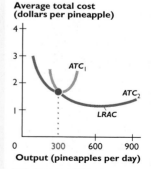

1c. If Tom produces up to 300 pineapples a day, he will operate with one field. If he produces more than 300 pineapples a day, he will operate with two fields.

1d. When Tom farms two fields and doubles his capital, average total cost increases at low outputs (up to 300 a day) and decreases at high outputs (greater than 300 a day).

1e. Tom experiences economies of scale up to an output of 740 pineapples a day because as he increases his plant and produces up to 740 pineapples a day, the average total cost of picking and packing a pineapple decreases.

CHAPTER CHECKPOINT

Key Points

1 **Explain how economists measure a firm's cost of production and profit.**

- Firms seek to maximize economic profit, which is total revenue minus total cost.
- Total cost equals opportunity cost—the sum of explicit costs plus implicit costs and includes normal profit.

2 **Explain the relationship between a firm's output and labor employed in the short run.**

- In the short run, the firm can change the output it produces by changing labor only.
- A total product curve shows the limits to the output that the firm can produce with a given quantity of capital and different quantities of labor.
- As the quantity of labor increases, the marginal product of labor increases initially but eventually decreases—the law of decreasing returns.

3 **Explain the relationship between a firm's output and costs in the short run.**

- As total product increases, total fixed cost is constant, and total variable cost and total cost increase.
- As total product increases, average fixed cost decreases and average variable cost, average total cost, and marginal cost decrease at small outputs and increase at large outputs. Their curves are U-shaped.

4 **Derive and explain a firm's long-run average cost curve.**

- In the long run, the firm can change the size of its plant.
- Long-run cost is the cost of production when all inputs have been adjusted to produce at the lowest attainable cost.
- The long-run average cost curve traces out the lowest attainable average total cost at each output when both capital and labor inputs can be varied.
- The long-run average cost curve slopes downward with economies of scale and upward with diseconomics of scale.

Key Terms

Average fixed cost, 305
Average product, 300
Average total cost, 305
Average variable cost, 305
Constant returns to scale, 312
Decreasing marginal returns, 298
Diseconomies of scale, 312
Economic depreciation, 293

Economic profit, 293
Economies of scale, 311
Explicit cost, 293
Implicit cost, 293
Increasing marginal returns, 298
Law of decreasing returns, 300
Long run, 296
Long-run average cost curve, 312

Marginal cost, 304
Marginal product, 298
Normal profit, 293
Short run, 296
Total cost, 303
Total fixed cost, 303
Total product, 297
Total variable cost, 303

myeconlab **Exercises**

1. Joe runs a shoeshine stand at the airport. With no skills and no job experience, Joe has no alternative employment. The other shoeshine stand operators that Joe knows earn $10,000 a year. Joe pays the airport $2,000 a year for the space he uses, and his total revenue from shining shoes is $15,000 a year. He spent $1,000 on a chair, polish, and brushes and paid for these items using his credit card. The interest on his credit card balance is 20 percent a year. At the end of the year, Joe was offered $500 for his business and all its equipment. Calculate Joe's
   a. Explicit costs.
   b. Implicit costs.
   c. Economic profit.

2. Sonya used to sell real estate and earn $25,000 a year, but she now sells greeting cards. Normal profit for the retailers of greeting cards is $14,000. Over the past year, Sonya bought $10,000 worth of cards from manufacturers of cards. She sold these cards for $58,000. Sonya rents a shop for $5,000 a year and spends $1,000 on utilities and office expenses. Sonya owns a cash register, which she bought for $2,000 with her savings account. Her bank pays 3 percent a year on savings accounts. At the end of the year, Sonya was offered $1,600 for her cash register. Calculate Sonya's
   a. Explicit costs.
   b. Implicit costs.
   c. Economic profit.

TABLE 1

Labor (workers per day)	Total product (body boards per day)
0	0
1	20
2	44
3	60
4	72
5	80
6	84
7	86

3. Len's body board factory rents equipment for shaping boards and hires students. Table 1 sets out Len's total product schedule.
   a. Construct Len's marginal product and average product schedules.
   b. Over what range of workers do marginal returns increase?
   c. After how many workers employed do marginal returns decrease?

4. Yolanda runs a bullfrog farm in Yuma, Arizona. When Yolanda employed one person, she produced 1,000 bullfrogs a week. When she hired a second worker, her total product doubled. Her total product doubled again when she hired a third worker. When she hired a fourth worker, her total product increased but by only 1,000 bullfrogs.
   a. Construct Yolanda's marginal product and average product schedules.
   b. Over what range of workers do marginal returns increase?
   c. After how many workers employed do marginal returns decrease?

5. Len, in exercise 3, pays $300 a week for equipment and $1,000 a week to each student he hires. Given his total product schedule in Table 1,
   a. Construct Len's total variable cost and total cost schedules.
   b. Calculate total cost minus total variable cost at each output rate. What does this quantity equal? Why?
   c. Construct the average fixed cost, average variable cost, and average total cost schedules.
   d. Construct the marginal cost schedule.
   e. Calculate the output at which Len's average total cost is a minimum.
   f. Calculate the output at which Len's average variable cost is a minimum.
   g. Explain why the output at which average variable cost is a minimum is smaller than the output at which average total cost is a minimum.

6. Yolanda, in exercise 4, pays $1,000 a week for equipment and $500 a week to each worker she hires. Given her description of how her total product changes as she hires more labor,
   a. Construct Yolanda's total variable cost and total cost schedules.
   b. Calculate total cost minus total variable cost at each output rate. What does this quantity equal? Why?
   c. Construct the average fixed cost, average variable cost, and average total cost schedules.
   d. Construct the marginal cost schedule.
   e. Calculate the output at which Yolanda's average total cost is a minimum.
   f. Calculate the output at which Yolanda's average variable cost is a minimum.
   g. Explain why the output at which average total cost is a minimum is larger than the output at which average variable cost is a minimum.

7. Table 2 shows the costs incurred at Pete's peanut farm. Complete the table.

   TABLE 2

L	TP	TVC	TC	AFC	AVC	ATC	MC
0	0	0	100				
1	10	35					
2	24	70					
3	38	105					
4	44	140					
5	47	175					

8. Table 3 shows some of the costs incurred at Bill's Bakery. Calculate the values of A, B, C, D, and E. Show your work.

   TABLE 3

L	TP	TVC	TC	AFC	AVC	ATC	MC
1	100	350	850	C	3.50	D	2.50
2	240	700	B	2.08	2.92	5.00	E
3	380	A	1,550	1.32	2.76	4.08	5.83
4	440	1,400	1,900	1.14	3.18	4.32	11.67
5	470	1,750	2,250	1.06	3.72	4.79	

9. Explain what the long-run average cost curve shows and how it is derived.

10. Can a firm that produces at the lowest possible average cost lower its average cost further by increasing production? Explain, using the long-run average cost curve.

11. Explain the sources of economies of scale and diseconomies of scale and illustrate these two situations in a graph.

12. Provide examples of industries in which you think economies of scale exist and explain why you think they are present in these industries.

13. Provide examples of industries in which you think diseconomies of scale exist and explain why you think they are present in these industries.

Critical Thinking

14. WorldCom, a global communications company, spent billions of dollars laying fiber-optic cables under the oceans. Is the cost of this communications network a short-run cost or a long-run cost? Is it a sunk cost or an opportunity cost? Explain your answer.

15. Study *Eye on the U.S. Economy* on p. 313 and then answer the following questions:
    a. What is the main difference, from a cost point of view, between human tellers and ATMs?
    b. Why do you think ATMs have become so popular?
    c. Would it ever make sense for a bank in the United States not to use ATMs?
    d. Do you think that ATMs are as common in China as they are in the United States? Explain why or why not.

16. Suppose the government put a tax on banks for each ATM transaction but did not put a similar tax on human teller transactions.
    a. How would the tax affect a bank's costs and cost curves?
    b. Would the tax change the number of ATMs and the number of tellers that banks hire? If so, explain how. If not, why not?

Web Exercises

Use the links on MyEconLab to work the following exercises.

17. Visit the Web site of Bullfrogs.louisiana and check out the prices of bullfrogs of various sizes. Assume that prices reflect the cost of production and answer the following questions:
    a. Does farming bullfrogs appear to display increasing marginal cost? Explain why or why not.
    b. Does farming bullfrogs appear to display decreasing marginal returns? Explain why or why not.
    c. Why might someone pay $20 for a large (6 inches plus) bullfrog when the price of a smaller (4 to 6 inch) bullfrog is only $12?

18. Visit the Federal Reserve Bank of St. Louis and read the article "Do Economies of Scale Exist in the Banking Industry?"
    a. What is the survivor technique for identifying whether the firms in an industry experience economies of scale?
    b. Why does the survivor technique work?
    c. What does the survivor technique imply about economies of scale in the banking industry?
    d. Sketch the long-run average cost curve of a bank that is consistent with what the survivor technique implies about economies of scale.

19. Obtain information about the cost of producing pumpkins.
    a. List all the costs referred to on the Web site.
    b. For each item, classify it as a fixed cost, a variable cost, or perhaps a combination of the two.
    c. Make some assumptions and sketch the average cost curves (*AFC*, *AVC*, and *ATC*) and the marginal cost curve.
    d. Identify the minimum points of the *AVC* and *ATC* curves in your graph.

Perfect Competition

CHAPTER CHECKLIST

When you have completed your study of this chapter, you will be able to

1 Explain a perfectly competitive firm's profit-maximizing choices and derive its supply curve.

2 Explain how output, price, and profit are determined in the short run.

3 Explain how output, price, and profit are determined in the long run and explain why perfect competition is efficient.

The sun is not yet up on a dark February morning as Don Harlow climbs into his truck. After a bumpy ride on unpaved forest tracks, he reaches a tank into which a few hundred gallons of maple sap have flowed from the 11,000 taps and 40 miles of plastic tubing that he has set up. Don carts the sap to a sugaring house, where he boils it down to become syrup. Don and his forebears have produced maple syrup for more than 100 years.

But Don faces tough competition from 10,000 other farms that produce maple syrup—the real thing, not the Aunt Jemima synthetic variety.

You're going to see how a firm in a highly competitive market operates. You'll see how the principles of rational choice, balancing costs and benefits at the margin, and responding to incentives enable us to understand and predict the decisions that Don and entrepreneurs like him make when the competitive environment is fierce.

MARKET TYPES

The four market types are

- Perfect competition
- Monopoly
- Monopolistic competition
- Oligopoly

■ Perfect Competition

Perfect competition exists when

- Many firms sell an identical product to many buyers.
- There are no restrictions on entry into (or exit from) the market.
- Established firms have no advantage over new firms.
- Sellers and buyers are well informed about prices.

Perfect competition
A market in which there are many firms, each selling an identical product; many buyers; no restrictions on the entry of new firms into the industry; no advantage to established firms; and buyers and sellers are well informed about prices.

These conditions that define perfect competition arise when the market demand for the product is large relative to the output of a single producer. And this situation arises when economies of scale are absent so the efficient scale of each firm is small. But a large market and the absence of economies of scale are not sufficient to create perfect competition. In addition, each firm must produce a good or service that has no characteristics that are unique to that firm so that consumers don't care from which firm they buy. Firms in perfect competition all look the same to the buyer.

Wheat farming, fishing, wood pulping and paper milling, the manufacture of paper cups and plastic shopping bags, lawn service, dry cleaning, and the provision of laundry services are all examples of highly competitive industries.

■ Other Market Types

Monopoly
A market for a good or service that has no close substitutes and in which there is one supplier that is protected from competition by a barrier preventing the entry of new firms.

Monopolistic competition
A market in which a large number of firms compete by making similar but slightly different products.

Oligopoly
A market in which a small number of firms compete.

Monopoly arises when one firm sells a good or service that has no close substitutes and a barrier blocks the entry of new firms. In some places, the phone, gas, electricity, and water suppliers are local monopolies—monopolies that are restricted to a given location. For many years, a global firm called DeBeers had a near international monopoly in diamonds.

Monopolistic competition arises when a large number of firms compete by making similar but slightly different products. Each firm is the sole producer of the particular version of the good in question. For example, in the market for running shoes, Nike, Reebok, Fila, Asics, New Balance, and many others make their own versions of the perfect shoe. The term "monopolistic competition" reminds us that each firm has a monopoly on a particular brand of shoe but the firms compete with each other.

Oligopoly arises when a small number of firms compete. Airplane manufacture is an example of oligopoly. Oligopolies might produce almost identical products, such as Kodak and Fuji film. Or they might produce differentiated products, such as the colas produced by Coke and Pepsi.

We study perfect competition in this chapter, monopoly in Chapter 14, monopolistic competition in Chapter 15, and oligopoly in Chapter 16.

13.1 A FIRM'S PROFIT-MAXIMIZING CHOICES

A firm's objective is to maximize *economic profit*, which is equal to *total revenue* minus the *total cost* of production. *Normal profit*, the return that the firm's entrepreneur can obtain in the best alternative business, is part of the firm's cost.

In the short run, a firm achieves its objective by deciding the quantity to produce. This quantity influences the firm's total revenue, total cost, and economic profit. In the long run, a firm achieves its objective by deciding whether to enter or exit a market.

These are the key decisions that a firm in perfect competition makes. Such a firm does *not* choose the price at which to sell its output. The firm in perfect competition is a **price taker**—it cannot influence the price of its product.

■ Price Taker

Price taker
A firm that cannot influence the price
of the good or service that it
produces.

To see why a firm in perfect competition is a price taker, imagine that you are a wheat farmer in Kansas. You have a thousand acres under cultivation—which sounds like a lot. But then you go on a drive through Colorado, Oklahoma, Texas, and back up to Nebraska and the Dakotas. You find unbroken stretches of wheat covering millions of acres. And you know that there are similar vistas in Canada, Argentina, Australia, and Ukraine. Your thousand acres are a drop in the ocean. Nothing makes your wheat any better than any other farmer's, and all the buyers of wheat know the price they must pay. If the going price of wheat is $4 a bushel, you are stuck with that price. You can't get a higher price than $4, and you have no incentive to offer it for less than $4 because you can sell your entire output at that price.

The producers of most agricultural products are price takers. We'll illustrate perfect competition with another agriculture example: the market for maple syrup. The next time you pour syrup on your pancakes, think about the competitive market that gets this product from the sap of the maple tree to your table!

Dave's Maple Syrup is one of the more than 11,000 similar firms in the maple syrup market of North America. Dave is a price taker. Like the Kansas wheat farmer, he can sell any quantity he chooses at the going price but none above that price. Dave faces a *perfectly elastic* demand. The demand for Dave's syrup is perfectly elastic because syrup from Don Harlow, Casper Sugar Shack, and all the other maple farms in North America are *perfect substitutes* for Dave's syrup.

We'll explore Dave's decisions and their implications for the way a competitive market works. We begin by defining some revenue concepts.

Wheat farmers and maple syrup farmers are price takers.

■ Revenue Concepts

Marginal revenue
The change in total revenue that
results from a one-unit increase in the
quantity sold.

In perfect competition, market demand and market supply determine the price. A firm's *total revenue* equals this given price multiplied by the quantity sold. A firm's **marginal revenue** is the change in total revenue that results from a one-unit increase in the quantity sold. In perfect competition, marginal revenue equals price. The reason is that the firm can sell any quantity it chooses at the going market price. So if the firm sells one more unit, it sells it for the market price and total revenue increases by that amount. But this increase in total revenue is marginal revenue. So marginal revenue equals price.

The table in Figure 13.1 illustrates the equality of marginal revenue and price. The price of syrup is $8 a can. Total revenue is equal to the price multiplied by the quantity sold. So if Dave sells 10 cans, his total revenue is 10 × $8 = $80. If the quantity sold increases from 10 cans to 11 cans, total revenue increases from $80 to $88, so marginal revenue is $8 a can, the same as the price.

Figure 13.1 illustrates price determination and revenue in the perfectly competitive market. Market demand and market supply in part (a) determine the market price. Dave is a price taker, so he sells his syrup for the market price. The demand curve for Dave's syrup is the horizontal line at the market price in part (b). Because price equals marginal revenue, the demand curve for Dave's syrup is Dave's marginal revenue curve (*MR*). The total revenue curve (*TR*), in part (c), shows the total revenue at each quantity sold. Because he sells each can for the market price, the total revenue curve is an upward-sloping straight line.

■ Profit-Maximizing Output

As output increases, total revenue increases. But total cost also increases. And because of *decreasing marginal returns* (see pp. 298–300), total cost eventually increases faster than total revenue. There is one output level that maximizes economic profit, and a perfectly competitive firm chooses this output level.

■ FIGURE 13.1

Demand, Price, and Revenue in Perfect Competition

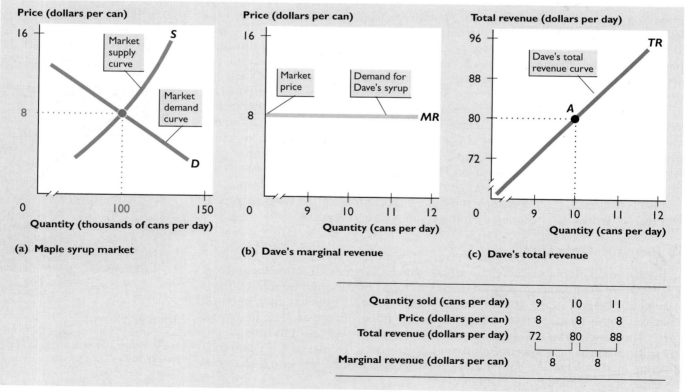

Quantity sold (cans per day)	9	10	11
Price (dollars per can)	8	8	8
Total revenue (dollars per day)	72	80	88
Marginal revenue (dollars per can)		8	8

Part (a) shows the market for maple syrup. The market price is $8 a can. The table calculates total revenue and marginal revenue.

Part (b) shows the demand curve for Dave's syrup, which is Dave's marginal revenue curve (*MR*).

Part (c) shows Dave's total revenue curve (*TR*). Point *A* corresponds to the second column of the table.

One way to find the profit-maximizing output is to use a firm's total revenue and total cost curves. Profit is maximized at the output level at which total revenue exceeds total cost by the largest amount. Figure 13.2 shows how to do this for Dave's Maple Syrup.

The table lists Dave's total revenue, total cost, and economic profit at different output levels. Figure 13.2(a) shows the total revenue and total cost curves. These curves are graphs of the numbers shown in the first three columns of the table. The total revenue curve (*TR*) is the same as that in Figure 13.1(c). The total cost curve (*TC*) is similar to the one that you met in Chapter 12 (p. 304). Figure 13.2(b) is an economic profit curve.

Dave makes an economic profit on outputs between 4 and 13 cans a day. At outputs of fewer than 4 cans a day and more than 13 cans a day, he incurs an economic loss. At outputs of 4 cans and 13 cans a day, total cost equals total revenue and Dave's economic profit is zero—Dave's *break-even points*.

The profit curve is at its highest when the vertical distance between the *TR* and *TC* curves is greatest. In this example, profit maximization occurs at an output of 10 cans a day. At this output, Dave's economic profit is $29 a day.

■ **FIGURE 13.2**

Total Revenue, Total Cost, and Economic Profit

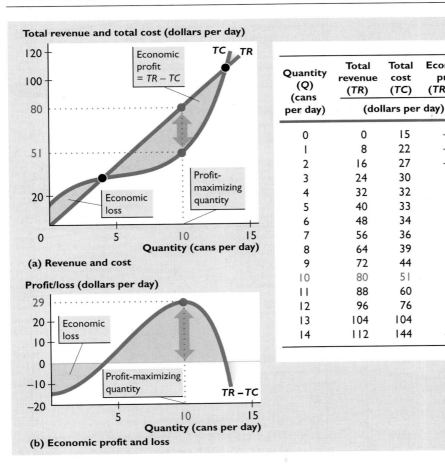

(a) Revenue and cost

(b) Economic profit and loss

Quantity (Q) (cans per day)	Total revenue (TR)	Total cost (TC)	Economic profit (TR – TC)
		(dollars per day)	
0	0	15	–15
1	8	22	–14
2	16	27	–11
3	24	30	–6
4	32	32	0
5	40	33	7
6	48	34	14
7	56	36	20
8	64	39	25
9	72	44	28
10	80	51	29
11	88	60	28
12	96	76	20
13	104	104	0
14	112	144	–32

In part (a), economic profit is the vertical distance between the total cost and total revenue curves. Dave's maximum economic profit is $29 a day ($80 − $51) when output is 10 cans a day.

In part (b), economic profit is the height of the profit curve.

■ Marginal Analysis and the Supply Decision

Another way to find the profit-maximizing output is to use *marginal analysis*, which compares marginal revenue, *MR*, with marginal cost, *MC*. As output increases, marginal revenue is constant but marginal cost eventually increases.

If marginal revenue exceeds marginal cost (if *MR* > *MC*), then the extra revenue from selling one more unit exceeds the extra cost incurred to produce it. Economic profit increases if output *increases*. If marginal revenue is less than marginal cost (if *MR* < *MC*), then the extra revenue from selling one more unit is less than the extra cost incurred to produce it. Economic profit increases if output *decreases*. If marginal revenue equals marginal cost (if *MR* = *MC*), economic profit is maximized. The rule *MR* = *MC* is a prime example of marginal analysis.

Figure 13.3 illustrates these propositions. The table records Dave's marginal revenue and marginal cost. If Dave increases output from 9 cans to 10 cans a day, marginal revenue is $8 and marginal cost is $7. Because marginal revenue exceeds marginal cost, economic profit increases. The last column of the table shows that economic profit increases from $28 to $29. The blue area in the figure shows this economic profit from the tenth can.

If Dave increases output from 10 cans to 11 cans a day, marginal revenue is still $8 but marginal cost is $9. Because marginal revenue is less than marginal cost, economic profit decreases. The last column of the table shows that economic profit decreases from $29 to $28. The red area in the figure shows this economic loss from the eleventh can.

Dave maximizes economic profit by producing 10 cans a day, the quantity at which marginal revenue equals marginal cost.

■ FIGURE 13.3
Profit-Maximizing Output

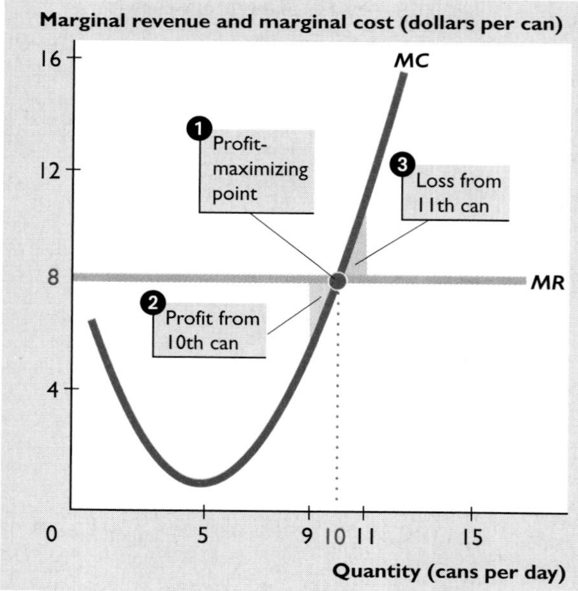

Quantity (Q) (cans per day)	Total revenue (TR) (dollars per day)	Marginal revenue (MR) (dollars per can)	Total cost (TC) (dollars per day)	Marginal cost (MC) (dollars per can)	Economic profit (TR – TC) (dollars per day)
8	64		39		25
		8		5	
9	72		44		28
		8		7	
10	80		51		29
		8		9	
11	88		60		28
		8		16	
12	96		76		20

❶ Profit is maximized when marginal revenue equals marginal cost at 10 cans a day. ❷ If output increases from 9 to 10 cans a day, marginal cost is $7, which is less than the marginal revenue of $8, and profit increases. ❸ If output increases from 10 to 11 cans a day, marginal cost is $9, which exceeds the marginal revenue of $8, and profit decreases.

In the example that we've just worked through, Dave's profit-maximizing output is 10 cans a day. This quantity is Dave's *quantity supplied* at a price of $8 a can. If the price were higher than $8 a can, he would increase production. If the price were lower than $8 a can, he would decrease production. These profit-maximizing responses to different prices are the foundation of the law of supply: *Other things remaining the same, the higher the price of a good, the greater is the quantity supplied of that good.*

■ Exit and Temporary Shutdown Decisions

Sometimes, the price falls so low that a firm cannot cover its costs. What does the firm do in such a situation? The answer depends on whether the firm expects the low price to be permanent or temporary.

If a firm is incurring an economic loss that it believes is permanent and sees no prospect of ending, the firm exits the market. We'll study the consequences of this action later in this chapter where we look at the long run (pp. 334–335).

If a firm is incurring an economic loss that it believes is temporary, it will remain in the market, and it might produce some output or temporarily shut down. To decide whether to produce or to shut down, the firm compares the loss it would incur in the two situations.

If the firm shuts down, it incurs an economic loss equal to total fixed cost. If the firm produces some output, it incurs an economic loss equal to total fixed cost *plus* total variable cost *minus* total revenue. If total revenue exceeds total variable cost, the firm's economic loss is less than total fixed cost. So it pays the firm to produce. But if total revenue were less than total variable cost, the firm's economic loss would exceed total fixed cost. So the firm would shut down temporarily. Total fixed cost is the largest economic loss that the firm will incur.

The firm's economic loss equals total fixed cost when price equals average variable cost. So the firm produces if price exceeds average variable cost and shuts down if average variable cost exceeds price.

■ The Firm's Short-Run Supply Curve

A perfectly competitive firm's short-run supply curve shows how the firm's profit-maximizing output varies as the price varies, other things remaining the same. This supply curve is based on the marginal analysis and shutdown decision that we've just explored.

Figure 13.4 derives Dave's supply curve. Part (a) shows the marginal cost and average variable cost curves, and part (b) shows the supply curve. There is a direct link between the marginal cost and average variable cost curves and the supply curve. Let's see what that link is.

If the price is above minimum average variable cost, Dave maximizes profit by producing the output at which marginal cost equals price. We can determine the quantity produced at each price from the marginal cost curve. At a price of $8 a can, the marginal revenue curve is MR_1 and Dave maximizes profit by producing 10 cans a day. If the price rises to $12 a can, the marginal revenue curve is MR_2 and Dave increases production to 11 cans a day.

The firm shuts down if the price falls below minimum average variable cost. The **shutdown point** is the output and price at which the firm just covers its total variable cost. In Figure 13.4(a), if the price is $3 a can, the marginal revenue curve is MR_0, and the profit-maximizing output is 7 cans a day at the shutdown point.

Shutdown point
The output and price at which the firm just covers its total variable cost.

But both price and average variable cost equal $3 a can, so total revenue equals total variable cost and Dave incurs an economic loss equal to total fixed cost. At a price below $3 a can, if Dave produces any positive quantity, average *variable* cost exceeds price and the firm's loss exceeds total fixed cost. So at a price below $3 a can, Dave shuts down and produces nothing.

Dave's short-run supply curve, shown in Figure 13.4(b), has two separate parts: First, at prices that exceed minimum average variable cost, the supply curve is the same as the marginal cost curve above the shutdown point (T). Second, at prices below minimum average variable cost, Dave shuts down and produces nothing. His supply curve runs along the vertical axis. At a price of $3 a can, Dave is indifferent between shutting down and producing 7 cans a day. Either way, he incurs a loss of $15 a day, which equals his total fixed cost.

So far, we have studied one firm in isolation. We have seen that the firm's profit-maximizing actions depend on the price, which the firm takes as given. In the next section, you'll learn how market supply is determined.

▨ FIGURE 13.4
Dave's Supply Curve

Part (a) shows that at $8 a can, Dave produces 10 cans a day; at $12 a can, he produces 11 cans a day; and at $3 a can, he produces either 7 cans a day or nothing. At any price below $3 a can, Dave produces nothing. The minimum average variable cost is the shutdown point.

Part (b) shows Dave's supply curve, which is made up of the marginal cost curve (part a) at all points *above* the shutdown point T (minimum average variable cost) and the vertical axis at all prices *below* the shutdown point.

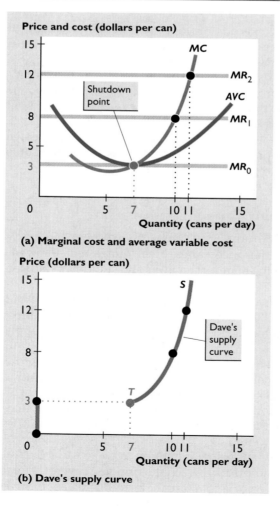

(a) Marginal cost and average variable cost

(b) Dave's supply curve

CHECKPOINT 13.1

1 Explain a perfectly competitive firm's profit-maximizing choices and derive its supply curve.

Practice Problems 13.1

1. Sarah's Salmon Farm produces 1,000 fish a week. The marginal cost is $30 a fish, average variable cost is $20 a fish, and the market price is $25 a fish. Is Sarah maximizing profit? If Sarah is not maximizing profit, to do so, will she increase or decrease the number of fish she produces in a week?

2. Trout farming is a perfectly competitive industry, and all trout farms have the same cost curves. The market price is $25 a fish. To maximize profit, each farm produces 200 fish a week. Average total cost is $20 a fish, and average variable cost is $15 a fish. Minimum average variable cost is $12 a fish.
   a. If the price falls to $20 a fish, will a trout farm continue to produce 200 fish a week? Explain why or why not.
   b. If the price falls to $12 a fish, what will the trout farmer do?
   c. What is one point on the trout farm's supply curve?

Exercise 13.1

1. Paula is an asparagus farmer, and the world asparagus market is perfectly competitive. The market price is $15 a box. Paula sells 800 boxes a week, and her marginal cost is $18 a box.
   a. Calculate Paula's total revenue.
   b. Calculate Paula's marginal revenue.
   c. Is Paula maximizing profit? Explain your answer.
   d. The price falls to $12 a box, and Paula cuts her output to 500 boxes a week. Her average variable cost and marginal cost fall to $12 a box. Is Paula maximizing profit? Is she making an economic profit or a loss?
   e. What is one point on Paula's supply curve?

Solutions to Practice Problems 13.1

1. Profit is maximized when marginal cost equals marginal revenue. In perfect competition, marginal revenue equals the market price and is $25 a fish. Because marginal cost exceeds marginal revenue, Sarah is not maximizing profit. To maximize profit, Sarah will decrease her output until marginal cost falls to $25 a fish (Figure 1).

2a. The farm will produce fewer than 200 fish a week. The marginal cost increases as the farm produces more fish. So to reduce its marginal cost from $25 to $20, the farm cuts production.

2b. If the price falls to $12 a fish, farms cut production to the quantity at which marginal cost equals $12. But because $12 is minimum average variable cost, this price puts farms at the shutdown point. Farms will be indifferent between producing the profit-maximizing output and producing nothing. Either way, each farm incurs an economic loss equal to total fixed cost.

2c. At $25 a fish, the quantity supplied is 200 fish; at $12 a fish, the quantity supplied might be zero; at a price below $12 a fish, the quantity supplied is zero.

FIGURE 1

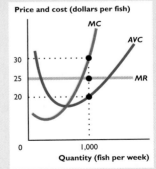

Price and cost (dollars per fish)

13.2 OUTPUT, PRICE, AND PROFIT IN THE SHORT RUN

To determine the price and quantity in a perfectly competitive market, we need to know how market demand and supply interact. We begin by studying a perfectly competitive market in the short run when the number of firms is fixed.

■ Market Supply in the Short Run

The market supply curve in the short run shows the quantity supplied at each price by a fixed number of firms. The quantity supplied at a given price is the sum of the quantities supplied by all firms at that price.

Figure 13.5 shows the supply curve for the competitive syrup market. In this example, the market consists of 10,000 firms exactly like Dave's Maple Syrup. The table shows how the market supply schedule is constructed. At prices below $3, every firm in the market shuts down; the quantity supplied is zero. At a price of $3, each firm is indifferent between shutting down and producing nothing or operating and producing 7 cans a day. The quantity supplied by each firm is *either* 0 or 7 cans, and the quantity supplied in the market is *between* 0 (all firms shut down) and 70,000 (all firms produce 7 cans a day each). At prices above $3, we sum the quantities supplied by the 10,000 firms, so the quantity supplied in the market is 10,000 times the quantity supplied by one firm.

At prices below $3, the market supply curve runs along the price axis. Supply is perfectly inelastic. At a price of $3, the market supply curve is horizontal. Supply is perfectly elastic. At prices above $3, the supply curve is upward sloping.

■ **FIGURE 13.5**

The Market Supply Curve

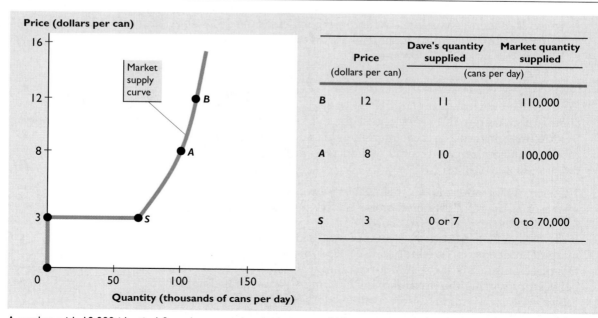

	Price	Dave's quantity supplied	Market quantity supplied
	(dollars per can)	(cans per day)	
B	12	11	110,000
A	8	10	100,000
S	3	0 or 7	0 to 70,000

A market with 10,000 identical firms has a supply schedule similar to that of the individual firm, but the quantity supplied is 10,000 times greater. At the shutdown price of $3 a can, each firm produces either 0 or 7 cans a day, but the market supply curve is perfectly elastic at that price.

■ Short-Run Equilibrium in Good Times

Market demand and market supply determine the price and quantity bought and sold. Figure 13.6(a) shows a short-run equilibrium in the syrup market. The supply curve S is the same as that in Figure 13.5.

If the demand curve D_1 shows market demand, the equilibrium price is $8 a can. Although market demand and market supply determine this price, each firm takes the price as given and produces its profit-maximizing output, which is 10 cans a day. Because the market has 10,000 firms, market output is 100,000 cans a day.

Figure 13.6(b) shows the situation that Dave faces. The price is $8 a can, so Dave's marginal revenue is constant at $8 a can. Dave maximizes profit by producing 10 cans a day.

Figure 13.6(b) also shows Dave's average total cost curve (ATC). Recall that average total cost is the cost per unit produced. It equals total cost divided by the quantity of output produced.

Here, when Dave produces 10 cans a day, his average total cost is $5.10 a can. So the price of $8 a can exceeds average total cost by $2.90 a can. This amount is Dave's economic profit per can.

If we multiply the economic profit per can of $2.90 by the number of cans, 10 a day, we arrive at Dave's economic profit, which is $29 a day.

The blue rectangle shows this economic profit. The height of that rectangle is the profit per can, $2.90, and the length is the quantity of cans, 10 a day, so the area of the rectangle (height × length) measures Dave's economic profit of $29 a day.

■ **FIGURE 13.6**
Economic Profit in the Short Run

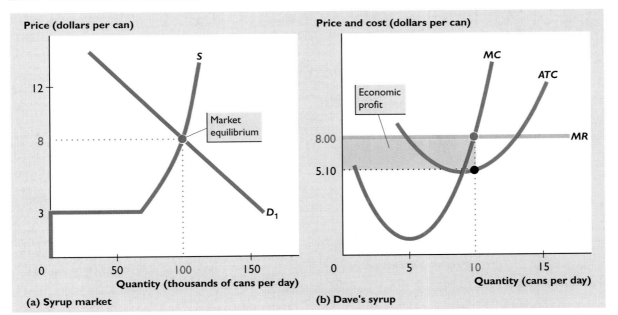

In part (a), with market demand curve D_1 and market supply curve S, the equilibrium market price is $8 a can.

In part (b), Dave's marginal revenue is $8 a can, so he produces 10 cans a day. At this quantity, price ($8) exceeds average total cost ($5.10), so Dave makes an economic profit shown by the blue rectangle.

■ Short-Run Equilibrium in Bad Times

In the short-run equilibrium that we've just examined, Dave is enjoying an economic profit. But such an outcome is not inevitable. Figure 13.7 shows the syrup market in a less happy state. The market demand curve is now D_2. The market still has 10,000 firms, and the costs of these firms are the same as before. So the market supply curve, S, is the same as before.

With the demand and supply curves shown in Figure 13.7(a), the equilibrium price of syrup is $3 a can and the equilibrium quantity is 70,000 cans a day.

Figure 13.7(b) shows the situation that Dave faces. The price is $3 a can, so Dave's marginal revenue is constant at $3 a can. Dave maximizes profit by producing 7 cans a day.

Figure 13.7(b) also shows Dave's average total cost curve (*ATC*), and you can see that when Dave produces 7 cans a day, his average total cost is $5.14 a can. So the price of $3 a can is less than average total cost by $2.14 a can. This amount is Dave's economic loss per can.

If we multiply the economic loss per can of $2.14 by the number of cans, 7 a day, we arrive at Dave's economic loss, which is $14.98 a day.

The red rectangle shows this economic loss. The height of that rectangle is the loss per can, $2.14, and the length is the quantity of cans, 7 a day, so the area of the rectangle measures Dave's economic loss of $14.98 a day.

■ **FIGURE 13.7**

Economic Loss in the Short Run

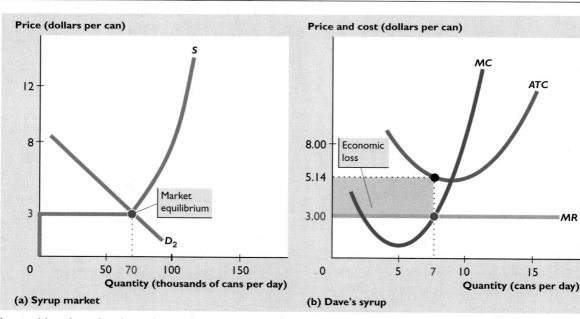

(a) Syrup market

(b) Dave's syrup

In part (a), with market demand curve D_2 and market supply curve S, the equilibrium market price is $3 a can.

In part (b), Dave's marginal revenue is $3 a can, so he produces 7 cans a day. At this quantity, price ($3) is less than average total cost ($5.14), so Dave incurs an economic loss shown by the red rectangle.

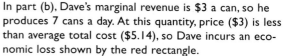

CHECKPOINT 13.2

2 Explain how output, price, and profit are determined in the short run.

Practice Problem 13.2

1. Tulip growing is a perfectly competitive industry, and all tulip growers have the same cost curves. The market price of tulips is $25 a bunch, and each grower maximizes profit by producing 2,000 bunches a week. The average total cost of producing tulips is $20 a bunch, and the average variable cost is $15 a bunch. Minimum average variable cost is $12 a bunch.
   a. What is the economic profit that each grower is making in the short run?
   b. What is the price at the grower's shutdown point?
   c. What is each grower's profit at the shutdown point?

Exercises 13.2

1. Tom's Tattoos is a tattooing business in a perfectly competitive market in Miami. The market price of a tattoo is $20. Table 1 shows Tom's total costs.
   a. How many tattoos an hour does Tom's Tattoos sell?
   b. What is Tom's Tattoos' economic profit in the short run?

2. In exercise 1, if the market price of a tattoo falls to $15,
   a. How many tattoos an hour does Tom's Tattoos sell?
   b. What is Tom's Tattoos' economic profit in the short run?

3. In exercise 1,
   a. At what market price will Tom's Tattoos shut down?
   b. At the shutdown point, what is Tom's Tattoos' economic loss?

TABLE 1

Quantity (tattoos per hour)	Total cost (dollars per hour)
0	30
1	50
2	65
3	75
4	90
5	110
6	140

Solution to Practice Problem 13.2

1a. The market price ($25) exceeds the average total cost ($20), so tulip growers are making an economic profit of $5 a bunch. Each grower produces 2,000 bunches a week, so each grower makes an economic profit of $10,000 a week (Figure 1).

1b. The price at which a grower will shut down is equal to minimum average variable cost—$12 a bunch (Figure 1).

1c. At the shutdown point, the grower incurs an economic loss equal to total fixed cost. $ATC = AFC + AVC$. When 2,000 bunches a week are grown, ATC is $20 a bunch and AVC is $15 a bunch, so AFC is $5 a bunch. Total fixed cost equals $10,000 a week—$5 a bunch × 2,000 bunches a week. So at the shutdown point, the grower incurs an economic loss equal to $10,000 a week.

FIGURE 1

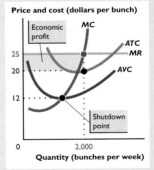

13.3 OUTPUT, PRICE, AND PROFIT IN THE LONG RUN

Neither good times nor bad times last forever in perfect competition. In the long run, a firm in perfect competition earns normal profit. It earns zero economic profit and incurs no economic loss.

Figure 13.8 shows the syrup market in a long-run equilibrium. The market demand curve is now D_3. The market still has 10,000 firms, and the costs of these firms are the same as before. So the market supply curve, S, is the same as before.

With the demand and supply curves shown in Figure 13.8(a), the equilibrium price of syrup is $5 a can and the equilibrium quantity is 90,000 cans a day.

Figure 13.8(b) shows the situation that Dave faces. The price is $5 a can, so Dave's marginal revenue is constant at $5 a can and Dave maximizes profit by producing 9 cans a day.

Figure 13.8(b) also shows Dave's average total cost curve (ATC), and you can see that when Dave produces 9 cans a day, his average total cost is $5 a can, which is also the minimum average total cost. That is, Dave can't produce syrup at an average total cost that is less than $5 a can no matter what his output is.

The price of $5 a can equals average total cost, so Dave has neither an economic profit nor an economic loss. He breaks even. But because his average total cost includes normal profit, Dave earns normal profit.

■ **FIGURE 13.8**

Long-run Equilibrium

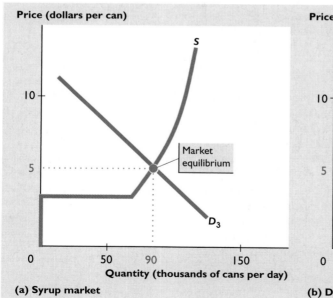

(a) Syrup market

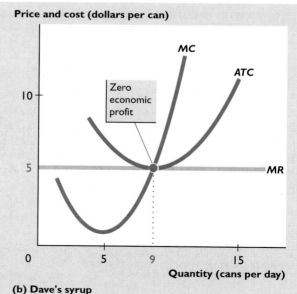

(b) Dave's syrup

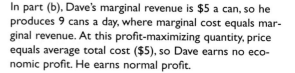

In part (a), with market demand curve D_3 and market supply curve, S, the equilibrium market price is $5 a can.

In part (b), Dave's marginal revenue is $5 a can, so he produces 9 cans a day, where marginal cost equals marginal revenue. At this profit-maximizing quantity, price equals average total cost ($5), so Dave earns no economic profit. He earns normal profit.

■ Entry and Exit

In the short run, a perfectly competitive firm might make an economic profit (Figure 13.6) or incur an economic loss (Figure 13.7). But in the long run, a firm earns normal profit (Figure 13.8).

In the long run, firms respond to economic profit and economic loss by either entering or exiting a market. New firms enter a market in which the existing firms are making an economic profit. And existing firms exit a market in which they are incurring an economic loss. Temporary economic profit or temporary economic loss, like a win or loss at a casino, does not trigger entry and exit. But the prospect of persistent economic profit or loss does.

Entry and exit influence price, the quantity produced, and economic profit. The immediate effect of the decision to enter or exit is to shift the market supply curve. If more firms enter a market, supply increases and the market supply curve shifts rightward. If firms exit a market, supply decreases and the market supply curve shifts leftward.

Let's see what happens when new firms enter a market.

The Effects of Entry

Figure 13.9 shows the effects of entry. Initially, the market is in long-run equilibrium. Demand is D_0, supply is S_0, the price is $5 a can, and the quantity is 90,000 cans a day. A surge in the popularity of syrup increases demand, and the demand curve shifts to D_1. The price rises to $8 a can, and the firms in the syrup market increase output to 100,000 cans a day and make an economic profit.

Times are good for syrup producers like Dave, so other potential syrup producers want some of the action. New firms begin to enter the market. As they do so, supply increases and the market supply curve shifts rightward to S_1. With the

---

■ FIGURE 13.9

The Effects of Entry

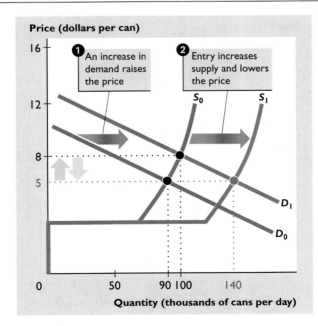

Starting in long-run equilibrium, ❶ demand increases and the demand curve shifts from D_0 to D_1. The price rises from $5 to $8 a can.

Economic profit brings entry. ❷ As firms enter the market, the supply curve shifts rightward, from S_0 to S_1. The equilibrium price falls from $8 to $5 a can, and the quantity produced increases from 100,000 to 140,000 cans a day.

greater supply and unchanged demand, the price falls from $8 to $5 a can and the quantity increases to 140,000 cans a day.

Market output increases, but because the price falls, Dave and the other producers decrease output, back to its original level. But because the number of firms in the market increases, the market as a whole produces more.

As the price falls, each firm's economic profit decreases. When the price falls to $5, economic profit disappears and each firm makes a normal profit. The entry process stops, and the market is again in long-run equilibrium.

You have just discovered a key proposition:

> **Economic profit is an incentive for new firms to enter a market, but as they do so, the price falls and the economic profit of each existing firm decreases.**

The Effects of Exit

Figure 13.10 shows the effects of exit. Again we begin on demand curve D_0 and supply curve S_0 in long-run equilibrium. Now suppose that the development of a new high-nutrition, low-fat breakfast food decreases the demand for pancakes, and as a result, the demand for maple syrup decreases. The demand curve shifts from D_0 to D_2. Firms' costs are the same as before, so the market supply curve is S_0.

With demand at D_2 and supply at S_0, the price falls to $3 a can and 70,000 cans a day are produced. The firms in the syrup market incur economic losses.

Times are tough for syrup producers, and Dave must seriously think about leaving his dream business and finding some other way of making a living. But other producers are in the same situation as Dave. And some start to exit the market while Dave is still thinking through his options.

■ **FIGURE 13.10**

The Effects of Exit

Starting in long-run equilibrium, ❶ demand decreases and the demand curve shifts from D_0 to D_2. The price falls from $5 to $3 a can.

Economic loss brings exit. ❷ As firms exit the market, the supply curve shifts leftward, from S_0 to S_2. The equilibrium price rises from $3 to $5 a can, and the quantity produced decreases from 70,000 to 40,000 cans a day.

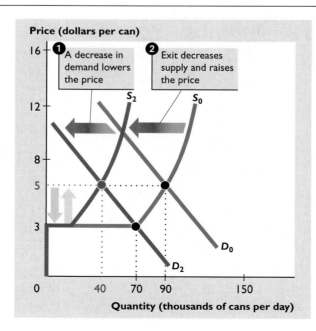

As firms exit, the market supply curve shifts leftward to S_2. With the decrease in supply, output decreases from 70,000 to 40,000 cans and the price rises from $3 to $5 a can.

As the price rises, Dave and each other firm that remains in the market move up along their supply curves and increase output. That is, for each firm that remains in the market, the profit-maximizing output *increases*. As the price rises and each firm sells more, economic loss decreases. When the price rises to $5, each firm makes a normal profit. Dave is happy that he can still make a living producing syrup.

You have just discovered a second key proposition:

Economic loss is an incentive for firms to exit a market, but as they do so, the price rises and the economic loss of each remaining firm decreases.

EYE ON THE U.S. ECONOMY

Entry in Personal Computers, Exit in Farm Machines

An example of entry and falling prices occurred during the 1980s and 1990s in the personal computer market. When IBM introduced its first PC in 1981, there was little competition; the price was $7,000 (a bit more than $14,000 in today's money), and IBM earned a large economic profit on the new machine. But new firms such as Compaq, NEC, Dell, and a host of others entered the market with machines that were technologically identical to IBM's. In fact, they were so similar that they came to be called "clones." The massive wave of entry into the personal computer market shifted the supply curve rightward and lowered the price and the economic profit for all firms. Today, a $1,000 computer is much more powerful than its 1981 ancestor that cost 14 times as much.

An example of a firm leaving a market is International Harvester, a manufacturer of farm equipment. For decades, people associated the name "International Harvester" with tractors, combines, and other farm machines. But International Harvester wasn't the only maker of farm equipment. The market became intensely competitive, and the firm began to incur an economic loss. Now the company has a new name, Navistar International, and it doesn't make tractors any more. After years of economic losses and shrinking revenues, it got out of the farm-machine business in 1985 and started to make trucks.

International Harvester exited because it was incurring an economic loss. Its exit decreased supply and made it possible for the remaining firms in the market to earn a normal profit.

■ Change in Demand

A competitive market is in long-run equilibrium and the firms are earning normal profit (zero economic profit). Then demand increases, the price rises, firms increase production to keep marginal cost equal to price, and firms are earning an economic profit. The market is now in short-run equilibrium but not in long-run equilibrium.

Economic profit is an incentive for new firms to enter the market. As firms enter, market supply increases and the price falls. With a lower price, firms decrease output to keep marginal cost equal to price.

Notice that as firms enter the market, market output increases, but each firm's output decreases. Eventually, enough firms enter to eliminate economic profit and the market is again in long-run equilibrium.

The key difference between the initial long-run equilibrium and the new long-run equilibrium is the number of firms. A permanent increase in demand increases the number of firms. Each firm produces the same output in the new long-run equilibrium as initially and earns normal profit. In the process of moving from the initial equilibrium to the new one, firms earn economic profits.

The demand for airline travel in the world economy increased during the 1990s, and the deregulation of the airlines freed up firms to seek profit opportunities in this market. The result was a massive rate of entry of new airlines. The process of competition and change in the airline market were similar to what we have just studied.

A decrease in demand triggers a similar response, except in the opposite direction. The decrease in demand brings a lower price, economic loss, and exit. Exit decreases market supply, raises the price, and eliminates the economic loss.

■ Technological Change

Firms are constantly discovering lower-cost techniques of production. For example, the cost of producing personal computers has tumbled. So have the cost of MP3 players and most other electronic products. Most cost-saving production techniques can be implemented only by investing in a new plant. Consequently, it takes time for a technological advance to spread through an industry. Firms whose plants are on the verge of being replaced are quick to adopt the new technology, while firms whose plants have recently been replaced continue to operate an old technology until they can no longer cover their average variable cost. Once average variable cost cannot be covered, a firm scraps even a relatively new plant (embodying an old technology) in favor of a plant with a new technology.

New technology lowers cost. So as firms adopt a new technology, their cost curves shift downward. With lower costs, firms are willing to supply a given quantity at a lower price, or, equivalently, they are willing to supply a larger quantity at a given price. In other words, market supply increases, and the market supply curve shifts rightward. With a given demand, the quantity produced increases and the price falls.

Firms that adopt the new technology make an economic profit, so new-technology firms enter. Firms that stick with the old technology incur economic losses, so they either exit or switch to the new technology. As new-technology firms enter and old-technology firms exit, the price falls and the quantity produced increases. Eventually, the market arrives at a long-run equilibrium in which all the firms use the new technology and each firm makes zero economic profit (a normal profit).

Because competition eliminates economic profit in the long run, technological change brings only temporary gains to firms. But the lower prices and better products that technological advances bring are permanent gains for consumers.

The process that we've just described is one in which some firms experience economic profits and others experience economic losses—a period of dynamic change for a market. Some firms do well, and others do badly. Often, the process has a geographical dimension—the expanding new-technology firms bring prosperity to what was once the boondocks, and with old-technology firms going out of business, traditional industrial regions decline. Sometimes, the new-technology firms are in a foreign country, while the old-technology firms are in the domestic economy. The information revolution of the 1990s produced many examples of changes like these. Commercial banking (a competitive but less than perfectly competitive industry), traditionally concentrated in New York, San Francisco, and

---

E Y E ON THE G L O B A L   E C O N O M Y

The North American Market in Maple Syrup

North American maple syrup production runs at about 8 million gallons a year. Most of this syrup is produced in Canada, but farms in Vermont, New York, Maine, Wisconsin, New Hampshire, Ohio, and Michigan together produce close to 20 percent of the total output.

The number of firms that produce maple syrup can only be estimated, because some are tiny and sell their output to a small local market. But there are around 9,500 producers in Canada and approaching 2,000 in the United States.

The syrup of each producer is not quite identical. And at the retail level, people have preferences about brands and sources of supply. But at the wholesale level, the market is highly competitive and a good example of perfect competition.

All of the events that can occur in a perfectly competitive market and that we've studied in this chapter have actually occurred in the maple syrup market over the past 20 years.

During the 1980s, the technology for extracting sap advanced as more taps that use a plastic tube vacuum technology were installed. During this period, farms exited the market and the average farm increased in scale. In 1980, the average farm had 1,400 taps; by 1990, this number was 2,000; and

by 1996, the number of taps had increased to 2,400.

During the 1990s, with a steady growth in the demand for maple syrup, new farms entered the market.

Through the past 20 years, total production has increased and the price has held remarkably stable at around $8 per half-gallon can. So increasing demand has brought economic profit, which in turn has brought entry and an increase in supply.

other large cities, now flourishes in Charlotte, North Carolina, which has become the nation's number three commercial banking city. Television shows and movies, traditionally made in Los Angeles and New York, are now made in large numbers in Orlando and Toronto.

Technological advances are not confined to the information and entertainment market. Food production has seen major technological change, and today, genetic engineering is fueling that change.

■ Is Perfect Competition Efficient?

Perfect competition is efficient. To see why, first recall the conditions for an efficient allocation of resources. Resources are used efficiently when it is not possible to get more of one good without giving up something that is valued more highly. To achieve this outcome, marginal benefit must equal marginal cost. That is what perfect competition achieves.

We derive a firm's supply curve in perfect competition from its marginal cost curve. The supply curve is the marginal cost curve at all points above the minimum of average variable cost (the shutdown price). Because the market supply curve is found by summing the quantities supplied by all the firms at each price, the market supply curve is the entire market's marginal cost curve.

The demand curve is the marginal benefit curve. And because the supply curve and demand curve intersect at the equilibrium price, that price equals both marginal cost and marginal benefit.

Figure 13.11 illustrates the efficiency of perfect competition. We've labeled the demand curve $D = MB$ and the supply curve $S = MC$ to remind you that these curves are also the marginal benefit (MB) and marginal cost (MC) curves.

■ FIGURE 13.11
The Efficiency of Perfect Competition

❶ Market equilibrium occurs at a price of $5 a can and a quantity of 90 cans a day.

❷ The supply curve is also the marginal cost curve.

❸ The demand curve is also the marginal benefit curve.

Because at the market equilibrium, marginal benefit equals marginal cost, the ❹ efficient quantity of syrup is produced. ❺ Total surplus (consumer surplus plus producer surplus) is maximized.

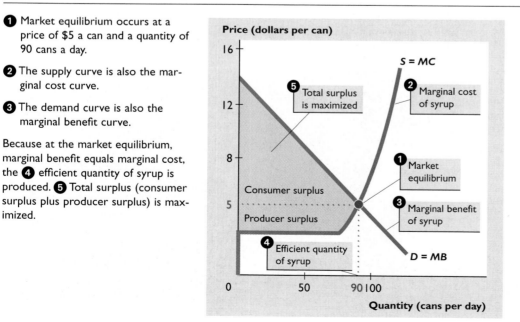

These curves intersect at the equilibrium price and quantity. The price equals marginal benefit and marginal cost. And the equilibrium quantity is efficient. The total surplus, which is the sum of consumer surplus and producer surplus, is maximized. Any departure from this outcome is inferior to it and brings an avoidable deadweight loss.

■ Is Perfect Competition Fair?

Perfect competition places no restrictions on anyone's actions. Everyone is free to try to earn an economic profit. And the process of competition eliminates economic profit and brings maximum attainable benefit to the consumer.

Fairness as equality of opportunity and fairness as equality of outcomes are achieved in perfect competition in long-run equilibrium.

But in the short run, economic profit and economic loss arise. So there are unequal outcomes in the short run. These inequalities might sometimes seem unfair.

REALITY CHECK

Perfect Competition in YOUR Life

You don't run into *perfect* competition very often. But you do see many markets that are highly competitive and almost perfectly competitive. And your entire life is influenced by and benefits immeasurably from the forces of competition. Adam Smith's invisible hand might be hidden from view, but it is enormously powerful.

Just about every good or service that you consume and take for granted is available because of the forces of competition. Your home, your food, your clothing, your books, your CDs, your MP3 files, your computer, your bike, your car, . . . , the list is endless.

No one organizes all the magic that enables you to consume this vast array of products. But competitive markets and entrepreneurs striving to earn the largest possible profit make it happen.

When either demand or technology changes and makes the current allocation of resources the wrong one, the market swiftly and silently acts. It sends signals to entrepreneurs that bring entry and exit and a new and efficient use of scarce resources.

3   **Explain how output, price, and profit are determined in the long run and explain why perfect competition is efficient.**

Practice Problem 13.3

1. Tulip growing is a perfectly competitive industry, and all tulip growers have the same cost curves. The market price of tulips is $15 a bunch, and each grower maximizes profit by producing 1,500 bunches a week. The average total cost of producing tulips is $21 a bunch. Minimum average variable cost is $12 a bunch, and the minimum average total cost is $18 a bunch.
   a. What is a tulip grower's economic profit in the short run?
   b. How does the number of tulip growers change in the long run?
   c. What is the price in the long run?
   d. What is a tulip grower's economic profit in the long run?

Exercise 13.3

1. Tom's Tattoos is a tattooing business in a perfectly competitive market in Miami. Table 1 shows Tom's total costs.
   a. If the market price is $20 per tattoo, what is Tom's economic profit?
   b. If the market price is $20 per tattoo, do new firms enter or do existing firms exit the industry in the long run?
   c. What is the price of a tattoo in the long run?
   d. How many tattoos per hour does Tom sell in the long run?
   e. What is Tom's economic profit in the long run?

TABLE 1

Quantity (tattoos per hour)	Total cost (dollars per hour)
0	30
1	50
2	65
3	75
4	90
5	110
6	140

Solution to Practice Problem 13.3

1a. The price is less than average total cost, so the tulip grower is incurring an economic loss in the short run. Because the price exceeds minimum average variable cost, the tulip grower continues to produce. The economic loss equals the loss per bunch ($21 minus $15) multiplied by the number of bunches (1,500), which equals $9,000 (Figure 1).

1b. Because firms in the industry are incurring a loss, some firms will exit in the long run. So the number of tulip growers will decrease.

1c. The price in the long run will be such that economic profit is zero. That is, as tulip growers exit, the price will rise until it equals minimum average total cost. The long-run price will be $18 a bunch (Figure 2).

1d. A tulip grower's economic profit in the long run will be zero because average total cost equals price. Each tulip grower will make a normal profit (Figure 2).

FIGURE 1

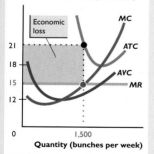

Price and cost (dollars per bunch)

FIGURE 2

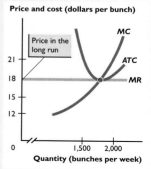

Price and cost (dollars per bunch)

CHAPTER CHECKPOINT

Key Points

1 **Explain a perfectly competitive firm's profit-maximizing choices and derive its supply curve.**

- A perfectly competitive firm is a price taker.
- Marginal revenue equals price.
- The firm produces the output at which price equals marginal cost.
- If price is less than minimum average variable cost, the firm temporarily shuts down.
- A firm's supply curve is the upward-sloping part of its marginal cost curve above minimum average variable cost and the vertical axis at all prices below minimum average variable cost.

2 **Explain how output, price, and profit are determined in the short run.**

- Market demand and market supply determine price.
- Firms choose the quantity to produce that maximizes profit, which is the quantity at which marginal cost equals price.
- In short-run equilibrium, a firm can make an economic profit or incur an economic loss.

3 **Explain how output, price, and profit are determined in the long run and explain why perfect competition is efficient.**

- Economic profit induces entry, which increases market supply and lowers price and profit. Economic loss induces exit, which decreases market supply, raises price, and lowers the losses.
- In the long run, economic profit is zero and there is no entry or exit.
- An increase in demand increases the number of firms and increases the equilibrium quantity.
- An advance in technology that lowers cost increases market supply, lowers the price, and increases the quantity.
- Perfect competition is efficient because it makes marginal benefit equal marginal cost, and it is fair in the sense that it provides equal opportunity for profit.

Key Terms

Marginal revenue, 321
Monopolistic competition, 320
Monopoly, 320
Oligopoly, 320

Perfect competition, 320
Price taker, 321
Shutdown point, 325

myeconlab Exercises

1. In what type of market is each of the following goods and services sold? Explain your answers.
   a. Wheat
   b. Jeans
   c. Camera film
   d. Toothpaste
   e. Taxi rides in a town with one taxi company

2. Explain why in a perfectly competitive market, the firm is a price taker. Why can't the firm choose the price at which it sells its good?

3. Table 1 shows the demand schedule for Lin's Fortune Cookies.
   a. In what type of market does Lin's Fortune Cookies operate? How can you tell?
   b. Calculate Lin's marginal revenue for each quantity demanded.
   c. Why does Lin's marginal revenue equal price?

4. Table 2 shows some cost data for Lin's Fortune Cookies, which operates in the market described in exercise 3. To answer these questions, draw Lin's short-run cost curves.

TABLE 1

Price (dollars per batch)	Quantity demanded (batches of fortune cookies per day)
50	0
50	1
50	2
50	3
50	4
50	5
50	6

TABLE 2

Total product (batches of cookies per day)	Average fixed cost	Average variable cost	Average total cost	Marginal cost
		(dollars per batch)		
1	84.0	51.00	135	
				37
2	42.0	44.00	86	
				29
3	28.0	39.00	67	
				27
4	21.0	36.00	57	
				32
5	16.8	35.20	52	
				40
6	14.0	36.00	50	
				57
7	12.0	39.00	51	
				83
8	10.5	44.50	55	

   a. At a price of $50 per batch of cookies, what quantity does Lin produce and what is the firm's economic profit? Do firms enter or exit the industry?
   b. At a price of $35.20 per batch, what quantity does Lin produce and what is the firm's economic profit? Do firms enter or exit the industry?
   c. At a price of $83 per batch, what quantity does Lin produce and what is the firm's economic profit? Do firms enter or exit the industry?

5. Use the data in Table 2 to create Lin's short-run supply schedule and make a graph of Lin's short-run supply curve.

6. Explain why Lin's supply curve is only part of his marginal cost curve. Why will Lin never consider producing two batches of fortune cookies a day?

7. Suppose there are 1,000 fortune cookie producers that are exactly like Lin's Fortune Cookies. Table 3 shows the demand schedule for fortune cookies.
   a. What is the short-run equilibrium price of fortune cookies?
   b. What is the short-run equilibrium quantity of fortune cookies?
   c. What is the economic profit earned or loss incurred by each firm?
   d. Do firms enter or exit the industry? Why?
   e. What is the price in long-run equilibrium?
   f. Approximately how many firms are in the industry in long-run equilibrium?

TABLE 3

Price (dollars per batch)	Quantity demanded (batches per day)
92	4,000
85	4,500
78	5,000
71	5,500
64	6,000
57	6,500
50	7,000
43	7,500
36	8,000

8. Suppose that the restaurant industry is perfectly competitive. Joe's Diner is always packed in the evening but rarely has a customer at lunchtime. Why doesn't Joe's Diner close—temporarily shut down—at lunchtime?

9. 3M created the sticky note, which 3M called the Post-it note. Soon many other firms entered the sticky note market and started to produce sticky notes.
   a. What was the incentive for these firms to enter the sticky note market?
   b. As time goes by, do you expect more firms to enter this market? Explain why or why not.
   c. Can you think of any reason why any of these firms might exit the sticky note market?

10. In 1969, when Rod Laver completed his tennis grand slam, all tennis rackets were made of wood. Today, tennis players use graphite rackets.
    a. Draw two graphs of the market for wooden tennis rackets in 1969: one that shows the market as a whole and one that shows an individual producer of rackets.
    b. Show in the graphs the effect of a permanent decrease in the demand for wooden rackets.
    c. How did the economic profit from producing wooden rackets change and what effects did the change in profit have on the number of producers of wooden rackets?

11. During the 1980s and 1990s, the cost of producing a personal computer decreased.
    a. Draw two graphs of the market for personal computers: one that shows the market as a whole and one that shows an individual producer.
    b. Show in the graphs the effect of a decrease in the cost of producing a computer on the price of a computer, the quantity of computers bought, and the economic profit of producers in the short run and in the long run.

12. Small aluminum scooters became popular during 2000. Sketch the cost and revenue curves of a typical firm in the scooter industry when
    a. The scooter fashion began.
    b. The scooter fashion was two years old.
    c. The scooter fashion faded.

Critical Thinking

13. Airport security was stepped up after the attacks on September 11, 2001, and much of the additional security service was provided by private firms that operate in a competitive market. Use the perfect competition model to answer the following questions.
    a. Do you think that airport security providers earned an economic profit or incurred an economic loss during 2002? Explain your answer.
    b. Would you expect the price of airport security services to have increased or decreased in 2003 and 2004? Why?

14. Review *Eye on the Global Economy* on p. 337.
    a. List the features of the maple syrup market that make it an example of perfect competition.
    b. Draw a graph to describe the maple syrup market and the cost and revenue of an individual firm in 1980, assuming that the industry was in long-run equilibrium.
    c. Use your answer to part **b** to explain the effects of the technological changes in maple syrup farming during the 1980s.
    d. Suppose that Aunt Jemima invents a new maple-flavored syrup that no one can distinguish, in a blind test, from the real thing and can produce it for $5 a gallon. What effect would this invention have on the market for real maple syrup? Illustrate the effects graphically.

15. The combination of the DVD player, the flat plasma screen, and surround sound has revolutionized watching a movie at home. At the same time, advances in technology in the movie theater have raised the standard that the home entertainment alternative must achieve. Think about the effects of these technological changes on competitive markets for goods and services that are influenced by movie going and home movie watching. Identify the market for one related good or service that will expand and one that will contract. Describe in detail the sequence of events as the two markets you've identified respond to the new technologies.

Web Exercise

Use the links on MyEconLab to work the following exercise.

16. Open the spreadsheet that provides information about the world market for wheat and then answer the following questions:
    a. Is the world market for wheat perfectly competitive? Why or why not?
    b. What happened to the price of wheat during the 1990s?
    c. What happened to the quantity of wheat produced during the 1990s?
    d. What do you think were the main influences on the demand for wheat during the 1990s?
    e. What do you think were the main influences on the supply of wheat during the 1990s?
    f. Do you think farmers entered or exited the wheat market during the 1990s? Explain your answer.

Monopoly

CHAPTER CHECKLIST

When you have completed your study of this chapter, you will be able to

1   Explain how monopoly arises and distinguish between single-price monopoly and price-discriminating monopoly.

2   Explain how a single-price monopoly determines its output and price.

3   Compare the performance of a single-price monopoly with that of perfect competition.

4   Explain how price discrimination increases profit.

5   Explain why monopoly can sometimes achieve a better allocation of resources than competition can.

From Boston to Baton Rouge to Sacramento, cable TV customers are fuming. AT&T Broadband rates are up 8 percent, Cox Communications rates are up 7 percent, Comcast standard rates are up 6.2 percent, and rates for premium packages are up by as much as 21 percent. But what can an angry customer do when there's no effective alternative to cable? Switch to satellite perhaps. But the switch isn't hassle-free.

The providers of cable TV services face little competition. They are the sole suppliers of these services in the regions they serve—they are monopolies. How does a monopoly choose the quantity to produce and the price at which to sell it? Does a monopoly charge too much?

In this chapter, we study monopolies such as your cable TV provider. We learn how a monopoly behaves, and we discover whether it is efficient and fair.

345

14.1 MONOPOLY AND HOW IT ARISES

A *monopoly* is a market with a single supplier of a good or service that has no close substitutes and in which a barrier to entry prevents competition from new firms.

Markets for local telephone service, gas, electricity, and water are examples of local monopoly. GlaxoSmithKline has a monopoly on AZT, a drug that is used to treat AIDS. DeBeers, a South African firm, controls 80 percent of the world's production of raw diamonds—close to being a monopoly but not quite one.

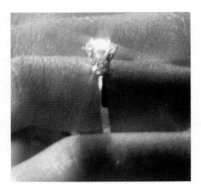

The market for diamonds is close to being a monopoly.

■ How Monopoly Arises

Monopoly arises when there are

- No close substitutes
- A barrier to entry

No Close Substitutes

If a good has a close substitute, even though only one firm produces it, that firm effectively faces competition from the producers of substitutes. Water supplied by a local public utility is an example of a good that does not have close substitutes. While it does have a close substitute for drinking—bottled spring water—it has no effective substitutes for doing the laundry, taking a shower, or washing a car.

The availability of close substitutes isn't static. Technological change can create substitutes and weaken a monopoly. For example, the creation of courier services such as UPS and the development of the fax machine and e-mail provide close substitutes for the mail-carrying services provided by the U.S. Postal Service and have weakened its monopoly. Broadband fiber-optic phone lines and satellite dishes have weakened the monopoly of cable television companies.

The arrival of a new product can also create a monopoly. For example, the IBM PC of the early 1980s provided an opportunity for Microsoft to become the monopoly supplier of DOS and Windows.

A Barrier to Entry

Anything that protects a firm from the arrival of new competitors is a **barrier to entry**. There are three types of barrier to entry:

- Natural
- Ownership
- Legal

Barrier to entry
A natural or legal constraint that protects a firm from competitors.

Natural monopoly
A monopoly that arises because one firm can meet the entire market demand at a lower average total cost than two or more firms could.

Natural Barrier to Entry A **natural monopoly** exists when the technology for producing a good or service enables one firm to meet the entire market demand at a lower average total cost than two or more firms could. One electric power distributor can meet the market demand for electricity at a lower cost than two or more firms could. Imagine two or more sets of wires running to your home so that you could choose your electric power supplier.

Figure 14.1 illustrates a natural monopoly in the distribution of electric power. Here, the demand curve for electric power is *D*, and the long-run average cost curve is *LRAC*. Economies of scale prevail over the entire length of this *LRAC* curve, indicated by the fact that the curve slopes downward. One firm can produce 4 million kilowatt-hours at 5 cents a kilowatt-hour. At this price, the quan-

■ FIGURE 14.1
Natural Monopoly

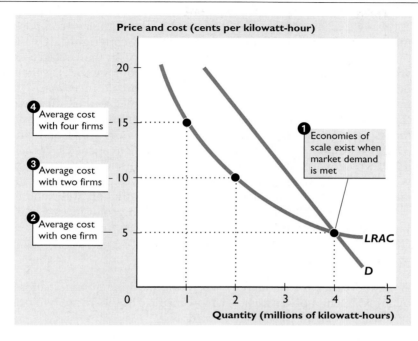

Price and cost (cents per kilowatt-hour)

④ Average cost with four firms — 15

③ Average cost with two firms — 10

② Average cost with one firm — 5

① Economies of scale exist when market demand is met

LRAC

D

Quantity (millions of kilowatt-hours)

The demand curve for electric power is *D*, and the long-run average cost curve is *LRAC*.

① Economies of scale exist over the entire *LRAC* curve. One firm can distribute 4 million kilowatt-hours at a **②** cost of 5 cents a kilowatt-hour. This same total output **③** costs 10 cents a kilowatt-hour with two firms and **④** 15 cents a kilowatt-hour with four firms. So one firm can meet the market demand at a lower cost than two or more firms can, and the market is a natural monopoly.

tity demanded is 4 million kilowatt-hours. So if the price was 5 cents, one firm could supply the entire market. If two or more firms shared the market, average total cost would be higher.

In Chapter 10 (p. 239), we said that a good that is nonrival but excludable is produced by a natural monopoly. You can now see why. If a good is nonrival, one more person can use it without any additional cost being incurred. The costs of producing the good are fixed costs, and the cost of supplying an additional user is zero. So for a nonrival good, the average total cost curve slopes downward like that in Figure 14.1. If the good is excludable as well as nonrival, it will be produced by a natural monopoly.

Ownership Barrier to Entry   A monopoly can arise in a market in which competition and entry are restricted by the concentration of ownership of a natural resource. DeBeers, which controls more than 80 percent of the world's production of raw diamonds, is an example of this type of monopoly. There is no natural barrier to entry in diamonds. Even though the diamond is a relatively rare mineral, its sources of supply could have many owners who compete in a global competitive auction market. Only by buying control over most of the world's diamonds was DeBeers able to prevent entry and competition.

Legal Barrier to Entry   A legal barrier to entry creates a legal monopoly. A **legal monopoly** is a market in which competition and entry are restricted by the granting of a public franchise, government license, patent, or copyright.

A *public franchise* is an exclusive right granted to a firm to supply a good or service, an example of which is the U.S. Postal Service's exclusive right to deliver

Legal monopoly
A market in which competition and entry are restricted by granting of a public franchise, government license, patent, or copyright.

first-class mail. A *government license* controls entry into particular occupations, professions, and industries. An example is Michael's Texaco in Charleston, Rhode Island, which is the only firm in the area licensed to test for vehicle emissions.

A *patent* is an exclusive right granted to the inventor of a product or service. A *copyright* is an exclusive right granted to the author or composer of a literary, musical, dramatic, or artistic work. Patents and copyrights are valid for a limited time period that varies from country to country. In the United States, a patent is valid for 20 years. Patents are designed to encourage the *invention* of new products and production methods. They also stimulate *innovation*—the use of new inventions—by encouraging inventors to publicize their discoveries and offer them for use under license. Patents have stimulated innovations in areas as diverse as soybean seeds, pharmaceuticals, memory chips, and video games.

Most monopolies are regulated by government agencies. We can better understand why governments regulate monopolies and what effects regulations have if we know how an unregulated monopoly behaves. So we'll first study an unregulated monopoly and then look at monopoly regulation at the end of this chapter.

A monopoly sets its own price, but in doing so, it faces a market constraint. Let's see how the market limits a monopoly's pricing choices.

■ Monopoly Price-Setting Strategies

A monopoly faces a tradeoff between price and the quantity sold. To sell a larger quantity, the monopoly must set a lower price. But there are two price-setting possibilities that create different tradeoffs:

- Single price
- Price discrimination

Single Price

Single-price monopoly
A monopoly that must sell each unit of its output for the same price to all its customers.

A **single-price monopoly** is a firm that must sell each unit of its output for the same price to all its customers. DeBeers sells diamonds (of a given size and quality) for the same price to all its customers. If it tried to sell at a higher price to some customers than to others, only the low-price customers would buy from DeBeers. Others would buy from DeBeers's low-price customers. So DeBeers is a *single-price* monopoly.

Price Discrimination

Price-discriminating monopoly
A monopoly that is able to sell different units of a good or service for different prices.

A **price-discriminating monopoly** is a firm that is able to sell different units of a good or service for different prices. Many firms price discriminate. Airlines offer a dizzying array of different prices for the same trip. Pizza producers charge one price for a single pizza and almost give away a second one. Different customers might pay different prices (like airfares), or one customer might pay different prices for different quantities bought (like the bargain price for a second pizza).

When a firm price discriminates, it appears to be doing its customers a favor. In fact, it is charging each group of customers the highest price it can get them to pay and is increasing its profit.

Not all monopolies can price discriminate. The main obstacle to the practice of price discrimination is resale by the customers who buy for a low price. Because of resale possibilities, price discrimination is limited to monopolies that sell services that cannot be resold.

CHECKPOINT 14.1

1 Explain how monopoly arises and distinguish between single-price monopoly and price-discriminating monopoly.

Practice Problems 14.1

1. Monopoly arises in which of the following situations?
    a. Coca-Cola cuts its price below that of Pepsi-Cola in an attempt to increase its market share.
    b. A single firm, protected by a barrier to entry, produces a personal service that has no close substitutes.
    c. A barrier to entry exists, but some close substitutes for the good exist.
    d. A firm offers discounts to students and seniors.
    e. A firm can sell any quantity it chooses at the going price.
    f. The government issues Tiger Woods, Inc. an exclusive license to produce golf balls.
    g. A firm experiences economies of scale even when it produces the quantity that meets the entire market demand.

2. Which of the cases **a** to **f** in practice problem 1 are natural monopolies and which are legal monopolies? Which can price discriminate, which cannot, and why?

Exercises 14.1

1. Which of the following are monopolies?
    a. A large shopping mall in downtown Houston
    b. Tiffany, the upscale jeweler
    c. Wal-Mart
    d. The Grand Canyon mule train
    e. The only shoe-shine stand licensed to operate in an airport
    f. The U.S. Postal Service

2. Which of the monopolies in exercise 1 are natural monopolies and which are legal monopolies? Which can price discriminate, which cannot, and why?

Solutions to Practice Problems 14.1

1. Monopoly arises when a single firm produces a good or service that has no close substitutes and a barrier to entry exists. Monopoly arises in **b**, **f**, and **g**. In **a**, there is more than one firm. In **c**, the good has some close substitutes. In **d**, a monopoly might be able to price discriminate, but other types of firms (for example, pizza producers and art museums) price discriminate and they are not monopolies. In **e**, the demand for the good that the firm produces is perfectly elastic and there is no limit to what the firm could sell if it wished. Such a firm is in perfect competition.

2. Natural monopoly exists when one firm can meet the entire market demand at a lower price than two or more firms could. So **g** is a natural monopoly, but **b** could be also. Legal monopoly exists when the granting of a right creates a barrier to entry. So **f** is a legal monopoly, but **b** could be also. Monopoly **b** could price discriminate because a personal service cannot be resold.

14.2 SINGLE-PRICE MONOPOLY

To understand how a single-price monopoly makes its output and price decisions, we must first study the link between price and marginal revenue.

■ Price and Marginal Revenue

Because in a monopoly there is only one firm, the demand for the firm's output is the market demand. Let's look at Bobbie's Barbershop, the sole supplier of haircuts in Cairo, Nebraska. The table in Figure 14.2 shows the demand schedule for Bobbie's haircuts. For example, at $12, consumers demand 4 haircuts an hour (row *E*).

Total revenue is the price multiplied by the quantity sold. For example, in row *D*, Bobbie sells 3 haircuts at $14 each, so total revenue is $42. *Marginal revenue* is the change in total revenue resulting from a one-unit increase in the quantity sold. For example, if the price falls from $16 (row *C*) to $14 (row *D*), the quantity sold increases from 2 to 3 haircuts. Total revenue rises from $32 to $42, so the change in total revenue is $10. Because the quantity sold increases by 1 haircut, marginal revenue equals the change in total revenue and is $10. Marginal revenue is placed between the two rows to emphasize that marginal revenue relates to the *change* in the quantity sold.

Figure 14.2 shows the market demand curve and Bobbie's marginal revenue curve (*MR*) and also illustrates the calculation that we've just made. Notice that at each output, marginal revenue is less than price—the marginal revenue curve lies below the demand curve. Why is marginal revenue less than price? It is because when the price is lowered to sell one more unit, two opposing forces affect total

---

■ **FIGURE 14.2**

Demand and Marginal Revenue

The table shows the market demand schedule and Bobbie's total revenue and marginal revenue schedules.

If the price falls from $16 to $14, the quantity sold increases from 2 to 3. ❶ Total revenue lost on 2 haircuts is $4; ❷ total revenue gained on 1 haircut is $14; and ❸ marginal revenue is $10.

	Price (dollars per haircut)	Quantity demanded (haircuts per hour)	Total revenue (dollars per hour)	Marginal revenue (dollars per haircut)
A	20	0	0	
				18
B	18	1	18	
				14
C	16	2	32	
				10
D	14	3	42	
				6
E	12	4	48	
				2
F	10	5	50	

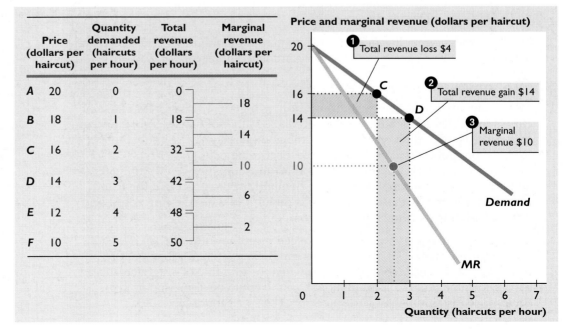

revenue. The lower price results in a revenue loss, and the increased quantity sold results in a revenue gain. For example, at a price of $16, Bobbie sells 2 haircuts (point C). If she lowers the price to $14 a haircut, she sells 3 haircuts and has a revenue gain of $14 on the third haircut. But she now receives only $14 a haircut on the first two—$2 a haircut less than before. So she loses $4 of revenue on the first 2 haircuts. To calculate marginal revenue, she must deduct this amount from the revenue gain of $14. So her marginal revenue is $10, which is less than the price.

■ Marginal Revenue and Elasticity

In Chapter 5 (p. 122), you learned about the *total revenue test*, which determines whether demand is elastic or inelastic. Recall that if a price fall increases total revenue, demand is elastic, but if it decreases total revenue, demand is inelastic.

We can use the total revenue test to see the relationship between marginal revenue and elasticity. Figure 14.3 illustrates this relationship. As the price falls from $20 to $10, the quantity demanded increases from 0 to 5 an hour. Total revenue increases (part b), so demand is elastic and marginal revenue is positive (part a). As the price falls from $10 to $0, the quantity demanded increases from 5 to 10 an hour. Total revenue decreases (part b), so demand is inelastic and marginal revenue is

---

■ FIGURE 14.3
Marginal Revenue and Elasticity

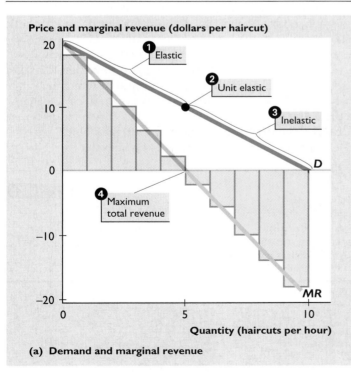

(a) Demand and marginal revenue

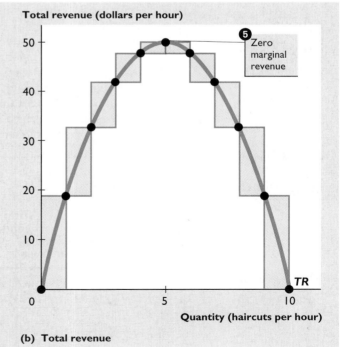

(b) Total revenue

Over the range from 0 to 5 haircuts an hour, marginal revenue is positive and ❶ demand is elastic. At 5 haircuts an hour, marginal revenue is zero and ❷ demand is unit elastic. Over the range 5 to 10 haircuts an hour, marginal revenue is negative and ❸ demand is

inelastic. At zero marginal revenue in part (a), ❹ total revenue is maximized. And at maximum total revenue in part (b), ❺ marginal revenue is zero.

negative (part a). When the price is $10, total revenue is at a maximum, demand is unit elastic, and marginal revenue is zero.

The relationship between marginal revenue and elasticity implies that a monopoly never profitably produces an output in the inelastic range of its demand curve. It could charge a higher price, produce a smaller quantity, and increase its profit. Let's look at a monopoly's output and price decision.

■ Output and Price Decision

To determine the output level and price that maximize a monopoly's profit, we study the behavior of both revenue and costs as output varies.

Table 14.1 summarizes the information we need about Bobbie's revenue, costs, and economic profit. Economic profit, which equals total revenue minus total cost, is maximized at $12 an hour when Bobbie sells 3 haircuts an hour for $14 each. If she sold 2 haircuts for $16 each, her economic profit would be only $9. And if she sold 4 haircuts for $12 each, her economic profit would be only $8.

You can see why 3 haircuts is Bobbie's profit-maximizing output by looking at the marginal revenue and marginal cost. When Bobbie increases output from 2 to 3 haircuts, her marginal revenue is $10 and her marginal cost is $7. Profit increases by the difference, $3 an hour. If Bobbie increases output yet further, from 3 to 4 haircuts, her marginal revenue is $6 and her marginal cost is $10. In this case, marginal cost exceeds marginal revenue by $4, so profit decreases by $4 an hour.

Figure 14.4 shows the information contained in Table 14.1 graphically. Part (a) shows Bobbie's total revenue curve (*TR*) and her total cost curve (*TC*). It also shows Bobbie's economic profit as the vertical distance between the *TR* and *TC* curves. Bobbie maximizes her profit at 3 haircuts an hour and earns an economic profit of $12 an hour ($42 of total revenue minus $30 of total cost).

Figure 14.4(b) shows the market demand curve (*D*) and Bobbie's marginal revenue curve (*MR*) along with her marginal cost curve (*MC*) and average total cost curve (*ATC*). Bobbie maximizes profit by producing the output at which marginal cost equals marginal revenue—3 haircuts an hour. But what price does she charge for a haircut? To set the price, the monopoly uses the demand curve and finds the highest price at which it can sell the profit-maximizing output. In Bobbie's case, the highest price at which she can sell 3 haircuts an hour is $14 a haircut.

■ TABLE 14.1
A Monopoly's Output and Price Decision

	Price (dollars per haircut)	Quantity demanded (haircuts per hour)	Total revenue (dollars per hour)	Marginal revenue (dollars per haircut)	Total cost (dollars per hour)	Marginal cost (dollars per haircut)	Profit (dollars per hour)
A	20	0	0		12		−12
				18		5	
B	18	1	18		17		1
				14		6	
C	16	2	32		23		9
				10		7	
D	14	3	42		30		12
				6		10	
E	12	4	48		40		8
				2		15	
F	10	5	50		55		−5

When Bobbie produces 3 haircuts an hour, her average total cost is $10 (read from the *ATC* curve) and her price is $14 (read from the *D* curve). Her profit per haircut is $4 ($14 minus $10). Bobbie's economic profit is shown by the blue rectangle, which equals the profit per haircut ($4) multiplied by the number of haircuts (3 an hour), for a total of $12 an hour.

A positive economic profit is an incentive for firms to enter a market. But barriers to entry prevent that from happening in a monopoly. So in a monopoly, the firm can make a positive economic profit and continue to do so indefinitely.

A monopoly charges a price that exceeds marginal cost, but does it always make an economic profit? The answer is no! Bobbie makes a positive economic profit in Figure 14.4. But suppose that Bobbie's landlord increases the rent she pays for her barbershop. If Bobbie pays an additional $12 an hour in shop rent, her fixed cost increases by that amount. Her marginal cost and marginal revenue don't change, so her profit-maximizing output remains at 3 haircuts an hour. Her profit decreases by $12 an hour to zero. If Bobbie pays more than an additional $12 an hour for her shop rent, she incurs an economic loss. If this situation were permanent, Bobbie would go out of business. But monopoly entrepreneurs are creative, and Bobbie might find another shop at a lower rent.

■ FIGURE 14.4

A Monopoly's Profit-Maximizing Output and Price   Ⓧ myeconlab

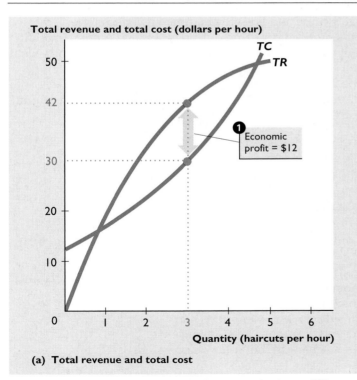

(a) Total revenue and total cost

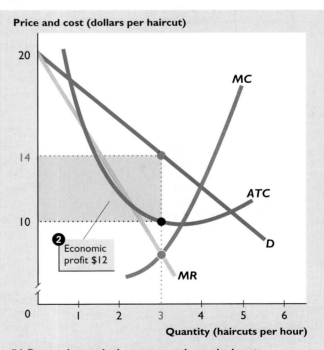

(b) Demand, marginal revenue, and marginal cost

In part (a), economic profit is maximized when total revenue (*TR*) minus total cost (*TC*) is greatest. ❶ Economic profit, the vertical distance between *TR* and *TC*, is $12 an hour at 3 haircuts an hour.

In part (b), economic profit is maximized when marginal cost (*MC*) equals marginal revenue (*MR*). The price is determined by the demand curve (*D*) and is $14. ❷ Economic profit, the blue rectangle, is $12—the profit per haircut ($4) multiplied by 3 haircuts.

2 **Explain how a single-price monopoly determines its output and price.**

Practice Problem 14.2

TABLE 1

Price (dollars per bottle)	Quantity (bottles per hour)	Total cost (dollars per hour)
10	0	1.0
9	1	1.5
8	2	2.5
7	3	5.5
6	4	10.5
5	5	17.5

1. Minnie's Mineral Springs is a single-price monopoly. The first two columns of Table 1 show the demand schedule for Minnie's spring water, and the middle and third columns show the firm's total cost schedule.
   a. Calculate Minnie's total revenue and marginal revenue schedules.
   b. Sketch the demand curve and Minnie's marginal revenue curve.
   c. Calculate Minnie's profit-maximizing output, price, and economic profit.
   d. If the owner of the water source that Minnie's uses increases the fee that Minnie's pays by $15.50 an hour, what are Minnie's new profit-maximizing output, price, and economic profit?
   e. If instead of increasing the fee that Minnie's pays by $15.50 an hour, the owner of the water source increases the fee that Minnie pays by $4 a bottle, what are Minnie's new profit-maximizing output, price, and economic profit?

Exercise 14.2

TABLE 2

Price (thousands of dollars per ride)	Quantity (rides per month)	Total cost (thousands of dollars per month)
220	0	80
200	1	160
180	2	260
160	3	380
140	4	520
120	5	680

1. Fossett's Round-the-World Balloon Rides is a single-price monopoly. The first two columns of Table 2 show the demand schedule for Fossett's rides, and the middle and third columns show the firm's total cost schedule.
   a. Calculate Fossett's total revenue and marginal revenue schedules.
   b. Sketch the demand curve and Fossett's marginal revenue curve.
   c. Calculate Fossett's profit-maximizing output, price, and economic profit.
   d. If the government places a fixed tax on Fossett's of $60,000 a month, what are the new profit-maximizing output, price, and economic profit?
   e. If instead of imposing a fixed tax on Fossett's, the government taxes Fossett's by $30,000 per ride, what are the new profit-maximizing output, price, and economic profit?

Solution to Practice Problem 14.2

TABLE 3

Quantity (bottles per hour)	Total revenue (dollars per hour)	Marginal revenue (dollars per bottle)
0	0	
1	9	9
2	16	7
3	21	5
4	24	3
5	25	1

1a. Total revenue equals price multiplied by quantity sold, and marginal revenue equals the change in total revenue when the quantity sold increases by one unit (Table 3).

1b. Figure 1 shows the demand curve and Minnie's marginal revenue curve.

1c. The profit-maximizing output is 3 bottles an hour, the quantity at which marginal revenue equals marginal cost. Marginal cost is the change in total cost when the quantity produced increases by 1 bottle. Minnie's profit-maximizing price is $7 a bottle, and its economic profit is $15.50 an hour.

1d. If the fee that Minnie's pays increases by $15.50 an hour, Minnie's fixed cost increases but its marginal cost doesn't change. Its profit-maximizing output and price are unchanged, but it now earns no economic profit.

1e. If Minnie's pays an extra $4 a bottle, its marginal cost increases by this amount. Its new profit-maximizing output is 2 bottles an hour; the price is $8 a bottle; and economic profit is $5.50 an hour.

FIGURE 1

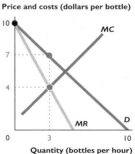

Price and costs (dollars per bottle)

14.3 MONOPOLY AND COMPETITION COMPARED

Imagine a market in which many small firms operate in perfect competition. Then a single firm buys out all these small firms and creates a monopoly. What happens in this market to the quantity produced, the price, and efficiency?

■ Output and Price

Figure 14.5 shows the market that we'll study. The market demand curve is D. Initially, with many small firms in the market, the market supply curve is S, which is the sum of the supply curves—and marginal cost curves—of the firms. The equilibrium price is P_C, which makes the quantity demanded equal the quantity supplied. The equilibrium quantity is Q_C. Each firm takes the price P_C and maximizes its profit by producing the output at which its own marginal cost equals the price.

A single firm now buys all the firms in this market. Consumers don't change, so the demand curve doesn't change. But the monopoly recognizes this demand curve as a constraint on its sales and knows that its marginal revenue curve is MR.

The market supply curve in perfect competition is the sum of the marginal cost curves of the firms in the industry. So the monopoly's marginal cost curve is the market supply curve of perfect competition—labeled $S = MC$. The monopoly maximizes profit by producing the quantity at which marginal revenue equals marginal cost, which is Q_M. This output is smaller than the competitive output, Q_C. And the monopoly charges the price P_M, which is higher than P_C. So

> **Compared to perfect competition, a single-price monopoly produces
> a smaller output and charges a higher price.**

■ **FIGURE 14.5**

Monopoly's Smaller Output and Higher Price

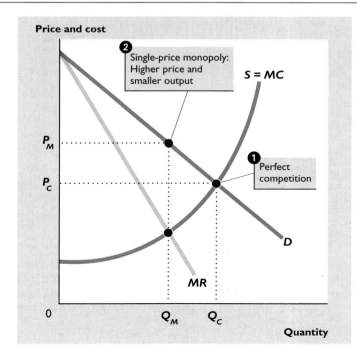

❶ A competitive industry produces the quantity Q_C at price P_C.

❷ A single-price monopoly produces the quantity Q_M at which marginal revenue equals marginal cost and sells that quantity for the price P_M. Compared to perfect competition, a single-price monopoly restricts output and raises the price.

■ Is Monopoly Efficient?

You learned in Chapter 6 that resources are used efficiently when marginal benefit equals marginal cost. Figure 14.6(a) shows that perfect competition achieves this efficient use of resources. The demand curve ($D = MB$) shows the marginal benefit to consumers. The supply curve ($S = MC$) shows the marginal cost (opportunity cost) to producers. At the competitive equilibrium, the price is P_C and the quantity is Q_C. Marginal benefit equals marginal cost, and resource use is efficient. Total surplus (Chapter 6, p. 150), the sum of *consumer surplus*, the green triangle, and *producer surplus*, the blue area, is maximized.

Figure 14.6(b) shows that monopoly is inefficient. Monopoly output is Q_M and price is P_M. Price (marginal benefit) exceeds marginal cost and the underproduction creates a *deadweight loss* (Chapter 6, p. 153), which is shown by the gray area. Consumers lose partly by getting less of the good, shown by the gray triangle above P_C, and partly by paying more for the good. Consumer surplus shrinks to the smaller green triangle. Producers lose by selling less of the good, shown by the part of the gray area below P_C, but gain by selling their output for a higher price, shown by the dark blue rectangle. Producer surplus expands and is larger in monopoly than in perfect competition.

■ **FIGURE 14.6**

The Inefficiency of Monopoly

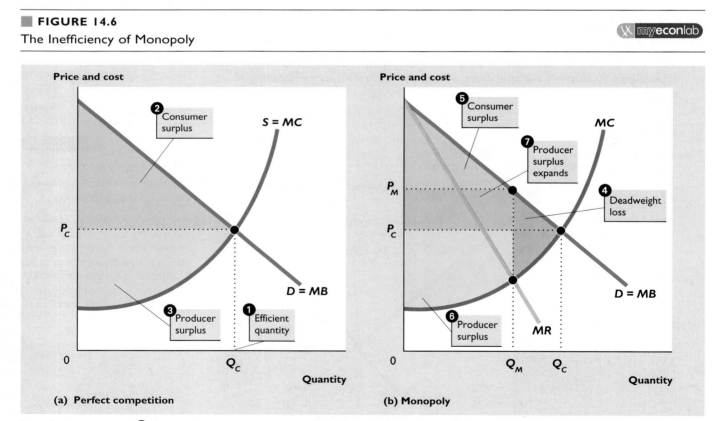

(a) Perfect competition

(b) Monopoly

In perfect competition, ❶ the equilibrium quantity is the efficient quantity, Q_C, because at that quantity, the price, P_C, equals marginal benefit and marginal cost. The sum of ❷ consumer surplus and ❸ producer surplus is maximized.

In a single-price monopoly, the equilibrium quantity, Q_M, is inefficient because the price, P_M, which equals marginal benefit, exceeds marginal cost. Underproduction creates a ❹ deadweight loss. ❺ Consumer surplus shrinks, and ❻ producer surplus ❼ expands.

■ Is Monopoly Fair?

Monopoly is inefficient because it creates a deadweight loss. But monopoly also *redistributes* consumer surplus. The producer gains, and the consumers lose.

Figure 14.6 shows this redistribution. The monopoly gets the difference between the higher price, P_M, and the competitive price, P_C, on the quantity sold, Q_M. So the dark blue rectangle shows the part of the consumer surplus taken by the monopoly. This portion of the loss of consumer surplus is not a loss to society. It is redistribution from consumers to the monopoly producer.

Are the gain for the monopoly and loss for consumers fair? You learned about two standards of fairness in Chapter 6: fair *results* and fair *rules*. Redistribution from the rich to the poor is consistent with the fair results view. So on this view of fairness, whether monopoly redistribution is fair or unfair depends on who is richer: the monopoly or the consumers of its product. It might be either. Whether the *rules* are fair depends on whether the monopoly has benefited from a protected position that is not available to anyone else. If everyone is free to acquire the monopoly, then the rules are fair. So monopoly is inefficient and it might be, but is not always, unfair.

The pursuit of monopoly profit leads to an additional costly activity that we'll now describe: rent seeking.

■ Rent Seeking

Rent seeking is the act of obtaining special treatment by the government to create economic profit or to divert consumer surplus or producer surplus away from others. ("Rent" is a general term in economics that includes all forms of surplus such as consumer surplus, producer surplus, and economic profit.) Rent seeking does not always create a monopoly, but it always restricts competition and often creates a monopoly.

Scarce resources can be used to produce the goods and services that people value or they can be used in rent seeking. Rent seeking is potentially profitable for the rent seeker but costly to society because it uses scarce resources purely to transfer wealth from one person or group to another person or group rather than to produce the things that people value.

To see why rent seeking occurs, think about the two ways in which a person might become the owner of a monopoly:

- Buy a monopoly
- Create a monopoly by rent seeking

Buy a Monopoly

A person might try to earn a monopoly profit by buying a firm (or a right) that is protected by a barrier to entry. Buying a taxicab medallion in New York is an example. The number of medallions is restricted, so their owners are protected from unlimited entry into the industry. A person who wants to operate a taxi must buy a medallion from someone who already has one. But anyone is free to enter the bidding for a medallion. So competition among buyers drives the price up to the point at which they earn only normal profit. For example, competition for the right to operate a taxi in New York City has led to a price of more than $165,000 for a taxi medallion, which is sufficiently high to eliminate economic profit for taxi operators and leave them with normal profit.

Rent seeking
The act of obtaining special treatment by the government to create economic profit or to divert consumer surplus or producer surplus away from others.

Create a Monopoly by Rent Seeking

Because buying a monopoly means paying a price that soaks up the economic profit, creating a monopoly by rent seeking is an attractive alternative to buying one. Rent seeking is a political activity. It takes the form of lobbying and trying to influence the political process to get laws that create legal barriers to entry. Such influence might be sought by making campaign contributions in exchange for legislative support or by indirectly seeking to influence political outcomes through publicity in the media or by direct contacts with politicians and bureaucrats. An example of a rent created in this way is the law that restricts the quantities of textiles that can be imported into the United States. Another is a law that limits the quantity of tomatoes that can be imported into the United States. These laws restrict competition, which decreases the quantity for sale and increases prices.

Rent-Seeking Equilibrium

Rent seeking is a competitive activity. If an economic profit is available, a rent seeker will try to get some of it. Competition among rent seekers pushes up the cost of rent seeking until it leaves the monopoly earning only a normal profit after paying the rent-seeking costs.

Figure 14.7 shows a rent-seeking equilibrium. The cost of rent seeking is a fixed cost that must be added to a monopoly's other costs. The average total cost curve, which includes the fixed cost of rent seeking, shifts upward until it just touches the demand curve. Consumer surplus is unaffected. But the deadweight loss of monopoly now includes the original deadweight loss triangle plus the economic profit consumed by rent seeking, which the enlarged gray area shows.

■ **FIGURE 14.7**
Rent-Seeking Equilibrium

Ⓧ myeconlab

① Rent-seeking costs exhaust economic profit. The firm's rent-seeking costs are fixed costs. They add to total fixed cost and to average total cost. The *ATC* curve shifts upward until, at the profit-maximizing price, the firm breaks even.

② Consumer surplus shrinks.

③ The deadweight loss increases.

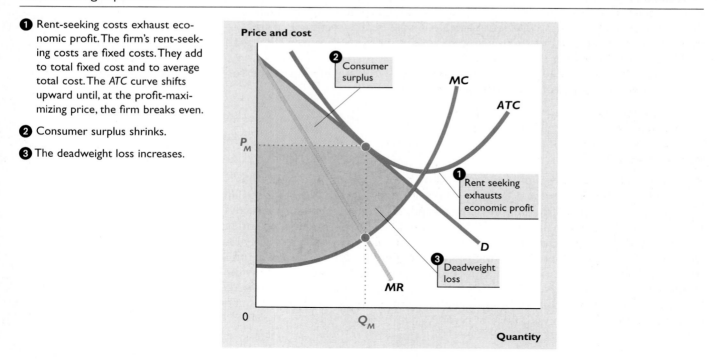

CHECKPOINT 14.3

3 Compare the performance of a single-price monopoly with that of perfect competition.

Practice Problem 14.3

1. Township is a small isolated community served by one newspaper that can meet the market demand at a lower cost than two or more newspapers could. There is no local radio or TV station and no Internet access. The *Township Gazette* is the only source of news. Figure 1 shows the marginal cost of printing the *Township Gazette* and the demand for it. The *Township Gazette* is a profit-maximizing, single-price monopoly.

   a. How many copies of the *Township Gazette* are printed each day?
   b. What is the price of the *Township Gazette*?
   c. What is the efficient number of copies of the *Township Gazette*?
   d. What is the price at which the efficient number of copies could be sold?
   e. Is the number of copies printed the efficient quantity? Explain why or why not.
   f. On the graph, show the consumer surplus that is redistributed from consumers to the *Township Gazette*.
   g. On the graph, show the deadweight loss that arises from the monopoly of the *Township Gazette*.

FIGURE 1

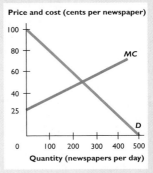

Exercise 14.3

1. Is Bobbie's Barbershop in Cairo, Nebraska, (on pp. 350–351) efficient? What is the consumer surplus that is transferred to Bobbie? What is the deadweight loss that she generates? How much would someone be willing to pay to buy Bobbie's monopoly?

Solution to Practice Problem 14.3

1a. The profit-maximizing quantity of newspapers for the *Township Gazette* is 150 a day, where marginal revenue equals marginal cost (Figure 2).
1b. The price is 70¢ a copy (Figure 2).
1c. The efficient quantity of copies is 250, where demand (marginal benefit) equals marginal cost (Figure 2).
1d. The efficient quantity would be bought at 50¢ a copy (Figure 2).
1e. The number of copies printed is not efficient because the marginal benefit of the 150th copy exceeds its marginal cost (Figure 2).
1f. The blue rectangle ❶ in Figure 2 shows the consumer surplus transferred from the consumers to the *Township Gazette*.
1g. The gray triangle ❷ in Figure 2 shows the deadweight loss.

FIGURE 2

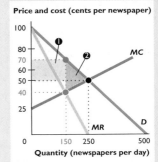

14.4 PRICE DISCRIMINATION

Price discrimination—selling a good or service at a number of different prices—is widespread. You encounter it when you travel, go to the movies, get your hair cut, buy pizza, or visit an art museum. At first sight, it appears that price discrimination contradicts the assumption of profit maximization. Why would a movie operator allow children to see movies at half price? Why would a hairdresser charge students and senior citizens less? Aren't these firms losing profit by being nice to their customers?

Deeper investigation shows that far from lowering profit, price discriminators make a bigger profit than they would otherwise. So a monopoly has an incentive to find ways of discriminating and charging each buyer the highest possible price. Some people pay less with price discrimination, but others pay more.

Most price discriminators are *not* monopolies, but monopolies do price discriminate when they can. To be able to price discriminate, a firm must

- Identify and separate different types of buyers.
- Sell a product that cannot be resold.

Price discrimination is charging different prices for a single good or service because the willingness to pay varies across buyers. Not all price *differences* are price *discrimination*. Some goods that are similar but not identical have different prices because they have different production costs. For example, the cost of producing electricity depends on time of day. If an electric power company charges a higher price for consumption between 7:00 and 9:00 in the morning and between 4:00 and 7:00 in the evening than it does at other times of the day, the company is not price discriminating.

■ Price Discrimination and Consumer Surplus

The key idea behind price discrimination is to convert consumer surplus into economic profit. To extract every dollar of consumer surplus from every buyer, the monopoly would have to offer each individual customer a separate price schedule based on that customer's own willingness to pay. Such price discrimination cannot be carried out in practice because a firm does not have enough information about each consumer's demand curve. But firms try to extract as much consumer surplus as possible, and to do so, they discriminate in two broad ways:

- Among groups of buyers
- Among units of a good

Discriminating Among Groups of Buyers

To price discriminate among groups of buyers, the firm offers different prices to different types of buyers, based on things such as age, employment status, or some other easily distinguished characteristic. This type of price discrimination works when each group has a different average willingness to pay for the good or service.

For example, a face-to-face sales meeting with a customer might bring a large and profitable order. For salespeople and other business travelers, the marginal benefit from an airplane trip is large and the price that such a traveler will pay for a trip is high. In contrast, for a vacation traveler, any of several different trips or even no vacation trip are options. So for vacation travelers, the marginal benefit of a trip is small and the price that such a traveler will pay for a trip is low. Because business travelers are willing to pay more than vacation travelers are, it is possible for an airline to profit by price discriminating between these two groups.

Discriminating Among Units of a Good

To price discriminate among units of a good, the firm charges the same prices to all its customers but offers a lower price per unit for a larger number of units bought. When Pizza Hut charges $10 for one home-delivered pizza and $14 for two, it is using this type of price discrimination. In this example, the price of the second pizza is only $4.

Let's see how an airline exploits the differences in demand by business and vacation travelers and increases its profit by price discriminating.

■ Profiting by Price Discriminating

Global Air has a monopoly on an exotic route. Figure 14.8 shows the demand curve (*D*) for travel on this route and Global Air's marginal revenue curve (*MR*). It also shows Global Air's marginal cost (*MC*) and average total cost (*ATC*) curves.

Initially, Global is a single-price monopoly and maximizes its profit by producing 8,000 trips a year (the quantity at which *MR* equals *MC*). The price is $1,200 a trip. The average total cost of a trip is $600, so economic profit is $600 a trip. On 8,000 trips, Global's economic profit is $4.8 million a year, shown by the blue rectangle. Global's customers enjoy a consumer surplus shown by the green triangle.

■ **FIGURE 14.8**
A Single Price of Air Travel

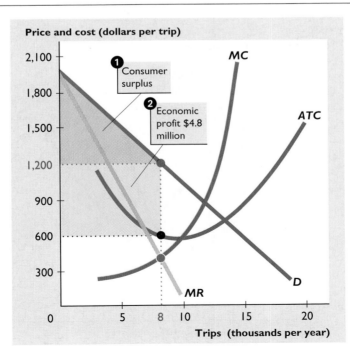

Global Air has a monopoly on an air route. The demand curve for travel on this route is *D*, and Global's marginal revenue curve is *MR*. Its marginal cost curve is *MC*, and its average total cost curve is *ATC*.

As a single-price monopoly, Global maximizes profit by selling 8,000 trips a year at $1,200 a trip. ❶ Global's customers enjoy a consumer surplus—the green triangle—and ❷ Global's economic profit is $4.8 million a year—the blue rectangle.

Global is struck by the fact that many of its customers are business travelers, and Global suspects that they are willing to pay more than $1,200 a trip. So Global does some market research, which tells Global that some business travelers are willing to pay as much as $1,800 a trip. Also, these customers almost always make their travel plans at the last moment. Another group of business travelers is willing to pay $1,600. These customers know a week ahead when they will travel, and they never want to stay over a weekend. Yet another group is willing to pay up to $1,400. These travelers know two weeks ahead when they will travel, and they don't want to stay away over a weekend.

So Global announces a new fare schedule. No restrictions, $1,800; 7-day advance purchase, non-refundable, $1,600; 14-day advance purchase, non-refundable, $1,400; 14-day advance purchase, must stay over weekend, $1,200.

Figure 14.9 shows the outcome with this new fare structure and also shows why Global is pleased with its new fares. It sells 2,000 trips at each of its four prices. Global's economic profit increases by the blue steps in the figure. Its economic profit is now its original $4.8 million a year plus an additional $2.4 million from its new higher fares. Consumer surplus has shrunk to the smaller green area.

■ Perfect Price Discrimination

Perfect price discrimination
Price discrimination that extracts the entire consumer surplus by charging the highest price that consumers are willing to pay for each unit.

But Global reckons that it can do even better. It plans to achieve **perfect price discrimination**, which extracts the entire consumer surplus by charging the highest price that consumers are willing to pay for each unit. To do so, Global must get creative and come up with a host of additional business fares ranging between $2,000 and $1,200, each one of which appeals to a small segment of the business market.

■ FIGURE 14.9
Price Discrimination

Global revises its fare structure. It now offers no restrictions at $1,800, 7-day advance purchase, non-refundable at $1,600, 14-day advance purchase, non-refundable at $1,400, and 14-day advance purchase, must stay over the weekend, at $1,200.

Global sells 2,000 units at each of its four new fares. Its economic profit increases by $2.4 million a year to $7.2 million a year, which is shown by the original blue rectangle plus the blue steps. Global's customers' consumer surplus shrinks.

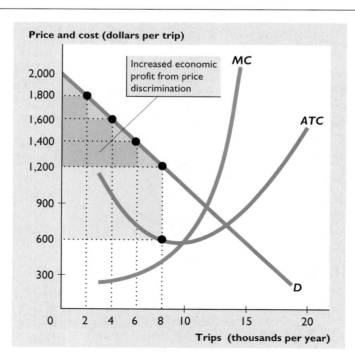

Once Global is discriminating finely between different customers and getting from each customer the maximum he or she is willing to pay, something special happens to marginal revenue. Recall that for the single-price monopoly, marginal revenue is less than price. The reason is that when the price is cut to sell a larger quantity, the price is lower on all units sold. But with perfect price discrimination, Global sells only the marginal seat at the lower price. All the other customers continue to buy for the highest price they are willing to pay. So for the perfect price discriminator, marginal revenue equals price and the demand curve becomes the marginal revenue curve.

With marginal revenue equal to price, Global can obtain yet greater profit by increasing output up to the point at which price (and marginal revenue) is equal to marginal cost.

So Global now seeks additional travelers who will not pay as much as $1,200 a trip but who will pay more than marginal cost. More creative pricing comes up with vacation specials and other fares that have combinations of advance reservation, minimum stay, and other restrictions that make these fares unattractive to Global's existing customers but attractive to a further group of travelers. With all these fares and specials, Global extracts the entire consumer surplus and maximizes economic profit.

Figure 14.10 shows the outcome with perfect price discrimination. The dozens of fares paid by the original travelers who are willing to pay between $1,200 and $2,000 have extracted the entire consumer surplus from this group and converted it into economic profit for Global. The new fares between $900 and $1,200 have attracted 3,000 additional travelers but have taken their entire consumer surplus also. Global is earning an economic profit of more than $9 million a year.

◼ FIGURE 14.10

Perfect Price Discrimination

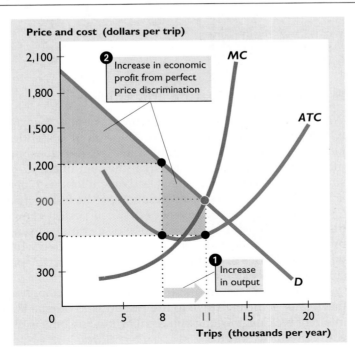

With perfect price discrimination, the demand curve becomes Global's marginal revenue curve. Economic profit is maximized when the lowest price equals marginal cost.

❶ Output increases to 11,000 passengers a year, and ❷ Global's economic profit increases to $9.35 million a year.

EYE ON THE U.S. ECONOMY

Airline Price Discrimination

The normal coach fare from San Francisco to Washington, D.C. is $1,400. Book 14 days in advance, and this fare is $550. On a typical flight, passengers might be paying as many as 20 different fares.

The airlines sort their customers according to their willingness to pay by offering a maze of advance-purchase and stayover restrictions that attract price-sensitive leisure travelers but don't get bought by business travelers.

Despite the sophistication of the airlines' pricing schemes, about 30 percent of seats fly empty. The marginal cost of filling an empty seat is close to

zero, so a ticket sold at a few dollars would be profitable.

Extremely low prices are now feasible, thanks to Priceline.com. Priceline's Web site gets 1.5 million hits a week. Shopping around airlines with bids from travelers, Priceline brokers several thousand tickets a day and gets the lowest possible fares for its customers.

Would it bother you to hear how little I paid for this flight?

From William Hamilton, "Voodoo Economics," © 1992 by the Chronicle Publishing Company, p. 3. Reprinted with permission of Chronicle Books.

■ Price Discrimination and Efficiency

With perfect price discrimination, the monopoly increases output to the point at which price equals marginal cost. This output is identical to that of perfect competition. Perfect price discrimination pushes consumer surplus to zero but increases producer surplus to equal the sum of consumer surplus and producer surplus in perfect competition. Deadweight loss with perfect price discrimination is zero. So perfect price discrimination produces the efficient quantity.

But there are two differences between perfect competition and perfect price discrimination. First, the distribution of the total surplus is different. It is shared by consumers and producers in perfect competition while the producer gets it all with perfect price discrimination. Second, because the producer grabs all the total surplus, rent seeking becomes profitable.

Rent seekers use resources in pursuit of monopoly, and the bigger the rents, the greater is the incentive to use resources to pursue those rents. With free entry into rent seeking, the long-run equilibrium outcome is that rent seekers use up the entire producer surplus.

CHECKPOINT 14.4

4 **Explain how price discrimination increases profit.**

Practice Problem 14.4

1. Village, a small isolated town, has one doctor. For a 30-minute consultation, the doctor charges a rich person twice as much as a poor person.
   a. Does the doctor practice price discrimination?
   b. Does the doctor's pricing system redistribute consumer surplus? If so, explain how.
   c. Is the doctor using resources efficiently? Explain your answer.
   d. If the doctor decided to charge everyone the maximum price that he or she would be willing to pay, what would be the consumer surplus?
   e. In part **d**, is the market for medical service in Village efficient?

Exercises 14.4

1. Under what conditions is price discrimination possible?

2. Which of the following is *not* an example of price discrimination?
   a. A diner offers senior citizens a discount on Tuesday lunches.
   b. An airline offers stand-by fares at a 75 percent discount.
   c. An airline offers a 25 percent discount on a round-trip ticket for a week-end stay.
   d. A supermarket sells water for $2 a bottle or $18 for a box of 12 bottles.
   e. A bank charges a higher interest rate on a loan to buy a motorcycle than the rate it charges the same person on a student loan.
   f. A California car wash pays a higher price for water than a California farmer pays.
   g. A cell phone company offers free calls on the weekend.
   h. A museum offers discounts to students and senior citizens.
   i. A power utility charges a steel smelter a higher price for electricity between 6:00 A.M. and 9:00 A.M. than it charges between midnight and 6:00 A.M.

Solution to Practice Problem 14.4

1a. The doctor practices price discrimination because rich people and poor people pay a different price for the same service: a 30-minute consultation.
1b. With price discrimination, the doctor takes some of the consumer surplus. So yes, consumer surplus is reduced and redistributed to the doctor as economic profit.
1c. No, the doctor creates a deadweight loss and so is not using resources efficiently.
1d. The doctor now practices perfect price discrimination. To maximize profit, the doctor increases the number of consultations to make the lowest price charged equal to marginal cost. The doctor takes the entire consumer surplus. So consumer surplus is zero.
1e. The doctor no longer creates a deadweight loss, so resources are being used efficiently.

14.5 MONOPOLY POLICY ISSUES

A single-price monopoly produces too little with marginal benefit greater than marginal cost. A price discriminating monopoly might produce the efficient quantity, but if it does so it converts the entire consumer surplus into economic profit. And all monopolies waste resources through rent seeking. If monopoly is so bad, why do we put up with it? Why don't we have laws that crack down on monopoly so hard that it never rears its head? We do indeed have laws that limit monopoly and regulate the prices that monopolies are permitted to charge. We explain the regulation of monopoly in Chapter 17.

But monopoly also brings some benefits. So society faces a tradeoff between these benefits and the inefficiency (and perhaps unfairness) that monopoly brings. We begin this review of monopoly policy issues by looking at the benefits of monopoly.

■ Benefits of Monopoly

Monopoly has two potential benefits over competition. Monopoly can lower the cost of production by enabling a firm to capture economies of scale. And by enabling a firm to earn an economic profit, monopoly provides an incentive to firms to innovate either by developing new products or by seeking lower-cost methods of production.

Capturing Economies of Scale

Economies of scale can lead to *natural monopoly*—a situation in which a single firm can produce at a lower average total cost than a larger number of smaller firms can. Examples of industries in which economies of scale are so significant that they lead to a natural monopoly include the distribution of electric power and natural gas, cable television, and water.

If a natural monopoly were broken into a number of competing firms, resources would be wasted. The cost of running not one but several cables through every neighborhood and to every home to deliver competitive cable television would be large. The cost of running several water pipes and gas pipes to bring competition to those industries would be even greater.

So here is the dilemma: Where economies of scale can be enjoyed only with a single producer, should we take the economies of scale and put up with monopoly, or should we forgo the economies of scale and make the industry competitive?

Breaking up a natural monopoly to create competition is almost never a good idea and is almost impossible to accomplish. It is a bad idea because it increases cost. It is hard to accomplish because each firm has an incentive to expand and try to take the entire market.

So the choice that most societies make is to operate natural monopolies but try to regulate them so that they operate at an efficient price and output level. You can study the regulation of natural monopoly in Chapter 17.

Strengthening the Incentive to Innovate

We take it for granted that every year will bring new and better products. Flat-screen television is gradually replacing the bulky old TV set. Pocket-sized MP3 players are replacing the Discman and a case of CDs. Ever faster and more powerful computer games keep appearing. Drug companies frequently announce yet another breakthrough in the treatment of some dreaded disease. Chemical companies routinely discover new compounds. Seed and fertilizer makers provide farmers with new products that lower the cost of food production.

But the process of invention and innovation that brings all these new goods and lower-cost technologies is not free. Firms spend billions of dollars in pursuit of the blockbuster product that will make their stockholders and managers rich.

Most (perhaps all) of these innovations bring greater benefits than they cost. Which type of market is likely to lead to more innovation: monopoly or competition? The answer is monopoly. If a firm can capture some economic profit from investing in a new product, it has an incentive to undertake the investment. But if a firm knows that competition will drive its economic profit to zero, it has a weak incentive to innovate.

So here's another dilemma: Where innovations can be enjoyed only with monopoly, should we take the innovations and put up with monopoly, or should we forgo the innovations and make markets competitive?

REALITY CHECK

Monopoly in YOUR Life

When Bill Gates decided to quit Harvard in 1975, he realized that PCs would need an operating system and applications programs to interact with the computer's hardware. He also knew that whoever owned the copyright on these programs would have a license to print money. And he wanted to be that person.

In less than 30 years, Bill Gates became the world's richest person. Such is the power of the right monopoly.

You, along with millions of other PC users, have willingly paid the monopoly price for Windows and Microsoft Office. Sure, the marginal cost of a copy of these programs is close to zero, so the quantity sold is way too few. There is a big deadweight loss.

Compared with the alternative of no Windows, you're better off. But are you better off than you would be if there were many alternatives to Windows competing for your attention? To answer this question, think about the applications—spreadsheets, word processing, and so on—that you need to make your computer useful. With lots of operating systems, what would happen to the cost of developing applications? Would you have more or less choice?

Patent law is the main tool that governments use to resolve this dilemma and to choose the point on the tradeoff between the gains from innovation and the efficiency loss from monopoly.

By granting a firm a patent, the law creates a legal monopoly and the innovator is able to earn an ongoing economic profit. But the patent eventually expires, and the market for the product then becomes competitive.

■ U.S. Patent Law

In the United States, the inventor of a new product or process may patent the invention and enjoy exclusive use of it for 20 years. At the end of 20 years, the patent expires and everyone is free to copy the original invention.

There is no deep economic science behind the 20-year time limit for a patent. The intent is to make the period long enough to provide a strong incentive to the innovator and short enough to avoid the deadweight loss from monopoly to persist for too long.

Although a patent expires after 20 years, patent holders sometimes try to extend their patent protection. One method of doing so is to make a small change to a patented product or process so that a new patent can by applied for. This activity is a form of rent seeking and, like other forms of rent seeking, it uses scarce resources and is a further source of inefficiency.

There is no neat bottom line on monopoly versus competition. Where competition is possible, it is more efficient. But often, the choice is between monopoly and nothing. Then monopoly might be better.

CHECKPOINT 14.5

myeconlab

5 **Explain why monopoly can sometimes achieve a better allocation of resources than competition can.**

Practice Problem 14.5

1. Major league baseball is a monopoly.
   a. Is it a natural monopoly?
   b. Can you think of a justification for baseball being a monopoly on the basis of either economies of scale or the incentive to innovate?

Exercise 14.5

1. The distribution of water is undertaken by a monopoly.
   a. Is water distribution a natural monopoly? Explain why or why not.
   b. Could water be distributed more efficiently by competitive water companies? Why or why not?

Solution to Practice Problem 14.5

1a. Major league baseball is a legal monopoly, not a natural monopoly.
1b. There is no justification for major league baseball being given monopoly status. It doesn't have economies of scale, and the rules of the game make innovation and product development irrelevant.

CHAPTER CHECKPOINT

Key Points

1 **Explain how monopoly arises and distinguish between single-price monopoly and price-discriminating monopoly.**

- A monopoly is a market with a single supplier of a good or service that has no close substitutes and in which legal or natural barriers to entry prevent competition.
- A monopoly can price discriminate when there is no resale possibility.
- Where resale is possible, a firm charges a single price.

2 **Explain how a single-price monopoly determines its output and price.**

- The demand for a monopoly's output is the market demand, and a single-price monopoly's marginal revenue is less than price.
- A monopoly maximizes profit by producing the output at which marginal revenue equals marginal cost and by charging the maximum price that consumers are willing to pay for that output.

3 **Compare the performance of a single-price monopoly with that of perfect competition.**

- A single-price monopoly charges a higher price and produces a smaller quantity than does a perfectly competitive market and creates a deadweight loss.
- Monopoly imposes a loss on society that equals its deadweight loss plus the cost of the resources devoted to rent seeking.

4 **Explain how price discrimination increases profit.**

- Perfect price discrimination charges a different price for each unit sold, obtains the maximum price that each consumer is willing to pay for each unit, and redistributes the entire consumer surplus to the monopoly.
- With perfect price discrimination, the monopoly produces the same output as would a perfectly competitive market, but rent seeking uses some of the surplus.

5 **Explain why monopoly can sometimes achieve a better allocation of resources than competition can.**

- A natural monopoly can produce at a lower price than competitive firms can, and monopoly strengthens the incentive to innovate.
- The U.S. patent law provides the creators of new products and technologies with a 20-year temporary monopoly.

Key Terms

Barrier to entry, 346
Legal monopoly, 347
Natural monopoly, 346

Perfect price discrimination, 362
Price-discriminating monopoly, 348

Rent seeking, 357
Single-price monopoly, 348

(X) myeconlab   # Exercises

1. What are the three types of barrier to entry that can create a monopoly? Provide an example of each type. Why can't barriers to entry simply be torn down so that all markets become competitive?

2. Technological change is constantly creating and destroying barriers to entry and is changing the competitive and monopoly landscapes.
   a. Provide three examples of technological changes that have occurred during the past 20 years that have created a new barrier to entry and resulted in monopoly.
   b. Provide three examples of technological changes that have occurred during the past 20 years that have destroyed a barrier to entry and resulted in competition where previously monopoly was present.

3. Why isn't the demand for the good or service produced by a monopoly perfectly elastic like the demand for the good or service produced by a firm in perfect competition?

4. What is price discrimination? Can any monopoly choose to price discriminate? Why or why not?

5. Explain why the marginal revenue curve of a single-price monopoly is downward sloping.

TABLE 1

Price (dollars per bottle)	Quantity (bottles per day)
10	0
9	1,000
8	2,000
7	3,000
6	4,000
5	5,000
4	6,000
3	7,000
2	8,000
1	9,000
0	10,000

6. Elixir Spring produces a unique and highly prized mineral water. The firm's total fixed cost is $5,000 a day, and its marginal cost is zero. Table 1 shows the demand schedule for Elixir water.
   a. Construct Elixir's total revenue schedule and marginal revenue schedule and make a graph of the demand and marginal revenue curves.
   b. Calculate and illustrate in a graph Elixir's profit-maximizing price, output, and economic profit.
   c. Compare Elixir's profit-maximizing price with the marginal cost of producing the profit-maximizing output.
   d. What is the elasticity of demand for Elixir water at the profit-maximizing quantity?

TABLE 2

Price (dollars per bunch)	Quantity (bunches per day)	Total cost (dollars per day)
80	0	80
72	1	82
64	2	88
56	3	100
48	4	124
40	5	160
32	6	208
24	7	268
16	8	340

7. The Blue Rose Company is the only flower grower to have cracked the secret of making a blue rose. The first two columns of Table 2 show the demand schedule for blue roses, and the middle and third columns show the total cost schedule for producing them.
   a. Construct Blue Rose's total revenue and marginal revenue schedule and make a graph of the demand and marginal revenue curves.
   b. Calculate Blue Rose's marginal cost schedule and add it to your graph.
   c. Calculate Blue Rose's profit-maximizing price, output, and economic profit.

8. Use the demand schedule for Elixir water in Table 1. Suppose that there are 1,000 springs, all able to produce this water at zero marginal cost. Suppose that for these firms, total fixed cost is also zero.
   a. What are the equilibrium price and quantity of Elixir water?
   b. Compare this equilibrium with the monopoly equilibrium in exercise 6.

c. What is the consumer surplus if Elixir water is produced in perfect competition?
d. What is the producer surplus if Elixir water is produced in perfect competition?
e. What are the consumer surplus and producer surplus from Elixir water if a monopoly produces it?
f. When the Elixir monopoly maximizes profit, what is the deadweight loss?

9. Suppose that 1,000 competitive firms produce Elixir water and that one of these firms begins quietly to buy the others.
   a. What is the most that a firm would be willing to pay to obtain a monopoly in Elixir water?
   b. Illustrate this maximum amount in a graph.
   c. If a firm pays the maximum amount it is willing to pay for a monopoly in Elixir water, what is the firm's economic profit? Explain.

10. Bobbie's Hair Care is a natural monopoly in a small isolated town. The first two columns of Table 3 show the demand schedule for Bobbie's haircuts, and the middle and third columns show Bobbie's total cost. Bobbie has done a survey and discovered that she gets four types of customer each hour: one woman who is willing to pay $18, one senior citizen who is willing to pay $16, one student who is willing to pay $14, and one boy who is willing to pay $12. If Bobbie price discriminates among the four types of customer,
    a. What is the price she charges to each type of customer?
    b. How many haircuts an hour does Bobbie sell?
    c. What is Bobbie's economic profit?
    d. Is the quantity of haircuts efficient? Explain why or why not.
    e. What are the consumer surplus and producer surplus?
    f. Who benefits from Bobbie's price discrimination?

TABLE 3

Price (dollars per haircut)	Quantity (haircuts per hour)	Total cost (dollars per hour)
20	0	20
18	1	21
16	2	24
14	3	30
12	4	40
10	5	54

11. A city art museum, which is a local monopoly, is worried that it is not generating enough revenue to cover its costs, and the city government is cutting the museum's budget. The museum charges $1 admission and $5 for special exhibitions. The museum director asks you to help him solve his problem. Can you suggest a pricing scheme that will bring in more revenue? At the same time, can you help the museum get even more people to visit it?

12. Big Top is the only circus in the nation. Table 4 sets out the demand schedule for circus tickets and the cost schedule for producing the circus.
    a. Calculate Big Top's total revenue and marginal revenue.
    b. Calculate Big Top's profit-maximizing price, output, and economic profit if it charges a single price for all tickets.
    c. In part **b**, what is the consumer surplus and producer surplus?
    d. When Big Top maximizes profit in part **b**, is the circus efficient? Explain why or why not.
    e. If the circus industry were perfectly competitive, how many tickets would be sold and what would be the price of a ticket?
    f. Big Top offers children a discount of 50 percent. How will this discount change the consumer surplus and producer surplus? Will Big Top be more efficient?

TABLE 4

Price (dollars per ticket)	Quantity (tickets per show)	Total cost (dollars per show)
20	0	1,000
18	100	1,600
16	200	2,200
14	300	2,800
12	400	3,400
10	500	4,000
8	600	4,600
6	700	5,200
4	800	5,800

Critical Thinking

13. The National Collegiate Athletic Association (NCAA) controls the market for college athletes. It sets the amounts paid to these athletes below what they would be in a competitive market and ensures that colleges do not violate the rules that it lays down.
    a. Is the NCAA a natural monopoly, a legal monopoly, or neither? Explain.
    b. Who benefits and who loses from the NCAA's control of the market for college athletes?
    c. Is the system operated by the NCAA efficient?

14. Major league baseball is exempt from laws designed to limit market power and operates as a monopoly.
    a. How might competition be introduced into the market for baseball?
    b. If the baseball market became competitive, what do you predict would happen to the number of teams and the economic profit of a team?
    c. If the baseball market became competitive, what do you predict would happen to the number of players and their average salaries?
    d. All things considered, would you favor or oppose the introduction of competition among leagues in baseball?

15. Before 1991, the eight Ivy League colleges (Brown, Columbia, Cornell, Dartmouth, Harvard, Princeton, the University of Pennsylvania, and Yale), along with MIT, shared information and agreed on rules for setting their prices of education (price equals tuition minus scholarship). Since 1991, these schools have set their prices in competition with each other. Compare the market for an Ivy League education before and after 1991. Predict what has happened to the efficiency of the market, to the distribution of producer and consumer surplus, and to deadweight loss.

Web Exercises

Use the links on MyEconLab to work the following exercises.

16. Visit the Web site of Robert Barro and read his article on competition and monopoly in the hi-tech sector.
    a. What is Robert Barro's central argument?
    b. Explain why you agree or disagree with Barro.
    c. What are the main implications of Barro's view for government policy toward monopoly?

17. Visit the Web site of the Department of Justice and review the information on the case of the United States versus Microsoft.
    a. Did the courts find Microsoft to be a monopoly?
    b. What are the main factors that the courts considered in reaching their conclusions about Microsoft?
    c. What remedies did the court propose?
    d. Compare the court's findings with Barro's views (in exercise 16).

18. Visit the Web site of United Airlines and get some prices for a trip from the major airport nearest you to anywhere in the world that interests you. Get the best fare possible and establish the restrictions on its use. Compare it with the normal fare. Explain how the restrictions increase United Airlines' total revenue.

CHAPTER 15

Monopolistic Competition

CHAPTER CHECKLIST

When you have completed your study of this chapter, you will be able to

1 Describe and identify monopolistic competition.

2 Explain how a firm in monopolistic competition determines its output and price in the short run and the long run.

3 Explain why advertising costs are high and why firms use brand names in monopolistic competition.

Raymond's end-of-term party had to be run on a a tight budget. But he knew that he'd be able to keep his costs down by using the coupons he'd saved from this week's papers. He would need to spend a bit of time running around Albertsons, Kroger, Safeway, Winn-Dixie, and Shop 'n Save to get each of their weekly "specials" and pay the lowest prices. But time was what he now had, and money was what he was short of.

The supermarkets that Raymond visited for his party shopping compete. But they are not like the firms in perfect competition that you studied in Chapter 13. There are no best deals, fliers, or specials in perfect competition. There is no gain from advertising or price cutting when you sell a product identical to that of your competitors.

To understand fliers, coupons, and the competition that we witness every day in the markets in which we buy, we need the model of monopolistic competition that is explained in this chapter.

15.1 WHAT IS MONOPOLISTIC COMPETITION?

Most real-world markets lie between the extremes of perfect competition in Chapter 13 and monopoly in Chapter 14. Most firms possess some power to set their prices as monopolies do, and they face competition from the entry of new firms as the firms in perfect competition do. We call the markets in which such firms operate *monopolistic competition*. (Another market that lies between perfect competition and monopoly is *oligopoly*, which we study in Chapter 16.)

Monopolistic competition is a market structure in which

- A large number of firms compete.
- Each firm produces a differentiated product.
- Firms compete on price, product quality, and marketing.
- Firms are free to enter and exit.

■ Large Number of Firms

In monopolistic competition, as in perfect competition, the industry consists of a large number of firms. The presence of a large number of firms has three implications for the firms in the industry.

Small Market Share

Each firm supplies a small part of the market. Consequently, while each firm can influence the price of its own product, it has little power to influence the average market price.

No Market Dominance

Each firm must be sensitive to the average market price of the product. But it does not pay attention to any one individual competitor. Because all the firms are relatively small, no single firm can dictate market conditions, so no one firm's actions directly affect the actions of the other firms.

Collusion Impossible

Firms sometimes try to profit from illegal agreements—collusion—with other firms to fix prices and not undercut each other. Collusion is impossible when the market has a large number of firms, as it does in monopolistic competition.

■ Product Differentiation

Product differentiation
Making a product that is slightly different from the products of competing firms.

Product differentiation is making a product that is slightly different from the products of competing firms. A differentiated product has close substitutes but does not have perfect substitutes. Some people will pay more for one variety of the product, so when its price rises, the quantity demanded decreases. For example, Adidas, Asics, Diadora, Etonic, Fila, New Balance, Nike, Puma, and Reebok all make differentiated running shoes. Other things remaining the same, if the price of Adidas running shoes rises and the prices of the other shoes remain constant, Adidas sells fewer shoes.

■ Competing on Quality, Price, and Marketing

Product differentiation enables a firm to compete with other firms in three areas: quality, price, and marketing.

Quality

The quality of a product is the physical attributes that make it different from the products of other firms. Quality includes design, reliability, the service provided to the buyer, and the buyer's ease of access to the product. Quality lies on a spectrum that runs from high to low. Go to the J.D. Power Consumer Center at jdpower.com, and you'll see the many dimensions on which this rating agency describes the quality of autos, boats, financial services, travel and accommodation services, telecommunication services, and new homes—all examples of products that have a large range of quality variety.

Price

Because of product differentiation, a firm in monopolistic competition faces a downward-sloping demand curve. So, like a monopoly, the firm can set both its price and its output. But there is a tradeoff between the product's quality and price. A firm that makes a high-quality product can charge a higher price than what a firm that makes a low-quality product can.

Marketing

Because of product differentiation, a firm in monopolistic competition must market its product. Marketing takes two main forms: advertising and packaging. A firm that produces a high-quality product wants to sell it for a suitably high price. To be able to do so, it must advertise and package its product in a way that convinces buyers that they are getting the higher quality for which they are paying. For example, drug companies advertise and package their brand-name drugs to persuade buyers that these items are superior to the lower-priced generic alternatives. Similarly, a low-quality producer uses advertising and packaging to persuade buyers that although the quality is low, the low price more than compensates for this fact.

■ Entry and Exit

In monopolistic competition, there are no barriers to entry. Consequently, a firm cannot make an economic profit in the long run. When firms make economic profits, new firms enter the industry. This entry lowers prices and eventually eliminates economic profits. When economic losses are incurred, some firms leave the industry. This exit increases prices and profits of the remaining firms and eventually eliminates the economic losses. In long-run equilibrium, firms neither enter nor leave the industry and the firms in the industry make zero economic profit.

■ Identifying Monopolistic Competition

Several factors must be considered to identify monopolistic competition and distinguish it from perfect competition on the one side and oligopoly and monopoly on the other side. One of these factors is the extent to which a market is dominated by a small number of firms. To measure this feature of markets, economists use two indexes called measures of concentration. These indexes are

- The four-firm concentration ratio
- The Herfindahl-Hirschman Index

The Four-Firm Concentration Ratio

Four-firm concentration ratio
The percentage of the total revenue in an industry accounted for by the four largest firms in an industry.

The **four-firm concentration ratio** is the percentage of the total revenue of the industry accounted for by the four largest firms in the industry. The range of the concentration ratio is from almost zero for perfect competition to 100 percent for monopoly. This ratio is the main measure used to assess market structure.

Table 15.1 shows two calculations of the four-firm concentration ratio: one for tire makers and one for printers. In this example, 14 firms produce tires. The largest four firms have 80 percent of the industry's total revenue, so the four-firm concentration ratio is 80 percent. In the printing industry, with 1,004 firms, the largest four firms have only 0.5 percent of the industry's total revenue, so the four-firm concentration ratio is 0.5 percent.

A low concentration ratio indicates a high degree of competition, and a high concentration ratio indicates an absence of competition. A monopoly has a concentration ratio of 100 percent—the largest (and only) firm has 100 percent of the total revenue. A four-firm concentration ratio that exceeds 60 percent is regarded as an indication of a market that is highly concentrated and dominated by a few firms in an oligopoly. A ratio of less than 40 percent is regarded as an indication of a competitive market—monopolistic competition.

■ **TABLE 15.1**

Concentration Ratio Calculations

(a) Firms' total revenue

Tire makers		Printers	
Firm	**(millions of dollars)**	**Firm**	**(millions of dollars)**
Top, Inc.	200	Fran's	4
ABC, Inc.	250	Ned's	3
Big, Inc.	150	Tom's	2
XYZ, Inc.	100	Jill's	1
Largest 4 firms	700	Largest 4 firms	10
Other 10 firms	175	Other 1,000 firms	1,990
Industry	**875**	Industry	**2,000**

(b) Four-firm concentration ratios

Tire makers		Printers	
Total revenue of largest 4 firms	700	Total revenue of largest 4 firms	10
Industry's total revenue	875	Industry's total revenue	2,000

Four-firm concentration ratio

$$\frac{700}{875} \times 100 = 80 \text{ percent}$$

Four-firm concentration ratio

$$\frac{10}{2,000} \times 100 = 0.5 \text{ percent}$$

The Herfindahl-Hirschman Index

The **Herfindahl-Hirschman Index**—also called the HHI—is the square of the percentage market share of each firm summed over the largest 50 firms (or summed over all the firms if there are fewer than 50) in a market. For example, if there are four firms in a market and the market shares of the firms are 50 percent, 25 percent, 15 percent, and 10 percent, the Herfindahl-Hirschman Index is

$$HHI = 50^2 + 25^2 + 15^2 + 10^2 = 3,450.$$

In perfect competition, the HHI is small. For example, if each of the largest 50 firms in an industry has a market share of 0.1 percent, the HHI is $0.1^2 \times 50 = 0.5$. In a monopoly, the HHI is 10,000—the firm has 100 percent of the market: $100^2 = 10,000$.

The HHI became a popular measure of the degree of competition during the 1980s, when the Justice Department used it to classify markets. A market in which the HHI is less than 1,000 is regarded as being competitive and an example of monopolistic competition. A market in which the HHI lies between 1,000 and 1,800 is regarded as being moderately competitive. It probably is an example of monopolistic competition. But a market in which the HHI exceeds 1,800 is regarded as being uncompetitive. The Justice Department scrutinizes any merger of firms in a market in which the HHI exceeds 1,000 and is likely to challenge a merger if the HHI exceeds 1,800.

Concentration measures are a useful indicator of the degree of competition in a market. But they must be supplemented by other information to determine a market's structure. Table 15.2 summarizes the range of other information, along with the measures of concentration that determine which market structure describes a particular real-world market.

Herfindahl-Hirschman Index
The square of the percentage market share of each firm summed over the largest 50 firms (or summed over all the firms if there are fewer than 50) in a market.

■ TABLE 15.2
Market Structure

Characteristics	Perfect competition	Monopolistic competition	Oligopoly	Monopoly
Number of firms in industry	Many	Many	Few	One
Product	Identical	Differentiated	Identical or differentiated	No close substitutes or regulated
Barriers to entry	None	None	Moderate	High
Firm's control over price	None	Some	Considerable	Considerable
Concentration ratio	0	Low	High	100
HHI	Close to 0	Less than 1,800	More than 1,800	10,000
Examples	Wheat, corn	Food, clothing	Cereals	Local water supply

Limitations of Concentration Measures

The two main limitations of concentration measures alone as determinants of market structure are their failure to take proper account of

- The geographical scope of the market
- Barriers to entry and firm turnover

Geographical Scope of the Market   Concentration measures take a national view of the market. Many goods are sold in a *national* market, but some are sold in a *regional* market and some in a *global* one. The ready-mix concrete industry consists of local markets. The four-firm concentration ratio for ready-mix concrete is 6.2, and the HHI is 26. These numbers suggest a market that is close to perfect competition. But there is a high degree of concentration in the ready-mix concrete industry in most cities, so this industry is not competitive despite its low measured concentration. The four-firm concentration ratio for automobiles is 87, and the HHI is 2,725. These numbers suggest a highly concentrated market. But competition from imports gives the auto market many of the features of monopolistic competition.

Barriers to Entry and Firm Turnover   Concentration measures don't measure barriers to entry. Some industries are highly concentrated but have easy entry and an enormous amount of turnover of firms. For example, many small towns have few restaurants, but there are no restrictions on opening a restaurant and many firms attempt to do so.

A market with a high concentration ratio or HHI might nonetheless be competitive because low barriers to entry create *potential competition*. The few firms in a market face competition from many firms that can easily enter the market and will do so if economic profits are available.

EYE ON THE U.S. ECONOMY

Examples of Monopolistic Competition

These ten industries are all examples of monopolistic competition. They have a large number of firms, shown in parentheses after the name of the industry. The bars measure the percentage of industry total revenue received by the 20 largest firms. The number on the right is the Herfindahl-Hirschman Index.

Industry (number of firms)	Herfindahl-Hirschman Index
Audio and video equipment (521)	415
Computers (1870)	465
Frozen foods (531)	350
Canned foods (661)	259
Book printing (690)	364
Men's and boy's clothing (1362)	462
Sporting goods (2477)	161
Fish and seafood (731)	105
Jewelry (2278)	81
Women's and girl's clothing (2927)	76

Percentage of industry total revenue

■ 4 largest firms   ■ Next 4 largest firms   ■ Next 12 largest firms

SOURCE OF DATA: U.S. Census Bureau.

CHECKPOINT 15.1

1 Describe and identify monopolistic competition.

Practice Problems 15.1

1. Table 1 shows the total revenue of the 50 firms in the tattoo industry.
   a. Calculate the four-firm concentration ratio.
   b. Calculate the HHI.
   c. What is the structure of the tattoo industry?
   d. How would your answer to part **c** change if the 50 firms in the tattoo industry operated in different cities spread across the nation?
   e. What additional information would you need about the tattoo industry to be sure that it is an example of monopolistic competition?

2. Suppose that a new tattoo technology makes it easier for anyone to enter the tattoo industry. How might the market structure of the tattoo industry change?

TABLE 1

Firm	Total revenue (dollars)
Bright Spots	450
Freckles	325
Love Galore	250
Native Birds	200
Next 16 firms (each)	50
Next 30 firms (each)	20
Total total revenue	2,625

Exercises 15.1

1. Table 2 shows the total revenue of the six firms that make fine chocolates.
   a. Calculate the four-firm concentration ratio.
   b. Calculate the HHI.
   c. What is the structure of the chocolate industry?
   d. Suppose that the firms in the chocolate industry face fierce competition from foreign suppliers. How does this information affect your answer to part **c**?
   e. What additional information would you need about the chocolate industry to be sure that it is an example of monopolistic competition?

2. Suppose that a new chocolate-making technology enables anyone with a kitchen to produce outstanding chocolates. How might the market structure of the chocolate industry change?

TABLE 2

Firm	Total revenue (dollars)
Mayfair	30
Bond	40
Magic	10
All Nature	30
Truffles	60
Gold	30
Total total revenue	200

Solution to Practice Problems 15.1

1a. The four-firm concentration ratio is 46.6. The market shares of the four largest firms are 17.1, 12.4, 9.5, and 7.6.

1b. The HHI is 671.14. The market shares from largest to smallest are 17.1, 12.4, 9.5, 7.6, 1.9, and 0.8 percent. Square these numbers to get
$292.41 + 153.76 + 90.25 + 57.76 + (3.61 \times 16) + (0.64 \times 30) = 671.14$.

1c. The four-firm concentration ratio and the HHI suggest that the tattoo industry is an example of monopolistic competition unless there are other reasons that would make the concentration measures unreliable guides.

1d. If each of the 50 firms in the tattoo industry operates in different cities spread across the nation, each firm is effectively without competition. The market might be a series of monopolies.

1e. We would want to know about product differentiation; to observe competition on price, quality, and marketing; and to see evidence of low barriers to the entry of new firms.

2. This new tattoo technology would most likely lead to the entry of more firms, greater product differentiation, and more competition.

15.2 OUTPUT AND PRICE DECISIONS

Think about the decisions that Tommy Hilfiger must make about Tommy jeans. First, the firm must decide on the design and quality of its jeans and on its marketing program. We'll suppose that Tommy Hilfiger has already made these decisions so that we can concentrate on the firm's output and pricing decision. But we'll study quality and marketing decisions in the next section.

For a given quality of jeans and a given amount of marketing activity, Tommy Hilfiger faces given costs and market conditions. How, given its costs and the demand for its jeans, does Tommy Hilfiger decide the quantity of jeans to produce and the price at which to sell them?

■ The Firm's Profit-Maximizing Decision

A firm in monopolistic competition makes its output and price decision just as a monopoly firm does. Figure 15.1 illustrates this decision for Tommy jeans. The demand curve for Tommy jeans is *D*. The *MR* curve shows the marginal revenue curve associated with this demand curve and is derived just like the marginal revenue curve of a single-price monopoly in Chapter 14. The *ATC* curve shows the average total cost of producing Tommy jeans, and *MC* is the marginal cost curve.

Tommy Hilfiger maximizes profit by producing the output at which marginal revenue equals marginal cost. In Figure 15.1, this output is 125 pairs of jeans a day. Tommy Hilfiger charges the price that buyers are willing to pay for this quantity, which is determined by the demand curve. This price is $75 a pair. When it produces 125 pairs of jeans a day, Tommy Hilfiger's average total cost is $25 a pair and it makes an economic profit of $6,250 a day ($50 a pair multiplied by 125 pairs a day). The blue rectangle shows Tommy Hilfiger's economic profit.

■ **FIGURE 15.1**

Output and Price in Monopolistic Competition

❶ Profit is maximized where marginal revenue equals marginal cost.

❷ The profit-maximizing quantity is 125 pairs of Tommy jeans a day.

❸ The price of $75 a pair exceeds the average total cost of $25 a pair, so the firm makes an economic profit of $50 a pair.

❹ The blue rectangle illustrates economic profit, which equals $6,250 a day ($50 a pair multiplied by 125 pairs).

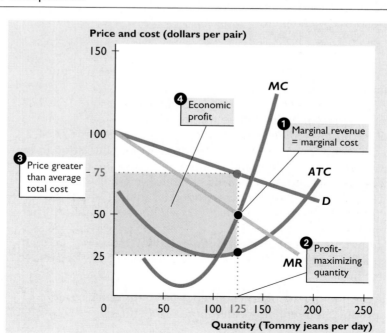

■ Profit Maximizing Might Be Loss Minimizing

Tommy Hilfiger in Figure 15.1 is earning a healthy economic profit. But such an outcome is not inevitable. The demand for a firm's product might be too low for it to earn an economic profit. Excite@Home was such a firm. Offering high-speed Internet service over the same cable that provides television, Excite@Home hoped to capture a large share of the Internet portal market in competition with AOL, MSN, and a host of other providers.

Figure 15.2 illustrates the situation facing Excite@Home in 2001. The demand curve for its portal service is *D*, the marginal revenue curve is *MR*, the average total cost curve is *ATC*, and the marginal cost curve is *MC*. Excite@Home maximizes profit—equivalently, it minimizes its loss—by producing the output at which marginal revenue equals marginal cost. In Figure 15.2, this output is 40,000 customers. Excite@Home charges the price that buyers are willing to pay for this quantity, which is determined by the demand curve and which is $40 a month. With 40,000 customers, Excite@Home's average total cost is $50 a customer, so Excite@Home incurs an economic loss of $400,000 a month ($10 a customer multiplied by 40,000 customers). The red rectangle shows the firm's economic loss.

The largest loss that a firm will incur is equal to total fixed cost. The reason is that if the profit-maximizing (loss-minimizing) price is less than average variable cost, the firm will shut down temporarily and produce nothing (just like a firm in perfect competition—see p. 325).

So far, the firm in monopolistic competition looks like a single-price monopoly. It produces the quantity at which marginal revenue equals marginal cost and then charges the highest price that buyers are willing to pay for that quantity. The difference between monopoly and monopolistic competition lies in what happens when firms either earn an economic profit or incur an economic loss.

■ FIGURE 15.2
Economic Loss in the Short Run

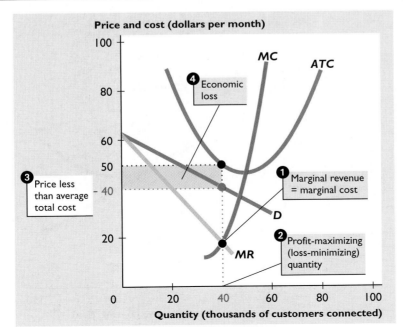

❶ Profit is maximized and loss is minimized where marginal revenue equals marginal cost.

❷ The loss-minimizing quantity is 40,000 customers connected.

❸ The price of $40 a month is less than average total cost of $50 a month, so the firm incurs an economic loss of $10 a customer.

❹ The red rectangle illustrates economic loss, which equals $400,000 a month ($10 a customer multiplied by 40,000 customers).

■ Long Run: Zero Economic Profit

A firm like Excite@Home is not going to incur an economic loss for long. Eventually, it goes out of business. Also, there is no restriction on entry in monopolistic competition, so if firms in an industry are making an economic profit, other firms have an incentive to enter that industry.

As the Gap and Calvin Klein start to make jeans similar to Tommy jeans, the demand for Tommy jeans decreases. The demand curve for Tommy jeans and the marginal revenue curve start to shift leftward. At each point in time, the firm maximizes its profit by producing the quantity at which marginal revenue equals marginal cost and by charging the highest price that buyers are willing to pay for this quantity. But as the demand curve shifts leftward, the profit-maximizing quantity and price fall.

Figure 15.3 shows the long-run equilibrium. The demand curve for Tommy jeans and the marginal revenue curve have shifted leftward. The firm produces 75 pairs of jeans a day and sells them for $50 each. At this output level, average total cost is also $50 a pair. So Tommy Hilfiger is making zero economic profit on its jeans. When all the firms in the industry are earning zero economic profit, there is no incentive for new firms to enter.

If demand is so low relative to costs that firms incur economic losses, exit will occur. As firms leave an industry, the demand for the products of the remaining firms increases and their demand curves shift rightward. The exit process ends when all the firms in the industry are making zero economic profit.

■ FIGURE 15.3
Output and Price in the Long Run

Economic profit encourages entry, which decreases the demand for each firm's product. Economic loss encourages exit, which increases the demand for each remaining firm's product.

When the demand curve touches the average total cost curve at the quantity at which marginal revenue equals marginal cost, the market is in long-run equilibrium. ❶ The output that maximizes profit is 75 pairs of Tommy jeans a day, and ❷ the price, $50 a pair, equals average total cost. ❸ Economic profit is zero.

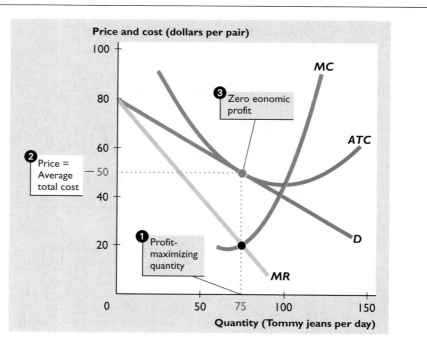

■ Monopolistic Competition and Perfect Competition

Figure 15.4 compares monopolistic competition and perfect competition and highlights two key differences between them: excess capacity and markup.

Excess Capacity

A firm has **excess capacity** if it produces below its **efficient scale**, which is the quantity at which average total cost is a minimum—the quantity at the bottom of the U-shaped *ATC* curve. In Figure 15.4(a), Tommy Hilfiger has *excess capacity*. Because the demand curve for Tommy jeans is downward sloping, zero profit occurs only where the average total cost curve is also downward sloping. In Figure 15.4(b), a firm in perfect competition has no excess capacity. Because the demand curve for a perfectly competitive firm's jeans is horizontal, zero profit occurs where the average total cost is a minimum.

Excess capacity
When the quantity that a firm produces is less than the quantity at which average total cost is a minimum.

Efficient scale
The quantity at which average total cost is a minimum.

Markup

A firm's **markup** is the amount by which price exceeds marginal cost. Figure 15.4(a) shows Tommy's markup. Figure 15.4(b) shows the zero markup of perfect competition. Buyers pay a higher price in monopolistic competition than in perfect competition and pay more than marginal cost.

Markup
The amount by which price exceeds marginal cost.

FIGURE 15.4

Excess Capacity and Markup

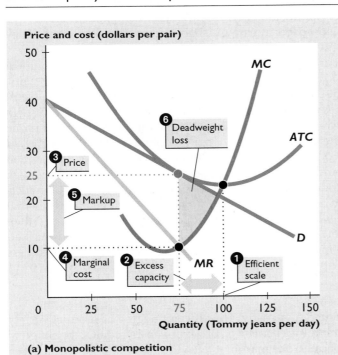

(a) Monopolistic competition

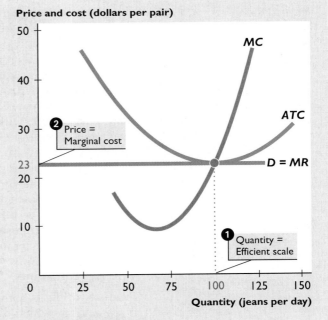

(b) Perfect competition

❶ The efficient scale is 100 pairs a day. In monopolistic competition in the long run, the firm has ❷ excess capacity. ❸ Price exceeds ❹ marginal cost by the amount of the ❺ markup and ❻ creates a deadweight loss.

In contrast, because in perfect competition demand for the firm's output is perfectly elastic, ❶ the quantity produced equals the efficient scale and ❷ price equals marginal cost.

■ Is Monopolistic Competition Efficient?

You've learned that resources are used efficiently when marginal benefit equals marginal cost. You've also learned that price measures marginal benefit. So if the price of a pair of Tommy jeans exceeds the marginal cost of producing them, the quantity of Tommy jeans produced is less than the efficient quantity. And you've just seen that in long-run equilibrium in monopolistic competition, price *does* exceed marginal cost.

Deadweight Loss

Because price exceeds marginal cost, monopolistic competition creates deadweight loss, just like monopoly. Figure 15.4(a) shows this deadweight loss. But is monopolistic competition less efficient than perfect competition?

Making the Relevant Comparison

Two economists meet in the street, and one asks the other how her husband is. "Compared to what?" is the quick reply. This bit of economic wit illustrates a key point: Before we can conclude that something needs fixing, we must check out the available alternatives.

The markup that drives a gap between price and marginal cost in monopolistic competition arises from product differentiation. It is because Tommy jeans are not quite the same as jeans from Banana Republic, CK, Diesel, DKNY, Earl Jeans, Gap, Levi, Ralph Lauren, or any of the other dozens of producers of jeans that the demand for Tommy jeans is not perfectly elastic. The only way in which the demand for jeans from Tommy Hilfiger might be perfectly elastic is if there were only one kind of jeans and Tommy along with every other firm made them. In this situation, Tommy jeans would be indistinguishable from all other jeans. They wouldn't even have identifying labels.

If there was only one kind of jeans, the marginal benefit of jeans would almost certainly be less than it is with variety. People value variety. And people value variety not only because it enables each person to select what he or she likes best but also because it provides an external benefit. Most of us enjoy seeing variety in the choices of others. Contrast a scene from the China of the 1960s when everyone wore a Mao tunic with the China of today when everyone wears the clothes of their own choosing. Or contrast a scene from the Germany of the 1930s when almost everyone who could afford a car owned a first-generation Volkswagen Beetle with the world of today with its variety of styles and types of automobiles.

If people value variety, why don't we see infinite variety? The answer is that variety is costly. Each different variety of any product must be designed, and then customers must be informed about it. These initial costs of design and marketing—called setup costs—mean that some varieties that are too close to others already available are just not worth creating.

The Bottom Line

Product variety is both valued and costly. The efficient degree of product variety is the one for which the marginal benefit of product variety equals its marginal cost. The loss that arises because the marginal benefit of one more unit of a given variety exceeds marginal cost is offset by a gain that arises from having an efficient degree of product variety. So compared to the alternative—complete product uniformity—monopolistic competition is efficient.

CHECKPOINT 15.2

2   Explain how a firm in monopolistic competition determines its output and price in the short run and the long run.

Practice Problem 15.2

1. Natti is a dot.com entrepreneur who has established a Web site at which people can design and buy a pair of way-cool sunglasses. Natti pays $4,000 a month for her Web server and Internet connection. The glasses that her customers design are made to order by another firm, and Natti pays this firm $50 a pair. Natti has no other costs. Table 1 shows the demand schedule for Natti's sunglasses.
    a. Calculate Natti's profit-maximizing output, price, and economic profit.
    b. Do you expect other firms to enter the Web sunglasses business and compete with Natti?
    c. What happens to the demand for Natti's sunglasses in the long run?
    d. What happens to Natti's economic profit in the long run?

TABLE I

Price (dollars per pair)	Quantity (pairs per month)
250	0
200	50
150	100
100	150
50	200
0	250

Exercise 15.2

1. Lorie restrings tennis racquets. Her fixed costs are $1,000 a month, and it costs her $15 of labor to string one racquet. Table 2 shows the demand schedule for Lorie's restringing services.
    a. Calculate Lorie's profit-maximizing output, price, and economic profit.
    b. Do you expect other firms to enter the tennis racquet restringing business and compete with Lorie?
    c. What happens to the demand for Lorie's restringing services in the long run?
    d. What happens to Lorie's economic profit in the long run?

TABLE 2

Price (dollars per racquet)	Quantity (racquets per month)
25	0
20	10
15	20
10	30
5	40
0	50

Solution to Practice Problem 15.2

1a. Marginal cost, *MC*, is $50 a pair—the price that Natti pays her supplier of glasses. To find marginal revenue, calculate the change in total revenue when the quantity increases by 1 pair of sunglasses. Figure 1 shows the demand curve, the marginal revenue curve, and the marginal cost curve. Profit is maximized when *MC* = *MR* and Natti sells 100 pairs a month. The price is $150, and average total cost, *ATC*, is $90—the sum of $50 marginal (and average variable) cost and $40 average fixed cost. Economic profit is $60 a pair on 100 pairs a month, so it is $6,000 a month.

1b. Because Natti is making an economic profit, other firms have an incentive to enter and will do so.

1c. Because firms will enter the market, the demand for Natti's sunglasses will decrease and the demand curve for Natti's sunglasses will shift leftward.

1d. As the demand for Natti's sunglasses decreases, her economic profit also decreases. In the long run, she will earn zero economic profit.

FIGURE I

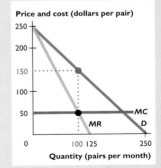

Price and cost (dollars per pair)

15.3 PRODUCT DEVELOPMENT AND MARKETING

When we studied a firm's output and price decisions, we supposed that the firm had already made its product quality and marketing decisions. We're now going to study these decisions and the impact they have on the firm's output, price, and economic profit.

■ Innovation and Product Development

To enjoy economic profits, firms in monopolistic competition must be continually developing new products because whenever economic profits are earned, imitators emerge and set up business. So to maintain its economic profit, a firm must seek out new products that will provide it with a competitive edge, even if only temporarily. A firm that manages to introduce a new and differentiated product will temporarily face a less elastic demand and will be able to increase its price temporarily. The firm will make an economic profit. Eventually, new firms that make close substitutes for the innovative product will enter and compete away the economic profit. So to restore economic profit, the firm must again innovate.

Cost Versus Benefit of Product Innovation

The decision to innovate is based on the same type of profit-maximizing calculation that you've already studied. Innovation and product development are costly activities, but they also bring in additional revenues. The firm must balance the cost and benefit at the margin. At a low level of product development, the marginal revenue from a better product exceeds the marginal cost. When the marginal dollar of product development expenditure (the marginal cost of product development) brings in a dollar of additional revenue (the marginal benefit from product development), the firm is spending the profit-maximizing amount on product development.

For example, when Eidos Interactive released "Lara Croft Tomb Raider: The Angel of Darkness," it was probably not the best game that Eidos could have created. But it was a game with features whose marginal benefit—and consumers' willingness to pay—equaled the marginal cost of those features.

Efficiency and Product Innovation

Is product innovation an efficient activity? Does it benefit the consumer? There are two views about the answers to these questions. One view is that monopolistic competition brings to market many improved products that bring great benefits to the consumer. Clothing, kitchen and other household appliances, computers, computer programs, cars, and many other products keep getting better every year, and the consumer benefits from these improved products.

But many so-called improvements amount to little more than changing the appearance of a product or giving a different look to the packaging. In these cases, there is little objective benefit to the consumer.

But regardless of whether a product improvement is real or imagined, its value to the consumer is its marginal benefit, which equals the amount the consumer is willing to pay. In other words, the value of product improvements is the increase in price that the consumer is willing to pay. The marginal benefit to the producer is marginal revenue, which in equilibrium equals marginal cost. Because price exceeds marginal cost in monopolistic competition, product improvement is not pushed to its efficient level.

■ Advertising

Firms differentiate their products by designing and developing features that are actually different from those of the other firms. But firms also attempt to create a consumer perception of product differentiation even when actual differences are small. Advertising and packaging are the principal means firms use to achieve this end. An American Express card is a different product from a Visa card. But the actual differences are not the main ones that American Express emphasizes in its marketing. The deeper message is that if you use an American Express card, you can be like Tiger Woods (or some other high-profile successful person).

Advertising Expenditures

Firms incur huge costs to ensure that buyers appreciate and value the differences between their own products and those of their competitors. So a large proportion of the prices that we pay cover the cost of selling a good. And this proportion is increasing. Advertising in newspapers and magazines and on radio, television, and the Internet is the main selling cost. But it is not the only one. Selling costs include the cost of shopping malls that look like movie sets; glossy catalogs and brochures; and the salaries, airfares, and hotel bills of salespeople.

The total scale of advertising costs is hard to estimate, but some components can be measured. A survey conducted by a commercial agency suggests that for liquor and real estate agents, around 15 percent of the price is spent on advertising. Figure 15.5 shows estimates for a wide range of goods and services.

■ **FIGURE 15.5**

Advertising Expenditures

X myeconlab

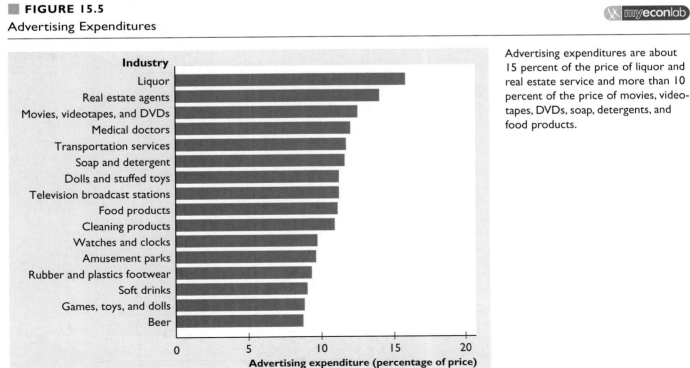

Advertising expenditures are about 15 percent of the price of liquor and real estate service and more than 10 percent of the price of movies, videotapes, DVDs, soap, detergents, and food products.

SOURCE OF DATA: Marketing Today, reported at http://www.marketingtoday.com/tools/ad_to_sales_2004.html.

For the U.S. economy as a whole, there are some 20,000 advertising agencies, which employ more than 200,000 people and have total revenue of $45 billion. But these numbers are only part of the total cost of advertising because many firms have their own internal advertising departments, the costs of which we can only guess.

Advertising expenditures and other selling costs affect firms' profits in two ways: They increase costs and they change demand. Let's look at these effects.

■ Selling Costs and Total Costs

Selling costs such as advertising expenditures increase the costs of a monopolistically competitive firm above those of a perfectly competitive firm or a monopoly. Advertising costs and other selling costs are fixed costs. They do not vary as total output varies. So, just like fixed production costs, advertising costs per unit decrease as output increases.

Figure 15.6 shows how selling costs and advertising expenditures change a firm's average total cost. The blue curve shows the average total cost of production. The red curve shows the firm's average total cost of production plus advertising. The height of the red area between the two curves shows the average fixed cost of advertising. The *total* cost of advertising is fixed. But the *average* cost of advertising decreases as output increases.

Figure 15.6 shows that if advertising increases the quantity sold by a large enough amount, it can lower average total cost. For example, if the quantity sold increases from 25 pairs of jeans a day with no advertising to 100 pairs of jeans a day with advertising, average total cost falls from $60 a pair to $40 a pair. The reason is that although the *total* fixed cost has increased, the greater fixed cost is spread over a greater output, so average total cost decreases.

■ FIGURE 15.6
Selling Costs and Total Costs

Selling costs such as the cost of advertising are fixed costs. ❶ When advertising costs are added to ❷ the average total cost of production, ❸ average total cost increases by more at small outputs than at large outputs.

❹ If advertising enables the quantity sold to increase from 25 pairs of jeans a day to 100 pairs a day, it *lowers* average total cost from $60 a pair to $40 a pair.

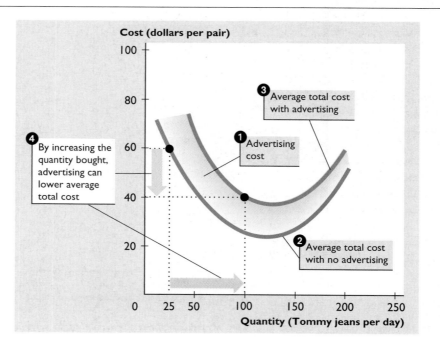

Selling Costs and Demand

Advertising and other selling efforts change the demand for a firm's product. But how? Does demand increase or does it decrease? The most natural answer is that advertising increases demand. By informing people about the quality of its products or by persuading people to switch from the products of other firms, a firm might expect to increase the demand for its own products.

But all firms in monopolistic competition advertise. And all seek to persuade customers that they have the best deal. If advertising enables a firm to survive, it might increase the number of firms in the market. And to the extent that it increases the number of firms, it *decreases* the demand for any one firm's products. It also makes the demand for any one firm's product more elastic. So advertising can end up not only lowering average total cost but also lowering the markup and the price.

Figure 15.7 illustrates this possible effect of advertising. In part (a), with no advertising, the demand for Tommy jeans is not very elastic. Profit is maximized at 75 pairs of jeans a day, and the markup is large. In part (b), advertising, which is a fixed cost, increases average total cost and shifts the average total cost curve upward from ATC_0 to ATC_1 but leaves the marginal cost curve unchanged at MC. Demand becomes much more elastic, the profit-maximizing quantity increases, and the markup shrinks.

■ FIGURE 15.7
Advertising and the Markup

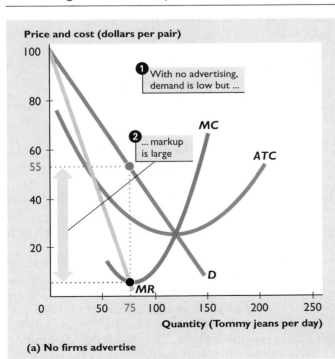

(a) No firms advertise

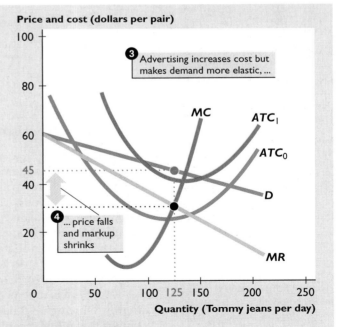

(b) All firms advertise

❶ With no firms advertising, demand is low and not very elastic, so the ❷ markup is large.

❸ Advertising shifts the average total cost curve upward from ATC_0 to ATC_1 and makes demand more elastic. ❹ With all firms advertising, the price falls and the markup shrinks.

Selling Costs in YOUR Life

When you buy a new pair of running shoes, you're buying materials that cost $9, production costs of $8, a U.S. import duty of $3, and selling costs of $50.

Running shoes are not unusual. Almost everything that you buy includes a selling cost component that exceeds one half of the total cost.

The table provides a detailed breakdown of the cost of a pair of shoes.

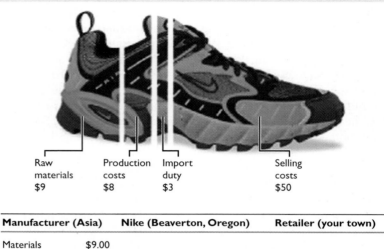

Raw materials $9   Production costs $8   Import duty $3   Selling costs $50

Manufacturer (Asia)		Nike (Beaverton, Oregon)		Retailer (your town)	
Materials	$9.00				
Cost of labor	$2.75	Cost of shoe to Nike	$20.00	Cost of shoe to retailer	$35.50
Cost of capital	$3.00	Sales, distribution, and administration	$5.00	Sales clerk's wages	$9.50
Profit	$1.75	Advertising	$4.00	Shop rent	$9.00
Shipping	$0.50	Research & development	$0.25	Retailer's other costs	$7.00
Import duty	$3.00	Nike's profit	$6.25	Retailer's profit	$9.00
Nike's cost	**$20.00**	**Retailer's cost**	**$35.50**	**Price paid by you**	**$70.00**

■ Using Advertising to Signal Quality

Some advertising, like the Tiger Woods' American Express card ads on television and in glossy magazines or the huge number of dollars that Coke and Pepsi spend, seems hard to understand. There doesn't seem to be any concrete information about a credit card in the glistening smile of a golfer. And surely everyone knows about Coke and Pepsi. What is the gain from pouring millions of dollars a month into advertising a well-known cola?

One answer is that advertising is a signal to the consumer of a high-quality product. A **signal** is an action taken by an informed person (or firm) to send a message to uninformed people. Think about two colas: Coke and Oke.

Oke knows that its cola is not very good and that its taste varies a lot depending on which cheap batch of unsold cola it happens to buy each week. So Oke knows that while it could get a lot of people to try Oke by advertising, they would all quickly discover what a poor product it is and switch back to the cola they bought before. The amount that Oke spent on advertising would exceed the revenue that came in.

Coke, in contrast, knows that its product has a high-quality consistent taste and that once someone has tried it, there is a good chance that they'll never drink

Signal
An action taken by an informed person (or firm) to send a message to uninformed people.

anything but Coke. If Coke ran a costly advertising campaign, more people would try Coke and most would stick with it. The revenue earned would exceed the cost of the advertising campaign.

On the basis of this reasoning, Oke doesn't advertise but Coke does. And Coke spends a lot of money to make a big splash.

Cola drinkers who see Coke's splashy ads believe that the firm would not spend so much money advertising if its product were not truly good. So the cola drinker reasons that Coke is indeed a really good product. The flashy expensive ad has signaled that Coke is really good without saying anything about Coke.

Notice that if advertising is a signal, it doesn't need any specific product information. It just needs to be expensive and hard to miss. That's what a lot of advertising looks like. So the signaling theory of advertising predicts much of the advertising that we see.

■ Brand Names

Many firms create a brand name and spend a lot of money promoting it. Why? What benefit does a brand name bring to justify the sometimes high cost of establishing it? The basic answer is that a brand name provides consumers with information about the quality of a product and the producer with an incentive to achieve a high and consistent quality standard.

To see how a brand name helps the consumer, think about how you use brand names to get information about quality. You're on a road trip, and it is time to find a place to spend the night. You see roadside advertisements for Holiday Inn and Embassy Suites and for Joe's Motel and Annie's Driver's Stop. You know about Holiday Inn and Embassy Suites because you've stayed in them before. And you've seen their advertisements. You know what to expect from them. You have no information at all about Joe's and Annie's. They might be better than the lodging you do know about, but without that knowledge, you're not going to chance them. You use the brand name as information and stay at Holiday Inn.

This same story explains why a brand name provides an incentive to the producer to achieve high and consistent quality. Because no one would know whether they were offering a high standard of service, Joe's and Annie's have no incentive to do so. But equally, because everyone expects a given standard of service from Holiday Inn, a failure to meet a customer's expectation would almost surely lose that customer to a competitor. So Holiday Inn has a strong incentive to deliver what it promises in the advertising that creates its brand name.

■ Efficiency of Advertising and Brand Names

To the extent that advertising and brand names provide consumers with information about the precise nature of product differences and about product quality, they benefit the consumer and enable a better product choice to be made. But the opportunity cost of the additional information must be weighed against the gain to the consumer.

The final verdict on the efficiency of monopolistic competition is ambiguous. In some cases, the gains from extra product variety unquestionably offset the selling costs and the extra cost arising from excess capacity. The tremendous varieties of books and magazines, clothing, food, and drinks are examples of such gains. It is less easy to see the gains from being able to buy brand-name drugs that have a chemical composition identical to that of a generic alternative. But many people do willingly pay more for the brand-name alternative.

3 **Explain why advertising costs are high and why firms use brand names in monopolistic competition.**

Practice Problem 15.3

1. Bianca bakes delicious cookies. Her total fixed cost is $40 a day, and her average variable cost is $1 a bag. Few people know about Bianca's Cookies, and she is maximizing her profit by selling 10 bags a day for $5 a bag. Bianca thinks that if she spends $50 a day on advertising, she can increase her market and sell 25 bags a day for $5 a bag. If Bianca's belief about the effect of advertising is correct,
   a. Can she increase her economic profit by advertising?
   b. If she advertises, will her average total cost increase or decrease at the quantity produced?
   c. If she advertises, will she continue to sell her cookies for $5 a bag or will she raise her price or lower her price?

Exercise 15.3

1. Bianca—the same Bianca as in the practice problem—changes the recipe that she uses and now bakes even more delicious cookies. Bianca's costs don't change, but people love her new cookies and think that they are much better than those of the other cookie producers.
   a. How will the change described here affect Bianca's price, quantity produced, and economic profit?
   b. Can she still increase her economic profit by advertising?

Solution to Practice Problem 15.3

1a. With no advertising, Bianca's total revenue is $50 (10 bags at $5 a bag) and her total cost is $50 (the sum of $40 total fixed cost and $10 total variable cost). So her economic profit is zero. With $50 a day advertising expenditure, Bianca has a total revenue of $125 (25 bags at $5 a bag) and total cost of $115 (total fixed cost is now $90, and total variable cost is now $25). Her economic profit with no price change is $10. So Bianca can increase her economic profit by advertising.

1b. If Bianca advertises, her average total cost will decrease. With no advertising, her average total cost is $5 a bag ($50 ÷ 10). With advertising, her average total cost is $4.60 a bag ($115 ÷ 25).

1c. We can't say if she will continue to sell her cookies for $5 a bag. It depends on how her demand curve shifts. Advertising costs are fixed costs, so they don't change marginal cost, which remains at $1 a bag. She will sell the profit-maximizing quantity (the quantity at which marginal revenue equals marginal cost) for the highest price she can charge for the quantity produced.

CHAPTER CHECKPOINT

Key Points

1 **Describe and identify monopolistic competition.**

- Monopolistic competition is a market structure in which a large number of firms compete; each firm produces a product that is slightly different from the products of its competitors; firms compete on price, quality, and marketing; and new firms are free to enter the industry.

- Monopolistic competition is identified by a low degree of concentration measured by either the four-firm concentration ratio or the HHI.

2 **Explain how a firm in monopolistic competition determines its output and price in the short run and the long run.**

- Firms in monopolistic competition face downward-sloping demand curves and produce the quantity at which marginal revenue equals marginal cost.

- Entry and exit result in zero economic profit and excess capacity in long-run equilibrium.

3 **Explain why advertising costs are high and why firms use brand names in monopolistic competition.**

- Firms in monopolistic competition innovate and develop new products to maintain economic profit.

- Advertising expenditures increase total cost, but they might lower average total cost if they increase the quantity sold by enough.

- Advertising expenditures might increase demand, but they might also decrease the demand facing a firm by increasing competition.

- Whether monopolistic competition is inefficient depends on the value people place on product variety.

Key Terms

Efficient scale, 383
Excess capacity, 383
Four-firm concentration ratio, 376
Herfindahl-Hirschman Index, 377

Markup, 383
Product differentiation, 374
Signal, 390

myeconlab

Exercises

1. Which of the following goods and services are sold by firms in monopolistic competition?
   a. Cable television service
   b. Wheat
   c. Athletic shoes
   d. Soda
   e. Shaving cream
   f. Toothbrushes
   g. Ready-mix concrete

   Explain your selections.

2. The four-firm concentration ratio for audio equipment makers is 30, and that for electric lamp makers is 89. The HHI for audio equipment makers is 415, and that for electric lamp makers is 2,850. Which of these markets is an example of monopolistic competition?

FIGURE 1

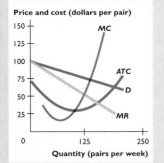

3. Figure 1 shows the demand curve, marginal revenue curve, and cost curves of Lite and Kool, Inc., a producer of running shoes in monopolistic competition.
   a. What quantity does Lite and Kool produce?
   b. What price does it charge?
   c. What is Lite and Kool's markup?
   d. How much profit does Lite and Kool make?
   e. Do firms in monopolistic competition always have excess capacity?
   f. Explain why Lite and Kool does or does not have excess capacity.
   g. Do you expect firms to enter the running shoes market or exit from that market in the long run? Explain your answer.

FIGURE 2

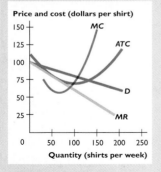

4. Figure 2 shows the demand curve, marginal revenue curve, and cost curves of Stiff Shirt, Inc., a producer of shirts in monopolistic competition.
   a. Show on the graph the quantity that Stiff Shirt produces.
   b. Show on the graph the price that Stiff Shirt charges.
   c. Show on the graph Stiff Shirt's markup.
   d. Show on the graph Stiff Shirt's profit.
   e. Does Stiff Shirt have excess capacity?
   f. If Stiff Shirt increased output, would its average total cost fall or rise?
   g. In light of your answer to part **f**, why doesn't Stiff Shirt increase its output?
   h. Do you expect firms to enter the shirt market or exit from that market in the long run? Explain your answer.
   i. Do you expect the price of a shirt to rise or fall in the long run? Explain your answer.

FIGURE 3

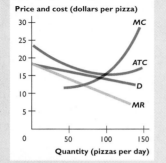

5. Figure 3 shows the demand curve, marginal revenue curve, and cost curves of La Bella Pizza, a firm in monopolistic competition.
   a. Show on the graph the quantity La Bella produces.
   b. Show on the graph the price La Bella charges.
   c. Show on the graph La Bella's economic profit.

   d. Does La Bella have excess capacity? Explain why or why not.
   e. Does La Bella have a price markup? Explain why or why not.
   f. Do you expect firms to enter the pizza market or exit from that market in the long run? Explain your answer.
   g. Do you expect the price of pizza to rise or fall in the long run?

6. Figure 4 shows the demand curve, marginal revenue curve, and cost curves of Bob's Best Burgers, a firm in monopolistic competition.
   a. What quantity of burgers does Bob produce?
   b. What price does Bob charge?
   c. What is Bob's economic profit?
   d. Do you expect other firms to enter the burger business and compete with Bob? Why or why not?
   e. Does Bob have excess capacity? Explain why or why not.
   f. Does Bob have a price markup? Explain why or why not.

FIGURE 4

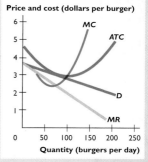

7. Jeb and George are discussing their respective businesses. Jeb says that there is no way he could lower his average total cost. He wouldn't be able to hold his costs to their current level if he either increased or decreased his production. George says that he is frustrated by the level of demand for his product and that he could cut his costs if only he could sell more. One of these people runs a diner, and the other is a wheat farmer.
   a. Who is which and why?
   b. What does this conversation imply about the efficiency of wheat farms and diners?
   c. What does this conversation imply about the economic profit earned by wheat farms and diners?

8. Mike's, a firm in monopolistic competition, produces running shoes. With no advertising, Mike's profit-maximizing output is 500 pairs a day and the price is $100 a pair. But the firms in this market begin to advertise, and so does Mike's. With advertising, Mike's profit-maximizing output increases to 1,000 pairs a day, but the price falls to $50 a pair.
   a. Sketch a demand curve, marginal revenue curve, average total cost curve, and marginal cost curve that are consistent with the no-advertising situation described.
   b. Sketch a demand curve, marginal revenue curve, average total cost curve, and marginal cost curve that are consistent with the advertising situation described.
   c. In which situation does Mike's have the larger markup?
   d. In which situation does Mike's have the larger excess capacity?

9. Some people happily pay more for Coke or Pepsi than they are willing to pay for a nonbranded cola. And some people happily pay more for Tylenol than they are willing to pay for generic acetaminophen.
   a. Does this behavior mean that such people are irrational?
   b. How do brand names help consumers?
   c. How do brand names change the behavior of producers?
   d. Why would it not be efficient to ban brand names?

Critical Thinking

10. "Advertising and brand names are a social waste. We would be better off if brand names were not protected and if advertising were banned." Discuss these assertions, and in doing so, use the analysis of the effects of advertising and brand names presented in this chapter.

11. What is your favorite television advertisement?
    a. Describe the advertisement.
    b. Is this advertisement a signal?
    c. How do you think this advertisement increases the profits of the producer?
    d. How do you think this advertisement benefits the consumer?
    e. In what ways do you think this advertisement creates deadweight loss?

12. The Xerox brand of photocopiers has become so common that people often use the name Xerox as a common noun (a xerox) and a verb (to xerox). Xerox launched an expensive campaign urging the public to use "Xerox" only as a proper noun (the Xerox brand photocopiers).
    a. Why is Xerox so concerned about the use of its brand name as a common noun or verb?
    b. Do consumers benefit if "Xerox" is not used as an everyday noun and verb?

Web Exercises

Use the links on MyEconLab to work the following exercises.

13. Go to the U.S. Census Bureau and get the latest (1997) data on concentration ratios in manufacturing.
    a. Find the four-firm concentration ratio and HHI for six consumer items that are examples of monopolistic competition.
    b. Find the four-firm concentration ratio and HHI for six consumer items that are too concentrated to be examples of monopolistic competition.
    c. Explain your selections.

14. Go to pricescan.com and check the prices of an item that interests you.
    a. What is the lowest price for which the item is available?
    b. What is the highest price for which the item is available?
    c. What is the high-price source offering that the low-price source isn't?
    d. If you were buying this item, from which source would you buy it and why?

15. Go to Brand Names Education Forum and read the article "Be a Smart Shopper."
    a. Summarize the article in about 100 words.
    b. Does the article correctly identify the benefits of brand names? Explain why or why not.
    c. Does the advice on being a smart shopper correctly identify the benefits to the consumer of using brand name information? Explain why or why not.

16. See what the Brand-naming Service at yourDictionary.com offers. On the basis of the economics of brand names explained in the chapter, do you think that the specific name chosen for a brand matters much? Explain why or why not.

Oligopoly

CHAPTER CHECKLIST

**When you have completed your study of this chapter,
you will be able to**

1. Describe and identify oligopoly and explain how it arises.

2. Explore the range of alternative price and quantity outcomes and describe the dilemma faced by firms in oligopoly.

3. Use game theory to explain how price and quantity are determined in oligopoly.

When you go shopping for a softball bat, you buy an Anderson, a DeMarini, an Easton, a Louisville Slugger, a Miken, or a Worth. When PC makers go shopping for chips, their choice is narrower. They buy from one of two firms: Intel or Advanced Micro Devices (AMD). And when the world's airlines go shopping for a large passenger jet, they buy a Boeing or an Airbus. In all of these markets, there is competition. But the competition is unlike perfect competition or monopolistic competition. It is unlike perfect competition because the producers of softball bats, computer chips, and airplanes are not price takers. They can influence their prices. It is unlike monopolistic competition because each firm is so big that its actions influence the profits of all the other firms, so it must consider how the other firms might react to its own decisions. To understand how the prices and quantities of softball bats, computer chips, and airplanes are determined, we need the models of oligopoly explained in this chapter.

16.1 WHAT IS OLIGOPOLY?

Oligopoly, like monopolistic competition, is a type of market that lies between perfect competition and monopoly. The firms in oligopoly might produce an identical product and compete only on price, or they might produce a differentiated product and compete on price, product quality, and marketing. The distinguishing features of oligopoly are that

- A small number of firms compete.
- Natural or legal barriers prevent the entry of new firms.

■ Small Number of Firms

In contrast to monopolistic competition and perfect competition, an oligopoly consists of a small number of firms. Each firm has a large share of the market, the firms are interdependent, and they face a temptation to collude.

Interdependence

With a small number of firms in a market, each firm's actions influence the profits of the other firms. To see how, suppose you run one of the three gas stations in a small town. If you cut your price, your market share increases, and your profits might increase too. But the market share and profits of the other two firms fall. In this situation, the other firms will most likely cut their prices too. If they do cut their prices, your market share and profit take a tumble. So before deciding to cut your price, you must predict how the other firms will react and take into account the effects of those reactions on your own profit. Your profit depends on the actions of the other firms, and their profit depends on your actions. You and the other two firms are interdependent.

Temptation to Collude

When a small number of firms share a market, they can increase their profits by forming a cartel and acting like a monopoly. A **cartel** is a group of firms acting together—colluding—to limit output, raise price, and increase economic profit. Cartels are illegal in the United States (and most other countries), but even when there is no formal cartel, firms might try to operate like a cartel. Also, international cartels can operate legally (see *Eye on the Global Economy* on p. 405).

For reasons that you'll discover in this chapter, cartels tend to be unstable and eventually break down.

Cartel
A group of firms acting together to limit output, raise price, and increase economic profit.

■ Barriers to Entry

Either natural or legal barriers to entry can create oligopoly. You saw in Chapter 14 how economies of scale and demand form a natural barrier to entry that can create a *natural monopoly*. These same factors can create a natural oligopoly.

Like natural monopoly, a natural oligopoly arises from the interaction of the demand for a good or service and the extent of economies of scale in its production. Figure 16.1 illustrates two natural oligopolies.

The demand curve, *D* (in both parts of the figure), shows the demand for taxi rides in a town. If the average total cost curve of a taxi company is ATC_1 in part (a), the market is a natural **duopoly**—a market with only two firms. You can prob-

Duopoly
A market with only two firms.

FIGURE 16.1
Natural Oligopoly

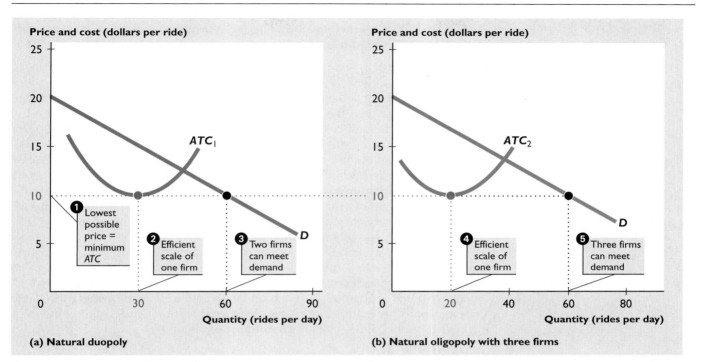

(a) Natural duopoly

(b) Natural oligopoly with three firms

❶ The lowest possible price is $10 a ride, which is the minimum average total cost. ❷ When a firm produces 30 rides a day, the efficient scale, ❸ two firms can satisfy the market demand. This natural oligopoly has two firms—a natural duopoly.

❹ When the efficient scale of one firm is 20 rides a day, ❺ three firms can satisfy the market demand at the lowest possible price. This natural oligopoly has three firms.

ably see some examples of duopoly where you live. Some cities have only two suppliers of milk, two local newspapers, two taxi companies, two car rental firms, two copy centers, or two college bookstores.

Notice in part (a) that the efficient scale of one firm is 30 rides a day. The lowest price at which the firm would remain in business is $10 a ride. At that price, the quantity of rides demanded is 60 a day, the quantity that can be provided by just two firms. There is no room in this market for three firms. To sell more than 60 rides a day, the price would have to fall below $10 a ride. But then the firms would incur an economic loss, and one of them would exit. If there were only one firm, it would earn an economic profit and a second firm would enter to take some of the business and economic profit.

If the average total cost curve of a taxi company is ATC_2 in part (b), the efficient scale of one firm is 20 rides a day. This market is large enough for three firms. But it is not large enough for a fourth firm. Economies of scale limit the market to three because firms would incur a loss if there were four of them. And this market will not operate with two firms because with only two, economic profit would encourage the entry of a third firm.

A legal oligopoly arises when a legal barrier to entry protects the small number of firms in a market. A city might license two taxi firms or two bus companies, for example, even though the combination of demand and economies of scale leaves room for more than two firms.

When barriers to entry create an oligopoly, firms can make an economic profit in the long run without fear of triggering the entry of additional firms.

■ Identifying Oligopoly

Identifying oligopoly is the flip side of identifying monopolistic competition. But the borderline between the two market types is hard to pin down. We need to know whether a market is an oligopoly or monopolistic competition for two reasons. First, we want to be able to make predictions about how the market operates and how price and quantity will respond to such factors as a change in demand or a change in costs. Second, we want to know whether the firms in a market are delivering an efficient outcome that serves the public interest.

The key features of a market that we need to identify are whether the firms are so few that they recognize the interdependencies among them and whether they are acting in a similar way to a monopoly.

As a practical matter, we try to identify oligopoly by looking at the four-firm concentration ratio and the Herfindahl-Hirschman Index, qualified with other information about the geographical scope of the market and barriers to entry.

As we noted in Chapter 15, a market in which the HHI lies between 1,000 and 1,800 is usually an example of monopolistic competition. And a market in which the HHI exceeds 1,800 is usually an example of oligopoly.

EYE ON THE U.S. ECONOMY

Examples of Oligopoly

You're pretty familiar with some of the industries shown in the figure. You probably know, for example, that Kellogg's makes most of the breakfast cereals consumed in the United States. It is said that Kellogg's does more business before eight o'clock in the morning than most firms do all day!

You probably also know that Phillip Morris and RJ Reynolds make most of the cigarettes sold in the United States. You also know that you see Duracell, Energizer, and not much else when you go shopping for a battery. And the washing machine and dryer in

your home were most likely made by General Electric, Maytag, or Whirlpool.

Some of these industries are less familiar, but you see a lot of their products without recognizing them. One of these industries is the manufacture of glass bottles and jars. When you buy anything that comes in glass, there's a good chance that the container was made in Toledo, Ohio, by Owens-Illinois, the world's largest glass packaging manufacturer.

There isn't much room for hesitation about identifying the first seven industries shown in the figure as oligopolies. They have a small number of firms, a high four-firm concentration

ratio, and an HHI that exceeds 2,000. All of these industries are ones in which the largest firms pay serious attention to each other and think hard about the impact of their decisions on their competitors and the repercussion they may themselves face from their competitors' reactions. The last three industries in the figure are less easily classified. They might be considered borderline between oligopoly and monopolistic competition. The four-firm concentration ratio and HHI are high. But there are many firms in these industries. And while a few of the firms are very large, they face tough competition from the many others.

CHECKPOINT 16.1

1 Describe and identify oligopoly and explain how it arises.

Practice Problems 16.1

1. What are the distinguishing features of oligopoly?

2. Why are breakfast cereals made by firms in oligopoly? Why isn't there monopolistic competition in that industry?

Exercises 16.1

1. Identify an oligopoly market in which you have bought something recently.

2. Why are the firms that make boxes of chocolates on the borderline between oligopoly and monopolistic competition?

Solution to Practice Problems 16.1

1. The distinguishing features of oligopoly are a small number of interdependent firms competing behind natural or legal barriers to entry.

2. Breakfast cereals are made by firms in oligopoly because economies of scale and demand limit the number of firms that can earn a profit in that market.

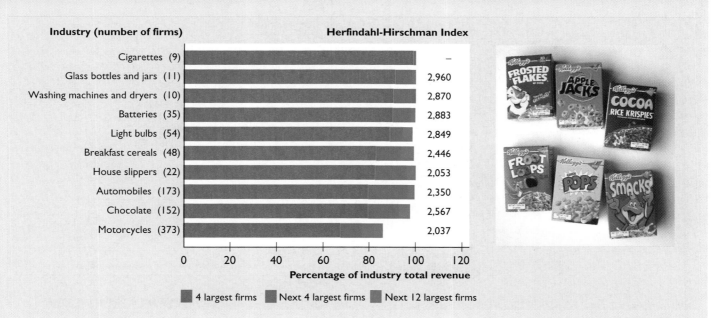

SOURCE OF DATA: U.S. Census Bureau.

16.2 ALTERNATIVE OLIGOPOLY OUTCOMES

Oligopoly might operate like monopoly, like perfect competition, or somewhere between these two extremes. To see these alternative possible outcomes, we'll study duopoly in the market for airplanes. Airbus and Boeing are the only makers of large commercial jet aircraft. Suppose that they have identical costs. To keep the numbers simple, assume that total fixed cost is zero and that regardless of the rate of production, the marginal cost of an airplane is $1 million.

Figure 16.2 shows the market demand schedule and demand curve for airplanes. Airbus and Boeing share this market. The total quantity sold and the quantities sold by each firm depend on the price of an airplane.

■ Monopoly Outcome

If this industry had only one firm operating as a single-price monopoly, its marginal revenue curve would be the one shown in Figure 16.2. Marginal revenue equals marginal cost when 6 airplanes a week are produced and the price is $13 million an airplane. Total cost would be $6 million and total revenue would be $78 million, so economic profit would be $72 million a week.

■ **FIGURE 16.2**

A Market for Airplanes

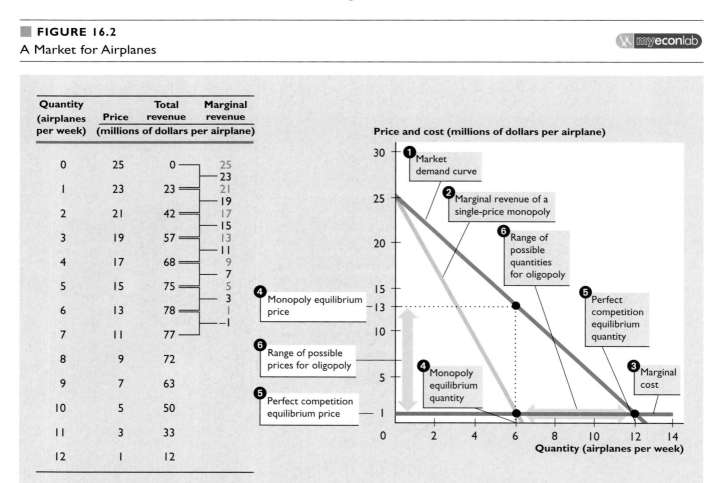

Quantity (airplanes per week)	Price	Total revenue	Marginal revenue
	(millions of dollars per airplane)		
0	25	0	25
			23
1	23	23	21
			19
2	21	42	17
			15
3	19	57	13
			11
4	17	68	9
			7
5	15	75	5
			3
6	13	78	1
			-1
7	11	77	
8	9	72	
9	7	63	
10	5	50	
11	3	33	
12	1	12	

Cartel to Achieve Monopoly Outcome

Can the two firms achieve the monopoly outcome that we've just found and maximize their joint profit? They can attempt to do so by forming a cartel.

Suppose that Airbus and Boeing agreed to limit the total production of airplanes to 6 a week. The market demand curve tells us that the price would be $13 million per airplane and economic profit would be $72 million a week. Suppose that the two firms also agree to split the market evenly and each produce 3 airplanes a week. They would each make an economic profit of $36 million a week—see Table 16.1.

Would it be in the self-interest of Airbus and Boeing to stick to their agreement and limit production to 3 aircraft a week each?

To begin answering this question, notice that with the price of an airplane exceeding marginal cost, if one firm increased production, it would increase its profit. But if both firms increased output whenever price exceeded marginal cost, the end of the process would be the same as perfect competition.

■ Perfect Competition Outcome

You can see the perfect competition outcome in Figure 16.2. The equilibrium is where the industry supply curve, which is the marginal cost curve, intersects the demand curve. The quantity is 12 million airplanes a week, and the price is the same as marginal cost—$1 million per airplane.

■ Other Possible Cartel Breakdowns

Because price exceeds marginal cost, a cartel is likely to break down. But a cartel might not unravel all the way to perfect competition. In *Eye on the Global Economy* on p. 405, you can see the brief history of a sometimes successful and sometimes unsuccessful cartel in the global market for oil. You can see why a cartel breaks down but not all the way to perfect competition by looking at some alternative outcomes in the airplane industry example.

Boeing Increases Output to 4 Airplanes a Week

Suppose that starting from a cartel that achieves the monopoly outcome, Boeing increases output by 1 airplane a week. Table 16.2 keeps track of the data. With Boeing producing 4 airplanes a week and Airbus producing 3 airplanes a week, total output is 7 airplanes a week. To sell 7 airplanes a week, the price must fall. The demand schedule in Figure 16.2 tells us that the quantity demanded is 7 airplanes a week when the price is $11 million an airplane.

Market total revenue would now be $77 million, total cost would be $7 million, and economic profit would fall to $70 million. But the distribution of this economic profit is now unequal. Boeing would gain, and Airbus would lose.

Boeing would now receive $44 million a week in total revenue, have a total cost of $4 million, and earn an economic profit of $40 million. Airbus would receive $33 million a week in total revenue, incur a total cost of $3 million, and earn an economic profit of $30 million.

So by increasing its output by 1 airplane a week, Boeing can increase its economic profit by $4 million and cause the economic profit of Airbus to fall by $6 million.

Because the two firms in this example are identical, we could rerun the above story with Airbus increasing production by 1 airplane a week and Boeing holding

TABLE 16.1 MONOPOLY OUTCOME

	Boeing	Airbus	Market total
Quantity (airplanes a week)	3	3	6
Price ($ million per airplane)	13	13	13
Total revenue ($ million)	39	39	78
Total cost ($ million)	3	3	6
Economic profit ($ million)	36	36	72

TABLE 16.2 BOEING INCREASES OUTPUT TO 4 AIRPLANES A WEEK

	Boeing	Airbus	Market total
Quantity (airplanes a week)	4	3	7
Price ($ million per airplane)	11	11	11
Total revenue ($ million)	44	33	77
Total cost ($ million)	4	3	7
Economic profit ($ million)	40	30	70

output at 3 a week. In this case, Airbus would earn $40 million a week and Boeing would earn $30 million a week.

Boeing is better off producing 4 airplanes a week if Airbus sticks with 3 a week. But is it in Airbus's interest to hold its output at 3 airplanes a week? To answer this question, we need to compare the economic profit Airbus makes if it maintains its output at 3 airplanes a week with the profit it makes if it produces 4 airplanes a week. How much economic profit does Airbus make if it produces 4 airplanes a week with Boeing also producing 4 airplanes a week?

Airbus Increases Output to 4 Airplanes a Week

With both firms producing 4 airplanes a week, total output is 8 airplanes a week. To sell 8 airplanes a week, the price must fall further. The demand schedule in Figure 16.2 tells us that the quantity demanded is 8 airplanes a week when the price is $9 million an airplane.

Table 16.3 keeps track of the data. Market total revenue would now be $72 million, total cost would be $8 million, and economic profit would fall to $64 million. With both firms producing the same output, the distribution of this economic profit is now equal.

Both firms would now receive $36 million a week in total revenue, have a total cost of $4 million, and earn an economic profit of $32 million. For Airbus, this outcome is an improvement on the previous one by $2 million a week. For Boeing, this outcome is worse than the previous one by $8 million.

This outcome is better for Airbus, but would Boeing go along with it? You know that Boeing would be worse off if it decreased its output to 3 airplanes a week because it would get the outcome that Airbus has in Table 16.2—an economic profit of only $30 million a week. But would Boeing be better off if it increased output to 5 airplanes a week?

Boeing Increases Output to 5 Airplanes a Week

Suppose now that Airbus maintains its output at 4 airplanes a week and Boeing increases output to 5 a week. Table 16.4 keeps track of the data. Total output is now 9 airplanes a week. To sell this quantity, the price must fall to $7 million an airplane. Market total revenue is $63 million and total cost is $9 million, so economic profit for the two firms is $54 million. The distribution of this economic profit is again unequal. But now both firms would lose.

Boeing would now receive $35 million a week in total revenue, have a total cost of $5 million, and earn an economic profit of $30 million—$2 million less than it would earn if it maintained its output at 4 airplanes a week. Airbus would receive $28 million a week in total revenue, incur a total cost of $4 million, and earn an economic profit of $24 million—$8 million less than before. So neither firm gains by increasing total output beyond 8 airplanes a week.

■ The Oligopoly Cartel Dilemma

With a cartel, both firms make the maximum available economic profit. If both increase production, both see their profit fall. If only one firm increases production, that firm makes a larger economic profit while the other makes a lower economic profit. So what will the firms do? We can speculate about what they will do. But to work out the answer, we need some game theory. That's our next task.

TABLE 16.3 AIRBUS INCREASES OUTPUT TO 4 AIRPLANES A WEEK

	Boeing	Airbus	Market total
Quantity (airplanes a week)	4	4	8
Price ($ million per airplane)	9	9	9
Total revenue ($ million)	36	36	72
Total cost ($ million)	4	4	8
Economic profit ($ million)	32	32	64

TABLE 16.4 BOEING INCREASES OUTPUT TO 5 AIRPLANES A WEEK

	Boeing	Airbus	Market total
Quantity (airplanes a week)	5	4	9
Price ($ million per airplane)	7	7	7
Total revenue ($ million)	35	28	63
Total cost ($ million)	5	4	9
Economic profit ($ million)	30	24	54

The OPEC Global Oil Cartel

The Organization of the Petroleum Exporting Countries (OPEC) is an international cartel of oil-producing nations. OPEC was created in 1960 by the governments of Iran, Iraq, Kuwait, Saudi Arabia, and Venezuela. Six other nations are now members of the organization: Qatar, Indonesia, Libya, United Arab Emirates, Algeria, and Nigeria.

OPEC describes its objective as being "to co-ordinate and unify petroleum policies among member countries in order to secure fair and stable prices, . . . an efficient, economic and regular supply of petroleum to consuming nations; and a fair return on capital to those investing in the industry." These words can be interpreted as being code for "restricting the production of oil to keep its price high."

During the 1960s, OPEC quietly built its organization and prepared the ground for its push to dominate the global oil market. Its first opportunity came in 1973 when, with an Arab-Israeli war raging, it was able to organize an embargo on oil shipments to the United States and Europe and drive the price of oil to four times its previous level.

OPEC's second opportunity came with a revolution in Iran in 1979 when the price of oil more than doubled.

The figure shows these two price hikes. To make the prices mean the same in terms of the value of money, the graph shows the price of oil in terms of the value of the dollar in 2000. You can see that the price went from about $7 a barrel in 1970 to more than $55 a barrel by 1981.

OPEC ministers meeting in Vienna

During the 1980s, many new sources of oil supply opened up and the OPEC cartel lost control of the global market. The cartel broke down, and the price of oil fell.

The price of oil remained remarkably stable during the 1990s, and the power of OPEC was countered by a large supply of oil from other sources.

But during 2004 and 2005, when the global demand for oil increased dramatically, with much of the increased demand coming from China and other developing Asian economies, OPEC was again able to dominate the market, restrict its own production, and raise the world price.

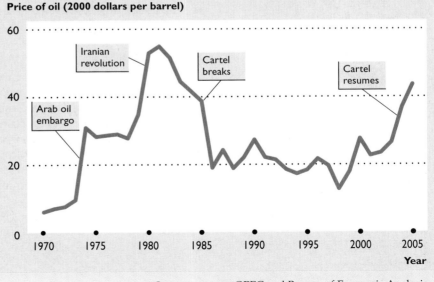

Price of oil (2000 dollars per barrel)

SOURCE OF DATA: OPEC and Bureau of Economic Analysis.

2 Explore the range of possible price and quantity outcomes and describe the dilemma faced by firms in oligopoly.

Practice Problem 16.2

TABLE 1

Price (dollars per unit)	Quantity demanded (units per day)
12	0
11	1
10	2
9	3
8	4
7	5
6	6
5	7
4	8
3	9
2	10
1	11
0	12

1. Isolated Island has two natural gas wells, one owned by Tom and the other owned by Jerry. Each well has a valve that controls the rate of flow of gas, and the marginal cost of producing gas is zero. Table 1 gives the demand schedule for gas on this island. What will the price of gas be on Isolated Island if Tom and Jerry
   a. Form a cartel and maximize their joint profit?
   b. Are forced to sell at the perfectly competitive price?
   c. Compete as duopolists?

Exercises 16.2

1. A third gas well is discovered on Isolated Island, and Joey owns it. There is no change in the demand for gas, and Joey's cost of production is zero, like Tom's and Jerry's costs. Now what is the price of gas on Isolated Island if Tom, Jerry, and Joey
   a. Form a cartel and maximize their joint profit?
   b. Are forced to sell at the perfectly competitive price?

2. Kodak and Fuji are the only major producers of high-speed photo film. Each company has developed a fast-speed film and aggressively advertises it. The two firms are locked in a duopolists' dilemma.
   a. Describe the dilemma facing Kodak and Fuji.
   b. Suppose that Kodak and Fuji were to secretly form a cartel. What do you predict would
      i.   Happen to the price of film?
      ii. Be the change in the two firms' advertising and research and development budgets?

TABLE 2

Quantity (units per day)	Total revenue (dollars per day)	Marginal revenue (dollars per unit)
0	0	
1	11	11
2	20	9
3	27	7
4	32	5
5	35	3
6	36	1
7	35	−1
8	32	−3
9	27	−5
10	20	−7
11	11	−9
12	0	−11

Solution to Practice Problem 16.2

1a. If Tom and Jerry form a cartel and maximize their joint profit, they will charge the monopoly price. This price is the highest price the market will bear when the quantity produced makes marginal revenue equal to marginal cost. Marginal cost is zero, so we need to find the price at which marginal revenue is zero. Marginal revenue is zero when total revenue is a maximum, which occurs when output is 6 units a day (Table 2) and price is $6 a unit (see the demand schedule in Table 1).

1b. The perfectly competitive price equals marginal cost, which is zero. In this case, output is 12 units a day.

1c. If Tom and Jerry compete as duopolists, they will increase production above the monopoly level, but they will not drive the price down to zero.

16.3 GAME THEORY

Game theory is the main tool that economists use to analyze *strategic behavior*—behavior that recognizes mutual interdependence and takes account of the expected behavior of others. John von Neumann invented game theory in 1937, and today it is a major research field in economics.

Game theory helps us to understand oligopoly and many other forms of economic, political, social, and even biological rivalries. We will begin our study of game theory and its application to the behavior of firms by thinking about familiar games that we play for fun.

■ What Is a Game?

What is a game? At first thought, the question seems silly. After all, there are many different games. There are ball games and parlor games, games of chance and games of skill. But what is it about all these different activities that make them games? What do all these games have in common? All games share three features:

- Rules
- Strategies
- Payoffs

Let's see how these common features of games apply to a game called "the prisoners' dilemma." The **prisoners' dilemma** is a game between two prisoners that shows why it is hard to cooperate even when it would be beneficial to both players to do so. This game captures the essential feature of the duopolists' dilemma that we've just been studying. The prisoners' dilemma also provides a good illustration of how game theory works and how it generates predictions.

■ The Prisoners' Dilemma

Art and Bob have been caught red-handed, stealing a car. During the district attorney's interviews with the prisoners, he begins to suspect that he has stumbled on the two people who committed a multimillion-dollar bank robbery some months earlier. But this is just a suspicion. The district attorney has no evidence on which he can convict them of the greater crime unless he can get them to confess. He makes the prisoners play a game with the following rules.

Rules

Each prisoner (player) is placed in a separate room and cannot communicate with the other player. Each is told that he is suspected of having carried out the bank robbery and that

- If both of them confess to the larger crime, each will receive a reduced sentence of 3 years for both crimes.
- If he alone confesses and his accomplice does not, he will receive an even shorter sentence of 1 year, while his accomplice will receive a 10-year sentence.
- If neither of them confesses to the larger crime, each will receive a 2-year sentence for car theft.

Game theory
The tool that economists use to analyze *strategic behavior*—behavior that recognizes mutual interdependence and takes account of the expected behavior of others.

Prisoners' dilemma
A game between two prisoners that shows why it is hard to cooperate even when it would be beneficial to both players to do so.

Strategies
All the possible actions of each player in a game.

Payoff matrix
A table that shows the payoffs for each player for every possible combination of actions by the players.

TABLE 16.5 PRISONERS' DILEMMA PAYOFF MATRIX

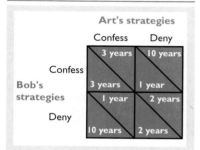

Each square shows the payoffs for the two players, Art and Bob, for each possible pair of actions. In each square, the red triangle shows Art's payoff and the blue triangle shows Bob's. For example, if both confess, the payoffs are in the top left square.

Nash equilibrium
An equilibrium in which each player takes the best possible action given the action of the other player.

Strategies

In game theory, **strategies** are all the possible actions of each player. Art and Bob each have two possible strategies:

- Confess to the bank robbery.
- Deny having committed the bank robbery.

Payoffs

Because there are two players, each with two strategies, there are four possible outcomes:

- Both confess.
- Both deny.
- Art confesses and Bob denies.
- Bob confesses and Art denies.

Each prisoner can work out exactly what happens to him—his *payoff*—in each of these four situations. We can tabulate the four possible payoffs for each of the prisoners in what is called a payoff matrix for the game. A **payoff matrix** is a table that shows the payoffs for every possible action by each player given every possible action by the other player.

Table 16.5 shows a payoff matrix for Art and Bob. The squares show the payoffs for each prisoner—the red triangle in each square shows Art's, and the blue triangle shows Bob's. If both prisoners confess (top left), each gets a prison term of 3 years. If Bob confesses but Art denies (top right), Art gets a 10-year sentence and Bob gets a 1-year sentence. If Art confesses and Bob denies (bottom left), Art gets a 1-year sentence and Bob gets a 10-year sentence. Finally, if both of them deny (bottom right), neither can be convicted of the bank robbery charge but both are sentenced for the car theft—a 2-year sentence.

Equilibrium

The equilibrium of a game occurs when each player takes the best possible action given the action of the other player. This equilibrium concept is called **Nash equilibrium**. It is so named because John Nash of Princeton University, who received the Nobel Prize for Economic Science in 1994, proposed it. (The same John Nash was portrayed in the popular movie *A Beautiful Mind*.)

In the case of the prisoners' dilemma, equilibrium occurs when Art makes his best choice given Bob's choice and when Bob makes his best choice given Art's choice. Let's find the equilibrium.

First, look at the situation from Art's point of view. If Bob confesses, it pays Art to confess because in that case, he is sentenced to 3 years rather than 10 years. If Bob does not confess, it still pays Art to confess because in that case, he receives 1 year rather than 2 years. So no matter what Bob does, Art's best action is to confess.

Second, look at the situation from Bob's point of view. If Art confesses, it pays Bob to confess because in that case, he is sentenced to 3 years rather than 10 years. If Art does not confess, it still pays Bob to confess because in that case, he receives 1 year rather than 2 years. So no matter what Art does, Bob's best action is to confess.

Because each player's best action is to confess, each does confess, each gets a 3-year prison term, and the district attorney has solved the bank robbery. This is the equilibrium of the game.

Not the Best Outcome

The equilibrium of the prisoners' dilemma game is not the best outcome for the prisoners. Isn't there some way in which they can cooperate and get the smaller 2-year prison term? There is not, because the players cannot communicate with each other. Each player can put himself in the other player's place and can figure out what the other will do. The prisoners are in a dilemma. Each knows that he can serve only 2 years if he can trust the other to deny. But each also knows that it is not in the best interest of the other to deny. So each prisoner knows that he must confess, thereby delivering a bad outcome for both.

Let's now see how we can use the ideas we've just developed to understand the behavior of firms in oligopoly. We'll start by returning to the duopolists' dilemma.

■ The Duopolist's Dilemma

The dilemma of Airbus and Boeing is similar to that of Art and Bob. Each firm has two strategies. It can produce airplanes at the rate of

- 3 a week
- 4 a week

Because each firm has two strategies, there are four possible combinations of actions for the two firms:

- Both firms produce 3 a week (monopoly outcome).
- Both firms produce 4 a week.
- Airbus produces 3 a week and Boeing produces 4 a week.
- Boeing produces 3 a week and Airbus produces 4 a week.

The Payoff Matrix

Table 16.6 sets out the payoff matrix for this game. It is constructed in exactly the same way as the payoff matrix for the prisoners' dilemma in Table 16.5. The squares show the payoffs for Airbus and Boeing. In this case, the payoffs are economic profits. (In the case of the prisoners' dilemma, the payoffs were losses.)

The table shows that if both firms produce 4 a week (top left), each firm makes an economic profit of $32 million. If both firms produce 3 a week (bottom right), they make the monopoly profit, and each firm earns an economic profit of $36 million. The top right and bottom left squares show what happens if one firm produces 4 a week while the other produces 3 a week. The firm that increases production makes an economic profit of $40 million, and the one that keeps production at the monopoly quantity makes an economic profit of $30 million.

Equilibrium of the Duopolist's Dilemma

What do the firms do? To answer this question, we must find the equilibrium of the duopoly game.

TABLE 16.6 DUOPOLISTS' DILEMMA PAYOFF MATRIX

Each square shows the payoffs from a pair of actions. For example, if both firms produce 3 airplanes a week, the payoffs are recorded in the bottom right square. The red triangle shows Airbus's payoff, and the blue triangle shows Boeing's.

TABLE 16.7 THE NASH EQUILIBRIUM

The Nash equilibrium is for each firm to produce 4 airplanes a week.

Using the information in Table 16.7, look at things from Airbus's point of view. Airbus reasons as follows: Suppose that Boeing produces 4 a week. If I produce 3 a week, I will make an economic profit of $30 million. If I also produce 4 a week, I will make an economic profit of $32 million. So I'm better off producing 4 a week. Airbus continues to reason: Now suppose Boeing produces 3 a week. If I produce 4 a week, I will make an economic profit of $40 million, and if I produce 3 a week, I will make an economic profit of $36 million. An economic profit of $40 million is better than an economic profit of $36 million, so I'm better off if I produce 4 a week. So regardless of whether Boeing produces 4 a week or 3 a week, it pays Airbus to produce 4 a week.

Because the two firms face identical situations, Boeing comes to the same conclusion as Airbus. So both firms produce 4 a week. The equilibrium of the duopoly game is that both firms produce 4 airplanes a week.

Collusion Is Profitable but Difficult to Achieve

In the duopolists' dilemma that you've just studied, Airbus and Boeing end up in a situation that is similar to that of the prisoners in the prisoners' dilemma game. They don't achieve the best joint outcome. Because each produces 4 airplanes a week, each earns an economic profit of $32 million a week.

If firms were able to collude, they would agree to limit their production to 3 airplanes a week each and they would each earn the monopoly profit of $36 million a week.

The outcome of the duopolists' dilemma shows why it is difficult for firms to collude. Even if collusion were a legal activity, firms in duopoly would find it difficult to implement an agreement to restrict output. Like the players of the prisoners' dilemma game, the duopolists would reach a Nash equilibrium in which they produce more than the joint profit-maximizing quantity.

If two firms have difficulty maintaining a collusive agreement, oligopolies with more than two firms have an even harder time. The operation of OPEC (see *Eye on the Global Economy* on p. 405) illustrates this difficulty. To raise the price of oil, OPEC must limit global oil production. The members of this cartel meet from time to time and set a production limit for each member nation. Almost always, within a few months of a decision to restrict production, some (usually smaller) members of the cartel break their quotas, production increases, and the price sags below the cartel's desired target. The OPEC cartel plays an oligopoly dilemma game similar to the prisoners' dilemma. Only in 1973, 1979–1980, and 2005 did OPEC manage to keep its members' production under control and raise the price of oil.

■ Advertising and Research Games in Oligopoly

Every month, Coke and Pepsi, Kodak and Fuji, Xerox and Canon, Nike and Reebok, Procter & Gamble and Kimberly-Clark, and hundreds of other pairs of big firms locked in fierce competition spend millions of dollars on advertising campaigns and on research and development (R&D). They make decisions about whether to increase or cut the advertising budget or whether to undertake a large R&D effort aimed at making the product more reliable (usually, the more reliable a product, the more expensive it is to produce but the more people are willing to pay for it) or at lowering production costs. These choices can be analyzed as games. Let's look at some examples of these types of games.

Advertising Game

A key to success in the soft drink industry is to run huge advertising campaigns. These campaigns affect market share but are costly to run. Table 16.8 shows some hypothetical numbers for the advertising game that Pepsi and Coke play. Each firm has two strategies: Advertise or don't advertise. If neither firm advertises, they each make $50 million (bottom right of the payoff matrix). If each firm advertises, each firm's profit is lower by the amount spent on advertising (top left square of the payoff matrix). If Pepsi advertises but Coke does not, Pepsi gains and Coke loses (top right square of the payoff matrix). Finally, if Coke advertises and Pepsi does not, Coke gains and Pepsi loses (bottom left square).

Pepsi reasons as follows: Regardless of whether Coke advertises, we're better off advertising. Coke reasons similarly: Regardless of whether Pepsi advertises, we're better off advertising. Because advertising is the best strategy for both players, it is the Nash equilibrium. The outcome of this game is that both firms advertise and make less profit than they would if they could collude to achieve the cooperative outcome of no advertising.

Research and Development Game

A key to success in the disposable diaper industry is to design a product that people value highly relative to the cost of producing it. The firm that develops the most highly valued product and also develops the least-cost technology for producing it gains a competitive edge, undercutting the rest of the market, increasing its market share, and increasing its profit. But the R&D that must be undertaken to achieve product improvements and cost reductions is costly. So the cost of R&D must be deducted from the profit resulting from the increased market share that lower costs achieve. If no firm does R&D, every firm can be better off, but if one firm initiates the R&D activity, all must follow.

Table 16.9 illustrates the dilemma (with hypothetical numbers) for the R&D game that Kimberly-Clark and Procter & Gamble play. Each firm has two strategies: Do R&D or do no R&D. If neither firm does R&D, Kimberly-Clark makes $30 million and Procter & Gamble makes $70 million (bottom right of the payoff matrix). If each firm does R&D, each firm's profit is lower by the amount spent on R&D (top left square of the payoff matrix). If Kimberly-Clark does R&D but Procter & Gamble does not, Kimberly-Clark gains and Procter & Gamble loses (top right square of the payoff matrix). Finally, if Procter & Gamble conducts R&D and Kimberly-Clark does not, Procter & Gamble gains and Kimberly-Clark loses (bottom left square).

Kimberly-Clark reasons as follows: Regardless of whether Procter & Gamble undertakes R&D, we're better off doing R&D. Procter & Gamble reasons similarly: Regardless of whether Kimberly-Clark does R&D, we're better off doing R&D.

Because R&D is the best strategy for both players, it is the Nash equilibrium. The outcome of this game is that both firms conduct R&D. They make less profit than they would if they could collude to achieve the cooperative outcome of no R&D.

The real-world situation has more players than Kimberly-Clark and Procter & Gamble. A large number of other firms strive to capture market share from Procter & Gamble and Kimberly-Clark. So the R&D effort by these two firms not only serves the purpose of maintaining shares in their own battle but also helps to keep barriers to entry high enough to preserve their joint market share.

TABLE 16.8 THE ADVERTISING GAME PAYOFF MATRIX

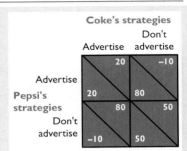

The red triangle shows Coke's payoff, and the blue triangle shows Pepsi's. If both firms advertise they earn less than if neither firm advertises. But each firm is better off advertising if the other doesn't advertise. The Nash equilibrium for this prisoners' dilemma advertising game is for both firms to advertise.

TABLE 16.9 THE R&D GAME PAYOFF MATRIX

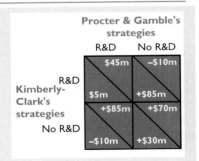

The red triangle shows Procter & Gamble's payoff, and the blue triangle shows Kimberly-Clark's. If both firms do R&D, they earn less than if neither firm undertakes R&D. But each firm is better off doing R&D if the other does no R&D. The Nash equilibrium for this prisoners' dilemma R&D game is for both firms to do R&D.

■ Repeated Games

The games that we've studied are played just once. In contrast, most real-world games get played repeatedly. This fact suggests that real-world duopolists might find some way of learning to cooperate so that they can enjoy a monopoly profit. If a game is played repeatedly, one player has the opportunity to penalize the other player for previous "bad" behavior. If Airbus produces 4 airplanes this week, perhaps Boeing will produce 4 next week. Before Airbus produces 4 this week, won't it take account of the possibility of Boeing producing 4 next week? What is the equilibrium of this more complicated dilemma game when it is repeated indefinitely?

The monopoly equilibrium might occur if each firm knows that the other will punish overproduction with overproduction, "tit for tat." Let's see why.

Table 16.10 keeps track of the numbers. Suppose that Boeing contemplates producing 4 airplanes in week 1. This move will bring it an economic profit of $40 million and will cut the economic profit of Airbus to $30 million. In week 2, Airbus will punish Boeing and produce 4 airplanes. But Boeing must go back to 3 airplanes to induce Airbus to cooperate again in week 3. So in week 2, Airbus makes an economic profit of $40 million, and Boeing makes an economic profit of $30 million. Adding up the profits over these two weeks of play, Boeing would have made $72 million by cooperating (2 × $36 million) compared with $70 million from producing 4 airplanes in week 1 and generating Airbus's tit-for-tat response.

What is true for Boeing is also true for Airbus. Because each firm makes a larger profit by sticking to the monopoly output, both firms do so and the monopoly price, quantity, and profit prevail.

In reality, whether a duopoly (or more generally an oligopoly) works like a one-play game or a repeated game depends primarily on the number of players and the ease of detecting and punishing overproduction. The larger the number of players, the harder it is to maintain the monopoly outcome.

TABLE 16.10 PAYOFFS WITH PUNISHMENT

Period of play	Cooperate		Overproduce	
	Boeing profit	Airbus profit	Boeing profit	Airbus profit
	(millions of dollars)			
I	36	36	40	30
2	36	36	30	40

■ Is Oligopoly Efficient?

The quantity produced of any good or service is the efficient quantity if the price (which measures marginal benefit) equals marginal cost. Does oligopoly produce efficient quantities of goods and services?

You've seen that if firms in oligopoly play a repeated prisoners' dilemma game, they can end up restricting output to the monopoly level and earning the same economic profit as a monopoly would earn. You've also seen that even when the firms don't cooperate, they don't necessarily drive the price down to marginal cost. So generally, oligopoly is not efficient. It suffers from the same source of inefficiency as monopoly.

Also, firms in oligopoly might end up operating at a higher average total cost than the lowest attainable cost because their advertising and research budgets are higher than the socially efficient level.

Because oligopoly creates inefficiency, antitrust laws and regulations are established that seek to reduce market power and move the outcome closer to that of competition and efficiency. We study these laws and regulations in Chapter 17.

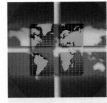

EYE ON THE GLOBAL ECONOMY

Duopoly in CPUs

The CPU in your computer or your game box—the brainpower of the machine—is made either by Intel Corporation or by Advanced Micro Devices, Inc. (AMD). Intel dominates this market, as the pie charts show.

The graph in part (c) shows the prices of some of the most popular CPU chips in May 2005. Notice that at comparable clock speeds, AMD chips are higher priced than Intel chips but Intel makes the fastest chips.

Competition between Intel and AMD is like the duopolists' dilemma that you've studied in this chapter. The game is played on both price and product design and quality and across a range of differentiated products.

SOURCE OF DATA: sharkyextreme.com.

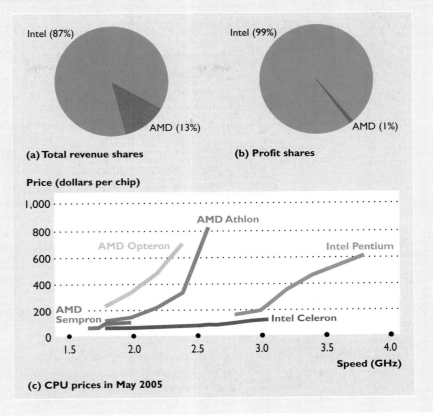

(a) Total revenue shares

(b) Profit shares

(c) CPU prices in May 2005

REALITY CHECK

A Game in YOUR Life

The payoff matrix here describes a game that might be familiar to you. But it isn't a prisoners' dilemma. It's a lovers' dilemma. Jane and Jim like to do things together. But Jane likes the movies more than the ball game, and Jim likes the ball game more than the movies. The payoff matrix describes how much they like the various outcomes (measured in units of utility). What do they do?

You can figure out that Jim never goes to the movies alone and Jane never goes to the ball game alone. You can also figure out that Jim doesn't go to the ball game alone and Jane doesn't go to the movies alone. So they go out together. But do they do the movies or the ball game? This game has no unique equilibrium. The payoffs tell you that they might go to either the game or the movies. In a repeated game, they'll probably alternate between the two!

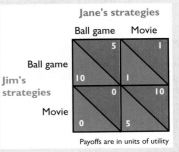

Payoffs are in units of utility

3 **Use game theory to explain how price and quantity are determined in oligopoly.**

Practice Problem 16.3

1. Bud and Wise are the only two producers of aniseed beer, a New Age product designed to displace root beer. Bud and Wise are trying to figure out how much of this new beer to produce. They know that if they both limit production to 10,000 gallons a day, they will make the maximum attainable joint profit of $200,000 a day—$100,000 a day each. They also know that if either of them produces 20,000 gallons a day while the other produces 10,000 a day, the one that produces 20,000 gallons will make an economic profit of $150,000 and the one that sticks with 10,000 gallons will incur an economic loss of $50,000. They also each know that if they both increase production to 20,000 gallons a day, they will both earn zero economic profit.
    a. Construct a payoff matrix for the game that Bud and Wise must play.
    b. Find the Nash equilibrium.
    c. What is the equilibrium if this game is played repeatedly?

Exercise 16.3

1. Bud and Wise are racing to develop a new brand of coconut milk that they both believe will be the next big soft drink. Bud and Wise know that if they both develop the new product, they will earn zero economic profit; if only one of them develops the new product, that firm will make an economic profit of $2 million a week and the other will incur an economic loss of $1 million a week; and if neither of them develops the new product, both will earn zero economic profit.
    a. Construct a payoff matrix for this game.
    b. Find the Nash equilibrium.
    c. Is there any chance of cooperation in this research and development game?

Solution to Practice Problem 16.3

TABLE 1

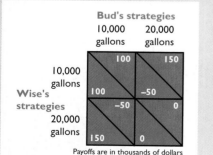

Payoffs are in thousands of dollars

1a. Table 1 shows the payoff matrix for the game that Bud and Wise must play.
1b. The Nash equilibrium is for both to produce 20,000 gallons. To see why, notice that regardless of the quantity that Bud produces, Wise makes more profit by producing 20,000 gallons. The same is true for Bud. So Bud and Wise each produce 20,000 gallons a day.
1c. If this game is played repeatedly, both Bud and Wise produce 10,000 gallons a day and earn maximum economic profit. They can achieve this outcome by playing a tit-for-tat strategy.

CHAPTER CHECKPOINT

Key Points

1 **Describe and identify oligopoly and explain how it arises.**

- Oligopoly is a market type in which a small number of interdependent firms compete behind a barrier to entry.
- The barriers to entry that create oligopoly are both natural (economies of scale and demand) and legal.

2 **Explore the range of possible price and quantity outcomes and describe the dilemma faced by firms in oligopoly.**

- Firms in oligopoly would make the same economic profit as a monopoly if they could act together to restrict output to the monopoly level.
- Each firm can make a larger profit by increasing production, but this action damages the economic profit of other firms.

3 **Use game theory to explain how price and quantity are determined in oligopoly.**

- Game theory is a method of analyzing strategic behavior.
- In a prisoners' dilemma, two prisoners acting in their own interests harm their joint interest.
- An oligopoly (duopoly) game is like the prisoners' dilemma.
- The firms might cooperate to produce the monopoly output or overproduce.
- In a one-play game, both firms overproduce and the price and economic profit are less than they would be in monopoly.
- Advertising and research and development create a prisoners' dilemma for firms in oligopoly.
- In a repeated game, a punishment strategy can produce a monopoly output, price, and economic profit.
- Oligopoly is usually inefficient because the price (marginal benefit) exceeds marginal cost and cost might not be the lowest attainable.

Key Terms

Cartel, 398
Duopoly, 398
Game theory, 407
Nash equilibrium, 408

Payoff matrix, 408
Prisoners' dilemma, 407
Strategies, 408

(X myeconlab) Exercises

1. When the first automobiles were built in 1901, they were manufactured by skilled workers using hand tools. Later, in 1913, Henry Ford introduced the moving assembly line, which lowered costs and speeded production. Over the years, the production line has become ever more mechanized, and today robots have replaced people in many operations.
   a. Sketch the average total cost curve and the demand curve for automobiles in 1901.
   b. Sketch the average total cost curve and the demand curve for automobiles in 1913.
   c. Sketch the average total cost curve and the demand curve for automobiles in 2006.
   d. Describe the changing barriers to entry in the automobile industry and explain how the combination of demand and economies of scale has changed the structure of the industry over the past 100 years.

2. Isolated Island has two taxi companies, one owned by Ann and the other owned by Zack. Figure 1 shows the demand curve for taxi rides, D, and the average total cost curve of one of the firms, ATC.
   a. If Ann and Zack produce the same quantity of rides as would be produced in perfect competition, what are the quantity of rides, the price of a ride, and the economic profit of Ann and Zack?
   b. If Ann and Zack form a cartel and produce the same quantity of rides as would be produced in monopoly, what are the quantity of rides, the price of a ride, and the economic profit of Ann and Zack?
   c. Would Ann and Zack have an incentive to break the cartel agreement and cut their price to increase the number of rides? Explain why or why not.

FIGURE 1

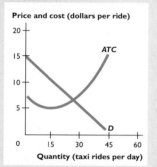

3. Use the information about the market for taxi rides on Isolated Island provided in exercise 2. Suppose that Ann and Zack have two strategies: collude, fix the monopoly price, and limit the number of rides or break the collusion, cut the price, and produce more rides.
   a. Create a payoff matrix for the game that Ann and Zack play.
   b. Find the Nash equilibrium for this game if it is played just once.
   c. Do the people of Isolated Island get the efficient quantity of taxi rides from Ann and Zack in the situation in part **b**?
   d. Find the Nash equilibrium for this game if it is played repeatedly and Ann and Zack use a tit-for-tat punishment strategy.
   e. Do the people of Isolated Island get the efficient quantity of taxi rides from Ann and Zack in the situation in part **d**?

4. Jenny loves the movies (payoff of +100) and hates the ball game (payoff of −100). Joe loves the ball game (payoff of +100) and hates the movies (payoff of −100). But both Jenny and Joe prefer to go out together (bonus payoff of +100 each in addition to the payoff from the activity they choose). If they go out separately, they get no bonus payoff.
   a. Make a payoff matrix of the game that Jenny and Joe play.
   b. Is this game similar to the prisoners' dilemma or different in some way?
   c. What is the Nash equilibrium? What do Jenny and Joe do? Does it make a difference if the game is repeated many times?
   d. Do Jenny and Joe get the best outcome for each of them?

5. The United States claims that Canada subsidizes the production of softwood lumber and that imports of Canadian lumber damage the interests of U.S. producers. The United States has imposed a high tariff on Canadian imports to counter the subsidy. Canada is thinking of retaliating by refusing to export water to California. Table 1 shows a payoff matrix for the game that the United States and Canada are playing.
   a. What is the United States' best strategy?
   b. What is Canada's best strategy?
   c. What is the outcome of this game? Explain.
   d. Is this game like a prisoners' dilemma or different in some crucial way? Explain.
   e. Which country would benefit more from a free trade agreement?

6. Agile Airlines is earning $10 million a year economic profit on a route on which it has a monopoly. Wanabe Airlines is considering entering the market and operating on this route. Agile warns Wanabe to stay out and threatens to cut the price to the point at which Wanabe will make no profit if it enters. Wanabe does some research and determines that the payoff matrix for the game in which it is engaged with Agile is that shown in Table 2.
   a. Does Wanabe believe Agile's assertion?
   b. Does Wanabe enter or not? Explain.

7. Coke and Pepsi know that they are spending millions of dollars on advertising just to counter each other's ads. The marketing managers of the two firms spend a weekend on the golf course plotting a collaboration that will cut the costs of both firms by $100 million a year. When they get back to the office on Monday morning, they begin to sell their scheme to their chief financial officers (CFOs), who have studied some economics. The CFOs tell the marketing managers that they are dreaming and that their plan has no chance of working.
   a. Why are the CFOs so sure?
   b. Sketch a payoff matrix that describes the advertising game played by Coke and Pepsi that supports the CFOs.
   c. Find and describe the Nash equilibrium for the game in part **b**.
   d. Sketch a payoff matrix that describes an advertising game played by Coke and Pepsi that does not support the CFOs and that makes the sales managers' plan possible.
   e. Find and describe the Nash equilibrium for the game in part **d**.

TABLE 1

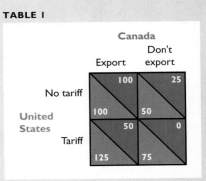

TABLE 2

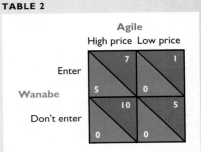

Critical Thinking

8. Adam Smith wrote in *The Wealth of Nations*, published in 1776, "People of the same trade seldom meet together, even for merriment and diversion, but the conversation ends in a conspiracy against the public, or in some contrivance to raise prices." What do you think this quotation implies about the predominant market structure in Adam Smith's world of the late 1700s? Why?

9. Dental care is big business and three firms, Procter & Gamble (which now owns Gillette), Colgate, and GlaxoKlineSmith are the dominant players. Check the dental care products in the supermarket. Describe how these firms differentiate their dental products. Do you think these firms are locked in an R&D game or an advertising game in dental products? Why?

10. Do you think the market for word-processing software such as Microsoft Word, Lotus WordPro, and WordPerfect is an example of oligopoly or monopolistic competition?
    a. Would consumers benefit from greater cooperation between software developers so that instead of having to choose among Microsoft Word, Lotus WordPro, and WordPerfect, they could buy just one word processor?
    b. What benefits do consumers enjoy with competition among software developers that would be lost from cooperation?
    c. Why (aside from the fact that it is illegal) is it impossible for software producers to collude and earn a larger economic profit?

11. Suppose that Google and Microsoft develop their own versions of an amazing new Web browser that allows advertisers to target consumers with greater precision than is now possible. Advertisers would pay Google or Microsoft a fee for providing this service. The new browser is easier and more fun to use than existing browsers. Each firm is trying to decide whether to sell the browser or to give it away.
    a. What are the possible benefits from each action?
    b. Sketch the payoff matrix for the game that Google and Microsoft must play.
    c. On the basis of the payoff matrix you've constructed, what do Google and Microsoft do?

Web Exercises

Use the links on MyEconLab to work the following exercises.

12. Visit the BBC and read the article on OPEC. Also visit OPEC and review the "About OPEC" pages.
    a. Is OPEC a cartel?
    b. What do you think OPEC's main objective is?
    c. What actions can OPEC take to achieve its main objective?
    d. What are the obstacles that OPEC must overcome?
    e. Use the ideas of the prisoners' dilemma to analyze the decisions of OPEC and its member countries.
    f. Use the ideas of the prisoners' dilemma to analyze the decisions of non-OPEC oil producers.
    g. Do you think the global market in crude oil is efficient or inefficient? Provide reasons.

13. Visit EV World and read the article on ethanol price fixing by Archer Daniels Midland.
    a. Would you describe the market for ethanol as an oligopoly?
    b. What does the news article claim about the price of ethanol?
    c. Use the ideas of the prisoners' dilemma to analyze the decisions of Archer Daniels Midland and other producers of ethanol.
    d. Do you think the market for ethanol is efficient or inefficient? Provide reasons.

Regulation and
Antitrust Law

CHAPTER CHECKLIST

**When you have completed your study of this chapter,
you will be able to**

1 Explain the effects of regulation of natural monopoly and oligopoly.

2 Describe U.S. antitrust law and explain three antitrust policy debates.

When you consume water or use the local telephone service, you are buying from a regulated monopoly. Why are the industries that produce these items regulated? How are they regulated? Do the regulations work in the public interest—the interest of all consumers and producers—or do they serve special interests—the interests of particular groups of consumers or producers?

The U.S. Department of Justice has accused Microsoft of violating the antitrust laws. What are the antitrust laws? How have they evolved over the years? How are they used today?

This chapter studies government regulation of monopolies and U.S. antitrust law that restricts the behavior of monopolies and oligopolies.

The chapter draws several threads together. It uses what you've learned about how markets work and your knowledge of consumer surplus and producer surplus. It shows how consumers and producers can redistribute these surpluses in the political marketplace, and it identifies who stands to win and who stands to lose from government regulation.

17.1 REGULATION

You learned in Chapter 6 and saw again in Chapter 13 that a competitive market produces the quantity at which marginal benefit equals marginal cost and is efficient. Because it is efficient, a competitive market doesn't need any government intervention. It is self-regulating. You also saw in Chapter 6 that underproduction creates a deadweight loss. In your detailed look at monopoly and oligopoly in Chapters 14 and 16, you saw that profit-maximizing firms in these types of markets chose to produce less than the efficient quantity. For this reason, governments regulate monopoly and oligopoly.

Regulation consists of rules administered by a government agency to influence economic activity by determining prices, product standards and types, and the conditions under which new firms may enter an industry. To implement its regulations, the government establishes agencies to oversee the regulations and ensure their enforcement.

The past 120 years have seen big changes in the way the U.S. economy is regulated. We're going to begin by examining these changes. Next, we'll turn to the regulatory process and examine how regulators control prices and other aspects of market behavior. Finally, we'll tackle the more difficult and controversial questions: Why do we regulate some things but not others? Who benefits from the regulations that we have: consumers or producers?

Regulation
Rules administered by a government agency to influence economic activity by determining prices, product standards and types, and the conditions under which new firms may enter an industry.

■ The Changing Scope of Regulation

The first national regulatory agency to be set up in the United States was the Interstate Commerce Commission (ICC), established in 1887. Its task was to control prices, routes, and the quality of service of interstate railroads. Its scope later expanded to cover trucking lines, bus lines, water carriers, and oil pipelines. Following the establishment of the ICC, the federal regulatory environment remained static until the years of the Great Depression. Then, during the 1930s, more agencies were established: the Federal Power Commission, the Federal Communications Commission, the Securities and Exchange Commission, the Federal Maritime Commission, the Federal Deposit Insurance Corporation, and, in 1938, the Civil Aeronautical Agency, which was replaced in 1940 by the Civil Aeronautics Board. There was a further lull until the establishment during the 1970s of the Copyright Royalty Tribunal and the Federal Energy Regulatory Commission. In addition to these, there are many state and local regulatory commissions.

Regulation peaked during the 1970s when almost a quarter of the nation's output was produced by regulated industries. Regulation applied to banking and financial services; telecommunications; gas and electric utilities; railroads, trucking, airlines, and buses; many agricultural products; and even haircutting and braiding. Since the late 1970s, there has been a tendency to deregulate the U.S. economy.

Deregulation
The process of removing restrictions on prices, product standards and types, and entry conditions.

Deregulation is the process of removing restrictions on prices, product standards and types, and entry conditions. During the past 25 years, deregulation has occurred in domestic air transportation, telephone service, interstate trucking, and banking and financial services. Cable TV was deregulated in 1984, re-regulated in 1992, and deregulated again in 1996.

What exactly do regulatory agencies do? How do they regulate?

■ The Regulatory Process

Though regulatory agencies vary in size and scope and in the detailed aspects of economic life that they control, all agencies have features in common.

First, the Administration, Congress, and state and local governments appoint the people who run the regulatory agencies. In addition, all agencies have a permanent bureaucracy made up of experts in the industry being regulated and often recruited from regulated firms. Agencies have budgets, voted by Congress or state or local legislatures, to cover the costs of their operations.

Second, each agency adopts a set of practices or operating rules for controlling prices and other aspects of economic performance. These rules and practices are based on well-defined physical and financial accounting procedures, but they are extremely complicated and, in practice, hard to administer.

In a regulated industry, individual firms are usually free to determine their production technology. But they are not free to determine the prices to charge, the quantities to produce, or the markets to serve. The regulatory agency certifies a company to serve a particular market and produce a particular line of goods and services, and it determines the prices that may be charged. In some cases, the agency also determines the scale of output permitted.

■ Economic Theory of Regulation

Two broad economic theories of regulation are

- Public interest theory
- Capture theory

Public Interest Theory

The **public interest theory** is that regulation seeks an efficient use of resources. Public interest theory assumes that the political process relentlessly seeks out deadweight loss and introduces regulations that eliminate it. For example, where monopoly exists, the political process will introduce price regulations to ensure that output increases and price falls to its competitive level.

Public interest theory
The theory that regulation seeks an efficient use of resources.

Capture Theory

The **capture theory** is that a regulated firm captures the regulator and makes a monopoly profit. Capture theory assumes that the cost of regulation is high and only those regulations that increase the surplus of small, easily identified groups and that have low organization costs are supplied by the political process. Because of rational ignorance (see Chapter 10, p. 247), even though these regulations impose costs on others, if the costs are spread thinly, they do not decrease votes.

The predictions of the capture theory are less clear-cut than those of the public interest theory. The capture theory predicts that regulations benefit cohesive interest groups, bring large and visible benefits to each member of the interest group, and impose a small cost on everyone else. The cost per person is so small that no one finds it worthwhile to incur the cost of organizing an interest group to avoid it.

Which theory of regulation best explains real-world regulations? Which regulations are in the public interest and which are in the interest of producers? To answer these questions, it is convenient to distinguish between the regulation of a natural monopoly and the regulation of a cartel. Let's begin with the regulation of a natural monopoly.

Capture theory
The theory that a regulated firm captures the regulator and makes a monopoly profit.

■ Natural Monopoly

We defined *natural monopoly* in Chapter 14 (pp. 346–347) as an industry in which one firm can supply the entire market at a lower price than two or more firms can. Examples of natural monopoly include local distribution of water, electricity and gas, and urban rail services. For these activities, most of the costs are fixed, so the larger the output, the lower is its average total cost. It is much more expensive to have two or more sets of pipes, wires, and train lines serving every neighborhood than it is to have a single set. What industry or market is a natural monopoly changes over time as technology changes. With the introduction of fiber-optic cables, both telephone companies and cable television companies can compete in urban areas that have a sufficiently dense population. So what were once natural monopolies are becoming more competitive industries. Direct satellite TV is a substitute, but not a close substitute, for cable TV, and in many parts of the country, cable TV remains a natural monopoly.

Figure 17.1 shows the market for cable TV in the 20 states served by Cox Communications based in Atlanta. The demand curve for cable TV is *D*. Cox's marginal cost curve is *MC*. That marginal cost curve is (assumed to be) horizontal at $10 per household per month—that is, the cost of providing each additional household with a month of cable programming is $10. Cox Communications has invested heavily in satellite receiving dishes, cables, and control equipment and so has large fixed costs. These fixed costs are part of the company's average total cost curve, shown as *ATC*. The average total cost curve slopes downward because

---

■ **FIGURE 17.1**

Natural Monopoly: Marginal Cost Pricing   **myeconlab**

A cable TV operator faces the demand curve *D*. Its marginal cost *MC* is a constant $10 per household per month. Its fixed cost is large, and the average total cost curve, which includes average fixed cost, is *ATC*.

❶ Price is set equal to marginal cost at $10 a month.

At this price, ❷ the efficient quantity (8 million households) is served.

❸ Consumer surplus is maximized as shown by the green triangle.

❹ The firm incurs a loss on each household, shown by the red arrow.

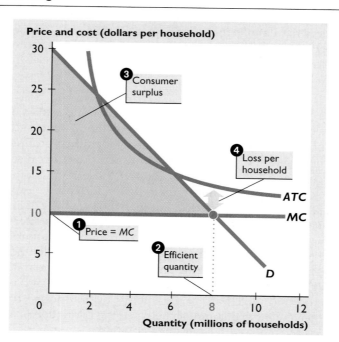

as the number of households served increases, the fixed cost is spread over a larger number of households. (If you need to refresh your memory on the average total cost curve, take a quick look back at Chapter 12, pp. 305–307.)

■ Public Interest or Private Interest Regulation?

According to public interest theory, regulation achieves an efficient use of resources, which occurs if marginal cost equals marginal benefit, which also equals price. A **marginal cost pricing rule**, which sets price equal to marginal cost, achieves an efficient output in a regulated industry.

Marginal cost pricing rule
A rule that sets price equal to marginal cost to achieve an efficient output in a regulated industry.

Marginal Cost Pricing

Figure 17.1 illustrates the marginal cost pricing rule. The efficient outcome occurs if the price is regulated at $10 per household per month and if 8 million households are served.

A natural monopoly that follows the marginal cost pricing rule incurs an economic loss. Because the average total cost curve of a natural monopoly is downward sloping, marginal cost is less than average total cost. Because price equals marginal cost, price is less than average total cost. Average total cost minus price is the loss per unit produced. It's pretty obvious that a cable TV company that is required to use a marginal cost pricing rule will not stay in business for long. How can a company cover its costs and, at the same time, obey a marginal cost pricing rule?

One possibility is price discrimination (see Chapter 14, pp. 360–364). Another possibility is to use a two-part price (called a *two-part tariff*). For example, local telephone companies charge consumers a monthly fee for being connected to the telephone system and then charge a price equal to marginal cost (zero) for each local call. A cable TV operator charges a one-time connection fee that covers its fixed cost and then charges a monthly fee equal to marginal cost.

But a natural monopoly cannot always cover its costs in these ways. If the price that a natural monopoly can charge its customers does not cover its total cost and if the government wants it to follow a marginal cost pricing rule, the government must subsidize the firm and raise the revenue for the subsidy by taxing some other activity. But as we saw in Chapter 8, taxes themselves generate deadweight loss. So the deadweight loss that results from additional taxes must be subtracted from the efficiency gained by forcing the natural monopoly to adopt a marginal cost pricing rule. As a result, it might be more efficient to permit the natural monopoly to charge a price that is higher than marginal cost. Doing so avoids taxing other parts of the economy to subsidize the natural monopoly and avoids creating deadweight loss in those parts of the economy.

Average Cost Pricing

For a natural monopoly to cover its total cost, its price must equal average total cost. And the pricing rule that delivers this outcome is called the **average cost pricing rule**, a rule that sets price equal to average total cost. Because average total cost exceeds marginal cost for a natural monopoly, when price equals average total cost, the quantity is less than the efficient quantity and a deadweight loss arises. Figure 17.2 illustrates the outcome for Cox Communications.

Average cost pricing rule
A rule that sets price equal to average total cost to enable a regulated firm to cover its costs.

FIGURE 17.2

Natural Monopoly: Average Cost Pricing

❶ Price is set equal to average total cost at $15 a month.

At this price, **❷** the quantity served (6 million households) is less than the efficient quantity (8 million households).

❸ Consumer surplus shrinks to the smaller green triangle.

❹ A producer surplus enables the firm to pay its fixed cost and break even.

❺ A deadweight loss, shown by the gray triangle, arises.

Price and cost (dollars per household)

❸ Consumer surplus

❹ Producer surplus

❺ Deadweight loss

ATC

MC

❶ Price = ATC

❷ Less than efficient quantity

D

Quantity (millions of households)

In Figure 17.2, to cover its costs, Cox charges $15 a month and serves 6 million households. A deadweight loss arises, which is shown by the gray triangle in the figure. This outcome is in the public interest—is efficient—if this deadweight loss is smaller than the deadweight loss from collecting the taxes to finance a subsidy under marginal cost pricing.

Implementing the pricing rules that we've just examined is difficult because the regulator does not directly observe the firm's costs and doesn't know how hard the firm is trying to minimize cost. So regulators use one of two practical rules:

- Rate of return regulation
- Price cap regulation

Let's see whether these practical rules deliver an outcome that is in the public interest or the private interest.

Rate of Return Regulation

Rate of return regulation
A regulation that sets the price at a level that enables a regulated firm to earn a specified target percent return on its capital.

Under **rate of return regulation**, a regulated firm must justify its price by showing that the price enables it to earn a specified target percent return on its capital. The target rate of return is determined with reference to what is normal in competitive industries. This rate of return is part of the opportunity cost of the natural monopoly and part of the firm's average total cost.

If the regulator were able to observe the firm's total cost and also know that the firm had minimized total cost, it would accept only a price proposal from the firm that was equivalent to average cost pricing.

The outcome would be like that in Figure 17.2, in which the regulated price is $15 a month and 6 million households are served. In this case, rate of return regulation would result in a price that favors the consumer and prevents the producer from making monopoly profit. The special interest group will have failed to capture the regulator, and the outcome will be closer to that predicted by the public interest theory of regulation.

But the managers of a regulated firm might not minimize cost. And if the firm is regulated to achieve a target rate of return, the managers have an incentive to inflate costs and raise price. One way to inflate the firm's costs is to spend on inputs that are not strictly required for the production of the good. On-the-job luxury in the form of sumptuous office suites, limousines, free baseball tickets (disguised as public relations expenses), company jets, lavish international travel, and entertainment are all ways in which managers can inflate costs.

Managers also have an incentive to use more capital than the efficient amount because the more capital they use, the larger is the total return they are permitted to earn. And they have an incentive to make larger-than-required charges for depreciation and losses from bad debts.

If the cable TV operator in our example persuades the regulator that its true costs are higher than the *ATC* curve in Figure 17.2, then rate of return regulation will raise the price and decrease the quantity and might end up enabling the firm to operate at the same price and quantity as those that would occur if the monopoly were unregulated.

EYE ON THE U.S. ECONOMY

Airline Deregulation

U.S. airline deregulation in 1979 lowered fares by an estimated 18 percent.

And fares have continued to fall in recent years with the arrival of new low-cost airlines such as AirTran, ATA, America West, Frontier, JetBlue, Southwest, and Spirit, which has put the traditional carriers under competitive pressure.

Fares were falling during 2001 well before 9/11 decreased the demand for air travel. And fares continued to fall through 2004.

The figure shows the average (inflation-adjusted) fare of a flight that cost $100 in the first quarter of 1985.

But air fares could be even lower. The reason is that the airline industry operates with barriers to entry that arise from the allocation of slots at major airports and legal restrictions on foreign airlines. Air fares would fall if these barriers to entry were lowered.

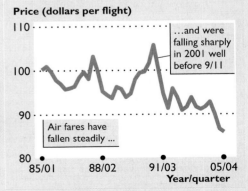

SOURCE OF DATA: Bureau of Transportation Statistic and the Bureau of Economic Analysis.

Price Cap Regulation

Price cap regulation
A rule that specifies the highest price that a firm is permitted to set—a price ceiling.

For the reason that we've just examined, rate of return regulation is increasingly being replaced by price cap regulation. A **price cap regulation** is a price ceiling—a rule that specifies the highest price the firm is permitted to set. This type of regulation gives a firm an incentive to operate efficiently and keep costs under control. Price cap regulation has become common for the electricity and telecommunications industries and is replacing rate of return regulation.

To see how a price cap works, let's suppose that the cable TV operator is subject to this type of regulation. Figure 17.3 shows that without regulation, the firm maximizes profit by serving 4 million households and charging a price of $20 a month. If a price cap is set at $15 a month, the firm is permitted to sell any quantity it chooses at that price or at a lower price. At 4 million households, the firm now incurs an economic loss. It can decrease the loss by *increasing* output to 6 million households. To increase output above 6 million households, the firm would have to lower the price and again it would incur a loss. So the profit-maximizing quantity is 6 million households—the same as with average cost pricing.

Notice that a price cap lowers the price and increases output. This outcome is in sharp contrast to the effect of a price ceiling in a competitive market that you studied in Chapter 7 (pp. 168–173). The reason is that in a monopoly, the unregulated equilibrium output is less than the competitive equilibrium output and the price cap regulation replicates the conditions of a competitive market.

Earnings sharing regulation
A regulation that requires firms to make refunds to customers when profits rise above a target level.

In Figure 17.3, the price cap delivers average cost pricing. In practice, the regulator might set the cap too high. For this reason, price cap regulation is often combined with **earnings sharing regulation**—a regulation that requires firms to make refunds to customers when profits rise above a target level.

FIGURE 17.3

Natural Monopoly: Price Cap Regulation

❶ With no regulation, a cable TV operator serves 4 million households at a price of $20 a month.

❷ A price cap regulation sets the maximum price at $15 a month.

❸ Only when 6 million households are served can the firm break even and earn a normal rate of return. (When fewer than 6 million households are served or more than 6 million households are served, the firm incurs an economic loss.) The firm has an incentive to keep costs as low as possible and to produce the quantity demanded at the price cap.

❹ The price cap regulation lowers the price and increases the quantity.

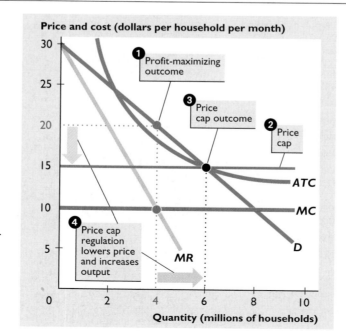

■ Oligopoly Regulation

A *cartel* is a collusive agreement among a number of firms that is designed to restrict output and achieve a higher profit for its members. Cartels are illegal in the United States and in most other countries. But international cartels can sometimes operate legally, such as the international cartel of oil producers known as OPEC (Organization of the Petroleum Exporting Countries).

Illegal cartels can arise in oligopoly. You saw in Chapter 16 that if firms in oligopoly can collude and behave like a monopoly, they will set the same price and sell the same total quantity as a monopoly firm would. But we also discovered that in such a situation, each firm is tempted to cheat, increasing its own output and profit at the expense of the other firms. Such cheating unravels the monopoly equilibrium and leads to a higher output rate, lower price, and smaller economic profit. Such an outcome benefits consumers at the expense of producers.

How is oligopoly regulated? Does regulation prevent monopoly practices or does it encourage those practices?

According to the public interest theory, oligopoly is regulated to ensure a competitive outcome. Consider, for example, the market for trucking tomatoes from the San Joaquin Valley to Los Angeles, illustrated in Figure 17.4. The market demand curve for trips is *D*. The industry marginal cost curve—and the competitive supply curve—is *MC*. Public interest regulation will regulate the price of a trip at $20, and there will be 300 trips a week.

How would this industry be regulated according to the capture theory? Regulation that is in the producer interest will maximize profit. To find the outcome in this case, we need to determine the price and quantity when marginal

---

■ **FIGURE 17.4**

Collusive Oligopoly

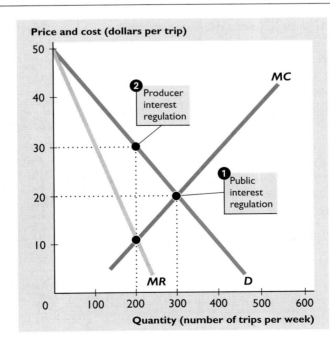

Ten trucking firms transport tomatoes from the San Joaquin Valley to Los Angeles. The demand curve is *D*, and the industry marginal cost curve is *MC*. Under competition, the *MC* curve is the industry supply curve.

❶ Public interest regulation will achieve the efficient competitive outcome: a price of $20 a trip and 300 trips a week.

❷ Producer interest regulation will limit output to 200 trips a week (where industry marginal revenue, *MR*, is equal to industry marginal cost, *MC*), and the price will be $30 a trip.

cost equals marginal revenue. The marginal revenue curve is *MR*. So marginal cost equals marginal revenue at 200 trips a week. The price of a trip is $30.

One way of achieving this outcome is to place an output limit on each firm in the industry. If there are 10 trucking companies, an output limit of 20 trips per company ensures that the total number of trips in a week is 200. Penalties can be imposed to ensure that no single producer exceeds its output limit.

All the firms in the industry would support this type of regulation because it helps to prevent cheating and maintain a monopoly outcome. Each firm knows that without effectively enforced production quotas, every firm has an incentive to increase output. (For each firm, price exceeds marginal cost, so a greater output brings a larger profit.) So each firm wants a method of preventing output from increasing above the industry profit-maximizing output, and the quotas enforced by regulation achieve this end. With this type of cartel regulation, the regulator enables a cartel to operate legally and in its own best interest.

Cartel-like behavior occurs in many regulated activities when the *purpose* of regulation is quality control but the *effect* of regulation is monopoly profit. One example is citrus fruit production in California and Florida, where the state citrus boards, whose purpose is to regulate the size and quality of fruit, also regulate the weekly sales of the producers. Another example is the provision of physicians' services. Regulation of the quality of doctors ends up regulating entry and achieving a monopoly price for their services.

EYE ON THE U.S. ECONOMY

Regulatory Roller Coaster

You are paying much more than marginal cost for your cable TV services. And until effective competition arrives from an improved wireless technology, it is difficult to see lower cable TV prices coming.

Cable television has been on a regulatory roller coaster. When cable first arrived, its prices were regulated. They were deregulated in 1984, but profits soared and in 1992, prices were again regulated. Congress passed yet another deregulation law in 1996 and set March 31, 1999, as the date when the Federal Communications

Commission (FCC) would stop regulating most cable TV prices. Federal price controls were removed from packages that include popular channels, such as CNN, Discovery, ESPN, and MTV.

Before the 1999 deregulation, consumers paid an average of $31 a month for cable TV services.

Back in 1996, when Congress set the date of March 31, 1999, it expected to see effective competition among cable companies, but competition did not develop.

When the 1992 regulated prices took effect in 1993, prices fell. But in 1994, the FCC loosened the rules and prices began to rise. In mid-1996, cable

rates increased sharply. Prices have continued to increase but the range and quality of service have improved as well.

CHECKPOINT 17.1

1 **Explain the effects of regulation of natural monopoly and oligopoly.**

Practice Problem 17.1

1. An unregulated natural monopoly bottles Elixir, a unique health product that has no substitutes. The monopoly's total fixed cost is $150,000, and its marginal cost is 10 cents a bottle. Figure 1 illustrates the demand for Elixir.
    a. How many bottles of Elixir does the monopoly sell?
    b. What is the price of a bottle of Elixir?
    c. Is the monopoly's use of resources efficient?
    d. How might the government regulate the monopoly in the public interest?
    e. If the government introduces a marginal cost pricing rule, what will be the price of a bottle of Elixir, the quantity of Elixir sold, and the monopoly's profit?

FIGURE 1

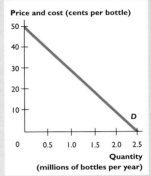

Exercise 17.1

1. An unregulated natural monopoly cans Mt. McKinley air, unique clean air that has no substitutes. The monopoly's total fixed cost is $30,000, and its marginal cost is 10 cents a can. Figure 2 illustrates the demand for Mt. McKinley air.
    a. How many cans of Mt. McKinley air does the monopoly sell?
    b. What is the price of a can of Mt. McKinley air?
    c. If the monopoly captures the regulator, how might the monopoly be regulated?
    d. If the monopoly can mislead the regulator about its costs, what is the maximum excess average total cost that it would claim?
    e. Would the regulated monopoly use resources efficiently?

FIGURE 2

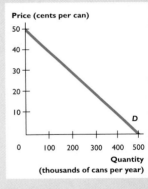

Solution to Practice Problem 17.1

1a. The monopoly will produce 1 million bottles a year—the quantity at which marginal revenue equals marginal cost (Figure 3).
1b. The price is 30 cents a bottle—the highest price at which the monopoly can sell the 1 million bottles a year (Figure 3).
1c. The monopoly's use of resources is inefficient. If resource use were efficient, the monopoly would produce the quantity at which price equals marginal cost: 2 million bottles a year.
1d. The government might use a marginal cost pricing rule or an average cost pricing rule to regulate the monopoly.
1e. With a marginal cost pricing rule, the price would be 10 cents a bottle and the monopoly would produce 2 million bottles a year. The monopoly would make an economic loss of $150,000 a year. The monopoly would need a subsidy from the government to keep it in business.

FIGURE 3

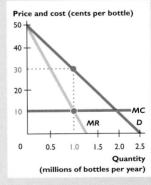

17.2 ANTITRUST LAW

Antitrust law
A law that regulates and prohibits certain kinds of market behavior, such as monopoly and monopolistic practices.

Antitrust law is the body of law that regulates and prohibits certain kinds of market behavior, such as monopoly and monopolistic practices. Antitrust law is enacted by Congress and enforced through the judicial system. Lawsuits under the antitrust laws may be initiated either by government agencies or by injured private parties. The main thrust of antitrust law is the prohibition of monopoly practices of restricting output to achieve higher prices and profits.

■ The Antitrust Laws

The U.S. antitrust laws are easily summarized. The first antitrust law, the Sherman Act, was passed in 1890 in an atmosphere of outrage and disgust at the actions and practices of J. P. Morgan, John D. Rockefeller, and W. H. Vanderbilt—the so-called "robber barons." Ironically, the most lurid stories of the actions of these great American capitalists are not of their monopolization and exploitation of consumers but of their sharp practices against each other. Nevertheless, monopolies did emerge—for example, the spectacular control of the oil industry by John D. Rockefeller.

A wave of mergers at the turn of the twentieth century produced stronger antitrust laws. The Clayton Act of 1914 supplemented the Sherman Act, and the Federal Trade Commission, an agency charged with enforcing the antitrust laws, was created.

Table 17.1 summarizes the two main provisions of the Sherman Act. Section 1 of the act is precise. Conspiring with others to restrict competition is illegal. But section 2 is general and imprecise. Just what is an "attempt to monopolize"? The Clayton Act and its two amendments, the Robinson-Patman Act of 1936 and Celler-Kefauver Act of 1950, which outlaw specific practices, answers this question. Table 17.2 describes these practices and summarizes the main provisions of these three acts.

■ **TABLE 17.1**

The Sherman Act, 1890

Section 1:

Every contract, combination in the form of trust or otherwise, or conspiracy, in restraint of trade or commerce among the several States, or with foreign nations, is hereby declared to be illegal.

Section 2:

Every person who shall monopolize, or attempt to monopolize, or combine or conspire with any other person or persons, to monopolize any part of the trade or commerce among the several States, or with foreign nations, shall be deemed guilty of a felony.

■ **TABLE 17.2**

The Clayton Act and Its Amendments

Clayton Act   1914

Robinson-Patman Act 1936

Celler-Kefauver Act   1950

These acts prohibit the following practices only if they substantially lessen competition or create monopoly:

1. Price discrimination.
2. Contracts that require other goods to be bought from the same firm (called tying arrangements).
3. Contracts that require a firm to buy all its requirements of a particular item from a single firm (called requirements contracts).
4. Contracts that prevent a firm from selling competing items (called exclusive dealing).
5. Contracts that prevent a buyer from reselling a product outside a specified area (called territorial confinement).
6. Acquiring a competitor's shares or assets.
7. Becoming a director of a competing firm.

■ Three Antitrust Policy Debates

Price fixing is *always* a violation of the antitrust law. If the Justice Department can prove the existence of price fixing, a defendant can offer no acceptable excuse. But other practices are more controversial and generate debate among antitrust lawyers and economists. We'll examine three of these practices:

- Resale price maintenance
- Tying arrangements
- Predatory pricing

Resale Price Maintenance

Most manufacturers sell their products to the final consumer indirectly through a wholesale and retail distribution system. **Resale price maintenance** occurs when a manufacturer agrees with a distributor on the price at which the product will be resold.

Resale price maintenance (also called vertical price fixing) *agreements* are illegal under the Sherman Act. But it isn't illegal for a manufacturer to refuse to supply a retailer who doesn't accept the manufacturer's guidance on what the price should be.

Attorneys general in 41 states alleged that Universal, Sony, Warner, Bertelsmann, and EMI kept CD prices artificially high between 1995 and 2000 with a practice called "minimum-advertised pricing." The companies denied the allegation but made a large payment to settle the case.

Resale price maintenance
An agreement between a manufacturer and a distributor on the price at which a product will be resold.

Does resale price maintenance create an inefficient or efficient use of resources? Economists can be found on both sides of this question.

Inefficient Resale Price Maintenance   Resale price maintenance is inefficient if it enables dealers to charge the monopoly price. By setting and enforcing the resale price, the manufacturer might be able to ensure that retailers don't try to undercut each other.

Efficient Resale Price Maintenance   Resale price maintenance might be efficient if it enables a manufacturer to induce dealers to provide the efficient standard of service. Suppose that SilkySkin wants shops to demonstrate the use of its new unbelievable moisturizing cream in an inviting space. With resale price maintenance, SilkySkin can offer all the retailers the same incentive and compensation. Without resale price maintenance, a cut-price drug store might offer SilkySkin products at a low price. Buyers would then have an incentive to visit a high-price shop and get the product demonstrated and then buy from the low-price shop. The low-price shop would be a free rider (like the consumer of a public good in Chapter 10, p. 241), and an inefficient level of service would be provided.

SilkySkin could pay a fee to retailers that provide good service and leave the resale price to be determined by the competitive forces of supply and demand. But it might be too costly for SilkySkin to monitor shops and ensure that they provided the desired level of service.

Tying Arrangements

Tying arrangement
An agreement to sell one product only if the buyer agrees to buy another, different product.

A **tying arrangement** is an agreement to sell one product only if the buyer agrees to buy another, different product. With tying, the only way the buyer can get the one product is to buy the other product at the same time. Microsoft has been accused of tying Internet Explorer and Windows (see next page). Textbook publishers sometimes tie a Web site and a textbook and force students to buy both. (You can't buy the book you're now reading, new, without the Web site. But you can buy the Web site access without the book, so these products are not tied.)

Could publishers of textbooks make more money by tying a book and access to a Web site? The answer is sometimes but not always. Think about what you are willing to pay for a book and access to a Web site. To keep the numbers simple, suppose that you and other students are willing to pay $40 for a book and $10 for access to a Web site. The publisher can sell these items separately for these prices or bundled for $50. There is no gain to the publisher from bundling.

But now suppose that you and only half of the students are willing to pay $40 for a book and $10 for a Web site. And suppose that the other half of the students are willing to pay $40 for a Web site and $10 for a book. Now if the two items are sold separately, the publisher can charge $40 for the book and $40 for the Web site. Half the students buy the book but not the Web site, and the other half buy the Web site but not the book. But if the book and Web site are bundled for $50, everyone buys the bundle and the publisher makes an extra $10 per student. In this case, bundling has enabled the publisher to price discriminate.

There is no simple, clear-cut test of whether a firm is engaging in tying or whether, by doing so, it has increased its market power and profit and created inefficiency.

Predatory Pricing

Predatory pricing is setting a low price to drive competitors out of business with the intention of setting a monopoly price when the competition has gone. John D. Rockefeller's Standard Oil Company was the first to be accused of this practice in the 1890s, and it has been claimed often in antitrust cases since then.

It is easy to see that predatory pricing is an idea, not a reality. Economists are skeptical that predatory pricing occurs. They point out that a firm that cuts its price below the profit-maximizing level loses during the low-price period. Even if the firm succeeds in driving its competitors out of business, new competitors will enter as soon as the price is increased. So any potential gain from a monopoly position is temporary. A high and certain loss is a poor exchange for a temporary and uncertain gain. No case of predatory pricing has been definitively found.

Predatory pricing
Setting a low price to drive competitors out of business with the intention of setting a monopoly price when the competition has gone.

◼ A Recent Antitrust Showcase: The United States Versus Microsoft

In 1998, the U.S. Department of Justice along with a number of states charged Microsoft, the world's largest producer of software for personal computers, with violations of both sections of the Sherman Act. A 78-day trial followed that pitched two prominent MIT economics professors against each other (Franklin Fisher for the government and Richard Schmalensee for Microsoft).

The Case Against Microsoft

The claims against Microsoft were that it

- Possessed monopoly power in the market for PC operating systems.
- Used *predatory pricing* and *tying arrangements* to achieve a monopoly in the market for Web browsers.
- Used other anticompetitive practices to strengthen its monopoly in these two markets.

It was claimed that with 80 percent of the market for PC operating systems, Microsoft had excessive monopoly power. This monopoly power arose from two barriers to entry: economies of scale and network economies. Microsoft's average total cost falls as production increases (economies of scale) because the fixed cost of developing an operating system like Windows is large while the marginal cost of producing one copy of Windows is small. Further, as the number of Windows users increases, the range of Windows applications expands (network economies), so a potential competitor would need to produce not only a competing operating system but also an entire range of supporting applications.

When Microsoft entered the Web browser market with its Internet Explorer (IE), it offered the browser for ⎽ zero price. This price was viewed as *predatory pricing*. Microsoft integrated IE with Windows so that anyone who uses this operating system would not need a separate browser such as Netscape Communicator. Microsoft's competitors claimed that this practice was an illegal *tying arrangement*.

Microsoft's Response

Microsoft challenged all these claims. It said that although Windows was the dominant operating system, it was vulnerable to competition from other operating systems such as Linux and Apple's Mac OS and that there was a permanent threat of competition from new entrants.

Microsoft claimed that integrating Internet Explorer with Windows provided a single, unified product of greater consumer value. Instead of tying, Microsoft said, the browser and operating system constituted a single product. It was like a refrigerator with a chilled water dispenser or an automobile with a stereo player.

The Outcome

The court agreed that Microsoft was in violation of the Sherman Act and ordered that it be broken into two firms: an operating systems producer and an applications producer. Microsoft successfully appealed this order. But in the final judgment, Microsoft was ordered to disclose details about how its operating system works to other software developers so that they could compete effectively against Microsoft. In the summer of 2002, Microsoft began to comply with this order.

We end this chapter by examining the rules that guide merger decisions.

■ Merger Rules

The Department of Justice uses guidelines to determine which mergers it will examine and possibly block on the basis of the Herfindahl-Hirschman index (HHI), which is explained in Chapter 15 (p. 378). A market in which the HHI is less than 1,000 is regarded as competitive. An index between 1,000 and 1,800 indicates a moderately concentrated market, and a merger in this market that would increase the index by 100 points is challenged by the Department of Justice. An index above 1,800 indicates a concentrated market, and a merger in this market that would increase the index by 50 points is challenged. Figure 17.5(a) summarizes these guidelines.

The Department of Justice used these guidelines to analyze two proposed mergers in the market for soft drinks in 1986. First, PepsiCo announced its intention to buy 7-Up for $380 million. A month later, Coca-Cola said that it would buy Dr Pepper for $470 million. Whether this market is concentrated depends on how it is defined. The market for all soft drinks, which includes carbonated drinks marketed by these four companies plus fruit juices and bottled water, has an HHI of 120, so it is highly competitive. But the market for carbonated soft drinks is highly concentrated. Coca-Cola has a 39 percent share, PepsiCo has 28 percent, Dr Pepper is next with 7 percent, then comes 7-Up with 6 percent. One other producer, RJR, has a 5 percent market share. So the five largest firms in this market have an 85 percent market share. If we assume that the other 15 percent of the market consists of 15 firms, each with a 1 percent market share, the Herfindahl-Hirschman index is

$$HHI = 39^2 + 28^2 + 7^2 + 6^2 + 5^2 + 15 = 2,430.$$

With an HHI of this magnitude, a merger that increases the index by 50 points is examined by the Department of Justice. Figure 17.5(b) shows how the HHI would have changed with the mergers. The PepsiCo and 7-Up merger would have increased the index by more than 300 points, the Coca-Cola and Dr Pepper merger would have increased it by more than 500 points, and both mergers together would have increased the index by almost 800 points. The Justice Department decided to define the market narrowly and, with increases of these magnitudes, blocked the mergers.

FIGURE 17.5
The HHI Merger Guidelines

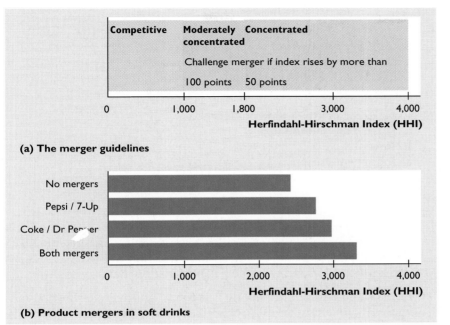

(a) The merger guidelines

(b) Product mergers in soft drinks

The Department of Justice scrutinizes proposed mergers if the HHI exceeds 1,000. Proposed mergers between producers of carbonated soft drinks were blocked in 1986 by application of these guidelines.

REALITY CHECK

Regulation in YOUR Life

Regulation and deregulation touch *your* life at many points. We have noted some of them already in this chapter.

Pay attention as you go about your everyday affairs and think about the regulation that you encounter. Before you open your eyes, you are awakened by an alarm clock that uses regulated electric power; you turn on the regulated cable news channel; you go to school on a regulated commuter train; you write your term paper on a laptop that runs Windows produced by a firm that has been pulled through the antitrust courts. It is hard to get away from regulation and laws designed to limit monopoly power.

Think hard about who benefits from and who bears the cost of the regulation that you encounter. Do we really need all the regulation we've got? And do we need more regulation in some areas?

2 **Describe U.S. antitrust law and explain three antitrust policy debates.**

Practice Problems 17.2

1. Since 1987, hundreds of hospital mergers have taken place in the United States. Rarely has the Federal Trade Commission (FTC) challenged a hospital merger. Use the link on MyEconLab to find out why the FTC decided not to challenge hospital mergers under U.S. antitrust law.

2. Explain each of the following terms:
   a. Attempt to monopolize
   b. Price fixing
   c. Predatory pricing
   d. Tying arrangements

Exercises 17.2

1. The FTC approved the $27 billion merger of BP Amoco PLC and ARCO only after it met the U.S. Federal Trade Commission's demands for substantial divestitures. Use the link on MyEconLab to find what some of the required divestitures were and why the FTC insisted on them.

2. In 1911, Standard Oil Company was found guilty under the Sherman Act and was ordered to divest itself. Some of the oil companies that were created as a result of the 1911 order have now merged to form large companies. Why do you think Standard Oil Company was found guilty under the Sherman Act while recent oil company mergers have been approved?

Solutions to Practice Problems 17.2

1. The FTC will not challenge a hospital merger if the merger will not substantially lessen competition. Such a situation arises if (1) the merger would not increase the likelihood of market power either because strong competitors exist or because the merging hospitals were sufficiently differentiated; (2) the merger would allow the hospitals to reduce cost; or (3) the merger would eliminate a hospital that otherwise would probably have failed and left the market.

2a. An attempt to monopolize is an attempt by a company to drive out its competitors so that it can operate as a monopoly.
2b. Price fixing is making an agreement with competitors to set a specified price and not to vary it.
2c. Predatory pricing is the attempt to drive out competitors by charging a price that is too low for anyone to earn a profit. (Economists think the practice is unlikely to be used.)
2d. Tying arrangements exist when a company does not offer a buyer the opportunity to buy one item without at the same time buying another item.

CHAPTER CHECKPOINT

Key Points

1 **Explain the effects of regulation of natural monopoly and oligopoly.**

- The Interstate Commerce Commission, established in 1887, was the first national regulatory agency.
- At the peak of regulation, in the late 1970s, almost a quarter of U.S. output was produced by regulated industries.
- Public interest theory predicts that regulation achieves an efficient use of resources. Capture theory predicts that regulation helps producers to maximize economic profit.
- A natural monopoly is efficient if its price equals marginal cost.
- A natural monopoly maximizes its profit if its marginal revenue equals marginal cost and price exceeds marginal cost.
- Rate of return regulation makes price equal to average cost.
- Price cap regulation motivates a firm to earn an economic profit by keeping costs under control.

2 **Describe U.S. antitrust law and explain three antitrust policy debates.**

- Antitrust law is used to control monopoly and monopolistic practices.
- The first U.S. antitrust law, the Sherman Act, was passed in 1890, and the law was strengthened in 1914 when the Clayton Act was passed and the Federal Trade Commission was created.
- All price-fixing agreements are in violation of the Sherman Act.
- Resale price maintenance might be efficient if it enables a producer to ensure the efficient level of service by distributors.
- Tying arrangements can enable a monopoly to price discriminate and increase profit, but in many cases, tying would not increase profit.
- Predatory pricing is unlikely to occur because it brings losses and only temporary potential gains.
- The Federal Trade Commission uses guidelines to determine which mergers to examine and possibly block on the basis of the Herfindahl-Hirschman Index.

Key Terms

Antitrust law, 430
Average cost pricing rule, 423
Capture theory, 421
Deregulation, 420
Earnings sharing regulation, 426

Marginal cost pricing rule, 423
Predatory pricing, 433
Price cap regulation, 426
Public interest theory, 421
Rate of return regulation, 424

Regulation, 420
Resale price maintenance, 431
Tying arrangement, 432

Exercises

1. When were the antitrust laws introduced? Why were they introduced? What practices do the laws make illegal? And why are these practices illegal?

2. What charges might be brought under the antitrust law in each of the following situations? And why, if at all, might a firm or firms want to take the actions described?
    a. The owners of the only two ready-mix concrete producers in a city are discovered holding secret meetings to fix their prices.
    b. Amazon.com proposes to buy Barnes & Noble and other major book retailers.
    c. A pharmaceutical manufacturer opens a chain of drug stores.
    d. Ford Motor Company installs a small refrigerator in all its cars, and GM accuses Ford of a tying arrangement.
    e. A video rental store requires customers to rent a B movie with every A movie they rent.

3. Hawaii Cable Television is a natural monopoly. Sketch a demand curve, a marginal revenue curve, an average total cost curve, and a marginal cost curve that illustrate Hawaii Cable's situation.

4. If Hawaii Cable (in exercise 3) is unregulated and maximizes profit, show in your graph the price, quantity, economic profit, consumer surplus, and deadweight loss.

5. If Hawaii Cable (in exercise 3) is regulated in the public interest, show in your graph the price, quantity, economic profit, consumer surplus, and deadweight loss.

6. If Hawaii Cable (in exercise 3) is subject to a price cap regulation that enables it to earn normal profit, show in your graph the price, quantity, economic profit, consumer surplus, and deadweight loss.

7. What would happen if the regulator set the price cap for Hawaii Cable (in exercise 3) too low for the firm to earn normal profit?

FIGURE 1

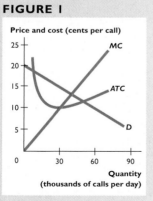

Price and cost (cents per call)

8. Land Line and Cellular City are the only two phone companies that offer local calls in an area. Figure 1 illustrates the market demand for calls and the marginal cost and average total cost of a call for each firm.
    a. If these firms behave as a cartel, show on the graph the price they charge for a call and the quantity of calls made.
    b. If the phone companies are regulated in the public interest, show on the graph the price of a call and the quantity of calls made.
    c. Show on the graph the price of a call and the quantity of calls if the phone companies capture the regulator.
    d. Show on the graph the deadweight loss that arises in part **c**.

9. Using the information in exercise 8,
    a. What regulation would lead to resource use being efficient?
    b. Would the firms incur an economic loss with efficient regulation? Why or why not?

   c. Show on the graph the price and quantity of calls if the firms were subject to an efficient price cap regulation.

   d. Show on the graph the deadweight loss that arises in part **c**.

10. In the market for local phone calls in which Land Line and Cellular City operate in exercise 8, suppose that the market is unregulated but that the price has been driven down to the competitive level because the firms are unable to form an effective cartel. Land Line would like to drive Cellular City out of business and considers practicing predatory pricing. Could Land Line succeed in eliminating competition in the short run and in the long run?

11. Explain why, during the 1980s, the antitrust authorities blocked a proposed merger between PepsiCo and 7-Up and between Coca-Cola and Dr Pepper. What do you predict would have happened to the price and quantity of soda if the mergers had occurred?

12. The Organization of the Petroleum Exporting Countries (OPEC) is an international cartel headquartered in Vienna, Austria, and operates outside the scope of the U.S. antitrust laws. OPEC controls about 40 percent of the world's crude oil production but owns about 75 percent of the world's known crude oil reserves. OPEC routinely meets to fix production quotas that are designed to change—usually to raise—the world price of oil.

   a. If the U.S antitrust laws could be extended to cover OPEC, would OPEC be in violation of the law? If so, explain which part of the law it would violate. If not, explain why not.

   b. What do you think would happen to the world price of oil and the quantity of oil consumed if OPEC were made to operate under antitrust laws like those of the United States?

13. Suppose that in the market for local phone calls described in exercise 8, Land Line and Cellular City propose a merger to create Land and Cell, Inc.

   a. What would happen to the price and quantity of local calls?

   b. What would happen to the consumer surplus, producer surplus, and deadweight loss in the market for local calls?

   c. Why would the antitrust authorities block this merger?

14. Suppose that Burger King, McDonald's, and Wendy's proposed a merger into a single Super Burger Chain.

   a. Do you think such a merger would be in the public interest? Explain.

   b. What do you think would happen to the price of a burger? Explain.

   c. What do you think would happen to consumer surplus, producer surplus, and deadweight loss if such a merger occurred?

   d. Would the antitrust authorities block such a merger? Why or why not?

   e. What is the main reason that, in reality, a merger would be in the interest of any of these firms?

Critical Thinking

15. Governments talk about regulating the Internet and taxing e-commerce. From what you know about how the Internet works and what e-commerce is,
    a. What problems might governments encounter in regulating the Internet?
    b. What difficulties do you think governments would have taxing e-commerce?
    c. Do you think that the arrival of the Internet has created more problems for the antitrust laws to solve or lessened the problems of monopoly?
    d. What parts of antitrust law do you think will be hard to enforce on companies that trade on the Internet?

16. Thinking about the Microsoft antitrust case,
    a. Do you agree that Microsoft attempted to monopolize the market for PC operating systems? Explain.
    b. Do you agree that Microsoft engaged in predatory pricing of Internet Explorer? Explain.
    c. Do you agree that Microsoft engaged in an illegal tying arrangement by bundling Internet Explorer with Windows? Explain.
    d. Do you think that the court's direction to Microsoft to share its code is an adequate way of achieving an efficient use of resources in the software market? Explain.

Web Exercises

myeconlab

Use the links on MyEconLab to work the following exercises.

17. Visit the Federal Trade Commission, where you can obtain information about Intel, the computer chip maker.
    a. Is Intel a natural monopoly?
    b. What was the problem that the FTC had with Intel?
    c. What did Intel agree to do?
    d. Explain how Intel's agreement will influence the price, quantity, consumer surplus, and producer surplus in the market for computer chips.

18. Visit the CNN Special on the California Electricity market.
    a. Describe how electricity utilities were regulated in California before 1996.
    b. Describe the changes in regulations that occurred in 1996.
    c. Identify at least three areas in which the electricity industry in California remained regulated after "deregulation."
    d. Explain the probable effects of the price cap on electricity generated in California.
    e. How do you think the situation in California would be different if, instead of a price cap, the state had introduced an earnings sharing plan?

19. Visit the U.S. Department of Justice Antitrust Division and look at the long list of antitrust cases listed on that Web site.
    a. Select a case that interests you.
    b. Describe the alleged violation of the antitrust laws.
    c. Explain the likely effects of the violation on price, quantity, producer surplus, consumer surplus, and deadweight loss.
    d. Describe the outcome of the case.
    e. Explain the likely effects of the settlement of the case on price, quantity, producer surplus, consumer surplus, and deadweight loss.

Demand and Supply in Factor Markets

CHAPTER CHECKLIST

When you have completed your study of this chapter, you will be able to

1 Describe the anatomy of the markets for labor, capital, and land.

2 Explain how the value of marginal product determines the demand for a factor of production.

3 Explain how wage rates and employment are determined.

4 Explain how interest rates, borrowing, and lending are determined.

5 Explain how rents and natural resource prices are determined.

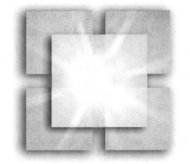

Bobby Stoops makes $2.2 million a year coaching the Sooners, the University of Oklahoma's football team. Deborah Watson, a Harvard Ph.D. physicist, is one of the University of Oklahoma's female professors who on the average earn $62,000 a year. What is going on? How can a football coach earn 37 times what a professor earns? You will learn in this chapter how factor markets answer these questions.

First, we'll describe the anatomy of the labor, capital, and land markets. Then we'll learn what determines the demand for a factor of production. We'll go on to study demand, supply, and equilibrium in factor markets. These markets determine the quantities of factors of production that are used to produce goods and services, which determine the prices and incomes of the factors of production and determine *for whom* goods and services get produced.

18.1 THE ANATOMY OF FACTOR MARKETS

The four factors of production that produce goods and services are

- Labor
- Capital
- Land
- Entrepreneurship

The first three factors—labor, capital, and land—are traded in markets that work like the markets for goods and services that you studied in Chapter 4. What a factor of production is paid—a **factor price**—is determined in a *factor market*. Entrepreneurship is different. Entrepreneurs create firms and hire labor, capital, and land in factor markets. The income of an entrepreneur is a profit (or a loss).

We'll begin by looking at the anatomy of the factor markets.

Factor price
The price of a factor of production. The wage rate is the price of labor, the interest rate is the price of capital, and rent is the price of land.

■ Labor Markets

Whether you're looking for a summer job or a permanent job after you graduate, you'll find it by searching in a labor market. Similarly, if you're running a business and want to hire some workers, you'll go to a labor market.

Labor consists of the work effort of people. And a **labor market** is a collection of people and firms who are trading labor services. Some labor is traded day by day, called casual labor. People who pick fruit and vegetables often just show up at a farm and take whatever work is available that day. But most labor is traded on a contract, called a **job**.

Labor market
A collection of people and firms who are trading labor services.

Job
A contract between a firm and a household to provide labor services.

Labor is supplied in combination with *human capital*—the skills obtained from education, on-the-job training, and work experience. Each person has a fixed (and equal) amount of time, but individual ability and human capital vary. Also, productivity depends on how well the skills of a worker match the skills required by an employer. For these reasons, a large amount of search activity takes place in labor markets. People search for the best job they can find, and firms search for the best person to fill a particular job.

People find jobs by using a variety of search devices, such as leads from friends and family members, help wanted advertisements, job centers, and job-clearing Web sites such as NationJob.com.

The price of labor is a wage rate, which is expressed as dollars per unit of time—dollars per hour, day, week, month, or year.

People find jobs from help wanted advertisements, at job centers, and on job-clearing Web sites.

■ Financial Markets

Capital consists of the tools, instruments, machines, buildings, and other constructions that have been produced in the past and that businesses now use to produce goods and services. These physical objects are themselves goods—*capital goods*—and are traded in markets, just as bottled water and toothpaste are. There are markets for earth-moving equipment, cranes, printing presses, Internet servers, and so on. The prices and quantities of capital goods are determined in markets just like those that you studied in Chapter 4.

Financial capital consists of the funds that firms use to buy and operate capital. The financial market is where firms get the funds that they use to buy capital. Firms are the demanders in the financial market. On the other side of a financial market are the people who have savings to lend.

A **financial market** is the collection of people and firms who are lending and borrowing to finance the purchase of physical capital. The price of financial capital, which is determined in the financial markets, is expressed as an interest rate (percent per year).

The two main types of financial market are

- Stock market
- Bond market

Stock Market

A **stock market** is a market in which shares in the stocks of companies are traded. A share in the stock of a company is an entitlement to a share in the profits of the company. The New York Stock Exchange and NASDAQ (the National Association of Security Dealers Automated Quotation System) are examples of stock markets. You can visit the Web sites of these stock markets and see the prices and the quantities of shares that are being traded minute by minute throughout the business day.

The growth of the Internet has created many new methods of participating in the stock market, and dozens of new firms offer services that enable anyone who is connected to the Internet to trade online.

Bond Market

A **bond market** is a market in which bonds issued by firms and governments are traded. A **bond** is a promise to pay specified sums of money on specified dates. To learn more about bond markets and how they are organized, you might visit the Bond Market Web site.

Financial capital
The funds that firms use to buy and operate physical capital.

Financial market
A collection of people and firms who are lending and borrowing to finance the purchase of physical capital.

Stock market
A market in which shares in the stocks of companies are traded.

Bond market
A market in which bonds issued by firms and governments are traded.

Bond
A promise to pay specified sums of money on specified dates.

Closing bell at the New York Stock Exchange.

■ Land Markets

Land consists of all the gifts of nature. So there are many different objects in this category of the factors of production. What we call *land* in everyday speech is just one of these. Raw materials that we dig or pump from beneath the ground or ocean, such as metal ores, coal, oil, and natural gas, are also called *land*.

The market for land as a factor of production is the market for the services of land (of all types). These services are rented, and the price that is determined in a land market is a rent expressed as dollars per unit. The market for a raw material is called a **commodity market**.

Commodity market
A market in which raw materials are traded.

■ Competitive Factor Markets

Factor markets vary in many ways. But most factor markets have one thing in common: many buyers and sellers. These markets are competitive markets.

In competitive factor markets, buyers and sellers are price takers—wage rate, interest rate, and rental rate takers—and market forces determine factor prices. We study competitive factor markets in this chapter.

CHECKPOINT 18.1

(X myeconlab)

1 Describe the anatomy of the markets for labor, capital, and land.

Practice Problem 18.1

1. To stage the 2004 Olympic Games, the Athens Organizing Committee
   a. Borrowed money and sold sponsorships.
   b. Built an Olympic Village and other venues.
   c. Hired and trained several thousand volunteers and security guards.
   d. Sold more than 7 million tickets.
   e. Built environmentally friendly water- and waste-recycling plants in the Olympic facilities.
   f. Set up an Internet site, which was able to receive 1 million hits a day.

   Which of these items are not factors of production? Divide those that are factors of production into land, labor, physical capital, human capital, financial capital, and entrepreneurship.

Exercise 18.1

1. Visit the Web site of the 2006 Winter Olympics: Torino 2006. What are some of the factors of production that the organizers are using to stage the 2006 Winter Olympic Games?

Solution to Practice Problem 18.1

1. The tickets sold are not a factor of production. The other items are factors of production. *Land* includes sites on which housing and facilities are built. *Labor* includes volunteers and guards. *Physical capital* includes Olympic Village, other venues, recycling plants, and Internet site. *Human capital* includes the skill of the security guards and the trained volunteers. *Financial capital* includes money borrowed and sponsorships sold. *Entrepreneurship* includes the Athens Organizing Committee.

18.2 THE DEMAND FOR A FACTOR OF PRODUCTION

The demand for a factor of production is a **derived demand**—it is derived from the demand for the goods and services that it is used to produce. You've seen, in Chapters 13 through 16, how a firm determines its profit-maximizing output. The quantities of factors of production demanded are a direct consequence of firms' output decisions. Firms hire the quantities of factors of production that maximize profit.

To decide the quantity of a factor of production to hire, a firm compares the cost of hiring an additional unit of the factor with its value to the firm. The cost of hiring an additional unit of a factor of production is the factor price. The value to the firm of hiring one more unit of a factor of production is called the factor's **value of marginal product**, which equals the price of a unit of output multiplied by the marginal product of the factor of production. To study the demand for a factor of production, we'll examine the demand for labor.

Derived demand
The demand for a factor of production, which is derived from the demand for the goods and services it is used to produce.

Value of marginal product
The value to a firm of hiring one more unit of a factor of production, which equals price of a unit of output multiplied by the marginal product of the factor of production.

■ Value of Marginal Product

Table 18.1 shows you how to calculate the value of the marginal product of labor at Max's Wash 'n' Wax car wash service. The first two columns show Max's *total product* schedule—the number of car washes per hour that each quantity of labor can produce. The third column shows the *marginal product* of labor—the change in total product that results from a one-unit increase in the quantity of labor employed. (See Chapter 12, pp. 293–297 for a refresher on product schedules.) Max can sell car washes at the going market price of $3 a wash. Given this information, we can calculate the value of marginal product (fourth column). It equals price multiplied by marginal product. For example, the marginal product of hiring the second worker is 4 car washes an hour. Each wash brings in $3, so the value of the marginal product of the second worker is $12 (4 washes at $3 each).

■ **TABLE 18.1**

Calculating the Value of Marginal Product

	Quantity of labor (workers)	Total product (car washes per hour)	Marginal product (washes per additional worker)	Value of marginal product (dollars per additional worker)
A	0	0		
			5	15
B	1	5		
			4	12
C	2	9		
			3	9
D	3	12		
			2	6
E	4	14		
			1	3
F	5	15		

The price of a car wash is $3. The value of the marginal product of labor equals the price of the product multiplied by marginal product of labor (column 3). The marginal product of the second worker is 4 washes, so the value of the marginal product of the second worker (in column 4) is $3 a wash multiplied by 4 washes, which is $12.

The Value of Marginal Product Curve

Figure 18.1 graphs the value of the marginal product of labor at Max's Wash 'n' Wax as the number of workers that Max hires changes. The blue bars that show the value of the marginal product of labor correspond to the numbers in Table 18.1. The curve labeled *VMP* is Max's value of marginal product curve.

■ A Firm's Demand for Labor

The value of the marginal product of labor and the wage rate determine the quantity of labor demanded by a firm. The value of the marginal product of labor tells us the additional revenue the firm earns by hiring one more worker. The wage rate tells us the additional cost the firm incurs by hiring one more worker.

Because the value of marginal product decreases as the quantity of labor employed increases, there is a simple rule for maximizing profit: Hire labor up to the point at which the value of marginal product equals the wage rate. If the value of marginal product of labor exceeds the wage rate, a firm can increase its profit by employing one more worker. If the wage rate exceeds the value of marginal product of labor, a firm can increase its profit by employing one fewer worker. But if the wage rate equals the value of the marginal product of labor, the firm cannot increase its profit by changing the number of workers it employs. The firm is making the maximum possible profit.

So the quantity of labor demanded by a firm is the quantity at which the wage rate equals the value of the marginal product of labor.

■ **FIGURE 18.1**

The Value of the Marginal Product at Max's Wash 'n' Wax

The blue bars show the value of the marginal product of the labor that Max hires based on the numbers in Table 18.1. The orange line is the firm's value of the marginal product of labor curve.

	Quantity of labor (workers)	Value of marginal product (dollars per additional worker)
A	1	15
B	2	12
C	3	9
D	4	6
E	5	3

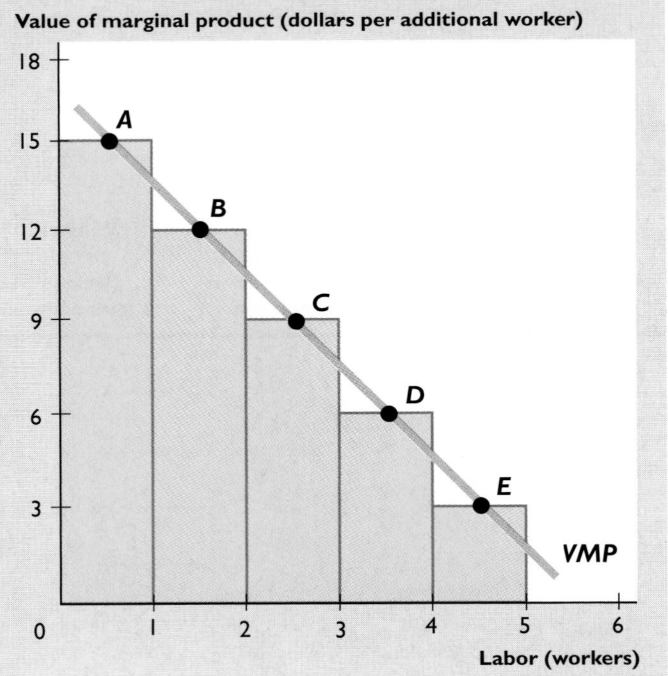

A Firm's Demand for Labor Curve

A firm's demand for labor curve is also its value of marginal product curve. If the wage rate falls and other things remain the same, a firm hires more workers. Figure 18.2 shows Max's value of marginal product curve in part (a) and demand for labor curve in part (b). The x-axis measures the number of workers hired in both parts. The y-axis measures the value of marginal product in part (a) and the wage rate—dollars per hour—in part (b).

Suppose the wage rate is $10.50 an hour. You can see in part (a) that if Max hires 1 worker, the value of the marginal product of labor is $15 an hour. Because this 1 worker costs Max only $10.50 an hour, he makes a profit of $4.50 an hour. If Max hires 2 workers, the value of the marginal product of the second worker is $12 an hour. So on this second worker, Max makes a profit of $1.50 an hour. Max's total profit per hour on the first two workers is $6 an hour—$4.50 on the first worker plus $1.50 on the second worker.

If Max hired 3 workers, his profit would fall. The third worker generates a marginal product of only $9 an hour but costs $10.50 an hour, so Max does not hire

---

■ FIGURE 18.2

The Demand for Labor at Max's Wash 'n' Wax

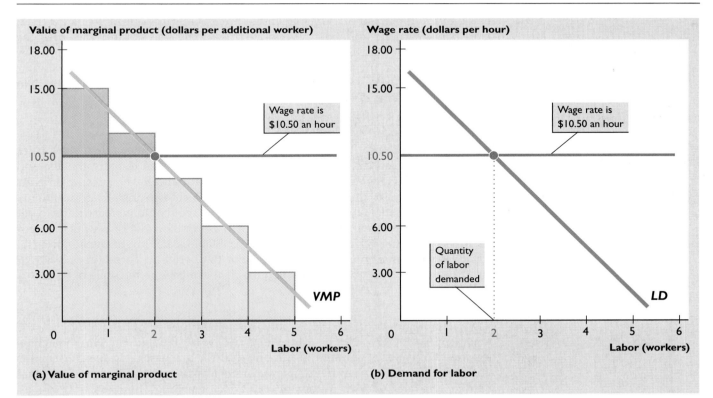

(a) Value of marginal product

(b) Demand for labor

At a wage rate of $10.50 an hour, Max makes a profit on the first 2 workers but would incur a loss on the third worker (part a), so the quantity of labor demanded is 2 workers (part b). Max's demand for labor curve in part (b) is the same as the value of marginal product curve. The demand for labor curve slopes downward because the value of the marginal product of labor diminishes as the quantity of labor employed increases.

3 workers. The quantity of labor demanded by Max when the wage rate is $10.50 an hour is 2 workers, which is a point on Max's demand for labor curve, *LD*, in Figure 18.2(b).

If the wage rate increased to $12.50 an hour, Max would decrease the quantity of labor demanded to 1 worker. If the wage rate decreased to $7.50 an hour, Max would increase the quantity of labor demanded to 3 workers.

A change in the wage rate brings a change in the quantity of labor demanded and a movement along the demand curve. A change in any other influence on a firm's labor-hiring plans changes the demand for labor and shifts the demand for labor curve.

■ Changes in the Demand for Labor

The demand for labor depends on

- The price of the firm's output
- The prices of other factors of production
- Technology

The Price of the Firm's Output

The higher the price of a firm's output, the greater is its demand for labor. The price of output affects the demand for labor through its influence on the value of marginal product. A higher price for the firm's output increases the value of the marginal product of labor. A change in the price of a firm's output leads to a shift in the firm's demand for labor curve. If the price of the firm's output increases, the demand for labor increases and the demand for labor curve shifts rightward.

For example, if the price of a car wash increased to $4, the value of the marginal product of Max's third worker would increase from $9 an hour to $12 an hour. At a wage rate of $10.50, Max would now hire 3 workers instead of 2.

The Prices of Other Factors of Production

If the price of using capital decreases relative to the wage rate, a firm substitutes capital for labor and increases the quantity of capital it uses. Usually, the demand for labor will decrease when the price of using capital falls. For example, if the price of a car wash machine falls, Max might decide to install an additional machine and lay off a worker. But the demand for labor could increase if the lower price of capital led to a sufficiently large increase in the scale of production. For example, with cheaper capital equipment available, Max might install an additional car wash machine and hire more labor to operate it. These types of factor substitution occur in the *long run* when the firm can change the scale of its plant.

Technology

New technologies decrease the demand for some types of labor and increase the demand for other types. For example, if a new automated car wash machine becomes available, Max might install one of these machines and fire most of his work force—a decrease in the demand for car wash workers. But the firms that manufacture and service automatic car wash machines hire more labor—an increase in the demand for these types of labor. During the 1980s and 1990s, the electronic telephone exchange decreased the demand for telephone operators and increased the demand for computer programmers and electronics engineers.

CHECKPOINT 18.2

2 **Explain how the value of marginal product determines the demand for a factor of production.**

Practice Problem 18.2

1. Kaiser's Ice Cream Parlor hires workers to produce smoothies. The market for smoothies is perfectly competitive, and smoothies sell for $4.00 each. The labor market is competitive, and the wage rate is $40 a day. Table 1 shows the workers' total product schedule.
    a. Calculate the marginal product of hiring the fourth worker.
    b. Calculate the value of the marginal product of the fourth worker.
    c. How many workers will Kaiser's hire to maximize its profit?
    d. How many smoothies a day will Kaiser's produce to maximize its profit?
    e. If the price rises to $5 a smoothie, how many workers will Kaiser's hire?
    f. Kaiser's installs a new soda fountain that increases the productivity of workers by 50 percent. If the price remains at $4 a smoothie and the wage rises to $48 a day, how many workers does Kaiser's hire?

TABLE 1

Workers	Smoothies per day
1	7
2	21
3	33
4	43
5	51
6	55

Exercise 18.2

1. Greg's Grooming hires workers to groom dogs. The market for dog grooming is perfectly competitive, and the price of a grooming is $20. The labor market is competitive, and the wage rate is $40 a day. Table 2 shows the workers' total product schedule.
    a. Calculate the marginal product of hiring the third worker.
    b. Calculate the value of the marginal product of the third worker.
    c. How many workers will Greg's hire to maximize its profit?
    d. How many dogs a day will Greg's groom to maximize its profit?
    e. If the wage rate rises to $60 a day, how many workers will Greg's hire?
    f. If Greg installs a machine that doubles the productivity of workers and the price of a grooming falls to $10, how many workers will Greg's hire at $40 a day?

TABLE 2

Workers	Groomings per day
1	4
2	7
3	11
4	16
5	20
6	23
7	25

Solution to Practice Problem 18.2

1a. The *MP* of hiring the fourth worker equals the *TP* of 4 workers (43 smoothies) minus the *TP* of 3 workers (33 smoothies), which is 10 smoothies.
1b. The *VMP* of the fourth worker equals the *MP* of the fourth worker (10 smoothies) multiplied by the price of a smoothie ($4), which is $40.
1c. Kaiser's maximizes profit by hiring the number of workers that makes *VMP* equal to the wage rate ($40 a day). Kaiser's hires 4 workers.
1d. Kaiser's hires 4 workers, and they produce 43 smoothies. When Kaiser's hires 4 workers, the *MP* of labor is 10 smoothies. The cost of a worker is $40 a day, so the *MC* of a smoothie is $40 ÷ 10 smoothies a day, which is $4 a smoothie. Kaiser's *MC* equals the price of a smoothie ($4 a smoothie) when Kaiser's produces 43 smoothies a day.
1e. Kaiser's maximizes its profit by hiring 5 workers.
1f. Kaiser's maximizes its profit by hiring 5 workers.

18.3 WAGES AND EMPLOYMENT

For most of us, the labor market is our only source of income. We work and earn a wage. What determines the amount of labor that we supply?

■ The Supply of Labor

People supply labor to earn an income. Many factors influence the quantity of labor that a person plans to provide, but a key factor is the wage rate.

To see how the wage rate influences the quantity of labor supplied, think about Larry's labor supply decision, which Figure 18.3 illustrates. Larry enjoys his leisure time, and he would be pleased if he didn't have to spend his evenings and weekends working at Max's Wash 'n' Wax. But Max pays him $10.50 an hour, and at that wage rate, Larry chooses to work 30 hours a week. The reason is that he is offered a wage rate that is high enough to make him regard this use of his time as the best available to him. If he were offered a lower wage rate, Larry would not be willing to give up so much leisure. If he were offered a higher wage rate, Larry would want to work even longer hours, but only up to a point. Offer Larry $25 an hour, and he would be willing to work a 40-hour week (and earn $1,000). With the goods and services that Larry can buy for $1,000, his priority would be a bit more leisure time if the wage rate increased further. If the wage rate increased above $25 an hour, Larry would cut back on his work hours and take more leisure. Larry's labor supply curve eventually bends backward.

■ **FIGURE 18.3**

An Individual's Labor Supply Curve

1 At a wage rate of $10.50 an hour, **2** Larry is willing to supply 30 hours a week of labor.

3 Larry's quantity of labor supplied **4** increases as the wage rate increases up to **5** a maximum, and then further increases in the wage rate **6** bring a decrease in the quantity of labor supplied. Larry's labor supply curve eventually bends backward.

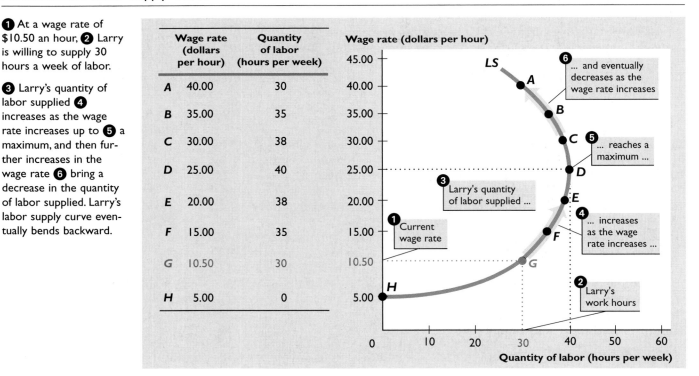

	Wage rate (dollars per hour)	Quantity of labor (hours per week)
A	40.00	30
B	35.00	35
C	30.00	38
D	25.00	40
E	20.00	38
F	15.00	35
G	10.50	30
H	5.00	0

Market Supply Curve

Larry's supply curve shows the quantity of labor supplied by one person as that person's wage rate changes. Most people behave like Larry. But different people have different wage rates at which they are willing to work and at which their labor supply curve bends backward. A market supply curve shows the quantity of labor supplied by all households in a particular job. It is found by adding together the quantities supplied by all households at each wage rate. Also, along a market supply curve, the wage rates available in other jobs remain the same. So, for example, along the supply curve of car wash workers, we hold constant the wage rates of car salespeople, mechanics, and all other types of labor.

Offer Larry more for car washing than for oil changing, and he will supply more of his labor to car washing. So the market supply curve in a given job slopes upward like the one in Figure 18.4, which shows the market supply curve for car wash workers in a large city.

■ Influences on the Supply of Labor

The supply of labor changes when influences other than the wage rate change. The key factors that change the supply of labor are

- Adult population
- Preferences
- Time in school and training

▨ FIGURE 18.4

The Supply of Car Wash Workers   Ⓧ myeconlab

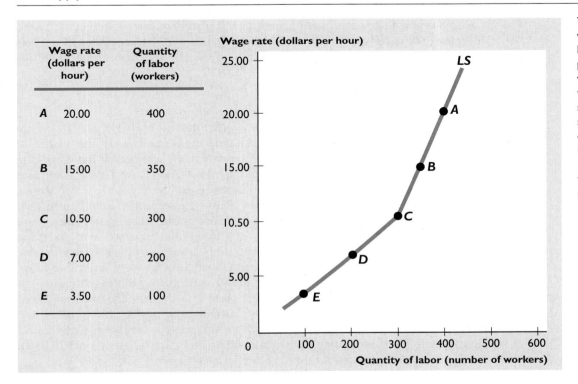

	Wage rate (dollars per hour)	Quantity of labor (workers)
A	20.00	400
B	15.00	350
C	10.50	300
D	7.00	200
E	3.50	100

The supply curve of car wash workers shows how the quantity supplied changes when the wage rate changes, other things remaining the same. In a market for a specific type of labor, the quantity supplied increases as the wage rate increases, other things remaining the same.

Adult Population

An increase in the adult population increases the supply of labor. Such an increase might occur because the birth rate exceeds the death rate. Or it might occur because of migration. Historically, the population of the United States has been strongly influenced by migration.

Preferences

In 1960, 34 percent of women had jobs. In 2005, 56 percent of women had jobs and the percentage was still rising. Many factors contributed to this change, which economists classify as a change in preferences. The result has been a large increase in the supply of female labor. At the same time, the percentage of men with jobs has shrunk, from 80 percent in 1960 to 73 percent in 2005.

Time in School and Training

The more people who remain in school for full-time education and training, the smaller is the supply of low-skilled labor. Today in the United States, almost everyone completes high school and more than 50 percent of high-school graduates enroll in college or university. Although many students work part time, the supply of labor by students is less than it would be if they were full-time workers. So when more people pursue higher education, other things remaining the same, the supply of low-skilled labor decreases. But time spent in school and training converts low-skilled labor into high-skilled labor. So the greater the proportion of people who receive a higher education, the greater is the supply of high-skilled labor.

When the amount of work that people want to do at a given wage rate changes, the supply of labor changes. So an increase in the adult population or an increase in the percentage of women with jobs increases the supply of labor. An increase in college enrollment decreases the supply of low-skilled labor. Later, it increases the supply of high-skilled labor. Changes in the supply of labor shift the supply of labor curve, just like the shifts of the supply curves that you studied in Chapter 4 (p. 97).

■ Labor Market Equilibrium

Labor market equilibrium determines the wage rate and employment. In Figure 18.5, the market demand curve for car wash workers is *LD.* Here, if the wage rate is $10.50 an hour, the quantity of labor demanded is 300 workers. If the wage rate rises to $14 an hour, the quantity demanded decreases to 200. And if the wage rate falls to $9 an hour, the quantity demanded increases to 350. Figure 18.5 also shows the supply curve of car wash workers, *LS,* which is the same as that in Figure 18.4.

Figure 18.5 also shows equilibrium in the labor market. The equilibrium wage rate is $10.50 an hour, and the equilibrium quantity is 300 car wash workers. If the wage rate exceeded $10.50 an hour, there would be a surplus of car wash workers. More people would be looking for car wash jobs than firms were willing to hire.

In such a situation, the wage rate would fall as firms found it easy to hire people at a lower wage rate. If the wage rate were less than $10.50 an hour, there would be a shortage of car wash workers. Firms would not be able to fill all the jobs they had available. In this situation, the wage rate would rise as firms found it necessary to offer higher wages to attract labor. Only at a wage rate of $10.50 an hour are there no forces operating to change the wage rate.

Reallocating Labor

Technological change destroys some jobs and creates others. But it creates more jobs than it destroys, and *on the average,* the new jobs pay more than the old ones did. But to benefit from technological change, people must acquire new skills and change their jobs. Between 2002 and 2012, the number of jobs in clothing manufacturing, tobacco, metal ore mining, and coal mining are expected to decline. But the number of jobs in services industries, especially in computer and data services, is expected to expand.

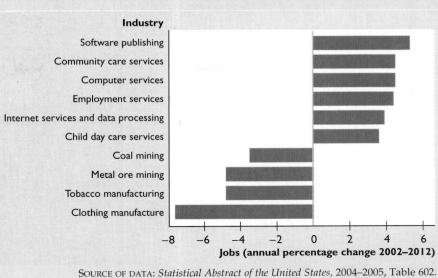

SOURCE OF DATA: *Statistical Abstract of the United States,* 2004–2005, Table 602.

Changes in demand and supply in these labor markets will change employment and the equilibrium wage rates.

■ **FIGURE 18.5**
Labor Market Equilibrium

(X) myeconlab

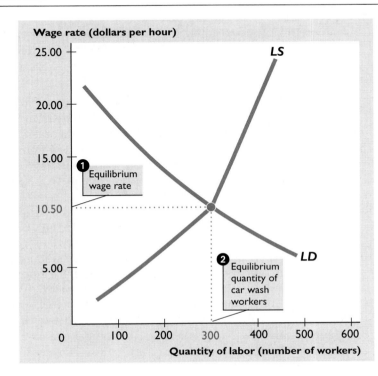

The labor market coordinates firms' demand for labor and households' supply of labor plans by changing the wage rate. The market is in equilibrium—the quantity of labor demanded equals the quantity supplied. ❶ The equilibrium wage rate is $10.50 an hour and ❷ the equilibrium quantity of labor is 300 workers.

If the wage rate exceeds $10.50 an hour, the quantity supplied exceeds the quantity demanded and the wage rate falls. If the wage rate is below $10.50 an hour, the quantity demanded exceeds the quantity supplied and the wage rate rises.

3 **Explain how wage rates and employment are determined.**

Practice Problem 18.3

1. Fast-food outlets in Greenville hire teenagers and retirees. In Greenville, the following events occur one at a time and other things remain the same. Explain the influence of each event on the market for fast-food workers.
    a. A new theme park opens and hires teenagers to sell tickets for its rides.
    b. The new theme park becomes the hottest tourist attraction in the state.
    c. Retirees from around the state flock to Greenville and make it their home.
    d. The demand for hamburgers decreases, and as a result, the price of a hamburger decreases.
    e. New technology in the fast-food industry decreases the marginal product of fast-food workers.

Exercises 18.3

1. Ski instructors are skilled workers. Consider the market for ski instructors in the greater Salt Lake City region and explain how that market would change if
    a. Ski holidays became more popular.
    b. New skis were invented that were much easier to use than the current ones.

2. What do you think the effect of Internet commerce has been on the markets for truck drivers, couriers, and sales clerks?

3. More and more people use the Internet. What are three types of labor for which the demand will continue to increase and three types for which the demand will continue to decrease? Explain your answer.

4. As more people go to college, what changes do you predict will occur in the markets for college graduates and low-skilled workers?

Solution to Practice Problem 18.3

FIGURE I

Wage rate (dollars per hour)

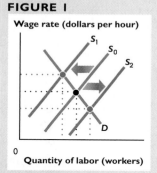

Quantity of labor (workers)

FIGURE 2

Wage rate (dollars per hour)

Quantity of labor (workers)

1a. Some teenagers prefer to work as ticket sellers, so the supply of labor in the fast-food market decreases. The supply curve shifts from S_0 to S_1 (Figure 1). The wage rate rises, and the number of fast-food workers employed decreases.

1b. The number of visitors to Greenville increases. The demand for fast food increases, so the demand for fast-food workers increases. The demand curve shifts from D_0 to D_1 (Figure 2). The wage rate increases, and the number of fast-food workers employed increases.

1c. An increase in the number of retirees increases the supply of fast-food labor. The supply curve shifts from S_0 to S_2 (Figure 1). The wage rate falls, and the number of fast-food workers employed increases.

1d. A decrease in the price of fast food decreases the demand for fast-food workers. The demand curve shifts from D_0 to D_2 (Figure 2). The wage rate decreases, and the number of fast-food workers employed decreases.

1e. A decrease in the marginal product of fast-food workers decreases the demand for fast-food workers. The demand curve shifts from D_0 to D_2 (Figure 2). The wage rate falls, and the number of fast-food workers employed decreases.

18.4 FINANCIAL MARKETS

Financial markets are the channels through which firms borrow financial resources to buy capital. These financial resources come from saving. The price of financial capital, which adjusts to make the quantity of capital supplied equal to the quantity demanded, is the interest rate.

For most of us, financial markets are where we make our biggest-ticket transactions. We borrow in a financial market to buy a home. And we lend in financial markets to build up a fund on which to live when we retire.

Let's look at demand and supply in financial markets.

■ The Demand for Financial Capital

A firm's demand for *financial* capital stems from its demand for *physical* capital to produce goods and services. And the quantity of *physical* capital that a firm plans to use depends on the price of *financial* capital—the interest rate.

Other things remaining the same, the higher the interest rate, the smaller is the quantity of capital demanded. The quantity of capital demanded decreases if the interest rate rises, other things remaining the same, because the marginal product of capital diminishes as the quantity of capital employed by a firm increases.

For example, suppose that the interest rate is 4 percent a year and Amazon.com is planning to build a $100 million warehouse. The cost of this capital is 4 percent of $100 million, or $4 million a year. Amazon reckons that the value of the marginal product of this warehouse is enough to earn the $4 million a year that the capital will cost. Now suppose that the interest rate rises to 6 percent a year while all other prices remain constant. If Amazon goes ahead with its plan, it will now incur a cost of $6 million a year. In this situation, Amazon scales back its warehouse plans and borrows less.

Two main factors that change the demand for capital are

- Population growth
- Technological change

As the population grows, the demand for all goods and services increases, so the demand for the physical capital that produces them increases. Advances in technology increase the demand for some types of physical capital and decrease the demand for other types. For example, the development of desktop computers increased the demand for office computing equipment, decreased the demand for electric typewriters, and increased the overall demand for capital in the office. So the demand for financial capital increased.

■ The Supply of Financial Capital

The quantity of financial capital supplied results from people's saving decisions. Other things remaining the same, the higher the interest rate, the greater is the quantity of saving supplied.

A dollar saved today grows into a dollar plus interest tomorrow. The higher the interest rate, the greater is the amount that a dollar saved today becomes in the future. Other things remaining the same, if the interest rate rises, the opportunity cost of current consumption increases, so people cut their consumption and increase their saving.

The supply of saving changes if the amount that people want to save at a given interest rate changes. The main influences on the supply of saving are

- Population
- Average income
- Expected future income

An increase in the population increases the supply of saving because it increases the number of potential savers.

Saving converts *current* income into *future* consumption potential. For example, saving can pay for a child's future college education or for consumption during retirement. The higher a household's income, the more it consumes both now and in the future. But to increase *future* consumption, the household must save. So other things remaining the same, the higher a household's income, the more it saves. Most households save a roughly constant proportion of their income. So as income increases, the supply of capital also increases.

Over their lives, most people try to achieve a level of consumption that fluctuates less than their income—that is, they try to smooth out the effects of income fluctuations on consumption. So the amount that a household saves depends not only on its current income but also on its *expected future income*. If a household's current income is high and its expected future income is low, the household will have a high level of saving. But if the household's current income is low and its expected future income is high, the household's saving will be low (perhaps even negative).

EYE ON THE U.S. ECONOMY

Interest Rate Fluctuations

The figure shows the *real interest rate*—which is the interest rate that people *really* earn and pay after adjusting for the fact that inflation lowers the value of money—earned in the stock market and in the bond market in the United States since 1964.

Interest rates fluctuate a lot because the demand for capital fluctuates much more than does the supply of capital. When rapid technological change brings an increase in the demand for capital, the real interest rate rises, as it did during the 1990s. When the demand for capital grows slowly or decreases temporarily, the real interest rate falls, as it did in 1975.

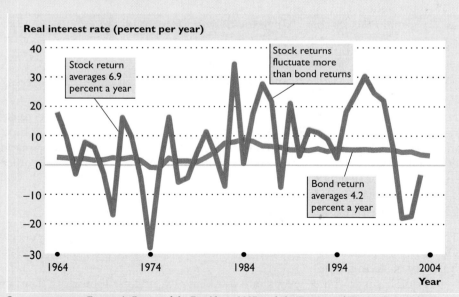

SOURCE OF DATA: *Economic Report of the President*, 2005 and the Bureau of Economic Analysis.

The real interest rate earned on stocks is more volatile than that on bonds, but the average real interest rate on stocks is higher.

Young people (especially students) usually have low current incomes compared with their expected future incomes. They often consume more than they earn and go into debt. In middle age, most people's incomes reach a peak. At this stage in life, their current income is large and their expected future income is small because they anticipate stopping full-time work during their sixties. At this stage of life, saving is at a maximum. After retirement, people spend part of the wealth they have accumulated during their working lives, so saving falls again.

■ Financial Market Equilibrium and the Interest Rate

Figure 18.6 illustrates financial market equilibrium. The demand curve, *KD*, shows the relationship between the total quantity of financial capital demanded and the interest rate, other things remaining the same. And the supply curve, *KS*, shows the relationship between the quantity of financial capital supplied and the interest rate, other things remaining the same. Here, the equilibrium interest rate is 6 percent a year, and the quantity of capital is $200 billion.

Over time, the demand for capital and the supply of capital increase and the demand curve and the supply curve shift rightward. Population growth increases the demand for capital. And as the increased population earns a larger income, the supply of capital increases. Technological advances increase the demand for capital and bring higher incomes, which in turn increase the supply of capital. Because both the demand for capital and the supply of capital increase over time, the quantity of capital increases but the interest rate does not persistently increase or decrease (see *Eye on the U.S. Economy* on p. 456).

▓ FIGURE 18.6
Financial Market Equilibrium

The demand for financial capital is *KD*, and the supply of financial capital is *KS*. Market equilibrium occurs at ❶ an interest rate of 6 percent a year with a ❷ quantity of financial capital of $200 billion.

4 Explain how interest rates, borrowing, and lending are determined.

Practice Problem 18.4

1. Wendy plans to open a Starbucks coffee shop. To do so, she will need $50,000 to buy the franchise and $20,000 to outfit the coffee shop. Wendy has $15,000 in her bank account, and the current interest rate is 5 percent a year.
   a. What is Wendy's opportunity cost of opening the coffee shop?
   b. What is the quantity of financial capital that Wendy plans to get from the financial market?
   c. What is the quantity of financial capital that Wendy plans to provide herself?
   d. If demand for financial capital increases just when Wendy plans to go to the financial market, what will happen to her opportunity cost of the coffee shop? Explain your answer.
   e. If the supply of financial capital increases just when Wendy plans to go to the financial market, what will happen to her opportunity cost of the coffee shop? Explain your answer.

Exercise 18.4

1. Lou operates an avocado orchard. He plans to buy trees that will cost $20,000. He also plans to hire some workers to help run the orchard. The wage rate for orchard workers is currently $8 an hour, and he will need to hire 100 hours of labor a week. The interest rate is 3 percent a year. Lou has no savings.
   a. What is the cost of the capital in Lou's orchard?
   b. Lou predicts that in the first 50 weeks, he will harvest no avocados. How much financial capital is Lou planning to get from the financial market?
   c. If an avocado-picking machine becomes available that allows Lou to replace the workers and that costs $10,000, how much financial capital will Lou now need to get from the financial market?

Solution to Practice Problem 18.4

1a. Wendy's opportunity cost is 5 percent of the cost of the coffee shop, which is 5 percent of $70,000 or $3,500 a year.
1b. Wendy needs $70,000 but has $15,000, so the quantity of financial capital that she requires is $55,000 ($70,000 minus $15,000).
1c. Wendy plans to provide $15,000 herself.
1d. An increase in the demand for capital will increase the interest rate. The interest rate that Wendy has to pay will exceed 5 percent a year and increase the opportunity cost of her coffee shop.
1e. An increase in the supply of capital will decrease the interest rate. Wendy will pay less than 5 percent a year for her financial capital and decrease the opportunity cost of her coffee shop.

18.5 LAND AND NATURAL RESOURCE MARKETS

All natural resources are called *land,* and they fall into two categories:

- Renewable
- Nonrenewable

Renewable natural resources are natural resources that can be used repeatedly such as forestland—land in its everyday sense. **Nonrenewable natural resources** are resources that can be used only once and that cannot be replaced once they have been used. Examples are coal, natural gas, and oil—called hydrocarbon fuels.

Let's look first at the market for a renewable natural resource.

■ The Market for Land (Renewable Natural Resources)

The demand for land is based on the same factors as the demand for labor and the demand for capital. The lower the rent, other things remaining the same, the greater is the quantity of land demanded.

But the supply of land is special: The quantity is fixed, so the quantity supplied cannot be changed by people's decisions. People can vary the amount of land they own. But when one person buys some land, another person sells it. The aggregate quantity of land supplied of a particular type and in a particular location is fixed. This fact means that the supply of each particular block of land is *perfectly inelastic.* Figure 18.7 illustrates the supply of a 10-acre block on Chicago's "Magnificent Mile." The quantity supplied is 10 acres regardless of the rent.

Renewable natural resources
Natural resources that can be used repeatedly.

Nonrenewable natural resources
Natural resources that can be used only once and that cannot be replaced once they have been used.

■ **FIGURE 18.7**

A Market for Land

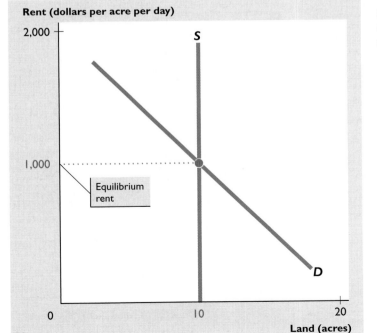

The demand curve for a 10-acre block of land is *D,* and the supply curve is *S.* Equilibrium occurs at a rent of $1,000 an acre per day.

Because the quantity of land supplied is fixed, the rent is determined by demand. In Figure 18.7, the demand curve is D and the equilibrium price (rent) is $1,000 an acre per day. The greater the demand, the higher is the rent.

■ Economic Rent and Opportunity Cost

Rent is a special kind of income because the resource that receives a rent would be available even if the rent were zero. Low demand would make the rent low, and high demand would make the rent high. But the quantity of land wouldn't change.

Land is not the only resource that is in fixed supply. Some human resources are too. There is only one Tiger Woods. This extraordinary golfer earns a large income because he has a high value of marginal product. A large part of Tiger Woods's income is called "economic rent." **Economic rent** is the income received by *any* factor of production over and above the amount required to induce a given quantity of the factor to be supplied. The income that is required to induce the supply of a given quantity of a factor of production is its *opportunity cost*—the value of the factor of production in its next best use.

Figure 18.8 illustrates the economic rent and opportunity cost components of a factor's income. Suppose that the demand curve for Tiger's time were D and his supply curve were S. The wage rate would be $50,000 an hour, and Tiger would work 40 hours a week. His income is the sum of the red and green areas. The red area below the supply curve measures opportunity cost, and the green area above the supply curve but below the resource price measures economic rent.

Economic rent
The income received by *any* factor of production over and above the amount required to induce a given quantity of the factor to be supplied.

■ **FIGURE 18.8**
Economic Rent and Opportunity Cost

Part of the income of a factor of production is ❶ opportunity cost (the red area), and part is ❷ economic rent (the green area). The figure shows the market for Tiger Woods's labor. At $50,000 an hour, Tiger is willing to work 40 hours a week. Tiger earns a large economic rent.

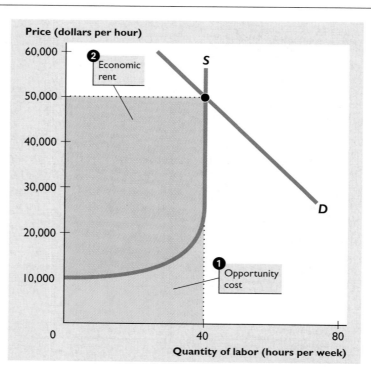

■ The Supply of a Nonrenewable Natural Resource

At a given time, the quantity of any natural resource is fixed and is independent of its price. Over time, the quantity of a nonrenewable natural resource decreases as it is used up. But the *known* quantity of a natural resource increases because advances in technology enable ever less accessible sources of the resource to be discovered.

Using a natural resource decreases its supply, which causes its price to rise. But new technologies that lead to the discovery of previously unknown reserves increase supply, which causes the price to fall. Also, new technologies that enable a more efficient use of a nonrenewable natural resource decrease demand, which causes the price to fall.

Historically, the forces that bring lower prices have outweighed those that bring higher prices and natural resource prices have fallen. Adjusted for inflation, the prices of metals, for example, fell by more than 50 percent between 1970 and 2005. Again, adjusted for inflation, even the price of crude oil was lower in 2005 than it had been at its peak in 1980.

You've now seen how competitive factor markets work. In the next chapter, we look more closely at the labor market and the reasons for earnings differences.

REALITY CHECK

Factor Markets in YOUR Life

Would you like to be a millionaire? If you would, it is in factor markets that you are going to make it happen.

You might come up with a $1 million idea that you develop with your entrepreneurial skills. In this case, you'll be hiring factors of production—borrowing to finance capital expenditures and hiring labor.

But the surest way of becoming a millionaire is by saving. If starting at age 25 you save $66 a week and earn an interest rate of 8 percent a year (which is less than the average of the past 30 years), how long do you think it will take you to accumulate $1 million? The answer is 40 years.

You will have saved $137,000—that is $66 multiplied by 2080 weeks—and you will have earned almost $870,000 in interest on your savings (and interest on your interest).

With a bit of financial planning, you can probably manage to save more than $66 a week, and much more if your earnings rise as you get older. By making the capital market work for you, you can grow a few dollars a week into $1 million.

5 **Explain how rents and natural resource prices are determined.**

Practice Problem 18.5

1. Which of the following items are nonrenewable natural resources, which are renewable natural resources, and which are not natural resources? Explain your answers.
    a. Beaches in Florida
    b. Lake Powell
    c. The Empire State Building
    d. Silver mines in Arizona
    e. The Great Lakes
    f. National parks
    g. Redwood forests
    h. The Statue of Liberty

Exercises 18.5

1. New technology has allowed oil to be pumped from much deeper offshore oil fields than before. For example, 28 deep ocean rigs operate in the deep waters of the Gulf of Mexico. What effect do you think deep ocean sources have had on the world oil price? Who will benefit from drilling for oil in the Gulf of Mexico? Explain your answer.

2. Water is a natural resource that is plentiful in Canada but not plentiful in Arizona and southern California. If Canadians start to export bulk water to Arizona and southern California, what do you predict will be the effect on the price of bulk water? Will Canada eventually run out of water?

3. In the 1970s, few people drank bottled spring water and the major producers of bottled spring water were in Europe. Today, lots of people drink bottled spring water. How has this increase in the demand for spring water been satisfied? Will this increase in demand lead to some springs running dry?

4. As cities grow, good farmland is being replaced by urban sprawl. Why do farmers sell their land to urban developers?

Solution to Practice Problem 18.5

1. Natural resources include all the gifts of nature. A nonrenewable natural resource is one that once used cannot be used again. A renewable natural resource is one that can be used repeatedly.

    Nonrenewable natural resources include silver mines in Arizona.

    Renewable natural resources include beaches in Florida, Lake Powell, the Great Lakes, national parks, and redwood forests.

    The Empire State Building and the Statue of Liberty are national landmarks, but they are not natural resources. Labor and capital were used to build the Empire State Building. The Statue of Liberty was a gift from France and not a gift of nature.

CHAPTER CHECKPOINT

Key Points

1 **Describe the anatomy of the markets for labor, capital, and land.**

- Labor is traded on job contracts.
- Financial markets provide the funds that are used to buy physical capital.
- Natural resources are traded in land markets and commodity markets.

2 **Explain how the value of marginal product determines the demand for a factor of production.**

- The demand for a factor of production is a derived demand—it is derived from the demand for the goods and services that the factor of production is used to produce.
- The quantity of a factor of production that is demanded depends on its price and the value of its marginal product, which equals the price of the product multiplied by marginal product.

3 **Explain how wage rates and employment are determined.**

- Wage rates are determined by demand and supply in labor markets.
- Changes in technology bring changes in the allocation of labor.

4 **Explain how interest rates, borrowing, and lending are determined.**

- Interest rates are determined by demand and supply in financial markets.
- Real interest rates on stocks are higher on the average but fluctuate by more than those on bonds.

5 **Explain how rents and natural resource prices are determined.**

- Rents and natural resource prices are determined by demand and supply in land and commodity markets.
- Nonrenewable natural resource prices have fallen because technological change has led to the discovery of new sources and made the use of natural resources more productive.

Key Terms

Bond, 443
Bond market, 443
Commodity market, 444
Derived demand, 445
Economic rent, 460

Factor price, 442
Financial capital, 443
Financial market, 443
Job, 442
Labor market, 442

Nonrenewable natural resources, 459
Renewable natural resources, 459
Stock market, 443
Value of marginal product, 445

<X> myeconlab   **Exercises**

1. Through the 1990s, the percentage of high school students who decided to go to college increased. What effect do you predict that this increase has had on the market for
   a. College graduates? Draw a demand-supply graph to illustrate your answer.
   b. College professors? Explain your answer.
   c. High school graduates? Draw a demand-supply graph to illustrate your answer.

2. If your college switched to online delivery of its courses, what changes do you predict would occur in the factor markets in the town where your college is located?

3. A California asparagus farmer is maximizing profit. The price of asparagus is $2 a box, a farm worker's wage rate is $12 an hour, and the asparagus farm employs six workers.
   a. What is the marginal product of the sixth farm worker?
   b. Is the marginal product of the fifth worker greater or less than the marginal product of the sixth?
   c. If, when the price of asparagus rises to $3 a box, the farm hires eight workers, what is the marginal product of the eighth worker?

4. Suppose that Palm Island is the world's largest grower of coconuts and the interest rate on Palm Island is 3 percent a year. The following events occur, one at a time:
   a. Palm Island plans to build a $100 million airport on 100 acres—its first airport.
   b. Palm Island plans to double its population in 3 years by hiring well-educated people from the United States.
   c. The world price of coconuts is expected to increase by 200 percent next year and remain high for the next decade.
   d. Palm Island is short of entrepreneurs and plans to allow anyone with $1 million to immigrate to Palm Island.

   Explain the influence of each event on Palm Island's financial market and land market.

5. Use the laws of demand and supply in factor markets to explain whether the following statements are true or false:
   a. New technology enables tomato growers to pick and pack tomatoes by machine. Tomato growers will now hire fewer workers and will be able to hire these workers at a lower wage rate than before.
   b. If soccer becomes more popular in the United States and basketball becomes less popular, basketball players will earn more than they do today.
   c. A recent new discovery of diamonds in the Yukon in Canada will lower the world price of diamonds and lower the wage rate paid to diamond workers in South Africa.
   d. As cars become more and more fuel efficient, the price of gasoline at the pump will fall.

6. Suppose that a tax is imposed on college and university tuition and the revenue generated is spent on making payments to firms that provide on-the-job training for low-skilled labor. Draw diagrams to show what happens to the demand for labor, the supply of labor, and the equilibrium wage rate in the markets for
   a. College graduates.
   b. Industrial workers with skills acquired on the job.
   c. College professors.
   d. Skilled industrial workers.

7. The personal saving rate has fallen in recent years in the United States.
   a. What are some of the factors that might have contributed to the fall?
   b. Of the factors that you identified in part **a**, which have changed the quantity of saving supplied and which have changed the supply of saving?
   c. How do you expect the fall in the saving rate to have affected the real interest rate?

8. During the years after World War II, there was a big increase in the birth rate that created the so-called baby boom generation. That generation is fast approaching retirement age.
   a. What do you predict will happen to the saving rate when the baby boom generation retires?
   b. How will the real interest rate be affected?
   c. Do you expect production to become more capital intensive?

9. Since 1983, the United States has borrowed $4 trillion from the rest of the world that has financed capital expenditures.
   a. Draw a demand-supply graph of the U.S. capital market to show the effects of this inflow of funds from abroad on the quantity of capital, the real interest rate, and the amount of domestic saving.
   b. Draw a graph of the U.S. labor market to show the effects of this inflow of funds from abroad on the quantity of labor employed and the real wage rate.
   c. Show the effects in your demand-supply graph of the U.S. capital market if the government restricted the amount that firms were permitted to borrow from abroad.
   d. Show the effects in your demand-supply graph of the U.S. labor market if the government restricted the amount that firms were permitted to borrow from abroad.

10. Hong Kong is much more densely populated than the United States is. How do you think the rent on land compares in Hong Kong with that in Chicago? Can you explain why the percentage of commercial buildings that are new in downtown Chicago is less than in Hong Kong?

11. "As more people buy Internet service, the price of Internet service will fall. The fall in the price of Internet service will lead to a fall in the wage rate paid to Web page designers." Is this statement true or false? Explain your answer.

12. Draw demand-supply graphs of the U.S. labor markets and capital markets to show the effects of the increased provision of airport security following the September 11, 2001, attacks.

Critical Thinking

13. In 1811, in England, the real wage rate of young, unskilled mill workers was cut. The workers, led by Ned Ludd and known as Luddites, broke into factories at night and destroyed the new machines that their employers were using.
    a. If technological change increases productivity, why didn't the development of new cotton and wool milling technologies at the beginning of the 1800s increase rather than decrease the wage rate of mill workers?
    b. Do you think any workers benefited from the advance in technology in the cotton and wool industries of the early 1800s?
    c. How do you think the actions of the Luddites affected the wage rate of unskilled mill workers?
    d. Write a note to Ned Ludd explaining why he would or would not be wise to encourage people to destroy machines. (Ignore the fact that the actions of the Luddites were illegal.)

14. What parallels can you see between the introduction of machines in the cotton mills and wool mills of the early 1800s and the introduction of computers in the telecommunications industry at the end of the 1900s? Consider the effects on the demand for labor in all the markets affected.

15. Explain why you think that technological changes that lower wage rates justify or do not justify minimum wage laws.

Web Exercises

Use the links on MyEconLab to work the following exercises.

16. Visit the Web site of monster.com.
    a. Create your free user account.
    b. Search for a job that interests you.
    c. Are there any jobs that match your interests?
    d. Who pays for monster.com?

17. Visit the Web site of the New York Stock Exchange.
    a. What happened to the prices of stocks on the average over this day?
    b. Find the price of the stock of a company that interests you.
    c. Is the stock of the company you've chosen performing better or worse than average? Why do you think that might be?

18. Visit the Web site of the U.S. Open tennis tournament and look at the prize money lists for men's and women's singles, doubles, and mixed doubles. Also visit the PGA to check the prize money for the 2005 PGA championship and the LPGA to check the prize money for the LPGA.
    a. What main differences and similarities do you notice between the earnings of women and men in tennis and golf?
    b. How might you use the theory of the labor market that you've learned in this chapter to explain the differences and similarities?
    c. In particular, why do you think women earn the same as men in tennis but much less than men in golf? (Note that in tennis, men play longer matches than women but in golf, both sexes play the same type of course.)

CHAPTER 19

Inequality and Poverty

CHAPTER CHECKLIST

When you have completed your study of this chapter, you will be able to

1 Describe the economic inequality and poverty in the United States.

2 Explain how economic inequality and poverty arise.

3 Explain why governments redistribute income and describe the effects of redistribution on economic inequality and poverty.

Billionaires Michael Bloomberg (New York City mayor) and Rupert Murdoch (CEO of News Corp, which owns Fox News and movie studios) are watching the sun setting across the Hudson River and the city skyline beyond from a penthouse high above Central Park. The temperature is falling and on the street below this mansion in the sky, a small group of men and women huddle in a shop doorway to escape the biting wind. Tonight, they will sleep in cardboard boxes and seek warmth from subway grates. They are frostbitten, hungry, and lonely. They have neither jobs, homes, nor hope.

Why are some people exceedingly rich while others are very poor? Are the rich getting richer and the poor getting poorer? How do taxes, social security, welfare, and health-care programs influence economic inequality?

The goal of this chapter is to examine these emotion-charged questions using the dispassionate tools of economics. You will learn how we measure economic inequality, how it arises, and how government actions influence it.

19.1 ECONOMIC INEQUALITY IN THE UNITED STATES

We measure economic inequality by looking at the distributions of income and wealth. A household's *income* is the amount that it receives in a given period. A household's *wealth* is the value of the things it owns at a point in time.

Imagine the population of the United States lined up from the lowest to the highest income earner. Now divide the line into five equal-sized groups, each with 20 percent of the population. Then share out total income among these groups so that the shares represent the U.S. income distribution. Table 19.1(a) lists the percentages received by each group. The lowest 20 percent receives 3.4 percent of total income, while the richest 20 percent receives 50 percent.

Next share out the pie of total wealth. Table 19.1(b) shows the percentages owned by each of seven groups. The poorest 40 percent owns 0.2 percent of total wealth, while the richest 1 percent owns 38.1 percent.

■ Lorenz Curves

Lorenz curve

A curve that graphs the cumulative percentage of income (or wealth) against the cumulative percentage of households.

A **Lorenz curve** graphs the cumulative percentage of income (or wealth) on the *y*-axis against the cumulative percentage of households on the *x*-axis. Figure 19.1 shows the Lorenz curves for income and wealth in the United States. Graphing the cumulative percentage of income against the cumulative percentage of households makes the Lorenz curve for income and the points *A* to *D* on the graph correspond to the rows identified by those letters in the table. For example, row *B* and point *B* show that the 40 percent of households with the lowest incomes received 12.1 percent of total income—3.4 percent plus 8.7 percent from Table 19.1(a).

■ TABLE 19.1

The Income Distribution and Wealth Distribution in the United States

(a) Income distribution in 2004: median household income $44,389

		Households		Income	
		Percentage	**Cumulative percentage**	**Percentage**	**Cumulative percentage**
A	Lowest 20	20		3.4	3.4
B	Second 20	40		8.7	12.1
C	Third 20	60		14.7	26.8
D	Fourth 20	80		23.2	50.0
E	Highest 20	100		50.0	100.0

(b) Wealth distribution in 1998: median household wealth $60,700

		Households		Wealth	
		Percentage	**Cumulative percentage**	**Percentage**	**Cumulative percentage**
A'	Lowest 40	40		0.2	0.2
B'	Next 20	60		4.5	4.7
C'	Next 20	80		11.9	16.6
D'	Next 10	90		12.5	29.1
E'	Next 5	95		11.5	40.6
F'	Next 4	99		21.3	61.9
G'	Highest 1	100		38.1	100.0

SOURCES OF DATA: DeNavas-Walt, Carmen, Bernadette D. Proctor, and Cheryl Hill Lee, U.S. Census Bureau, Current Population Reports, P60–229, *Income, Poverty, and Health Insurance Coverage in the United States: 2004*, U.S. Government Printing Office, Washington, DC, 2005, and Edward N. Wolff, "Recent Trends in Wealth Ownership, 1983–1998," Jerome Levy Economics Institute Working Paper No. 300, April 2000.

FIGURE 19.1

Lorenz Curves for Income and Wealth in the United States

Cumulative percentage of		
Households	**Income**	**Wealth**
20	A 3.4	0
40	B 12.1	A' 0.2
60	C 26.8	B' 4.7
80	D 50.0	C' 16.6
90		D'29.1
95		E' 40.6
99		F' 61.9

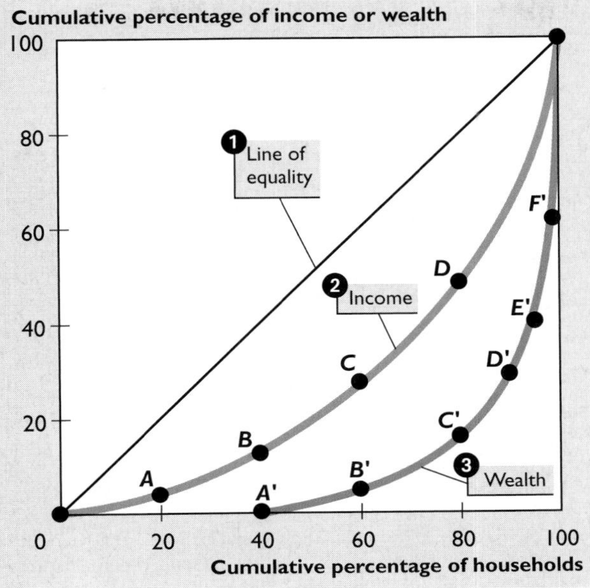

① If income and wealth were distributed equally, the Lorenz curve would lie along the straight line labeled "Line of equality."

② The income Lorenz curve shows the cumulative percentage of income graphed against the cumulative percentage of households. The 20 percent of households with the lowest incomes received 3.4 percent of total income, and the 20 percent of households with the highest incomes received 50 percent.

③ The wealth Lorenz curve shows the cumulative percentage of wealth graphed against the cumulative percentage of households. The poorest 40 percent of households owned 0.2 percent of total wealth, and the richest 1 percent owned 38.1 percent.

SOURCES OF DATA: See Table 19.1.

Graphing the cumulative percentage of wealth against the cumulative percentage of households makes the Lorenz curve for wealth and the points A' to F' on the graph correspond to the rows identified by those letters in the table of Figure 19.1. For example, row C' and point C' show that the poorest 80 percent of households owned 16.6 percent of total wealth—0.2 percent plus 4.5 percent plus 11.9 percent from Table 19.1(b).

If income (or wealth) were distributed equally, each 1 percent of households would receive 1 percent of total income (or own 1 percent of total wealth), and the cumulative percentage of income received (or wealth owned) by a given cumulative percentage of households would fall along the straight line labeled "Line of equality." The Lorenz curve is always below this line, and the closer the Lorenz curve is to the line of equality, the more equal is the distribution. You can see that the Lorenz curve for wealth is much farther away from the line of equality than is the Lorenz curve for income. The distribution of wealth is much more unequal than the distribution of income.

■ Inequality over Time

Has U.S. income inequality increased or decreased over the past few decades? It has increased. The highest incomes have increased much faster than the lower incomes and the gap between the rich and the poor has widened.

Figure 19.2(a) shows this widening gap by looking at the average incomes of each 20 percent (or quintile) group between 1967 and 2004. The numbers are expressed in 2004 dollars, which means that the effects of rising prices have been removed from the data. These numbers show us the changes in the real volumes of goods and services that people can afford to buy.

■ FIGURE 19.2

Trends in the Distribution of Income and Economic Mobility

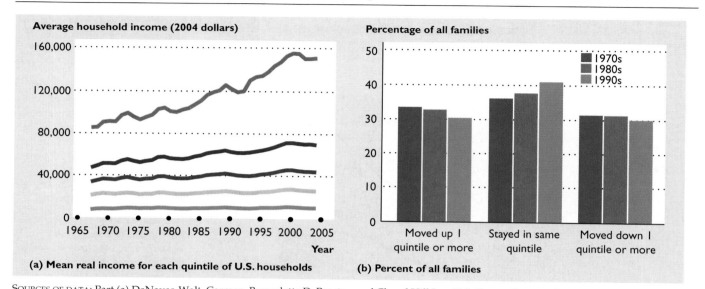

(a) Mean real income for each quintile of U.S. households

(b) Percent of all families

Sources of data: Part (a) DeNavas-Walt, Carmen, Bernadette D. Proctor, and Cheryl Hill Lee, U.S. Census Bureau, Current Population Reports, P60-229, *Income, Poverty, and Health Insurance Coverage in the United States: 2004,* U.S. Government Printing Office, Washington, DC, 2005; part (b) Katharine Bradbury and Jane Katz, "Are lifetime incomes becoming more unequal? Looking at new evidence on family income mobility," *Regional Review,* Federal Reserve Bank of Boston, Volume 12, Number 4, Quarter 4 2002, pp. 2–5.

In part (a), the average income of the highest 20 percent group increased from $85,000 a year in 1967 to $152,000 a year in 2004, a 77 percent increase. The average income of the lowest 20 percent group increased from $7,700 a year in 1967 to $10,300 a year in 2004, a 34 percent increase. The average income of the three middle groups also increased by 34 percent between 1967 and 2004.

In part (b), over a ten-year period, about 30 percent of families move up a quintile or more and a similar percentage move down a quintile or more. Between 35 and 40 percent of families remain in the same quintile. Mobility through the quintiles has decreased over the 1980s and 1990s.

You can see that the highest quintile have seen their incomes grow from about $85,000 a year in 1967 to $152,000 a year in 2004, a 77 percent increase. In contrast, the lowest quintile have seen their incomes grow from about $7,700 a year in 1967 to $10,300 a year in 2004, a 34 percent increase. The three middle quintiles have seen their incomes increase by a similar percentage to that of the lowest quintile.

■ Economic Mobility

Economic mobility is the movement of a family up or down the income ladder and through the income quintiles. If there were no economic mobility, a family would be stuck at a given point in the income distribution and be persistently poor, or rich, or somewhere in the middle. Also, in such a situation, the data on annual income distribution would be a good indicator of life-time inequality.

But if there is economic mobility, families move upward or downward through the income distribution and life-time inequality is not as severe as the inequality apparent in the data for a single year. How much economic mobility is there?

Katharine Bradbury and Jane Katz, economists at the Federal Reserve Bank of Boston, have provided an answer to this question and Figure 19.2(b) shows what they found. The figure shows the percentages of families that moved up or down the income ladder by one quintile or more over a ten-year period. It also shows the percentage of families that remained in the same quintile.

You can see from Figure 19.2(b) that there is quite a lot of economic mobility. About 30 percent of families move up by a quintile or more during a decade and a slightly smaller percentage move down by a quintile or more. Between 35 percent and 40 percent of families remain in the same quintile.

What is the source of economic mobility? Much of it arises from normal changes over a family's life cycle. Most families start out with a low income and are in one of the bottom three quintiles. Many of these families experience income growth as their workers become more skilled and experienced and in some cases, income grows by enough to move the family up a quintile or more. As a family continues to get older and its workers retire, its income falls. At this stage, some families move down a quintile or more.

So if we look at three households that have identical lifetime incomes—that are *economically equal*—but one is young, one is middle-aged, and one is old, we will see a great deal of inequality. Inequality of annual incomes overstates the degree of lifetime inequality.

You've seen that income inequality is increasing. But is economic mobility also increasing? The data in Figure 19.2(b) answer this question. And they show a

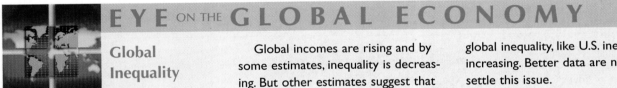

EYE ON THE GLOBAL ECONOMY

Global Inequality

Global incomes are rising and by some estimates, inequality is decreasing. But other estimates suggest that global inequality, like U.S. inequality, is increasing. Better data are needed to settle this issue.

There is much more income inequality in the global economy than in the United States. The Lorenz curves in this figure provide a comparative picture. You can see that the global Lorenz curve lies much farther from the line of equality than does the U.S. Lorenz curve.

Numbers that highlight the comparison are the percentages of families that get a half (50 percent) of the income. In the United States, the top 20 percent of families get a half of the income and the remaining 80 percent share the other half. In the global economy the top 10 percent of families get a half of the income and the remaining 90 percent share the other half.

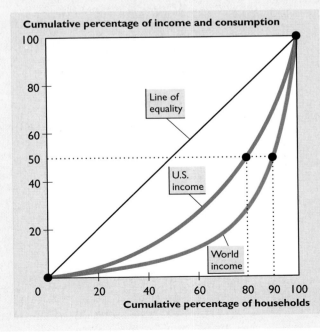

Sources of data: U.S. see Figure 19.1. World, Branko Milanovic, "True World Income Distribution, 1988 and 1993: First Calculation Based on Household Surveys Alone", *Economic Journal*, 112, 2002.

trend toward less economic mobility, not more. A decreasing percentage of families is moving either up or down a quintile or more and an increasing percentage of families is remaining in the same quintile. Why economic mobility has decreased remains a question for future research.

■ Who Are the Rich and the Poor?

The lowest-income household in the United States today is likely to consist of a black woman over 65 years of age who lives alone somewhere in the South and has fewer than nine years of elementary school education. The highest-income household in the United States today is likely to consist of a college-educated white married couple between 45 and 54 years of age living together with two children somewhere in the Northeast or the West.

These snapshot profiles are the extremes in Figure 19.3. That figure illustrates the importance of education, size of household, marital status, age of householder, race, and region of residence in influencing the size of a household's income. The range arising from education differences is the largest—from $18,800 a year for people with less than grade 9 to $76,000 a year for people with a bachelor's degree or higher. Household size, marital status, and age are also important. Race and region of residence have much smaller effects than do these first four factors.

■ **FIGURE 19.3**

The Distribution of Income by Selected Household Characteristics in 2004

Education is the single biggest factor affecting the distribution of household income, but size of household, marital status, and age of householder are also important. Race and region of residence also play a role.

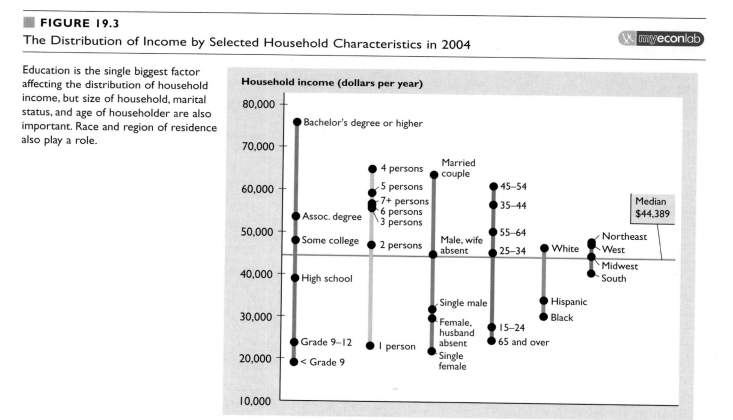

SOURCE OF DATA: U.S. Bureau of the Census, Current Population Reports, P60–218, 2001; P60–229, 2004 (see Table 19.1 for details.)

■ Poverty

Households with very low incomes are so poor that they are considered to be living in poverty. What is poverty? How do we measure it, how much is there, and is the amount of poverty decreasing or increasing?

Poverty Defined

Poverty is a state in which a household's income is too low to be able to buy the quantities of food, shelter, and clothing that are deemed necessary. Poverty is a *relative* concept. Millions of people living in Africa and Asia survive on incomes of less than $400 a year. Almost no one in the United States experiences this degree of poverty. But there are some very poor people in the United States compared with the average.

Poverty
A state in which a household's income is too low to be able to buy the quantities of food, shelter, and clothing that are deemed necessary.

Measurement, Incidence, and Trends

To measure the degree of poverty, the Census Bureau considers a household to be living in poverty if its income is less than some defined level. The level varies with household size and is updated each year. In 2004, the poverty level for a household with 2 adults and 2 children was an income of $19,157. In that year, 37 million or 12.7 percent of Americans lived in households that had incomes below the poverty level.

Figure 19.4 shows the level, trends in, and distribution by race of poverty in the United States. Black and Hispanic households are more than twice as likely to be poor as are white households. In 2004, the poverty rates were 10.8 percent for whites, 24.7 percent for blacks, and 21.9 percent for Hispanics.

▓ FIGURE 19.4
Poverty Rates in the United States

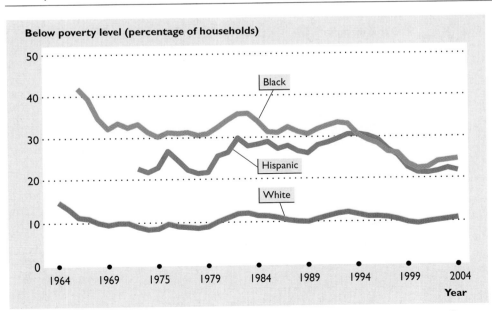

Poverty rates for blacks and Hispanics were about double those for whites in 2004. The poverty rate of black households has fallen in two waves: the late 1960s and the late 1990s. The poverty rate of Hispanics also fell during the late 1990s, but it had previously increased. The poverty rate of whites fell during the 1960s but then remained fairly steady.

Source of data: U.S. Bureau of the Census, *Income, Poverty, and Health Insurance Coverage in the United States: 2004,* Current Population Reports, P60–229.

The trends in poverty have been downward—and strikingly so during the late 1990s for black and Hispanic households. The poverty rate of black households had also fallen during the late 1960s. So between 1965 and 2004, the poverty rate for blacks halved. The fall in the poverty rate of Hispanic households during the late 1990s came after a previous increase, so the poverty rate of this group was the same in 2004 as it had been 30 years earlier.

Poverty Duration

Another dimension of poverty is its duration. If a household is in poverty for a few months it faces serious hardship during those months, but it faces a less serious problem than it would if its poverty persisted for several months or, worse yet, for several years.

Because the duration of poverty is an important additional indicator of the hardship that poverty brings, the Census Bureau has provided measures of duration for the years 1996 to 1999. Figure 19.5 shows these data.

It turns out that more than 50 percent of poverty lasts for between 2 and 4 months. So for about a half of poor families, their most severe problems are not persistent. But almost 30 percent of poverty lasts for more than 9 months. So a seriously large number of households experience chronic poverty.

In the next sections, we look at the sources of inequality and poverty and the policies that aim to redistribute income and lift the living standard of the poor.

■ **FIGURE 19.5**

The Duration of Poverty Spells in the United States

More than 50 percent of the people who fall below the poverty level remain in that state for 2 to 4 months. Almost 30 percent of the people who fall below the poverty level remain in that state for more than 9 months.

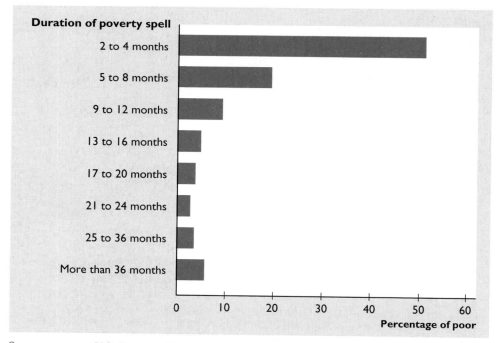

SOURCE OF DATA: U.S. Bureau of the Census, *Dynamics of Economic Well-Being: Poverty 1996–1999,* Current Population Reports, P70–91.

CHECKPOINT 19.1

1   **Describe the economic inequality and poverty in the United States.**

Practice Problem 19.1

1. Table 19.1(a) on page 468 shows the distribution of income in the United States. Table 1 shows the distribution of income in Canada:
   a. Create a table that shows the cumulative percentages of households and income in Canada.
   b. Draw the Lorenz curves for Canada and the United States.
   c. Compare the distribution of income in Canada with that in the United States. Which distribution is more unequal?

TABLE 1

Households	Income (percentage)
Lowest 20 percent	7.4
Second 20 percent	13.2
Third 20 percent	18.1
Fourth 20 percent	24.9
Highest 20 percent	36.4

Exercise 19.1

1. Table 19.1(a) on page 468 shows the distribution of income in the United States, the table in the practice problem above shows the distribution of income in Canada, and Table 2 shows the distribution of income in the United Kingdom:
   a. Create a table that shows the cumulative percentages of households and income in the United Kingdom.
   b. Draw the Lorenz curves for the United Kingdom, Canada, and the United States.
   c. Compare the distribution of income in the United Kingdom with that in the United States. Which distribution is more unequal?
   d. Compare the distribution of income in the United Kingdom with that in Canada. Which distribution is more unequal?

TABLE 2

Households	Income (percentage)
Lowest 20 percent	3
Second 20 percent	5
Third 20 percent	14
Fourth 20 percent	25
Highest 20 percent	53

Solution to Practice Problem 19.1

1a. The following table shows the cumulative percentages of households and income.

Households	Income (percentage)	Cumulative percentage of Households	Cumulative percentage of Income
Lowest 20 percent	7.4	Lowest 20	7.4
Second 20 percent	13.2	Lowest 40	20.6
Third 20 percent	18.1	Lowest 60	38.7
Fourth 20 percent	24.9	Lowest 80	63.6
Highest 20 percent	36.4	100	100.0

1b. Lorenz curve plots the cumulative percentage of income against the cumulative percentage of households. The blue curve in Figure 1 plots these data.

1c. The line of equality shows an equal distribution. The Canadian Lorenz curve lies closer to the line of equality than does the U.S. Lorenz curve, so the distribution of income in the United States is more unequal than that in Canada.

FIGURE 1

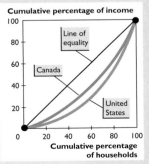

19.2 HOW INEQUALITY AND POVERTY ARISE

Economic inequality and poverty arise from a wide variety of factors. The five key ones that we'll examine here are

- Human capital
- Discrimination
- Financial and physical capital
- Entrepreneurial ability
- Personal and family characteristics

■ Human Capital

Human capital is the accumulated skill and knowledge of human beings. To see how human capital differences affect economic inequality, we'll study an economy with two levels of human capital, which we'll call *high-skilled labor* and *low-skilled labor*. Low-skilled labor might be law clerks, hospital orderlies, or bank tellers, and high-skilled labor might be attorneys, surgeons, or bank CEOs.

The Demand for High-Skilled and Low-Skilled Labor

High-skilled workers can perform tasks that low-skilled workers would perform badly or couldn't even perform at all. Imagine an untrained person doing surgery or piloting an airplane. High-skilled workers have a higher value of marginal product (*VMP*) than low-skilled workers do. As we learned in Chapter 18, a firm's demand for labor curve is derived from and is the same as the firm's value of marginal product of labor curve.

Figure 19.6(a) shows the demand curves for high-skilled and low-skilled labor. At any given employment level, firms are willing to pay a higher wage rate to a high-skilled worker than to a low-skilled worker. The gap between the two wage rates measures the value of marginal product of skill—for example, at an employment level of 2,000 hours, firms are willing to pay a high-skilled worker $25 an hour and a low-skilled worker only $10 an hour, a difference of $15 an hour. Thus the value of marginal product of skill is $15 an hour.

The Supply of High-Skilled and Low-Skilled Labor

Skills are costly to acquire. The opportunity cost of acquiring a skill includes actual expenditures, such as tuition, and costs in the form of lost or reduced earnings while the skill is being acquired. When a person goes to school full time, that cost is the total earnings forgone. But some people acquire skills on the job. Such skill acquisition is called on-the-job training. Usually, a worker who is undergoing on-the-job training is paid a lower wage rate than one who is doing a comparable job but not undergoing training. In such a case, the cost of acquiring the skill is equal to the wage paid to a person not being trained minus the wage paid to a person being trained.

Because skills are costly to acquire, a high-skilled person is not willing to work for the same wage that a low-skilled person is willing to accept. The position of the supply curve of high-skilled workers reflects the cost of acquiring the skill. Figure 19.6(b) shows two supply curves: one of high-skilled workers and the other of low-skilled workers. The supply curve of high-skilled workers is S_H, and that of low-skilled workers is S_L.

■ **FIGURE 19.6**
Skill Differentials

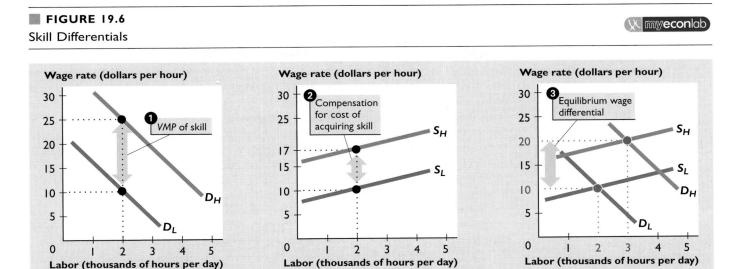

(a) Demand for high-skilled and low-skilled labor

(b) Supply of high-skilled and low-skilled labor

(c) Markets for high-skilled and low-skilled labor

In part (a), D_L is the demand curve for low-skilled labor and D_H is the demand curve for high-skilled labor. ❶ The vertical distance between these two curves is the value of marginal product of the skill.

In part (b), S_L is the supply curve of low-skilled workers and S_H is the supply curve of high-skilled workers. ❷ The vertical distance

between these two curves is the required compensation for the cost of acquiring a skill.

In part (c), in equilibrium, low-skilled workers earn a wage rate of $10 an hour and high-skilled workers earn a wage rate of $20 an hour. ❸ The $10 wage differential is the equilibrium effect of acquiring skill.

The high-skilled worker's supply curve lies above the low-skilled worker's supply curve. The vertical distance between the two supply curves is the compensation that high-skilled workers require for the cost of acquiring the skill. For example, suppose that the quantity of low-skilled labor supplied is 2,000 hours at a wage rate of $10 an hour. This wage rate compensates the low-skilled workers mainly for their time on the job. Consider next the supply of high-skilled workers. To induce high-skilled labor to supply 2,000 hours, firms must pay a wage rate of $17 an hour. This wage rate for high-skilled labor is higher than that for low-skilled labor because high-skilled labor must be compensated not only for the time on the job but also for the time and other costs of acquiring the skill.

Wage Rates of High-Skilled and Low-Skilled Labor

To work out the wage rates of high-skilled and low-skilled labor, we have to bring together the effects of skill on the demand for and supply of labor.

Figure 19.6(c) shows the demand curves and the supply curves for high-skilled and low-skilled labor. These curves are the same as those plotted in parts (a) and (b). Equilibrium occurs in the market for low-skilled labor where the supply and demand curves for low-skilled labor intersect. The equilibrium wage rate is $10 an hour, and the quantity of low-skilled labor employed is 2,000 hours. Equilibrium in the market for high-skilled workers occurs where the supply and demand curves for high-skilled workers intersect. The equilibrium wage rate is $20 an hour, and the quantity of high-skilled labor employed is 3,000 hours.

As you can see in Figure 19.6(c), the equilibrium wage rate of high-skilled labor is higher than that of low-skilled labor. There are two reasons why this occurs: First, high-skilled labor has a higher value of marginal product than does low-skilled labor, so at a given wage rate, the quantity of high-skilled labor demanded exceeds that of low-skilled labor. Second, skills are costly to acquire, so at a given wage rate, the quantity of high-skilled labor supplied is less than that of low-skilled labor. The wage differential (in this case, $10 an hour) depends on both the value of marginal product of the skill and the cost of acquiring it. The higher the value of marginal product of the skill, the larger is the vertical distance between the demand curves. The more costly it is to acquire a skill, the larger is the vertical distance between the supply curves. The higher the value of marginal product of the skill and the more costly it is to acquire, the larger is the wage differential between high-skilled and low-skilled workers.

Education and on-the-job training enable people to acquire skills and move up through the income distribution. But education is the most important contributor to a higher income, as you can see in *Eye on the U.S. Economy* below.

Discrimination, which we examine next, is another possible source of economic inequality.

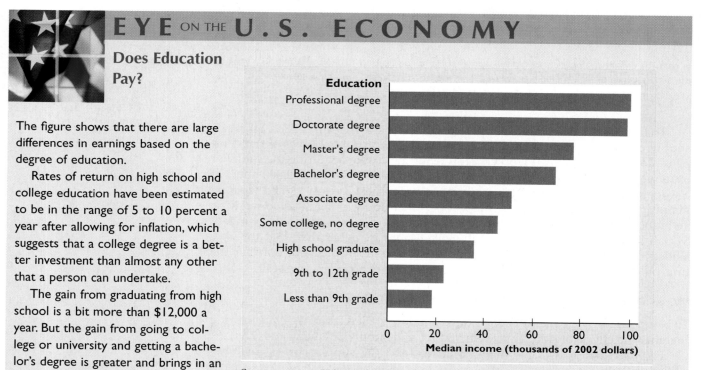

EYE ON THE U.S. ECONOMY

Does Education Pay?

The figure shows that there are large differences in earnings based on the degree of education.

Rates of return on high school and college education have been estimated to be in the range of 5 to 10 percent a year after allowing for inflation, which suggests that a college degree is a better investment than almost any other that a person can undertake.

The gain from graduating from high school is a bit more than $12,000 a year. But the gain from going to college or university and getting a bachelor's degree is greater and brings in an additional $18,000 a year.

Remaining at the university to complete a master's degree (usually one more year of study) brings in an extra

SOURCE OF DATA: U.S. Bureau of the Census, *Statistical Abstract of the United States*, 2004, Table 667.

$7,000 a year, and working for a professional degree or doctorate increases income by more than $22,000 a year.

■ Discrimination

Large and persistent earnings differences exist between women and men and among the races. You can see them in *Eye on the U.S. Economy* below. Does discrimination contribute to these differences? It might. But economists do not yet have the ability to isolate and measure the effect of discrimination, so we can't say exactly whether or by how much the differences arise from this source.

For discrimination to bring persistent wage differences, people must be willing to pay to indulge their prejudices. If they are not willing to pay, then any wage difference would encourage people who are prejudiced to hire (or buy from) the people against whom they are prejudiced. This force would eliminate the wage differences.

But if people are willing to pay to indulge their prejudices, wage differences can persist. For example, suppose that black women and white men have identical abilities as investment advisors. With everyone free of prejudice about race and sex, the two groups have the same value of marginal product, face the same demand curve for their services, and earn the same wage. But if some people are so prejudiced that they are not willing to pay as much for the investment advice of a black woman as they are for that of a white man, then the value of marginal product of black women is lower than that of white men. And the demand for investment advice from black women is lower than that from white men. The result is a lower equilibrium wage rate (and fewer high-paying jobs) for black women than for white men.

EYE ON THE U.S. ECONOMY

Sex and Race Earnings Differences

The figure shows the earnings of different race and sex groups expressed as a percentage of the earnings of white men.

In 2003, white women earned, on the average, 79 percent of what white men earned. Black men earned 78 percent, and black women earned 69 percent. The lowest-income groups, men and women of Hispanic origin, earned only 65 percent and 57 percent, respectively, of white men's wages.

These earnings differentials have persisted over many years, and only those of women have begun to narrow in a significant way.

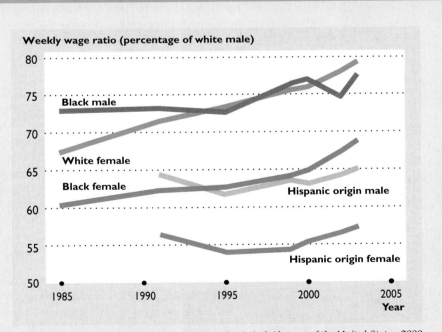

Source of data: U.S. Bureau of the Census, *Statistical Abstract of the United States:* 2000, Table 696 and 2004, Table 623.

■ Financial and Physical Capital

The people with the highest incomes are usually those who own large amounts of financial capital and physical capital. These people receive incomes in the form of interest and dividend payments and from capital gains—increases in the stock market value.

Families with a large amount of capital tend to become even more wealthy across generations for two reasons. First, they bequeath wealth to their children and second, rich people marry rich partners (on the average).

Saving, and the wealth accumulation that it brings, is not inevitably a source of increased inequality and can even be a source of increased equality. When a household saves to redistribute an uneven income over the life cycle, it enjoys more equal consumption. Also, if a lucky generation that has a high income saves a large amount and makes a bequest to a generation that is unlucky, this act of saving also decreases the degree of inequality.

■ Entrepreneurial Ability

Some of the most spectacularly rich people have benefited from unusual entrepreneurial talent. Household names such as Bill Gates (Microsoft), Michael Dell (Dell Computers), and Sam Walton (Wal-Mart) are examples of people who began life with modest amounts of wealth and modest incomes and through a combination of hard work, good luck, and outstanding entrepreneurship have become extremely rich.

But some very poor people, and some who fall below the poverty level, have also tried their hands at being entrepreneurs. We don't hear much about these people. They are not in the headlines. But they have put together a business plan, borrowed heavily, and through a combination of hard work, bad luck, and in some cases poor decisions have become extremely poor.

■ Personal and Family Characteristics

Each individual's personal and family characteristics play a crucial role, for either good or ill, in influencing economic well-being.

People who are exceptionally good looking and talented with stable and creative families enjoy huge advantages over the average person. Many movie stars, entertainers, and extraordinarily talented athletes are in this category. These people enjoy some of the highest incomes because their personal or family characteristics make the value of the marginal product of their labor very large.

Success often breeds yet further success. A large income can generate a large amount of saving, which in turn generates yet more interest income.

Adverse personal circumstances, such as chronic physical or mental illness, drug abuse, or an unstable home life possibly arising from the absence of a parent or from an abusive parent, place a huge burden on many people and result in low incomes and even poverty.

A tough life, just like its opposite, can be self-reinforcing. Weak physical or mental health makes it difficult to study and obtain a skill and results in a low labor income or no income because a job is just too hard to hold down. And the children of the poorest people find it hard to get into college and university and so find it difficult to break the cycle of poverty.

CHECKPOINT 19.2

2 **Explain how economic inequality and poverty arise.**

Practice Problem 19.2

1. In the United States in 2000, 30 million people had full-time managerial and professional jobs that paid an average of $800 a week. At the same time, 10 million people had full-time sales positions that paid an average of $530 a week.
    a. Explain why managers and professionals are paid more than salespeople.
    b. Explain why, despite the higher weekly wage, more people are employed as managers and professionals than as salespeople.
    c. Shopping online has become popular and more and more firms offer their goods and services for sale online. If this trend continues, how do you think the market for salespeople will change in coming years?

Exercises 19.2

1. In the United States in 2000, 2 million people worked full-time in protective services and were paid an average of $600 a week. At the same time, 7 million people worked as full-time machine operators and were paid an average of $450 a week.
    a. Explain why people who are employed in protective services are paid more than machine operators.
    b. Explain why fewer people are employed in protective services than as machine operators.

2. In Canada and Australia, the manager of a manufacturing plant earns 20 times what the factory floor worker earns. In Hong Kong and Malaysia, such a manager earns 40 times what the factory floor worker earns. Can you explain this difference?

Solution to Practice Problem 19.2

1a. A typical manager or professional has incurred a higher cost of education and on-the-job training than has the typical salesperson. The supply curve of managers and professionals, S_H, lies above that of salespeople, S_L (Figure 1). The better education and more on-the-job training result in managers and professionals having more human capital and a higher value of marginal product than that of a salesperson. The demand curve for managers and professionals, D_H, is greater than the demand for salespeople, D_L. Figure 1 shows that the combination of demand and supply leads to a higher wage rate for managers and professionals than for salespeople.

1b. Figure 1 shows that the demand and supply for each type of labor leads to a greater employment for managers and professionals than for salespeople.

1c. As shopping online continues to grow, firms will hire fewer salespeople. The demand for salespeople will decrease, and fewer people will work in sales. What will happen to their wage rate will depend on how the supply of salespeople will change.

FIGURE 1

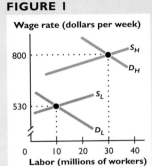

Wage rate (dollars per week)

Labor (millions of workers)

19.3 INCOME REDISTRIBUTION

We've described the distribution of income and wealth in the United States and examined the five main sources of economic inequality and poverty. Our task in the final section of this chapter is to study the *redistribution* of income by government.

How do governments redistribute income? What is the scale of redistribution? Why do we vote for policies that redistribute income? What are the challenges in designing policies that achieve a fair and efficient distribution of income and reduction of poverty?

■ How Governments Redistribute Income

The three main ways in which governments in the United States redistribute income are

- Income taxes
- Income maintenance programs
- Subsidized services

Income Taxes

Income taxes may be progressive, regressive, or proportional (see Chapter 8, p. 197). A *progressive income tax* is one that taxes income at an average rate that increases with the level of income. A *regressive income tax* is one that taxes income at an average rate that decreases with the level of income. A *proportional income tax* (also called a *flat-rate income tax*) is one that taxes income at a constant rate, regardless of the level of income.

The income tax rates that apply in the United States are composed of two parts: federal and state taxes. Some cities, such as New York City, also have an income tax. There is variety in the detailed tax arrangements in the individual states, but the tax system, at both the federal and state levels, is progressive. The poorest working households receive money from the government through an earned income tax credit. The middle-income households pay 15 percent of each additional dollar they earn, and successively richer households pay 25 percent, 28 percent, 33 percent, and 35 percent of each additional dollar earned.

Income Maintenance Programs

Three main types of programs redistribute income by making direct payments (in cash, services, or vouchers) to people in the lower part of the income distribution. They are

- Social Security programs
- Unemployment compensation
- Welfare programs

Social Security Programs   Social Security is a public insurance system paid for by compulsory payroll taxes on employers and employees. Social Security has two main components: Old Age, Survivors, Disability, and Health Insurance or OASDHI, which provides monthly cash payments to retired or disabled workers or their surviving spouses and children; and Medicare, which provides hospital and health insurance for the elderly and disabled. In 2005, Social Security supported 48 million people, who received average monthly checks of $874.

Unemployment Compensation   To provide an income to unemployed workers, every state has established an unemployment compensation program. Under these programs, a tax is paid that is based on the income of each covered worker and such a worker receives a benefit when he or she becomes unemployed. The details of the benefits vary from state to state.

Welfare Programs   The purpose of welfare programs is to provide incomes for people who do not qualify for Social Security or unemployment compensation. The programs are

1. Supplementary Security Income (SSI) program, which is designed to help the neediest elderly, disabled, and blind people

2. Temporary Assistance for Needy Families (TANF) program, which is designed to help families that have inadequate financial resources

3. Food Stamp program, which is designed to help the poorest households obtain a basic diet

4. Medicaid, which is designed to cover the costs of medical care for households that receive help under the SSI and TANF programs

Subsidized Services

A great deal of redistribution takes place in the United States through the provision of subsidized services—services provided by the government at prices far below the cost of production. The taxpayers who consume these goods and services receive a transfer in kind from the taxpayers who do not consume them. The two most important areas in which this form of redistribution takes place are education—both kindergarten through grade 12 and college and university—and health care. But neither necessarily redistributes from the rich to the poor.

In 2005–2006, students who were enrolled in the University of California system who were not residents of California paid a tuition of $12,627 per semester. This amount is probably close to the cost of providing a semester's education at UCLA or Berkeley. But California residents paid tuition of only $3,717. So California households with a member enrolled at the University of California received a benefit from the government of almost $9,000 a semester. Many of these households have above-average incomes.

Government provision of health-care services has grown to equal the scale of private provision. Medicaid provides high-quality and high-cost health care to millions of people who earn too little to buy such services themselves. Medicaid redistributes from the rich to the poor. Medicare, which is available to all over 65 years of age, is not targeted at the poor.

■ The Scale of Income Redistribution

A household's income in the absence of government redistribution is called **market income.** We can measure the scale of income redistribution by calculating the percentage of market income paid in taxes minus the percentage received in benefits at each income level. The available data include redistribution through taxes and cash and noncash benefits to welfare recipients. The data do not include the value of subsidized services such as a college education, which might decrease the total scale of redistribution from the rich to the poor.

Figure 19.7 shows how government actions change the distribution of income. The blue Lorenz curve describes the market distribution of income. It is not the

Market income
A household's income earned from the markets for factors of production and with no government redistribution.

Money income

Market income plus money benefits paid by the government.

same as that in Figure 19.1, which is based on money income. **Money income** is market income plus money benefits paid by the government. The green Lorenz curve shows the income distribution based on this measure. The orange Lorenz curve shows the distribution of income after all taxes and benefits, including Medicaid and Medicare benefits. The distribution after taxes and benefits is more equal than the market distribution of income.

Figure 19.7(b) shows that redistribution increases the share received by the lowest 60 percent of households and decreases the share received by the highest 40 percent of households.

The sources of income at different income levels provide another measure of the scale of redistribution. The poorest 20 percent of households receive 80 percent of their income from the government. The second 20 percent receive around 33 percent of their income from the government. In contrast, the richest 20 percent receive almost nothing from the government but receive a third of their income from capital—interest and dividends from financial assets.

■ **FIGURE 19.7**

The Scale of Income Redistribution

Taxes and income maintenance programs reduce the degree of inequality that the market generates. In part (a), the Lorenz curve moves closer to the line of inequality.

Part (b) shows the redistribution in 2001 (the most recent year for which this type of income distribution data are available). The 20 percent of households with the lowest incomes received net benefits that increased their share of total income from 0.9 percent to 4.5 percent. The 20 percent of households with the highest incomes paid taxes that decreased their share of total income from 55.7 percent to 46.6 percent of total income.

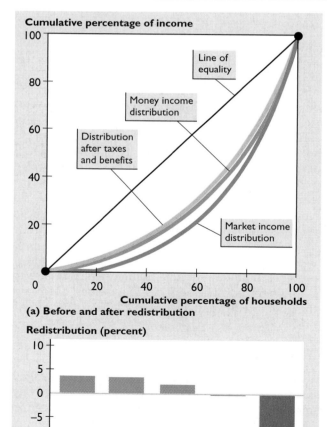

(a) Before and after redistribution

(b) Redistribution

SOURCE OF DATA: U.S. Bureau of the Census, *Money Income in the United States: 2001,* Current Population Reports, P60–218.

■ Why We Redistribute Income

Why do we vote for government polices that redistribute income? Why don't we leave everyone to make voluntary contributions to charities that help the poor?

There are two ways of approaching these questions: normative and positive. The normative approach discusses why we *should* compel everyone to help the poor and looks for principles to guide the appropriate scale of redistribution. The positive approach seeks reasons why we *do* compel everyone to help the poor and tries to explain the actual scale of redistribution.

Normative Theories of Income Redistribution

Philosophy and politics, not economics, are the subjects that consider the normative theories of redistribution. And not surprisingly, there are several different points of view on whether income should be redistributed and, if so, on what scale.

Utilitarianism points to the ideal distribution being one of equality. But efficiency is also desirable. And greater equality can be achieved only at the cost of greater inefficiency—the *big tradeoff* (defined in Chapter 6, p. 158). The redistribution of income creates the big tradeoff because it uses scarce resources and weakens incentives, which decreases the total size of the economic pie to be shared.

A dollar collected from a rich person does not translate into a dollar received by a poor person. Some of it gets used up in the process of redistribution. Tax-collecting agencies such as the Internal Revenue Service and welfare-administering agencies (as well as tax accountants and lawyers) use skilled labor, computers, and other scarce resources to do their work. The bigger the scale of redistribution, the greater is the opportunity cost of administering it.

But the cost of collecting taxes and making welfare payments is a small part of the total cost of redistribution. A bigger cost arises from the inefficiency—*excess burden*—of taxes and benefits (see Chapter 8, p. 192). Greater equality can be achieved only by taxing productive activities such as work and saving. Taxing people's income from their work and saving lowers the after-tax income they receive. This lower income makes them work and save less, which in turn results in smaller output and less consumption not only for the rich who pay the taxes but also for the poor who receive the benefits.

Benefit recipients as well as taxpayers face weaker incentives. In fact, under the welfare arrangements that prevailed before the 1996 reforms, the weakest incentives to work were those faced by households that benefited from welfare. When a welfare recipient got a job, benefits were withdrawn and eligibility for programs such as Medicaid ended, so the household in effect paid a tax of more than 100 percent on its earnings. This arrangement locked poor households in a welfare trap.

Recognizing the tension between equality and efficiency, John Rawls proposed the principle that income should be redistributed to the point at which it maximizes the size of the slice of the economic pie received by the person with the smallest slice (see Chapter 6, p. 159).

Libertarian philosophers such as Robert Nozick say that any redistribution is wrong because it violates the sanctity of private property and voluntary exchange. (see Chapter 6, p. 159).

Modern political parties stand in the center of the extremes that we've just described. Some favor a bit more redistribution than others, but the major political parties are broadly happy with the prevailing scale of redistribution.

Positive Theories of Income Redistribution

A good positive theory of income redistribution would explain why some countries have more redistribution than others and why redistribution has increased over the past 200 years. We don't have such a theory. But economists have proposed a promising idea called the median voter theory. The **median voter theory** is that the policies that governments pursue are those that make the median voter as well off as possible. If a proposal can be made that improves the well-being of the median voter, a political party that makes the proposal can improve its standing in an election.

Median voter theory
The theory that governments pursue policies that make the median voter as well off as possible.

The median voter theory arises from thinking about how a democratic political system such as that of the United States works. In this system, governments must propose policies that appeal to enough voters to get them elected. And in a majority voting system, the voter whose views carry the most weight is the one in the middle—the median voter.

The median voter wants income to be redistributed to the point at which her or his own after-tax income is as large as possible. Taxing the rich by too much would weaken their incentives to create businesses and jobs and lower the median voter's after-tax income. But taxing the rich by too little would leave some money on the table that could be transferred to the median voter.

The median voter might be concerned about the poor and want to reduce poverty. Unselfishly, the median voter might simply be concerned about the plight of the poor and want to help them. Self-interestedly, the median voter might believe that if there is too much poverty, there will be too much crime and some of it will touch her or his life.

If for either reason the median voter wants to help the poor, the political process will deliver a greater scale of redistribution to reflect this voter preference.

■ The Major Welfare Challenge

Among the poorest people in the United States (see p. 472) are young women who have not completed high school, have a child (or children), live without a partner, and are more likely to be black or Hispanic than white. These young women and their children present the major welfare challenge.

There are about 10 million single mothers, and a quarter of them receive no support from their children's fathers. The long-term solution to the problem of these women is education and job training—acquiring human capital. The short-term solution is welfare. But welfare must be designed in ways that strengthen the incentive to pursue the long-term solution. And a change in the U.S. welfare programs introduced during the 1990s pursues this approach.

The Current Approach: TANF

Passed in 1996, the Personal Responsibility and Work Opportunities Reconciliation Act created the Temporary Assistance for Needy Families (TANF) program. TANF is a block grant that is paid to the states, which administer payments to individuals. It is not an open-ended entitlement program. An adult member of a household receiving assistance must either work or perform community service. And there is a five-year limit for assistance.

These measures go a long way toward removing one of the most serious poverty problems while being sensitive to the potential inefficiency of welfare. But some economists want to go further and introduce a negative income tax.

Negative Income Tax

The negative income tax is not on the political agenda. But it is popular among economists, and it is the subject of several real-world experiments. A **negative income tax** provides every household with a guaranteed minimum annual income and taxes all earned income above the guaranteed minimum at a fixed rate. Suppose the guaranteed minimum annual income is $10,000 and the tax rate is 25 percent. A household with no earned income receives the $10,000 guaranteed minimum income from the government. This household "pays" income tax of *minus* $10,000, hence the name "negative income tax."

A household that earns $40,000 a year pays $10,000—25 percent of its earnings—to the government. But this household also receives from the government the $10,000 guaranteed minimum income, so it pays no income tax. It has the break-even income. Households that earn between zero and $40,000 a year receive more from the government than they pay to the government. They "pay" a negative income tax.

A household that earns $60,000 a year pays $15,000—25 percent of its earnings—to the government. But this household receives from the government the $10,000 guaranteed minimum income, so it pays an income tax of $5,000. All households that earn more than $40,000 a year pay more to the government than they receive from it. They pay a positive amount of tax.

A negative income tax doesn't eliminate the excess burden of taxation. But it improves the incentives to work and save at all levels of income.

Negative income tax
A tax and redistribution scheme that provides every household with a guaranteed minimum annual income and taxes all earned income above the guaranteed minimum at a fixed rate.

REALITY CHECK

Redistribution in YOUR Life

You are on both sides of the redistribution equation. But what's your bottom line? Are you a net receiver or a net payer? Try to figure out which.

First work out how much tax you're paying. If you have a job, your payslip shows the amount of income tax you're paying. You can calculate the sales taxes you pay by keeping a note for a week every time you buy something. You can work out how much gas, tobacco, and alcohol tax you pay by checking the scale of these taxes in your state at www.taxadmin.org.

Now for the benefits. If you're receiving any direct cash payments such as unemployment benefits, these are easy to identify. But most likely, you don't receive any money from the government. You do, though, receive the benefits of services provided by government. Your education costs more than the tuition you're paying. One estimate of the value of your education is the tuition paid by an out-of-state student minus the tuition paid by a state resident. Try to estimate what all the government-provided services are worth to you and then work out your bottom line.

3 **Explain why governments redistribute income and describe the effects of redistribution on economic inequality and poverty.**

Practice Problem 19.3

1. Table 1 shows the distribution of market income in an economy. The government redistributes income by collecting income taxes and paying benefits shown in Table 2.
   a. Calculate the income shares of each 20 percent of households after tax and redistribution.
   b. Draw this economy's Lorenz curve before and after taxes and benefits.

Exercises 19.3

1. In the economy in the practice problem, the government lowers the tax rate on the third 20 percent to 15 percent, on the fourth 20 percent to 25 percent, and on the highest 20 percent to 30 percent but benefits are unchanged.
   a. Calculate the income shares of each 20 percent of households after tax and redistribution.
   b. Draw this economy's Lorenz curve before and after taxes and benefits.

2. In the economy in the practice problem, the government increases the benefits paid to the lowest 20 percent to $12 million, to the second 20 percent to $10 million, and to the third 20 percent to $5 million but keeps the tax rates unchanged. Calculate the income shares of each 20 percent of households after tax and redistribution.

Solution to Practice Problem 19.3

1a. To find the distribution of income, multiply the market incomes by the tax rates, subtract the taxes paid, and add the benefits received to obtain the income after tax and benefits. Then calculate each group's income as a percentage of total income. The following table summarizes the calculations.

TABLE 1

Households	Income (millions of dollars per year)
Lowest 20 percent	5
Second 20 percent	10
Third 20 percent	18
Fourth 20 percent	28
Highest 20 percent	39

TABLE 2

Households	Income tax (percent)	Benefits (millions of dollars)
Lowest 20 percent	0	10
Second 20 percent	10	8
Third 20 percent	18	3
Fourth 20 percent	28	0
Highest 20 percent	39	0

Households	Market Income (millions of dollars)	Tax paid (millions of dollars)	Benefits received (millions of dollars)	Income after tax and benefits (millions of dollars)	Income (percentage)
Lowest 20 percent	5	0.0	10	15.0	16.0
Second 20 percent	10	1.0	8	17.0	18.1
Third 20 percent	18	3.2	3	17.8	19.0
Fourth 20 percent	28	7.8	0	20.2	21.5
Highest 20 percent	39	15.2	0	23.8	25.4

1b. To draw the Lorenz curves, calculate the cumulative shares. For example, before taxes and benefits, the lowest 20 percent have 5 percent of total income and the lowest 40 percent have 15 percent (5 + 10) of total income. After taxes and benefits, the lowest 20 percent have 16 percent of total income and the lowest 40 percent have 34.1 percent (16 + 18.1) of total income. Figure 1 plots the Lorenz curves.

FIGURE 1

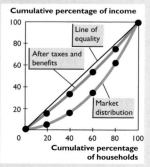

Cumulative percentage of income

Line of equality

After taxes and benefits

Market distribution

Cumulative percentage of households

CHAPTER CHECKPOINT

Key Points

1 **Describe the economic inequality and poverty in the United States.**

- The richest 1 percent of Americans own almost one third of the total wealth in the country.
- Income is distributed less unevenly than wealth. Throughout the 1970s and 1980s, inequality increased.
- The poorest people in the United States are single black women over 65 years of age with less than nine years of schooling who live in the South. The richest people live in the West and are college-educated, middle-aged, white families in which husband and wife live together.
- The distribution of wealth exaggerates the degree of inequality because it excludes human capital.
- The distribution of annual income exaggerates lifetime inequality.

2 **Explain how economic inequality and poverty arise.**

- Economic inequality arises from inequality of labor market outcomes, ownership of capital, entrepreneurial ability, and personal and family characteristics.
- In labor markets, skill differences result in earnings differences. Discrimination might also contribute to earnings differences.
- Inherited capital, unusual entrepreneurial talent, and personal or family good fortune or misfortune widen the gaps between rich and poor.

3 **Explain why governments redistribute income and describe the effects of redistribution on economic inequality and poverty.**

- Governments redistribute income through progressive income taxes, income maintenance programs, and provision of subsidized services.
- Normative theories of redistribution recognize the tension between equality and efficiency—the big tradeoff—and seek principles to guide the political debate.
- The main positive theory of redistribution is the median voter theory.
- The negative income tax is a proposal for addressing the big tradeoff.

Key Terms

Lorenz curve, 468
Market income, 483
Median voter theory, 486

Money income, 484
Negative income tax, 487
Poverty, 473

myeconlab

Exercises

1. Table 1 shows the distribution of income in Australia.
    a. Create a pie chart to illustrate the distribution of income in Australia.
    b. Calculate the cumulative distribution of income for Australia.
    c. Draw the Lorenz curve for Australian income.
    d. Compare the distribution of income in Australia with that in the United States.
    e. Which distribution is more unequal?

TABLE 1

Households	Income (percentage)
Lowest 20 percent	1
Second 20 percent	3
Third 20 percent	15
Fourth 20 percent	26
Highest 20 percent	55

2. Table 2 shows the distribution of prize money among the top 20 professional golfers.
    a. Create a pie chart to illustrate the distribution of income of these golfers.
    b. Calculate the cumulative distribution of income of these golfers.
    c. Draw the prize money distribution Lorenz curve of these golfers.
    d. Compare the distribution of income of these golfers with that in the United States as a whole.
    e. Which distribution is more unequal?
    f. Which distribution is more desirable? Why?

TABLE 2

Professional golfers	Income (percentage)
Lowest 20 percent	15
Second 20 percent	16
Third 20 percent	18
Fourth 20 percent	20
Highest 20 percent	31

3. Figure 1 shows the market for low-skilled workers. With on-the-job training, low-skilled workers can become high-skilled workers. The value of the marginal product of high-skilled workers at each employment level is twice the value of the marginal product of low-skilled workers. But the cost of acquiring the skill adds $2 an hour to the wage rate that will attract high-skilled labor. What is the equilibrium
    a. Wage rate of low-skilled labor.
    b. Number of low-skilled workers employed.
    c. Wage rate of high-skilled labor.
    d. Number of high-skilled workers employed.

FIGURE 1

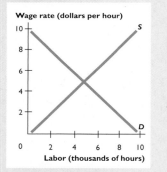

4. Suppose the cost of acquiring a skill increases and the value of the marginal product of skill increases. Draw demand-supply graphs of the labor markets for high-skilled and low-skilled labor to explain what happens to the equilibrium
    a. Wage rate of low-skilled labor.
    b. Number of low-skilled workers employed.
    c. Wage rate of high-skilled labor.
    d. Number of high-skilled workers employed.

TABLE 3

Households	Income (percentage)
Lowest 20 percent	5
Second 20 percent	9
Third 20 percent	20
Fourth 20 percent	30
Highest 20 percent	36

5. Table 3 shows the distribution of market income in an economy. If the government redistributes income by taxing the 60 percent of households with the highest incomes 10 percent; and paying the tax collected as benefits to the 40 percent of the population with the lowest market income,
    a. Calculate the distribution of income after taxes and benefits.
    b. Draw the Lorenz curve before and after taxes and benefits.
    c. If the cost of administrating the redistribution scheme takes 50 percent of the taxes collected, calculate the new distribution of income.
    d. If the people whose incomes are taxed cut their work hours and their incomes fall by 10 percent, what now is the distribution of income? (Ignore the cost of administrating the redistribution scheme.)

6. In the United States in 2002, 130,000 aircraft mechanics and services technicians earned an average of $20 an hour, while 30,000 elevator installers and
   repairers earned an average of $25 an hour. The skill and training for these
   two jobs are very similar.
   a. Draw the demand and supply curves for these two types of labor.
   b. Describe the feature of your graph that accounts for the differences in the
      wage rates of these two groups.
   c. Describe the feature of your graph that accounts for the differences in the
      quantities of labor employed of these two groups.
   d. Why do you think these demand for labor curves differ?
   e. Why do you think these supply of labor curves differ?
   f. Suppose that a government law required both groups to be paid $22.50 an
      hour. What would happen in the two markets?

Critical Thinking

7. Why do economists think that discrimination in the labor market based on
   prejudice against visible minorities or women is an unlikely explanation for
   the persistent inequality in earnings of these two groups compared to white
   males?

8. How do you think the minimum wage influences the distribution of
   income?

9. What is the big tradeoff? How does the 1996 Personal Responsibility and
   Work Opportunities Reconciliation Act address the big tradeoff and how
   might a negative income address it?

10. What were the features of U.S. redistribution prior to 1996 that created
    weaker incentives for benefit recipients and taxpayers? What does it mean to
    say that the scheme "locked poor people in a welfare trap"?

11. Do you think the distributions of income and wealth in the United States
    today are too unequal, too equal, or about right? Provide a detailed justifica-
    tion for your opinion using the ideas of economic efficiency, the two views
    of fairness explained in Chapter 6, the concept of the big tradeoff, and the
    data presented in the tables in this chapter.

12. What practical changes would you suggest to the government actions that
    redistribute income and wealth in the United States today? Provide a
    detailed justification for your suggestions using the ideas of economic effi-
    ciency, the two views of fairness explained in Chapter 6, the concept of the
    big tradeoff, and the data presented in the tables in this chapter.

13. "The distribution of income within a country is only a small part of the story
    of economic inequality. The truly disturbing inequality is that among
    nations. The rich countries must do much more to help the poor ones."
    Appraise this statement. Do you agree or disagree with it? Provide a
    detailed justification for your opinion using the ideas of economic efficiency,
    the two views of fairness explained in Chapter 6, the concept of the big
    tradeoff, and the data presented in the tables in this chapter.

Web Exercises

Use the links on MyEconLab to work the following exercises.

14. Obtain data on the salaries of the major league baseball players or download the spreadsheet.
    a. Calculate the cumulative distribution of income for the major league players.
    b. Is the distribution of income among the major league players more unequal or less unequal than that for the United States?
    c. Which distribution of income, the major league players or the United States, is better? Why?

15. Visit the Economic Policy Institute's page on the living wage.
    a. What is the concept of the living wage?
    b. How does the concept of the living wage relate to the concept of poverty that you've studied in this chapter?
    c. How does the concept of the living wage relate to the concept of the minimum wage that you studied in Chapter 7?
    d. Do you think that the living wage solves the problem of low income?

16. Visit the Center on Budget and Policy Priorities and other sites and obtain information on President George W. Bush's tax cut proposals.
    a. What are the main elements in the President's tax plan?
    b. How do you think the President's proposals would change the Lorenz curve? Explain in detail.

17. Read the article "Reengineering Social Security in the New Economy" by Thomas F. Siems, an economist at the Dallas Federal Reserve.
    a. What does Dr. Siems say is wrong with Social Security?
    b. How does he suggest that the problems with Social Security be fixed?
    c. How would Dr. Siems's suggestions influence the distribution of income?

International Trade

CHAPTER CHECKLIST

When you have completed your study of this chapter, you will be able to

1 Describe the patterns and trends in international trade.

2 Explain why nations engage in international trade and why trade benefits all nations.

3 Explain how trade barriers reduce international trade.

4 Explain the arguments used to justify trade barriers and show why these arguments are incorrect but also why some barriers are hard to remove.

We live in a global economy, but wages in most nations are lower than wages in the United States. How can we compete with countries that pay their workers a fraction of U.S. wages?

Would it be better if we isolated our economy from the rest of the world? Or are there some gains from trading with other nations that are worth the macroeconomic disturbances and international competition that they bring?

In this chapter, you are going to learn about international trade. You will discover how all nations can gain by specializing in producing the goods and services in which they have a comparative advantage and trading with other countries. You will discover that all countries can compete, no matter how high their wages are. And you'll learn why, despite the fact that international trade brings benefits to all countries, they nevertheless restrict trade.

20.1 TRADE PATTERNS AND TRENDS

The goods and services that we buy from people in other countries are called **imports**. The goods and services that we sell to people in other countries are called **exports**. What are the most important things that we import and export?

Imports
Goods and services that we buy from other countries.

Exports
Goods and services that we sell in other countries.

■ U.S. Exports and Imports

Most people would probably guess that a rich nation such as the United States imports raw materials and exports manufactured goods. Although that is one feature of U.S. international trade, it is not its most important feature. The vast bulk of U.S. exports and imports are manufactured goods and services. We sell to other countries automobiles, airplanes, supercomputers, scientific equipment, and financial, insurance, and education services. And we buy from other countries DVD players, T-shirts, and technical and professional services. See *Eye on the Global Economy* (p. 495) for the relative importance of broad categories of U.S. international trade.

Trade in Goods

In 2004, manufactured goods accounted for 54 percent of U.S. exports and for 66 percent of U.S. imports. Minerals and fuels accounted for 2 percent of U.S. exports and for 12 percent of U.S. imports, and agricultural products accounted for only 5 percent of U.S. exports and 3 percent of U.S. imports. The largest U.S. export *and* import item in 2004 (and for many years) was automobiles and auto parts.

But goods accounted for only 70 percent of U.S. exports and 83 percent of U.S. imports in 2004. The rest of U.S. international trade was in services.

Trade in Services

You might be wondering how a country can export and import services. Here are some examples.

If you take a vacation in France and travel there on an Air France flight from New York, the United States imports transportation services from France. The money you spend in France on hotel bills and restaurant meals is also classified as a U.S. import of services. Similarly, the vacation taken by a French student in the United States counts as a U.S. export of services to France.

When we import TV sets from South Korea, the owner of the ship that transports them might be Greek and the company that insures them might be British. The payments that we make for the transportation and insurance are U.S. imports of services. Similarly, when a U.S. shipping company transports California wine to Tokyo, the transportation cost is a U.S. export of a service to Japan. U.S. international trade in these types of services is large and growing.

■ The Outsourcing Trend

In 1960, we exported 5 percent of total output and imported 4 percent of the goods and services that we bought. By 2005, these percentages had jumped to 10.5 for exports and 16 for imports. Some of the increase arises from what has come to be called *offshore outsourcing*—buying a good or services from a lower-cost overseas supplier. This activity has received a lot of public attention as jobs have been lost in services such as data processing, computer programming, customer support, and telemarketing to providers in places as far afield as India and Ireland.

EYE ON THE GLOBAL ECONOMY

The Major Items That We Trade with Other Nations

The figure shows the U.S. volume of trade and balance of trade for the 20 largest traded items in 2004. If a bar has more red (imports) than blue (exports), the United States has a trade deficit in that item.

The largest traded item is automobiles and parts. Other private services (education and technical services are examples), fuels, consumer durables (TV sets, DVD players, and kitchen equipment are examples) travel, computers, and aircraft and parts are also large traded items. Notice that other private services and travel are larger than most goods.

SOURCE OF DATA: Bureau of Economic Analysis.

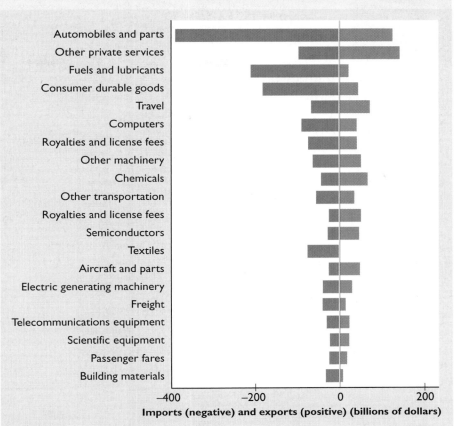

Trading Partners and Trade Agreements

The United States has trading links with every part of the world and is a member of the World Trade Organization (or WTO), an organization that seeks to promote free international trade. The United States has also negotiated trade agreements with several individual countries and with some regional groups of countries.

U.S. Trading Partners

Canada is the United States' biggest trading partner. Mexico and China are the next biggest and almost equal. Our other large trading partners are Japan, Germany, and the United Kingdom. But we also have significant volumes of trade with the other rapidly expanding Asian economies such as South Korea, Taiwan, Singapore, and Hong Kong. *Eye on the Global Economy* on p. 496 shows the data for our 17 largest trading partners.

Trade Agreements

Trade agreements are treaties between two countries (called bilateral agreements) or among a number of countries (called multilateral agreements) designed to promote greater trade and economic cooperation, and sometimes, additionally, to promote political and social goals. The United States has entered into bilateral trade agreements with Australia, Bahrain, Chile, Israel, Jordon, Morocco, Oman,

The Major U.S. Trading Partners and Volumes of Trade

The figure shows the U.S. volume of trade and balance of trade with its 17 largest trading partners in 2004. If a bar has more red (imports) than blue (exports), the United States has a trade deficit with that country.

Canada is the major trading partner of the United States by a big margin. Mexico comes next. China overtook Japan in 2003 to take the third place. Of the newly industrialized countries of Asia, South Korea and Taiwan have much more trade with the United States than do Singapore and Hong Kong. Trade with Germany and the United Kingdom is large.

SOURCE OF DATA: Bureau of Economic Analysis.

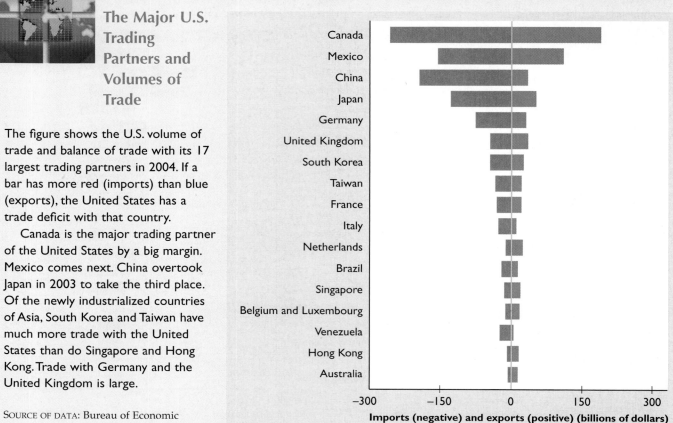

Imports (negative) and exports (positive) (billions of dollars)

Singapore, and Thailand. And the United States is a member of three multilateral regional groups that arise from the North American Free Trade Agreement, the Central American Free Trade Agreement, and Asia-Pacific Economic Cooperation. A larger Free Trade Area of the Americas is a possible future development.

North American Free Trade Agreement (NAFTA) NAFTA is an agreement among the United States, Canada, and Mexico to make trade among the three countries easier and freer. This agreement came into effect in 1994. During the years since then, trade among these three nations has expanded rapidly.

Central American Free Trade Agreement (CAFTA) CAFTA is a comprehensive trade agreement between Costa Rica, the Dominican Republic, El Salvador, Guatemala, Honduras, Nicaragua, and the United States. The agreement has both trade and political goals, the latter to promote freedom and democracy in Central America.

Asia-Pacific Economic Cooperation (APEC) APEC is a group of 21 nations that border the Pacific Ocean. The largest of these are the United States, China, and Japan, but other significant members are Australia, Canada, Indonesia, and the dynamic new industrial Asian economies. The APEC nations conduct 50 percent of world trade.

Free Trade Area of the Americas (FTAA) The American continents consist of 35 nations, and the governments of the 34 democracies (which exclude Cuba) have begun a Free Trade Area of the Americas process. The objective of this process is to achieve free international trade among all the nations of the Americas.

■ Balance of Trade and International Borrowing

The value of exports minus the value of imports is called the **balance of trade**. In 2005, the United States imported more than it exported. When a country imports more than it exports, it has a trade deficit and pays by borrowing from foreigners or selling some of its assets. When a country exports more than it imports, it has a trade surplus and lends to other countries or buys more foreign assets to enable the rest of the world to pay its trade deficit.

Balance of trade
The value of exports minus the value of imports.

CHECKPOINT 20.1

(X) myeconlab

1 **Describe the patterns and trends in international trade.**

Practice Problem 20.1

1. Use the spreadsheet on MyEconLab to answer the following questions:
   a. In 1990, what percentage of Canadian production was exported to the United States and what percentage of total goods and services bought by Canadians was imported from the United States?
   b. In 2005, what percentage of Canadian production was exported to the United States and what percentage of total goods and services bought by Canadians was imported from the United States?

Exercise 20.1

1. Use the spreadsheet on MyEconLab to answer the following questions:
   a. In 1990, what percentage of Mexican production was exported to the United States and what percentage of total goods and services bought by Mexicans was imported from the United States?
   b. In 2005, what percentage of Mexican production was exported to the United States and what percentage of total goods and services bought by Mexicans was imported from the United States?

Solution to Practice Problem 20.1

1a. In 1990, Canada exported 19 percent of total production to the United States and imported 19 percent of total goods and services purchased from the United States.
1b. In 2005, Canada exported to the United States 28 percent of total production and imported from the United States 24 percent of goods and services purchased.

20.2 THE GAINS FROM INTERNATIONAL TRADE

Comparative advantage is the fundamental force that generates international trade. And comparative advantage arises from differences in opportunity costs. You met this idea in Chapter 3 (pp. 77–78), but we're now going to put some flesh on the bones of the basic idea. We'll begin by looking at an item that we export.

■ Why the United States Exports Airplanes

Boeing produces many more airplanes each year than airlines in the United States buy. Most of Boeing's production goes to airlines in other parts of the world. The United States is an exporter of airplanes. Why?

The answer is that the United States has a comparative advantage in the production of airplanes. The opportunity cost of producing an airplane is lower in the United States than in most other countries. So buyers can obtain airplanes from Boeing for a lower price than the price at which they could buy them from other potential suppliers. And Boeing can sell airplanes to foreigners for a higher price than it could obtain from an additional U.S. buyer.

So both countries gain. The foreign buyer gains from lower-priced airplanes. And Boeing's stockholders, managers, and workers gain from higher-priced airplanes. A win-win situation!

Figure 20.1 illustrates the effects of international trade in airplanes. The demand curve *D* shows the demand for airplanes in the United States. This curve tells us the quantity of airplanes that U.S. airlines are willing to buy at various prices. The demand curve also tells us the most that an additional airplane is worth to a U.S. airline at each quantity.

The supply curve *S* shows the supply of airplanes in the United States. This curve tells us the quantity of airplanes that U.S. aircraft makers are willing to sell at various prices. The supply curve also tells us the opportunity cost of producing an additional airplane at each quantity.

No Trade

First, let's see what happens in the market for airplanes if there is no international trade. Figure 20.1(a) shows the situation. The airplane market is in equilibrium when 400 airplanes are produced by U.S. aircraft makers and bought by U.S. airlines. The price is $80 million an airplane.

Trade

Second, let's see what happens in the market for airplanes if international trade takes place. Figure 20.1(b) shows the situation. The price of an airplane is determined in the world market, not the U.S. domestic market. Suppose that world demand and world supply determine a world equilibrium price of $100 million per airplane. In Figure 20.1(b), the world price line shows this price.

The U.S. demand curve, *D*, tells us that at $100 million an airplane, U.S. airlines buy 300 airplanes a year. The U.S. supply curve, *S*, tells us that at $100 million per airplane, U.S. aircraft makers produce 800 airplanes a year. So domestic production at 800 a year exceeds domestic purchases of 300 a year.

The quantity produced in the United States minus the quantity purchased by U.S. airlines is the quantity of U.S. exports, which is 500 airplanes a year.

FIGURE 20.1

An Export

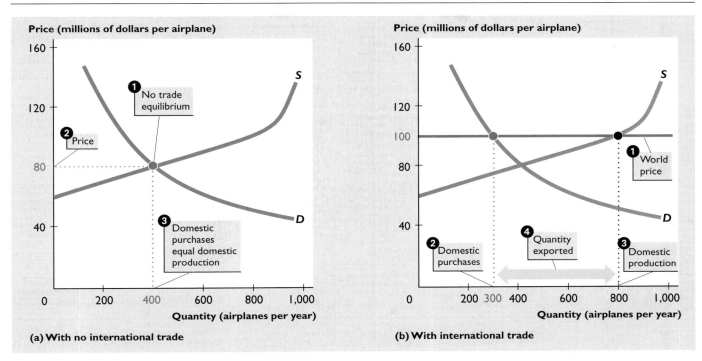

(a) With no international trade

(b) With international trade

With no international trade in airplanes, ❶ equilibrium at the intersection of the domestic demand and supply curves determines ❷ the price at $80 million an airplane and ❸ the quantity at 400 airplanes a year.

With international trade, world demand and supply determine ❶ the world price, which is $100 million an airplane. ❷ Domestic purchases decrease to 300 a year, and ❸ domestic production increases to 800 a year; ❹ 500 airplanes a year are exported.

Comparative Advantage

You can see that U.S. aircraft makers have a comparative advantage in producing airplanes by comparing the U.S. supply curve and the world price line. At the equilibrium quantity of 800 airplanes a year, the world opportunity cost of producing an airplane is $100 million. But the U.S. supply curve tells us that only the 800th airplane has an opportunity cost of $100 million. Each of the other 799 airplanes has an opportunity cost of less than $100 million.

■ Why the United States Imports T-Shirts

Americans spend more than twice as much on clothing as the value of U.S. apparel production. That is, more than half of the clothing that we buy is manufactured in other countries and imported into the United States. Why?

The answer is that the rest of the world (mainly Asia) has a comparative advantage in the production of clothes. The opportunity cost of producing a T-shirt is lower in Asia than in the United States. So buyers can obtain T-shirts from Asia for a lower price than the price at which they could buy them from U.S. garment makers. And Asian garment makers can sell T-shirts to Americans for a higher price than they could obtain from an additional Asian buyer.

So again, both countries gain. The U.S. buyer gains from lower-priced T-shirts, and Asian garment makers gain from higher-priced T-shirts. Another win-win situation!

Figure 20.2 illustrates the effects of international trade in T-shirts. Again, the demand curve *D* and the supply curve *S* show the demand and supply in the U.S. domestic market only.

The demand curve tells us the quantity of T-shirts that Americans are willing to buy at various prices. The demand curve also tells us the most that an additional T-shirt is worth to an American at each quantity.

The supply curve tells us the quantity of T-shirts that U.S. garment makers are willing to sell at various prices. The supply curve also tells us the opportunity cost of producing an additional T-shirt in the United States at each quantity.

No Trade

Again, we'll first look at a market with no international trade, shown in Figure 20.2(a). The T-shirt market is in equilibrium when 20 million shirts are produced by U.S. garment makers and bought by Americans. The price is $8 a shirt.

FIGURE 20.2

An Import

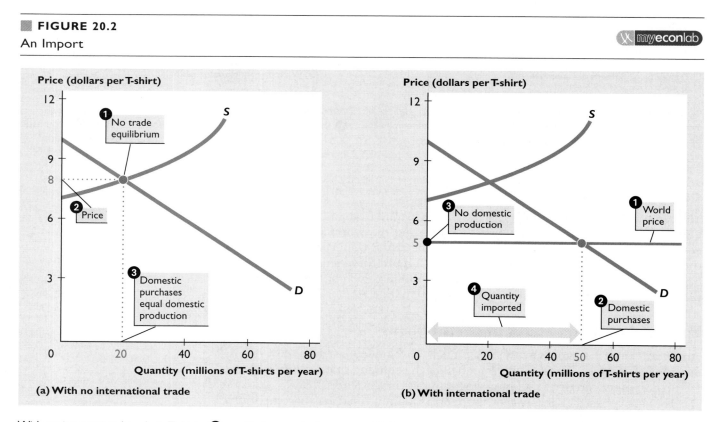

(a) With no international trade

(b) With international trade

With no international trade in T-shirts, ❶ equilibrium at the intersection of the domestic demand and supply curves determines ❷ the price at $8 a shirt and ❸ the quantity at 20 million shirts a year.

With international trade, world demand and supply determine the ❶ world price, which is $5 a shirt. ❷ Domestic purchases increase to 50 million shirts a year, and ❸ domestic production decreases to zero. ❹ The entire 50 million shirts a year are imported.

Trade

Figure 20.2(b) shows what happens in the market for T-shirts if international trade takes place. Now the price of a T-shirt is determined in the world market, not the U.S. domestic market. Suppose that world demand and world supply determine a world equilibrium price of $5 a shirt. In Figure 20.2(b), the world price line shows this price.

The U.S demand curve, *D*, tells us that at $5 a shirt, Americans buy 50 million shirts a year. The U.S. supply curve, *S*, tells us that at $5 a shirt, U.S. garment makers produce no T-shirts. So there is no domestic production, and domestic purchases are 50 million T-shirts a year. The entire quantity of T-shirts purchased in the United States is the quantity imported.

Comparative Advantage

Now you can see that Asian garment makers have a comparative advantage in producing T-shirts by comparing the U.S. supply curve and the world price line. At the equilibrium quantity of 50 million T-shirts a year, the world opportunity cost of producing a T-shirt is $5. But the U.S. supply curve tells us that no U.S. garment maker has such a low opportunity cost, not even at smaller outputs. So Asian garment makers have a comparative advantage in producing T-shirts.

■ Gains from Trade and the *PPF*

The demand and supply model that you've just studied makes it clear why we export some goods and import others. But it doesn't show directly the gains from international trade. Another way of looking at comparative advantage uses the production possibilities frontier (*PPF*) that you learned about in Chapter 3. This approach shows the gains from trade in a powerful way, as you're about to discover.

Let's explore comparative advantage using the production possibilities approach.

Production Possibilities in the United States and China

To focus on the essential idea, we'll assume that the United States can produce only two goods: airplanes and T-shirts. China can also produce only these same two goods. But production possibilities and opportunity costs are different in the two countries.

Table 20.1 shows U.S. production possibilities. If the United States uses all of its resources to produce airplanes, its output is 10 airplanes per year and no T-shirts. If it uses all of its resources to produce T-shirts, its output is 100 million T-shirts a year and no airplanes. We'll assume that the U.S. opportunity cost of producing an airplane is constant. To produce 10 airplanes, the United States must forgo 100 million T-shirts, which means that to produce 1 airplane, the United States must forgo 10 million T-shirts. That is,

The U.S. opportunity cost of producing 1 airplane is 10 million T-shirts.

Table 20.2 shows China's production possibilities. If China uses all of its resources to make airplanes, it can produce 2 airplanes a year and no T-shirts. And if it uses all of its resources to make T-shirts, it can produce 100 million T-shirts a year and no airplanes. We'll assume that China's opportunity cost of producing an

TABLE 20.1 U.S. PRODUCTION POSSIBILITIES

Item	Quantity per year
Airplane	10
T-shirt	100,000,000

TABLE 20.2 CHINA'S PRODUCTION POSSIBILITIES

Item	Quantity per year
Airplane	2
T-shirt	100,000,000

airplane is constant. To produce 2 airplanes, China must forgo 100 million T-shirts, which means that to produce 1 airplane, China must forgo 50 million T-shirts. That is,

China's opportunity cost of producing 1 airplane is 50 million T-shirts.

Figure 20.3(a) illustrates the production possibilities for the United States, and Figure 20.3(b) shows the production possibilities for China. The assumption that the opportunity costs are constant means that the two *PPFs* are linear.

We are assuming that the opportunity costs are constant so that we can illustrate the gains from trade in the simplest and cleanest way. We could assume that opportunity cost increases (as it does in Chapter 3) and we would reach the same conclusion that we'll reach here, but the story would be more complicated and the point wouldn't jump out as clearly as it does with constant opportunity costs.

Along the U.S. *PPF*, 1 airplane costs 10 million T-shirts. And along China's *PPF*, 1 airplane costs 50 million T-shirts. You can check these opportunity costs by calculating the slopes of the two *PPFs*: −10 for the U.S. *PPF* and −50 for China's *PPF*.

■ **FIGURE 20.3**

Production Possibilities in the United States and China

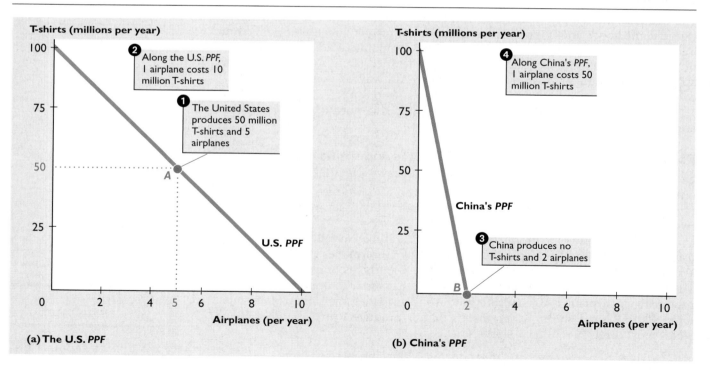

(a) The U.S. *PPF*

(b) China's *PPF*

❶ The United States produces at point *A* on its *PPF* (part a).
❷ The opportunity cost of an airplane is 10 million T-shirts.
❸ China produces at point *B* on its *PPF* (part b). ❹ The opportunity cost of an airplane is 50 million T-shirts.

The opportunity cost of an airplane is lower in the United States than in China, so the United States has a comparative advantage in producing airplanes. The opportunity cost of a T-shirt is lower in China than in the United States, so China has a comparative advantage in producing T-shirts.

No Trade

With no international trade, we'll suppose that the United States produces 5 airplanes and 50 million T-shirts at point *A* on its *PPF*. And we'll suppose that China produces 2 airplanes and no T-shirts at point *B* on its *PPF*.

Comparative Advantage

In which of the two goods does China have a comparative advantage? Recall that comparative advantage is a situation in which one nation's opportunity cost of producing a good is lower than another nation's opportunity cost of producing that same good. China has a comparative advantage in producing T-shirts. The opportunity cost of a T-shirt is 1/50,000,000 of an airplane in China and 1/10,000,000 of an airplane in the United States.

You can see China's comparative advantage by looking at the *PPF*s for China and the United States in Figure 20.3. China's *PPF* is steeper than the U.S. *PPF*. To produce an additional 1 million T-shirts, China must give up fewer airplanes than does the United States. So China's opportunity cost of a T-shirt is less than the U.S. opportunity cost of a T-shirt. This means that China has a comparative advantage in producing T-shirts.

The United States has a comparative advantage in producing airplanes. In Figure 20.3, the U.S. *PPF* is less steep than China's *PPF*. This means that the United States must give up fewer T-shirts to produce an additional airplane than does China. The U.S. opportunity cost of producing an airplane is 10 million T-shirts, which is less than China's 50 million T-shirts. So the United States has a comparative advantage in producing airplanes.

Because China has a comparative advantage in producing T-shirts and the United States has a comparative advantage in producing airplanes, both China and the United States can gain from specialization and trade. China specializes in T-shirts, and the United States specializes in airplanes.

The Gains Available from Trade

If the United States, which has a comparative advantage in producing airplanes, allocates all of its resources to that activity, it can produce 10 airplanes a year. If China, which has a comparative advantage in producing T-shirts, allocates all of its resources to that activity, it can produce 100 million T-shirts a year. By specializing, the United States and China together can produce 10 airplanes and 100 million T-shirts. With no trade, their total production had been 7 airplanes (5 from the United States and 2 from China) and 50 million T-shirts (all produced by the United States). The production of airplanes can increase by 3 and the production of T-shirts can increase by 50 million.

So both countries can end up with more of both goods. But to achieve the gains from specialization, the United States and China must trade with each other.

Achieving the Gains from Trade

Suppose that the world market price of an airplane is $100 million and that the world market price of a T-shirt is $5. Then on the world market, 1 airplane costs 20 million T-shirts.

Recall that the United States can produce an airplane at a cost of 10 million T-shirts. So by selling airplanes for 20 million T-shirts, the United States can get more T-shirts per airplane than it can by producing T-shirts. So the United States produces as many airplanes as it can and sells some in exchange for T-shirts. The United States produces 10 airplanes and no T-shirts.

Recall that China can produce an airplane at a cost of 50 million T-shirts. So by buying airplanes for 20 million T-shirts, China can get an airplane for fewer T-shirts than it can by producing airplanes. So China produces as many T-shirts as it can and sells some of them in exchange for airplanes. China produces 100 million T-shirts and no airplanes.

The quantities that people buy depend on their preferences, which influence demand. Suppose that at the world market price of 20 million T-shirts per airplane, U.S. residents and firms want to buy 60 million T-shirts and 7 airplanes. They can do so by devoting all their resources to producing airplanes and then sell 3 of these airplanes to China in exchange for T-shirts. Americans end up with 60 million T-shirts and 7 airplanes (10 produced minus 3 sold)—a gain of 10 million T-shirts and 2 airplanes. China sells 60 million T-shirts and buys 3 airplanes. The Chinese end up with 40 million T-shirts (100 million produced minus 60 million sold) and 3 airplanes—a gain of 40 million T-shirts and 1 airplane.

Figure 20.4 shows these gains from trade. The United States moves from point A with no trade to point A' with trade. China moves from point B to point B'.

As a result of specialization and trade, both countries consume outside their production possibilities frontiers and both countries gain from trade.

■ FIGURE 20.4

The Gains from Trade

❶ If the United States specializes in airplanes, it produces 10 a year at point P.

❷ If China specializes in T-shirts, it produces 100 million T-shirts a year at point Q.

❸ If T-shirts and airplanes are traded at 20 million T-shirts per airplane, both countries can increase their consumption of both goods and consume at points A' and B'. The gains from trade are the increases in consumption of the two countries.

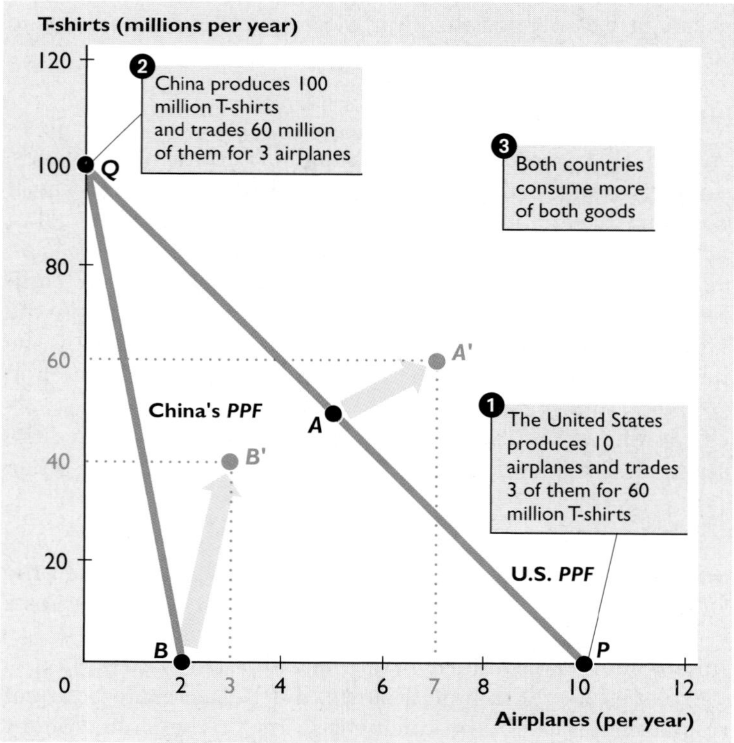

❷ China produces 100 million T-shirts and trades 60 million of them for 3 airplanes

❸ Both countries consume more of both goods

❶ The United States produces 10 airplanes and trades 3 of them for 60 million T-shirts

China's PPF

U.S. PPF

T-shirts (millions per year)

Airplanes (per year)

■ Offshoring and Outsourcing

If you have seen Lou Dobbs on the CNN evening news, you know that he is very concerned about what he calls "exporting America"—the phenomenon of jobs that were previously done in the United States now being done in some other country. Lou is worried about *offshoring*. What exactly is offshoring?

What Is Offshoring?

A firm in the United States can obtain the things that it sells in any of four ways:

1. Hire U.S. labor and produce in the United States.
2. Hire foreign labor and produce in other countries.
3. Buy finished goods, components, or services from other firms in the United States.
4. Buy finished goods, components, or services from other firms in other countries.

Activities 3 and 4 are **outsourcing**, and activities 2 and 4 are **offshoring**. Activity 4 is *offshore outsourcing*. Notice that offshoring includes activities that take place inside U.S. firms. If a U.S. firm opens its own facilities in another country, then it is offshoring.

Offshoring has been going on for hundreds of years. But the activity expanded rapidly and became a source of concern during the 1990s when it began to cover activities that went beyond manufacturing to include information technology services and general office services such as finance, accounting, and human resources management.

Outsourcing
A firm buying finished goods, components, or services from other firms.

Offshoring
A U.S. firm either producing in another country or outsourcing to a firm in another country.

Why Did Offshoring of Services Boom During the 1990s?

A dramatic fall in the cost of telecommunication generated the offshoring services boom of the 1990s. The gains from specialization and trade that you saw in the previous section must be large enough to make it worth incurring the costs of communication and transportation. If the cost of producing a T-shirt in China isn't lower than the cost in the United States by an amount that exceeds the cost of transporting a shirt from China to the United States, then it is more efficient to produce shirts in the United States and avoid the transportation costs.

If services are to be produced offshore, then the cost of delivering those services must be low enough to leave the buyer with an overall lower cost. Until the 1990s, the cost of communicating across large distances was too high to make the offshoring of business services efficient. But when satellites, fiber-optic cables, and computers cut the cost of a phone call between the United States and India to less than a dollar an hour, a huge base of offshore resources became competitive with similar resources in the United States.

What Are the Benefits of Offshoring?

Offshoring brings gains from trade that are identical to those of any other type of trade. We could easily change the names of the items traded from airplanes and T-shirts (the example in the previous section of this chapter) to banking services and call center services (or any other pair of services). A U.S. bank might export banking services to Indian firms, and Indians might provide call center services to U.S. firms. This type of trade would benefit both Americans and Indians provided the

United States has a comparative advantage in banking services and India has a comparative advantage in call center services.

Comparative advantages like these emerged during the 1990s. India has the world's largest educated English-speaking population and it is located at a time zone a half a day ahead of the United States, which facilitates 24 × 7 operations. When the cost of communicating with a worker in India was several dollars a minute, as it was before the 1990s, tapping these vast resources was just too costly. But at today's cost of a long-distance telephone call, resources in India can be used to produce services in the United States at a lower cost than those services can be produced by using resources located in the United States. And with the incomes that Indians earn from exporting services, they buy services (and goods) produced in the United States.

Why Is Offshoring a Concern?

Despite the obvious gain from specialization and trade that offshoring brings, many people believe that it also brings costs that swamp the gains. Why?

One reason is that jobs growth has slowed since 2001, which some people say is a consequence of offshoring stealing U.S. jobs in both manufacturing and services. The loss of manufacturing jobs to other countries has been going on for decades. But the U.S. service sector has always expanded by enough to create new jobs to replace the lost manufacturing jobs. Now that service jobs are also going overseas, the fear is that there will not be enough jobs for Americans.

This fear is misplaced. It is true that *some* service jobs are going overseas. But many service jobs are expanding. The United States imports call center services, but it exports education, health care, legal, and a host of other types of services. Jobs in these sectors are expanding and will continue to expand.

The numbers reinforce this view that the fear of job loss is misplaced. Exact numbers of jobs that have moved to lower-cost offshore locations are not known, and estimates vary. The best guess is that 200,000 jobs a year are going offshore. Some estimates are as high at 400,000 (and some are much lower). Assume that the 400,000 a year number is correct, and put it in perspective. Since 2000, each *month* on the average, 4.5 million people in the United States have been fired or quit their jobs, 4.6 million have started a new job, and the number of people employed has increased by 100,000. In 2005, 142 million Americans had jobs, the highest number in U.S. history. Set against these total job market numbers, the jobs going offshore are a drop in the ocean.

A second reason for concern about offshoring is that U.S. imports have grown faster than U.S. exports. You will learn in Chapter 21 what causes an overall deficit in our international trade and that offshoring is not one of the reasons.

Winners and Losers

Gains from trade do not bring gains for every single individual. Americans on the average gain from offshoring. But some lose. The losers are those who have invested in human capital to do a specific job that has now gone offshore.

Unemployment benefits provide short-term temporary relief for these displaced workers. But long-term solutions require retraining and the acquisition of new skills. Beyond providing short-term relief through unemployment benefits, there is a large role for government education and training policies to ensure that the labor force of the twenty-first century becomes increasingly flexible and capable of retooling to take on new jobs that today we can't foresee.

CHECKPOINT 20.2

2 Explain why nations engage in international trade and why trade benefits all nations.

Practice Problem 20.2

1. During most of the Cold War, the United States and Russia (then known as
the Soviet Union) did not trade with each other. Both countries produced
manufactured goods and farm produce. Suppose that in the last year of the
Cold War, the United States could produce 100 million units of manufactured goods or 50 million units of farm produce and Russia could produce
30 million units of manufactured goods or 10 million units of farm produce.
   a. What was the U.S. opportunity cost of 1 unit of farm produce?
   b. What was the Russian opportunity cost of 1 unit of farm produce?
   c. Which country had a comparative advantage in producing farm produce?
   d. With the end of the Cold War and the opening up of trade between
      Russia and the United States, which good did the United States import
      from Russia?
   e. Did the United States gain from this trade? Explain why or why not.
   f. Did Russia gain from this trade? Explain why or why not.

Exercise 20.2

1. In 2005, the United States does not trade with Cuba. Suppose that the
United States can produce 1,000 million units of manufactured goods or 500
million units of food. Suppose that Cuba can produce 2 million units of
manufactured goods or 5 million units of food.
   a. What is the U.S. opportunity cost of 1 unit of food?
   b. What is the Cuban opportunity cost of 1 unit of food?
   c. Which country has a comparative advantage in producing food?
   d. Suppose that the United States opens up trade with Cuba. Which good
      will the United States import from Cuba?
   e. Will the United States gain from this trade? Explain why or why not.
   f. Will Cuba gain from this trade? Explain why or why not.

Solution to Practice Problem 20.2

1a. The U.S. opportunity cost of 1 unit of farm produce was 2 units of manufactured goods.

1b. The Russian opportunity cost of 1 unit of farm produce was 3 units of manufactured goods.

1c. The United States had a comparative advantage in producing farm produce
because the U.S. opportunity cost of a unit of farm produce was less than
the Russian opportunity cost of a unit of farm produce.

1d. The United States imported from Russia the good in which Russia had a
comparative advantage. The United States imported manufactured goods.

1e. and **1f.** Both the United States and Russia gained because each country
ended up with more of both goods. When countries produce the good in
which they have a comparative advantage and trade, both countries gain.

20.3 INTERNATIONAL TRADE RESTRICTIONS

Governments use two main tools to restrict international trade and protect domestic industries from foreign competition. They are

- Tariffs
- Nontariff barriers

Tariff
A tax on a good that is imposed by the importing country when an imported good crosses its international boundary.

Nontariff barrier
Any action other than a tariff that restricts international trade.

A **tariff** is a tax on a good that is imposed by the importing country when an imported good crosses its international boundary. A **nontariff barrier** is any action other than a tariff that restricts international trade. Examples of nontariff barriers are quantitative restrictions and health and safety standards.

■ Tariffs

The temptation for governments to impose tariffs is a strong one. First, tariffs provide revenue to the government. Second, they enable the government to satisfy special interest groups in import-competing industries. But as we will see, free international trade brings enormous benefits that are reduced when tariffs are imposed. Let's see how.

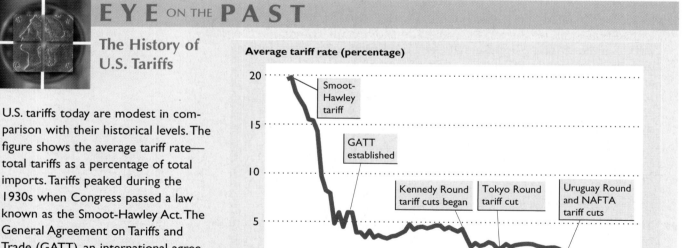

EYE ON THE PAST

The History of U.S. Tariffs

U.S. tariffs today are modest in comparison with their historical levels. The figure shows the average tariff rate—total tariffs as a percentage of total imports. Tariffs peaked during the 1930s when Congress passed a law known as the Smoot-Hawley Act. The General Agreement on Tariffs and Trade (GATT), an international agreement to eliminate trade restrictions that was signed in 1947, resulted in a series of rounds of negotiations that have brought wide-spread tariff cuts. Today, the World Trade Organization (WTO) continues the work of GATT.

The United States is a party to the North American Free Trade Agreement (NAFTA), which became effective

Average tariff rate (percentage)

Smoot-Hawley tariff

GATT established

Kennedy Round tariff cuts began

Tokyo Round tariff cut

Uruguay Round and NAFTA tariff cuts

SOURCES OF DATA: The Budget for Fiscal Year 2006, Historical Tables, Table 2.5 and Bureau of Economic Analysis.

on January 1, 1994, and under which barriers to international trade between the United States, Canada, and Mexico will be virtually eliminated after a 15-year phasing-in period.

To analyze how tariffs work, let's return to the example of U.S. T-shirt imports. Figure 20.5 shows the market for T-shirts in the United States. Part (a) is the same as Figure 20.2(b) and shows the situation with free international trade. The United States produces no T-shirts and imports 50 million shirts a year at the world market price of $5 a shirt.

Now suppose that under pressure from U.S. garment makers, the U.S. government imposes a tariff on imported T-shirts. In particular, suppose that a tariff of 50 percent is imposed. What happens?

- The price of a T-shirt in the United States rises.
- The quantity of T-shirts bought in the United States decreases.
- The quantity of T-shirts produced in the United States increases.
- The quantity of T-shirts imported by the United States decreases.
- The U.S. government collects the tariff revenue.
- U.S. consumers lose.

FIGURE 20.5

The Effects of a Tariff

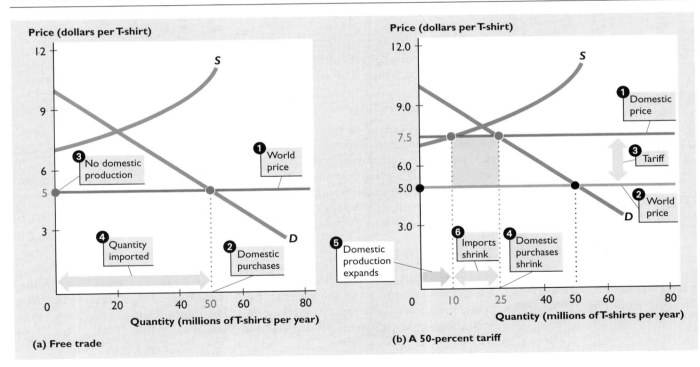

(a) Free trade

(b) A 50-percent tariff

With free trade (part a), ❶ the world price is $5 a T-shirt and ❷ the United States buys 50 million T-shirts. ❸ The United States produces no T-shirts and ❹ imports 50 million T-shirts.

In part (b), the United States imposes a tariff on imports of T-shirts. ❶ The domestic price equals ❷ the world price plus ❸ the tariff, so the tariff raises the price that Americans pay for a T-shirt.

❹ The quantity of T-shirts purchased by Americans decreases, ❺ the quantity produced in the United States increases, and ❻ the quantity imported decreases. The U.S. government collects tariff revenue shown by the purple rectangle.

Rise in Price of a T-Shirt

To buy a T-shirt, Americans must pay the world market price plus the tariff. So the price of a T-shirt rises by 50 percent to $7.50. Figure 20.5(b) shows the domestic price line, which lies 50 percent (or $2.50) above the world price line.

Decrease in Purchases

The higher price of a T-shirt brings a decrease in the quantity demanded, which Figure 20.5(b) shows as a movement along the demand curve for T-shirts from 50 million a year at $5 a shirt to 25 million a year at $7.50 a shirt.

Increase in Domestic Production

The higher price of a T-shirt stimulates domestic production, which increases from zero to 10 million shirts a year—a movement along the supply curve in Figure 20.5(b).

Decrease in Imports

T-shirt imports decrease by 35 million from 50 million to 15 million a year. Both the decrease in purchases and the increase in domestic production contribute to this decrease in imports.

Tariff Revenue

The government collects tariff revenue of $2.50 per shirt on the 15 million shirts imported each year, a total of $37.5 million, as shown by the purple rectangle.

U.S. Consumers Lose

A T-shirt costs only $5 to produce—the opportunity cost of that shirt is $5. But the American consumer pays $7.50 for a T-shirt. So the consumer pays $2.50 a shirt more than its opportunity cost. Consumers are willing to buy up to 50 million T-shirts a year at a price that equals the opportunity cost of a shirt. The tariff makes people pay more than the opportunity cost and deprives them of items they are willing to buy at a price that exceeds the opportunity cost.

   Let's now look at the other tools for restricting trade: nontariff barriers.

■ Nontariff Barriers

Quota
A specified maximum amount of a good that may be imported in a given period of time.

A **quota**, which is a quantitative restriction on the import of a good that specifies the maximum amount of the good that may be imported in a given period, is a widely used nontariff barrier. The United States imposes quotas on many items, including sugar, tomatoes, bananas, and textiles.

How a Quota Works

Figure 20.6 shows how a quota works. Begin by identifying the situation with free international trade. The United States produces no T-shirts and imports 50 million shirts a year at the world market price of $5 a shirt.

   Now suppose that the United States imposes a quota that restricts imports to 15 million T-shirts a year. The total of the imports permitted under the quota and the quantity produced in the United States is the market supply in the United States. This market supply curve is the one labeled $S + quota$ in Figure 20.6.

FIGURE 20.6

The Effects of a Quota

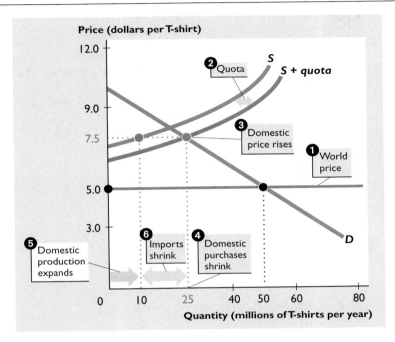

❶ The world price is $5 a T-shirt.
❷ A quota of 15 million shirts a year is added to the U.S. supply to give the market supply curve, S + *quota*.
❸ The equilibrium domestic price rises to $7.50 a shirt, and ❹ domestic purchases decrease. ❺ The United States produces 10 million shirts a year, and ❻ U.S. imports equal the quota of 15 million a year.

With this new supply curve, the U.S. price of a T-shirt is $7.50, the price that makes the quantity demanded by Americans equal the quantity supplied by U.S. producers plus imports. This quantity is 25 million shirts a year.

At a price of $7.50, U.S. garment makers produce 10 million shirts a year and U.S. imports equal the quota of 15 million a year.

We've made the outcome with a quota in Figure 20.6 the same as that with a tariff in Figure 20.5(b). But there is a difference between a tariff and a quota. In the case of a tariff, the U.S. government collects tariff revenue. In the case of a quota, there is no tariff revenue and the difference between the world price and the U.S. price goes to the person who has the right to import T-shirts under the import quota regulations.

Health, Safety, and Other Nontariff Barriers

Thousands of detailed health, safety, and other regulations restrict international trade. Here are just a few examples. All U.S. imports of food products are examined by the Food and Drug Administration to determine whether the imported food is "pure, wholesome, safe to eat, and produced under sanitary conditions." The discovery of BSE in just one U.S. cow in 2003 was enough to close down international trade in U.S. beef. The European Union has banned imports of most genetically modified foods, such as U.S.-produced soybeans and Canadian granola. Australia has banned the import of U.S. grapes to protect its domestic grapes from a virus that is present in California. Restrictions also apply to many nonfood items. Although regulations of the type we've just described are not designed to limit international trade, they have that effect.

3 **Explain how trade barriers reduce international trade.**

Practice Problems 20.3

1. Before 1995, the United States imposed tariffs on goods imported from Mexico and Mexico imposed tariffs on goods imported from the United States. In 1995, Mexico joined NAFTA. U.S. tariffs on imports from Mexico and Mexican tariffs on imports from the United States are gradually being removed. Explain how the removal of tariffs will change
   a. The price that U.S. consumers pay for goods imported from Mexico.
   b. The quantity of U.S. imports from Mexico.
   c. The quantity of U.S. exports to Mexico.
   d. The U.S. government's tariff revenue from trade with Mexico.

2. In 2000, the U.S. government placed a ban on potato imports from Canada. Explain how this ban influences
   a. The price that U.S. consumers pay for potatoes.
   b. The quantity of potatoes consumed in the United States.
   c. The price received by Canadian potato growers.
   d. The U.S. and Canadian gains from trade.

Exercises 20.3

1. In 2000, the U.S. Congress and Senate extended an arrangement that limits the tariffs on imports from China. If the United States imposed higher tariffs on imports from China, explain how a higher tariff on toys will change
   a. The price that U.S. consumers pay for toys imported from China.
   b. The quantity of U.S. imports of toys from China.
   c. The quantity of toys produced in the United States.
   d. The U.S. government's tariff revenue from trade in toys with China.
   e. The U.S. and Chinese gains from trade.

2. Australia has a comparative advantage in producing beef. Explain how a quota on U.S. imports of beef from Australia influences
   a. The price that U.S. consumers pay for beef.
   b. The quantity of beef produced in the United States.
   c. The U.S. and Australian gains from trade.

Solutions to Practice Problems 20.3

1a. The price that U.S. consumers pay for goods imported from Mexico will fall.
1b. The quantity of U.S. imports from Mexico will increase.
1c. The quantity of U.S. exports to Mexico will increase.
1d. The U.S. government's tariff revenue from trade with Mexico will fall to zero.

2a. The price that U.S. consumers pay for potatoes will rise.
2b. The quantity of potatoes consumed in the United States will fall.
2c. The price received by Canadian potato growers will fall.
2d. Both the U.S. and Canadian gains from trade will decrease.

20.4 THE CASE AGAINST PROTECTION

For as long as nations and international trade have existed, people have debated whether free international trade or protection from foreign competition is better for a country. The debate continues, but most economists believe that free trade promotes prosperity for all countries while protection reduces the potential gains from trade. We've seen the most powerful case for free trade: All countries benefit from their comparative advantage. But there is a broader range of issues in the free trade versus protection debate. Let's review these issues.

■ Three Traditional Arguments for Protection

Three traditional arguments for protection and restricting international trade are

- The national security argument
- The infant-industry argument
- The dumping argument

Let's look at each in turn.

The National Security Argument

The national security argument for protection is that a country must protect industries that produce defense equipment and armaments and those on which the defense industries rely for their raw materials and other intermediate inputs. This argument for protection can be taken too far.

First, it is an argument for international isolation, for in a time of war, there is no industry that does not contribute to national defense. Second, if the case is made for boosting the output of a strategic industry—say aerospace—it is more efficient to achieve this outcome with a subsidy financed out of taxes than with a tariff or quota. A subsidy would keep the industry operating at the scale that is judged appropriate, and free international trade would keep the prices faced by consumers at their world market levels.

The Infant-Industry Argument

The **infant-industry argument** for protection is that it is necessary to protect a new industry to enable it to grow into a mature industry that can compete in world markets. The argument is based on the idea of dynamic comparative advantage, which can arise from learning-by-doing.

Learning-by-doing is a powerful engine of productivity growth, and comparative advantage evolves and changes because of on-the-job experience. But these facts do not justify protection.

For example, there are huge productivity gains from learning-by-doing in the manufacture of aircraft. But almost all of these gains benefit the stockholders and workers of aircraft producers such as Boeing. Because the people making the decisions, bearing the risk, and doing the work are the ones who benefit, they take the dynamic gains into account when they decide on the scale of their activities. Only if some of the benefits spill over to other parts of the economy would government assistance be needed to achieve an efficient outcome.

The historical evidence is against the protection of infant industries. Countries in East Asia that have not given such protection have performed well. Countries that have protected infant industries, as India once did, have performed poorly.

Infant-industry argument
The argument that it is necessary to protect a new industry to enable it to grow into a mature industry that can compete in world markets.

Dumping
When a foreign firm sells its exports at a lower price than its cost of production.

The Dumping Argument

Dumping occurs when a foreign firm sells its exports at a lower price than its cost of production. A firm that wants to gain a global monopoly might use dumping. In this case, the foreign firm sells its output at a price below its cost to drive domestic firms out of business. When the domestic firms have gone, the foreign firm takes advantage of its monopoly position and charges a higher price for its product. Dumping is usually regarded as a justification for temporary tariffs and the WTO and NAFTA and CAFTA permit such tariffs. Consequently, anti-dumping tariffs have become important in today's world.

But there are powerful reasons to resist the dumping argument for protection. First, it is virtually impossible to detect dumping because it is hard to determine a firm's costs. As a result, the test for dumping is whether a firm's export price is below its domestic price. But this test is a weak one because it can be rational for a firm to charge a lower price in markets in which the quantity demanded is highly sensitive to price and a higher price in a market in which demand is less price-sensitive.

Second, it is hard to think of a good that is produced by a natural global monopoly. So even if all the domestic firms were driven out of business in some industry, it would always be possible to find several and usually many alternative foreign sources of supply and to buy at prices determined in competitive markets.

Third, if a good or service were a truly global natural monopoly, the best way to deal with it would be by regulation—just as in the case of domestic monopolies. Such regulation would require international cooperation.

The three arguments for protection that we've just examined have an element of credibility. The counterarguments are in general stronger, so these arguments do not make the case for protection. But they are not the only arguments that you might encounter. There are many others, five of which we'll now examine.

■ Five Newer Arguments for Protection

Five newer but commonly made arguments for restricting international trade are that protection

- Saves jobs
- Allows us to compete with cheap foreign labor
- Brings diversity and stability
- Penalizes lax environmental standards
- Protects national culture

Saves Jobs

The argument is that when we buy shoes from Brazil or shirts from Taiwan, U.S. workers lose their jobs. With no earnings and poor prospects, these workers become a drain on welfare and spend less, causing a ripple effect of further job losses. The proposed solution to this problem is to ban imports of cheap foreign goods and to protect U.S. jobs. The proposal is flawed for the following reasons.

First, free trade does cost some jobs, but it also creates other jobs. It brings about a global rationalization of labor and allocates labor resources to their highest-valued activities. Because of international trade in textiles, tens of thousands of workers in the United States have lost jobs because textile mills and other factories have closed. But tens of thousands of workers in other countries now have jobs because textile mills have opened there. And tens of thousands of U.S.

workers now have better-paying jobs than as textile workers because other export industries have expanded and created more jobs than have been destroyed.

Second, imports create jobs. They create jobs for retailers that sell imported goods and for firms that service those goods. They also create jobs by creating incomes in the rest of the world, some of which are spent on imports of U.S.-made goods and services.

Protection saves some particular jobs, but it does so at a high cost. For example, until 2005, textile jobs in the United States were protected by quotas imposed under an international agreement called the Multifiber Arrangement (or MFA). The U.S. International Trade Commission (ITC) estimated that because of quotas, 72,000 jobs existed in textiles that would otherwise disappear and annual clothing expenditure in the United States was $15.9 billion, or $160 per family, higher than it would be with free trade. In other words, the ITC estimated that each textile job saved costs consumers $221,000 a year. The end of the MFA led to the destruction of a large number of textile jobs in the United States and Europe in 2005.

Allows Us to Compete with Cheap Foreign Labor

With the removal of protective tariffs in U.S. trade with Mexico, some people said that jobs would be sucked into Mexico and that the United States would not be able to compete with its southern neighbor. Let's see what's wrong with this view.

The labor cost of a unit of output equals the wage rate divided by labor productivity. For example, if a U.S. auto worker earns $30 an hour and produces 15 units of output an hour, the average labor cost of a unit of output is $2. If a Mexican auto worker earns $3 an hour and produces 1 unit of output an hour, the average labor cost of a unit of output is $3. Other things remaining the same, the higher a worker's productivity, the higher is the worker's wage rate. High-wage workers have high productivity. Low-wage workers have low productivity.

Although high-wage U.S. workers are more productive, on the average, than lower-wage Mexican workers, there are differences across industries. U.S. labor is relatively more productive in some activities than in others. For example, the productivity of U.S. workers in producing movies, financial services, and customized computer chips is relatively higher than their productivity in the production of metals and some standardized machine parts. The activities in which U.S. workers are relatively more productive than their Mexican counterparts are those in which the United States has a comparative advantage. By engaging in free trade, increasing our production and exports of the goods and services in which we have a comparative advantage, and decreasing our production and increasing our imports of the goods and services in which our trading partners have a comparative advantage, we can make ourselves and the citizens of other countries better off.

Brings Diversity and Stability

A diversified investment portfolio is less risky than one that has all of its eggs in one basket. The same is true for an economy's production. A diversified economy fluctuates less than an economy that produces only one or two goods.

But big, rich, diversified economies like those of the United States, Japan, and Europe do not have this type of stability problem. Even a country such as Saudi Arabia that produces almost only one good (in this case, oil) can benefit from specializing in the activity at which it has a comparative advantage and then investing in a wide range of activities in other countries to bring greater stability to its income and consumption.

Penalizes Lax Environmental Standards

A new argument for protection is that many poorer countries, such as Mexico, do not have the same environmental standards that we have, and because they are willing to pollute and we are not, we cannot compete with them without tariffs. So if they want free trade with the richer and "greener" countries, they must clean up their environments to our standards.

This argument for trade restrictions is not entirely convincing. A poor country is less able than a rich one to devote resources to achieving high environmental standards. So if free trade helps a poor country to become richer, it will also help that country to develop the means to improve its environment. But there probably is a case for using the negotiation of free trade agreements such as NAFTA and CAFTA to hold member countries to higher environmental standards. There is an especially large payoff from using such bargaining to try to avoid irreversible damage to resources such as tropical rainforests.

Protects National Culture

The national culture argument for protection is not heard much in the United States, but it is a commonly heard argument in Canada and Europe.

The expressed fear is that free trade in books, magazines, movies, and television programs means U.S. domination and the end of local culture. So, the reasoning continues, it is necessary to protect domestic "culture" industries from free international trade to ensure the survival of a national cultural identity.

Protection of these industries is common and takes the form of nontariff barriers. For example, regulations often require local content on radio and television broadcasting and in magazines.

The cultural identity argument for protection is used most aggressively by writers, publishers, and broadcasters who want to limit foreign competition so that they can earn larger incomes. Many of the creators of so-called American cultural products are not Americans, but the talented citizens of other countries, ensuring the survival of their national cultural identities in Hollywood! Also, if national culture in Canada and Europe is in danger, it is not clear that preventing competition is the best way to restore it to health. Competition among cultures might be a source of strength.

So none of the five common arguments that we've just considered provide overwhelming support for protection. They all have flaws and leave the case for free international trade a strong one.

■ Why Is International Trade Restricted?

Why, despite all the arguments against protection, is international trade restricted? There are two key reasons:

- Tariff revenue
- Rent seeking

Tariff Revenue

Government revenue is costly to collect. In developed countries, such as the United States, well-organized tax collection systems exist that can generate billions of dollars of income tax and sales tax revenues. These tax collection systems are made possible by the fact that firms that must keep properly audited financial records do most economic transactions. Without such records, the revenue collection agencies (such as the Internal Revenue Service in the United States) would be severely hampered in their work. Even with audited financial accounts, some proportion of potential tax revenue is lost. Nonetheless, for industrialized countries, the income tax and sales taxes are the major sources of revenue and the tariff plays a very small role.

But governments in developing countries have a difficult time collecting taxes from their citizens. Much economic activity takes place in an informal economy with few financial records. So these countries collect only a small amount of revenue from income taxes and sales taxes. The one area in which economic transactions are well recorded and audited is international trade. So this activity is an attractive base for tax collection in these countries and is used much more extensively than it is in the developed countries.

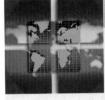

EYE ON THE GLOBAL ECONOMY

Competing with Low-Wage Nations

New Balance athletic shoes are made in two ways:

(1) At a New Balance factory in Norridgewock, Maine, skilled workers who earn $14 an hour operate "see-and-sew" machines—$100,000 automated sewing machines guided by cameras. It costs $4 to make a pair of shoes in Maine.

(2) At a subcontractor's factory in China, low-skilled women in their teens and early twenties who earn 40 cents an hour operate ordinary sewing machines. It costs $1.30 to make a pair of shoes in China.

China and other Asian economies have a comparative advantage in making athletic shoes. Even though New Balance has invested heavily in equipment to make its U.S. work force much more productive than the Chinese work force, it costs three times as much to make a pair of shoes in Maine as it costs in China.

Given this cost difference, Nike and other makers of athletic shoes produce their entire output in Asia.

But New Balance produces 25 percent of its output in the United States and the rest in Asia.

Why is New Balance willing to pay three times as much to produce shoes in Maine?

First, the cost of production is a small part of the retail price.

Second, some people are willing to pay more for a product with a label that says "Made in the United States." If 25 percent of New Balance's customers are willing to pay just a few dollars more for a pair of "Made in the United States" shoes, New Balance profits by producing some shoes in Maine.

Rent Seeking

Rent seeking is lobbying and other political activity that seeks to capture the gains from trade. Free trade increases consumption possibilities on the average, but not everyone shares in the gain and some people even lose. Free trade brings benefits to some and imposes costs on others, with total benefits exceeding total costs. It is the uneven distribution of costs and benefits that is the principal source of impediment to achieving more liberal international trade.

Suppose that we had a tariff on T-shirts, as in the example that you studied earlier in this chapter. A few thousand (perhaps a few hundred) garment makers and their employees who must switch to some other activity would bear the cost of the United States moving to free trade. The millions of T-shirt buyers would reap the benefits of moving to free trade. The number of people who gain will, in general, be enormous in comparison with the number who lose. The gain per person will therefore be small. The loss per person to those who bear the loss will be large.

Because the loss that falls on those who bear it is large, it will pay those people to incur considerable expense to lobby against free trade. On the other hand, it will not pay those who gain to organize to achieve free trade. The gain from trade for any one individual is too small for that individual to spend much time or money on a political organization to lobby for free trade. The loss from free trade will be seen as being so great by those bearing that loss that they will find it profitable to join a political organization to prevent free trade. Each group is

When the United States and Canada negotiated the Canada-U.S. Free Trade Agreement (the predecessor of NAFTA), U.S. President Ronald Reagan (hand outstretched on the right) and Canadian Prime Minister Brian Mulroney (maple-leafed figure on the left), were able to go only as far as their national self-interested rent seekers would allow them to go in dismantling tariffs and other barriers to free trade between the world's two largest trading partners.

Cartoon by Alan King, The Ottawa Citizen, Canwest News Service.

weighing benefits against costs and choosing the best action for themselves. But the anti-free-trade group will undertake a larger quantity of political lobbying than will the pro-free-trade group.

Compensating Losers

If, in total, the gains from free international trade exceed the losses, why don't those who gain compensate those who lose so that everyone is in favor of free trade? To some degree, such compensation does take place. When Congress approved the NAFTA deal with Canada and Mexico, it set up a $56 million fund to support and retrain workers who lost their jobs because of the new trade agreement. During the first six months of the operation of NAFTA, only 5,000 workers applied for benefits under this scheme.

It is difficult to identify and compensate the losers from free international trade. But if we don't make a better effort to do so, protectionism will remain a popular and permanent feature of our national economic and political life.

REALITY CHECK

International Trade in YOUR Life

International trade plays an extraordinarily large role in *your* life in three broad ways.

First, as a consumer, you benefit from the availability of a wide range of low-cost, high-quality goods and services that are produced in other countries. Look closely at the labels on the items you buy. Where was your computer made? Where were your shirt and your shoes made? Where are the fruits and vegetables that you buy, especially in winter, grown?

Second, as a producer (or as a potential producer if you don't yet have a job) you benefit from huge global markets for U.S. products. Your job prospects would be much dimmer if the firm for which you work didn't have global markets in which to sell its products. Even if you were to become a college professor, you would benefit if your school could sell its education services to foreign students.

Third, as a voter, you have a big stake in the politics of free trade versus protection. As a buyer, your self-interest is hurt by tariffs on imported goods. Each time you buy a $20 sweater, you contribute $5 to the government in tariff revenue. But as a worker, your self-interest might be hurt by offshoring and by freer access to U.S. markets for foreign producers. As a voter, you must decide what trade policy serves your self-interest and what best serves the social interest.

4 Explain the arguments used to justify trade barriers and show why these arguments are incorrect but also why some barriers are hard to remove.

Practice Problems 20.4

1. Japan sets quotas on imports of rice. California rice growers would like to export more rice to Japan. What are Japan's arguments for restricting imports of Californian rice? Are these arguments correct? Who loses from this restriction in trade?

2. The United States has, from time to time, limited imports of steel from Europe. What argument has the United States used to justify this quota? Who wins from this restriction? Who loses?

3. The United States maintains a quota on imports of sugar. What is the argument for this quota? Is this argument flawed? If so, explain why.

Exercises 20.4

1. Venezuelan president Hugo Chavez opposes the creation of a Free Trade Area of the Americas (FTAA). Why? Who does he think will gain and lose? Do you think he is correct?

2. The Summit of the Americas in November 2005, President George W. Bush made no progress in his bid to create the FTAA. What are the main obstacles to establishing the FTAA?

3. Hong Kong has never restricted trade. What gains has Hong Kong reaped by unilaterally adopting free trade with all nations? Is there any argument for restricted trade that might have benefited Hong Kong?

Solutions to Practice Problems 20.4

1. The main arguments are that Japanese rice is a better quality rice and that the quota limits competition faced by Japanese farmers. The arguments are not correct. If Japanese consumers do not like the quality of Californian rice, they will not buy it. The quota does limit competition but allows Japanese farmers to use their land less efficiently. The big losers are the Japanese consumers who pay about three times the U.S. price for rice.

2. The U.S. argument is that European producers dump steel on the U.S. market. With a quota, U.S. producers will face less competition in the market for steel and U.S. jobs will be saved. Workers in the steel industry and owners of steel companies will win at the expense of U.S. buyers of steel.

3. The argument is that the quota protects the jobs of U.S. workers. The argument is flawed because the United States does not have a comparative advantage in producing sugar and so a quota allows the U.S. sugar industry to be inefficient. With free trade in sugar, the U.S. sugar industry would exist but it would be much smaller and more efficient.

CHAPTER CHECKPOINT

Key Points

1 **Describe the patterns and trends in international trade.**

- Large flows of trade take place between countries; most trade is in manufactured goods exchanged among rich industrialized countries.
- Since 1960, the volume of U.S. trade has more than doubled and offshore outsourcing has expanded.
- The United States has trading links with every part of the world and is a member of several international organizations and treaties that seek to promote free international trade.

2 **Explain why nations engage in international trade and why trade benefits all nations.**

- When opportunity costs between countries diverge, comparative advantage enables countries to gain from international trade.
- By increasing production of goods in which it has a comparative advantage and then trading some of the increased output, a country can consume at points outside its production possibilities frontier.

3 **Explain how trade barriers reduce international trade.**

- Countries restrict international trade by imposing tariffs and quotas.
- Trade restrictions raise the domestic price of imported goods, lower the volume of imports, and reduce the total value of imports.

4 **Explain the arguments used to justify trade barriers and show why these arguments are incorrect but also why some barriers are hard to remove.**

- The arguments that protection is necessary for national security, for infant industries, and to prevent dumping are weak.
- Arguments that protection saves jobs, allows us to compete with cheap foreign labor, makes the economy diversified and stable, protects national culture, prevents rich countries from exploiting developing countries, and is needed to offset the costs of environmental policies are flawed.
- Trade is restricted because tariffs raise government revenue and because protection brings a small loss to a large number of people and a large gain per person to a small number of people.

Key Terms

Balance of trade, 497
Dumping, 514
Exports, 494
Imports, 494
Infant-industry argument, 513

Nontariff barrier, 508
Offshoring, 505
Outsourcing, 505
Quota, 510
Tariff, 508

FIGURE 1

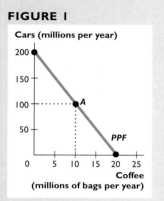

Exercises

1. Suppose that with no international trade between the United States and Brazil, Figure 1 shows the U.S. production possibilities and the quantities of coffee and cars produced (point *A*). Figure 2 shows Brazil's production possibilities and the quantities of coffee and cars produced (point *B*).
   a. What is the opportunity cost of a bag of coffee in the United States?
   b. What is the opportunity cost of a bag of coffee in Brazil?
   c. Which country has a comparative advantage in producing coffee?
   d. Which country has a comparative advantage in producing cars?
   e. With free trade between Brazil and the United States, what does the United States import from Brazil and what does it export to Brazil? Explain your answer.
   f. Does Brazil gain from trade with the United States? Why or why not?

2. When free trade occurs in exercise 1, the world price of a bag of coffee is 1/25th of a car. If Brazil completely specializes in coffee and exports half of it to the United States,
   a. Show on Figure 2 the quantities of the two goods that Brazil consumes.
   b. Show on Figure 1 the quantities of the two goods that the United States consumes.

3. The table provides information about production possibilities in Kenya and Morocco.

FIGURE 2

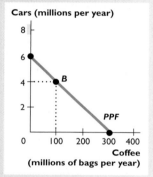

| | Kenya's production possibilities | | | |
Item	A	B	C	D
Coffee (millions of bags per year)	0	2	4	6
Oranges (millions per year)	3	2	1	0

| | Morocco's production possibilities | | | |
Item	A	B	C	D
Coffee (millions of bags per year)	0	1	2	3
Oranges (millions per year)	6	4	2	0

   a. What is the opportunity cost of producing a bag of coffee in Kenya?
   b. What is the opportunity cost of producing a bag of coffee in Morocco?
   c. What is the opportunity cost of producing an orange in Kenya?
   d. What is the opportunity cost of producing an orange in Morocco?
   e. Suppose that Kenya and Morocco do not trade and that in each country, production and consumption are 2 million bags of coffee and 2 million oranges. Make a graph of the two *PPFs* and mark on them the point at which each country produces and consumes.

    f. Now suppose that the two countries specialize and trade. What now are the total quantities of coffee and oranges produced?

    g. If one bag of coffee exchanges for one orange on the world market, what are the volumes of exports and imports of Kenya and Morocco?

    h. What are the consumption of coffee and oranges in Kenya and Morocco?

4. Look at the information provided in *Eye on the Global Economy* on p. 495.
    a. Select an item from the figure in which the United States has a comparative advantage.
    b. Select an item from the figure in which the rest of the world has a comparative advantage.
    c. Make some assumptions about prices and quantities and draw your own figures similar to Figure 20.1 and 20.2 to illustrate the situation in the markets for the two items you chose in parts **a** and **b**.
    d. Make some assumptions about opportunity costs and draw your own figures similar to the two parts of Figure 20.3 to illustrate the U.S. *PPF* and the rest-of-the-world *PPF* for the two items you chose in parts **a** and **b**.

5. Figure 3 shows the car market in Brazil when Brazil places no restriction on imports of cars. The world price of a car is $10,000. If the government of Brazil introduces a 20 percent tariff on car imports, what will be
    a. The price of a car in Brazil?
    b. The quantity of cars imported into Brazil?
    c. The quantity of cars produced in Brazil?
    d. The government's tariff revenue?

6. Suppose that in exercise 5, the Brazilian government introduces a quota of 50 million cars a year. Show on Figure 3
    a. The price of a car in Brazil.
    b. The quantity of cars imported into Brazil.
    c. The quantity of cars produced in Brazil.

7. If the tariff described in exercise 5 is imposed,
    a. Who will gain and who will lose?
    b. Why might a tariff be imposed?

8. If the quota described in exercise 6 is imposed,
    a. Who will gain and who will lose?
    b. Why might a quota be imposed?

FIGURE 3

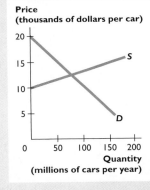

9. In the 1950s, Ford and General Motors established a small car-producing industry in Australia and argued for a high tariff on car imports. The tariff has remained through the years. In 2000, the tariff was cut from 22.5 percent to 15 percent. What might have been the argument for the high tariff? Is the tariff the best way to achieve the goals of the argument?

10. The Canadian government argues against free trade in magazines and movies. Why is the Canadian government concerned about the quantity of U.S. magazines and movies that Canadians see? What is wrong with the Canadian government's argument? Who in Canada gains from the government's argument?

11. The U.S. government imposes a quota on lamb imports from New Zealand and Australia. New Zealand and Australia have lobbied the U.S. government for an increase in the quota. What is the argument put forward by the New Zealand and Australian governments? What is the counterargument put forward by the U.S. government? Which argument is really an example of rent seeking?

12. In 1845, French economist Frédéric Bastiat wrote a satirical "petition of the candlemakers" in which he argued that competition from the sun was unfair to the makers of artificial lighting. He suggested that to level the playing field, boost the production of artificial light, and create much employment and economic activity, the government should pass a law ordering the shutting up of all windows, openings, and chinks through which sunlight may enter buildings.
    a. Explain why passing the law called for in Bastiat's petition would create inefficiency.
    b. Explain why the argument presented in Bastiat's petition is similar to that of people who argue for protection from foreign competition.

Web Exercises

Use the links on MyEconLab to work the following exercises.

13. Visit the Web site of the World Trade Organization (WTO).
    a. What is the WTO?
    b. Review the ten benefits of the WTO trading system listed on the Web site. Do you agree that these are benefits? Who benefits?
    c. Review the ten common misunderstandings about the WTO listed on the Web site. Do you agree that these are misunderstandings? Explain why or why not.

14. Visit the Agriculture Negotiations page of the WTO Web site.
    a. What are the problems facing international trade in agricultural products?
    b. How does the WTO plan to deal with these problems?
    c. If international trade in agricultural products becomes freer, do you expect U.S. farms to expand or contract? Why?

15. Visit the Global Trade Watch page on the Web site of the Public Citizen.
    a. What are the views expressed by Global Trade Watch?
    b. Are these views among the ten common misunderstandings about the WTO?
    c. Are the views of Global Trade Watch consistent with the ideas about the gains from international trade that you've studied in this chapter?
    d. Explain why you agree or disagree with the views of Global Trade Watch.

16. Visit the Web site of the U.S. International Trade Commission (USITC).
    a. What are the main functions and responsibilities of the USITC?
    b. How does the role of the USITC differ from that of the WTO?
    c. Review the page on effects of the proposed Free Trade Agreement between the United States and the Southern Africa Customs Union. Who do you think would gain from such an agreement and why?

CHAPTER 21

International Finance

CHAPTER CHECKLIST

**When you have completed your study of this chapter,
you will be able to**

1 Describe a country's balance of payments accounts and explain what
determines the amount of international borrowing and lending.

2 Explain how the exchange rate is determined and why it fluctuates.

Every single year since 1982, the United States
has spent more on imports than it has earned
on exports. By the end of 2004, the accumulated deficit exceeded $4 trillion! How can a
nation spend more than it earns? What determines the balance of international payments?

The world's four big currencies are the U.S.
dollar, the Japanese yen, the British pound, and
the European euro. Most of the world's international trade
and finance are conducted in terms of these four currencies.
But another currency—the Chinese yuan—is important for
the United States. The values of most currencies fluctuate.
For example, since 1998, the U.S. dollar has fluctuated
between a high of 145 yen and a low of 103 yen. But our
dollar bought the same 8.28 yuan every month from January
1998 through June 2005. Why is our dollar permitted to fluctuate against some currencies but is fixed against others? Is a
fluctuating currency better or worse than a fixed one?

In this chapter, you are going to learn about international
finance. You will discover how nations keep their international accounts and what determines the balance of payments and the value of the dollar.

21.1 FINANCING INTERNATIONAL TRADE

When Apple Computer, Inc. imports iPods that it manufactures in Taiwan, it pays for them using Taiwanese dollars. When a French construction company buys an earthmover from Caterpillar, Inc., it uses U.S. dollars. Whenever we buy things from another country, we pay in the currency of that country. It doesn't make any difference what the item being traded is; it might be a consumption good or a service or a capital good, a building, or even a firm.

We're going to study the markets in which different types of currency are bought and sold. But first we're going to look at the scale of international trading and borrowing and lending and at the way in which we keep our records of these transactions. These records are called the balance of payments accounts.

■ Balance of Payments Accounts

Balance of payments accounts
The accounts in which a nation records its international trading, borrowing, and lending.

A country's **balance of payments accounts** record its international trading, borrowing, and lending. There are in fact three balance of payments accounts:

- Current account
- Capital account
- Official settlements account

Current account
Record of international receipts and payments—current account balance equals exports minus imports, plus net interest and transfers received from abroad.

The **current account** records receipts from the sale of goods and services to other countries (exports), minus payments for goods and services bought from other countries (imports), plus the net amount of interest and transfers (such as foreign aid payments) received from and paid to other countries. The **capital account** records foreign investment in the United States minus U.S. investment abroad. The **official settlements account** records the change in official U.S. reserves. **U.S. official reserves** are the government's holdings of foreign currency. If U.S. official reserves increase, the official settlements account balance is negative. The reason is that holding foreign money is like investing abroad. U.S. investment abroad is a minus item in the capital account and in the official settlements account. (By the same reasoning, if official reserves decrease, the official settlements account balance is positive.)

Capital account
Record of foreign investment in the United States minus U.S. investment abroad.

Official settlements account
Record of the change in U.S. official reserves.

U.S. official reserves
The government's holdings of foreign currency.

The sum of the balances on the three accounts always equals zero. That is, to pay for our current account deficit, we must either borrow more from abroad than we lend abroad or use our official reserves to cover the shortfall.

Table 21.1 shows the U.S. balance of payments accounts in 2004. Items in the current account and capital account that provide foreign currency to the United States have a plus sign; items that cost the United States foreign currency have a minus sign. The table shows that in 2004, U.S. imports exceeded U.S. exports and the current account deficit was $668 billion. We paid for imports that exceeded the value of our exports by borrowing from the rest of the world. The capital account tells us by how much. We borrowed $1,440 billion (foreign investment in the United States) but made loans of $860 billion (U.S. investment abroad). So our measured net foreign borrowing was $580 billion. Measurement error (recorded in the balance of payments accounts as a statistical discrepancy) was $85 billion. Our official reserves decreased by $3 billion and are shown in Table 21.1 as a positive $3 billion, a convention that makes the three accounts sum to zero.

You might better understand the balance of payments accounts and the way in which they are linked if you think about the income and expenditure, borrowing and lending, and bank account of an individual.

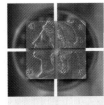

The U.S. Balance of Payments

The numbers in Table 21.1 provide a snapshot of the U.S balance of payments in 2004. The figure puts this snapshot into perspective by showing how the balance of payments evolved from 1980 to 2004.

(Because the economy grows and the price level rises, changes in the dollar value of the balance of payments do not convey much information. To remove the influences of growth and inflation, the figure shows the balance of payments as a percentage of GDP.)

The capital account balance is almost a mirror image of the current account balance because the official settlements balance is very small in comparison with the balances on these other two accounts. A large cur-

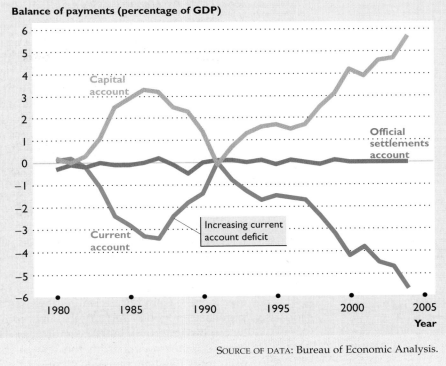

Balance of payments (percentage of GDP)

SOURCE OF DATA: Bureau of Economic Analysis.

rent account deficit (and capital account surplus) emerged during the 1980s but declined from 1987 to

1991. Throughout the 1990s and 2000s, the current account deficit increased.

■ **TABLE 21.1**

The U.S. Balance of Payments Accounts in 2004

Current account	(billions of dollars)
Exports of goods and services	+1,152
Imports of goods and services	−1,769
Net interest	30
Net transfers	−81
Current account balance	−668
Capital account	
Foreign investment in the United States	+1,440
U.S. investment abroad	−860
Statistical discrepancy	85
Capital account balance	+665
Official settlements account	
Official settlements account balance	3

SOURCE OF DATA: Bureau of Economic Analysis.

Personal Analogy

You have a set of personal balance of payments accounts that parallel those of a nation. You have a current account, a capital account, and a settlements account.

Your current account records your income from supplying the services of factors of production and your expenditure on goods and services. Consider, for example, Joanne. She worked in 2005 and earned an income of $25,000. Joanne has $10,000 worth of investments that earned her interest of $1,000. Joanne's current account shows an income of $26,000. Joanne spent $18,000 buying goods and services for consumption. She also bought a new house, which cost her $60,000. So Joanne's total expenditure was $78,000. The difference between her expenditure and her income is $52,000 ($78,000 minus $26,000).

To pay for expenditure of $52,000 in excess of her income, Joanne has to use the money that she has in the bank or she has to take out a loan. Suppose that Joanne took a mortgage of $50,000 to help buy her house. This mortgage was the only borrowing that Joanne did, so her capital account surplus was $50,000. With a current account deficit of $52,000 and a capital account surplus of $50,000, Joanne is still $2,000 short. She got that $2,000 from her own bank account. Her cash holdings decreased by $2,000. Joanne's settlements balance was $2,000.

Joanne's income from her work is like a country's income from its exports. Her income from her investments is like a country's interest from foreigners. Her purchases of goods and services, including her purchase of an apartment, are like a country's imports. Joanne's mortgage—borrowing from someone else—is like a country's borrowing from the rest of the world. The change in Joanne's bank account is like the change in a country's official reserves.

Check that the sum of Joanne's balances is zero. Her current account balance is −$52,000, her capital account balance is +$50,000, and her settlements account balance is +$2,000, so the sum of the three balances is zero.

■ Borrowers and Lenders, Debtors and Creditors

A country that is borrowing more from the rest of the world than it is lending to the rest of the world is called a **net borrower**. Similarly, a **net lender** is a country that is lending more to the rest of the world than it is borrowing from it.

The United States is a net borrower, but it is a relative newcomer to the ranks of net borrower nations. Throughout the 1960s and most of the 1970s, the United States was a net lender to the rest of the world. It had a surplus on its current account and a deficit on its capital account. It was not until 1983 that the United States became a significant net borrower from the rest of the world. Between 1983 and 1987, U.S. borrowing increased each year. Then it decreased and was briefly zero in 1991. After 1991, U.S. borrowing started to increase again. The average net foreign borrowing by the United States between 1983 and 2004 was $183 billion a year.

Most countries are net borrowers like the United States. But a small number of countries, including Japan and oil-rich Saudi Arabia, are net lenders.

A net borrower might be reducing its net assets held in the rest of the world, or it might be going deeper into debt. A nation's total stock of foreign investment determines whether the nation is a debtor or creditor. A **debtor nation** is a country that during its entire history has borrowed more from the rest of the world than it has lent to the rest of the world. It has a stock of outstanding debt to the rest of the world that exceeds the stock of its own claims on the rest of the world. A **creditor nation** is a country that during its entire history has invested more in the rest of the world than other countries have invested in it.

Net borrower
A country that is borrowing more from the rest of the world than it is lending to the rest of the world.

Net lender
A country that is lending more to the rest of the world than it is borrowing from the rest of the world.

Debtor nation
A country that during its entire history has borrowed more from the rest of the world than it has lent to the rest of the world.

Creditor nation
A country that during its entire history has invested more in the rest of the world than other countries have invested in it.

Flows and Stocks

Borrowing and lending are flows—amounts per unit of time. Debts are stocks—amounts at a point in time. The flow of borrowing and lending changes the stock of debt.

The United States was a debtor nation through the nineteenth century as we borrowed from Europe to finance our westward expansion, railroads, and industrialization. We paid off our debt and became a creditor nation for most of the twentieth century. But following a string of current account deficits, we became a debtor nation again in 1989.

The largest debtor nations are the capital-hungry developing countries (as the United States was during the nineteenth century). The international debt of these countries grew from less than a third to more than a half of their gross domestic product during the 1980s and created what is called the "Third World debt crisis."

Should we be concerned that the United States is a net borrower? The answer is probably not. Our international borrowing finances the purchase of new capital goods, which adds to the nation's capital, and increases productivity. Governments also purchase education and health care services, which increase human capital so our international borrowing is financing private and public investment, not consumption.

EYE ON THE GLOBAL ECONOMY

Current Account Balances Around the World

The U.S. current account deficit in 2004 is the major international payments deficit. No other country has a deficit remotely similar to that of the United States.

For every deficit, there must be a corresponding surplus. The figure shows that the U.S. deficit is reflected in a large number of small surpluses spread around the world. No single country or group of countries has a surplus to match the U.S. deficit.

Notice in particular how small China's surplus is. The other advanced nations were the ones with the largest surpluses in 2004. Other large surpluses are earned by the oil-exporting Middle East and by Japan and other industrialized Asian economies.

SOURCE OF DATA: International Monetary Fund, *World Economic Outlook*, April 2005.

1   **Describe a country's balance of payments accounts and explain what determines the amount of international borrowing and lending.**

Practice Problem 21.1

1. It is 2006, and the U.S. economy records the following transactions: Imports of goods and services, $2,000 billion; interest paid to the rest of the world, $500 billion; interest received from the rest of the world, $400 billion; decrease in U.S. official reserves, $10 billion; capital account balance, $330 billion; net transfers, zero.

   a. Calculate the current account balance, the official settlements account balance, and exports of goods and services.
   b. Is the United States a debtor or a creditor nation in 2006?
   c. If interest payments to the rest of the world increase by $100 billion, what would happen to the current account balance?

Exercise 21.1

1. It is 2007, and the U.S. economy records the following transactions: Exports of goods and services, $1,800 billion; interest payments to the rest of the world, $550 billion; interest received from the rest of the world, $350 billion; decrease in U.S. official reserves, $10 billion; capital account balance, $600 billion; net transfers are zero.

   a. Calculate the current account balance, the official settlements account balance, and imports of goods and services.
   b. Has the United States become a larger or smaller debtor or creditor nation in 2007 than it was in 2006 (practice problem 21.1)?
   c. If imports increase by $100 billion, what would happen to the capital account balance?

Solution to Practice Problem 21.1

1a. The U.S. official reserves fell by $10 billion, so the official settlements account balance is a *surplus* of $10 billion. To find the current account balance, use the fact that the sum of the current account, capital account, and official balance account is zero. The capital account balance is $330 billion and the official settlements balance is $10 billion, so the current balance is −$340 billion. To calculate exports of goods and services, use the fact that the current account balance (−$340 billion) equals exports (the number we seek) minus imports ($2,000 billion) plus net interest (−$100 billion) plus net transfers (zero). Exports of goods and services equal $1,760 billion.

1b. The United States is a debtor nation in 2006 because it pays out more in interest to the rest of the world than it receives from the rest of the world.

1c. If interest paid to the rest of the world increased by $100 billion, the current account deficit would increase to $440 billion.

21.2 THE EXCHANGE RATE

When we buy foreign goods or invest in another country, we pay using that country's currency. When foreigners buy U.S.-made goods or invest in the United States, they pay in U.S. dollars. We get foreign currency, and foreigners get U.S. dollars in the foreign exchange market. The **foreign exchange market** is the market in which the currency of one country is exchanged for the currency of another. The foreign exchange market is not a place like a downtown flea market or produce market. It is made up of thousands of people: importers and exporters, banks, and specialist traders of foreign exchange, called foreign exchange brokers. The foreign exchange market opens on Monday morning in Hong Kong, which is still Sunday evening in New York. As the day advances, markets open in Singapore, Tokyo, Bahrain, Frankfurt, London, New York, Chicago, and San Francisco. As the U.S. West Coast markets close, Hong Kong is only an hour away from opening for the next business day. Dealers around the world are in continual contact, and on a typical day in 2005, $2 trillion changed hands.

Foreign exchange market
The market in which the currency of one country is exchanged for the currency of another.

The price at which one currency exchanges for another is called a **foreign exchange rate**. For example, in August 2005, one U.S. dollar bought 111 Japanese yen. The exchange rate was 111 yen per dollar. We can also express the exchange rate in terms of dollars (or cents) per yen, which in August 2005 was a bit less than 1 cent per yen.

Foreign exchange rate
The price at which one currency exchanges for another.

Currency depreciation is the fall in the value of one currency in terms of another currency. For example, if the dollar falls from 100 yen to 80 yen, the dollar depreciates by 20 percent.

Currency depreciation
The fall in the value of one currency in terms of another currency.

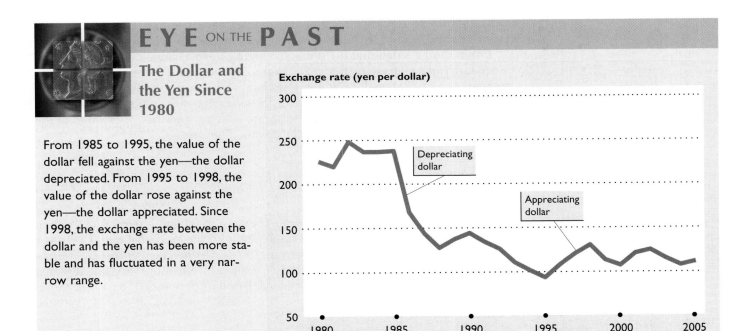

EYE ON THE PAST

The Dollar and the Yen Since 1980

From 1985 to 1995, the value of the dollar fell against the yen—the dollar depreciated. From 1995 to 1998, the value of the dollar rose against the yen—the dollar appreciated. Since 1998, the exchange rate between the dollar and the yen has been more stable and has fluctuated in a very narrow range.

Exchange rate (yen per dollar)

Depreciating dollar

Appreciating dollar

SOURCE OF DATA: PACIFIC FX Service, University of British Columbia.

Currency appreciation
The rise in the value of one currency in terms of another currency.

Currency appreciation is the rise in the value of one currency in terms of another currency. For example, if the dollar rises from 100 yen to 120 yen, the dollar appreciates by 20 percent. When the U.S. dollar appreciates against the yen, the yen depreciates against the dollar.

Why does the U.S. dollar fluctuate in value? Why does it sometimes depreciate and sometimes appreciate?

The exchange rate is a price. And like all prices, demand and supply determine the exchange rate. So to understand the forces that determine the exchange rate, we need to study demand and supply in the foreign exchange market. We'll begin by looking at the demand side of the market.

■ Demand in the Foreign Exchange Market

The quantity of U.S. dollars demanded in the foreign exchange market is the amount that traders plan to buy during a given time period at a given exchange rate. This quantity depends on many factors, but the main ones are

- The exchange rate
- Interest rates in the United States and other countries
- The expected future exchange rate

Let's look first at the relationship between the quantity of dollars demanded in the foreign exchange market and the exchange rate.

■ The Law of Demand for Foreign Exchange

People do not buy dollars because they enjoy them. The demand for dollars is a *derived demand.* People demand dollars so that they can buy U.S.-made goods and services (U.S. exports). They also demand dollars so that they can buy U.S. assets such as bank accounts, bonds, stocks, businesses, and real estate. Nevertheless, the law of demand applies to dollars just as it does to anything else that people value.

Other things remaining the same, the higher the exchange rate, the smaller is the quantity of dollars demanded. For example, if the price of the U.S. dollar rises from 100 yen to 120 yen but nothing else changes, the quantity of U.S. dollars that people plan to buy decreases. Why does the exchange rate influence the quantity of dollars demanded? There are two separate reasons, and they are related to the two sources of the derived demand for dollars. They are

- Exports effect
- Expected profit effect

Exports Effect

The larger the value of U.S. exports, the larger is the quantity of dollars demanded. But the value of U.S. exports depends on the exchange rate. The lower the exchange rate, other things remaining the same, the cheaper are U.S.-made goods and services to people in the rest of the world, the more the United States exports, and the greater is the quantity of U.S. dollars demanded to pay for them.

Expected Profit Effect

The larger the expected profit from holding dollars, the greater is the quantity of dollars demanded in the foreign exchange market. But expected profit depends on the exchange rate. The lower the exchange rate, other things remaining the same, the larger is the expected profit from holding dollars and the greater is the quantity of dollars demanded on the foreign exchange market.

FIGURE 21.1
The Demand for Dollars

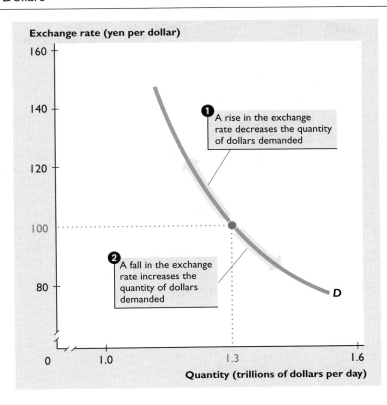

Exchange rate (yen per dollar)

1 A rise in the exchange rate decreases the quantity of dollars demanded

2 A fall in the exchange rate increases the quantity of dollars demanded

D

Quantity (trillions of dollars per day)

Other things remaining the same, the quantity of dollars that people plan to buy depends on the exchange rate.

1 If the exchange rate rises, the quantity of dollars demanded decreases and there is a movement up along the demand curve for dollars.

2 If the exchange rate falls, the quantity of dollars demanded increases and there is a movement down along the demand curve for dollars.

To understand this effect, suppose that you think the dollar will be worth 120 yen by the end of the month. If a dollar costs 115 yen today, you buy dollars. But a person who thinks that the dollar will be worth 115 yen at the end of the month does not buy dollars. Now suppose that the exchange rate falls to 110 yen per dollar. More people think that they can profit from buying dollars, so the quantity of dollars demanded increases.

Figure 21.1 shows the demand curve for U.S. dollars in the foreign exchange market. For the two reason we've just reviewed, when the foreign exchange rate rises, other things remaining the same, the quantity of dollars demanded decreases and there is a movement up along the demand curve, as shown by the arrow. When the exchange rate falls, other things remaining the same, the quantity of dollars demanded increases and there is a movement down along the demand curve, as shown by the arrow.

Changes in the Demand for Dollars

A change in any other influence on the quantity of U.S. dollars that people plan to buy in the foreign exchange market brings a change in the demand for dollars, and the demand curve for dollars shifts. These other influences are

- Interest rates in the United States and other countries
- The expected future exchange rate

Interest Rates in the United States and Other Countries

U.S. interest rate differential
The U.S. interest rate minus the foreign interest rate.

If you can borrow in another country and lend in the United States at a higher interest rate, you will make a profit. What matters is not the level of foreign and U.S. interest rates, but the gap between them. This gap, the U.S. interest rate minus the foreign interest rate, is called the **U.S. interest rate differential**. The larger the U.S. interest rate differential, the greater is the demand for U.S. assets and the greater is the demand for dollars.

The Expected Future Exchange Rate

Suppose you are Toyota's finance manager. The exchange rate is 100 yen per dollar, and you expect that by the end of the month, it will be 120 yen per dollar. You spend 100,000 yen today and buy $1,000. At the end of the month, the dollar equals 120 yen, as you predicted, and you sell the $1,000. You get 120,000 yen. You've made a profit of 20,000 yen. The higher the expected future exchange rate, the greater is the expected profit and the greater is the demand for dollars.

Figure 21.2 summarizes the influences on the demand for dollars. A rise in the U.S. interest rate differential or a rise in the expected future exchange rate increases the demand for dollars today and shifts the demand curve rightward from D_0 to D_1. A fall in the U.S. interest rate differential or a fall in the expected future exchange rate decreases the demand for dollars today and shifts the demand curve leftward from D_0 to D_2.

■ **FIGURE 21.2**

Changes in the Demand for Dollars

❶ The demand for dollars increases if:

■ The U.S. interest rate differential increases.
■ The expected future exchange rate rises.

❷ The demand for dollars decreases if:

■ The U.S. interest rate differential decreases.
■ The expected future exchange rate falls.

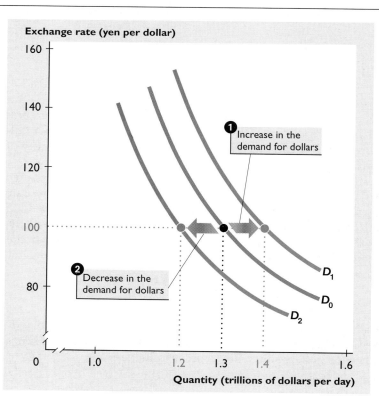

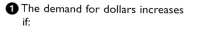

■ Supply in the Foreign Exchange Market

The quantity of U.S. dollars supplied in the foreign exchange market is the amount that traders plan to sell during a given time period at a given exchange rate. This quantity depends on many factors, but the main ones are

- The exchange rate
- Interest rates in the United States and other countries
- The expected future exchange rate

Does this list of factors seem familiar? It should: It is the same list as that for demand. The demand side and the supply side of the foreign exchange market are influenced by all the same factors. But the ways in which these three factors influence supply are the opposite of the ways in which they influence demand.

Let's look first at the relationship between the quantity of dollars supplied in the foreign exchange market and the exchange rate.

■ The Law of Supply of Foreign Exchange

Traders supply U.S. dollars in the foreign exchange market when people and businesses buy other currencies. And they buy other currencies so that they can buy foreign-made goods and services (U.S. imports). They also supply dollars and buy foreign currencies so that they can buy foreign assets such as bank accounts, bonds, stocks, businesses, and real estate. The law of supply applies to dollars just as it does to anything else that people plan to sell.

Other things remaining the same, the higher the exchange rate, the greater is the quantity of dollars supplied in the foreign exchange market. For example, if the price of the U.S. dollar rises from 100 yen to 120 yen but nothing else changes, the quantity of U.S. dollars that people plan to sell in the foreign exchange market increases. Why does the exchange rate influence the quantity of dollars supplied?

There are two reasons, and they parallel the two reasons on the demand side of the market. They are

- Imports effect
- Expected profit effect

Imports Effect

The larger the value of U.S. imports, the larger is the quantity of foreign currency demanded to pay for these imports. And when people buy foreign currency, they supply dollars. So the larger the value of U.S. imports, the greater is the quantity of dollars supplied on the foreign exchange market. But the value of U.S. imports depends on the exchange rate. The higher the exchange rate, other things remaining the same, the cheaper are foreign-made goods and services to Americans. So the more the United States imports, the greater is the quantity of U.S. dollars supplied on the foreign exchange market to pay for these imports.

Expected Profit Effect

The larger the expected profit from holding a foreign currency, the greater is the quantity of that currency demanded and the greater is the quantity of dollars supplied in the foreign exchange market. But the expected profit from holding a foreign currency depends on the exchange rate. The higher the exchange rate, other things remaining the same, the larger is the expected profit from selling dollars and the greater is the quantity of dollars supplied on the foreign exchange market.

■ FIGURE 21.3

The Supply of Dollars

Other things remaining the same, the quantity of dollars that people plan to sell depends on the exchange rate.

① If the exchange rate rises, the quantity of dollars supplied increases and there is a movement up along the supply curve of dollars.

② If the exchange rate falls, the quantity of dollars supplied decreases and there is a movement down along the supply curve of dollars.

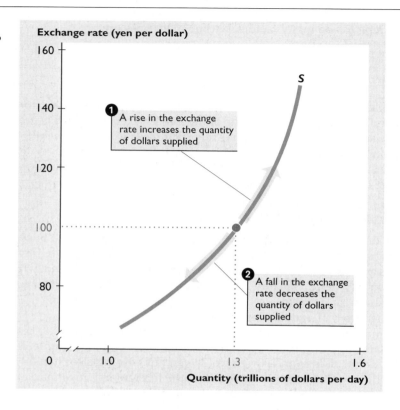

Exchange rate (yen per dollar)

S

① A rise in the exchange rate increases the quantity of dollars supplied

② A fall in the exchange rate decreases the quantity of dollars supplied

Quantity (trillions of dollars per day)

For the two reasons we've just reviewed, other things remaining the same, when the foreign exchange rate rises, the quantity of dollars supplied increases, and when the foreign exchange rate falls, the quantity of dollars supplied decreases. Figure 21.3 shows the supply curve of U.S. dollars in the foreign exchange market. In this figure, when the foreign exchange rate rises, other things remaining the same, there is an increase in the quantity of dollars supplied and a movement up along the supply curve, as shown by the arrow. When the exchange rate falls, other things remaining the same, there is a decrease in the quantity of dollars supplied and a movement down along the supply curve, as shown by the arrow.

■ Changes in the Supply of Dollars

A change in any other influence on the quantity of U.S. dollars that people plan to sell in the foreign exchange market brings a change in the supply of dollars, and the supply curve of dollars shifts. Supply either increases or decreases. These other influences on supply parallel the other influences on demand but have exactly the opposite effects. These influences are

- Interest rates in the United States and other countries
- The expected future exchange rate

Interest Rates in the United States and Other Countries

The larger the U.S. interest rate differential, the smaller is the demand for foreign assets and the smaller is the supply of dollars on the foreign exchange market.

The Expected Future Exchange Rate

Other things remaining the same, the higher the expected future exchange rate, the smaller is the supply of dollars. To see why, suppose that the dollar is trading at 100 yen per dollar today and you think that by the end of the month, the dollar will trade at 120 yen per dollar. You were planning on selling dollars today, but you decide to hold off and wait until the end of the month. If you supply dollars today, you get only 100 yen per dollar. But at the end of the month, if the dollar is worth 120 yen as you predict, you'll get 120 yen for each dollar you supply. You'll make a profit of 20 percent. So the higher the expected future exchange rate, other things remaining the same, the smaller is the expected profit from selling U.S. dollars today and the smaller is the supply of dollars today.

Figure 21.4 summarizes the above discussion of the influences on the supply of dollars. A rise in the U.S. interest rate differential or a rise in the expected future exchange rate decreases the supply of dollars today and shifts the supply curve leftward from S_0 to S_1. A fall in the U.S. interest rate differential or a fall in the expected future exchange rate increases the supply of dollars today and shifts the supply curve rightward from S_0 to S_2.

■ FIGURE 21.4

Changes in the Supply of Dollars

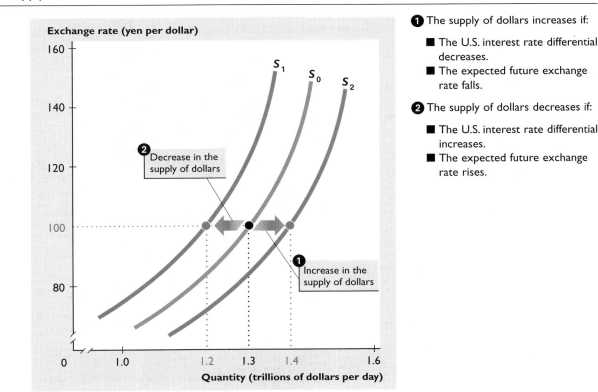

❶ The supply of dollars increases if:

- The U.S. interest rate differential decreases.
- The expected future exchange rate falls.

❷ The supply of dollars decreases if:

- The U.S. interest rate differential increases.
- The expected future exchange rate rises.

■ Market Equilibrium

Figure 21.5 shows how demand and supply in the foreign exchange market determine the exchange rate. The demand curve is *D*, and the supply curve is *S*. Just as in all the other markets you've studied, the price (the exchange rate) acts as a regulator. If the exchange rate is too high, there is a surplus—the quantity supplied exceeds the quantity demanded. For example, in Figure 21.5, if the exchange rate is 120 yen per dollar, there is a surplus of dollars.

If the exchange rate is too low, there is a shortage—the quantity supplied is less than the quantity demanded. For example, in Figure 21.5, if the exchange rate is 80 yen per dollar, there is a shortage of dollars.

At the equilibrium exchange rate, there is neither a shortage nor a surplus. The quantity supplied equals the quantity demanded. In Figure 21.5, the equilibrium exchange rate is 100 yen per dollar. At this exchange rate, the quantity demanded equals the quantity supplied and is $1.3 trillion a day.

The foreign exchange market is constantly pulled to its equilibrium by the forces of supply and demand. Foreign exchange dealers are constantly looking for the best price they can get. If they are selling, they want the highest price available. If they are buying, they want the lowest price available. Information flows from dealer to dealer through the worldwide computer network, and the price adjusts second by second to keep buying plans and selling plans in balance. That is, price adjusts second by second to keep the market at its equilibrium.

▨ FIGURE 21.5

Equilibrium Exchange Rate

⟨X⟩ myeconlab

The demand curve for dollars is *D*, and the supply curve is *S*.

❶ If the exchange rate is 120 yen per dollar, there is a surplus of dollars and the exchange rate falls.

❷ If the exchange rate is 80 yen per dollar, there is a shortage of dollars and the exchange rate rises.

❸ If the exchange rate is 100 yen per dollar, there is neither a shortage nor a surplus of dollars and the exchange rate remains constant. The market is in equilibrium.

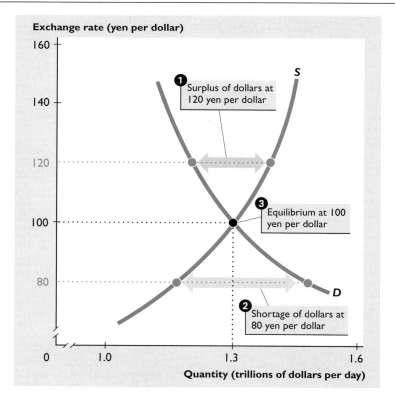

■ Changes in the Exchange Rate

A change in either the demand for dollars or the supply of dollars (or both) changes the exchange rate. Let's look at two episodes during the 1990s.

A Depreciating Dollar: 1994–1995

Between 1994 and the summer of 1995, the exchange rate fell from 100 yen to a low of 84 yen per dollar. Figure 21.6(a) explains this fall. In 1994, the demand and supply curves were those labeled D_{94} and S_{94}. The exchange rate was 100 yen per dollar. During 1994, traders expected the U.S. dollar to depreciate. They expected a lower exchange rate. As a result, the demand for dollars decreased and the supply of dollars increased. The demand curve shifted leftward to D_{95}, and the supply curve shifted rightward to S_{95}. The exchange rate fell to 84 yen per dollar.

An Appreciating Dollar: 1995–1998

Between 1995 and 1998, the dollar appreciated against the yen. It rose from 84 yen to 130 yen per dollar. Figure 21.6(b) explains why this happened. In 1995, the

---

■ **FIGURE 21.6**
Exchange Rate Fluctuations

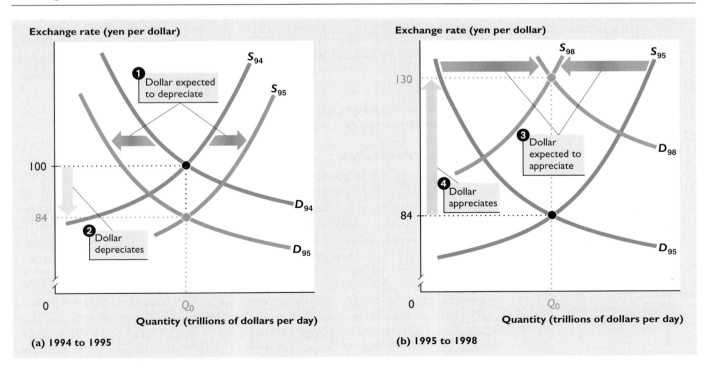

(a) 1994 to 1995

(b) 1995 to 1998

❶ The dollar is expected to depreciate, so the supply of dollars increases and the demand for dollars decreases.

❷ An excess supply of dollars brings a falling exchange rate.

❸ The dollar is expected to appreciate so the supply of dollars decreases and the demand for dollars increases.

❹ An excess demand for dollars brings a rising exchange rate.

demand and supply curves were those labeled D_{95} and S_{95}. The exchange rate was 84 yen per dollar—where the supply and demand curves intersect. During the next two years, Japan was in recession and the U.S. economy was expanding. Interest rates in Japan fell, and the yen was expected to depreciate. The demand for yen decreased, and the demand for dollars increased. The demand curve shifted from D_{95} to D_{98}. The supply of dollars decreased, and the supply curve shifted from S_{95} to S_{98}. These two shifts reinforced each other, and the exchange rate increased to 130 yen per dollar.

Why the Exchange Rate Is Volatile

You've seen that sometimes the dollar depreciates and at other times it appreciates. But the quantity of dollars traded each day barely changes. Why? Because in the foreign exchange market, supply and demand are not independent.

When we studied the demand for dollars and the supply of dollars, we saw that unlike other markets, the demand side and the supply side of the market have common influences. A change in the expected future exchange rate or a change in the U.S. interest rate differential changes *both* demand and supply, and they change in *opposite directions*. These common influences on both demand and supply explain why the exchange rate can be volatile at times, even though the quantity of dollars traded does not change.

Everyone in the market is potentially either a demander or a supplier. Each has a price above which he or she will sell and below which he or she will buy.

■ Exchange Rate Expectations

The changes in the exchange rate that we've just examined occurred in part because the exchange rate was expected to change. This explanation sounds a bit like a self-fulfilling forecast. But what makes expectations change? The answer is new information about the deeper forces that influence the value of money. There are two such forces:

- Purchasing power parity
- Interest rate parity

Purchasing Power Parity

Money is worth what it will buy. But two kinds of money, U.S. dollars and Canadian dollars, for example, might buy different amounts of goods and services. Suppose a Big Mac costs $4 (Canadian) in Toronto and $3 (U.S.) in New York. If the Canadian dollar exchange rate is $1.33 Canadian per U.S. dollar, the two monies have the same value. You can buy a Big Mac in either Toronto or New York for either $4 Canadian or $3 U.S.

Purchasing power parity
Equal value of money—a situation in which money buys the same amount of goods and services in different currencies.

The situation we've just described is called **purchasing power parity**, which means equal value of money. If purchasing power parity does not prevail, some powerful forces go to work. To understand these forces, suppose that the price of a Big Mac in New York rises to $4 U.S., but in Toronto the price remains at $4 Canadian. Suppose the exchange rate remains at $1.33 Canadian per U.S. dollar. In this case, a Big Mac in Toronto still costs $4 Canadian or $3 U.S. But in New York, it costs $4 U.S. or $5.32 Canadian. Money buys more in Canada than in the United States. Money is not of equal value in both countries.

If all (or most) prices have increased in the United States and not increased in Canada, then people will generally expect that the U.S. dollar exchange rate is going to fall. The demand for U.S. dollars decreases, and the supply of U.S. dollars increases. The U.S. dollar exchange rate falls, as expected. If the U.S. dollar falls to $1.00 Canadian and there are no further price changes, purchasing power parity is restored. A Big Mac now costs $4 in either U.S. dollars or Canadian dollars in both New York and Toronto.

If prices increase in Canada and other countries but remain constant in the United States, then people will generally expect that the value of the U.S. dollar on the foreign exchange market is too low and that the U.S. dollar exchange rate will rise. The demand for U.S. dollars increases, and the supply of U.S. dollars decreases. The U.S. dollar exchange rate rises, as expected.

Ultimately, the value of money is determined by prices. So the deeper forces that influence the exchange rate have tentacles that spread throughout the economy. If prices in the United States rise faster than those in other countries, the exchange rate falls. And if prices in the United States rise more slowly than those in other countries, the exchange rate rises.

EYE ON THE GLOBAL ECONOMY

Purchasing Power Parity

Purchasing power parity (PPP) is a long-run phenomenon. In the short run, deviations from PPP can be large.

The figure shows the range of deviations from PPP in November 2002. At that time, the Norwegian krone was overvalued by 45 percent and the Japanese yen was overvalued by 22 percent. The yen has been overvalued for most of the past 10 years. An overvalued currency is one that, according to PPP, will depreciate at some point in the future.

The most undervalued currency in November 2002 was the Polish zloty. An undervalued currency is one that, according to PPP, will appreciate at some time in the future. But PPP does not predict *when* a currency will depreciate or appreciate.

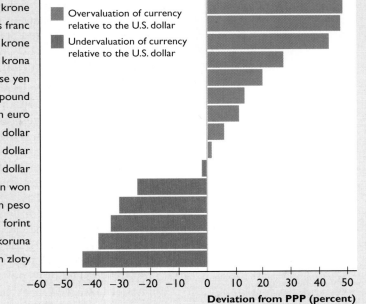

SOURCE OF DATA: PACIFIC FX Service, University of British Columbia, August 7, 2005.

Interest Rate Parity

Suppose a Canadian dollar bank deposit in a Toronto bank earns 5 percent a year and a U.S. dollar bank deposit in a New York bank earns 3 percent a year. Why does anyone deposit money in New York? Why doesn't all the money flow to Toronto? The answer is: Because of exchange rate expectations. Suppose people expect the Canadian dollar to depreciate by 2 percent a year. This 2 percent depreciation must be subtracted from the 5 percent interest to obtain the net return of 3 percent a year that an American can earn by depositing funds in a Toronto bank. The two returns are equal. This situation is one of **interest rate parity**—equal interest rates when exchange rate changes are taken into account.

Interest rate parity always prevails. Funds move to get the highest return available. If the Canadian dollar was higher than its interest rate parity level, the return expected in Toronto would be lower than in New York. In seconds, traders would sell the Canadian dollar, its exchange rate would fall, and the expected return from lending in Toronto would rise to equal that in New York.

Interest rate parity
Equal interest rates—a situation in which the interest rate in one currency equals the interest rate in another currency when exchange rate changes are taken into account.

■ Monetary Policy and the Exchange Rate

The Fed's monetary policy influences the interest rate so its actions influence the interest rate differential and the exchange rate. If the Fed increases the U.S. interest rate and other central banks keep interest rates in other countries unchanged, the value of the U.S. dollar rises on the foreign exchange market. If other central banks increase their interest rates and the Fed keeps the U.S. interest rate unchanged, the value of the U.S. dollar falls on the foreign exchange market. So exchange rates fluctuate in response to changes and expected changes in monetary policy in the United States and around the world.

■ Pegging the Exchange Rate

Some central banks try to avoid exchange rate fluctuations by pegging the value of their currency against another currency. Suppose the Fed wanted to keep the dollar pegged at 100 yen per dollar. If the exchange rate rose above 100 yen, the Fed would sell dollars. If the exchange rate fell below 100 yen, the Fed would buy dollars.

Figure 21.7 illustrates foreign exchange market intervention. The supply of dollars is S, and initially, the demand for dollars is D_0. The equilibrium exchange rate is 100 yen per dollar, which is also the Fed's target—the horizontal red line.

If the demand for dollars increases to D_1, the Fed increases the supply of dollars—sells dollars—and prevents the exchange rate from rising. If the demand for dollars decreases to D_2, the Fed decreases the supply of dollars—buys dollars—and prevents the exchange rate from falling.

When the Fed buys dollars, it uses its reserves of yen. And when the Fed sells dollars, it takes yen in exchange and its reserves of yen increase. As long as the demand for dollars fluctuates around and, on the average, remains at D_0, the Fed's reserves of yen fluctuate but neither run dry nor persistently increase.

But if the demand for dollars decreased permanently to D_2, to maintain the exchange rate at 100 yen per dollar, the Fed would have to buy dollars and sell yen every day. The Fed would soon run out of yen. And when it did, the dollar would sink. If the demand for dollars increased permanently to D_1, the Fed would have to sell dollars and buy yen every day. The Fed would be piling up unwanted yen and at some point would let the dollar rise.

FIGURE 21.7

Foreign Exchange Market Intervention

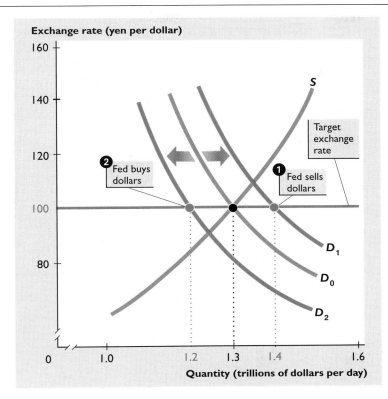

Initially, the demand for dollars is D_0, the supply of dollars is S, and the exchange rate is 100 yen per dollar. The Fed can intervene in the foreign exchange market to keep the exchange rate close to its target rate (100 yen in this example).

❶ If demand increases from D_0 to D_1, the Fed sells dollars to increase supply.

❷ If demand decreases from D_0 to D_2, the Fed buys dollars to decrease supply.

Persistent intervention on one side of the market cannot be sustained.

■ The People's Bank of China in the Foreign Exchange Market

Although the Fed could peg the value of the dollar, it chooses not to do so. But China's central bank, the People's Bank of China, does intervene to peg the value of its currency—the yuan. *Eye on the Global Economy* on page 545 shows the result of this intervention.

During much of the period that the yuan has been pegged to the U.S. dollar, China has piled up U.S dollar reserves. Figure 21.8(a) shows the numbers. You can see that in 2004 and 2005, China's reserves increased by $200 billion a year.

Figure 21.8(b), which shows the market for U.S. dollars priced in terms of the yuan, explains why China's reserves increased. The demand curve D and supply curve S intersect at 5 yuan per dollar. If the People's Bank of China took no actions in the foreign exchange market, this exchange rate would be the equilibrium rate. (This particular value is only an example. No one knows what the yuan-dollar exchange rate would be with no intervention.)

By intervening in the market and buying U.S. dollars, the People's Bank can peg the yuan at 8.28 yuan per dollar. But to do so, it must keep holding the dollars that it buys. In Figure 21.8(b), the People's Bank buys $200 billion a year.

Only by allowing the yuan to appreciate can China stop accumulating dollars. That is what the People's Bank decided to do in July 2005. But China continues to intervene in the foreign exchange market to manage the rate of appreciation of the yuan. Eventually, when China's foreign exchange market becomes more accustomed to a floating yuan, it is likely that the People's Bank will lessen its intervention and the value of the yuan will be determined by market forces.

■ FIGURE 21.8

China's Foreign Exchange Market Intervention

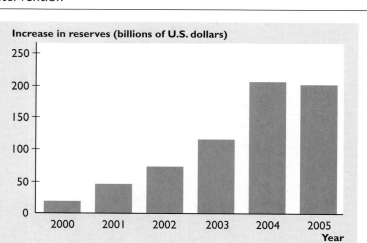

(a) Increase in U.S. dollar reserves

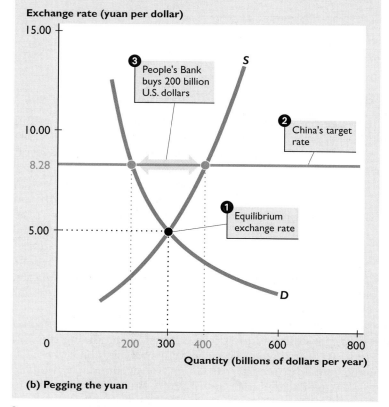

(b) Pegging the yuan

China has been piling up reserves of U.S. dollars since 2000. In 2004 and 2005, the build-up of reserves was very large. Part (a) shows the numbers.

Part (b) shows the market for the U.S. dollar in terms of the Chinese yuan. Note that a higher exchange rate (yuan per dollar) means a lower value of the yuan and a higher value of the dollar. The yuan appreciates when the number of yuan per dollar decreases.

❶ With demand curve *D* and supply curve *S*, the equilibrium exchange rate is 5 yuan per dollar. (The equilibrium value is not known, and the value assumed is only an example.)

❷ The People's Bank of China has a target exchange rate of 8.28 yuan per dollar. At this exchange rate, the yuan is *undervalued*.

❸ To keep the exchange rate pegged at its target level, the People's Bank of China must buy U.S. dollars in exchange for yuan, and China's reserves of dollars piles up.

SOURCE OF DATA: The People's Bank of China.

EYE ON THE GLOBAL ECONOMY

The Fixed Yuan

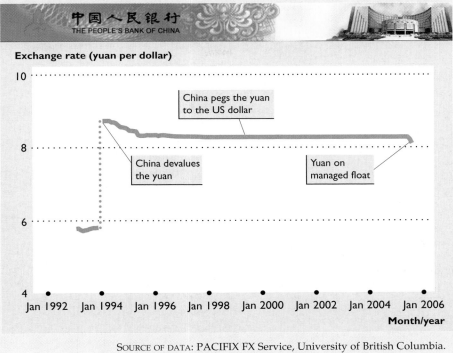

The Chinese central bank, the People's Bank of China, has pegged the value of the yuan in terms of the U.S. dollar for more than 10 years.

The figure shows the value of the yuan (yuan per dollar) from the early 1990s to 2005.

The yuan was devalued in January 1994. It appreciated a bit during 1994 and 1995. But it was then pegged at 8.28 yuan per U.S. dollar, a value that was maintained for more than 10 years. In July 2005, the yuan began a managed float.

SOURCE OF DATA: PACIFIX FX Service, University of British Columbia.

REALITY CHECK

International Finance in YOUR Life

If you go to Europe for a vacation, you will need some euros. What is the best way to get euros? One way is to just take your cash card to use an ATM in Europe. You get euros from the cash machine, and your bank account in the United States gets charged for the cash you obtain.

When you get euros, the number of euros you request is multiplied by the exchange rate to determine how many dollars to take from your bank account.

You have just made a transaction in the foreign exchange market. You have exchanged dollars for euros.

The exchange rate that you paid was probably costly. Your bank took a commission for helping you get euros. Some banks charge as much as 5 percent. Check in advance. It might be better to buy euros from your bank before you leave on your trip.

2 **Explain how the exchange rate is determined and why it fluctuates.**

Practice Problem 21.2

1. Suppose that yesterday, the U.S. dollar was trading on the foreign exchange market at 100 yen per dollar. Today, the U.S. dollar is trading at 105 yen per dollar.
   a. Which of the two currencies (the dollar or the yen) has appreciated and which has depreciated today?
   b. List the events that could have caused today's change in the value of the U.S. dollar on the foreign exchange market.
   c. Did the events that you listed in part **b** change the demand for U.S. dollars, the supply of U.S. dollars, or both the demand for and supply of U.S. dollars?
   d. If the Fed had tried to stabilize the value of the U.S. dollar at 100 yen per dollar, what action would it have taken?
   e. In part **d**, what effect would the Fed's actions have had on U.S. official reserves?

Exercise 21.2

1. Suppose that yesterday, the Canadian dollar ($C) was trading on the foreign exchange market at $0.85 U.S. per $C. Today, the Canadian dollar is trading at $0.80 U.S. per $C.
   a. Which of the two currencies (the Canadian dollar or the U.S. dollar) has appreciated and which has depreciated today?
   b. List the events that could have caused today's change in the value of the Canadian dollar on the foreign exchange market.
   c. Did the events that you listed in part **b** increase or decrease the demand for Canadian dollars, the supply of Canadian dollars, or both the demand for and supply of Canadian dollars?
   d. If the Bank of Canada had tried to stabilize the value of the Canadian dollar at $0.85 U.S., what action would it have taken?
   e. In part **d**, what effect would the Bank of Canada's actions have had on Canadian official reserves?

Solution to Practice Problem 21.2

1a. Because the U.S. dollar costs a larger number of yen, the U.S. dollar has appreciated. The yen has depreciated because it buys fewer dollars.

1b. The main events might be an increase in the U.S. interest rate, a decrease in the Japanese interest rate, or a rise in the expected future exchange rate of the U.S. dollar.

1c. The events that you listed in part **b** change both the demand for and supply of dollars. They increase demand and decrease supply.

1d. To stabilize the value of the U.S. dollar, the Fed would have sold U.S. dollars to increase the supply of U.S. dollars in the foreign exchange market.

1e. When the Fed sells U.S. dollars, it buys foreign currency. U.S. official reserves would have increased.

CHAPTER CHECKPOINT

Key Points

1 **Describe a country's balance of payments accounts and explain what determines the amount of international borrowing and lending.**

- Foreign currency is used to finance international trade.
- A country's balance of payments accounts record its international transactions.
- Historically, the United States has been a net lender to the rest of the world, but in 1983, that situation changed and the United States became a net borrower, and in 1989 the United States became a debtor nation.
- Net exports are equal to the private sector balance plus the government sector balance.

2 **Explain how the exchange rate is determined and why it fluctuates.**

- Foreign currency is obtained in exchange for domestic currency in the foreign exchange market.
- The exchange rate is determined by demand and supply in the foreign exchange market.
- The lower the exchange rate, the greater is the quantity of dollars demanded. A change in the exchange rate brings a movement along the demand curve for dollars.
- Changes in the expected future exchange rate and the U.S. interest rate differential change the demand for dollars and shift the demand curve.
- The lower the exchange rate, the smaller is the quantity of dollars supplied. A change in the exchange rate brings a movement along the supply curve of dollars.
- Changes in the expected future exchange rate and the U.S. interest rate differential change the supply of dollars and shift the supply curve.
- Fluctuations in the exchange rate occur because fluctuations in the demand for and supply of dollars are not independent.
- A central bank can intervene in the foreign exchange market to smooth fluctuations in the exchange rate.

Key Terms

Balance of payments accounts, 526
Capital account, 526
Creditor nation, 528
Currency appreciation, 532
Currency depreciation, 531
Current account, 526

Debtor nation, 528
Foreign exchange market, 531
Foreign exchange rate, 531
Interest rate parity, 542
Net borrower, 528
Net lender, 528

Official settlements account, 526
Purchasing power parity, 540
U.S. interest rate differential, 534
U.S. official reserves, 526

Exercises

1. The following data describe the economy of Antarctica in 2050:

Item	(billions of Antarctica dollars)
Imports of goods and services	150
Exports of goods and services	50
Net interest	−10
Net transfers	35
Foreign investment in Antarctica	125
Antarctica's investment abroad	55

   a. Calculate Antarctica's current account balance.
   b. Calculate Antarctica's capital account balance.
   c. Calculate the increase in Antarctica's official reserves.
   d. Is Antarctica a debtor nation or a creditor nation?
   e. Are Antarctica's international assets increasing or decreasing?
   f. Can you determine whether Antarctica is borrowing to finance investment or consumption? Why or why not?

2. The U.S. dollar appreciates, and the nation's official holdings of foreign currency increase. State which of the following events could have caused these
   changes to occur and why.
   a. The Fed intervened in the foreign exchange market and sold dollars.
   b. The Fed conducted an open market operation and sold bonds.
   c. People began to expect the dollar to appreciate.
   d. The U.S. interest rate differential narrowed.
   e. The U.S. current account went into deficit.

3. The U.S. dollar depreciates. State which of the following events could have
   caused the depreciation and why.
   a. The Fed intervened in the foreign exchange market and sold dollars.
   b. The Fed intervened in the foreign exchange market and bought dollars.
   c. People began to expect the dollar to depreciate.
   d. The U.S. interest rate differential increased.
   e. Foreign investment in the United States increased.

4. The euro appreciates. State which of the following events could have caused
   the appreciation and why.
   a. The ECB intervened in the foreign exchange market and sold euros.
   b. The Fed intervened in the foreign exchange market and bought dollars.
   c. People began to expect the euro to depreciate.
   d. The EU interest rate differential increased.
   e. The EU interest rate differential decreased.
   f. Profits increased in Europe, and foreign investment in European companies surged.

5. If Japan has a lower inflation rate than the United States and the difference
   in inflation rates persists for some years, will
   a. The dollar appreciate or depreciate against the yen?
   b. The yen appreciate or depreciate against the dollar?

c. Purchasing power parity be violated? Why or why not?
d. Interest rate parity hold? Why or why not?
e. U.S. interest rates be higher or lower than Japanese interest rates? Why or why not?
f. The inflation difference influence the expected future exchange rate? Why or why not?
g. The inflation difference influence the U.S. current account balance? Why or why not?

6. Suppose that the euro keeps rising and hits $2 U.S. At this point, the Fed decides to stop the euro from rising (stop the dollar from falling) by intervening in the foreign exchange market.
   a. What actions might the Fed take in the foreign exchange market?
   b. Could the Fed take the actions you described in part **a** forever if necessary?
   c. Would the Fed's actions prevent interest rate parity from being achieved? Why or why not?
   d. Are there any other actions that the Fed could take to raise the foreign exchange value of the dollar? Explain your answer.

Critical Thinking

7. Many people think that a current account deficit is a sign that a nation is not able to compete in international markets. Explain why this view is incorrect and describe the factors that create a current account deficit.

8. For most of the 1990s, Argentina pegged the value of its currency, the peso, to the U.S. dollar. 1 peso equaled 1 U.S. dollar. Then, at the end of 2001, the peso was allowed to find its own value on the foreign exchange market and it fell dramatically.
   a. Why might it be difficult for Argentina to peg the value of its currency to the U.S. dollar?
   b. Why, nonetheless, might it be a good idea for Argentina to peg the value of its currency to the U.S. dollar? What are the potential benefits to Argentina?
   c. On balance, do you think a country such as Argentina should peg its currency to the U.S. dollar?

9. Now that Europe has replaced its national currencies (such as the French franc, German mark, and Italian lira) with a new single currency, the euro, some people say that North America should do the same. The suggestion is that the Mexican peso and Canadian dollar be scrapped and that the entire NAFTA area use the U.S. dollar for all transactions.
   a. What are some of the differences between the European and North American situations that might mean that the European solution would not work in North America?
   b. What are some of the similarities between the European and North American situations that might mean that the European solution *would* work in North America?

ⓧmyeconlab   ## Web Exercises

Use the links on MyEconLab to work the following exercises.

10. Visit FRED, the Federal Reserve Economic Database, and find data on the exchange rate and international trade.
    a. When did the United States last have a current account surplus?
    b. Does the United States have a surplus or a deficit in trade in goods?
    c. Does the United States have a surplus or a deficit in trade in services?
    d. What has happened to foreign investment in the United States during the past 10 years?
    e. Do you think the U.S. balance of payments record is a matter for concern? Why or why not?

11. Visit the PACIFIC Exchange Rate Service and obtain data on the exchange rate of the U.S. dollar against two other currencies.
    a. Use the demand and supply model to explain the changes (or absence of changes) in the exchange rates.
    b. What specific events might have changed exchange rate expectations?
    c. What forces might have prevented the exchange rate from changing?
    d. What information would you need to have to determine whether the central bank intervened in the foreign exchange market to limit the change in the exchange rate?

Glossary

Ability-to-pay principle The proposition that people should pay taxes according to how easily they can bear the burden. (p. 206)

Absolute advantage When one person is more productive than another person in several or even all activities. (p. 78)

Allocative efficiency A situation in which the quantities of goods and services produced are those that people value most highly—it is not possible to produce more of a good or service without giving up some of another good that people value more highly. (p. 68)

Antitrust law A law that regulates and prohibits certain kinds of market behavior, such as monopoly and monopolistic practices. (p. 430)

Average cost pricing rule A rule that sets price equal to average cost to enable the firm to cover its costs. (p. 423)

Average fixed cost Total fixed cost per unit of output. (p. 305)

Average product Total product divided by the quantity of an input. The average product of labor is total product divided by the quantity of labor employed. (p. 300)

Average tax rate The percentage of income that is paid in tax. (p. 197)

Average total cost Total cost per unit of output, which equals average fixed cost plus average variable cost. (p. 305)

Average variable cost Total variable cost per unit of output. (p. 305)

Balance of payments accounts The accounts in which a nation records its international trading, borrowing, and lending. (p. 526)

Balance of trade The value of exports minus the value of imports. (p. 497)

Barrier to entry A natural or legal constraint that protects a firm from competitors. (p. 346)

Benefit The benefit of something is the gain or pleasure that it brings. (p. 11)

Benefits principle The proposition that people should pay taxes equal to the benefits they receive from public goods and services. (p. 206)

Big tradeoff A tradeoff between efficiency and fairness that recognizes the cost of making income transfers. (p. 158)

Black market An illegal market that operates alongside a government-regulated market. (p. 169)

Bond A promise to pay specified sums of money on specified dates; it is a debt for the issuer. (p. 443)

Bond market A financial market in which bonds issued by firms and governments are traded. (p. 443)

Budget line A line that describes the limits to consumption possibilities and that depends on a consumer's budget and the prices of goods and services. (p. 262)

Capital Tools, instruments, machines, buildings, and other items that have been produced in the past and that businesses now use to produce goods and services. (p. 38)

Capital account Record of foreign investment in the United States minus U.S. investment abroad. (p. 526)

Capital goods Goods that are bought by businesses to increase their productive resources. (p. 34)

Capture theory The theory that a regulated firm captures the regulator and makes a monopoly profit. (p. 421)

Cartel A group of firms acting together to limit output, raise price, and increase economic profit. (p. 398)

Ceteris paribus Other things remaining the same (often abbreviated as *cet. par.*). (p. 15)

Change in demand A change in the quantity that people plan to buy when any influence on buying plans other than the price of the good changes. (p. 90)

Change in the quantity demanded A change in the quantity of a good that people plan to buy that results from a change in the price of the good. (p. 92)

Change in the quantity supplied A change in the quantity of a good that suppliers plan to sell that results from a change in the price of the good. (p. 99)

Change in supply A change in the quantity that suppliers plan to sell when any influence on selling plans other than the price of the good changes. (p. 97)

Circular flow model A model of the economy that shows the circular flow of expenditures and incomes that result from decision makers' choices and the way those choices interact to determine what, how, and for whom goods and services are produced. (p. 42)

Coase theorem The proposition that if property rights exist, only a small number of parties are involved, and transactions costs are low, then private transactions are efficient and the outcome is not affected by who is assigned the property right. (p. 220)

Command system A system that allocates resources by the order of someone in authority. (p. 140)

Commodity market A market in which raw materials are traded. (p. 444)

Common resource A resource, one unit of which, can be used only once but no one can be prevented from using what is available. (p. 239)

Comparative advantage The ability of a person to perform an activity or produce a good or service at a lower opportunity cost than someone else. (p. 77)

Complement A good that is consumed with another good. (p. 90)

Complement in production A good that is produced along with another good. (p. 97)

Constant returns to scale A condition in which, when a firm increases its plant size and labor employed by the same percentage, its output increases by the same percentage and its average total cost remains constant. (p. 312)

Consumer surplus The marginal benefit from a good or service minus the price paid for it, summed over the quantity consumed. (p. 145)

Consumption goods and services Goods and services that are bought by individuals and used to provide personal enjoyment and contribute to a person's standard of living. (p. 34)

Copyright A government-sanctioned exclusive right granted to the inventor of a good, service, or productive process to produce, use, and sell the invention for a given number of years. (p. 231)

Correlation The tendency for the values of two variables to move in a predictable and related way. (p. 16)

Creditor nation A country that during its entire history has invested more in the rest of the world than other countries have invested in it. (p. 528)

Cross elasticity of demand A measure of the responsiveness of the demand for a good to a change in the price of a substitute or complement when other things remain the same. (p. 131)

Cross-section graph A graph that shows the values of an economic variable for different groups in a population at a point in time. (p. 24)

Currency appreciation The rise in the value of one currency in terms of another currency. (p. 532)

Currency depreciation The fall in the value of one currency in terms of another currency. (p. 531)

Current account Record of international receipts and payments—current account balance equals exports minus imports, plus net interest and transfers received from abroad. (p. 526)

Deadweight loss The decrease in total surplus that results from an inefficient underproduction or overproduction. (p. 153)

Debtor nation A country that during its entire history has borrowed more from the rest of the world than it has lent to it. (p. 528)

Decreasing marginal returns When the marginal product of an additional worker is less than the marginal product of the previous worker. (p. 298)

Demand The relationship between the quantity demanded and the price of a good when all other influences on buying plans remain the same. (p. 87)

Demand curve A graph of the relationship between the quantity demanded of a good and its price when all the other influences on buying plans remain the same. (p. 88)

Demand schedule A list of the quantities demanded at each different price when all the other influences on buying plans remain the same. (p. 88)

Deregulation The process of removing restrictions on prices, product standards and types, and entry conditions. (p. 420)

Derived demand The demand for a factor of production, which is derived from the demand for the goods and services it is used to produce. (p. 445)

Diminishing marginal rate of substitution The general tendency for the marginal rate of substitution to decrease as the consumer moves down along the indifference curve, increasing consumption of the good measured on the *x*-axis and decreasing consumption of the good measured on the *y*-axis. (p. 286)

Diminishing marginal utility The general tendency for marginal utility to decrease as the quantity of a good consumed increases. (p. 269)

Direct relationship A relationship between two variables that move in the same direction. (p. 26)

Diseconomies of scale A condition in which, when a firm increases its plant size and labor employed by the same percentage, its output increases by a smaller percentage and its average total cost increases. (p. 312)

Dumping When a foreign firm sells its exports at a lower price than its cost of production. (p. 514)

Duopoly A market with only two firms. (p. 398)

Earnings sharing regulation A regulation that requires firms to make refunds to customers when profits rise above a target level. (p. 426)

Economic depreciation An opportunity cost of a firm using capital that it owns—measured as the change in the market value of capital over a given period. (p. 293)

Economic growth The sustained expansion of production possibilities. (p. 75)

Economic profit A firm's total revenue minus total cost. (p. 293)

Economic rent The income received by any factor of produc-

tion over and above the amount required to induce a given quantity of the factor to be supplied. (p. 460)

Economics The social science that studies the choices that we make as we cope with *scarcity* and the *incentives* that influence and reconcile our choices. (p. 3)

Economies of scale A condition in which, when a firm increases its plant size and labor employed by the same percentage, its output increases by a larger percentage and its average total cost decreases. (p. 311)

Efficient scale The quantity at which average total cost is a minimum. (p. 383)

Elastic demand When the percentage change in the quantity demanded exceeds the percentage change in price. (p. 116)

Elastic supply When the percentage change in the quantity supplied exceeds the percentage change in price. (p. 126)

Entrepreneurship The human resource that organizes labor, land, and capital. (p. 39)

Equilibrium price The price at which the quantity demanded equals the quantity supplied. (p. 101)

Equilibrium quantity The quantity bought and sold at the equilibrium price. (p. 101)

Excess burden The amount by which the burden of a tax exceeds the tax revenue received by the government—the deadweight loss from a tax. (p. 192)

Excess capacity When the quantity that a firm produces is less than the quantity at which average total cost is a minimum. (p. 383)

Excess demand A situation in which the quantity demanded exceeds the quantity supplied. (p.101)

Excess supply A situation in which the quantity supplied exceeds the quantity demanded. (p. 101)

Excludable A good, service, or resource is excludable if it is possible to prevent someone from enjoying its benefits. (p. 238)

Explicit cost A cost paid in money. (p. 293)

Exports Goods and services that we sell in other countries. (p. 494)

Externality A cost or a benefit that arises from production that falls on someone other than the producer or a cost or benefit that arises from consumption that falls on someone other than the consumer. (p. 214)

Factor markets Markets in which factors of production are bought and sold. (p. 42)

Factor price The price of a factor of production. The wage rate is the price of labor, the interest rate is the price of capital, and rent is the price of land. (p. 442)

Factors of production The productive resources that are used to produce goods and services— land, labor, capital, and entrepreneurship. (p. 36)

Financial capital The funds that firms use to buy and operate physical capital. (p. 443)

Financial markets The collection of people and firms who are lending and borrowing to finance the purchase of physical capital. (p. 443)

Firms The institutions that organize the production of goods and services. (p. 42)

Foreign exchange market The market in which the currency of one country is exchanged for the currency of another. (p. 531)

Foreign exchange rate The price at which one currency exchanges for another. (p. 531)

Four-firm concentration ratio The percentage of the total revenue of an industry accounted for by the four largest firms in the industry. (p. 376)

Free lunch A gift—getting something without giving up something else. (p. 61)

Free rider A person who enjoys the benefits of a good or service without paying for it. (p. 241)

Functional distribution of income The distribution of income among the factors of production. (p. 40)

Game theory The tool that economists use to analyze strategic behavior—behavior that recognizes mutual interdependence and takes account of the expected behavior of others. (p. 407)

Goods and services The objects (goods) and the actions (services) that people value and produce to satisfy human wants. (p. 3)

Goods markets Markets in which goods and services are bought and sold. (p. 42)

Herfindahl-Hirschman Index The square of the percentage market share of each firm summed over the largest 50 firms (or summed over all the firms if there are fewer than 50) in a market. (p. 377)

Horizontal equity The requirement that taxpayers with the same ability to pay should pay the same taxes. (p. 206)

Households Individuals or groups of people living together. (p. 42)

Human capital The knowledge and skill that people obtain from education, on-the-job training, and work experience. (p. 37)

Implicit cost An opportunity cost incurred by a firm when it uses a factor of production for which it does not make a direct money payment. (p. 293)

Imports Goods and services that we buy from other countries. (p. 494)

Incentive A reward or a penalty—a "carrot" or a "stick"—that encourages or discourages an action. (p. 13)

Income elasticity of demand A measure of the responsiveness of the demand for a good to a change in income when other things remain the same. (p. 132)

Increasing marginal returns When the marginal product of an additional worker exceeds the marginal product of the previous worker. (p. 298)

Indifference curve A line that shows combinations of goods among which a consumer is *indifferent*. (p. 285)

Individual transferable quota (ITQ) A production limit that is assigned to an individual, who is free to transfer the quota to someone else. (p. 255)

Inelastic demand When the percentage change in the quantity demanded is less than the percentage change in price. (p. 116)

Inelastic supply When the percentage change in the quantity supplied is less than the percentage change in price. (p. 126)

Infant-industry argument The argument that it is necessary to protect a new industry to enable it to grow into a mature industry that can compete in world markets. (p. 513)

Inferior good A good for which demand decreases when income increases. (p. 91)

Intellectual property rights The property rights of the creators of knowledge and other discoveries. (p. 231)

Interest Income paid for the use of capital. (p. 39)

Interest rate parity Equal interest rates—a situation in which the interest rate in one currency equals the interest rate in another currency when exchange rate changes are taken into account. (p. 542)

Inverse relationship A relationship between two variables that move in opposite directions. (p. 27)

Job A contract between a firm and a household to provide labor services. (p. 442)

Labor The work time and work effort that people devote to producing goods and services. (p. 37)

Labor force The number of people employed plus the number unemployed. (p. 442)

Land The "gifts of nature," or natural resources, that we use to produce goods and services. (p. 36)

Law of decreasing returns As a firm uses more of a variable input, with a given quantity of fixed inputs, the marginal product of the variable input eventually decreases. (p. 300)

Law of demand Other things remaining the same, if the price of a good rises, the quantity demanded of that good decreases; and if the price of a good falls, the quantity demanded of that good increases. (p. 87)

Law of market forces When there is a shortage, the price rises; when there is a surplus, the price falls. (p. 101)

Law of supply Other things remaining the same, if the price of a good rises, the quantity supplied of that good increases; and if the price of a good falls, the quantity supplied that good decreases. (p. 94)

Legal monopoly A market in which competition and entry are restricted by the granting of a public franchise, government license, patent, or copyright. (p. 347)

Linear relationship A relationship that graphs as a straight line. (p. 26)

Long run The time frame in which the quantities of all resources can be varied. (p. 296)

Long-run average cost curve A curve that shows the lowest average cost at which it is possible to produce each output when the firm has had sufficient time to change both its plant size and labor employed. (p. 312)

Lorenz curve A curve that graphs the cumulative percentage of income (or wealth) against the cumulative percentage of households. (p. 468)

Loss Income earned by an entrepreneur for running a business when that income is negative. (p.39)

Macroeconomics The study of the aggregate (or total) effects on the national economy and the global economy of the choices that individuals, businesses, and governments make. (p. 14)

Margin A choice on the margin is a choice that is made by comparing *all* the relevant alternatives systematically and incrementally. (p. 12)

Marginal benefit The benefit that arises from a one-unit increase in an activity. The marginal benefit of something is measured by what you *are willing* to give up to get one additional unit of it. (p. 12)

Marginal cost The opportunity cost that arises from a one-unit increase in an activity. The marginal cost of something is what you *must* give up to get one more unit of it. (p. 12) The marginal cost of producing a good is the change in total cost that results from a one-unit increase in output. (p. 304)

Marginal cost pricing rule A rule that sets price equal to marginal cost to achieve an efficient output in a regulated industry. (p. 423)

Marginal external benefit The benefit from an additional unit of a good or service that people other than the consumer of the good or service enjoy. (p. 226)

Marginal external cost The cost of producing an additional unit of a good or service that falls on people other than the producer. (p. 216)

Marginal private benefit The benefit from an additional unit of a good or service that the consumer of that good or service receives. (p. 226)

Marginal private cost The cost of producing an additional unit of a good or service that is borne by the producer of that good or service. (p. 216)

Marginal product The change in total product that results from a one-unit increase in the quantity of labor employed. (p. 298)

Marginal rate of substitution The rate at which a person will give up good y (the good measured on the y-axis) to get more of good x (the good measured on the x-axis) and at the same time remain on the same indifference curve. (p. 286)

Marginal revenue The change in total revenue that results from a one-unit increase in the quantity sold. (p. 321)

Marginal social benefit The marginal benefit enjoyed by society—by the consumers of a good or service and by everyone else who benefits from it. It is the sum of marginal private benefit and marginal external benefit. (p. 226)

Marginal social cost The marginal cost incurred by the entire society—by the producer and by everyone else on whom the cost falls. It is the sum of marginal private cost and marginal external cost. (p. 216)

Marginal tax rate The percentage of an additional dollar of income that is paid in tax. (p. 197)

Marginal utility The change in total utility that results from a one-unit increase in the quantity of a good consumed. (p. 269)

Marginal utility per dollar The marginal utility from a good relative to the price paid for the good. (p. 273)

Market Any arrangement that brings buyers and sellers together and enables them to get information and do business with each other. (p. 42)

Market demand The sum of the demands of all the buyers in a market. (p. 89)

Market equilibrium When buyers' and sellers' plans are in balance—the quantity demanded equals the quantity supplied. (p. 101)

Market income A household's income earned from the markets for factors of production and with no government redistribution. (p. 483)

Market supply The sum of the supplies of all the sellers in the market. (p. 96)

Markup The amount by which price exceeds marginal cost. (p. 383)

Median voter theory The theory that governments pursue policies that make the median voter as well off as possible. (p. 486)

Microeconomics The study of the choices that individuals and businesses make and the way these choices interact and are influenced by governments. (p. 14)

Minimum wage law A government regulation that makes hiring labor for less than a specified wage illegal. (p. 176)

Money income Market income plus money benefits paid by the government. (p. 484)

Monopolistic competition A market in which a large number of firms compete by making similar but slightly different products. (p. 320)

Monopoly A market for a good or service that has no close substitutes and in which there is one supplier that is protected from competition by a barrier preventing the entry of new firms. (p. 320)

Nash equilibrium An equilibrium in which each player takes the best possible action given the action of the other player. (p. 408)

Natural monopoly A monopoly that arises because one firm can meet the entire market demand at a lower average total cost than two or more firms could. (p. 346)

Negative externality A production or consumption activity that creates an external cost. (p. 214)

Negative income tax A tax and redistribution scheme that provides every household with a guaranteed minimum annual income and taxes all earned income above the guaranteed minimum at a fixed rate. (p. 487)

Negative relationship A relationship between two variables that move in opposite directions. (p. 27)

Net borrower A country that is borrowing more from the rest of the world than it is lending to the rest of the world. (p. 528)

Net lender A country that is lending more to the rest of the world than it is borrowing from the rest of the world. (p. 528)

Nonexcludable A good, service, or resource is nonexcludable if it is impossible to prevent someone from benefiting from it. (p. 238)

Nonrenewable natural resources Natural resources that can be used only once and that cannot be replaced once they have been used. (p. 459)

Nonrival A good, service, or resource is nonrival if its use by one person does not decrease the quantity available to someone else. (p. 238)

Nontariff barrier Any action other than a tariff that restricts international trade. (p. 508)

Normal good A good for which demand increases when income increases. (p. 91)

Normal profit The return to entrepreneurship. Normal profit is part of a firm's opportunity cost because it is the cost of not running another firm. (p. 293)

Official settlements account Record of the change in U.S. official reserves. (p. 526)

Offshoring A U.S. firm either producing in another country or outsourcing to a firm in another country. (p. 505)

Oligopoly A market in which a small number of firms compete. (p. 320)

Opportunity cost The opportunity cost of something is the best thing you must give up to get it. (p. 11)

Outsourcing A firm buying finished goods, components, or services from other firms. (p. 505)

Patent A government-sanctioned exclusive right granted to the inventor of a good, service, or productive process to produce, use, and sell the invention for a given number of years. (p. 231)

Payoff matrix A table that shows the payoffs for each player for every possible combination of actions by the players. (p. 408)

Perfect competition A market in which there are many firms, each selling an identical product; many buyers; no restrictions on the entry of new firms into the industry; no advantage to established firms; and buyers and sellers who are well informed about prices. (p. 320)

Perfect price discrimination Price discrimination that extracts the entire consumer surplus by charging the highest price that consumers are willing to pay for each unit. (p. 362)

Perfectly elastic demand When the quantity demanded changes by a very large percentage in response to an almost zero percentage change in price. (p. 116)

Perfectly elastic supply When the quantity supplied changes by a very large percentage in response to an almost zero percentage change in price. (p. 126)

Perfectly inelastic demand When the quantity demanded remains constant as the price changes. (p. 116)

Perfectly inelastic supply When the quantity supplied remains the same as the price changes. (p. 126)

Personal distribution of income The distribution of income among households. (p. 40)

Positive externality A production or consumption activity that creates an external benefit. (p. 214)

Positive relationship A relationship between two variables that move in the same direction. (p. 26)

Poverty A state in which a household's income is too low to be able to buy the quantities of food, shelter, and clothing that are deemed necessary. (p. 473)

Predatory pricing Setting a low price to drive competitors out of business with the intention of setting a monopoly price when the competition has gone. (p. 433)

Price cap A government regulation that places an upper limit on the price at which a particular good, service, or factor of production may be traded. (p. 168)

Price cap regulation A rule that specifies the highest price that a firm is permitted to set—a price ceiling. (p. 426)

Price ceiling A government regulation that places an upper limit on the price at which a particular good, service, or factor of production may be traded. (p. 168)

Price-discriminating monopoly A monopoly that is able to sell different units of a good or service for different prices. (p. 348)

Price elasticity of demand A measure of the responsiveness of the quantity demanded of a good to a change in its price when all other influences on buyers' plans remain the same. (p. 114)

Price elasticity of supply A measure of the responsiveness of the quantity supplied of a good changes to a change in its price when all other influences on sellers' plans remain the same. (p. 126)

Price floor A government regulation that places a lower limit on the price at which a particular good, service, of factor of production may be traded. (p. 175)

Price support A price floor in an agricultural market maintained by a government guarantee to buy any surplus output at that price. (p. 181)

Price taker A firm that cannot influence the price of the good or service that it produces. (p. 321)

Principle of minimum differentiation The tendency for competitors to make themselves identical to appeal to the maximum number of clients or voters. (p. 246)

Prisoners' dilemma A game between two prisoners that shows why it is hard to cooperate, even when it would be beneficial to both players to do so. (p. 407)

Private good A good or service that can be consumed by only one person at a time and only by the person who has bought it or owns it. (p. 238)

Producer surplus The price of a good minus the marginal cost of producing it, summed over the quantity produced. (p. 148)

Product differentiation Making a product that is slightly different from the products of competing firms. (p. 374)

Production efficiency A situation in which we cannot produce more of one good or service without producing less of something else—production is at a point *on* the *PPF*. (p. 60)

Production possibilities frontier The boundary between the combinations of goods and services that can be produced and the combinations that cannot be produced, given the available factors of production and the state of technology. (p. 58)

Profit Income earned by an entrepreneur for running a business. (p. 39)

Progressive tax A tax whose average rate increases as income increases. (p. 197)

Property rights Legally established titles to the ownership, use, and disposal of factors of production and goods and services that are enforceable in the courts. (p. 219)

Proportional tax A tax whose average rate is constant at all income levels. (p. 197)

Public good A good or service that can be consumed simultaneously by everyone and from which no one can be excluded. (p. 239)

Public interest theory The theory that regulation seeks an efficient use of resources. (p. 421)

Public provision The production of a good or service by a public authority that receives most of its revenue from the government. (p. 228)

Purchasing power parity Equal value of money—a situation in which money buys the same amount of goods and services in different currencies. (p. 540)

Quantity demanded The amount of any good, service, or resource that people are willing and able to buy during a specified period at a specified price. (p. 87)

Quantity supplied The amount of any good, service, or resource that people are willing and able to sell during a specified period at a specified price. (p. 94)

Quota A specified maximum amount of a good that may be imported in a given period of time. (p. 510)

Rate of return regulation A regulation that sets the price at a level that enables a regulated firm to earn a specified target percent return on its capital. (p. 424)

Rational choice A choice that uses the available resources to most effectively satisfy the wants of the person making the choice. (p. 10)

Rational ignorance The decision not to acquire information because the marginal cost of doing so exceeds the marginal benefit. (p. 247)

Regressive tax A tax whose average rate decreases as income increases. (p. 197)

Regulation Rules administered by a government agency to influence economic activity by determining prices, product standards and types, and the conditions under which new firms can enter an industry. (p. 420)

Relative price The price of one good in terms of another good— an opportunity cost. It equals the price of one good divided by the price of another good. (p. 266)

Renewable natural resources Natural resources that can be used repeatedly. (p. 459)

Rent Income paid for the use of land (p. 39)

Rent ceiling A regulation that makes it illegal to charge more than a specified rent for housing. (p. 168)

Rent seeking The act of obtaining special treatment by the government to create economic profit or to divert consumer surplus or producer surplus away from others. (p. 357)

Resale price maintenance An agreement between a manufacturer and a distributor on the price at which a product will be resold. (p. 431)

Rival A good, service, or resource is rival if its consumption by one person decreases the quantity available to someone else. (p. 238)

Scarcity The condition that arises because wants exceed the ability of resources to satisfy them. (p. 2)

Scatter diagram A graph of the value of one variable against the value of another variable. (p. 24)

Search activity The time spent looking for someone with whom to do business. (p. 170)

Self-interest The choices that are best for the individual who makes them. (p. 4)

Shortage A situation in which the quantity demanded exceeds the quantity supplied. (p. 101)

Short run The time frame in which the quantities of some resources are fixed. In the short run, a firm can usually change the quantity of labor it uses but not its technology and quantity of capital. (p. 296)

Shutdown point The output and price at which the firm just covers its total variable cost. p. 325)

Signal An action taken by an informed person (or firm) to send a message to uninformed people. (p. 390)

Single-price monopoly A monopoly that must sell each

unit of its output for the same price to all its customers. (p. 348)

Slope The change in the value of the variable measured on the y-axis divided by the change in the value of the variable measured on the x-axis. (p. 29)

Social interest The choices that are best for society as a whole. (p. 4)

Stock market A financial market in which shares in the stocks of companies are traded. (p. 443)

Strategies All the possible actions of each player in a game. (p. 408)

Subsidy A payment by the government to producers to cover part of the cost of production. (pp. 181, 229)

Substitute A good that can be consumed in place of another good. (p. 90)

Substitute in production A good that can be produced in place of another good. (p. 97)

Sunk cost A previously incurred and irreversible cost. (p. 11)

Supply The relationship between the quantity supplied and the price of a good when all other influences on selling plans remain the same. (p. 94)

Supply curve A graph of the relationship between the quantity supplied of a good and its price when all the other influences on selling plans remain the same. (p. 95)

Supply schedule A list of the quantities supplied at each different price when all the other influences on selling plans remain the same. (p. 95)

Surplus A situation in which the quantity supplied exceeds the quantity demanded. (p. 101)

Tariff A tax on a good that is imposed by the importing country when an imported good crosses its international boundary. (p. 508)

Taxable income Total income minus a personal exemption and a standard deduction (or other allowable deductions). (p. 196)

Tax incidence The division of the burden of a tax between the buyer and the seller. (p. 190)

Time-series graph A graph that measures time on the x-axis and the variable or variables in which we are interested on the y-axis. (p. 24)

Total cost The cost of all the factors of production used by a firm. (p. 303)

Total fixed cost The cost of the firm's fixed factors of production—the cost of land, capital, and entrepreneurship. (p. 303)

Total product The total quantity of a good produced in a given period. (p. 297)

Total revenue The amount spent on a good and received by sellers and equals the price of the good multiplied by the quantity of the good sold. (p. 122)

Total revenue test A method of estimating the price elasticity of demand by observing the change in total revenue that results from a price change (with all other influences on the quantity sold remaining unchanged). (p. 123)

Total surplus The sum of consumer surplus and producer surplus. (p. 151)

Total utility The total benefit that a person gets from the consumption of a good or service. Total utility generally increases as the quantity consumed of a good increases. (p. 268)

Total variable cost The cost of the firm's variable factor of production—the cost of labor. (p. 303)

Tradeoff An exchange—giving up one thing to get something else. (p. 61)

Tragedy of the commons The absence of incentives to prevent the overuse and depletion of a commonly owned resource. (p. 250)

Transactions costs The opportunity costs of making trades in a market. (pp. 155, 220)

Trend A general tendency for the value of a variable to rise or fall. (p. 24)

Tying arrangement An agreement to sell one product only if the buyer agrees to buy another, different product. (p. 432)

Unit elastic demand When the percentage change in the quantity demanded equals the percentage change in price. (p. 116)

Unit elastic supply When the percentage change in the quantity supplied equals the percentage change in price. (p. 126)

U.S. interest rate differential The U.S. interest rate minus the foreign interest rate. (p. 534)

U.S. official reserves The government's holdings of foreign currency. (p. 526)

Utilitarianism A principle that states that we should strive to achieve "the greatest happiness for the greatest number." (p. 158)

Utility The benefit or satisfaction that a person gets from the consumption of a good or service. (p. 268)

Utility-maximizing rule The rule that leads to the greatest total utility from all the goods and services consumed. The rule is: 1. Allocate the entire available budget. 2. Make the marginal utility per dollar equal for all goods. (p. 272)

Value of marginal product The value to a firm of hiring one more unit of a factor of production, which equals price of a unit of output multiplied by the marginal product of the factor of production. (p. 445)

Vertical equity The requirement that taxpayers with a greater ability to pay bear a greater share of the taxes. (p. 207)

Voucher A token that the government provides to households that can be used to buy specified goods or services. (p. 230)

Wages Income paid for the services of labor. (p. 39)

Index

Credits

Figures and Tables

Chapter 5: Some Price Elasticities of Demand, p. 121, Sources of Data: Ahsan Mansur and John Whalley, "Numerical Specification of Applied General Equilibrium Models: Estimation, Calibration, and Data," in *Applied General Equilibrium Analysis,* eds. Herbert E. Scarf and John B. Shoven (New York: Cambridge University Press, 1984), and Henri Theil, Ching-Fan Chung, and James L. Seale, Jr., Advances in Econometrics, Supplement I, 1989, International Evidence on Consumption Patterns (Greenwich, Conn.: JAI Press Inc., 1989). Reprinted with permis-sion; Income Elasticities of Demand, p. 133, Sources of Data: Ahsan Mansur and John Whalley, "Numerical Specification of Applied General Equilibrium Models: Estimation, Calibration, and Data", in *Applied General Equilibrium Analysis,* eds. Herbert E. Scarf and John B. Shoven (New York: Cambridge University Press, 1984), and Henri Theil, Ching-Fan Chung, and James L. Seale, Jr., Advances in Econometrics, Supplement I, 1989, International Evidence on Consumption Patterns (Greenwich, Conn.: JAI Press Inc., 1989). Reprinted with permission.

The Addison-Wesley Series in Economics

Abel/Bernanke
Macroeconomics

Bade/Parkin
Foundations of Economics

Bierman/Fernandez
Game Theory with Economic Applications

Binger/Hoffman
Microeconomics with Calculus

Boyer
Principles of Transportation Economics

Branson
Macroeconomic Theory and Policy

Bruce
Public Finance and the American Economy

Byrns/Stone
Economics

Carlton/Perloff
Modern Industrial Organization

Caves/Frankel/Jones
World Trade and Payments: An Introduction

Chapman
Environmental Economics: Theory, Application, and Policy

Cooter/Ulen
Law and Economics

Downs
An Economic Theory of Democracy

Ehrenberg/Smith
Modern Labor Economics

Ekelund/Ressler/Tollison
Economics

Fusfeld
The Age of the Economist

Gerber
International Economics

Ghiara
Learning Economics

Gordon
Macroeconomics

Gregory
Essentials of Economics

Gregory/Stuart
Russian and Soviet Economic Performance and Structure

Hartwick/Olewiler
The Economics of Natural Resource Use

Hubbard
Money, the Financial System, and the Economy

Hughes/Cain
American Economic History

Husted/Melvin
International Economics

Jehle/Reny
Advanced Microeconomic Theory

Johnson-Lans
A Health Economics Primer

Klein
Mathematical Methods for Economics

Krugman/Obstfeld
International Economics

Laidler
The Demand for Money

Leeds/von Allmen/Schiming
Economics

Leeds/von Allmen
The Economics of Sports

Lipsey/Courant/Ragan
Economics

Melvin
International Money and Finance

Miller
Economics Today

Miller
Understanding Modern Economics

Miller/Benjamin
The Economics of Macro Issues

Miller/Benjamin/North
The Economics of Public Issues

Mills/Hamilton
Urban Economics

Mishkin
The Economics of Money, Banking, and Financial Markets

Parkin
Economics

Perloff
Microeconomics

Phelps
Health Economics

Riddell/Shackelford/Stamos/Schneider
Economics: A Tool for Critically Understanding Society

Ritter/Silber/Udell
Principles of Money, Banking, and Financial Markets

Rohlf
Introduction to Economic Reasoning

Ruffin/Gregory
Principles of Economics

Sargent
Rational Expectations and Inflation

Scherer
Industry Structure, Strategy, and Public Policy

Stock/Watson
Introduction to Econometrics

Studenmund
Using Econometrics

Tietenberg
Environmental and Natural Resource Economics

Tietenberg
Environmental Economics and Policy

Todaro/Smith
Economic Development

Waldman
Microeconomics

Waldman/Jensen
Industrial Organization: Theory and Practice

Weil
Economic Growth

Williamson
Macroeconomics

Microeconomic Data

These microeconomic data series show some of the trends in what, how, and for whom goods and services are produced — the central questions of microeconomics. You will find these data in a spreadsheet that you can download from your MyEconLab Web site.

		1983	1984	1985	1986	1987	1988	1989	1990	1991	1992
WHAT WE PRODUCE											
Percentage of gross domestic product											
1	Agriculture, forestry, fishing, and hunting	1.3	1.6	1.5	1.4	1.7	1.6	1.7	1.7	1.5	1.6
2	Mining	1.9	1.8	1.5	1.0	1.5	1.4	1.4	1.5	1.3	1.1
3	Construction	3.7	3.9	4.1	4.4	4.6	4.6	4.5	4.3	3.8	3.7
4	Durable goods	9.8	10.3	9.8	9.5	10.2	10.2	9.9	9.4	9.0	8.9
5	Nondurable goods	7.8	7.4	7.2	6.6	6.9	7.0	7.0	7.0	6.9	6.8
6	Utilities	4.4	4.3	4.2	4.1	2.6	2.4	2.5	2.5	2.5	2.5
7	Wholesale trade	6.1	6.3	6.2	6.1	6.0	6.2	6.2	6.0	6.0	6.0
8	Retail trade	8.5	8.6	8.7	8.7	7.4	7.2	7.1	6.9	6.8	6.8
9	Transportation and warehousing	2.7	2.8	2.7	2.7	3.2	3.2	3.0	2.9	3.0	2.9
10	Finance, insurance, real estate, rental, and leasing	13.4	13.4	13.6	14.0	17.7	17.8	17.8	18.0	18.4	18.6
11	Professional and business services	—	—	—	—	8.7	9.1	9.4	9.8	9.7	9.9
12	Information	—	—	—	—	3.9	3.8	3.8	3.9	3.9	4.0
13	Educational services, health care, and social assistance	—	—	—	—	6.0	6.1	6.3	6.7	7.1	7.3
14	Arts, entertainment, recreation, accommodation, and food services	—	—	—	—	3.2	3.3	3.3	3.4	3.4	3.4
15	Other services, except government	—	—	—	—	2.4	2.4	2.4	2.5	2.4	2.4
HOW WE PRODUCE											
16	Average weekly hours	34.9	35.1	34.9	34.7	34.7	34.6	34.5	34.3	34.1	34.2
Employment (percentage of total)											
17	Agriculture	3.3	3.1	2.9	2.7	2.6	2.6	2.4	2.4	2.4	2.4
18	Mining	0.9	0.9	0.8	0.7	0.6	0.6	0.6	0.6	0.6	0.5
19	Construction	4.0	4.3	4.5	4.5	4.5	4.6	4.5	4.4	4.1	3.9
20	Manufacturing	16.9	17.1	16.6	16.0	15.7	15.6	15.3	14.9	14.5	14.2
21	Services	67.6	67.7	69.0	69.5	69.9	70.8	71.6	72.2	72.9	73.1
22	Other	7.2	7.0	6.2	6.7	6.7	5.9	5.6	5.5	5.6	5.9
FOR WHOM WE PRODUCE											
23	Wage rate (dollars per hour)	8.19	8.48	8.73	8.92	9.13	9.43	9.80	10.19	10.50	10.76
24	Real wage rate (2000 dollars per hour)	12.56	12.53	12.52	12.52	12.47	12.46	12.48	12.49	12.43	12.46
25	Stock price index (Dow Jones)	1,190	1,178	1,328	1,793	2,276	2,061	2,509	2,679	2,929	3,284
26	Real stock price index (2000 dollars)	1,825	1,742	1,905	2,516	3,109	2,723	3,194	3,283	3,469	3,802
27	Interest rate Aaa (percent per year)	12.0	12.7	11.4	9.0	9.4	9.7	9.3	9.3	8.8	8.1
28	Real interest rate (percent per year)	8.1	9.0	8.3	6.8	6.6	6.3	5.5	5.5	5.3	5.8
GOVERNMENT IN THE ECONOMY											
29	Government receipts (billions of dollars)	1,008	1,121	1,222	1,299	1,414	1,513	1,639	1,724	1,774	1,860
30	Government expenditures (billions of dollars)	1,206	1,308	1,434	1,534	1,617	1,695	1,816	1,970	2,069	2,225
31	Government surplus(+)/deficit(-) (billions of dollars)	−198	−187	−212	−234	−203	−182	−177	−246	−295	−366
32	Government debt (billions of dollars)	1,137	1,307	1,507	1,741	1,890	2,052	2,191	2,412	2,689	3,000